WELFARE IN AMERICA

Welfare in America

Christian Perspectives on a Policy in Crisis

Edited by

Stanley W. Carlson-Thies and James W. Skillen

William B. Eerdmans Publishing Company
Grand Rapids, Michigan / Cambridge, U.K.

255 Jefferson Ave. S.E., Grand Rapids, Michigan 49503 /
P. O. Box 163, Cambridge CB3 9PU U.K.

Printed in the United States of America

00 99 98 97 96 7 6 5 4 3 2 1

Library of Congress Cataloging-in-Publication Data

Welfare in America: Christian perspectives on a policy in crisis /
edited by Stanley W. Carlson-Thies and James W. Skillen.

p. cm.

Includes bibliographical references.

ISBN 0-8028-4127-9 (alk. paper)

1. Public welfare — United States. 2. Public welfare — Religious aspects — Christianity.
3. Church and social problems — United States.
I. Carlson-Thies, Stanley W. II. Skillen, James W.

HV97.A3C484 1995

362.5′8′0973 — dc20 95-42240

CIP

Contents

II. Foundations for a Christian Approach

III. Social Complexity and Diverse Responsibilities

Foreword

THE ESSAYS in this book represent a truly unusual collaborative effort of Christian scholars and practitioners. The chapters not only range over a wide terrain, but they show a team at work, digging beneath the surface of an amazingly complex set of problems. Welfare reform has become one of the topmost challenges facing the federal and state governments. It stands at the critical juncture where unemployment, poor education, hunger, family instability, social disorder, and crime intersect and reinforce one another. And yet the process of trying to reform a government welfare system widely regarded as deeply flawed has not produced many studies that have gone to the root of the basic assumptions guiding past and present policymaking. Moreover, there appears to be no other similarly wide-ranging study undertaken by a team that has aimed to reflect critically and creatively on these matters from a Christian point of view.

This book by no means manifests complete convergence of view-points and conclusions. It is an exploratory venture. It reveals Christians in serious discussion and argument with one another, grappling with life-and-death issues. Their aim is not to win applause or to further their careers. The concern that drove both the project behind this book and the writing of it is an urgently practical one: how can Christians help to promote justice for real people in a broken society by seeking truth, however complex, by exposing fundamental sources of injustice, and by trying to break through ideological blinders and patterns of self-interest that inhibit meaningful reform? We hope that this volume will help people in many vocations and with many different kinds of responsibility to understand the welfare crisis in a more profound way.

Those of us at the Center for Public Justice also hope this book will serve as a launching pad for ever more serious Christian reflection on the urgent public questions of our day. Increasingly, those questions—including welfare—require an understanding of the global dynamics at work in economic, social, and political life. But whether they require consideration of larger or smaller contexts, questions about justice, fairness, health, and well-being require intense, ongoing team efforts to arrive at good answers. Furthermore, in this day of multiple competing visions of life, if Christians expect to make a significant contribution to the well-being of society, an integral and coherent Christian vision must be developed through cooperative scholarship, political reform, and social service. This book represents one example of such an effort.

On behalf of the Center for Public Justice, I want to say thank you to all those who contributed to this book—most of all to Stanley Carlson-Thies—and to others who helped with the project that undergirded it.

James W. Skillen
Executive Director
Center for Public Justice

Introduction

The American Welfare Policy Crisis: A Challenge to Christian Reflection

Stanley W. Carlson-Thies

"Sure, you've phrased it as a welfare policy change that will help the poor escape their poverty, but in reality it's an attack on people who have already suffered so much."

"Well, what you're advocating only sounds compassionate. In fact your position presumes that the poor are just victims who are incapable of change."

THE QUESTION was whether suitable jobs are available to inner-city residents. Or was the dispute this time about welfare benefit levels: so generous that they entice people into dependency, or so miserly that people are left poor? Or were we going around yet again about single-parent families: to say that children should have two parents sounds like an attack on single mothers, but ignoring the fragmentation of the family makes it impossible even to describe the real challenges facing the children—and the mothers. Whatever the specific topic was, beneath the debate lurked highly charged intimations of bad faith, a lack of compassion, excuses for inexcusable behavior, perhaps even racism. . . . Tempers flared, voices were raised, unspoken threats to walk out charged the air.

But the combatants were neither strangers nor political enemies. They were Christian leaders—scholars and activists—all dedicated to finding better ways to help the needy. We were a team, consciously on the same side. We met periodically for weekends of deep and broad debate, and in between reviewed each other's manuscripts and critiqued drafts of a new argument about how to understand poverty and how to reform welfare. We had joined together because we were each convinced that conventional interpretations and options are deeply flawed. And we had joined together because we were each convinced that only a Christian perspective on persons, society, and government makes possible accurate understanding and fruitful reform.

Nevertheless, we often found ourselves in opposite corners during our three-year journey to dig to the roots of the crisis of American welfare policy. Indeed, the polarities that recurred during our discussions, we came to see, are located right at the heart of that crisis. Yet over the months of our working together we also began to grasp together a new understanding of the dimensions of poverty and a new perspective on how poverty can more effectively be redressed. Along the way others joined us to bring their insights and to critique the work we had started.

The outcome of our wrestling constitutes this book. It is neither a collection of empirical studies of poverty nor a series of evaluations of welfare programs with proposals for technical adjustments. We offer instead studies that approach a range of welfare and poverty issues at the level of moral, philosophical, and theological inquiry. For what has gone wrong with American welfare runs far deeper than programmatic deficiencies or insufficient funding. In some way the very approach has been deeply flawed. If so, then to reform welfare we must reconsider first principles. In order to address poverty adequately, we need a more accurate — a biblical — view of human nature, the appropriate ordering of society, and the limited but constructive responsibilities of government.

Our wrestling together yielded no pat answers. It did show us a direction to go forward. By means of this book we invite you to join us in an exploration to dig below the polarities that stymie the Christian and national debate about how we may best respond to the requirement that we love our needy neighbors.

Uncertain Responses to a Clear Command

Welfare reform has over the past two decades pushed to the top of the national and state political agendas. However, there has been little distinctive Christian contribution to the growing concern over the dilemmas, waste, injustices, and counterproductive effects of current welfare programs. Christian voices have too often been either silent or only echoes of positions adopted with little regard for biblical insight into persons, society, and government. But surely this absence of a clear and distinct Christian alternative in the debates over poverty and welfare is a scandal. For the confused and swirling welfare debate needs exactly the clarifying illumination of scriptural wisdom. And without a doubt, one of the clearest themes of the Scriptures is the command to care for the needy.

Loving our neighbors as we love ourselves ranks second only to loving God entirely, according to Jesus' summary of the Law of God (Matt. 22:37-40). God's people in the Old Testament are continually reminded that even as God had come to their aid when they were oppressed, they are to be merciful to the needy around them. Serving those who need help is such a central aspect of truly knowing God that Proverbs can say, "kindness shown to the poor is an act of worship" (14:31). Similarly, in the New Testament we are instructed that taking care of "orphans and widows in their distress" is an important aspect of "pure and faultless" religion (James 1:27). Throughout the Bible, helping the helpless is a central theme, a bright thread.

Christians in the United States have responded to this imperative in a multitude of ways. Many devote much time, energy, money, and prayer to the suffering, the sick, and the poor. They provide meals to families hit by sickness or financial setback. They give to the church's fund for helping the needy. They tutor at-risk kids in the evenings. They help build houses for low-income families. They may be careful to block myths about the lazy poor or slurs about minorities. They have organized, or support with their energy or money, a wide range of church-based and parachurch service ministries.

Yet, when the issue of helping the poor is enlarged much beyond the immediate circle, beyond our physical neighbor or our congregation, our certainty about the imperative to serve the needy becomes confusion. What kind of help is really helpful, we wonder. Don't we just foster dependency if we give aid to a poor person? Shouldn't the poor be taking more responsibility for their own problems? If we really love the needy, shouldn't we favor a generous government welfare system, even though it would cost us higher taxes? Or is assistance to the poor the responsibility of the church and not government at all? But what if the churches don't come to the rescue of the needy? In the end, just whose responsibility is it to help the poor? And what kind of assistance is it that is truly helpful? On such basic questions, communities of Christian conviction in the United States today speak with contrary voices, or are just silent.

Such uncertainty is doubly tragic at this moment when the American polity is struggling to find a new direction for welfare. If at one time the question was whether government could be moved sufficiently to fight poverty with vigor, now citizens, politicians, and experts alike quarrel over whether government does more harm than good, whether welfare is the problem or the solution, and whether the key issue is poverty, dependency, or out-of-wedlock births. These are disagreements not just about means and not even only about ends. They are disputes that extend to underlying questions about human nature, the structures of society, and the tasks of government. On such matters, Christians should have something solid to say. Instead, believers seem to be as unsure, divided, and wavering as everyone else when it comes to understanding and responding to the challenge of reforming welfare and renewing the fight against poverty in America.

This is the background and the rationale for this book. Our hope is to offer to our fellow believers, and to our fellow citizens, a serious wrestling with the deep questions concerning welfare and poverty. We are convinced that only by going to the roots can we find a place to stand in order to help address poverty. We seek to listen to the biblical witness about life, poverty, and assistance, not in order to shield our work from criticism by hiding behind religion, but rather because it is in the Scriptures that we find the only reliable source of light for human life in this world. We offer these studies of various aspects of American welfare and poverty in the hope of illuminating these complex issues and showing a fruitful direction for change.

Welfare in Crisis

Welfare in America over the past sixty years has come to encompass a wide range of government programs.[1] At the core are four major programs:

1. As of this writing in mid-1995, Congress was brimming with enthusiasm to change the welfare system radically by "devolving" almost all program design and administration from the federal government to state governments. But whether or not states begin playing a larger role, it is likely that an array of programs roughly like those built during the past decades will remain at least for the near future. For further discussion of the core welfare programs and of the objectives of American welfare, see John Mason, "Biblical Teaching and the Objectives of Welfare Policy in the United States," 145-85 in this volume. For an overview of welfare in America, see, e.g., Sheldon H. Danziger, Gary D. Sandefur, and Daniel H. Weinberg, eds., *Confronting Poverty: Prescriptions for Change*

AFDC (Aid to Families with Dependent Children), a federal/state program providing cash benefits mainly to single-parent mothers and their children; the federal Food Stamps program; Medicaid, another federal/state program, which provides access to medical care to the poor; and public housing and subsidies for low-income renters. Around this core are clustered many specialized programs, for example, WIC (Women, Infants, and Children) —nutrition assistance for poor mothers and their young children; Head Start—providing poor children with a solid foundation for schooling; and the school breakfast and lunch programs—designed to ensure that poor children are not kept from learning by inadequate nutrition.

The list is longer. For the disabled and the elderly poor, there is SSI (Supplemental Security Income), part of Social Security. The earned income tax credit (EITC) program provides a wage supplement to workers whose wages are very low. Other programs, such as Community Development Block Grants and enterprise or empowerment zones, seek to assist the poor by promoting the development of their economic and social environment. Some states operate General Assistance programs to provide aid to the needy who are ineligible for federal help. There are even more initiatives: job training or job preparation courses, summer jobs programs for poor urban youth, child care assistance. . . .

This is the collection of programs—calling it a welfare system or an American welfare state implies too much coordination—that is in deep crisis. The legitimacy of government programs to assist the poor has always been somewhat suspect in America; our sense of government as a useful and needed means to aid citizens has always been at war with a robust conviction that government is likely to restrict liberty.[2] Nevertheless, with public support, and sometimes enthusiasm, American governments have built a wide variety of welfare programs. But skepticism about the programs has expanded even as the effort has been enlarged. And now, to a growing

---

(Cambridge: Harvard Univ. Press, 1994); James T. Patterson, *America's Struggle Against Poverty, 1900-1985* (Cambridge: Harvard Univ. Press, 1986); Theodore Marmor, Jerry L. Mashaw, and Philip L. Harvey, *America's Misunderstood Welfare State: Persistent Myths, Enduring Realities*, paperback ed. (New York: BasicBooks, 1992); and Sar Levitan, *Programs in Aid of the Poor*, 6th ed. (Baltimore: Johns Hopkins Univ. Press, 1990).

2. Cf. Hugh Heclo, "General Welfare and Two American Traditions," *Political Science Quarterly* 101 (1986): 179-96.

number of citizens, officials, and experts, it is not only one or another welfare program but the very idea of government action on behalf of the needy that is deeply in doubt.

For a long time, welfare and social politics in this country were, at bottom, very simple: one side urged government to greater activism to overcome the scandal of poverty in an affluent nation, and they tagged those on the other side—the critics of expanded programs and expenditures—as uncompassionate tightwads. But advocates of an activist government no longer occupy the moral high ground in this dispute. Three decades of experiences with expanding and expensive federal and state social programs, which have often enough been ineffective and too often even counterproductive, have exploded the easy equation of greater government effort with increased compassion for the needy. The terrain of antipoverty analysis and action is now riven by disputes about pathways into and out of poverty, about whether good or harm is done by welfare programs, and about the relative importance of cultural or religious forces as opposed to economic factors.

It is no longer plausible simply to urge government to greater effort on behalf of the poor. But what is it about welfare that is mistaken? What is it that requires reform? On these essential questions there is great disagreement, rooted in broader disputes about underlying issues.

Consider, for example, the work of David Ellwood. In his influential 1988 book *Poor Support,* Ellwood, then a public policy professor at Harvard, argued that welfare programs gave ineffective assistance to the poor. Program improvements were the solution: a wide range of changes should be made to welfare and other policies affecting the needy so that the poor would be enabled to overcome their poverty.[3] By 1993, Ellwood was a key welfare official in the Clinton administration, helping to craft and defend a plan to "end welfare as we know it," in the President's memorable phrase. The new presumption was that dependence on welfare is the core problem; reforms were supposed to strengthen work requirements and put time limits on benefits. But then again, just before joining the administration, Ellwood had co-authored a book entitled *Welfare Realities* that argued that the key to the welfare problem was to end the epidemic of family breakdown and out-of-wedlock births.[4]

3. David T. Ellwood, *Poor Support* (New York: Basic, 1988).

4. Mary Jo Bane and David T. Ellwood, *Welfare Realities: From Rhetoric to Reform*

Insufficient help, welfare dependency, the fostering of illegitimate births—three very different analyses of why welfare does not work as it should, requiring three different strategies for reform. Should welfare be made better so that it helps people more effectively? Or should welfare be limited because it enslaves rather than strengthens the needy? Or is the fundamental issue how to prevent mistaken personal choices that create the need for welfare in the first place? Taken one by one, these positions are incompatible, even contradictory; they rest on different views of why people become and stay poor and different views of what kind of help will be effective. The positions may, in fact, all be correct, in some measure; Ellwood himself does not hold any single one to the exclusion of the others. But this just adds another level of complexity: in what way do the different diagnoses cohere? What kind of reform can address all of them? The welfare debate now reaches far beyond any simple dispute about how much assistance government should offer the poor. But in becoming more nuanced, more realistic, the debate has become more polarized, not less.[5]

Going to the Roots: The Welfare Responsibility Project

American welfare is, then, in a twofold crisis. The tragic first level of crisis is the ineffectiveness, and sometimes even counterproductiveness, of welfare policies: people who may desperately need help too often receive assistance that is insufficient or misguided. The second level of crisis is different in kind but equally serious in its consequences: rather than a consensus about the direction to take in order to make welfare work, there are deep disagreements about what welfare should be and insistent argu-

---

(Cambridge: Harvard Univ. Press, 1994). See the discussion of the book in Jean Bethke Elshtain, "Why End 'Welfare as We Know It'?" pp. 3-19 in this volume.

5. For an extended analysis of conflicting positions in the welfare debate, see Stanley W. Carlson-Thies, "The Crises of American Welfare: Issues, Theses, Resources," background study for the project Welfare Responsibility: An Inquiry into the Roots of America's Welfare Policy Crisis, Center for Public Justice (January 1993); a portion of this study has been published as Carlson-Thies, "Welfare Responsibility: Surveying the Territory," *Public Justice Report*, March/April 1993, pp. 4-5. See also my "Ending Welfare As We Know It? Time for a New Vision to Guide Welfare Reform," *Prism*, June 1994, pp. 16-19.

ments that government welfare mainly only exacerbates the very problems it is supposed to be redressing.

Decades of programs and spending have yielded not only a welfare crisis, but a crisis of welfare policy—a depth of disagreement about poverty and welfare that leads to completely opposed proposals for the direction of reform. "The critical situation we face," in other words, "is not merely in the factual degradation of human beings in many urban areas, but in the thinking of religious (and other) leaders about how to address these dire circumstances." The crises of welfare and of welfare policy are too advanced to be any longer "addressed as isolable, technical problems set within a framework of confident liberalism and conservatism. Instead, the very foundations of pragmatic liberalism and conservatism are being called into question."[6]

What is vital in these circumstances is not so much additional empirical analyses or more statistics but a fresh look at the foundations, a renewal of understanding about persons, society, and government. Such an assessment of the depth of the crisis of welfare policy gave birth to the research project of which this volume is a fruit. "Welfare Responsibility: An Inquiry into the Roots of America's Welfare Policy Crisis" was designed to dig down to the religious and moral confusions underlying the paralysis and polarities concerning how to redress persistent poverty and urban degradation.

The Welfare Responsibility Inquiry, which ran from late 1992 until early 1995, was a project of the Center for Public Justice, a Christian civic-education and public-policy research organization. James Skillen, the Center's executive director, initiated the project. Major funding was provided by The Pew Charitable Trusts, a national philanthropy based in Philadelphia. The Coalition for Christian Colleges and Universities provided administrative support and a point of contact with many of the key evangelical institutions of higher education.

At the heart of the project was a team of Christian scholars who met periodically for intensive discussion about basic questions concerning human nature, society, responsibility, government, and welfare. Most team

6. James W. Skillen, "American Social Welfare: Resolving Confusion at the Religious and Moral Foundations of a Growing Public Policy Conflict: A Proposal to The Pew Charitable Trusts," Dec. 31, 1991 (Washington, D.C., Center for Public Justice), p. 2.

members concurrently completed studies of some aspect of welfare or poverty. Their papers are key chapters in this volume.

The team members were Charles Glenn, an expert on school policy reform at Boston University and formerly director of the anti-discrimination office for the Massachusetts Department of Education; Bob Goudzwaard, an economist and poverty analyst from the Free University, Amsterdam, and co-author of the recent study *Beyond Poverty and Wealth: Toward an Economy of Care* (with H. de Lang, 1994); Jerry Herbert, head of the American Studies Program of the Coalition for Christian Colleges and Universities; Gina Barclay McLaughlin, former executive director of The Center for Successful Child Development in Chicago's Robert Taylor public housing project, now completing graduate studies at the University of Michigan; John Mason, an economist at Gordon College, Massachusetts, and cofounder of the Association of Christian Economists; Lawrence Mead, author of two influential books on welfare: *The New Politics of Poverty* (1992) and *Beyond Entitlement* (1986); James Skillen, executive director of the Center for Public Justice, author most recently of *Recharging the American Experiment* (1994), and editor of a reprinting of Abraham Kuyper's pathbreaking 1891 challenge to Christians, *The Problem of Poverty* (1991); Max Stackhouse, ethicist at Princeton Theological Seminary and noted author of many studies on issues ranging from business ethics to politics and from family life to voluntary associations, including *Public Theology and Political Economy: Christian Stewardship in Modern Society* (1987); Mary Stewart Van Leeuwen, professor of psychology and resident scholar at the Center for Christian Women in Leadership at Eastern College, co-author of *After Eden: Facing the Challenge of Gender Reconciliation* (1993), among other works; and Stanley Carlson-Thies, the director of the project and Fellow of the Center for Public Justice.

One fruit of the intensive team dialogues was an extended argument about the nature of persistent poverty, the character of human responsibility, the normative ordering of society, and the responsibilities of government to address poverty and injustice. Successive drafts were co-authored by James Skillen and the project director and discussed intensively by the team. A wider group of commentators also provided valuable critique. The argument was published in early 1994 as *A New Vision for Welfare Reform: An Essay in Draft*. It is reprinted in the appendix to this volume. A final version is scheduled to be prepared in the near future.

The project also invited another fifteen Christian scholars, representing a variety of disciplines, to prepare studies based on their own work on poverty and welfare and taking into account a late draft of *A New Vision for Welfare Reform*. Most of these studies are also included here.

In May 1994, the project hosted a conference on "Public Justice & Welfare Reform" in Washington, D.C. The major contentions of *A New Vision for Welfare Reform* were the focus of panels comprised of team members, the additional authors, and other invited scholars, policy analysts, and political leaders. Team members and the other invited authors then revised their papers in the light of the intensive discussions at the conference.

This Book

This book of collected essays is the outcome, then, of a lengthy process of communal dialogue in which successive drafts of *A New Vision for Welfare Reform* provided a focal point for interchange. The book suggests a different approach to welfare and poverty, an approach shaped by a conscious desire to be guided by biblical assumptions.

No attempt was made to enforce consensus among the contributors to this book. These chapters not only cover a wide range of topics but begin from varied starting points. However, all are guided by the conviction that the crisis of American welfare policy requires a serious reexamination of approaches to understanding poverty and to assisting the poor. All rest on the conviction that biblical wisdom provides the only sure foundation for correct understanding and effective compassionate action. All reject, pointedly or by implication, the conventional polarities of the welfare debate. All seek to show a better way by looking more truthfully at persons, society, and government.

The chapters have been divided into four sections: "Background and Context" of the crisis of American welfare policy; "Foundations for a Christian Approach" to welfare; the "Social Complexity and Diverse Responsibilities" that must be acknowledged in any effective effort to help the poor; and several proposals that point the way "Toward Lasting Reform." The distribution of chapters is somewhat arbitrary. Most of the essays could be placed with good justification in several of the sections. However, this categorization usefully emphasizes the various dimensions or levels of a new approach to welfare in Christian perspective. In the concluding chapter, I trace the outlines of that new approach developed through the separate essays of this book.

The goal of the Welfare Responsibility Inquiry was to "articulate a public philosophy of human moral responsibility that is at once both individual and corporate."[7] Persons are neither autonomous competitors in the marketplace nor citizens who may legitimately demand that government resolve all of their problems; they are, instead, responsible for themselves and each other in a wide variety of institutions and groups, ranging from families and schools through business enterprises and governments, to churches, charities, ethnic groups, and neighborhood organizations.

How can government welfare policy be changed so that it supports, rather than weakens or supplants, persons and institutions in carrying out their own responsibilities? That is the key question for meaningful welfare reform. We offer this book to the Christian community, and to the American public and American policymakers, as a contribution to the critical debate that we hope may answer this question.

7. Skillen, "American Social Welfare" project proposal, pp. 3-4.

I. BACKGROUND AND CONTEXT

Why End "Welfare as We Know It"?

Jean Bethke Elshtain

ONE OF THE most poignant films I know is Frederick Wiseman's 1975 documentary, *Welfare.* Filmed in a New York City welfare office, the movie records the comings and goings, the long waits, the frustrating encounters, the angry outbursts, the utter perplexity as to what some case worker is requiring or demanding — on and on. One elderly couple, clearly bewildered, sits quietly on chairs in the waiting area. Their names are on a list. They will be called "as soon as possible." We see the clock on the wall. It is 9 A.M. We notice the couple, a silent, stoical chorus of two, throughout the day, still sitting. We see them again, forlorn and confounded, leaving their location in bureaucratic purgatory at closing time. The clock on the wall now shows 5 P.M. They have talked to no one. Whatever sadness or need or trouble drove them to the welfare office they take home with them again, and to it is added a painful layer of humiliation and frustration.

I have used this film, in conjunction with readings from Hannah Arendt, to illustrate to students the loss of the precondition necessary to any democratic politics worthy of the name: a place in the world in which one's opinions can be made significant and one's actions effective. The utter occlusion of such space is what makes *Welfare* a frightening document.

Should we not then be buoyed by Bill Clinton's stated declaration that he would, as President, move with all deliberate speed to end "welfare as we know it"? Should we not be buoyed by the even louder promises of the ascendent Republicans' "Contract with America" more rapidly and thoroughly to revolutionize our public welfare system? I doubt very much that grounds for optimism exist. The current system, despite the fact that everyone — especially "clients" or "recipients" or "welfare users" themselves — professes to despise it, is not likely to go away any time soon. For we cannot make the needed changes without a fundamentally new dedication to marriage and family. And notwithstanding all our talk about "family values," we seem to lack the moral will and wit needed to firm up our crumbling institutions.

But if we have, in some sense, the kind of welfare system that we deserve, why do we despise it so much? The reasons are many and they are historically deep. Here are two: (1) state-down social provision seems to many Americans to create welfare programs that swell to look too much like a "welfare state"; (2) many Americans are sharply suspicious of welfare provisions that seem simply to be underwriting a typical welfare family that takes the form of a never-married mother and her children.

But why? Do Americans lack compassion? Or is something else going on? What might that "something else" be? There can be no doubt that the "current system discourages clients from working not only through its financial incentives but also through its bureaucratic impediments."[1] And, while it is possible to imagine a culture in which permanent welfare use would not automatically be disparagingly labeled as "dependency" by clients and taxpayers, that labeling is the strong tendency in American culture.

A defining feature of the welfare apparatus built up over the past half century is what the public policy experts call an "eligibility-compliance culture." Benefits are the prize, and meeting eligibility criteria is the price for those benefits. So welfare workers must vigorously police the applicants, their forms, and their documents, and applicants and recipients alike must so comport themselves as not to slip off the narrow way either to the left or to the right.[2] Such a system, an apparatus geared in this fashion, seems to Americans to be fatally flawed. But why? And why, if we are so convinced of its evils, is it so difficult to change?

The answer to the first question begins with an understanding of human dignity. Being cast in the role of a supplicant, a person with entitlements that are nonetheless revocable and continuously scrutinized, strikes us as an assault on, or a diminution of, human dignity. The internal culture

1. Mary Jo Bane and David Ellwood, *Welfare Realities: From Rhetoric to Reform* (Cambridge: Harvard Univ. Press, 1994), xi.

2. Bane and Ellwood, ch. 1.

of a welfare office is a Kafkaesque nightmare, all the more chilling for its seeming ordinariness. Welfare case workers are placed in the unhappy role of double agents: obliged to gain the trust of recipients yet required constantly to verify their eligibility at the same time.[3] Paradoxically and perversely, clients who show some spunk and initiative are rewarded with the classification of "error prone": bureaucratic lingo for a welfare recipient who, because she combines work with her welfare check, too easily may end up violating the strict rules of eligibility for welfare help.

This constricting and contradictory welfare apparatus and the negative behavior it facilitates are deeply troubling to Americans. The late Judith Shklar may help us see why. In one of her last books, devoted to the theme of political standing, Shklar uncontroversially locates the franchise as *primus inter pares*, the defining emblem of standing within the political community. But there is more. Shklar talks about the heavy premium put on standing on one's own two feet, an ideal tied to the dignity of labor, which is an essential part of citizenship in America.[4] Americans loathe welfare "dependence," Shklar continues, in part because for millions who flooded these shores, the possibility of being able to work and to receive a fair return for the sweat of one's brow was a promise of freedom, not a sentence to a lifetime of drudgery.

Long-term welfare dependents are severed, then, from one of the key features of political standing. They are forced to "go public" as victims rather than as citizens.[5] Political theorists, since at least John Locke, have fretted that state-down social provision may undermine free citizenship, and hence erode the necessary preconditions and presuppositions of the democratic state's own existence. So a worry about dependence on the state is nothing new. But it must become a matter for deeper consideration when reliance on state provision has become only one part of a pattern of debilitation. Persons whose every "need" is defined for them and whose lives have become chiefly a quest for "eligibility" are scarcely in a position to enact other sorts of human projects.

Perhaps a story of the sort told "on the ground" is apt at this juncture. I hailed a taxi outside one of the congressional office buildings a few years

3. Bane and Ellwood, 9.

4. Judith Shklar, *The Quest for Inclusion* (Cambridge: Harvard Univ. Press, 1991).

5. It should be noted that Shklar finds much of our preoccupation with welfare dependence to be "irrational," but she does not help us sort the matter out, for she herself has located work as an essential feature of human dignity and political standing.

ago, running a bit late on my trip to National Airport. My cab driver, a Nigerian woman, asked me what I had been up to. I told her I had attended a meeting about what is happening to the American family. She began to talk. I fumbled for paper and pen and began to take notes. The story she told me went like this:

> America has to sort this mess out. America is ruining the family. I tell you, if they don't tidy this thing up it is all over. I am thinking of going back to Nigeria. My son, I think, may be using drugs. And my daughter, she is just eleven, she said to me the other day, "When I'm twelve I'll have a baby and be independent." This is impossible. One baby is a job. The second is a promotion.

My cab driver-mother respondent's fear is twofold. She fears the erosion of family life in the American cultural climate, to be sure. But overlaid on that concern about general cultural decline is a very specific fear that our way of providing for the "welfare" of people who need help instead generates further deterioration, undermining responsible choices and elevating drug use, out-of-wedlock childbearing, detachment from the workforce.

A considerable amount of public policy and social science evidence buttresses my respondent's fears. Mary Jo Bane and David Ellwood's data show unmistakably that young women who enter AFDC as never married are those who will have the longest duration on welfare. Having a child or two to raise, lacking any support from a spouse, with little or no work experience, typically having dropped out of high school, these young women have every reason to resort to AFDC for their sustenance but very few forces to help them to get out of the program.

However, having noted all of this in careful detail, Bane and Ellwood, now policymakers coresponsible for welfare and welfare reform, in their book *Welfare Realities* pretty much just throw up their hands. The best cure for "welfare as we know it," they pronounce, would be prevention: to forestall the "formation of new single-parent families." The likelihood of this, they imply, is near to nil. And the consequence? "Absent an ability to change family formation and dissolution patterns dramatically, we will be forced to rely on methods to help single parents move off of welfare if the goal is to reduce long-term welfare use."[6] But the sad tale does not yet end.

6. Bane and Ellwood, 55.

For, corresponding to the fears expressed by my cab driver, the data Bane and Ellwood have analyzed — from many different perspectives, using many different models and techniques — are persuasive in cataloguing multiple failed attempts over the years to move people through the welfare system and out again once they are long-term "users." Bane and Ellwood call for "further study" of the matter. But we must do better in naming precisely what the problem is and what we might do about it.

Here is the deep challenge of welfare reform: how can we be both fair and compassionate? How can we help without generating dependency? How can we, at one and the same time, help those who need help, bolster the structures and habits that sustain healthy life, and also shore up the delicate webs of social responsibility without which no forms of assistance would exist in the first place? These are central questions of welfare and welfare reform. However, the more common question of welfare politics instead is this: Why should I, working my eight-hour day (or more), consider myself in any way responsible to sustain someone abusing drugs, having babies without a dependable father, or abandoning school?

Did we agree to that kind of responsibility when America adopted that "new social contract" called the New Deal? The answer is no, for clearly the ideal of Social Security was to help those who have been hardworking, responsible citizens, and the ideal of the other forms of "relief" was precisely that it was . . . "relief," a temporary hand-up for folks "down on their luck." The vast majority of Americans still today endorse enthusiastically this notion of social assistance. But, increasingly, they resist the repetition and retrenchment and deepening over time of that culture of compliance-dependency I have already noted. Should this resistance grow, my worry is that it may spill over — indeed, I fear it already has — into other areas: Why should I pay for public schools if I don't myself have young children? Why should I support public welfare at all if some of it fosters self-defeating choices? Why should I trust public programs and government action at all if they are not merely wasteful but even counterproductive?

A historical treatment of the particular political origins of American social policy may help us to take our bearings. In her bold book, *Protecting Soldiers and Mothers,* Theda Skocpol offers a fundamental rethinking of the origins and course of social provision in the United States.[7] She notes the

7. Skocpol, *Protecting Soldiers and Mothers* (Cambridge: Harvard Univ. Press, 1992).

frequent lament on the part of scholars, particularly those of a social democratic bent, that the United States failed to create a "paternalist welfare state, in which male bureaucrats would administer regulations and social insurance 'for the good' of bread winning industrial workers." Instead of this, Skocpol demonstrates, the United States "came close" to creating a "maternalist welfare state, with female-dominated public agencies implementing regulations and benefits for the good of women and their children."[8] Rather than social provisions to bolster heads of (intact) households, a system was crafted to aid women and children absent their husband and father. What is the origin of this remarkable development, one that exploded from 1900 through the early 1920s? The early and, at least at first glance, unlikely precedent, Skocpol argues, is post–Civil War assistance to soldiers of the Army of the Republic. She writes: "Through Civil War benefits, the federal government — long before the New Deal — became the source of generous and honorable social provision for a major portion of the American citizenry."[9]

Provision for soldiers emerged because the young men, many of them badly wounded, had earned aid — for themselves and their dependents — by serving their country. It was the Republican Party in this epoch that served as "the special vehicle" for delivering help. Coded into this post–Civil War provision was the presumption that assistance went to those who were, in some abiding sense, civically deserving. Taking their cue, then, from this Civil War precedent, a nationwide network of women activists pushed for mothers' pensions during the Progressive Era. Most states enacted the pensions and most as well instituted protections for women in the workplace. Aid would flow to mothers and their children who, through no fault of their own, had been thrown into penury upon the death or desertion of a spouse.

Skocpol is insistent on the importance and drama of these developments and on the way they have, for better or for worse, continued to shape the horizon for the politics of social provision in the United States. The move to "mothers' pensions" represented a decisive move away from earlier models of private charity. Public provision would now be the chief source of help, and entitlement based on need — without regard to the issues of responsible choice or rebuilding healthy patterns — would become the dominant mode.

8. Skocpol, 2.
9. Skocpol, 101.

Skocpol concludes her helpful volume by challenging contemporary scholars, especially feminists, to rethink their own presumption in favor of "maternalist" social reform because, from the perspective of gender egalitarianism, social policy that idealizes "separate spheres for the genders does not look progressive."[10] But we must go much further, I am convinced. The ways in which current welfare policy deepens and virtually guarantees and requires "separate spheres" is part of the problem ordinary American citizens have with it. This is not a matter of ideological prejudice; most Americans simply are morally troubled by social policies that provide long-term support for households of never-married women with their children. It goes against the grain of our sense of both fairness and responsibility to subsidize the sundering of the human community at its most basic level: the family. For fatherlessness — there seems no way around this — is bad for children.

The evidence has been mounting for years of the baneful effects of widespread familial fragmentation. Fatherlessness is bad for children, even if we control for all other factors. To this empirical evidence Christians add a firm normative conviction, namely, for us, the starting point for all considerations of social policy, including welfare, must be that we are all born *in* and *to* community. When community breaks down, or when it has already broken down, the Christian urgency is to reweave those community ties. No one should be outside the banquet table of life, and that includes children bereft of their fathers and fathers cut adrift from their children. What contemporary American welfare policy does is to *subsidize* the consequences of broken community in the hope of making amends for the loss of community. But this is a task it cannot do, certainly not in its current benefits/compliance bureaucratic form.

For the crisis of the family, although it contributes to and is worsened by our system of social provision, is not just a welfare problem, and it will not be solved with narrow changes to welfare policy. The Council on Families in America has made the case in these strong terms:

> We see, first, a frightening array of expanding social pathologies, from drive-by shootings to children bearing children, all reflecting the deterioration of childhood, and all inextricably linked to the rapid disintegration of marriage as society's baseline institution for child rearing and,

10. Skocpol, 524.

second, a strange inability, even reluctance, to name the problem. Our society is engaged in vigorous discussions of symptoms — from the effects of divorce on children to welfare reform to deadbeat dads to the increase of single mothers by choice — while maintaining a remarkable silence regarding the root cause. The root cause is the deinstitutionalization of marriage as society's principal childrearing institution. The solution is the reinstitutionalization of marriage in the interest of children. Yet this issue has hardly emerged on the public agenda.[11]

Although this statement is not quite as accurate a reflection of public discourse as it was just a year or two ago — now that a host of administration figures from President Clinton on down have declared their proximity to former Vice President Dan Quayle on the matter — it remains the case that even the most capable and inventive analysts and would-be reformers of welfare, like Mary Jo Bane and David Ellwood, profess utter perplexity about how to put the Humpty Dumpty of marital deinstitutionalization back together again.

Yet put it back together we must. For, as Ernesto Cortez, Jr., of the Texas Industrial Areas Foundation Network has written, in a piece on the Catholic tradition of family rights,

> Families teach us the first lessons of relationships among persons, some of which are essential not only to private but to public life as well. Within the family, one learns to act upon others and to be acted upon. It is in the family that we learn to identify ourselves with others or fail to learn to love. It is in the family that we learn to give and take with others — or fail to learn to be reciprocal. It is in the family that we learn to trust others as we depend on them or learn to distrust them. We learn to form expectations of others and to hold them accountable. We also learn to hold ourselves accountable. These lessons of reciprocity, trust, discipline, and self-restraint are important to the forming of relationships in public life.[12]

If children — and adults — fail to learn these lessons, there are twin harmful consequences. There will be more "welfare as we know it": more

11. Council on Families in America, *Marriage in America: A Report to the Nation* (Institute on Families in America, 1995).

12. Quoted in Jean Bethke Elshtain, "Family Matters," *Christian Century,* July 14–21, 1993, 711.

children and mothers coming to depend on welfare, more children and mothers stuck on welfare. Simultaneously, ordinary citizens' support for social provision will continue to plummet, for they are increasingly loathe to continue to finance what Senator Daniel Patrick Moynihan recently dubbed "defining deviancy down." Told they are being repressive if they question the effects of what some insist is merely an "alternative lifestyle," voters become sullen and susceptible to those who advocate shortcut solutions to the problems generated, in part, by the current welfare system: criminalizing a wider range of activities in the hope thereby of minimizing their incidence; compelling welfare mothers to work — as if sustaining jobs were readily available for people who are in some instances so disoriented and unschooled that it takes massive intervention just to teach fundamental competence and skills at the most basic level; or even dismantling public welfare as such, with the argument that the offer of help is itself the cause of people needing help.

These are solutions only in name and sound-bite promise. But the dysfunctional patterns and perverse programs that make them seductive cannot be permitted to continue, not if we hope to remain a society remarkably open and egalitarian in its general tendency and self-understanding; not if we are as concerned for the plight and well-being of those who end up on "the dole" as we proclaim ourselves to be; and not if we hope to mitigate the daily brutalities now routinized on the mean streets of American cities. But what is it that we must do?

I propose a thought experiment. Suppose we had full funding for Head Start, a generous expansion of the earned income tax credit program, guaranteed health care for all children, mandatory identification of paternity and efficient extraction of child-support payments, extensive family-leave programs, wide availability of good yet inexpensive child care, and all the rest of the social liberal agenda. What would change? Undoubtedly the well-being of children — at least those not already harmed permanently, so far as we can predict — would be marginally improved. But it seems important to confront the reality that even as total annual social spending by all levels of government (in constant 1990 dollars) rose from $144 billion to $787 billion over the past three decades and total annual inflation-adjusted spending on welfare increased 630 percent,[13] simultaneously child

13. William J. Bennett, *The Index of Leading Cultural Indicators,* vol. 1 (Washington, D.C.: Heritage Foundation and Empower America, 1993), i.

well-being was declining and family deinstitutionalization was growing at hitherto unimaginable rates.

The Council on Families in America's report, *Marriage in America,* rightly concludes that "no amount of public investment in children could possibly offset the enormous private disinvestment that has accompanied family fragmentation and the decline of marriage." It goes on to ask, "If you were a child, would you rather have massive economic subsidies from the government or a mother and a committed father?" But this is only a rhetorical question. We know what children would say. Children want parents. They tell us they want two parents. When they do not have two parents they wonder why. It is a source of longing, even torment. And it lies at the heart of our concerns about ending "welfare as we know it."

Children lost to society in increasing numbers may be a growing phenomenon but it is one we must name for what it is: a loss, a crying shame. Protecting, preserving, and strengthening family integrity and the well-being of mothers and fathers is a way of affirming our commitment to the human person and to that democratic society which best speaks to the aspirations of such persons. The rights of persons are fundamentally social. What is at stake in the family debate and our response to it is nothing less than our capacity for human sociality. We cannot separate family matters from welfare concerns and policy.

We notice, then, and welcome certain policy innovations, including a welfare reform initiative that

> grapples for the first time with the needs of a group usually pushed to the periphery of the welfare system: unwed low-income fathers. Staking a claim to welfare reform and family values, the [Clinton] Administration wants to train these men for jobs while giving them a sense of responsibility as fathers. The goal is to involve them in their children's lives and increase what the fathers can earn in order to help lift their children out of poverty.[14]

This sort of initiative provides a welcome beginning. I also support reforms such as an enhanced earned income tax credit, revision of the federal tax code to provide more favorable treatment for married couples with chil-

14. Susan Chira, "Novel Idea in Welfare Plan: Helping Children by Helping Their Fathers," *New York Times,* Mar. 30, 1994, sec. A, p. 10.

dren, and creative new efforts to give parents and children the means to fight back against violence, housing deterioration, the drug culture, and childhood pregnancies. A preferential option for the child requires no less.

But it requires much more. A bold conceptual shift — a veritable wrenching of the old welfare *Weltanschauung* — is required if we are really going to make progress, if we are going to redesign the welfare system so that marriage and the family are bolstered rather than weakened. I will take up three matters in turn, issues with which we must grapple if we are to end "welfare as we know it" and find some way to recuperate community and restore human dignity.

Covenantal Faithfulness

The family is, as John Paul II argued in a recent "Letter to Families" during the "Year of the Family," a "civilization of love." Love is *covenanted:* it is not utilitarian, it is not romantic. It is an expression of our "social nature," and in a family "thus constituted there appears a new unity in which the relationship of communion between the parents attains complete fulfillment."[15] This is both an opportunity and a challenge in a culture such as ours. Marriage and family offer intimations of a *common* good not reducible to the interests of each member.

Now let us segue to the growing American phenomenon of out-of-wedlock births to teenaged, never-married mothers. The rates vary, going as high as 75 percent for African-American teenagers in some of America's cities, but they are soaring for every group. Betty Rollins, who did a special NBC report on this phenomenon among white unmarried teen mothers, described her experience this way:

> I am still trembling from the profound dopiness of these girls. They *want* to have these babies. They think it's neat. All their friends have babies, so they want babies. Of course, there are profound social reasons that make them want to do this, but make no mistake, they don't want condoms. They want babies. . . . Talk to any worker in the field and they will tell you that these girls are not doing it for the welfare money. But if the money were not there, that would be a major disincentive. They

15. John Paul II, "Letter to Families," *Origins* 23, no. 37 (Mar. 3, 1994): 640-41.

know that the baby is going to be paid for. They know that their mother is not going to get too mad, because the baby will be paid for.[16]

What is going on here? What "profound social reasons" are these young women responding to? Why is having a baby at age fourteen "neat," as if the baby were a new toy or a living doll that will put one in the club because one has earned a merit badge of some sort? I submit that narrow econometric analyses cannot get at this issue. It is a profound ethical matter and it speaks, I am convinced, to the breakdown of community, hence the occlusion of a horizon of meaning that would locate these young people in the world in a way that would seem to them intelligible and meaningful. "Babies having babies" is, then, both cause and consequence of a spreading disaster — the drying up of the wellsprings of social meaning and trust, the atrophy of all institutions, but first and foremost among them, the family.

I spend a lot of time talking to young people. Not that long ago, I gave a talk at a fine institution, a good two-and-a-half-hour drive from the nearest airport. Those who fetched me at the airport to drive me to the university and then, later in the day, returned me to the airport were students. They told me they have no really clear ideas about what lies ahead or what they want to be. I was struck by one young man in particular — very bright and quite perturbed by the recent suicide death of Kurt Cobain, front man for the group "Nirvana," tagged the group that embodied the lost "X" generation. He said — and, remember, he is among the privileged — that his generation was cynical. "If you have a thought that doesn't seem cynical you have to get cynical about your own noncynicism so you can be safely cynical again and not seem like a dweeb or optimist of some sort." He hailed from a rather volatile private world of once feuding parents, then a "broken home." He was thoughtful but completely at sea, and he envied earlier generations because they seemed to have "purpose." I told him I thought it wasn't so much "purpose" as that my generation grew up with adult examples of "steadiness" and "competence," and that these were fast disappearing, too. It was a sobering drive to the airport.

I was reminded of the conundrum Rousseau presents in his *Social*

16. Reported in the transcript of the question-and-answer session with William Galston following his presentation, "Beyond the Murphy Brown Debate," at the Family Policy Symposium, New York City, Dec. 10, 1993.

Contract when he notes that the good morals that would result from the founding of a just polity must, in some way, be there at the founding moment in order to guide the minds and hearts of those creating a political order. Rousseau just left it hanging there — an unresolved paradox — but maybe we need not. On, then, to "worldview" shift number two.

Rights and Wrongs

Rights properly understood are social and transitive; they are ways we acknowledge the existence and integrity of others. But in America this is less and less true. Rights have become the way we sever ourselves one from another. Rights are construed as something "I" possess, and I jealously guard them "against" you — against *all* other you's. Why must this be so?

Consider the current debate over the legitimacy of the police making unannounced sweeps of housing projects where "danger is a constant presence." The people who live in these sites, and who are striving with what can only be called heroism to protect their children, *welcome* such police initiatives and can point to concrete beneficial results when they are undertaken. Mike Barnicle, the populist columnist for the *Boston Globe,* tells the story of one 31-year-old mother with her three children. She had been calling the police for months with stories of kids on her block "who were dealing daily in guns and drugs and creating such a climate of fear that anyone interested in living normally found it an impossible task." She would line the walls and windows of her apartment with mattresses to try to hide and perhaps to absorb bullets. When police implemented a policy called "Stop and Search," she and other project mothers rejoiced: maybe, at long last, things would get better.

But, in Barnicle's words, "it ended almost as quickly as it began after lawyers [he has the ACLU in mind] and editorial writers came to the conclusion that it was a tremendous abridgment of the Constitution." So "terrorists prosper" because "simple items like a curfew" get dismissed as coercive! Barnicle goes on to list a few rights not currently

> accorded a young black mother and her three children: The right to sit on a stoop or at a playground. The right to walk to a store at any reasonable time . . . without the fear of getting caught in the cross fire. The right to spend a peaceful evening inside their own apartment. The

> right to stare out a window. The right of free association. The right to use a swing set whenever the whim strikes. The right to complain publicly about gangsters in their midst. The right to be rid of crack and cocaine in the hallway and vestibule. The right to life.

But while kids with 9 millimeter guns — or worse — have their rights, "a mother of three children has her mattresses in front of the windows of her apartment."[17]

Here Barnicle offers a powerful statement from the front lines of America's embattled neighborhoods in favor of a notion of *communal* and not simply *individual* rights. A wholesale tilting toward a narrow and then yet narrower construal of the "individual" who possesses rights has evacuated the rights of their sociality and their transitive nature.

It is time for a major restoration project, one that would help enormously in *reframing* the welfare debate toward a more ecological or communal perspective. Why not start with "tenant rights" to self-governance in their homes and community? It is they who require protection, not the drug-dealing, gun-wielding children to whose defense misguided outsiders rush with an appeal to immunity from "unlawful search and seizure" as the highest good, a trump card that defeats every familial and social imperative. Something has gone haywire in a big way here and it is time to put it right, beginning with a preferential option for the child and a recognition of the need for familial and community ties to be nourished. Perhaps if more meaning could be found in local associations, in schools, and in friendship networks not marred by drugs, violence, and precocious childbearing, those girls presently tempted to think it is "neat" to have a baby of one's own would not seek such a desperate badge as the only sign of their worth. As community responsibility grew among the poor — as we who need not struggle against the same desperate circumstances helped to lift the siege — then voters would grow heartened and more generous in their attitude about (reformed) social provisions for the poor. This ties, in turn, to worldview alteration number three.

17. Mike Barnicle, "A Plea for Family Rights," *Boston Globe*, Apr. 12, 1994, p. 21.

Ending Welfare, Expanding Well-Being

Ending "welfare as we know it" means ending welfare provision as we know it. I refer to the entire overbloated self-justifying culture of welfare as presently constituted. The *New York Times* some time ago ran a frightening piece on a disabilities program that "got out of hand." The story, highly condensed, goes like this — and it involves the privileged, not the poor, thus underscoring the dynamic in all such programs. A wealthy socialite donates money in order to make provision for "bright youngsters with learning disabilities" and she chooses an elite Manhattan school for this purpose. The program starts out in a modest way but things quickly get out of hand. A school of four hundred children suddenly finds itself with fourteen full- and part-time learning disability specialists. The "need" to prescreen all children is institutionalized. More money comes in for this freshly minted "need." As the article notes, "the disabilities field has boomed" as all sorts of people, with training that is often more than a little suspect, bill themselves as experts on "language problems" or "reading problems" or "self-esteem" problems and the like.

What happened at the Dalton school is that remedial specialists "suddenly began finding enormous numbers of bright little children with learning problems." In one three-year period fully 77 of Dalton's 215 five-year-olds were labeled "at risk." Parents panicked when told that a child tested as being at risk for "sequencing ability deficits" or "potential visual motor problems." A "learning disability industry grew at Dalton." Yet more specialists came in, at higher prices, to handle the growing caseload — a caseload determined by the specialists themselves, given their techniques for ferreting out every problem under the sun and inventing new ones. Finally, some of the teachers "battled back, refusing to let the specialists in their rooms." The upshot was an out-of-control "welfare bureaucracy," of sorts, with a huge stake in keeping its clientele at high numbers. The more learning disabilities they found, the more their own jobs were justified. The whole thing turned rapidly into a bloated mess.[18]

What has this to do with "welfare as we know it"? The analogy should be obvious. Welfare, too, professionalizes care and counsel and "turns citizens into clients," in the words of John McKnight in a series of radio interviews

18. "A Disabilities Program that 'Got Out of Hand,'" *New York Times*, Apr. 8, 1994, p. 1 and sec. B, p. 6.

entitled "Community and its Counterfeits."[19] Modern institutions, McKnight claims, are machines that redefine human beings, locating us as entities in a system rather than people in a place. When the professionals move in on communities to "solve a problem," people grow weaker, not stronger, for their "needs" are authoritatively defined by sources outside themselves.

Needs, in other words, become "the resources of the service sector of contemporary economies — what iron ore is to the steel industry, needs are to those who propose to meet them." This "never-ending search for new needs," McKnight goes on to observe, "is always at the cost of diminished citizenship. So that as these systems of service colonize your life and my life, saying that we are bundles of needs and there are institutionalized services there to meet the needs to make us whole, to make us real, what we become is less and less powerful."

McKnight sums up four "universal and inevitable" side effects of such bureaucratic and professionalized intrusion: (1) a person's life is defined by deficiencies rather than capacities; (2) the majority of all public investments in the poor goes not to the poor but to "non-poor people, who are called service providers." Thus many welfare programs are jobs programs for middle-class providers and change nothing — or make matters worse — for the poor themselves; (3) the associations of local communities atrophy as agencies and systems move in on the scene; and (4) aggregating services around people creates "new environments that will guarantee deviant behavior by the people who receive the services," for only such behavior brings forth institutionalized services.

We have come full circle to Bane and Ellwood's definition of the "eligibility-compliance" culture with which I began. What John McKnight offers to our thinking and understanding is a recognition that a family "that is a collection of clients" has "no purpose other than procreation." No wonder, then, that family fragments, the world of "mothers and children only" that is expanding so rapidly in America today, perform that procreative function. That is their mode of existence. It is a world that emerges out of fear and futility, not strength, power, and communal commitment. The world of "welfare as we know it" makes and needs clients, not citizens.

19. "Community and its Counterfeits," *Ideas* (Canadian Broadcasting Corporation), Jan. 3, 10, 17, 1994.

But as John McKnight points out, the "awakened energies" of a community can become "dissipated in a maze of government regulations" and "resources [can become] tied up in social programs which deliver services to people whose real need is income." Why not, then, make a really bold move? Why not end "welfare as we know it" by ensuring that low-income people actually get the money designated for programs designed to help low-income people? Concludes McKnight: "Let them generate economies, rather than building compulsory service economies on their backs. Governments function best . . . when they transfer resources that enable people to act on their own behalf."

Let me sum up my argument in a nutshell: to end welfare as we know it, we need the energy of revitalized communities. To revitalize communities, people need the opportunity to define their own needs and the means to realize fruitful beginnings. To have anything resembling a community, there must be a core of adult human beings committed to the task of child rearing and to loving and enduring relationships with one another.

If we want to end "welfare as we know it," this is what is necessary. I doubt, quite frankly, that we want any such thing. We will fiddle at the margins. But we lack the moral faith and vision to do more.

Beneath and beyond the State: Social, Global, and Religious Changes That Shape Welfare Reform

Max L. Stackhouse

THE LIKELIHOOD of a viable welfare policy has changed with the election of a new Congress, but it continues to depend upon three issues that are rooted in the nature and changing character of civil society. These issues reside in the background of most debates about legislative directions, yet they could blunt the force of even the best reform of welfare programs. All three are at stake in the Republicans' "Contract with America," but they were already brought into public focus by President Clinton in his address to the Fall Convocation of the Church of God in Christ in 1993. In the context of comments on crime and joblessness in our cities, Clinton spoke of the crisis of the family, the changing role of the United States in the world, and the responsibilities of the churches. He said: "Where there are no families, where there is no order, where there is no hope, where we are reducing the size of the armed services because we have won the Cold War, who will be there to give structure, discipline and love to these children? You [the clergy] must do that and we [the government] must help."[1]

The statement is quite direct, and the themes it summarizes run through the whole address. The implications are vast, although it is doubtful that the President and his welfare advisors were fully aware of everything that his remarks imply for his own programs. He sees social and economic distress as realities rooted in the breakdown of family life, the changing

1. "Excerpts from Clinton's Speech to Black Ministers," *New York Times*, Nov. 14, 1993, p. 24.

character of international life, and the loss of moral and spiritual vision — themes that were also decisive in the 1994 election and that brought proposals for even more radical restructuring of welfare programs. What Clinton suggested is what his critics are also saying: the inner fabric of the common life is threatened for future generations.

Significantly, Clinton also noted the role that religion must play in upholding the structure of the common life, a role that inevitably has a decisive if disputed relation to government and public policy. At another meeting with religious leaders, Clinton referred with great enthusiasm to the book *The Culture of Disbelief* by Professor Stephen Carter of Yale Law School.[2] Carter argues that present interpretations of the separation of church and state, which blot out overt acknowledgment of the role of religion in society, are contrary to the intent of the First Amendment of the Constitution. In his speech to the pastors, President Clinton put it this way: "There are changes we can make from the outside in — that's the job of the President and the Congress and the governors and the mayors and the social service agencies. And then, there are some changes we're going to have to make from the inside out, or the others won't matter."[3]

A great issue is raised for this society at the very moment when the twentieth-century struggles against the totalitarianism of the fascist right and the communist left seem to be at an end. A participatory, democratic, compassionate, and inclusive society, one would expect, could now flourish with fewer challenges. But the glories of historical triumph are brief. If they shunt us away from one terror, we lurch toward others. Moreover, as Clinton's statement suggests, for at least some people — the least advantaged, including particularly racial minorities and many on welfare — civil society is dissolving. Life is experienced as a social void marked by isolation, violence, dependency, and uselessness.

Clinton's statement further recognizes the limits of what government can do, even if its leaders take their duties very seriously and seek to reverse the forces of disintegration. The reason for government's limited power is that every government, and especially a democratic one, depends on "society," on what many call "civil society." States cannot themselves generate or sustain the delicate but indispensable attitudes of mutual regard, the frail but necessary habits of responsibility, or those feeble but

2. Carter, *The Culture of Disbelief* (New York: Basic Books, 1993).

3. "Excerpts from Clinton's Speech."

essential institutions of practical trust, interaction, productivity, and exchange that sustain the viability of social life. Most important, states cannot produce the necessary but fragile and fundamental sense of meaning that sustains hope, discipline, and love.

Today the social fabric of the common life is being ripped apart in many places. New tissues of interdependency may also be forming, but some people are being left out of the new connections. Clinton recognizes that transformations are taking place at local levels that exacerbate the current crises in family life and thus in personality formation. Further, he recognizes the changes in the global situation that fundamentally alter our national role in the world. We are not bound together by a common enemy as we have been in the past, and some citizens who were useful in facing that threat are now no longer needed.[4] Thus, established assumptions about who "we" are, on which many policies have been based, are subject to doubt. Members of the "we" have become again a "they."

One underlying problem is the diminishing legitimacy of the "social contract" theory by which modern America has understood itself. This is the view that a religiously, metaphysically, and morally neutral rationality will be exercised by citizens in calculating what is good for each as individuals and for the society as a collectivity organized into a state, with the presumption that the good of each and the good of the whole will harmonize. In fact, no civil society, certainly not that of the United States, has ever been based on this rationalistic theory alone.[5] It neither grasps how things are nor tells us how they ought to be. Such a view simply cannot account for those reasonable patterns of order and meaning around which civil societies are in fact formed, and thus on which states are founded, laws are based, personal loyalties are sustained, and common senses of obligation, purpose, and dignity are known.

The defeat of fascism and the collapse of communism in our century surely reveal, among other things, that even total state control "for the sake

4. I am indebted to my colleague Peter Paris for this point. In "The Dream of an Inter-racial Society — Thirty Years After," a paper delivered at the American Academy of Religion Annual Meeting, Fall 1993, he suggested that those who built America by supplying the manual labor and who later joined the army to find jobs are now less necessary for the well-being of the future. A sense of uselessness tragically infects large portions of our citizenry.

5. See Adam Seligman, *The Idea of Civil Society* (New York: Free Press, 1992). Seligman argues convincingly that the core of contemporary civil society was grounded in philosophical theology, although he is skeptical about it today.

of 'the people'" (whether a nation or a class) cannot generate a civil society. In fact, the heavy hand of statism seems to arise where civil society is confused with government and where the state's domination smothers society. Massive efforts at reconstruction are required to revive this vital fabric of social life when it is damaged, as we easily see in Eastern Europe today. But it seems equally clear from the present condition of many urban areas in the United States that a rationalistic individualism cannot build and sustain civil society either. Furthermore, the external pressures from globally linked systems of technology, commerce, finance, communication, and law make the construction or reconstruction of a civil society within the boundaries of a single state more and more difficult. Thus, the question before the "triumphant" West after the collapse of modern "statism," left and right, is whether anything can create and sustain, renew or reform, a civil society under the changed conditions we now face, for it is only within a civil society that a consensus about the why, how, wherefore, and for whom of welfare can be formed.

We may well have to face the fact: much of what has been thought to be private turns out to be decisive for public life, and much of what was thought to be rational turns out to be dependent on public commitments and institutions that are nongovernmental and incapable of enforcement by states. Some vital social realities are, in other words, neither individual and private nor governmental and public. They stand, instead, between individuals and collectivities, beneath and beyond the state.

These social realities are often religious in root and character. We easily notice the religious dimension when we look elsewhere, even if we deny it at home. One cannot understand the life of South Asia without considering Hinduism, of the Arabic world without Islam, or of central and southern Africa without taking the traditions of tribal religion into account. Nor would we think of trying to explain the realities of Japan, Korea, or China — even contemporary post-Maoist China — without explicit reference to Confucianism and Buddhism.[6] Similarly, one cannot

6. One must also mention that new studies have been appearing documenting how changes of religion bring about altered forms of civil society. See, for example, David Martin, *Tongues of Fire* (New York: Free Press, 1990); M. Rubinstein, *The Protestant Community on Modern Taiwan* (Armonk, N.Y.: Sharpe, 1991); and P. Berger and Hsin-Huang Michael Hsiao, eds., *In Search of an Asian Development Model* (Rutgers, N.J.: Transaction Books, 1988).

understand what Europe is without recognizing the formative roles of Catholicism and Protestantism. Of course, in each case these religious influences are well mixed with many social, cultural, and historical forces, including various attempts to reject or deny the role of religion. But the denial cannot be sustained. In spite of widespread secularization, religion is more decisive than any other institution over time for the social environments of people, the channels of real and perceived opportunities, and the capacity of individuals and collective groups to cope with what they experience. These realities, indeed, shape the way in which science, law, technology, philosophy, and government, as well as other religions, are perceived and treated. And so it is here.[7]

Recognizing that these "supra-personal," "supra-communal," and "supra-national" religious realities are a powerful force does not say that all religions are good, or that they are all equal in merit. It does pose issues that are very difficult for many, for it forces us to reconsider the role that religion might play in public discourse and political decisions.[8] But failure to treat religion as a factor in forming and sustaining the common life will produce a failure in social policy.

The problem is this: below the state, civil society is being deconstructed — as we can see especially in the breakdown of the family; and beyond the state, a wider civilization is being reconstructed — as we can see in new patterns of transnational technological and economic interaction. On the one hand, individuals interact emotionally and sexually on the basis of a new serial monogamy, which produces all sorts of blended and partial or alternative, often quite temporary, "families." On the other hand,

7. I am indebted to Lewis S. Mudge on this point, especially his new work (in progress). Tentatively titled *Seeking the Good in Common,* it treats the reality, necessity, and difficulties of religion in civil society today. For contrasting views of how it should be done, even if there is agreement that it can and should be done, see Richard J. Neuhaus, *The Naked Public Square,* 2nd ed. (Grand Rapids, Mich.: Eerdmans, 1984), and A. J. Reichley, *Religion in American Public Life* (Washington, D.C.: Brookings, 1985).

8. See Samuel P. Huntington, "The Clash of Civilizations?" *Foreign Affairs,* Summer 1993, 22-49, with "Comments" by K. Mahbubani, R. L. Bartley, L. Binyan, J. J. Kirkpatrick, et al., *Foreign Affairs,* Sept.–Oct. 1993, 10-26, and "Response" by Huntington, *Foreign Affairs,* Nov.–Dec. 1993, 186-94. Cf. especially Roland Robertson and W. R. Garrett, eds. *Religion and Global Order* (New York: Paragon House, 1991); W. C. Roof, ed., *World Order and Religion* (Albany, N.Y.: SUNY, 1991); and my *Creeds, Society and Human Rights: A Study in Three Cultures* (Grand Rapids, Mich.: Eerdmans, 1985).

modern networks of corporations are creating flexible and interactive systems of production and distribution, domination and dependency, fads and standards of excellence. Such changes redesign our love lives and our work lives; they reduce popular interest in political problems and erode confidence in government programs' capacity to address social problems. Even more, they invite a reexamination of the causes of poverty and of the kinds of needs that can and should be met through public policy.[9]

The transformations of civil society, which some experience as a breakdown at local levels and which others see as a geoeconomic reconstruction at international levels, render some people functionally powerless in the face of forces they do not understand and cannot control. It makes, particularly, the near poor — the "working poor" — more vulnerable, at least in the short run, even if it promises to bring wider populations around the world into the middle classes in the long run. The global market puts some people in more intense competition with workers internationally, and reduces the willingness to raise taxes for social services, lest it make corporations less competitive or more inclined to move elsewhere. Even more, it invites further automation of a range of jobs, a fact that makes whole categories of labor dispensable. Again, the sense of having common values, interests, or purposes that would prompt "us" to take care of "our own" is eroded by the fact that the "we" with whom we share our most immediate values, interests, or purposes is redefined.

Compounding the problem is the growing religious heterogeneity of societies. For the sense of what ought to be done about the poor is inevitably influenced by religion, the chief bearer of ethical values. Views of wealth or of poverty as blessing or curse, as deserved or unmerited, as something to be resisted as temptation or accepted as preordained lot, vary widely in religions. And the place of charity, almsgiving, benevolence, diligence, thriftiness, stewardship, work, and equality as marks of fidelity or virtue varies widely in the world's religious ethics. The fact of pluralism further disinclines many from attending to religion as a factor.[10] Yet religious ethics

9. See Gertrude Himmelfarb, *Poverty and Compassion* (New York: Knopf, 1991), for a fascinating account of the changing reputation of poverty, its nature, causes, and cures, with special reference to the Victorian era, when social work was established as a profession.

10. Contemporary thought is, however, very inconsistent on the matter of pluralism. A variety of political theories and parties is thought to be healthy for politics;

remains as an inevitable and indispensable, even if disputatious, factor in human society.[11] Further, the kind of religious ethic that forms persons and informs the structures of the common life will shape the entire social system. Any approach to welfare policy that does not comprehend the reality and power of religion will be self-defeating.

Religion, in this view, is any deep belief in or honoring of an ultimate source or norm of meaning that evokes dedication to higher principles or purposes and generates bonds or associations between people that would not otherwise be present. Obviously, religion comes in many forms and thus shapes personal lives and civilizations differently, for each religion bears distinct implications for the several capacities of human personality and sociality. Each religion, in short, bonds people into particular kinds of relationships that sustain identity and community and thus shapes a society as a whole. Although each aspect of society — the family or the economy, for example — has its own relative integrity, and although the whole of society does not always recognize how dependent its fabric is on its own moral and spiritual center, religion is the core of civilization that gives distinctive shape to the other aspects of life.[12]

It is important to stress this factor in the current context, in part because

---

the competition of many corporations and products is held to be good for the economy; the availability of a variety of colleges and philosophies of learning is celebrated in education; but pluralism in religion is often taken to discredit this aspect of human social existence.

11. The fact that people argue about religion, and think that arguments count — that utter unreasonableness or obvious injustice discredits one religious position in the face of another — indicates that religions can be evaluated by theology and ethics in public discourse.

12. On this point, "liberal" Ernst Troeltsch's *The Social Teachings of the Christian Churches* (New York: Macmillan, 1931) suggests that ecclesiology is the clue to the development of civilizations and that ecclesiology is informed by both religious commitments and the practical demands of the various "departments of life" that constitute society. His view correlates with those of "conservative" Abraham Kuyper, who developed a theory of the "spheres" of society in *Lectures on Calvinism* (Grand Rapids, Mich.: Eerdmans, 1931). Without citing these theologians, John F. A. Taylor, in *Masks of Society* (New York: Appleton-Century Crofts, 1966), and Michael Walzer, in *Spheres of Justice* (New York: Basic Books, 1983), argue similar points. Cf. also my "Religion, Society and the Independent Sector: Key Elements of a General Theory," in Conrad Cherry and Rowland A. Sherrill, eds., *Religion, The Independent Sector and American Culture* (Atlanta: Scholars Press, 1992), esp. 11-30.

it is so often neglected.[13] But it is neglected to our peril. The cross-cultural and historical evidence is quite compelling: if religion is not present or its influence is minimal, selves and societies suffer. Further, the character of a religion counts. A religion that stresses as marks of faith a mutually supportive family life, disciplined learning, a global vision, and the formation of independent institutions for the production of wealth will shape persons and societies in a way that is quite distinct from one that stresses individual meditation, ecstatic experience, sacred places, and an economy centered in the palace. For these reasons, we shall pay particular attention to religious influences as we look at the two markers of change in contemporary civil society, the family and the corporation, as these bear on welfare policy.

Civil Society and Family Life

A recent cross-cultural analysis of the difficulties of civil society and its relationship to welfare policy, family life, and the changing patterns of economic life can be found in Alan Wolfe's *Whose Keeper?*[14] Wolfe argues that modern civil societies have been eroded by a dependence on paternalistic government, on the one hand, and by an ideology of individualistic self-fulfillment that appears particularly in market economies, on the other. This is true all over the West, he thinks, but Sweden, with its extensive welfare state provisions within a basically capitalist framework, serves as the paradigm of how these two tendencies have converged in modern "progressive" welfare policy. Indeed, Sweden has been seen as an ideal for democratic thinkers with a social conscience for many decades. It has undertaken extensive social planning while maximizing freedom in personal life. For instance, few countries in the world are more permissive with regard to sexual ethics and living arrangements or have greater provision

13. In the massive collection of major current debates about "Poverty, the Underclass, and Public Policy" edited by Mary Corcoran and Sheldon Danziger at the University of Michigan (Digicopy Corporation, 1993; 1162 pp.), there is no substantive reference to religion. Yet any worker in the minority communities in the city, or in areas of rural poverty, knows that the most influential institutions are religious. This is in addition to the fact stated above that religion shapes the response of the society to people in need.

14. Wolfe, *Whose Keeper? Social Science and Moral Obligation* (Berkeley: Univ. of California Press, 1989).

for child care, support of single-parent families, and availability of social services.

Wolfe sympathetically studies this society and comes to the reluctant conclusion that, despite its good intentions, this "third way" between statist policy and individualistic lifestyle erodes civil society and damages people. Here we do not find either an unfettered free market or a harsh command economy, and those who think that evil resides in one or another of these must look again. But neither is it a place where things visibly improve for the weaker segments of society. To be sure, most "basic needs" are met, but it is not clear that people therefore find it possible to establish deeper, more enduring relationships or to live more satisfying lives. In fact, suicide, alcoholism, and crime rates continue to rise, and begin to approach those of American cities. Further, the government finds that funds for its programs become more difficult to obtain as both capital and jobs begin to flee the tax rates necessary to provide the extensive social services. More problematic is the fact that the people lose heart with what they do have. He concludes that this model of a semisocialized, democratic, mixed (capitalist) economy is in difficulty.[15] The center is not holding.

Wolfe sees Sweden as representative in small of the larger patterns that are taking shape in the West more generally. Segments of the population become permanent wards of the state, which serves as provider and protector. This establishes a pervasive bureaucratic paternalism, especially in the case of single-parent mothers. Similarly, males are engaged in serial monogamy, and children are afflicted with problems of motivation and concentration that cause great difficulties in school. More and more people develop consumption-driven lifestyles detached from civic participation, stable families, and productive economic units.

What is missing is the capability to form and sustain those enduring habits, commitments, relationships, and institutions that enable people to participate fully in the common life and to support public policies of compassion and social justice for those in distress. Thus, Wolfe calls upon us to heed the appeals of the communitarian voices in contemporary social

15. Similar comparative studies reporting the deleterious effects of modernity on family life cross-culturally can be found in David Popenoe, *Disturbing the Nest* (New York: de Gruyter, 1988) and Richard Posner, *Sex and Reason* (Cambridge: Harvard Univ. Press, 1992). In different ways, they both see problems in the Swedish linkage of permissive family life and socialistic politics.

theory. "We need," he writes, "civil society — families, communities, friendship networks, solidaristic workplace ties, voluntarism, spontaneous groups and movements . . . to complete the project of modernity."[16] Later he writes that the sense of fellowship found in the "small town, the voluntary association, the spirit of the people — these aspects of how Americans viewed themselves contained such an emphasis on trust, friendship, and community that people simply assumed that they would always be there."[17] It is just these qualities that allow persons to develop a degree of independence from parents and the state, to form committed relationships, and to become productive members of society — a source of support for neighbors in need. And it is these qualities that must be cultivated in the next generation if we are to reduce the percentage of dependent persons and increase the percentage of integrated, contributing members of society.

However, Wolfe's telling study is problematic just at this point. As wide-ranging as his analysis is, it does not seem to grasp what in fact it takes to form and sustain a civil society. It simply is not clear that the community spirit he seeks was "always there." It was not "there," in the sense he intends, in Native American life, and it was not there in the relationships between masters and slaves, in Daniel Boone's Kentucky, or Wyatt Earp's boom towns, or in the factories of the robber barons, any more than it was always there among the ancient warring tribes of Europe, or during the feudal period of Western history. And it is not there in many parts of the world today. Such a social fabric has to be created. The commitment to and support for responsible relationships in responsive organizations has to be nurtured for such a social fabric to be sustained. Indeed, if we look at many places around the globe, we find not some natural benevolent community spirit, but the closing of ranks against those who do not fit our enclave, or even the genocidal clash of ethnic, class, or status groups. And if extensive welfare provisions are not sustainable in a homogenous country like Sweden, it seems likely that something other than state action has to create a spirit of responsibility and care.

At this point we can discover one of the great problems of much modern social theory as it bears on welfare. Arguments for the just and compassionate care of the neighbor often presume that there is an innate propensity to establish nurturing families, productive work habits, and a

16. Wolfe, 20.
17. Wolfe, 77.

hospitable mutuality that shares the bounty of nature. Many also presume that these impulses and resources are maliciously disrupted by the demands of modern life, which have turned some into rich victors and others into poor victims, and that we should return to a previous form of life. This romantic view has little understanding of how cruel and unstable primary communities and families can be, or of the real foundations for those human associations that do transcend group egoism, harness interests to mutual projects that develop resources beyond those needed for subsistence, and engender a commitment to care for or empower the needy neighbor.

In fact, such attitudes and bonds are created by certain kinds of religion more than by any other set of forces. They are, to put it another way, supernatural, not natural. Organized religion established the civil society of America, as Tocqueville and others have suggested, just as organized religions in quite different forms civilized India, China, and the Mid-East in quite different directions long before America was discovered. And in only some civilizations was civil society in anything like the pattern that Wolfe praises developed, for in only some of these was the religion of a sort that nurtured and developed the formation of voluntary communities that engendered the associational forms he seeks.[18]

The problem, however, is not only the failure of one scholar who ignores decisive forces that actually formed the tissues of civil society on which families, corporations, and responsible politics depend.[19] The problem is that this widespread view shows little comprehension of the socioreligious foundations on which basic human bonding, creative economic cooperation, and social interdependence rests.[20] Wolfe exempli-

18. No other single American author has developed this theme as fully as James Luther Adams. See his *Voluntary Associations*, ed. J. R. Engel (Chicago: Exploration Press, 1986) and *Voluntary Associations: The Study of Groups in Free Societies*, ed. D. B. Robertson (Richmond: John Knox Press, 1966). See also the sources cited in notes 5, 6, and 12 above, and my *Creeds, Society, and Human Rights.*

19. We shall deal with some of these questions later, but it is important to note here that the corporation is based on very complex cooperative values. See Max Stackhouse et al., eds., *On Moral Business: Classical and Contemporary Resources on Ethics and Economic Life* (Grand Rapids, Mich.: Eerdmans, 1995) and my "The Moral Roots of the Modern Corporation," *Theology and Public Policy* 5, no. 1 (1993): 29-39.

20. This point is recognized in the volume that is perhaps the best single cross-cultural overview of the multiple factors that shape the family: Alan Tapper, *The Family in the Welfare State* (North Sydney, N.S.W.: Allen & Unwin, 1990).

fies a postreligious obliviousness to the key factor in the very topic he is investigating. He knows that something more is necessary, for modern civil societies are using up their moral and spiritual capital without replacing it. But he holds that humans build their morality out of their felt social needs since there are no objective sources of meaning or guidelines to be discovered.[21] Thus the message becomes thin: since we now know that we construct our own morality, and it is the basis of civil society, let us henceforth construct a nice one.[22]

Wolfe knows that politics, with its inevitable lust for power, and economics, with its inescapable desire for gain, cannot alone or together form the moral center of society, any more than sexuality itself can hold family life together — even though power, wealth, and sex are necessary to human existence. In fact, welfare policies are necessary in part because power, wealth, and sex do not and cannot evoke a sustaining love at the most intimate level, a social generosity at the institutional level, or a sense of justice at an international level. But it is precisely enduring and reliable bonding along these dimensions that is essential if the world that is aborning is to be humane. What is required for public life is a spiritual and moral awareness, one that awakens a capacity for transcendence, touches the core of the individual's being, and creates the vision of a new kind of relationship. This is what constitutes a significant community spirit and establishes the foundation for a civil society, and hence for responsible persons, the family, the economy and, finally, the state itself. In other words, the morality Wolfe wants requires religion. Without religion, or with an inadequate one, civil society will break down or become either impervious to need or incapable of drawing people into creative participation in the common life.

21. See esp. ch. 8, "The Social Construction of Morality." He explores the theme of the human construction of meaning more extensively in *The Human Difference: Animal, Computer and the Necessity of Social Science* (Berkeley: Univ. of California Press, 1993).

22. Although Wolfe cites Robert Bellah et al., *The Good Society* (New York: Knopf, 1991) as a model of what he is after, he appears to be closer to Amitai Etzioni, *The Moral Dimension: Toward a New Economics* (New York: Free Press, 1988), but without awareness of Etzioni's appreciation of Martin Buber.

The Family Crisis

Wolfe is surely correct that many of the problems of civil society appear in the data about family life. The transformations that have taken place in the last generation are dramatic. The most commonly cited figures for the U.S. are these:

- In 1960, 15% of the households did not constitute a "family"; in 1990, 30% did not.
- "Nonfamily" households are those headed by divorced people, widows, students, the unmarried, and single parents (although labeling this last group as "nonfamily" has been heatedly disputed). Only a quarter of all households now comprise a married couple with children.
- One-third of all married couples with children are "blended" families, with "step" relatives.
- People marry later, and although cohabitation fills the gap, it correlates with a higher divorce rate. Two-thirds of 1970's birth cohort are likely to end their first marriage.
- Rates of venereal disease, of pregnancy and childbearing by unmarried teens, and of AFDC receipt by young mothers are up sharply.
- Rates of domestic and child abuse are up, and families are increasingly being abandoned by males.
- The crisis of the family is most dramatic in the black population, but it is increasingly a problem also in other minority groups and in the less-educated levels of the white community.

Such data are summarized in a number of recent publications, from the widely regarded work of Sara McLanahan to a recent more popular article by Barbara Dafoe Whitehead. Whitehead's article brought to a wider audience what has been debated in leading research centers for a decade.[23]

23. S. McLanahan and Gary Sandefur, *Growing Up with a Single Parent* (Cambridge: Harvard Univ. Press, 1994) and Barbara Dafoe Whitehead, "Dan Quayle Was Right," *Atlantic Monthly*, Apr. 1993, 47ff. The wider scholarly debate is summarized in the presidential address at the annual meeting of the Population Association of America by Larry L. Bumpass, "What's Happening to the Family? Interactions Between Demographic and Institutional Change," *Demography* 27, no. 4 (1990): 483-98. See also the Poponoe and Posner books cited in n. 15.

She offers, further, an argument about why these negative trends have occurred. Many of the factors are political and economic in nature, but one is essentially cultural: the attempt, since the 1960s, to construct a new morality for family life by invoking a no-fault theory of individual fulfillment not subject to social, communal, ethical, or religious constraint. Whitehead believes that this drive for self-fulfillment has augmented every problem of family breakdown and proven to be a disaster for society — especially for children. In a recent interview, she summarized these widely held conclusions:

> The absence of a two-parent family . . . [is] a central cause of many of our most vexing social problems. . . . Children of divorce and children in single-parent households are more likely than other children to be poor, to have emotional and behavioral problems, to drop out of high school, to abuse drugs and to be in trouble with the law. . . . Family diversity . . . dramatically weakens and undermines society, placing new burdens on schools, courts, prisons and the welfare system.[24]

There is great disagreement about why stable two-parent families have become so endangered and rare, although the reality of the trends is widely acknowledged. Some blame welfare programs,[25] while others blame the cultural ideologies that have brought notions of liberation to modern women.[26] Opponents of these two positions argue that some, especially minority youth, have declining wage opportunities, which undermines their ability to support a family.[27] Still others speak of the increased material independence of women made possible by new avenues of access to education, birth control, and the job market; no longer having to rely on permanent attachments to men for their economic well-being, women have gradually empowered themselves in building alternative models of family life.[28]

24. "Bad News for Kids of Divorce," by Charles Kenney, *Boston Globe,* April 6, 1993, pp. 63-64.

25. Charles Murray, *Losing Ground: American Social Policy 1950–1980* (New York: Basic Books, 1984).

26. See George Gilder, *Men and Marriage* (Gretna: Pelican, 1986).

27. William J. Wilson, *The Truly Disadvantaged* (Chicago: Univ. of Chicago Press, 1987).

28. Carolyn Johnston, *Sexual Power: Feminism and the Family in America* (Tuscaloosa: Univ. of Alabama Press, 1992).

Obviously economic factors play a role. These were recently summarized in Alice Rivlin's *Reviving the American Dream.*[29] She identifies two negative trends that are related to the deteriorating condition of marriages and families in America. First, while the real income of American families in the post–World War II period rose at a rate of about 3 percent per year until about 1973, since then it has stopped growing. At the same time, the gap between the higher and the lower brackets has been widening, putting pressure on the American family. Families would be in even worse economic shape than they are were it not for the unprecedented entry of women into the paid workforce — a change that is itself sure to shape the next generation, if in unpredictable ways.

The second, and related, economic problem stems from current shifts in the technology of production. With the further automation of production and the shift of some kinds of production overseas, where workers will labor for much less, the demand for low-skill workers in America is likely to continue to decline, making it harder for such workers to find sufficiently remunerative work, or any work at all. At the same time, immigrant populations are eager to enter the United States to do jobs that U.S. workers are reluctant to do; but while many immigrants flourish, others fall into the same patterns that attend the least advantaged already. Such economic trends suggest the possibility that more families will break up, leaving more scars on people and the civil society while putting more demands on social services.

No consensus has emerged concerning the relative effect of economic factors as distinct from ideational ones — cultural, ideological, and intellectual trends and forces. What caused what? It would be strange if the joblessness of minority males was not related to both cultural and economic forces, or if the dramatic movement of women into the workforce was not brought about by both material and ideological influences and did not have both material and cultural consequences. However, we do not know which chicken laid which egg and which egg hatched which chicken. In any event, the overall effect is the restructuring of the American family, leading toward more dual-career families, more single parents, and fewer children at all levels of the economic scale. And parents at the lower end of the ladder are

29. Rivlin, *Reviving the American Dream* (Washington, D.C.: Brookings, 1993). See also Robert Solow's discerning review in the *New York Review of Books,* Mar. 25, 1993, pp. 12ff.

finding it increasingly difficult to afford child care and to gain the educational advantages by which they and their children may prepare themselves for the world of the future.

It is curious and worthy of note that one factor is often overlooked in this research: religion. Many researchers simply assume that religion is a consequence or by-product of social forces and is not an independent causative influence. Nevertheless, the data are rather clear that strongly religious Jewish, Catholic, evangelical, Muslim, Confucian, and Hindu families have a lower incidence of single parenthood and higher rate of children going to college and into higher-paying jobs than do nonreligious families of the same ethnic, class, and educational status. Stable families tend also to support community involvements, while both parents and children of one-parent families more frequently become dropouts from religious and community organizations.[30] Further, the kind of family life that fosters fullest participation in the society, according to contemporary social research, is precisely the family advocated by the overwhelming majority of church teachings.[31]

Such findings are directly pertinent to questions of public policy regarding welfare, for they raise the issue of whether it is possible to devise government policies that would support and not inhibit those institutions that teach people how to love, and thus how to form viable networks of reliability, mutuality, trust, and trustworthiness. Leaving aside for the moment the question of whether or not the various teachings of those institutions are true in an ultimate or metaphysical sense, such patterns nurture generations after generations and enable them to study, stay healthy, get to

30. Linda Waite, "Present Trends in Family Studies: An Address to the Religion and the American Family Conference," Chicago, Sept. 12, 1992. See also William D'Antonio, *Religion and Family* (New York: Free Press, 1982) and Arland Thornton, *Religion and the Family Connection* (New York: Crossroad, 1993).

31. See J. Gordon Melton, *The Churches Speak on Sex and Family Life* (Detroit: Gale Research, 1991). See also Robert Wuthnow and Virginia Hodgkinson, *Faith and Philanthropy in America* (San Francisco: Jossey-Bass, 1991). I do not take up here the enormous battles now taking place in the ecumenical Protestant ("liberal") churches about sexuality and the new forms of family life. Lutherans, Presbyterians, Episcopalians, Methodists, and many others are embroiled in controversy about what the churches should teach and preach about homosexual marriages, divorce, premarital intercourse, abortion, etc. I intend to investigate the implications of these debates for the economic status of the family in *For Richer and for Poorer* (forthcoming).

school or work on time, become productive members of the community and, in brief, to participate in the tissues of civil society in ways that sustain souls and civilizations. Without these, we face the awful prospect of becoming a brutal society, marked by distrust, instability, drug abuse, casual liaisons, economic exploitation, neglected children, and violence. Such a degeneracy would correspond to the new nihilism that tends toward the barbaric, the social corollary of those contemporary philosophies advocating deconstruction of everything normative.[32]

Influences beyond the State

It is not, however, only at the levels of family — beneath the state — that we confront critical issues of civil society; it is also in the international arena — beyond the state. And here we are in a new era, the full significance of which we have only begun to grasp. The fall of the Berlin Wall marked the end of the era in which the state was understood to be the decisive instrument to guide the whole of life, the guarantor of the social and economic well-being of the citizenry. Some have suggested that we have come to the end of the period that began with the Peace of Westphalia.[33] That pact ended the "wars of religion" in 1648 and established for modernity the principle of national sovereignty. Thereafter, the state took responsibility for the welfare of the people in its territory and established, under the doctrine *cuius regio, eius religio,* a national faith to legitimate its common life — thereby echoing the practices of ancient pagan tribes and regimes. In spite of the fact that we have surpassed the establishment of religion under the impress of various separatist, independent, and "free church" movements, so that freedom of religion is now widely recognized as a human right, we have not surpassed the presumed moral priority of the state's responsibility for those in a territory or the notion that every social crisis must be resolved by a policy of state. For many the government

32. See G. Himmelfarb, *On Looking into the Abyss* (New York: Knopf, 1994) and R. H. Girgenti et al., *Religious Responses to Violence* (N.Y. State Religious Leaders Conference, 1993).

33. This was the theme of a presentation by Brian Hehir at a meeting of the Harvard Business and Harvard Divinity schools faculties, January 1993. See also R. D. Kaplan, "The Coming Anarchy," *Atlantic Monthly,* Feb. 1994, 44ff.

remains the most comprehensive horizon of morality imaginable, the frame within which all social morality is considered.

However, it turns out that states shed as much blood as does religion — if not more. And the great story of the twentieth century has been the rise and defeat of various socialisms. Socialism shared with religion the notion that something is prior to the state, but it seldom had much tolerance for religion. Twentieth-century socialism came in many varieties: national socialism in Central Europe, proletarian socialism in Eastern Europe, liberationist socialism in former colonies, democratic socialism in Western Europe. Each variety was marked by the use of state powers to restrict nonstate corporate developments, both religious and economic, and to engineer social objectives within a political framework. But they have all failed. And this universal failure is forcing painful reconsideration of what the state can and should do in regard to welfare.

These matters of course are much debated around the world, and no small amount of conflict persists as to what should be done by government and what should be left to other institutions. It is no longer new news whatsoever to note that, except for Cuba, North Korea, and Burma, every government around the world is discussing the merits of deregulation and privatization, and is seeking to attract transnational corporations. Indeed, the NAFTA and GATT agreements of 1993 and 1994 signal the political acknowledgment that worldwide trade by corporations is more necessary to the well-being of more people than protectionist impulses based on nation, class, government, or ideology. Geoeconomics is the new name for geopolitics, and any government that does not recognize this agenda is quickly replaced.

But religion has become even more central to the public agenda, to the great surprise and consternation of many. It appears not only that organized religion played a decisive role in the fall of the Wall,[34] but that the resurgent religions of the world are among the critical forces that are reshaping international life. Indeed, the great traditions now shape the deep political cultures of great clusters of states — the Islamic, the Confucian,

34. See, e.g., my "White Candles vs Red Flags," *Religion in Eastern Europe* (formerly *Occasional Papers on Religion in Eastern Europe*) 12, no. 5 (Oct. 1992): 1-18; Barbara Green, "Looking Back on a Closing Chapter," *Religion in Eastern Europe* 12, no. 6 (Dec. 1992): 1-13; and William Everett, *Neue Öffentlichkeit in neuem Bund: Theologische Reflexionen zur Kirche in der Wende* (Forschungsstätte der Evangelischen Studiengemeinschaft, Reihe B, Nr. 18, Dez., 1992).

the Hindic worlds — that can be compared to civilizational versions of tectonic plates. They move very slowly, but they engender social earthquakes when they clash.[35] Further, with the demise of socialism as the most militant antireligious humanism of our era, we face a plethora of "New Age" religions (mostly revitalized old paganisms or new syncretistic faiths) that are external to the capacity of every government and every "classic" religious tradition to control. We find not only a world market of commerce and corporations, but a world bazaar of convictions and creeds.[36] Each constitutes a much larger public than any national citizenry or any cultural-linguistic group. Certain spiritual forces, in other words, have an affinity with multinational material ones, which are themselves generating the foundations for a new civilization outside the confines of any state, and these are together reshaping our sense of what is public and what could count as basic principles to guide the common life.[37] A new convergence of conviction and interest now impacts our ethos and influences what we shall have to consider in regard to any reform of welfare, for one offers a vision of how the good life ought to be lived, and the other enlarges the means by which the good life, insofar as it is to be had on earth, might be gained.

Thanks to a number of highly regarded scholars,[38] we can identify a number of consequences of these developments:

- The United States has, with considerable uncertainty, become the policeman of the world, requiring highly mobile and technically trained military forces, but not massive numbers of ground troops, thereby throwing many ordinary soldiers into the job market — or unemployment.

35. See Samuel Huntington's article and the responses to it, cited in note 8, above.

36. See, for example, R. Robertson and W. R. Garrett, eds., *Religion and Global Order: Religion and the Political Order,* vol. 4 (New York: Paragon House, 1991), and David Krieger, *The New Universalism* (Maryknoll, N.Y.: Orbis Books, 1991).

37. See, e.g., A. W. Musschenga and B. Boorzanger, eds., *Morality, Worldview and the Law* (Assen, Netherlands: Van Gorcum, 1992); M. Featherstone, ed., *Global Culture: Nationalism, Globalization and Modernity* (London: Sage, 1990); and G. Outka and J. P. Reeder, eds., *Prospects for a Common Morality* (Princeton: Princeton Univ. Press, 1992).

38. See especially Robert Reich, *The Work of Nations* (New York: Knopf, 1991); Paul Kennedy, *Preparing for the 21st Century* (New York: Random House, 1993); and Roger J. Vaughan, *Making Work Pay* (Washington, D.C.: Corporation for Enterprise Development, 1992).

- Less-skilled workers face direct competition from the workers of less-developed countries, which attract labor-intensive industries, while info-tech and bio-tech capability spreads and exposes other segments of the population also to the pressures of competition.
- Both Europe and the Pacific Rim countries offer competitive human, technological, and organizational resources that require U.S. businesses to reduce their workforces and develop worldwide management and marketing capacities. Nationalistic policies mean obsolescence.
- Electronic information and communication systems as well as new corporate structures require fewer managers to gather and process information, mediate instructions, and coordinate operations. Teams are replacing hierarchies, demanding new personality skills.
- The skills most demanded and rewarded in the future will be those involving higher education, capacities for abstract, symbolic thinking, and the ability to work cross-culturally and with multiple subcultures.
- Most workers will have to find positions in smaller firms that support or supply larger ones, develop products for distinct consumer niches, or provide services to firms or families and individuals.
- The international, and sometimes worldwide, coordination of corporate activities means that if a government tries to impose constraints or obligations on corporations, their resources, jobs, and operations may be transferred to another area.
- Everywhere that these global trends are afoot, evangelical and Pentecostal Christian groups, or Islamic, Hindu, and Buddhist renewal groups, are growing at geometric rates.

Such developments indicate, according to Roland Robertson, the first major scholar to use the term "globalization" in an analytical and systematic way, that we face a fresh "compression of the world, a new interdependency, and a transformation of consciousness."[39] Indeed, he stresses that the very debate over what is going on in the world is now itself an encompassing process characterized by a new, dynamic pluralism within the world seen as a single place. It involves a common destiny where multicultural possibilities, emerging novelties, and greater diversities are increasingly present

39. R. Robertson, *Globalization: Social Theory and Global Culture* (London: Sage, 1992).

everywhere. Only some religious and ethical traditions are capable of responding creatively to this new world.

Many forces converge in this global reality — technology, ecological awareness, mass media, international law, and the historical memories of world wars and nuclear threat, as well as the new transnational corporations and religious movements. But according to Pope John Paul II's *Centesimus Annus*,[40] the two key forces likely to have the most direct bearing on the future are corporations and religion. Corporations are the instrument of economic productivity for the foreseeable future, and religion is the bearer of those decisive values by which we guide our production, distribution, and consumption of whatever wealth is generated. Those who do not fully participate in the economic side of this will find development taking place "over their heads," tragically to be left in perpetual poverty. And those who are not rooted in the moral demands of profound religion are likely to be consumed by consumerism and led to an emptiness that will further destroy family and the community life of civil society.

Of Firms and Faiths

We should have no doubt about the fact that corporations, like the family and the state and even organized religious groups, can become demonic. They can ride roughshod over persons and cultures, destroy the beauties of creation for the sake of gain, reduce every issue and principle to a calculation of profit, buy their way out of legal accountability, exploit workers, corrupt governments, and become an idolatrous temple for the mad pursuit of Mammon.[41] Advocates for the poor, including those involved in public policy formation, are aware that corporations can do, have done, and likely will again do all these things — just as the family can become a locus of sexual abuse or a center for the patriarchal celebration

40. John Paul II, *Centesimus Annus (On the Hundredth Anniversary)* (Boston: St. Paul Books, 1991). For particularly interesting commentaries on this encyclical, see George Weigel, ed., *A New Worldly Order* (Washington, D.C.: Ethics and Public Policy Center, 1992).

41. Some of the specifics of such charges can be found in Richard J. Barnet and John Cavanagh, *Global Dreams: Imperial Corporations and the New World Order* (New York: Simon & Schuster, 1993).

of the "bull-power" of Ba'al, or just as states can become tyrannies and empires, a terror to the people or a cult dedicated to Mars. The sin of idolatry remains in institutions that sustain us.

But the fact of corruptibility in all human institutions does not negate the possibility that precisely these worldly organizations can also become instruments of preservation and creativity when they are justly ordered. Indeed, they can become occasions of grace. At least some religious traditions lead us to believe that concretely, and thus in limited, material and temporal, ways, corporations can become as much a covenanted means of faithful, hopeful, and loving existence as families or governments. It is increasingly obvious that the corporation is potentially an instrument of social change, able to generate resources for the common life. It establishes a sphere of cooperative economic activity offering goods, services, and/or jobs to an area, and it demands reliable behavior and a degree of mutual trust. Insofar as it does these things and successfully generates wealth by which individuals and families, communities and states, are sustained, it is a valued member of society. It may take its place with the university, the hospital, and the law court as a center of potential grace in human life. Although corporate modes of production can be very disturbing to traditional cultures, it has quickly become a simple fact: where more corporations are present and accessible to a population, people are better off. Where they are absent, the people suffer.

This fact is a matter much denied or resisted by many contemporary religious bodies. Although many Christians are involved in organizing and managing corporations, and the majority of church members work in them, it is striking that very few analyses of corporations exist in the theological literature. In a new study of the public statements about social issues by church groups from the 1960s to the 1990s, Mark Ellingsen identifies more than 120 substantive statements by denominations and councils of churches from around the world on topics of economic life, poverty, development, and unemployment. But only three of these statements treat the corporation as a positive contributor to human well-being, and an enormous number express grave doubt about any genuine moral or spiritual contribution.[42] This means that the laity who are leading the corporations around the world, overwhelmingly Christian, are largely isolated from, or even treated with contempt by, the leaders of their religious traditions, and this despite the fact that these traditions have, more than any other single

42. M. Ellingsen, *The Cutting Edge* (Grand Rapids, Mich.: Eerdmans, 1993).

source, generated the social, legal, and moral precedent for the development and the moral constraint of the corporation. At present nothing like a "theology of the corporation" is widely enough held in leading Protestant or Catholic circles to prompt sustained preaching and teaching or deep moral and spiritual reflection on its possible contributions to the fabric of civil society or to the solution of welfare problems.[43]

Nor has the nature and character of the modern corporation been the subject of substantive ethical or spiritual analysis by Hindu or Islamic writers — although it is not difficult to find strong expressions of hostility to multinational or transnational corporations as part of generally anti-Western or anti-American polemics. However, the influence of Confucianism, Buddhism, and Shinto on East Asian corporations has been more widely recognized.[44]

Nevertheless, wherever it goes the corporation is increasingly recognized as a decisive instrument to generate the resources necessary to overcome poverty and dependency, and everywhere we see it evoke an array of international legal arrangements that require the quest for intercontextual definitions of justice, fresh patterns of cross-cultural cooperation, and more universalistic modes of interaction than previously. In several ways, humans are learning through the modern corporation to relate to one another in a wide variety of styles, situations, cultures, and locales.

One absolutely key consequence of the rise of corporations is this: the nation state is no longer the chief organizing institution of this cosmopolitan world. Thus, whatever is attempted in regard to welfare will inevitably be influenced by the global impact of the corporations. They are

43. Several efforts have been made to develop one. See, e.g., Michael Novak and J. W. Cooper, eds., *The Corporation: A Theological Inquiry* (Washington, D.C.: American Enterprise Institute for Public Policy Research, 1981); Oliver Williams and J. Houck, *The Judeo-Christian Vision and the Modern Business Corporation* (Notre Dame: Univ. of Notre Dame, 1982); Robert Dickie and L. Rouner, eds., *Corporations and the Common Good* (Notre Dame: Univ. of Notre Dame, 1986); Bruce Grelle and D. Krueger, *Christianity and Capitalism* (Chicago: Center for the Scientific Study of Religions, 1986); and "Spirituality and the Corporation," in my *Public Theology and Political Economy* (Lanham, Md.: University Press of America, 1992).

44. See Gordon Redding, *The Spirit of Chinese Capitalism* (New York: de Gruyter, 1990); Stewart Clegg and Gordon Redding, eds., *Capitalism in Contrasting Cultures* (New York: de Gruyter, 1990); Roy Hofheinz and Kent Calder, *The Eastasia Edge* (New York: Basic Books, 1982); and Berger and Hsiao, eds., *In Search of an Asian Development Model.* An article in *India Today,* July 15, 1994, reports that new courses for managers are being based on the *Gita.*

not only the chief bearers, generators, and consumers of technology[45] but the chief sources of jobs, wealth, and hope for earthly well-being.[46] Simultaneously, the great religions are challenged to discern the meaning of these developments, to give moral guidance to these new global institutions, to provide the motivation and vision for people in them, and to aid the reconstruction of the common life on this new and vaster scale.

In the short run, it is likely that these larger religious movements and corporations will only indirectly affect the life of the very poor. Only some of the least advantaged will be converted to one or another of these faiths, and only a few will have a chance to work in these corporations or to benefit from their goods or services in any quantity. But the general health of the civil society and its particular forms in the cities, countries, and regions of the world are likely to make a considerable difference in their lives. The presence or absence of positive religious movements and productive corporations will influence what resources are available to the communities of the future, and thus to any who seek a disciplined lifestyle, to find real opportunities to contribute to the commonwealth, to establish greater justice in the civil society, and to find ways to help those in distress.

Further, it is quite likely that religions and corporations will shape the prospects not only of those portions of the population that are below the poverty line, but also of those just above it: the working poor. The formal institutions that are present in a neighborhood make a great deal of difference to people who have few resources of their own. Crime, drugs, shootings, and sexual exploitation are present at every level of society and among all kinds of people, in many schools and on many streets. But they are less prominent, less threatening, less life-defining where viable religious institutions provide meaning and hope, and where operating companies provide employment and goods. These material/spiritual institutions deeply influence whether people think it is possible to hold their families and lives together. In these institutions people develop capacities for cooperation that allow them to join with others in common tasks. Without

45. Nathan Rosenberg, Ralph Landau, and David Mowery, eds., *Technology and the Wealth of Nations* (Stanford: Stanford Univ. Press, 1992).

46. Robert B. Nelson makes a compelling argument that this has become the chief quasi-theological presupposition of economics, as this "secular science" echoes the classic philosophic and theological traditions of the past. See his *Reaching for Heaven on Earth* (Savage, Md.: Rowman and Littlefield, 1992).

them, people are isolated in the cosmos and on earth. Such institutions thus often determine what kind of participation in the common life is conceivable. Both economic and religious participation concretely provide opportunity and motivation, ideals and principles that guide behavior, chances to develop habits of discipline and responsiveness, networks of trust, and demands for mutuality that form character, reduce alienation, actualize value in the common life, and generate civil society.

Implications

Pressures from beneath the state and from beyond the state are likely to converge in the next decades in ways that will profoundly influence what we can do with regard to welfare. How they combine will be fateful. These pressures already are rearranging our mental maps. We can no longer speak of the "First," "Second," and "Third" worlds because they no longer have clear locations. And it may become increasingly unhelpful to focus on race and sex as distinctive indicators of opportunity and meaning. Although racial and sexual discrimination remain, they are weaker than they have been in centuries, and attributing all social problems to them has decreasing credibility. It is more likely that we shall have to begin to think about humanity in terms of a complex, stratified pyramid that encompasses everyone in the world. It is both frightening and quite plausible to imagine that some 60 percent of the population of North America will join some 40 percent of the population of Europe, 20 percent of the Asian Rim and Latin American countries, and 10 percent of Africa and the island cultures to occupy the higher echelons of wealth, income, diet, health care, educational opportunity, and longevity. Such a scenario implies, of course, that some 10 percent of the American population will join some 80 percent of Africa, perhaps 60 percent of Asia and Latin America, and 40 percent of Eastern Europe to occupy the lower echelons of the world economy in the foreseeable future. If we are to prevent such a system from freezing into a new feudal or caste system with ever-increasing distance between the top and the bottom, we shall have to form a new global civil society. And for the reasons already stated, we shall have to follow President Clinton's advice to the religious leaders: "You [the clergy] must do that and we [the government] must help."

In the long run, what will be decisive is not, as previous generations thought, more and more state programs, although some carefully refined ones will surely be necessary. Nor will the decisive factor be, as previous ideologies taught, a warfare between two classes, although tensions between multiple strata are likely to remain. Nor need there be, as previous ages held, a blind resignation to inherited station, although some ranking of status is probably inevitable.[47]

What happens in regard to stratification, however, is likely to depend on whether people of faith assume — or better, resume — their role in the formation of a moral consensus about civil society with full awareness of interpersonal connectedness and the transnational fabric behind it. It depends also on the creation of institutions at each level to meet the direct spiritual, social, and material needs of the people at that level, and to provide the contexts in which persons are invited to a conversion of heart and a discernment of vocation. Thus the formation of community-based cooperatives, corporations, and service centers would be part of the ministry of the church at the lower echelons of modern civilization's global pyramid, while instruction about and legal advocacy of responsible social investment, equal opportunity, inclusiveness, and cultural diversity in the workplace would be part of the agenda at higher levels. Both the exterior formation and the interior conversion would be guided by an ethical discipline focused on the deeper, wider, and higher understanding of duty, purpose, and responsibility in family, community, and professional life. Experimental efforts in these directions are already in place, wherever people have begun to develop an articulate theology that gives moral or spiritual definition to the expanded civil society of our times. It requires a "public theology" — a system of normative theory about the nature and character of holiness in relation to the structures and processes of human existence, one that not only guides the practical work of the church, but is capable of entering the public arenas of discourse.[48]

47. See Louis Dumont, *Homo Hierarchicus* (Chicago: Univ. of Chicago Press, 1970). Dumont argues that the Indian traditions of caste recognize something that is true of all societies, including Western ones, and that the denial of this fact brings disastrous results.

48. The term "public theology" was first used by Reinhold Niebuhr and John Courtney Murray and was later developed by David Tracy and others. These efforts represent today the long traditions of public discourse about the most important matters as found in writers from Augustine, Thomas, and Calvin to Edwards. The main contours of these developments are found in the new overview by Robert Benne, *The Paradoxical Vision* (Minneapolis: Augsburg Press, 1994).

Such a general theory would have to be linked with a quite concrete analysis of what a religion does in society. And each religion is distinct in its social ethical effects. From its earliest days, for example, Christianity formed the church beyond the national borders of the established regimes, drew in people marginal to the society, and began to alter the ruling patterns of ancient societies — including the dominant practices of family life and economy. It has ever been an agent of transformation. When Rome fell and ancient thought faltered, the church picked up the pieces and rebuilt society. Later, as city life began to develop around cathedrals, the markets at their base, and sometimes the garrisons on the next hill or the harbors at the next bay, the Reformation recovered and recast the basic understandings of Christianity to construct a new civil society. And it did so once more in the taming of the raw, often vicious collection of cowboys, adventurers, crooks, opportunists, and misfits who settled the American frontier. In each case, it pressed simultaneously for the renewed sanctity of the family, a new morality for economic life, and a redefinition of inclusion in society. It modulated American culture in these directions again in our century under the influence of the social gospel of Walter Rauschenbusch, the Christian realism of Reinhold Niebuhr, the civil rights movement of Martin Luther King, Jr., and the formation of a worldwide ecumenical movement. That sort of thing now has to be done again, with a new focus — a global civil society.

Central to the faith throughout has been an ethic of sharing, love and sacrifice for others, and a calling to see that the world can be converted to relative degrees of justice and compassion — ultimately toward a new graceful city where all stand equally in the presence of holiness. At the same time, each movement has recognized the sin and wickedness that has to be contained until that ultimate vision is made actual, for a willingness to exploit the neighbor is a temptation that reaches to the hearts of all. Just as striking as these aspects of the classic ethic is an ethic of stewardly participation in the common life, in production, in the prudent management of that which we have been given. The ancient monks believed that the holy life consisted not only of prayer but also of work *(orare et laborare).* All Christians believe that humans can and should participate in the transformation of the world to the glory of God and the service of all peoples in ways that support (but do not require participation in) family life and that simultaneously honor and also surpass the authority of any state. The formation of well-ordered families and disciplined participation in productive economic institutions are part of the contemporary vocation of every able adult.[49]

The implications of this analysis may well be clear: the churches ought to be about the task of rebuilding the tissues of civil society on a firm religious foundation, guided by a public theology. Struggling models are present in nearly every center city and in many impoverished regions. Where effective, they generate human confidence and develop social competence. They draw isolated persons into responsible families and creative economic opportunities. They alter habituated patterns of living that disrupt families and lead to criminality. Corporations are superior to gangs. Two-parent families are superior to families with only a single parent. Religious convictions are superior to psychological and sociological doctrines that do not motivate the soul, reform lives, or evoke commitment to truth, justice, hope, and love. Thus clergy and layfolk who are guided by a profound public theology are more decisive for the future of people on welfare than are social workers.

Religion may well prove to be more able to perform services, generate confidence, overcome addictions, evoke interest in education, teach how to live with others, and promote a work ethic than any other group or program in civilization. Thus, efforts should be made to secure greater resources for those religious organizations that develop schools, nursery care, drug programs, job training, and parenting skills at the grass roots. The funding of religiously based social service agencies, organized into capital-generating corporations at the local level, organizationally distinct from communities of worship but building on the spiritual, moral, and social resources of those communities, would recognize the fact that certain changes in people's lives will only come when a religious impetus becomes incarnate, and that certain changes in the common ethos take place only when religious convictions are lived out in society with appropriate material support.

Religious groups can also become the mothers of enterprise. Indeed, what Black Muslims, Korean evangelicals, and Hispanic Pentecostals have already done shows this. Government contracting could further encourage the formation of grassroots corporations that perform social services, such as the home visitation of those who have various disability, dependency, or rehabilitation needs, those in family crises, or those on probation from prisons. Government could also make local empowerment programs more

49. See Melton; John Paul II.

effective by giving tax breaks and low-interest loans to corporations that are linked with religious communities and that subcontract with regional businesses and provide the social skills and job training necessary to enable people to find channels into the larger corporate world.[50]

Charity and justice, as they are dealt with by welfare, in other words, need a new institutional form. No doubt, child services for victims of neglect, substance abuse recovery centers, emergency medical care, subsidized housing, and remedial education will always be necessary in a complex modern society. But it is religious organizations that, more than any other single set of organizations, generate the commitment and compassion to undertake these jobs. Similarly, the social world of the future will need law enforcement specialists, and all that implies in terms of security and paralegal services, prisoner education, and halfway houses. Without these our cities will be further decivilized. But such services need people with both a realistic sense of sin and a hope for the redemption of each soul. Welfare provisions could be redesigned to maintain, at public expense, religiously rooted independent institutions that enable people to take responsibility themselves for the social demands of charity and justice.

In sum, the first priority of government welfare programs should not be support for individuals but the creation of the conditions under which morally active groups are encouraged and enabled to develop those institutions that care for people in a personal way, using means that are appropriate to the new shape of a global civil society. And such conditions would also foment those habits of life and sustain those patterns of reliable cooperation that draw people into responsible and productive corporate institutions. Thus, in the final analysis, the full weight of reform does not and cannot fall on government alone. It falls also on religious leadership and on religious institutions. The only thing that can bring people to pour their lives out for such purposes is religion. Religion is what offers a governing vision of how the world is, how it ought to be, and how, given the means, it can be improved. Civil society and the possibility of a global civilization, and with them the welfare of all peoples, rests on the rock of religion. Nothing else reaches as high, deep, or wide.

50. I have in mind the kind of thing done in the Boston area by the Christian Economic Coalition, under the leadership of Roger Dewey, which is utilizing a modified form of the Mondragon Cooperative Movement.

Who Cares? Poverty and the Dynamics of Responsibility: An Outsider's Contribution to the American Debate on Poverty and Welfare

Bob Goudzwaard

Prologue

I WOULD LIKE to begin with a personal note about the intent of this chapter.

It is a real honor to be invited as a European academician to join a team studying the roots of America's welfare crisis, and the honor is even greater because the team is composed of such outstanding members. But such an invitation can pose something of a problem: how to be, as a European, of real service to the readers and to the other members of the team?

I had to reject from the start the notion of framing my contribution in terms of the problem of poverty in Third-World countries, which usually occupies the center of my attention. It is almost impossible, and even unfair, to try to find a common denominator between the poverty in southern countries and the situation of the "truly disadvantaged"[1] within our own rich northern societies. More useful would be a comparison of the current American situation with the Western European one, examining the present crisis of the European welfare state and the recent emergence of a so-called new poverty within the European Union. In the following pages I will indeed pay some attention to the latter phenomenon. Nevertheless, I de-

1. William Julius Wilson, *The Truly Disadvantaged: The Inner City, the Underclass, and Public Policy,* 1987 (Chicago: Univ. of Chicago Press paperback, 1990).

cided not to adopt this as my main framework, because I believe the comparisons would not be very illuminating. The European nations differ so much from each other; more important, the American debate on welfare and poverty is so different from the European debate. Different choices have been made, different positions adopted, and different issues appear to be at stake.

So I decided it was best to follow another path. "Outsider" status becomes an asset instead of a liability if and where a perspective external to a situation is desirable. Such a perspective is useful, for instance, if in an ongoing debate the various positions are merely repeated over and over or if the participants begin to desire to see new options. Now, it so happens that some of the participants in the debate on American welfare have noted just such things.[2]

This gives me the freedom to offer this outsider's view on the debate on America's welfare policy. This chapter can best be read as the view of a highly interested European economist and ex-politician who is puzzled about the many deep disagreements about America's welfare policy, and who is looking for ways not only to understand these disagreements but also to help to overcome them.

Introduction

Observing the debate on American welfare, what strikes the outsider almost immediately is how often the word "crisis" is used in reference to the welfare system. Clearly a point has been reached in its history where a new kind of deadlock has presented itself and new choices have to be made. For this sense of a crisis *of* a system is, of course, far more serious than suggestions of a lack of effectiveness *within* a system. If the problem was merely the latter, then it could be solved by the introduction of better devices or techniques. But in the case of a real crisis, such measures do not help. The word "crisis" indicates situations or developments that are at least partly beyond our control, in which outcomes are becoming unpredictable and might even be paradoxical. And when it comes to alleviating poverty or

2. See, e.g., Robert Haveman and Isabel Sawhill, "The Nature, Causes, and Cures of Poverty: Accomplishments from Three Decades of Poverty Research and Policy," *Focus* (Institute for Research on Poverty) 14, no. 3 (Winter 1992–1993): 9-12.

deprivation, it is just such phenomena of unpredictability and paradox that now seem to be prevalent, at least in the view of many participants in the present debate.

We can observe these elements of unpredictability and paradox in, for instance, the types of questions that are asked. An increasing number of questions today concern how it is possible that poverty persists despite so many well-meant measures to combat it. Consider the title of Isabel Sawhill's well-known article: "Poverty in the U.S.: Why Is It So Persistent?"[3] In such a title lies the suggestion that, at least to some degree, poverty seems now to have adopted its own course, as if it possesses an internal power to resist our efforts, just like insects that have become immune to most kinds of insecticides.[4]

Other experts on American poverty and welfare have expressed similar views. Sheldon Danziger and Daniel Weinberg, surveying for a 1992 conference the facts on poverty since the federal government began its antipoverty fight, expressed puzzlement about the trajectory of poverty after 1983. They even term this period "anomalous" because, while mean income increased rapidly, so did inequality. As a result, poverty, rather than declining as before, remained above the 1973 level.[5]

3. *Journal of Economic Literature* 26 (1988): 1073-119.

4. Such immunity is suggested by Sawhill's article. After stating that "poverty has declined over the past 20 to 25 years but . . . progress more or less came to a halt after 1970" (p. 1082), Sawhill deals mainly with the question of how this persistence was possible despite the many programs intended to increase the productivity and the earnings of the poor. In trying to answer this question, she is able to link the persistence of poverty to a number of possible causes, such as demographic changes, the growth of unemployment, the rise of an "underclass" in urban areas, growing earnings inequality, and other factors. But in all honesty she also points out the insufficient explanatory power of many of these "causes." "The demographic trends are difficult to explain," she admits (p. 1112); and writing of the growth of the "underclass," she notes that "[t]he reasons for these trends are not well understood and remain controversial" (p. 1109). Similarly, Sawhill does not include growing earnings inequality in her final list of explanatory variables, "even though it has been a prominent finding in some recent work," because it is merely a "measure of our ignorance": "to say that poverty has increased because inequality has increased simply substitutes one puzzle for another" (p. 1110). Thus one of her final conclusions is that the "rather modest progress [in the struggle against poverty] in the face of a large increase in real spending for income transfers and for human capital programs targeted on the poor is difficult to explain" (p. 1113). The mystery of persistent poverty may be somewhat reduced, but it is not really solved.

5. Their findings are summarized in Sheldon H. Danziger, Gary D. Sandefur, and

It would be easy to attribute this "anomaly" or paradox to peculiarities of American society or to a possible American naiveté in thinking about poverty. But this would be a grave error. For in the first half of the 1980s, a similar "anomalous" growth of poverty became evident also in Europe, where it came to be called the "new poverty." The label "new" was used not to indicate that unprecedented types or forms of deprivation had appeared, but rather because the level of poverty itself had risen at an unexpected time and an unexpected rate, and despite the many efforts to fight it.

An excellent overview of this development is provided in the Council of Europe publication, based on a December 1991 colloquium, *Towards Greater Social Justice in Europe,* which places it in the context of a diminishing effect of all antipoverty measures. According to this report, in the twelve member states of the European Union (then called the European Community) in 1985, no fewer than 44 million people (14 percent of the total population) lived in poverty, and the projection was for even greater poverty in the future. "The optimistic expectation has been," according to the report, "that poverty can be eliminated smoothly by applying more or less radical measures of redistribution under conditions of economic growth. However, reality seems to be different" (p. 6). "Poverty is no longer an accidental, or rather a contingent, phenomenon," the report emphasizes (p. 82). And as new elements in the European context, it notes factors such as the rise of long-term unemployment (more than half of the unemployed in the European Union are now out of work longer than a year); the increase in the divorce rate; the growth of migratory movements; and the increase of consumption-oriented behavior. We can conclude, therefore, that for the European Union, too, the hardness and growing immunity of poverty obviously came as a nasty surprise.

Such a situation of crisis, both in the United States and in Europe, necessitates reflection in depth. What obviously is required is a kind of reflection that considers not only possible mistakes and shortcomings in the goals that have been adopted and the particular tools employed. We should at least be ready to entertain the possibility of far more basic shortcomings in our approach and/or analysis. But what could be their character, and how can we go about trying to find such basic defects?

Daniel H. Weinberg, "Introduction," in Danziger, Sandefur, and Weinberg, eds., *Confronting Poverty: Prescriptions for Change* (Cambridge: Harvard Univ. Press, 1994), 7.

Perhaps a metaphor is useful here. If a medical team is confronted with a patient whose illness seems to progress no matter what treatment is administered, then such a case of "persistency" can obviously have several causes. One possible reason is that the chosen treatments were incorrect, perhaps because of flawed diagnoses or because the members of the team could not reach consensus on the best therapy. But a second reason could be that the illness itself is not well understood, because the general medical insight into this type of disease is not adequate. The medical consensus may even be deficient because certain "blinders" hamper the profession or, in extreme cases, because it is simply impossible for the needed medical knowledge to be obtained.

A parallel with the persistency of contemporary poverty can easily be drawn. The first possibility noted corresponds with what can go wrong in the implementation of the various existing antipoverty programs. Problems here can be due simply to practical mistakes, or they could be due to the ideological differences between the political parties. The second option concerns insight into poverty itself, and corresponds with the possibility of general elements of blindness or distortion.

It goes without saying that finding the real causes of the hardening of poverty in modern societies is of great importance, in part because poverty has begun to manifest paradoxical traits. Our attention will be drawn, therefore, first to the possible role of political differences and of the general political debate on poverty (section 2). Then we will turn to the difficult matter of possible common basic biases or misunderstandings of poverty (section 3). The possibility that there might be impassable barriers to further progress in our knowledge will be touched on (section 4), but it will be set aside as being too sweeping a contention, despite its recent academic popularity.[6]

6. In the postmodernist camp, for instance, an author like Jean Baudrillard defends with great eloquence the position that in the present postmodern situation we should abandon the hope for accurate knowledge of the objective world itself, for the world has now developed its own fate-full laws and reasons, which as a type of black hole cannot be caught by the light of the human subjective mind. In his opinion the modern subjective mind even has lost completely the battle with the world of objects; the world proceeds autonomously to fufill its own fated strategies. I resist this position because it is one without any ray of hope. However, I have noted it because Baudrillard makes an important point in relating our present society and its problems, including its problem of poverty, to the modern era itself and to the modernistic fashion in which our society was formed. I hope to return to this point later.

Political Controversies

The first possible explanation of the impasse, as indicated above, is that the concrete proposals designed to fight poverty have been faulty, or short-sighted, or have been derived from political premises that are superficial or too narrow. In this context we also have to discuss the possibility that political differences played an adverse role by doing unnecessary harm to the "patient" — the American poor.

In considering the possible reasons for the persistence of poverty, we have to accept from the start a sharp limitation of possible arguments. There is no reason to depart from the almost universally accepted view of the experts on American poverty that poverty has been hardening and becoming persistent for longer than just the past decade. Already in the 1960s and 1970s an increasing number of references were made to the rise of new or resistant types of poverty, usually in the context of the emergence of a so-called underclass in the urban setting, or of an emerging "culture of poverty." Note, for instance, the opening sentence of William Julius Wilson's *The Truly Disadvantaged:* "In the mid-1960s, urban analysts began to speak of a new dimension to the urban crisis in the form of a large subpopulation of low-income families and individuals whose behavior contrasted sharply with the behavior of the general population." But if persistent poverty goes back that far, then it is impossible to blame it on the acts or omissions of any one political party. Neither policymaking under the Democrats nor governance by the Republicans can be held exclusively accountable for persistent poverty. This contention is further strengthened by the recent experience in Europe, as noted above. Most West European countries have had their own distinctive set of social and welfare policies that are more "progressive" than even the American Democratic tradition. But in these countries, too, persistent poverty, the "new poverty," has appeared.

That does not mean, of course, that social or welfare policies do not matter. They certainly do, especially for the very poor and with respect to the severity of unemployment. But up to now all of these policies have not been able to prevent the growth of hard-core poverty, which seems, in fact, to increase when the wealth of the society increases.

It may seem strange, but the unavoidable consequence of these considerations is that, when it comes to the significance of political views for the impasse about poverty, we should look primarily not to their differences, but rather to their points of agreement. If possible causes for the growing persistence of poverty are to be found in this realm, then they will be found in this area of underlying political consensus. But can those common factors be isolated and delineated?

In fact, indications of such underlying points of consensus can be found here and there in the literature. Ken Auletta, for instance, has pointed out that both the conservative explanation and the liberal explanation for the limited achievements of the Great Society can be characterized as too narrowly economic. Both explain the current problems of the poor as merely a matter of an excess or a deficiency of (transferred) resources.[7] Moreover, Lawrence Mead has pointed out that Great Society policymaking was, by and large, "consensual" between conservatives and liberals. At the same time, both camps ignored behavioral problems among the poor. According to him, since the early 1960s the poor mainly have been understood to be conditioned by their environment.[8]

These are important points. For there is no doubt a link between the two observations. Citizens who are seen as conditioned by external circumstances (whether these are good or bad, and whether they originate from their own culture or have external sources, such as government programs) are obviously in all such cases primarily seen and treated as "objects," in the same way that science studies objects. But when persons are treated as objects (whether of analysis or of assistance), they cease, we might say, to "act." They can only be supposed to "react" — in response to some impulse such as the stimulus of a transfer of financial means. But is not this far too narrow an approach? In the next section we will try to unearth the root of this way of looking at reality. But we can already conclude here that it would be unwise to exclude the possibility that this peculiar view of human beings has contributed to the growth of hard-core poverty, particularly since it could give the poor the sense of having been "objectified" by both political streams.

There is, however, more to be said. Elsewhere in his book, Mead remarks that conservatives and liberals can both be labeled, as far as their welfare policies are concerned, as economic conservatives. "There was no desire to remake American society, even to the extent of democratic social-

7. See Lawrence M. Mead, *Beyond Entitlement: The Social Obligations of Citizenship* (New York: Free Press, 1986), 47-48.

8. Mead, 49, 55.

ism seen in Western Europe," he says. "The Great Society was not economically radical, as the New Deal had been."[9] These remarks suggest this key question: might we find in the structure, unfolding, and direction of our modern societies a distinct cause for the rapid emergence of new types of poverty? Can we say for sure that neither the structure nor the orientation of modern society is culpable in the process of the hardening of poverty? Perhaps this factor went unnoticed by the main political traditions but was nevertheless quite important.

This possibility, too, will be examined more carefully later, in section 4. But I want to emphasize here that a critical examination of the specific structure and direction of modern society is not necessarily a leftist project, nor should it be presumed to be rooted in Marxism or communism. Far from it. In the heart of the Reformation tradition of Dutch Calvinism, in 1891, the Dutch statesman and theologian Abraham Kuyper urged the necessity of an ongoing "architectonic critique" of the foundations of modern Western society, and linked these faulty foundations to the social crisis — increasing poverty — of his own day.[10] Social illnesses, we should note, do not always have just a technical or economic character. They may be the fruit of very deep structural distortions or even of directional distortions, that is, the fruit of a wrong spiritual orientation of the society as a whole.

In Search of Analytical Biases

What factors might possibly have contributed to some sort of general bias in the analysis of, and thus remedies for, contemporary poverty in the United States — biases that are possibly related to distorted analytical views or common blinding factors? This is not an easy question to answer, and any answers are themselves subject to heated dispute. The best way to approach the question seems to be, therefore, to propose a hypothesis that can be verified or falsified, at least to some extent.

My hypothesis is that, in the American context, economists and social scientists have had a disproportionate influence in the poverty debate and

9. Mead, 20, 33.

10. See Abraham Kuyper, *The Problem of Poverty,* ed. and introduced by James W. Skillen (Grand Rapids, Mich.: Baker Book House, and Washington, D.C.: The Center for Public Justice, 1991).

have carried into that debate their overly narrow and restrictive way of looking at poverty. Their style of analysis consequently shaped public opinion in a lopsided manner.

Some initial evidence for the first part of this hypothesis can readily be found. Wilson, for instance, remarks, "In the final analysis, the policy agenda set by the architects of the Great Society, that is, the labor economists and sociologists who fashioned the War on Poverty in the 1960s, established the vision for the subsequent research and analysis of minority poverty."[11] Similarly, Isabel Sawhill begins her article "Poverty in the U.S." with the comment that, when in the mid-1960s the United States embarked on a war on poverty, the generals "enlisted economists and other social scientists to help them define and measure poverty, to plan programs, and later to evaluate them and to measure the progress achieved."[12] Sawhill gives further support to the hypothesis when she and Robert Haveman suggest that one reason why poverty researchers have such a narrowed vision is that economists have largely framed the debate. Especially harmful, Sawhill and Haveman judge, is the economists' inclination toward "marginal thinking," to always be asking, "What is the effect of adding a little bit more of a single input to a process in which all the other inputs are held constant?"[13] Others have pointed to sociologists as exercising a deleterious influence. Lawrence Mead, for example, asking why the Great Society achieved so little, points to "the sociological approach," shaped by Talcott Parsons, Robert K. Merton, C. Wright Mills, and others. In this approach, "the poor and disadvantaged were understood to be so conditioned by their environment that to expect better functioning from them, such as work, became almost inconceivable."[14]

This initial evidence is valuable because it makes it clear that, in addition to the specific influence of particular economists or other social scientists, a general style or framework for analysis may have become influential. But this, of course, is insufficient to validate a broader claim that the perspective of economists and other social scientists may have comprehensively distorted the analysis of poverty and the fight against poverty. So what more may be said?

Here I would like to make at least two fundamental observations. The

11. Wilson, 131.
12. Sawhill, 1073.
13. Haveman and Sawhill, 11.
14. Mead, 55.

first (A) is related to the specificity of science itself. The second (B) is related to the influence of modernity especially on the social sciences.

(A) The way in which scientists as analysts observe and perceive reality is, of course, quite different from the way in which all of us in our daily lives perceive reality. This difference generally presents no problem because we are aware of it and deal with it in an intuitive way. But in the case of social phenomena like poverty, a distinct and important difficulty may develop because of this perceptual or analytical difference. We understand that, due to the different roles involved, a scientist observing poverty will perceive it differently than does the person who is poverty-stricken. But there is a further and critical difference that cannot be explained away in terms of social-role distinctions. Living in a situation of poverty leads to experiences and forms of awareness that cannot fully be grasped by any scientific approach and that must not be discounted by the scientific observer.[15]

The scientific approach is inherently oriented toward generalization, even when the empirical material is highly specific. To generalize, scientists must take a modally specific approach, focusing on a single dimension of the multidimensional reality. Poverty, for instance, is studied as a social phenomenon, or as an anthropological phenomenon, or as an economic phenomenon. In each case the unity and consistency of the approach is guaranteed by, and created only by, the very unidimensionality of the framework. For the economist, for instance, poverty is seen as a scarcity of means in relation to essential needs, which then dictates the necessity of some different (micro or macro) allocation of resources.

Such an aspect-oriented, or unidimensional, approach can lead to very valuable conclusions. But the conclusions are always constrained by the limitations of the aspect-oriented approach itself, which can never grasp the full, multidimensional, reality of poverty as it really exists and is experienced by the poor themselves. For the poor, poverty has simultaneously

15. The great Dutch Christian philosopher Herman Dooyweerd, in his treatment of the differences between the so-called naive, or direct, experience and the scientific way of looking at reality, explicitly warned against an undervaluation of the former mode of perception. To deny that both of these have a legitimate place, he argued, is to adopt a rationalism that cannot be accepted from a Christian philosophical point of view. See Dooyeweerd, *A New Critique of Theoretical Thought*, trans. David H. Freeman, William S. Young, and H. De Jongste, four volumes published as two books (n.p.: Presbyterian and Reformed, 1969), vol. 1, pp. 83ff.

and in an interconnected way a multitude of dimensions or manifestations: physical (hunger, sickness), psychological (fear, stress), social (isolation or acceptance), juridical (subjection to discrimination or crime), ethical (shifting mores or loyalties), and even spiritual (living between hope and despair, searching for meaning). Even if scientists believe that they have adopted a holistic approach, they must beware that a summation of results from different disciplines or the addition of various unidimensional accounts will never lead to the creation of the same vivid unity of perception as it is found and seen in the reality itself.

The concrete significance of this inner limitation of every social science is that the scientific approach will usually tend to underestimate those forms of human or social development that have an intermodal or multidimensional character — those phenomena that cross the boundaries of the different disciplines. The economist, for instance, will tend to ignore those cases where a new economic need is created for a person or family by a social consequence of poverty, such as growing isolation.[16] Such "circularity" is not studied by economists because in the neoclassical tradition they are accustomed to start with the principle of given human needs. But poverty, especially prolonged poverty, has just this confounding character that can lead social-scientific analyses astray. In inner cities, for example, people are not just poor. They may also be subjected to extreme threats and violence. A person acting responsibly in such circumstances cannot respond only in accordance with a narrow economic calculation. The single parent raising a child in this setting may rightly judge that her responsibility to assure the physical safety of her child must take precedence over accepting employment that would require her absence from the house and neighborhood. When need has this multidimensional character, then the normal disciplinary point of view can hardly comprehend it or make any valid predictions about it.

Poverty that becomes manifest in those multiple dimensions can indeed develop a persistence that, from the scientific, aspect-oriented per-

16. An illuminating European treatment of the intermodal aspect of poverty is given in the well-known but quite unorthodox report of Father Wresinski, "Extreme Poverty," published in the *Journal officiel de la Republique Francaise* (28 Feb. 1987). Here we find, for instance, the introduction of the term "hypermaterial poverty" to refer to those states of poverty in which the material needs are accompanied by new needs of a nonmaterial or relational nature. Extrication of a person from this kind of poverty requires measures that address all of the dimensions of need.

spective, will seem largely a mystery. For its dynamic carries it across the barriers between the various sciences with their characteristic approaches. At the same time, the scientists' solutions are likely to fail or to have little positive effect.

(B) If we are to think about the possibility of some general bias in our perceptions of poverty, we must be willing to go even beyond this inherent general limitation of the scientific approach. We should be open to the possibility that the development of particularly the social sciences has created specific "blind spots" — not only in the eyes of those social scientists but also to some extent in the vision of the politicians who were advised by them.

Here I would like to call attention especially to the consequences of the rise of the modern, mechanical world-and-life view for the social sciences. We will have to go back to the sixteenth and seventeenth centuries, when, according to Stephen Toulmin and other social philosophers, the first traces of modernity can be detected. This takes us back a very long time, but the detour may be worthwhile.

These were times of great insecurity as former certainties crumbled. If Galileo was right, for instance, then apparently when people thought they were seeing a sunset their very eyes were misleading them. Confronted by such paradoxes, Hannah Arendt says, Western society was driven in that time to search for a firmer ground of certainty than was offered by past interpretations of the world, such as Christianity. A new, modern foundation for certainty had to be found, and was eventually found in a new Cosmo-polis (Toulmin), based on the autonomy of human reason (Descartes). For only human reason could function simultaneously as the expression of the full subjective freedom of humankind and as the path leading reliably to a controlling and unified knowledge of nature. (It was only somewhat later, at the time of the Enlightenment, that people began to see that these two motives or poles of modernity might conflict.)

What is critical for our topic is this: such a drive for a new, absolute kind of security in all scientific efforts required more than just another way of understanding reality. For if only what can be grasped logically is trustworthy, because science can or should no longer accept any idea of a God-given structure of reality, then there is indeed no other way for the scientist than to pave his or her own path of logical security step by step in the midst of the chaos of perceptions (Kant's so-called Copernican revolution). For then one can trust only what can be derived from fixed laws, which can be logically proven, and which have to be based on objective measurements.

It is no wonder, then, that from the early days of modernity the metaphor of a clock is so often used. For the clock, a human-made mechanism, runs in a predictable way, obeying natural laws that can be fully understood by reason. It measures time, but is simultaneously a wonderful example of precise human technical craftsmanship. So we see, from the start of modernity, early economists and other social scientists searching for a way of understanding society as if it was a complex clockwork: a mechanical world working on its own, and in continual motion. It might wobble or need to be repaired, but such repair could be successful only if guided by the laws inherent in its functioning. In later days the steam engine served as a similarly central metaphor.[17] In this search for understanding, God either is absent or is reduced to the role of the great clockmaker who went into retirement after his great creative act. For the universe has now become a universe of mechanical self-sufficiency.

But how is it possible for social scientists to arrive at universally acceptable statements about immutable laws, based on objective, measurable facts, if their domain of investigation is not the regularity of nature but rather the bewildering field of human society? For in social and economic life people again and again demonstrate very irregular types of behavior! This question leads us to the roots of those theoretical fallacies and shortcomings that have so handicapped the scientific observation, analysis, and treatment of poverty. For if the certainty of knowledge has to be maintained at all costs, but the scientist is studying a chaotic and whimsical reality, then only one strategy is available: social scientists must construct their own orderly image of social reality with predictable outcomes. If so, then social scientists must indeed organize what they observe in such a way that possible disturbing factors are excluded from the analysis before it even begins. And that is, in fact, the strategy that was adopted both by the young science of economics and

17. Cf. Adam Smith's comment about intellectual systems such as his own analysis of capitalism: "Systems in many respects resemble machines. . . . A system is an imaginary machine, invented to connect together in the fancy those different movements and effects which are already in reality performed." Quoted by Andrew Skinner in his introduction to Adam Smith, *The Wealth of Nations, Books I-III,* Penguin English Library (Harmondsworth, Middlesex, Eng.: Penguin Books, 1982), 12.

by the even younger science of sociology, albeit with different nuances in each case.

Economic science attempted to achieve the desired security by creating a kind of laboratory situation, called the "market mechanism." In this artificial universe of prices and quantities, reality is represented in such a way that all irregularities are "externalized": they are shifted to the so-called domain of "data," or given factors, so that only regular and fully predictable phenomena remain. Human behavior, of course, is the most unpredictable and disturbing factor in the working of the market. Therefore it is "frozen" into given wants and given attitudes, leading to the stereotyped behavior of all individuals. Economic science has in this way developed into a kind of natural science, which studies only those phenomena that result from the (disturbed or undisturbed) working of the market *qua* mechanism, including the phenomenon of poverty. In its rationally constructed cosmos, of course, "disturbances" can take place — unemployment, say, or a rapid increase in poverty. But in this self-created world, no one will ever ask the question: Who or which agency has caused that phenomenon? For the only accepted question is: What factor has caused this event?[18] Within a mechanical universe, no person or agent can be responsible or accountable. Everyone's behavior is presupposed to be stereotypical, to be always the same if other factors are constant (the so-called *ceteris paribus* clause). But then the question remains, and becomes even more pointed, whether such an approach can ever lead to a real understanding of what poverty is and how it can be cured.

The path of sociology has been different, but only relatively, only insofar as here greater attention is paid to human behavior itself. So we find that a wider set of hypotheses has been developed in this field to explain the behavior. But the explanations are still in terms of general rules, laws, or statements. Remarkable in this context is Mead's assessment that the most striking characteristic of the "sociological approach" to poverty has been its determinism. And he goes on to say, "Any science must assume

18. For a further elaboration of this difference, see John Hicks's book *Causality in Economics* (Oxford: Blackwell, 1979), where the distinction is made between the old concept of causality, in which "causes are always thought of as actions by someone," and a "new causality," comprising "the search for 'laws' or generalizations." Economics, according to this Nobel Prize winner, has been, since Adam Smith, committed to this new causality (p. 9).

that the phenomena under study are 'caused' in some sense by identifiable outside forces." But "[q]uantified social science applied that assumption to human problems more literally than before. . . . Poor children's learning problems in school, for example, were 'caused' by their parents' own limited background, plus the deficiencies of public programs."[19] So here too we can see the striking absence of any sense of causality that would search for possible causes in the actions of accountable persons.

It is quite clear from this that we should not expect that when economists and sociologists cooperate in the search for explanations of poverty or for remedies either group would correct the one-sidedness of the other. More likely is a mutual reinforcement of biases. And their very cooperation made it more likely that their way of approaching issues like poverty did become the standard approach, inclusive of all their biases.

All of these are not just abstract, theoretical concerns. This becomes quite clear if we ask about the general consequences of such a mechanistic understanding of economic and political life, and try to relate these consequences to the analysis of the specific phenomenon of poverty. At least five consequences can then be noted:

1. Looking to social reality as if it were just a physical mechanism implies, in the first place, the necessity of measurement. Science, in this mechanistic conception, consists of measurement, because without measuring no laws or tendencies can be formulated and verified. In this world-and-life view, therefore, social and economic phenomena can only be observed and studied as a quantifiable reality.
2. Moreover, the basic units or fundamental elements must be comparable in origins and in results. Therefore human behavior will at bottom be understood as the actions of distinct and disconnected persons, as the very term "individual behavior" indicates.[20]
3. In a mechanistic world, laws are operative, but they have a specific character. They guide processes to equilibrium or disequilibrium. Equilibria are preferred if one wants to maintain the system and prevent chaos. In a mechanistic world-and-life view, therefore, social

19. Mead, 55.

20. The word "individual" became widely used during the Enlightenment and the years of the French Revolution, employed to point to the smallest (i.e., in-divisible) element of society, the atoms out of which the whole structure is created.

and economic stability tend to be interpreted as equilibrium situations. Equilibria are desirable, in markets and in the very functioning of society itself (thus Talcott Parsons).

4. In a mechanistic worldview, "responsibility" and "accountability" are meaningless concepts. Mechanical consequences can be explained only in terms of mechanical causes. It is not human will or responsibility that sets processes in motion; processes are precisely and only ruled by objective factors, which in their turn determine human behavior. In other words, humans are not assumed to act in either responsible or irresponsible ways; they are assumed, rather, to react, like automatons, any of which in similar circumstances would provide the same "responses." Such responses are presumed to be expressions of self-interest.[21]
5. In a mechanistic view of the world, it is also of no use to talk about deeper human causes if one is confronted with a concrete socio-economic problem. The problem has to be taken as it is, as it presents itself now, specifically as a disturbance in the working of the mechanism. Either it will solve itself, if the (mechanical) laws of nature are permitted to operate, or it can be solved by taking the best and most efficient engineering approach to redress it (just as a car is repaired). The mechanistic world, therefore, is not only a world without moral good and evil. It is in fact also a world without a real history.

If we examine this list of five peculiarities of a fully mechanistic interpretation of human society, then indeed our suspicion must grow that they have already exercised a large influence on the public and conventional way of analyzing poverty and on our views of how to deal with it. Here we can trace without any doubt reasons why poverty now looks so "persistent" or intractable to us. For poverty is just the kind of phenomenon that confounds every mechanistic approach. Has not poverty many aspects that cannot be measured? And is it not primarily a social phenomenon, instead

21. Note the following statement of Amartya Sen in his *On Ethics and Economics* (Oxford: Blackwell, 1987): "Perhaps the economist might be personally allowed a moderate dose of friendliness, provided in his economic models he keeps the motivations of human beings pure, simple and hard-headed, and not messed up by such things as goodwill or moral sentiments. . . . Economics . . . has characterized . . . human motivation in spectacularly narrow terms" (p. 1).

of a fate descending on disconnected individuals? And what should be said or done if poverty seems to be the natural outcome of some kind of economic or social equilibrium? It leads immediately to the question whether breaking the current equilibrium — for instance, breaking the equilibrium of a constant general increase in our standard of living — would not be too high a price, or too "unnatural" a step, to overcome the rise of poverty. And what should we say if the persistence of poverty seems to be in some way related to any sort of lack of responsible, nonselfish human behavior, either by the poor themselves or by others who have contributed to their condition? Science is then under the command to keep silent, and usually we with it. Further, if people would suggest that injustice might be involved in the origins or causes of poverty today, the mechanistic framework can offer no response. And finally, if there are any indications that poverty might have its own special history and its own type of dynamics, this would also seem utterly irrelevant from the mechanistic perspective.

Thus the narrowness of the mechanistic world-and-life view, which has come to us via the current intellectual framework of economists and sociologists, has to be seen as a prime cause of the present impasse in the debate about the persistence of poverty in the context of the American welfare system. It explains many forms of distortion in the diagnoses and the therapies. It makes clear, as well, why the "objectification" of the poor, which we noticed in the previous section as a common trait in the liberal and conservative approaches to poverty, could so easily creep in. We can even say that it would obscure any possible causes of the persistence of poverty that are due to the structure or direction of Western society itself. Especially this last point, raised earlier, seems to be of the utmost importance. But can it be sustained and demonstrated?

Questions of Societal Structure and Direction

The idea that the direction or structure of our modern, capitalistic society might itself play a central causative role in persistent poverty seems immediately to collide with a simple counterargument: persistent poverty is a relatively new phenomenon, originating in the 1960s or so, while the order and dynamic of modern society are obviously older than that. As a mixed economy it took its main form not later than in the 1930s. It seems therefore fully inadequate to make the structure and direction of modern society in one or another way "accountable" for the emergence of persistent types of "new" poverty in the United States and Europe.

But this reaction, however appealing at first glance, is superficial. It would hold if, indeed, as is often presumed in the mechanical view of life and society, reality consisted of nothing other than human-made goods and human-made systems that are impervious to any other influences or constraints and in which humans act just like atoms or gears. But that kind of autonomy or self-sufficiency is not given to humankind nor to our systems. Human societies are always bound to a created reality that they must obey and that imposes on them restrictions that cannot simply be overcome by self-generated dynamics.

It is therefore quite possible that an existing social and economic structure, by the power of its own internal dynamics, at a particular moment can run against the wall of persistent problems and insurmountable paradoxes. For dynamic evolution cannot be the rule of everything in creation. Some features of nature and of humankind tend to remain the same, and they block the path of a kind of progress that has eternity and unlimited expansion as its only possible horizon.

Let us consider these suggestions further by treating poverty as a phenomenon shaped both by the structure of modern society and by its main cultural direction.

Since the time of the French Revolution and the industrial revolution, we have been living in a society that is itself to a large extent a mechanical artifact. It is a society founded on two key mechanisms: the market mechanism and the mechanism of democracy. But these two mechanisms do not just exist; they are, and were from the start, clear expressions of a new, formative world-and-life view. For the new cosmopolis, the new mechanistic society, was not only devoutly intended to be, but also constructed as, a project to bring more wealth and more power. It was created to guarantee, by its very structure, an ever-increasing "wealth of nations." And not only this. In the utopian images of the early days, with their expectations of the eternal progress of humankind and of the civic right of each person to pursue his or her own happiness, there was also a deep trust that all forms of poverty and exploitation would automatically fade away, and that the human race would, without fail, improve morally. That was the faith of modernity, the faith in the coming of a new era, constructed on the powers of economic and technological progress, and guaranteed by the correct economic and political institutions or mechanisms of society.

We now know that, despite that faith and despite well-constructed institutions, many serious problems did appear. When these successively appeared — the "social question," unemployment, the environmental problem — society attempted, and still attempts, to deal with them the best way. But it is remarkable that as soon as problems like these have appeared, they have been almost always addressed either by attempting to improve the prevailing mechanisms or by trying to adapt people more closely to the imperatives of what was thought to be an always progressing society. But the most basic questions were not asked, much less answered: Are there creational limits on human efforts? Could it be that the fundamental societal drives for increased power and material goods would finally deprive us of the most basic and deepest values of human life?

It seems that exactly here one of the most fundamental causes can be found for the unexpected rise and persistence of modern poverty. And the reason for this is not difficult to formulate. A society that has set its heart and staked its fate on the promotion of the highest possible economic growth as the means toward wealth and happiness is for that precise reason a very vulnerable society. It must increase its market efficiency and productivity at all costs, even if that requires extruding from the production process many potential workers. It is a well-known fact that all over the world since the beginning of the 1970s the former "natural" correlation between economic growth and expanding employment collapsed, at least partially. Forms of economic growth have appeared, especially in the industrial field, that can be achieved only if employment is cut (the growth of so-called structural or technological unemployment). Multinational concerns such as the Dutch Philips corporation achieved in the 1970s an increase in labor productivity of more than 10 percent annually, which, despite a sales increase of about 8 percent per year, was reached only with the dismissal of about 2 percent of its workforce. But poverty often follows rising unemployment, especially in the absence of good unemployment insurance provisions.

But the relationship between the societal quest for wealth and the structural increase in poverty goes even deeper. Income increases made possible by productivity gains can easily increase poverty in a society. Say that productivity in the industrial sector increases 4 percent annually on average. This gain will be translated into an increase in industrial-sector incomes, legitimately enough. However, if everywhere in society hearts are set on increasing incomes and abundance (for, as John Kenneth Galbraith observed in *The New Industrial State*, "a rising standard of living is an article of faith in western society"), then employees in other sectors will expect and demand income gains that match those in industry. But no corresponding productivity gains are possible in the service sector. A nurse in the hospital cannot help 4 percent more patients every year; a policeman cannot guarantee the safety of more citizens each year. If incomes are raised anyway, then service-sector costs will be driven continually upward. Vital services like health care, public safety, and education will become more and more costly, while industrial products are priced the same or become cheaper. And here we see, indeed, irresistible consequences for poor people, which lead to a kind of paradoxical persistence of poverty.

In the first place, this is true because the increasing costs per unit in all service sectors, by driving prices higher, diminish the demand for those services. One consequence is a contraction of employment, with the elimination especially of the many forms of low-skilled labor that are performed in these sectors. People are becoming too "costly" to be kept in those tasks and offices. But growing unemployment is directly linked to increased poverty.

Second, there is the influence of the increased costs themselves. Vital services like education and medical care become too expensive for the poor. The higher prices of these services may place them beyond the reach of increasing numbers of people. Many people, for instance, will no longer be able to afford adequate health care or will be unable to assure for their children the necessary schooling. A subculture of unhealthy and insufficiently educated people can in this way gradually be generated.

Finally, the government itself, which performs mainly services and has no direct part in industrial activities, is, in effect, "driven out of the market." Its yearly productivity increase is low, lower than the yearly increase of the salaries it must pay. And because society is usually not willing to pay ever-higher taxes, the government has no other choice than to cut its expenditures. And among those expenditures are, no doubt, programs meant to uphold the poor.

This threefold process of less demand for low-skilled labor, higher costs for education and medical care, and the ongoing process of cutting social expenditures has now become visible in all countries of the north, in America just as in Europe. And in its tri-unity it clearly contributes to the growth of persistent poverty in the midst of plenty. More people are becoming poor, or becoming vulnerable to poverty, or becoming mired in poverty. In the midst of our modern industrial societies, a devastating economic and social dynamic favoring poverty has been started.[22]

Given all of this, the conclusion seems indeed inescapable: poverty-increasing tendencies are built into the structure of modern society, but even more into the direction, the orientation, of our society. And these tendencies can no longer be overcome or neutralized by any of the technical devices that are in the tool boxes of either the liberals or the conservatives.

The basic problem is far more than a mechanical problem. At root it is a cultural and even spiritual problem.

An Alternative Approach

Let us try to summarize what we have discovered so far. With the help of a medical analogy — the treatment of a persistent disease — we began with a search for possible explanations of the deadlock in the American debate on poverty, in particular the puzzle of persistent poverty. In this search we looked especially at two promising candidates: the possibility of superficiality and/or narrowed vision in measures to deal practically with poverty, and the possibility of biases in the theoretical understanding of poverty. Our initial investigation of these two possibilities has already led us to some partial conclusions, which can be summarized as follows:

- Our deep faith in the judgment of scientists, including economists and other social scientists, has no doubt led us to undervalue essential insights into poverty and its alleviation that the poor themselves possess.
- The analytical framework used in economics and the other social sciences could easily, because of its mechanistic character, produce blind spots in the view of poverty held by the public and by government. An especially distorting influence we have noted is the objectification of people: regarding them to be conditioned by their culture or by external circumstances.

22. See the discussion in Goudzwaard and Harry de Lange, *Beyond Poverty and Affluence: Toward an Economy of Care,* trans. Mark R. Vander Vennen (Grand Rapids, Mich.: Eerdmans, and Geneva: WCC Publications, 1995).

- The public discussion about poverty and welfare, moreover, has largely fallen into the trap of mutually exclusive, yet also superficial, conservative and liberal views. This has turned attention away from possible deeper reasons for the growth and persistence of poverty.
- An important candidate for the explanation of the growth of hardcore poverty in modern society is society's obsession with rapid economic growth and an ever-increasing standard of living.

These conclusions are partial and even preliminary. But they seem nevertheless valuable, especially if they can point the way to another approach: to another diagnosis and a different way of addressing poverty.[23] That potential seems indeed to be present, at least to some degree. For these conclusions imply at least two possible paths forward.

The first path is related to the deep impact of the modernistic or mechanistic world-and-life view on the social sciences, which has contributed so much to blind spots or biases in the antipoverty fight. Perhaps these blind spots and biases can be attacked or removed by a reorientation of our outlook on poverty in accordance with a broader world-and-life view. If so, we will be able to find new options, also for political practice (I).

In the second place, we saw that the structure and direction of society as a whole might be deeply involved in the process of deepening and hardening American poverty. But this implies, at least, that a partial reorientation or reconstruction of society could contribute to alleviating poverty or at least to ending its growing persistency (II).

Two paths, two possible ways of renewal. But can they really be effective?

23. It must be emphasized here that we may never minimize or legitimize the sufferings of so many people in our society on the grounds that we are unable to conceive of any means to diminish those sufferings. This holds even more when the problem of impoverishment is accompanied by the problem of enrichment — which is a problem especially when it is not thought to be one. Mary Norman Tillman and James Tillman, Jr., two black sociologists, wrote in the late 1960s an impressive study of poverty, which they entitled *Why American Needs Racism and Poverty* (1972). One could certainly say that such a provocative statement is not the best way to start a public discussion on the topic. But the serious charge of the title should give us food for thought. Has perhaps the struggle for enrichment become part of our national character?

A New Understanding of Poverty

The first path has to do with changing our analytical approaches, and it immediately raises the question whether it really can make a difference in our way of dealing with welfare and poverty. What could be the real benefit if the dominant mechanical view of society, with its tendency to objectify people and to see them as determined by circumstances, was replaced by a more "organic," living, view of human society, in which each member of society has to fulfill his or her own roles of responsibility? Can this really lead to a different approach? For example, economics and the other social sciences currently employ mainly a "what-has-caused-this" type of causality. Would it really make a significant difference to broaden this into a "who-has-caused-this" idea of causality? Such a change seems so divorced from the world of political practice. Nevertheless, there are indeed indications that such a change could help. Consider somewhat more precisely, for instance, the character of the present debate between liberals and conservatives on how to fight poverty.

Even a first look reveals that in this debate only two options are in reality entertained, albeit in endless variations. To find good solutions, it is suggested, either something has to be changed in the external — that is, the objectively determined — surroundings of poor people (this is usually termed their "opportunity structure"), or else something has to change in the behavior and attitudes of the poor themselves (i.e., the poor need to adapt themselves better to the present societal system). In the first case (the liberal option that stresses the lack of sufficient opportunities), the various solutions can range between the extremes of a reconstruction of society on the macro level to the (re)equipping of the poor on the micro level (work training, remedial education, employment support services like child care). In the second case (the conservatives' contention that the poor lack initiative or engage in inappropriate behavior), the solutions can range from the option of enforcement (workfare), at one end, to the opposite extreme of simply exposing the poor to the incentives and punishments of the market. In this dialogue, however, we can hear the far echoes of a commonly shared mechanical view of society. According to this consensus, if the outcome of the mechanism is to be improved (in this case, by "producing" less poverty), then the quarrel indeed must be about whether the structures need to be improved or whether the separate parts need change so they will be better adapted to the functioning of the existing whole. But is not such a discussion far too meager and even insulting when we are dealing with responsible beings within an organic society?

Let us therefore start with the concept of living subjects within a society of differentiated responsibilities. In this conception, people who have become poor can never be seen as entirely "determined" in their actions either by external situations or by inner behavioral necessities. In one or another way they themselves, as conscious subjects, react either responsibly or irresponsibly to the impulses from outside. But in making their own subjective decisions, they as living subjects have of course far more to consider and far more at stake than, for instance, just the objective opportunities that do exist (the quality of the *opportunity structure*). At least as important for responsible subjects is what we could call the actual *motivational structure*, which has both an *internal* and an *external* side.[24]

A demotivating *external* context exists if the option of pursuing some specific opportunity is substantially hampered by strongly negative social (public or private) realities or circumstances. In the case of pursuing work, for instance, there may be no one to whom one may safely entrust the children. Public services like garbage collection or health care can be wholly inadequate, or the neighborhood may be crime-ridden. Next to these external factors, there may also be a demotivating *internal* structure. This is related to a person's possible lack of the attitudes and/or motivation needed to escape from poverty. (This could be due to simple laziness, but also to strong influences from a broken past, which simply cannot be overcome on one's own. The idea of a demotivational internal structure therefore carries no intention of blaming or stigmatizing people.)

These simple distinctions, which are derived from a view of causality that is subject-oriented and therefore somewhat broader than the mechanical one, are already helpful in distinguishing between several entirely different situations. There are situations in which either the liberal or the conservative option would be useful. But there are also situations in which neither would work. In fact, at least four different cases have to be distinguished.

24. An analysis that comes quite close to what I mean here is Reginald Clark's beautiful book, *Family Life and School Achievement: Why Poor Black Children Succeed or Fail* (1983; Chicago: Univ. of Chicago Press paperback, 1984). Here the central role of parents and their responsibility is studied in this nuanced fashion. Similarly, in Wilson's analysis of the problems of the "truly disadvantaged," we find concepts like "social buffer" and "concentration effects," which can be understood as ways of dealing with conscious human reactions to impulses from the outside.

1. In the first case there are no hindrances in the internal and external motivational structures, but the opportunity structure is deficient. For instance, people desire to work and are able to work, but cannot find employment. In such a clearly distinguishable situation, obviously the creation of better opportunities, such as the creation of more jobs, should form the heart of the fight against poverty. The "liberal" program is suitable here, and its measures will naturally correspond with the real needs and the responsible insights of those who are poor.
2. It can be that the opportunity side is not distorted (jobs are available) and the external motivational structure is not negative (people are equipped for work), and yet poverty exists and even grows. In this case, the real problem obviously is a negative internal motivational structure. Here a combination of social support services and an emphatic work obligation may indeed be the most responsible measure. And we may expect, in this case, too, that responsible poor people will understand and support such measures, with the proviso that such measures should never be implemented without seeking their insight and advice.
3. A very different situation and challenge exists when there is some combination of two negative elements. This third case combines a lack of opportunities either with a demotivating external context (when, for instance, no work is available and the neighborhood is socially disintegrating) or with a clear lack of internal motivation (e.g., there is no job and no motivation to find employment). In such cases it will be clear that neither the standard conservative nor the standard liberal solutions will work. Even worse, in such cases we must expect that conventional liberal or conservative remedies will make the problem even more intense than it was. In the case of a lack of internal motivation, for instance, a simple transfer of money will certainly not diminish the negative motivation, but may even strengthen it. On the other hand, in the case of a strong external demotivating circumstance, a policy of obligatory workfare will likely make people bitter, because it seems to force them into patterns of irresponsible behavior. In those circumstances, poor people may well interpret workfare as an attack on their personal dignity.
4. The final case is where both the internal and external motivational structures are negative. In this case, we can indeed speak of a cultural

(or perhaps urban) crisis. Precisely because of its cultural character, neither the standard liberal nor the standard conservative approaches will be helpful.

Now, it may be said that the mere existence today of various forms of persistent poverty, both within and outside inner cities, makes it almost impossible for anyone in the poverty debate to deny that what may be at work is more than the simple cases 1 and 2. At least some combination of negative elements in both the opportunity and the motivational structures is present (cases 3 and 4). In most of the material about present hard-core poverty, in Europe, but even more in the United States, we find clear indications either of a lack of jobs combined with unfavorable external circumstances or of a mutual reinforcement of negative internal and external motivational forces, and sometimes of a combination of the two.

But this implies that only measures that have more than one track can be successful. The good policies are those that try to deal both with the possible lack of labor opportunities and with the internal and external factors that tend to demotivate people.

In summary, therefore, three things can be said about what is needed. First, in contrast with the usual liberal and conservative approaches, programs to fight hard-core poverty should be multiple-purpose programs from the outset, combining elements of job creation and/or better public services with the building up of a better community life. Second, it must be stressed that it is impossible to improve particularly problems in the motivational structure without the active input of the poor themselves. Third, all relevant groups and institutions — including schools, churches, labor unions, government agencies, and corporations — should be involved and addressed in their respective differentiated responsibilities to prevent and to overcome poverty. For living up to the measure of each one's personal and institutional responsibility is the foundational layer of society, not only for the creation of adequate opportunities, but also for the healing of a deficient human motivation.[25]

25. Here, too, Clark's important study, *Family Life and School Achievement,* should be noted, because it displays real insight into the possible influences of both the opportunity structure and the motivational structures. This insight leads Clark to the conclusion that "[a]t some point, an escalating societal disenchantment with the overall quality of life in our communities will *move* us to address ourselves to the inattention of our

Renewing Society

With this last remark we are already approaching a discussion of the last possible — and necessary — way to fight against persistent poverty: changing the structure and direction of society itself. The connection of this with the issue of responsibility is direct and unavoidable.

This is not difficult to explain. I have noted already a number of critical issues of responsibility for poverty and its alleviation: a responsibility of the poor themselves to react fruitfully to impulses; a responsibility, also of others, to create and maintain an external context that motivates rather than demobilizes; and a responsibility to prevent a shifting of burdens from the rich and powerful to the poor and weak. But all of these charges to engage in responsible action are doomed to remain unanswered — to be mere moralistic hot air — if they are not in one way or another bound to specific human agents and to various social institutions, both public and nongovernmental. Further, even if this linkage with the institutional side of society is made, there still is no guarantee of a good outcome — people escaping poverty — unless there is what we might call a common "willingness of direction": a general intention in society as a whole to eliminate this fundamental social disease, which represents at the same time a fundamental waste of human economic resources.

In the previous section, however, it became already clear that the present direction of our modern society — its yearning for an always higher material standard of living — acts as an enormous stumbling block. For this acquisitive mood aggravates especially the persistent types of poverty — taking away jobs in the sector of services and low-skilled labor, increasing the costs and prices of particularly medical care and education, and leading every government to the necessity of a continual process of cutting social expenditures. So indeed not only the institutional structure of modern society requires discussion, but also its greedy direction. And we must remind ourselves that this is our own society, the one for which we are co-responsible.

To explore these two dimensions of modern society, structure and

---

public institutions to (1) the hideous degree of stress many parents undergo in their daily psychological and emotional routines, (2) the massive social and economic decline in low-income American families, [and] (3) state-sanctioned stereotypes and assumptions about family cultural patterns and needs" (p. 209).

direction, more carefully in their relation to poverty, we take a short and final look at the ideals and blueprints of modernity, where, of course, the sources of our modern society are found.

In the classical ideals of modernity, the problem of the best structure for society has always been framed as the question of what kind of social, economic, and political mechanisms (the mechanisms of the market, planning, and democracy) would best benefit a society consisting of individuals. Further, this strategy of deciding on a societal structure by working with these two poles — the mechanisms, on one side, and the individual "gears," on the other — was at the same time determinative for the development and direction of society. For in this modern societal project, the individuals themselves have, by definition, nothing to do other than to look after their own self-interest. Their autonomy consists of seeking individual pleasure and avoiding individual pain. For it was precisely the idea of a full and free interplay between the autonomous feedback mechanisms of society, on the one side, and the autonomously self-interested individuals, on the other, that fascinated Enlightenment thinkers like Adam Smith and Rousseau. The former was concerned about the mechanism of the market, the latter with the mechanism of democracy in the state, but both predicted a beautiful outcome of that interplay. But more: these ideas also became the basic formula for the rational construction of modern society itself. The formula is thus still present with us in many respects.

But this formula lacks two elements essential for the good and harmonious development of human society. First, it lacks the element of the responsibility and accountability of persons. In this model, the individuals are not supposed to take any specific care for their neighbors; well-functioning mechanisms themselves provide such care. The only thing required of the individuals is to stick to the rules of the mechanisms. Second, the element of the diversity of social institutions is missing. Families, schools, churches: these were for the great thinkers of modernity never necessary and valuable building blocks, but rather were usually seen merely as remnants from an earlier, a premodern, era. Strong social ties between persons were even thought likely to decrease the chances of good outcomes — either to distort the free interplay between the individual citizen and the mechanism of the state, or to hamper the free interplay between individual producers and consumers within the market mechanism.

Such a permissive, pleasure-oriented society, lacking any call to persons to take care for others and with a total neglect of the possible contribution of social groups, communities, and institutions — is that not just asking for the growing isolation and deprivation of those persons who have no helper and who are too weak to become full participants in the economic or political mechanisms? The question answers itself. But this answer also makes it clear that in these two missing elements the point of entry has to be found for structural ways of dealing with poverty, other than the conventional ones. Then neither the (conservative) strategy of fitting individual behavior more closely to the existing mechanisms of state and market, nor the (liberal) prescription of a better adaptation of these mechanisms to the needs of the individual will be adequate. To the contrary, the strengthening and building up of a common public consciousness then becomes essential, with "habits of the heart" that go deeper than any form of "ontological individualism."[26] And they have to be combined with the strengthening and building up of institutions and communities (especially in poor areas) that can fill the vacuum of the many almost forgotten responsibilities.[27]

But what does this view imply for institutions like the state and the market? Should they be abolished or be tightly constrained because they are in themselves simply inadequate mechanisms? Of course not. These worthwhile social institutions have been reduced to mere mechanisms by modern thinkers and modern society. But that is not their necessary and essential character. No culture on earth exists without the presence of some kind of market and some kind of state. For humans need exchange, they need each other's economic (productive) services to keep alive, just as they need a system of governance to deal with conflicts. The problem, therefore, does not lie in the institutions of the market and state as such. It lies in the fact that both of them have been cut loose from their original and intrinsic meanings and characteristics. The market and its participants have been cut loose from their task of carefully administering society's resources, and the state from its task of administering a society's public justice. And at the same time, these institutions, because of their "mechanization," have been removed from, or lifted out of, the broad domain of equal but differentiated social institutions and responsibilities. For it is here that both the state and the institutions of the market belong: within the panoply of all other social institutions, like families, farms, corporations, schools, churches, and voluntary groups, each with its own calling.

26. Robert N. Bellah et al., *Habits of the Heart* (Berkeley: Univ. of California Press, 1985).

27. Wilson, 143.

The implications of this insight for the struggle against poverty are twofold. The first implication is that we together, as citizens of a rich and increasingly rich society, must understand that the necessary expansion of efforts to fight poverty will not be possible if we maintain our incessant quest for higher and higher income and consumption levels. For how can our economic institutions — corporations, other enterprises, and labor unions — fight poverty more directly, for example by maintaining and creating meaningful work, if all economic margins and degrees of freedom are absorbed in advance in the name of promoting greater incomes and consumption? Our society will be able to fulfill its economic duties to the poor and to nature only if it becomes willing to save a part of its productive efforts explicitly for the purpose of caring for the needy. For this, it must change its economic horizon from the unlimited expansion of income and consumption to an "economy of enough."

The second implication is directly related to the institution of the state. It is far more than just a democratic mechanism. It is, as a human institution, tied to the service of public justice in society. That means that it must deal with poverty along the path of justice. Three or four dimensions of responsibility can be distinguished in this role or mandate of the state.

1. The first dimension is the responsibility of *public arbitration*, of intervening between groups or institutions in society. This task is especially important when there is not merely a collision of interests but when a misuse of power takes place that threatens the life-possibilities of a weaker group. In the case of poverty, we can point here not only to the problem of racial discrimination but also to the efforts of some social and economic interest groups to shift publicly the burdens to the weak, for instance, by regressive tax changes or by excessive wage and price demands.
2. The second dimension is the responsibility of *public provision*. I have stressed above the great importance, for the poor as well as others, of healthy opportunity and motivational structures. Their formation is not the sole responsibility of government. But government does have a responsibility, in the name of public justice, if there is a lack of something crucial to the public welfare, for instance elementary schooling, the maintenance of peace in the streets, the removal of garbage, the availability of primary health care. If such things are not supplied privately and/or they are not accessible to the poor, then the

government is obligated to step in, just to be a shield for the poor in the name of justice. Public provision also means that the government is entitled to obligate all citizens to contribute proportionately to social insurance so that all citizens have access to the necessary financial means to cope with personal and family emergencies.

3. The third dimension is the responsibility of *public regard.* Governments cannot solve all the problems of society. Most activities of life are not, certainly not in the first place, the responsibility of government nor the product of its motion. They are rather the domain of families, friends, farmers, artists, educators, entrepreneurs, employees, and more. But it can happen that some essential tasks are not institutionalized, or that society has so degenerated that persons and various institutions are unable or unwilling to fulfill their respective and diverse responsibilities.

   Here again we meet the issue of the direction of society as a whole. That direction can be so much restricted by, and closed in to, the pursuit of private material interests that there is a concrete and explicit denial of original human callings and mandates. People who can work may refuse all kinds of work; companies that are bound, just because of the nature of normative economic activity, to take good care of all human and natural resources, can spoil and misuse those resources; schools can carry out their educative task so poorly that students are not prepared for adult responsibilities. In such cases, government must act to ensure, as far as that is in its power, the fulfillment of responsibilities. However, the government is never entitled to full control of private lives or organizations. This does not mean that it must remain silent, because gross dereliction of responsibilities damages the entire commonwealth, and government may never idly stand by when this happens. It must act to defend and preserve the commonwealth.

4. In acting to bolster the fulfillment of responsibilities, government may take several paths. It may need in some instances only to educate people and institutions about their responsibilities. But in other cases it may need to stimulate positive alternatives. In extreme cases, government may even need to engage in *public enforcement.* Such action may, for instance, be necessary when irresponsibility causes violation of the norms of public justice themselves. This is the case, for example, if a person rejects employment in order to receive welfare

benefits, while also earning money off the books, or if a corporation does damage to the health of its employees or of the community surrounding its plants. In such cases government must use its legal power to enforce responsible action.

With this short overview of the possible positive tasks of government I have completed the sketch I had in mind in writing this essay. This does not mean that I have supplied a complete picture. But I hope that the scene that has now become visible shows that poverty, even if it grows paradoxically and persistently in the midst of societies of material abundance, is neither a fated outcome nor an unexplainable mystery. It is, rather, a challenge to think and to act responsibly.

What's Wrong with Welfare Rights?

Mary Ann Glendon

EVERY advanced democratic state is currently grappling in its own way with a common set of challenges: how to provide humanitarian aid without undermining personal responsibility; how to maintain a healthy mix in a mixed economy; how to preserve a just balance among individual freedom, equality, and social solidarity. In the case of welfare, the basic problem is nothing less than the great dilemma of how to hold together the two halves of the divided soul of liberalism: our love of individual liberty and our sense of a community for which we accept a common responsibility.

In the United States, these weighty questions are being debated in an alarmingly simplistic fashion. Advocates of public assistance as an entitlement wrangle endlessly with proponents of reduced public responsibility for the needy. Meanwhile, spreading social disarray threatens the very foundations of our democratic experiment. More and more members of the next generation of Americans are caught up in a culture of dependency and despair from which many will never escape.

It is easy to see why many well-meaning people frustrated with our nation's lack of success in fighting poverty are attracted to the idea of a "right" to at least a subsistence level of public benefits. The idea of a "welfare right" sounds respectful of human dignity; it helps to counter the stigma associated with reliance on government assistance; and it fits nicely into familiar political categories. In an era of flourishing suspicion of welfare recipients and expanding scepticism about government social programs, it is not surprising that many advocates for the poor cling to the concept of a government guarantee of welfare benefits for the needy. How else will the poor be assured of protection and care? But a right to welfare is not the right way to ensure the welfare of the poor. Nations with a more robust political commitment than ours to assisting the poor do not, we will see, ground their commitment in civil-rights types of constitutional guarantees. And we will discover that a careful examination of the American rejection of the concept of welfare rights can guide us toward a better way of ensuring assistance for the poor.

The Failed Welfare Rights Revolution

In the United States of the late 1960s and early 1970s, when the judicial rights revolution was in full swing, poverty lawyers and allied legal scholars were convinced that the time for welfare rights had come. They urged the courts to supplement our expanding catalog of political and civil rights with certain social and economic rights — to housing, education, and a minimum decent subsistence. The advocates of welfare rights were not deterred by the absence of pertinent constitutional language. After all, if the Court could find a right to privacy in the "penumbra" of the Bill of Rights, who knew what else might be discovered there?

Those efforts to constitutionalize what were historically matters of legislative discretion had only partial success. The Supreme Court did hold that, once legislatures bring into being certain entitlements such as welfare and disability benefits, the recipients have a constitutional right not to be deprived of those benefits without procedural due process.[1] The Court declined, however, to find that the entitlements themselves were constitutionally required.[2] The Justices were not impressed with the argument that affirmative government duties could be teased out of the "equal protection" language of the Fourteenth Amendment.

That result is hardly surprising in view of the fact that the welfare state was not even a twinkle in the eye of the drafters of the Civil War Amendments,

1. *Goldberg v. Kelly,* 397 U.S. 254 (1970) (welfare entitlements); *Mathews v. Eldridge,* 424 U.S. 319 (1976) (social security disability payments).

2. For example, *Lindsey v. Normet,* 405 U.S. 56 (1972) (no constitutional right to housing); *San Antonio Independent School District v. Rodriguez,* 411 U.S. 1 (1973) (no constitutional right to education).

much less the Founding Fathers. Failed constitutional arguments, though, have a way of reappearing. And though the welfare rights banner attracts few marchers at the moment, proponents of welfare as a pure entitlement have the same notion at heart. So it is important carefully to consider whether or not a contrary outcome in the 1960s and 1970s would have yielded greater progress in the antipoverty fight. The experience of other liberal democracies is illuminating in that connection, for most of their constitutions *do* contain welfare rights or solemn acknowledgments of collective responsibility to provide minimum decent subsistence to needy citizens.[3]

The first lesson to be learned from examining the way welfare is imagined in foreign legal systems is that, in this area as in so many others, the United States is in a class by itself. Our regime of constitutional rights was over a century old when the New Deal transformed the classical-liberal night-watchman state into a social-liberal regulatory welfare state. In most of the nations with which we ordinarily compare ourselves, the sequence was just the reverse: the foundations of the welfare system were in place well before the appearance of regimes of judicially enforceable constitutional rights.[4] Another element of American distinctiveness is the refusal of American governments to ratify international human rights instruments containing social and economic rights. And finally there is the unusual structure of our welfare state, which, to a much greater extent than elsewhere, leaves pensions, health, and other benefits to be organized privately, mainly through the workplace, rather than directly through the public sector. A brief elaboration of these points will suffice to show how differently rights and responsibilities are understood in America as compared to other North Atlantic countries.

Rights before Welfare

Americans are justly proud of the fact that, prior to 1945, we were one of very few countries where constitutional rights were protected by the insti-

3. Louis Favoreu, "La protection des droits economiques et sociaux dans les constitutions," in *Conflict and Integration: Comparative Law in the World Today* (Tokyo: Chuo Univ. Press, 1988), 691-92.

4. E.g., France adopted a limited form of constitutional control only in 1958; constitutional review did not become a significant feature of the German legal order until 1951; and Canada did not acquire judicial review until 1982.

tution of judicial review. However, our courts seldom exercised their power of reviewing governmental action for conformity to constitutional norms until the turn of the century. American judges then began energetically striking down factory laws and other early social legislation — just as legislatures in the rest of the industrialized world were laying the foundations of their welfare states with statutes broadly similar in spirit to those our courts were nullifying.

It was not until the active period of constitution making following World War II that bills of rights and institutional mechanisms to enforce them were widely adopted by other nations.[5] Nevertheless, most liberal democracies did not adopt the American method of judicial review; they opted instead for variants of a system that has come to be known as the "European model" of constitutional control. The principal feature that distinguishes the European from the American model is that, under the former, constitutional questions must be referred to a special tribunal that deals only or mainly with such matters. In sharp contrast, in the United States, and in the handful of countries that have imitated our system, ordinary courts have the power to rule on constitutional issues in regular lawsuits. Even among the nations that have adopted a form of the American model — Canada, Japan, and the Republic of Ireland — the United States remains unique. For no other country's courts have exercised their power to declare executive or legislative action unconstitutional with such frequency and boldness as their American counterparts.

What Counts as a Right?

A renowned European legal historian recently compiled a "basic inventory" of rights that have been accepted by most Western countries at the present time.[6] The list included, first and foremost, human dignity. Next came personal freedom. Following that were fair procedures to protect against arbitrary governmental action, active political rights (especially the right to

5. For a concise survey, see Louis Favoreu, "American and European Models of Constitutional Justice," in David Clark, ed., *Comparative and Private International Law: Essays in Honor of John Henry Merryman* (Berlin: Duncker & Humblot, 1990), 105.

6. Franz Wieacker, "Foundations of European Legal Culture," *American Journal of Comparative Law* 37, no. 1 (1990): 29.

vote), equality before the law, and then society's responsibility for the social and economic conditions of its members.

It is hard to say what would strike most American readers of that list as more strange — the omission of property rights or the inclusion, in a catalog of "rights," of affirmative welfare *obligations.* Yet the list is an accurate one. Welfare rights have been accorded a place beside traditional political and civil liberties in the national constitutions of most liberal democracies.[7] It is the eighteenth-century United States Constitution that, with the passage of time, has become anomalous in this respect.

The fact that welfare rights have been accorded constitutional status in so many countries cannot be attributed exclusively to the relatively recent vintage of their constitutions. It represents, rather, the confluence of Christian social thought (via Christian political parties), democratic socialist thought, and the kind of conservatism that is organic or social rather than individualistic or libertarian. Continental Europeans, whether of the right or the left, are not in principle so antagonistic toward the state as are Anglo-Americans, and are much more likely than Americans to take for granted that governments have affirmative duties to actively promote the well-being of their citizens.[8] Even the leading European conservative parties espouse openly what American conservatives have only accepted grudgingly and *sub silentio:* a mixed economy and a moderately interventionist state. A broad social consensus in Europe supports the subsidization of child-raising families and accepts the public funding of health care, higher education, unemployment compensation, and old age insurance at levels most Americans find scarcely imaginable.[9] American politicians of both the right and the left, by contrast, find it obligatory to profess mistrust of government.

7. The formulations vary from the bare recitation in the German Basic Law of 1949 that the Federal Republic of Germany is a "social" state (*Basic Law,* Article 20), to detailed lists of specific social and economic rights such as those contained in the constitutions of France, Italy, Japan, Spain, and the Nordic countries. See Paul Marshall, "Rights Talk and Welfare Policy," appendix II, 296f. in this volume.

8. Gerhard Casper, "European Convergence," *Univ. of Chicago Law Review* 58 (1991): 441, 445.

9. See William Pfaff, *Barbarian Sentiments: How the American Century Ends* (New York: Hill & Wang, 1989), 25.

International Welfare Rights

Continental European thinking about welfare prevailed in the principal post–World War II international human rights documents. Article 25 of the *United Nations Universal Declaration of Human Rights,* adopted by the General Assembly in 1948, provides that

> Everyone has the right to a standard of living adequate for the health and well-being of himself and his family, including food, clothing, housing and medical care and necessary social services, and the right to security in the event of unemployment, sickness, disability, widowhood, old age or other lack of livelihood in circumstances beyond his control.

To implement that principle, the U.N. *Covenant on Economic, Social, and Cultural Rights* was opened for signatures in 1966. The *Covenant* came into force a decade later, after being ratified by nearly ninety countries. The United States is the only one of the liberal democracies that has failed to ratify that instrument. Neither have we ratified its companion, the U.N. *Covenant on Civil and Political Rights.*[10]

A chief reason for this reticence on the part of Republican and Democratic administrations alike resides in our prudent unwillingness to subject ourselves to the jurisdiction of international organizations dominated by enemies or critics of the United States. Republicans, moreover, have been opposed in principle to characterizing a vast new range of social and economic interests as fundamental rights. A further and highly significant reason concerns the adverse legal consequences that would almost certainly follow from the uniquely American understanding of what it means to have a right. That understanding, about which I shall have more to say presently, would convert the sort of "right" that is understood elsewhere as purely aspirational into a basis for innumerable individual claims and lawsuits.

10. Richard Lillich, "United States Ratification of the United Nations Covenants," *Georgia Journal of International and Comparative Law* 20 (1990): 279. The United States did, however, sign the *Universal Declaration* and the Helsinki *Final Act* of 1975, which (like the *Universal Declaration*) calls for a nonbinding commitment to stated international norms of human rights.

Welfare Rights and Welfare States

What then has been the experience of liberal democracies that have enshrined welfare rights in their constitutions? Does that experience shed any light on what might have happened here if the Supreme Court had ruled in favor of welfare rights? What does it suggest might be the likely outcome if we seek progress in the antipoverty fight by a firmer entrenchment of more generous government benefits for the needy?

It is, upon reflection, not difficult to see why entitlement advocates in America have not put the spotlight on welfare rights elsewhere. In the first place, no liberal democracy has ever placed social and economic rights on precisely the same legal footing as the familiar civil and political liberties.[11] In some countries, for example, constitutional welfare language is so cryptic as to remain meaningless without extensive legislative specification (e.g., the declaration that the German republic is a "social" state).[12] More commonly, the various social and economic rights are specifically enumerated, but their special nature is flagged by presenting them as statements of political principles and goals to guide the organs of government as they carry out their respective functions. For example, the Swedish Instrument of Government provides, in a section entitled "The Basic Principles of the Constitution" that "[t]he personal, economic and cultural welfare of the individual shall be fundamental aims of the activities of the community. In particular, it shall be incumbent on the community to secure the right to work, to housing and to education and to promote social care and security as well as a favorable living environment."[13]

Continental lawyers call such rights "programmatic" to emphasize that they do not give rise to directly enforceable individual claims but await implementation through legislative or executive action and budgetary ap-

11. Favoreu, "La protection des droits economiques et sociaux," puts it this way: "[T]here are two categories of fundamental rights: immutable and absolute rights that exist whatever the epoch or the reigning ideology; and other rights, known as economic and social rights, that 'carry a certain coefficient of contingency and relativity' and whose recognition is a function of the state of society and its evolution" (p. 701). See Marshall, "Rights Talk and Welfare Policy," 277ff. in this volume, for further discussion of these different kinds of rights.

12. German *Basic Law* (1949), Art. 20.

13. Gisbert H. Flanz, "Sweden," in Albert P. Blaustein and Gisbert H. Flanz, eds., *Constitutions of the World* (Dobbs Ferry, N.Y.: Oceana, 1985), 9-11.

propriations. Such programmatic rights figure prominently in the constitutions of the Nordic countries as well as in the French, Greek, Italian, Japanese, and Spanish constitutions. It is striking that in all those countries the welfare state has been constructed by legislation through ordinary political processes — just as it has in the United States. Thus, in practice, the contrast between the United States and countries where welfare rights have been constitutionalized is much less sharp than it appears on paper.

One cannot conclude, however, that "programmatic" rights and obligations are of no practical significance. One important legal effect is that they endow the statutes enacted to carry out the constitutional "program" with a strong presumption of constitutionality. Nor can one discount the likelihood that these aspirational statements have a modest influence on public, judicial, and legislative deliberation about rights and welfare, especially in countries where constitutional welfare commitments have issued from, or were grafted onto, a well-established tradition of an affirmatively acting state. The idea that securing some form of governmental guarantee of provision for the needy is a positive gain has some merit.

However, at the most practical level there does not appear to be any strong correlation between the presence of, or the degree of emphasis on, welfare rights in the constitutions of affluent democracies and the generosity of welfare states as measured by the proportion of national expenditures devoted to health, housing, social security, and social assistance. That is the perhaps surprising conclusion we must take from examining evidence such as that in Table 1 on page 89.

As the table indicates, the United Kingdom, with no constitutional welfare rights (and no single-document constitution), devotes proportionately more of its resources to social expenditures than its richer "neighbor" Denmark, where rights to work, education, and social assistance are constitutionally guaranteed. And social expenditures consume considerably more of the budget of the Federal Republic of Germany, whose constitution merely announces that it is a "social" state, than they do in Sweden or Italy, where welfare rights are spelled out in some detail. The peculiar structure of our own welfare state makes it difficult to fit the United States into such statistical comparisons. But most analyses give us a relatively poor showing on most counts, and perhaps especially with respect to assistance to families raising children.[14]

14. See Sheila Kammerman and Alfred Kahn, *Income Transfers for Families with Children: An Eight-Country Study* (Philadelphia: Temple Univ. Press, 1983); Samuel

Table 1 Proportion of Central Government Expenditures Devoted to Health, Housing, Social Security, and Welfare in Selected Countries in 1988.

	Central Government Expenditures for Social Purposes (percentage)
Federal Republic of Germany	67.6
Sweden	55.3
Norway	46.8
Italy	45.8
United Kingdom	44.5
United States	44.0
Canada	43.2
Ireland	42.7
Denmark	42.4

Source: *World Development Report 1990,* Table 11, pp. 198-99.

If there *is* a relation between the constitutional status of welfare rights and the type and strength of welfare commitments in a given society, it seems to be but a loose relationship of consanguinity, with both the constitution and the welfare system influenced by such factors as the homogeneity or diversity of the population; the degree to which mistrust of government has figured in the country's political history; the vitality of political parties; the health of the legislative process; and the degree of individualism in the culture.

This kind of inconclusive speculation seems to lead only to the sort of conclusions that make sociology so unsatisfying to many people. It is difficult to become excited about the idea that a host of mutually conditioning factors, of which the constitutional status of welfare rights may be

---

Preston, "Children and the Elderly in the U.S.," *Scientific American,* Dec. 1984, 44-49; and Timothy Smeeding and Barbara Torrey, "Poor Children in Rich Countries," *Science,* Nov. 1988, 873.

both cause and consequence, are involved in determining the shape of a given country's welfare state — its basic commitments, the priorities among those commitments, the spirit in which it is administered, the degree of support and approval it wins from taxpayers, and the extent to which it disables or empowers those who resort to it.

What If . . . ?

That very inconclusiveness, though, might be taken by American rights enthusiasts as a basis for arguing that social and economic rights should be constitutionalized here or that the United States should adhere to international instruments providing for such rights. If the experience of other liberal democracies is any guide, one might argue, there is unlikely to be any harm in granting constitutional status to social and economic rights, and there might be some beneficial effects. However, those would be risky inferences to draw from cross-national comparisons, for reasons that reside not in the foreign experience, but in our own distinctive American culture of rights.

We Americans, for better or worse, take rights very seriously. Not only the term, but the very idea, of "programmatic" rights is unfamiliar and uncongenial to us. It is almost inconceivable that constitutional welfare rights, had they appeared in the United States, would be regarded by the public or treated by the legal community as mere statements of legislative and executive goals. Americans are accustomed to the notion that if we have a constitutional right to something, we can go to court to enforce that right, and that standing behind the court's order are sheriffs, marshalls, and the National Guard, if necessary.

Yet as soon as we begin to imagine constitutional welfare rights that are other than programmatic guides for legislative action we are headed down a road that no other country, including the former socialist states, has in fact traveled. However seriously programmatic welfare rights are treated by legislatures, executives, courts, and publics in other nations, they are not understood to be identical with immediately enforceable civil and political rights.[15] But what if, nonetheless, welfare benefits were to become a constitutionally guaranteed entitlement in the United States?

15. For a fuller discussion of this point, see Marshall, "Rights Talk and Welfare Policy," 277ff. in this volume.

The most directly foreseeable consequence of according constitutional status to social and economic rights would be a litigation explosion of heroic proportions. Would the benefits of that litigation outweigh the disadvantages? It is sometimes said that such lawsuits will prod government agencies into being more responsive and responsible. But under conditions of scarcity, the costs of legal defense (in dollars and morale) plus the occasional high damage award would more likely prod financially strapped local providers in the other direction, toward service cutbacks or eliminating some programs altogether.

No other country has had any experience that can guide us here. The fact is that we Americans place a unique degree of reliance on the system of damage awards (in both ordinary personal litigation and constitutional tort litigation) to perform certain social tasks that other advanced industrial nations handle with a more diverse range of techniques, including, notably, direct health and safety regulation and more comprehensive systems of social insurance.[16] But a potential litigation explosion is not the main reason we should avoid the welfare rights route. A more robust guarantee of government benefits to the needy is the wrong path to take in reforming welfare if what we seek is to fight poverty more effectively.

Finding Our Own Path

Other countries may have little to teach us about the serious consequences of extreme litigiousness, but their experience may help us to find a path to real welfare reform by heightening our awareness of positive indigenous resources that we ourselves are inclined to overlook or underrate. In recent years, policymakers in more highly centralized welfare states have begun to gaze wistfully at the American capacity for cooperation between governmental and nongovernmental organizations in the areas of health, education, and welfare, and at the ability our kind of federalism gives us to innovate and experiment creatively with diverse approaches to stubborn social problems.

The United States represents a rare working example, albeit an incomplete and imperfect one, of the principle of "subsidiarity": the notion

16. Basil S. Markesinis, "Litigation-Mania in England, Germany and the USA: Are We So Very Different?" *Cambridge Law Journal* 49 (1990): 233, 242-43, 263.

that no social task should be allocated to a body larger than the smallest one that can effectively do the job. The theory of subsidiarity, which is rooted in Christian social thought, provides a basis for more nuanced ways of thinking about the state, the market, civil society, and the individual than are available to us if we rely on the standard liberal and conservative mental frameworks that dominate public policy debate and analysis.

How unfortunate it would be if we Americans were to permit essential features of our system to atrophy just when they were most needed! Yet that is precisely the danger of our current impoverished political discourse, a discourse conducted only in terms of individuals, the state, and the market — leaving out all the intermediate institutions of civil society. A welfare debate that remains confined to shouting matches between proponents of more government social entitlements and advocates of chopping welfare because it only enables irresponsibility is a debate that mistakes the real contours of life and diverts us from resources that make possible real reform. Worse yet, guided by an impoverished social ontology, many government policies over the past few decades have actually helped to weaken the nation's families, schools, churches, neighborhoods, workplace associations, and other social groups.

What those who place excessive reliance on the state or the market have failed to appreciate is the extent to which both states and markets depend on cultural foundations. Below the surface of the sterile debate between hard-hearted libertarians and ham-fisted statists festers a long neglected political problem. Liberal democratic states require of their citizens certain kinds of excellence. They must ask men and women to possess and practice certain virtues that are not easy to acquire: respect for the dignity and worth of one's fellow human beings, self-restraint, self-reliance, and compassion. The fact is that neither a strong commitment to individual and minority rights nor a commitment to public assistance — not even America's modest one — can long be sustained without the active support of a citizenry that is willing to respect the rights of others, not just in the abstract but often at some cost to themselves; that is prepared to accept some responsibility for the poorest and most vulnerable members of society; and that is prepared to take significant responsibility for themselves and their own dependents.

The essential question, however, and one that seldom gets asked, is this: Where do such qualities come from? Where do people acquire an internalized willingness to view others with genuine regard for their dignity and concern for their well-being, rather than as objects, means, or obstacles? These qualities cannot be generated by governments or instilled by fear and force. The fact is that our welfare state, minimal though it may be, our market-based economy, and our experiment in democratic government all rest to a great extent on habits and practices formed within fragile social structures — families, neighborhoods, schools, religious and workplace associations, and other communities of memory and mutual aid — structures that must bear great weight just at a time when they themselves are in faltering condition.

The question then becomes: What, if anything, can be done to create and maintain, or at least to avoid undermining or destroying, social conditions that foster the peculiar combination of qualities that are required to sustain our commitments to the rule of law, individual freedom, and compassionate welfare provision? In a large, heterogeneous nation like the United States, the question is particularly urgent. America is especially well endowed with social resources, but we have tended to take that social wealth for granted, consuming our inherited capital at a faster rate than we are replenishing it. Like an athlete who develops the muscles in his upper body but lets his legs grow weak, we have nurtured our strong rights tradition while neglecting the cultural foundation upon which that tradition rests.

But to recognize that our crisis is a cultural one is only the beginning of awareness. In America religion is and always has been at the heart of culture. Thus recent attempts to deliberate weighty public matters while banishing religiously grounded moral convictions from public argument have separated Americans from their deepest springs of meaning, as well as from fertile sources of renewal. Until religious voices regain their rightful places in the public square, political discourse will remain impoverished. And until religion is restored to its rightful place as the first of freedoms, the United States risks destroying the groups that have proved time and again their capacity to deliver education, health care, and other social services more efficiently, effectively, and humanely than the state.

If the seedbeds of civic virtue are to be revitalized, it will be necessary to take a fresh look at our constitutional framework, and to recall that individual rights are but one set of elements in a larger constitutional structure. The parts of the constitutional design that have been neglected by constitutional lawyers in recent years — federalism, the legislative branch, and the ideal of government by the people — have an important bearing on the maintenance of the social capital upon which individual rights and the general welfare ultimately depend. The parts of the Bill of Rights that elites would like to forget protect not only individuals, but also institutions and associations — churches, citizen militias, and juries. The first of freedoms, the free exercise of religion, has been severely curtailed by the maximalist version of the separation of church and state that took rise in the Supreme Court's decisions beginning in the 1940s.

And so, by a circuitous route, a cross-national approach to rights and the welfare state points back toward the American Constitution and toward the "Madisonian understanding that individual liberty and strong local institutions need not be at cross-purposes with one another."[17] If America's endangered social environments do indeed hold the key to simultaneously maintaining a liberal-democratic regime of rights and a compassionate social safety net, then we need to start thinking about the effect of both rights and welfare, as currently conceived, on the settings where we first learn to respect the rights of, and care for, the needs of others. We need to recall that an active government often acts best by strengthening the rights and responsibilities of other institutions within a just social order, and by "call[ing] people and institutions to healthy patterns of life in society."[18]

Reflection on our own tradition, moreover, should give us pause concerning the disdain for politics that underlies so much current American thinking about legal and social policy. For one of the most important lessons of 1789 is the same one the world learned anew in 1989: that politics is a way not only of advancing the interest of a self or a group, but of transcending individual and factional interest. That transformative potential of the art through which we order our lives together represents our best hope for living up to our rights ideals and our welfare aspirations in coming years.

17. Akhil Amar, "The Bill of Rights as a Constitution," *Yale Law Journal* 100 (1991): 1136.

18. Center for Public Justice, *A New Vision for Welfare Reform: An Essay in Draft* (Washington, D.C.: Center for Public Justice, 1994), reprinted in the Appendix to this volume, Thesis 4, 569.

Defining Poverty through the Welfare Debate: Limitations for Policy and Program Response

Stephanie Baker Collins

POVERTY, homelessness, violence, and despair are typical characterizations of inner-city life in the United States. John Perkins describes the youth of the inner city as those lacking a "moral compass": "they cannot distinguish the value difference between a life and a tennis shoe." In addition, he says, those who live in the inner city no longer believe in a good future: "we believe society has exhausted both the means and the will to intervene for us."[1]

The pain of life in the inner city is matched in the surrounding society by a growing sense of powerlessness to prevent or to alleviate the suffering there. This sense of an impasse has led to a reexamination of traditional approaches to poverty. Leaders in the Christian community are calling for a new framework to address the situation, one that recognizes both the personal and the structural dimensions of brokenness and injustice.[2] The traditional dichotomy between "conservative behaviorists" and "liberal structuralists" has not served us well, and we must move beyond it.[3]

1. John M. Perkins, "Culture of Despair," *Prism*, Nov. 1993, 10.

2. See John Alexander, "Murphy Brown and the Looters," *Other Side*, Sept.–Oct. 1992, 44-45; Jennifer Turner, "The Social Conscience of Personal Morality," *Zadok Perspectives*, Dec. 1992, 18-19; and Walter Wink, "All Will Be Redeemed," *Other Side*, Nov.–Dec. 1992, 17-23.

3. Cornel West, *Race Matters*, cited in Jim Wallis, "The Meaning of Politics," *Sojourners*, Jan. 1994, 50.

In The Center for Public Justice's "essay in draft," *A New Vision for Welfare Reform,* the necessity of a fresh approach is put in these terms:

> The welfare debate is paralyzed in part . . . by what appears to be an irreconcilable tension between the assumption that poor people are responsible for their poverty and the assumption that they are helplessly trapped by adverse conditions. . . . From a biblical point of view, that false dilemma cannot stand.[4]

The intent of the essay is to outline an approach that transcends the unproductive traditional dichotomies. Yet the analysis of the causes of and remedies for poverty may be more deeply rooted in conventional assumptions than is apparent. Stating the need for a new framework will not by itself produce new assumptions.

As R. L. Warren points out, for example, it is difficult to establish a new framework that goes beyond definitions to actual program implementation. Technical competence in a policy area has usually been developed within *existing* frameworks. In addition, the new framework initially lacks an institutionalized thought structure and strategy through which it can be supported and implemented.[5]

In *A New Vision for Welfare Reform,* the concern about welfare policy is the entry point for a broader discussion of poverty, hopelessness, inner-city decay, institutional breakdown, and dependency. The condition of life in American inner cities is the primary concern driving the discussion. It is significant, however, that in the United States this concern is often addressed through welfare reform, even though welfare caseload dynamics have been fairly stable in the last decade.

The question that will be addressed in this chapter is the effect on our understanding of poverty of defining the problem, assessing the program response, and selecting a policy framework in accordance with the terms of the current welfare debate in the United States. What are the implications of addressing the problem of poverty and inner-city decay through the debate about welfare reform? Can this approach successfully

4. Center for Public Justice, *A New Vision for Welfare Reform: An Essay in Draft* (Washington, D.C.: Center for Public Justice, 1994), reprinted in the Appendix to this volume, 561.

5. R. L. Warren, "The Sociology of Knowledge and the Problem of the Inner Cities," *Social Science Quarterly* 52 (Sept. 1971): 479-82.

overcome the dilemmas of the individual/structural deficiency framework?

Problem Identification

Theories to Explain Poverty

The goal, clearly, must be to move beyond the limitations of defining poverty either from an individual deficiency framework or from a structural deficiency framework. A helpful first step in moving beyond this dichotomy is to recognize that more than two types of theories about poverty are available. In fact there are at least three distinct theories concerning the definition of poverty and program response to it.[6]

One of the theories is the familiar individual/cultural deficiency model. This theory explains poverty as the result of inadequacies on the part of the poor themselves. The poor display individual deficiencies in behavior,[7] or have become trapped in a subculture characterized by family disintegration, alcoholism, and welfare dependency.[8]

The social policy/program response to this definition of poverty is to oppose large-scale institutionalized welfare since the goal is changes in individual behavior.[9] What is required, instead, are small-scale programs that are targeted to specific subgroups and that provide only limited benefits in order to discourage dependence on government assistance. The programs would be designed to rehabilitate, educate, and train the poor in order to instill regular work habits and other appropriate behavior.[10]

Another theory about poverty is termed the "reformist" or "en-

6. See, for example, David Gil, *Unraveling Social Policy* (Cambridge, Mass.: Schenkman Publishing Company, 1981), 40, and Peter Taylor-Gooby and Jennifer Dale, *Social Theory and Social Welfare* (London: Arnold, 1981), 32.

7. Taylor-Gooby and Dale, 32, and Maxine Baca Zinn, "Family, Race and Poverty in the Eighties," *Signs: Journal of Women in Culture and Society* 14 (Summer 1989): 856-57.

8. Baca Zinn, 861, 863; Taylor-Gooby and Dale, 34; and Patricia Hill Collins, "A Comparison of Two Works on Black Family Life," *Signs: Journal of Women in Culture and Society* 14 (Summer 1989): 877.

9. Taylor-Gooby and Dale, 36; Warren, 472.

10. Warren, 473.

vironmental reality" theory.[11] The first label reflects the emphasis on reforming the institutions of the welfare system itself, and the latter an emphasis on reforming the distribution of resources. The common assumption behind the two emphases is that poverty can be addressed by reforms within the boundaries of the prevailing social structure.[12]

According to the reformist theory, poverty is the result of environmental factors such as economic depressions, extended unemployment, and changes in the makeup of the labor force and in the location of jobs.[13] Another factor is the inadequacy of welfare programs (lack of comprehensiveness or difficulty of access), which constrains their responses to these environmental changes.[14]

The social policy/program response to this conception of poverty is to reform the welfare system (better coordination, comprehensiveness, and service delivery) so that it can more effectively redistribute resources through in-kind or direct benefits,[15] and to address the environmental factors through income supplements, minimum wage laws, and work-guarantee programs.[16]

A third theory about poverty looks to structural causes of poverty rather than environmental or individual causes. According to this theory, poverty is the result of "socially structured and legitimated inequalities with respect to the allocation of statuses and the distribution of rights in a society."[17] Poverty is caused by inequality, which is rooted in the political, racial, and economic structure of society.[18] In fact, the existence of poverty serves the social system, for example by providing a low-wage flexible labor force.[19]

The social policy/program response to this theory of poverty is twofold. Some argue that poverty cannot be solved without radical changes in society, such as organizing the poor and transferring power to them.[20] Others argue that inequalities can be addressed. Economic inequality can be addressed through macroeconomic policies such as a comprehensive

11. These terms are used by Taylor-Gooby and Dale at 32 and Gil at 40.
12. Taylor-Gooby and Dale, 32.
13. Gil, 40, and Baca Zinn, 864.
14. Taylor-Gooby and Dale, 33, and Warren, 474-75.
15. Taylor-Gooby and Dale, 33, 37, and Warren, 474-75.
16. Gil, 41.
17. Gil, 40.
18. Taylor-Gooby and Dale, 44-45, Baca Zinn, 871, and Hill Collins, 883.
19. Taylor-Gooby and Dale, 47.
20. Taylor-Gooby and Dale, 32, 43, and Warren, 489.

industrial and job development plan.[21] Racial and gender inequality can be addressed through antidiscrimination policies and other policies that remove obstructions to equal access.[22]

Theories of Poverty in the Current Debate

The current welfare reform debate in the United States concentrates on the hard-core welfare dependent. The focus is on what Carol Prager calls "micro-level phenomena," the perspective of individuals living in poverty.[23] This is an example of the individual/cultural deficiency theory, which looks to characteristics of the poor themselves to explain poverty. New versions of this framework have been proposed that take as the villain the culture of poverty, changes in family structure, or the incentives of welfare programs.[24]

An example of the reformist model is Maxine Baca Zinn's analysis, which looks at environmental factors and at social programs' capacity to respond to these factors. She identifies numerous current environmental factors as generators of poverty, such as the decline of the manufacturing sector, the shift in the geographic location of jobs from the central city to the suburbs, and demographic changes in the makeup of the inner city.[25]

The structural model is not prominent in the current welfare reform debate. This theory looks for causes of poverty deeper in the fabric of society in terms of how access to the resources of society is determined by race, gender, and social class. According to this theory, as Patricia Hill Collins explains, social class is not an *outcome* variable based on cultural values and family structure, but a *causal* variable.[26] When social class is combined with inequities attached to race and gender, environmental factors have a disproportionately negative effect on some groups in society.

Because the problem of poverty in the welfare reform debate focuses on the chronic poor, adopting the debate's focus results in a definition of poverty

21. Hill Collins, 883.

22. Gil, 41, and Hill Collins, 883.

23. Carol A. L. Prager, "Poverty in North America: Losing Ground?" *Canadian Public Policy* 14 (Jan. 1988): 54-55.

24. Baca Zinn, 857.

25. Baca Zinn, 864-69. Since Baca Zinn acknowledges only the individual deficiency and structural deficiency models, she classifies these as structural factors.

26. Hill Collins, 862.

with the following three primary dimensions: poverty is identified as persistent, long-term, chronic poverty; it is identified as poverty linked to dependence on government assistance; and it is identified as poverty linked to social degradation and dysfunction. Each of these descriptions is rooted in the individual/cultural deficiency theory of poverty with its attempt to explain poverty by reference to characteristics of the poor themselves. But how well do these descriptions fit the whole range of the welfare poor?

Characteristics of the Long-Term Welfare Poor

1. Patterns of welfare use There are two ways of examining welfare use by recipients. Point-in-time samples describe the proportion of long-term and short-term users in the caseload at a particular point in time. Longitudinal studies look at individual spells of welfare use or lifetime use. These long-term studies indicate the general pattern of welfare use and the behavioral impact of welfare use. Grave misunderstanding results when point-in-time samples are used to draw inferences about the long-term nature of welfare use.[27] A brief summary of the findings in several literature reviews on long-term welfare use patterns follows.

Among the population of all welfare recipients, occasional welfare use is common, persistent welfare use is not.[28] Individual spell studies by Mary Jo Bane and David Ellwood show that a majority of welfare spells are short-term, lasting two years or less. Fewer than one out of six are long-term, defined as lasting eight years or more.[29]

When longitudinal studies consider lifetime welfare use, a different pattern of long-term use emerges. Bane and Ellwood estimate that 30 percent of new recipients will experience a lifetime welfare use of one to two years. The median lifetime welfare use for all recipients is four years. However, 30 percent of new recipients will experience a lifetime welfare use

27. Greg J. Duncan and Saul D. Hoffman, "The Use and Effects of Welfare: A Survey of Recent Evidence," *Social Service Review* 62 (June 1988): 242.

28. See Duncan and Hoffman, 239, and Prager, 56.

29. Mary Jo Bane and Daniel Ellwood, "The Dynamics of Dependence and the Routes to Self-Sufficiency" (Cambridge, Mass.: Urban Systems Research and Engineering, 1983), and June O'Neil, Douglas Wolf, Laurie J. Bassie, and Michael T. Hannon, "An Analysis of Time on Welfare" (Washington, D.C.: Urban Institute, 1984), cited in Duncan and Hoffman, 241-42.

of more than eight years. One quarter of new recipients will spend ten years or more in total on welfare.[30]

The conclusion that can be drawn from longitudinal studies is that long-term welfare use does not characterize the general population of welfare recipients. About one-quarter to one-third of the welfare caseload, however, does experience long-term welfare use during their lifetime.

2. Family structure The primary group eligible for welfare in the United States (Aid to Families with Dependent Children) is female heads of families with dependent children. The original purpose of the program was to provide income support to allow mothers to care for their children. Husband-wife families with an unemployed primary earner may also qualify for welfare assistance, but this caseload is extremely small due to strict eligibility requirements.[31]

Family composition changes are an important factor in welfare caseload dynamics. Studies show that family composition changes account for the majority of entrances into the AFDC caseload. This should not be surprising, since eligibility for AFDC is, in part, based on family composition. Bane and Ellwood report that 75 percent of all AFDC spells begin with a family-composition change: 45 percent due to divorce, separation, or widowhood, and 30 percent because of giving birth out-of-wedlock. They point out that those who enter due to out-of-wedlock births tend to have longer episodes of welfare use.[32]

Theories of Poverty Applied to the Welfare Reform Debate

An examination of the individual and group characteristics of the long-term poor does reveal some important trends. As noted above, a significant group of the welfare poor are poor for long periods of time, and female-headed families are particularly vulnerable to long-term poverty. Analysis

30. David T. Ellwood, "Targeting Would-Be Long Term Recipients of AFDC" (Princeton, N.J.: Mathematica Policy Research, 1986), cited in Duncan and Hoffman, 241-43, and in Robert Moffitt, "Incentive Effects of the U.S. Welfare System: A Review," *Journal of Economic Literature* 30 (Mar. 1992): 24-25.

31. Moffitt, 4.

32. Duncan and Hoffman, 244, 246.

of such trends can show the severe consequences of mistaken choices and also reveal how welfare programs fail to help people move out of poverty, or even worsen their circumstances.

There are dangers, however, in viewing the poor exclusively through the optic of the welfare caseload. The rise in the AFDC caseload, for example, has been linked to the general increase in the number of female-headed families in the United States. However, the proportion of all female-headed families who participate in the AFDC program has declined continuously since 1973. Thus, the tendency to participate in AFDC by virtue of being a female head has actually declined.[33] However, because it is primarily female-headed single-parent families that are eligible for welfare in the United States, the welfare caseload naturally will emphasize the poverty of female-headed families. Different eligibility rules would produce a different caseload and a different picture of the poor.

A caseload-driven analysis also misses important environmental factors in the explanation of poverty. William Julius Wilson and Kathryn M. Neckerman have argued, for example, that joblessness among young black males could be the most important cause of the increase in unwed motherhood among poor black women. Economic changes have decreased economic opportunity for young black men and the consequence has been declining labor-force participation and increasing mortality and rates of incarceration. At the same time, poverty among young black women is linked to their marital status. And their marital status, in turn, is directly affected by the labor-force problems of young black men.[34]

A caseload-driven analysis can also miss important structural factors. Research by Mary Jo Bane, for example, has demonstrated that the link between family breakup and poverty is different for whites than it is for blacks. Of white families transformed into a female-headed or single-person household, three-quarters became poor at the time of the change (event-caused poverty). Of black families who were poor after the same transition, two-thirds already had been poor before the transition (reshuffled poverty). Moreover, 55 percent of the difference in overall poverty rates between blacks and whites results from higher poverty rates *within* household types

33. Moffitt, 8.

34. William Julius Wilson and Kathryn M. Neckerman, "Poverty and Family Structure," in Sheldon Danziger and Daniel H. Weinberg, eds., *Fighting Poverty: What Works and What Doesn't* (Cambridge, Mass.: Harvard Univ. Press, 1986), 242-47, 252-59.

for blacks, compared to only 44 percent that stems from differences in household composition.[35]

Such important differences in poverty patterns based on race suggest a need to examine structural factors affecting access to economic opportunity for different racial groups. Bane herself concludes that, although the poverty of blacks is concentrated among women, children, and split-up families, "its roots cannot be found in decisions about family structure."[36] Analyses that focus only on family composition patterns (an individual/cultural factor) or on improving the labor market status of black males (an environmental factor) fail to address "the fundamental question of the scarcity of economic resources available to poor Blacks of both sexes" (a structural factor).[37]

Program Response

Is Program Failure the Problem?

A focus on the poor who are dependent on government assistance for long periods leads naturally to questions regarding the effectiveness of government programs. Clearly, poverty has not been adequately addressed in the United States by income security programs. The persistence and even growth of poverty despite significant welfare spending can lead to the general conclusion that welfare programs are failures. But such a sweeping conclusion is not warranted by the facts.

Opposite views of the success or failure of government programs can also be the consequence of different explanations of the phenomenon of poverty. An exclusive focus on intractable and persistent welfare poverty, for instance, will lead naturally to an examination of the failure of welfare programs to move people out of poverty and dependence. To the extent that the AFDC program itself becomes a trap rather than a needed temporary source of income support, such an examination is warranted. However, as we saw, long-term welfare use characterizes only about one-quarter to one-third of the total welfare population. For the rest — the large ma-

35. Mary Jo Bane, "Household Composition and Poverty," in Danziger and Weinberg, 214-16, 227.

36. Bane, 231.

37. Hill Collins, 883.

jority — the program has succeeded as an essential but temporary income replacement.

Moreover, an evaluation of the success of welfare programs must take into account the context in which the program is operating. A plausible image is to picture welfare programs as an attempt to walk up a downward moving escalator, with the escalator representing broad economic trends that increase poverty. In this case, a focus on program failure that ignores the larger picture would lead to the false conclusion that the entire exercise has been futile. Thus, to truly assess program failure, we must look beyond programs to the social and economic conditions they were meant to address.

In a situation in which economic and social conditions for the poor are generally becoming worse, welfare programs can function to help offset these worsening conditions. Poverty may not have decreased, but the programs may have prevented it from increasing. As Michael Mendelson expresses it, "Income security programs can only be judged to have failed to prevent increased poverty if the underlying rates of poverty would have been unchanged had there been no such program."[38]

In fact, the evidence suggests that the poor in the United States have indeed faced increasing income inequality, which has contributed to a rise in poverty in recent years. The *Financial Times* noted the following trends:

- Average weekly earnings for U.S. workers (in 1982 dollars) climbed from $261.92 in 1960 to $315.38 in 1982 but have now dropped below the 1960 level to $255.99.
- Wage declines were felt disproportionately by workers in the bottom wage bracket, whose incomes fell by 10.3 percent, while those of the highest wage earners rose by 4.4 percent.
- In 1993, 18 percent of America's full-time workers earned less than a poverty wage, compared with only 12 percent in 1979.[39]

In a situation of increasing inequality in earned income, poverty programs may function to offset these trends, even though poverty will not have been measurably reduced.

38. Michael Mendelson, "Can We Reform Canada's Income Security System?" (paper presented at the Canada/UK Colloquium on The Future of Social Welfare Systems, Ottawa, Canada, October 1986), 6.

39. "Lack of Training Shuts Door to Poor," *Financial Times,* Mar. 14, 1994, p. 4.

Program Adequacy

The ability of welfare programs to have a positive impact on the level of poverty is determined as well by the adequacy of their benefits. An important contribution of *A New Vision for Welfare Reform* is its description of the multidimensional nature of human well-being and of poverty in general. Poverty is more than a lack of income. Nevertheless, benefit levels and the comprehensiveness of income support programs are important issues.

Although income support is not a *sufficient* response to long-term poverty, it is for many households a *necessary* response. International comparisons with the level of poverty in the United States and of the effectiveness of income support programs ought to raise concerns among Americans about the adequacy of their programs. In a comparative study of the rich countries belonging to the Organization for Economic Cooperation and Development, the United States had one of the higher rates of pretax and pretransfer poverty among families and single parents, and also the highest poverty rate for both groups after taxes and transfers were taken into account.[40]

A study done by Rebecca M. Blank and Maria J. Hanratty tested the extent to which differences in social welfare institutions in the United States and Canada account for differences in poverty outcomes between the two countries. Their findings indicated that "the Canadian transfer system is substantially more effective than the US transfer system in raising people out of poverty."[41] The Canadian transfer system had a significantly greater impact on reducing poverty for single-parent families, reducing their poverty gap by 62 percent compared to 40 percent for the United States.[42] In a simulation that applied Canadian antipoverty programs to the United States and U.S. antipoverty programs to Canada, the authors concluded

40. Michael J. Foster, "Measurements of Low Incomes and Poverty in a Perspective of International Comparisons," *Occasional Paper no. 14* (Paris: OECD, 1994), cited in David P. Ross, E. Richard Shillington, and Clarence Lochhead, *The Canadian Fact Book on Poverty — 1994* (Ottawa: Canadian Council on Social Development, 1994), 113.

41. Rebecca M. Blank and Maria J. Hanratty, "Responding to Need: A Comparison of Social Safety Nets in Canada and the United States," in David Card and Richard B. Freeman, eds., *Small Differences That Matter: Labor Markets and Income Maintenance in Canada and the United States* (Chicago: Univ. of Chicago Press, 1993), 205.

42. Blank and Hanratty, 205.

that the poverty rate among single parents would decline from 43 percent to 16 percent in the United States if the nation adopted the typical Canadian program.[43]

The differences in program effectiveness, though not large, are enough to ensure that the growing inequality in market incomes in Canada was largely offset in the last decade by tax and transfer programs, whereas the same was not true for the United States. A study by Keith Banting compared the impact of income support programs on the level of child poverty in Canada and the United States. Table 1 on p. 107 illustrates his findings.

Based on such figures, Banting concluded that the weak redistributive role of the government in the United States could not compensate for the growing inequality in market incomes. In contrast, the tax-transfer system in Canada largely offset the growing inequality in market incomes there.[44]

These comparisons are all the more striking because Canada does not have a very expansive welfare state. Among OECD countries, it ranks second lowest in terms of the proportion of GDP spent on social programs, with only the United States spending a smaller proportion.[45]

Thus any effort at welfare program reform in the United States must address program adequacy. As noted by Blank and Hanratty, "There is nothing inherently unchangeable in the current poverty rates among women and children in the United States. They are, at least in part, a result of the policy choices that we have made."[46]

43. Blank and Hanratty, 192.

44. Keith Banting, "Economic Integration and Social Policy: Canada and the United States," in Terrence M. Hunsley, ed., *Social Policy in the Global Economy* (Kingston, Ontario: School of Policy Studies, Queen's University, 1992), 38. Banting cites as his source for the table T. Smeeding, "Cross National Perspectives on Trends in Child Poverty and the Effectiveness of Government Policies in Preventing Poverty among Families with Children: the First Evidence from LIS," as reported in U.S. House of Representatives, Committee on Ways and Means, *Overview of Entitlement Programs: 1991 Greenbook* (Washington, D.C.: GPO), 1155.

45. Oxley and Martin, "Controlling Government Spending and Deficits: Trends in the 1980s and Prospects for the 1990s," OECD Economic Studies, cited in Linda McQuaig, "Canada's Social Programs: Under Attack," special report for *Toronto Star,* Nov. 9, 1992, p. B1.

46. Blank and Hanratty, 219.

Table 1 Effects of Taxes and Transfers on Levels of Child Poverty in Canada and the United States in the 1980s (percent poor)

	Canada		United States	
	1981	**1987**	**1979**	**1986**
Pretax & pretransfer	15.5	15.7	19.0	22.3
Posttax & posttransfer	10.2	9.3	14.7	20.4
Reduction	5.3	6.4	4.3	1.9
Percent reduction	*34.2*	*40.8*	*24.2*	*8.5*

Program Reform

Although important environmental and structural factors must be addressed in welfare reform, there are also important changes to be made within welfare programs themselves. Changes are needed to make the transition from welfare to work easier, such as lowering the tax-back rate on earned income or providing continued health and other benefits for those who move to employment. It may be necessary to provide greater flexibility within the program for a combination of paid employment and income assistance, especially for single-parent families.

Holding fathers financially responsible for their children is a matter of equity and of encouraging parental accountability. Changing the rules so that the custodial parent can retain a significant portion of child support payments could provide an incentive to both parents to establish child support agreements. Providing training and/or employment programs could enhance employability for recipients and could function to increase self-esteem by providing work opportunities.

Program reform must examine how current welfare programs function for those who develop a long-term dependency on income assistance. But program reform cannot focus exclusively on solutions that stay *within* the parameters of social programs themselves. Program reform must also address changing economic conditions, growing market income inequality, and the overall impacts of tax and transfer policies.

Policy Framework

While welfare programs need internal reform and their benefit levels ought to be increased, such changes are not a sufficient response to poverty. As *A New Vision for Welfare Reform* argues, "Public policies should not serve to legitimize irresponsibility."[47] This means, for example, that the tax-transfer system should not have to compensate for economic institutions that create insecure, low-paying jobs with poor working conditions. Governments and other institutions must do more than respond to negative economic effects; they "should pursue more fundamental reforms, seeking to restore effective action on the part of all who bear responsibility for poverty."[48] This requires an examination of the total policy framework, including nonwelfare policies, to assess how they slow or speed a fall into poverty.

One barrier to serious policy reform identified in *A New Vision for Welfare Reform* is a political climate that discourages judgments about human responsibility in various arenas. Human responsibility must be addressed in the multidimensional way the essay proposes, by calling individuals, institutions, and governments to responsibility.

Some would argue that the current political climate does not allow for a discussion of individual responsibility. This certainly rings true of the general public discussion around moral accountability. However, when it comes to poverty and welfare, the debate in the United States is typically conducted in terms of the individual responsibilities of the poor, in contrast to the social focus of the Canadian and European discussions. Welfare programs have always struggled for legitimacy in the United States. The emphasis has been less on developing a welfare system that would provide a range of basic services to all citizens and more on helping individuals and groups to function more effectively within the existing structures of society. This focus prompted one author to state that "the major thrust of American effort in the 1960s was towards eradicating the 'culture of poverty' rather than poverty as such."[49]

In a comparison of the program implementations of the individual deficiency versus structural theories of poverty, Warren found that an institutionalized framework does exist to implement reforms based on the

47. Center for Public Justice, 569.

48. Center for Public Justice, 560.

49. Ramesh Mishra, *The Welfare State in Crisis: Social Thought and Social Change* (Brighton, Eng.: Wheatsheaf Books, 1984), 5.

"culture of poverty" theory in the United States. There is not, however, an institutionalized framework that can operate to implement structural change, even though structural factors are generally acknowledged to be partly responsible for causing poverty.[50] In his analysis of the Model Cities programs of the late 1960s, Warren found a constant drift in program implementation toward changing organizations and programs so they would more effectively serve poor people, rather than changing the social structures that generated poverty.[51]

All the dimensions of human responsibility need to be addressed, but often individual responsibility is addressed to the exclusion of other dimensions of responsibility. One reason is the prevalence of the "culture of poverty" theory in the United States. Another reason is that it is easier to make changes to social programs so that individuals will be required to seek employment than to make the institutional reforms needed to address environmental and structural factors. Responding to the high unemployment of young black males or the changing demographics of the inner city is more complex, and requires participation from more institutions in society, than changing the rules of an income support program. Public discourse tends to focus on the responsibilities of individuals and/or governments. Discussions of the responsibilities of corporations, unions, schools, churches, and neighborhood associations are less common.

A Policy Framework Based on the Integration of Social and Economic Policy

The limitations of addressing the problem of poverty primarily through the vehicle of welfare reform, with its focus on the long-term poor, have been discussed in this chapter. The tendency, as we have seen, is to focus on making improvements *within* current program parameters rather than to address environmental and structural factors that also impact program effectiveness and the level of poverty. If *A New Vision for Welfare Reform*'s intention to "strengthen the accountability structures that constitute the warp and woof of society"[52] is to be met, a broader approach is required.

50. Warren, 478-79.
51. Warren, 480-84.
52. Center for Public Justice, 569.

Some aspects of the debate in Canada can provide a helpful illustration for broadening the scope of the policy framework. At the same time as welfare reform is being debated in the United States, Canada is undergoing a comprehensive review of its income security programs. Income security programs in Canada are more generous and have a broader eligibility base than those in the United States. The caseload includes unemployed individuals, couples without children, and two-parent families, along with single-parent families. The focus of the discussion in Canada, therefore, is less on single-parent families and more on the employability of individuals, couples, and two-parent families.

The concern behind the Canadian review is that income security programs were not designed to respond to the fundamental changes in the labor market that have taken place in Canada in the last decade. The current social security system was based on the assumption that most citizens could rely on the job market for their primary source of income. Unemployment insurance was intended to provide income for Canadians suffering a temporary job loss. The social assistance program was designed to provide income assistance for those unable to work due to disability or a responsibility to care for children. The programs were not equipped to deal with the long-term, structural, and chronic unemployment that has rapidly increased the caseloads of both programs. The negative economic changes that have generated new levels of poverty include high unemployment in the midst of strong economic growth; longer periods of unemployment for older workers; and a fast-growing, low-wage, nontraditional job market. As the economy and the labor market have changed, the face of poverty has changed. More households are poor despite employment, poverty is increasing among young families, and families that rely on one earner are particularly vulnerable.[53]

The fear of the social policy community in Canada is that the government will reform social programs without ever addressing these changing conditions. But social programs cannot be expected to single-handedly address the growing inequity of the labor market. They do not have the capacity to do so and they should not, in any case, take on a responsibility that properly belongs to the actors and institutions of the labor market. As

53. Citizens for Public Justice, *Working Together for Justice,* Submission to the Standing Committee on Human Resources Development, Toronto (March 9, 1994), appendix D.

stated in *A New Vision for Welfare Reform,* "an open market, which is increasingly global in character, entails its own distinct moral obligations on the part of individuals, corporations, governments, and other actors."[54]

If social programs ought not to be responsible for inequities that originate elsewhere, such as in the labor market, then how can other sectors of society be held responsible? The Canadian Christian public policy organization Citizens for Public Justice (CPJ) has contributed to defining a new direction for social program reform in Canada by advocating that social and economic policy be redesigned so that they work together.[55]

Welfare reform requires an examination of both social and economic policy, for these are interconnected policies. They can either function together in a way that promotes justice or work at cross-purposes. For example, if Canada develops social programs to enhance the employability of social assistance recipients, but leaves in place a tax expenditure system for business that encourages capital- rather than labor-intensive industry, economic policy and social policy will be working in opposite directions. Individuals will be receiving training for a diminishing pool of employment opportunities.

Current approaches to integration of the two areas are based on the idea that social policy is bound by principles that promote human well-being, while economic policy is bound by principles that promote material prosperity. Most discussion revolves around the question of which set of principles should have priority. However, as stated in *A New Vision for Welfare Reform,*

> If government simply concentrates on promoting economic growth and giving a little aid to the needy, it may remain blind to the ways in which even its growth and assistance policies may contribute to the forces of greed and corruption that help cause poverty.[56]

Trends in the labor market in Canada and other industrialized nations, for example, cast doubt on the assumption that economic growth guarantees expanding employment opportunity. In the midst of strong

54. Center for Public Justice, 560.

55. Citizens for Public Justice is a national citizens organization that seeks to promote justice in Canadian public affairs. CPJ responds to God's call for love, justice, and stewardship through research, education, and advocacy.

56. Center for Public Justice, 567.

economic growth and a strong job-creation record in the 1980s, unemployment remained high in Canada.[57] One explanation may lie in the fact that between 1970 and 1990 Canadians more than doubled the nation's wealth by using only 50 percent more labor.[58]

CPJ urges that *both* social and economic policies should be bound by the same requirements of justice and stewardship. Economic policies must ensure that sufficient human and other resources are available to meet social needs. Economic policies should support the proper role of families and other social institutions, and not result in harmful side effects for society. Social policies must encourage job creation and enable people to make a useful contribution to society. Social policies should also be structured to enable people to develop their skills and abilities. A socioeconomic policy framework based on this two-way integration provides a framework in which institutions can be called to responsibility.

An example of the application of this approach to the Canadian situation is a policy proposal for changing the way that unemployment insurance is funded in Canada. Currently, a company's share of unemployment insurance (UI) premiums is based on the number of workers it employs. This system costs less for companies that use capital-intensive methods of production than for those that use labor-intensive methods. A company that reduces its workforce has its UI premiums reduced, while the fund strains to provide assistance for the workers the company has laid off. Companies that operate in a labor-intensive manner and save jobs thus bear the greater burden of funding the unemployment costs generated by companies that take the capital-intensive path and shed jobs.

CPJ has proposed that responsibility for funding income security programs be shared more equitably among all those participants in the economy whose actions affect the income security of Canadian households. One way to move in this direction is to alter how employer contributions for income security are levied. If the employer premiums for UI are based on the net added value of the company (the company's volume minus the

57. Gordon Ternowetsky and Graham Riches, "Labour Market Restructuring and the Public Safety Net" (paper presented at the December 1992 conference of the Association for Canadian Studies in Australia and New Zealand, Wellington, New Zealand), 4.

58. Armine Yalnizyan, "Defining Social Security, Defining Ourselves" (Canadian Centre for Policy Alternatives, May 1993), 6.

costs of raw materials and components), it will remove the incentive in the UI system to reduce payroll costs by shedding employees.[59]

Since the primary concern in Canada's review of social security programs is unemployment, this proposal provides a model in the Canadian context in which both social and economic institutions accept responsibility for increasing employment opportunities.

Social Support for Families

Given the concern in the United States welfare reform debates about chronic poverty among single-parent families, an even more pertinent model for the U.S. context concerns social support for families. *A New Vision for Welfare Reform* has identified the way in which the belief in human beings as autonomous, self-interested individuals has produced a framework that is not adequate to address the problem of poverty.[60] Human freedom has been misconstrued not only as freedom from any standards not devised by humans themselves, but as freedom from obligations to others. When such an emphasis on independence and self-sufficiency combines with an emphasis on material prosperity, the goal of public policy can become one of removing any barriers (such as obligations to others) that stand in the way of the pursuit of material gain.

The biblical perspective on human nature, as outlined by *A New Vision for Welfare Reform,* describes human beings not as autonomous individuals but as image bearers of God and stewards of creation, who are morally responsible for one another.[61] Dependence on God and interdependence with others is part of created human nature. Thus dependence and independence should not be defined in strictly economic terms, as when dependence is defined as receiving government income support and independence is defined as earning an income in the paid labor force.

Such a definition fails to recognize that meeting the responsibilities of caring for family members requires the support of other institutions in

59. For a discussion, see Bob Goudzwaard and Harry de Lange, *Beyond Poverty and Affluence: Toward an Economy of Care,* trans. Mark R. Vander Vennen (Grand Rapids, Mich.: Eerdmans, and Geneva: WCC Publications, 1995), 147-48.

60. Center for Public Justice, 556-57.

61. Center for Public Justice, 559.

society. The world of paid employment, for example, often does not give sufficient opportunity for meeting obligations to family and neighbors. In the marketplace work is generally valued in terms of what it yields financially. The tasks of caring for children or for disabled or elderly members of one's family are often undervalued in that context. If fulfilling one's responsibilities is defined primarily in terms of paid work, the work of caring for other members of the family will not be adequately supported.

According to the biblical perspective that undergirds the Center for Public Justice's welfare work, persons are called to responsibility to take up their various vocations, and institutions and governments are called to account to fulfill their diverse responsibilities. One of the primary vocations for parents is that of caring for and nurturing their children. This vocation is no less important for parents who receive income assistance. For most households on assistance, this vocation must be pursued without help from a spouse. If we are to honor this vocation, we must ask how the obligation to a parent is best balanced with the obligation to economically support one's family.

Without other supports in place, families — especially single-parent families — whose earned income is at the poverty level have a difficult time properly fulfilling their parenting responsibilities. Is a family in which a single parent works full-time at a minimum wage job, must rely on unsafe and inadequate child care, and lacks protection for medical emergencies more responsible than a family enabled by government assistance to have an at-home parent and access to Medicaid? The minimum-wage family may be economically "independent," but the price may be neglected or inadequately fulfilled parental responsibilities.

When such nonwelfare supports for families as health care or child care are not available, or are linked to welfare receipt, families face a double bind. Families that stand to lose valuable in-kind assistance find it difficult to move off welfare. At the same time, working poor families are not supported in their parenting vocation. To the extent that supports for families are not part of what the *New Vision for Welfare Reform* terms "a just social order," they will necessarily become part of what it calls the government's "emergency relief" efforts through such services as child protection.[62]

62. See Center for Public Justice, 570ff.

Raising children is generally viewed as an individual responsibility in the United States. Families with children in other industrialized nations are supported by income and in-kind benefits not available to U.S. parents — programs such as paid maternity leave for working parents, a child benefit available to all families to assist with the costs of raising children, medical care and financial assistance for pregnant women, national public health insurance, and public child care.[63] Part of a response to poverty among families should be an examination of the adequacy of income supports that can help families fulfill their parenting responsibilities. *A New Vision for Welfare Reform*'s suggestion of a direct public allowance coupled with income tax relief for the working poor is a good example of such support.[64]

Part of a response to poverty among families should also be an examination of the social supports that can help families fulfill their parenting responsibilities. The well-being of families is enhanced when support services such as child care, quality education, libraries, and recreation facilities are available in a community. Parents are assisted in their task through these formal support systems as well as through informal supports such as community associations, churches, parent support groups, and neighborhood associations. Therefore policies should encourage and support interdependence by building healthy communities. This approach addresses the concerns of family poverty in a more integrated way than just focusing on the employability of parents or on income assistance. A healthy informal support system can decrease the need for formal income support programs.

Conclusion

Recognizing that we need to move past traditional arguments, this chapter has also tried to point out how theories about poverty shape the identification of the problems to be solved in welfare reform and the proposed program response. The three poverty theories outlined earlier seek explanations in the individual or cultural attributes of the poor themselves, in environmental factors such as changing economic conditions, or in structural factors that cause economic and social changes to impact some in-

63. Linda McQuaig, "Canada's Social Programs: Under Attack," special report for *Toronto Star,* Nov. 8, 1992, pp. B1, B7.

64. Center for Public Justice, 571-72.

dividuals or groups disproportionately due to such characteristics as race or gender.

An analysis of poverty and welfare reform that begins with the long-term dependent poor may be shaped too strongly by the individual/cultural deficiency model, if it locates an explanation of poverty exclusively in the characteristics of the poor. This chapter has proposed the importance of examining environmental and structural factors as well. Each of the three theories accounts for an important piece of the explanation of poverty. Is it possible to bring these perspectives together?

The biblical view of human nature and responsibility offered in *A New Vision for Welfare Reform* can help us move beyond the unhelpful debate about who or what is to blame for the persistence of poverty. The concept of multiple, simultaneous vocations provides a framework for individual accountability in vocations. This is applied in the policy suggestion that fathers should be held responsible for the nurture and financial support of their children.[65]

The concept of diverse institutional and governmental responsibilities provides a framework for the institutional and public policy support that is needed in order for vocations to be fulfilled. This is applied in the policy suggestions of a national system of health insurance, public assistance to nongovernmental organizations that provide various relief and remediation services, and public support for parenting.[66]

Given the emphasis on the plurality of responsibilities, one addition to this framework would be to examine ways in which aspects of the structure of society such as racial or gender bias, which are not restricted to any one institution, may be operating in each of the institutions to create inequities.

65. Center for Public Justice, 571.
66. Center for Public Justice, 571.

II. FOUNDATIONS FOR A CHRISTIAN APPROACH

The Question of Being Human in Assessing the Requirements of Welfare Policy Reform

James W. Skillen

Progress or Regress in Understanding?

DO WE KNOW more or less today about what it means to be human? On the face of it this question sounds foolish. Who can doubt that we know much more today about human experience than people knew fifty or one hundred or five hundred years ago? The sciences are still developing, and they provide us with new data every year; people continue to explore everything in the cosmos, including themselves, and they learn new things every day; human inventiveness and creativity show no sign of letting up. Speaking both quantitatively and qualitatively, it appears that humans know more today than ever before in history about what it means to be human.

Despite all the gains in knowledge and experience, however, much evidence suggests that regress has also occurred over the centuries in at least some dimensions of human experience and self-understanding. Human degradation, political injustice, and individual hopelessness have been as ample in this century as in any earlier period. It seems clear, therefore, that to assess the evidence of progress and regress we will have to choose carefully the point of view from which to make such judgments.

If, for instance, one assumes that human beings are the kind of animal whose identity and behavior patterns can eventually be explained exhaustively by means of the natural sciences, and if one also assumes that whatever cannot be known scientifically is not important, then one might read a great deal into the "progress" of science during the past two hundred years. Scientists do know more today than they did even fifty years ago about stimulus-response mechanisms, psycho-physical disorders, mass psychology, group dynamics, and countless other aspects of human behavior.

If, by contrast, one assumes that human beings are more than psychobiological animals and that the quality of human life and self-understanding must be measured, at least in part, by the depth of practical human wisdom and by the kind of moral, political, legal, and aesthetic responsibility humans exhibit, then a great deal of ambiguity comes into view. One must then take careful notice of the signs of increasing degradation of human life — suicide and murder rates, levels of child abuse and starvation, rates of divorce and joblessness, the destructiveness of wars and other episodes of organized brutality. Some critics also judge that a great deal of art and music, literature and journalism, legal thinking and ecclesiastical life are of a lower quality today than they were two or three centuries ago. Many wonder whether human beings as religious, moral, and political creatures have made any progress at all.

The late Eric Voegelin, to take just one example, develops his entire political philosophy around the argument that the differentiation and expansion of human experience from the ancient Hebrews and Greeks through the European high Middle Ages displayed a certain kind of growth in human self-understanding and wisdom — a progress in the experience of what it means to be human, in community, in relation to God.[1] With the overwhelming impact of modern scientism and the application of natural scientific methods to human studies, however, human beings began to experience a regression in self-understanding because that reductionistic mindset refused to recognize that human beings are more than self-interested, self-seeking, psychobiological animals. We may know more today than our ancestors did about certain bodily and psycho-social functions, Voegelin would say, but we know less about ourselves as moral, philosophical, aesthetic, political, and religious creatures. We hold less of the truth and we hold it less firmly; the deeper meaning of what it is to be human is more opaque to us — is marked increasingly by uncertainty. We are less fully, less richly human now than were our ancestors who lived out their lives in exploratory openness before God in what they believed to be

1. See, e.g., Eric Voegelin, *The New Science of Politics* (Chicago: Univ. of Chicago Press, 1952); and Voegelin, *From Enlightenment to Revolution*, ed. John H. Hallowell (Durham, N.C.: Duke Univ. Press, 1975).

an ordered cosmos. Humans today have lost or forgotten a great deal of what our ancestors once knew and experienced.[2]

One need not adopt Voegelin's point of view to have some sense that all is not well in the arena of knowing what it means to be human. The question of being human is not narrowly about how many discrete, abstract details one can learn about various human functions and activities. The broader, more basic question concerns human identity as a whole and at its foundations. This includes the personal, existential questions that each of us asks not as a scientific observer or policymaker, but as a living person: Who am I? What is the meaning of life? To what purposes should I give myself? Shall I assume that I and other human beings are fundamentally physical, or psychical, or rational, or social, or economic, or political, or religious creatures? How do I arrive at an answer to a question like this? Depending on how I answer these questions, all the diverse functions and activities of human life will appear in a different light. Moreover, I cannot wait until all the "facts" are in to decide what it means to be human. I must live today and tomorrow on the basis of assumptions and beliefs about what it means to be human. My presuppositions, whether correct or incorrect, will guide not only the way I seek to learn *about* human life but also the way I choose to live my life.

If, for example, one lives and interprets life's meaning from a biblical perspective, believing that human beings have been created in the image of God and that they are marked to the core by their relation to God, then one's point of view will be radically different from the view that human meaning is confined within the course of natural, animal cycles that lack any transcendent meaning or purpose. These contrasting points of view, to name just two, lead to significantly different judgments about what is good

2. Others who are critics of the idea of human progress or who question the belief that the modern expansion of knowledge has created or coincided with an advance in the quality of human self-understanding include Leszek Kolakowski, *Modernity on Endless Trial* (Chicago: Univ. of Chicago Press, 1990); Harold J. Berman, *Law and Revolution: The Formation of the Western Legal Tradition* (Cambridge: Harvard Univ. Press, 1983); Michael Polanyi, *The Study of Man* (Chicago: Univ. of Chicago Press, 1959) and *Personal Knowledge: Towards a Post-Critical Philosophy* (Chicago: Univ. of Chicago Press, 1958), esp. 327-80; David Novak, *Jewish Social Ethics* (New York: Oxford Univ. Press, 1992); Vigen Guroian, *Ethics After Christendom: Toward an Ecclesial Christian Ethic* (Grand Rapids, Mich.: Eerdmans, 1994), esp. 11-52; George Parkin Grant, *Technology and Justice* (Notre Dame: Univ. of Notre Dame Press, 1986).

and bad in our contemporary society, about what it means to be human, and about the proper aim of public policies.

Why, for example, do we, or should we, believe that something is wrong when people are locked into poverty, crime, ill health, and hopelessness? What basis is there for making such a judgment and for believing that human life should *not* be characterized by those conditions? Why not assume that some people are simply fated for such lives? Nature is harsh at times. Evolutionary destiny requires the survival of the fittest. Some make it, some do not. Some rise to the top and others sink to the bottom. That is a simple, natural fact for humans just as it is for animals. Why not accept the truth that human experience is constituted by such power struggles?

Obviously, to judge that certain living conditions are good or bad, acceptable or unacceptable, is to take for granted certain *standards* or *principles* by which to judge the quality and meaning of human life. But where do such standards come from, and which suppositions about human identity point us to the correct standards or principles? The fact that human beings can discuss such matters and make judgments in the course of deliberative argument would seem to suggest that we ought to reflect critically on our presuppositions, especially at a time when people in our society have reached something like gridlock in their disagreements over the causes of and the cures for poverty.[3]

Examining the Anthropological Presuppositions of Welfare Policy

American welfare policies as we have known them for about three decades have been created by governments to try to overcome or to alleviate circumstances judged to be unhealthy or morally unacceptable in some way.[4]

3. Some of those on whom I depend for my philosophical anthropology and method of critical reflection on basic presuppositions include Herman Dooyeweerd, *In the Twilight of Western Thought* (Philadelphia: Presbyterian and Reformed, 1960); G. C. Berkouwer, *Man: The Image of God,* trans. Dirk W. Jellema (Grand Rapids, Mich.: Eerdmans, 1962); Mary Stewart Van Leeuwen, ed., *After Eden: Facing the Challenge of Gender Reconciliation* (Grand Rapids, Mich.: Eerdmans, 1993).

4. Numerous studies of welfare policy and its history are developed or referred to elsewhere in this volume. The immediate backdrop for my comments here can be found in Center for Public Justice, *A New Vision for Welfare Reform,* reprinted in the

In creating such policies, governments have presumed that the relationships and nongovernment institutions in which poor people find themselves are either not responsible for, or are insufficiently capable of dealing with, their predicament. Generally speaking, one of the key standards of judgment undergirding government policies has been that no citizen should have to live below the poverty line without receiving material assistance from the government. Our welfare policies have never had as their aim to try to make the poorest citizens as rich as the richest citizens or even as comfortable as middle-class citizens. Government welfare policies, if we ignore all the rhetoric, are an extension of "poor relief," namely, an attempt to alleviate joblessness, insufficient income, and helplessness in the face of ill health and other treatable degradations in order to bring the poorest people up from unacceptable poverty to acceptable poverty, but not up to middle-class comfort. Government's direct responsibility goes only so far. For the poorest citizens governments have tried to do something more, but not too much more, than they do regularly for all citizens through standard public operating policies.

With the words "something more" in the previous sentence I wish to highlight the fact that poor relief comes on top of other laws and programs designed to sustain or improve the general welfare of all citizens: tax-supported education for every child, income tax deductions for dependents, unemployment compensation for those temporarily unemployed, and much more. Furthermore, the well-being of most citizens is generally assumed to be the consequence not of particular government efforts but of the routine actions of persons and families going about their daily tasks of working, child rearing, studying, and more, supported in their fulfillment of these responsibilities by friendships, neighborhoods, churches, and places of employment.

A primary presupposition of welfare policies has been that if the typical

---

Appendix to this volume; David T. Ellwood, *Poor Support: Poverty in the American Family* (New York: Basic Books, 1988); Daniel Patrick Moynihan, *Family and Nation* (New York: Harcourt Brace Jovanovich, 1986); Charles Murray, *Losing Ground: American Social Policy 1950–1980* (New York: Basic Books, 1984); William Julius Wilson, *The Truly Disadvantaged: The Inner City, the Underclass, and Public Policy* (Chicago: Univ. of Chicago Press, 1987); Hugh Heclo, "The Political Foundations of Antipoverty Policy," in Sheldon H. Danziger and Daniel H. Weinberg, eds., *Fighting Poverty: What Works and What Doesn't* (Cambridge: Harvard Univ. Press, 1986), 312-40.

choices made by most individuals, families, employers, and governments are not sufficient to assure everyone of the material outcomes that even lower-middle class citizens enjoy, then government ought to do something extra for the poorest citizens to help them escape from an unacceptable standard of living. Very poor citizens, regardless of the reasons for their poverty, should, in other words, receive public assistance that will give them more freedom of movement than they would have without such assistance.

Notice the web of assumptions about human identity and meaning here. People are assumed to be social creatures, but judgments about their well-being are largely judgments about their relative economic positions in society. Governments ought to step in directly to help the poor even if the poor themselves and all other human institutions have failed to keep them from falling below an arbitrarily defined poverty line. Citizens and governments can feel that they have fulfilled their responsibility as long as they have given the poor a few benefits to help them reach a lower-class level of economic existence, but the public does not need to feel obligated to help the poor beyond that point. Many questions about other qualities of human life and about justice, love, and responsibility before God are left entirely unaddressed. Why is this? Why do citizens and governments in our society operate within this framework of assumptions and presuppositions?

One of the curious facts about prevailing assumptions undergirding modern welfare politics is that the aim to increase individual freedom is interpreted in quite different ways even by those who share many of the same assumptions. Many, for example, who emphasize the principle of economic *equality* (or at least fairness) in their view of human nature typically consider the poorest Americans to be in need of goods, services, and money that will allow them to act more like people who are not so poor. It is the considerable distance between wealth and poverty that pains them. Unequal outcomes offend them. On the other hand, many who stress the standard of *freedom* in their view of human nature urge that poor people should be treated in ways that will make them more accountable for their own actions — just like everyone else is treated. In other words, the gap of inequality in our society between responsibility and irresponsibility is what offends those who want people to act independently rather than dependently. If the truth about human identity is that people ought to be free, then let them accept the responsibilities of freedom.

Those with an equality-oriented viewpoint more often stress the larger, economic/social conditions of inequality that keep people from enjoying a better standard of living. Those with a freedom-oriented perspective more often emphasize the behavioral habits that free individuals ought to learn and exhibit. Both groups may favor special government action on behalf of the poorest citizens, but the first will be more sympathetic to longer-term, public financial support of the poor without judging too closely the decisions that individuals themselves make, while the second will be more sympathetic to temporary policies that help get individuals working again and off the dole.[5]

In both cases, however, similar assumptions about human nature and society are at work. The aim is a liberal aim: to make people more free and equal — more autonomous as individuals and more equal, materially, in comparison to fellow citizens. The taken-for-granted context is that of individuals in a larger public order — a context in which unencumbered individuals should, ideally, be free to act on their own initiative and in which governments should use policies to adjust the social and economic outcomes to keep the poorest from losing out altogether. Humans, from this point of view, are economically acquisitive animals, destined to desire maximum individual autonomy while also bearing a public-moral sense that is triggered when the poorest people have to endure circumstances that the middle classes do not find acceptable.

But is something missing here? How do these hypothetically free human beings achieve the capability of acting autonomously? Do they create themselves? What is the nature of human growth and development from birth to adulthood? How does it happen? Who is responsible for it? Do individuals alone exist, apart from governments, and do individuals act in response to their moral conscience only through government? Where do families, schools, churches, business enterprises, and voluntary organizations fit into this picture? For example, can human life develop in a healthy fashion outside the circle of an enduring family? With respect to the most basic assumptions about human identity, what is the nature and meaning of family life? Is there a sense in which human beings are fundamentally

5. The contrasting equality-oriented and freedom-oriented approaches are exemplified, for example, by Theodore R. Marmor, Jerry L. Mashaw, and Philip L. Harvey, *America's Misunderstood Welfare State* (New York: Basic Books, 1990), in the first instance, and Marvin Olasky, *The Tragedy of American Compassion* (Wheaton, Ill.: Crossway Books, 1992), in the second instance.

interdependent family creatures — social creatures — before they are acquisitive individuals and civic egalitarians?[6]

I ask these questions not to imply that there is an obvious and universal answer to them. Rather, the purpose of the questions is to suggest the opposite: the answers will be quite different depending on what one assumes, at bottom, to be the identity and meaning of human life. Additional questions can easily be added to the list. Is there anything besides economic advancement, individual freedom, and material equality that properly motivates individuals and satisfies their sense of purpose and well-being? Should freedom be thought of primarily as maximum individual independence — the maximum freedom to change commitments in minimum time, to consume an ever-widening array of goods and services, and to remain unbound by enduring institutional obligations? Is there something else humans must do in order to achieve fulfillment? And what should we make of the fact that humans quite often violate the standards of behavior that they generally profess to accept? Individuals do not always appear to act even in their own best interests.

6. Questions about human society beyond those about the state and the economy are urgent ones for the reconstruction of public policy. A recent article by management guru Peter F. Drucker highlights this urgency: "The Age of Social Transformation," *Atlantic Monthly*, Nov. 1994, 53-80. Who accomplishes community tasks in the "knowledge society?" Drucker asks. It is not the government and it is not the large business enterprise (as Drucker once thought it would be). Rather, it is the "social sector," including families, schools, churches, and increasingly the diverse array of nonprofit organizations, many of which are religious. In contemporary society, Drucker argues, we now have increasing differentiation: "Organizations must competently perform the one social function for the sake of which they exist — the school to teach, the hospital to cure the sick, and the business to produce goods, services, or the capital to provide for the risks of the future." But in such a society the questions of integration and human meaning become all the more important, since all organizations must accept social responsibility and together they constitute "the community." Government's role in this has never been more important, but it cannot perform the social-sector tasks any more than it can perform the economic tasks. And yet, Drucker concludes, "we do not have even the beginnings of political theory or the political institutions needed for effective government in the knowledge-based society of organizations."

More detailed sociological/philosophical assessments of the social and personal challenges of differentiated societies, in which government and the market contend with the "social sector" (or what others call the "civil society"), can be found in Alan Wolfe, *Whose Keeper? Social Science and Moral Obligation* (Berkeley: Univ. of California Press, 1989), and Michael Schluter and David Lee, *The R Factor* (London: Hodder and Stoughton, 1993).

If we turn our attention from the individual to the larger society, we must ask additional questions: is equality really the primary public standard bearing on human conscience? Or are there other standards that suffer diminution if equality is overemphasized or absolutized? Furthermore, if equality is so important, why should we accept welfare policies that do little more than lift people from underclass status to lower-class status? Why should government not lift people to a condition of genuine equality? Do welfare recipients actually experience a greater sense of equality as a consequence of benefiting from welfare programs, or is the sense of justice felt only by those who design and deliver the welfare support?

All of these questions lead in a definite direction — to the following question: should the debate over welfare policies today be redirected instead to a debate over the presuppositions that helped to give rise to those policies in the first place? If the standard operating policies by which government deals with education, health care, families, civil rights, employment security, social security, and crime are insufficient to keep everyone out of life-threatening poverty, and if, after three decades of additional programs targeted at the poorest citizens, we still have not overcome or fundamentally alleviated poverty in this country, then is it perhaps time to turn our attention to the basic framework and presuppositions of government's responsibility? Could it be that our laws and governance patterns are helping to produce the very poverty that welfare policies cannot adequately handle? Could it be that the liberal presuppositions about human nature — about individual autonomy and civic equality — are so flawed and inadequate that they require radical revision or supplementation before we can even begin to engage in disputes over the finer points of welfare policies?

If the answer to these questions is affirmative, as I believe it is, then it is incumbent upon us to turn a critical mind toward our fundamental assumptions and presuppositions about human identity and meaning in this world.

The Complexity of What It Means to Be Human

Today almost everyone in the United States takes for granted the existence of a differentiated society. We no longer live in tight clans in which decisions about everything in life come under the authority of a single head. We no longer live in a society in which church and state alone are able to make the rules for every other relationship and institution. While it is true that we often hear claims of omnicompetence coming from either "the people" or Congress (in the name of the people) — claims that may lead government to try to act on almost everything under the sun — we generally experience life in a manifold of relatively independent associations and institutions. Families, churches, businesses, scientific and artistic organizations, universities, newspapers, book publishers, and thousands of non-profit voluntary associations all follow their own courses, acting not at all like mere branches of government. Whether or not we think much about it, we take for granted that human life entails a diverse array of relationships and organizations.[7]

Even though liberal ideology interprets all institutions and relationships as artificial, that is, as reducible to contracts among supposedly autonomous individuals, the fact remains that many of the strongest and oldest social entities exhibit lives of their own, structuring and defining the behavior of individuals rather than the other way around. The endurance and marked diversity of institutions and associations belie the myth that they derive from mere contractualism. A publishing firm is something quite different from a farm; a church is quite distinct from an art club; a family has a character markedly different from a business enterprise. Each of these, with its own history of development, is a rich composite of received tradition, creative innovation, response to transcendent principles, and a sense of shared obligation.

The differentiated character of our social experience demonstrates the inadequacy of a political philosophy that reduces every human problem to the relative economic condition and equality (or inequality) of supposedly autonomous individuals. Individuals do not actually manifest self-sufficient, self-defining capabilities. To the contrary, in almost every situation in life individuals bear mutual responsibility with and for one another in homes, schools, churches, employment, politics, and so forth. This is one of the reasons why the so-called communitarians criticize "rights talk" that has become abstracted from the responsibilities and obligations of real

7. The argument here relates to Drucker's point (see n. 6 above) and is foundational to my social and political philosophy. See James W. Skillen, *Recharging the American Experiment: Principled Pluralism for Genuine Civic Society* (Grand Rapids, Mich.: Baker Book House, 1994), and James W. Skillen and Rockne M. McCarthy, eds., *Political Order and the Plural Structure of Society* (Atlanta: Scholars Press, 1991).

people in real communities and institutions.[8] There are very few rights one may legitimately claim and exercise that do not go hand in hand with obligations.

Moreover, on the responsibility side of this equation, it is not only, or even usually, the state and its laws to which one is responsible. Parents and children in a home bear responsibility to and for one another; church members and leaders bear mutual responsibility for each other; employers and employees, teachers and students, friends and neighbors all bear distinct types of mutual responsibility defined by those distinct relationships and institutions. A concern for the freedom and relative economic standing of citizens can never adequately lead to justice for citizens if it fails to take into account the fact that citizens are always *more than* citizens. Meaningful citizenship in a differentiated society depends on the fact that human beings exercise a variety of other (and often prior) responsibilities. The hypothetically autonomous individual who is supposed to be free to enjoy certain rights does not exist solely in relation to the state but exists first of all in relation to family members, neighbors, employer or employees, and more. The question, then, is how should public law take into account all of the obligations people have for one another — obligations that are not simply public-legal obligations of a civic character? How should government do justice to citizens (political creatures) who necessarily are more than citizens and who are not, in fact, autonomous individuals but thoroughly interdependent social creatures?

One cannot address this unavoidable question without revealing one's basic religious/philosophical assumptions. One cannot deal with the issues at stake without making (or presuming) a case for what humans are and how they *ought* to live. Part of the reason for the crisis in welfare policy, I believe, is that the dominant liberal/conservative mindset in America leads people to take for granted the truthfulness of certain presuppositions that are actually quite faulty. On the basis of those faulty assumptions people then make policies, utilizing cost-benefit analyses and a pragmatic-utilitarian calculus, which mistakenly assume that the alle-

8. Cf. Mary Ann Glendon, *Rights Talk: The Impoverishment of Political Discourse* (New York: Free Press, 1991); William A. Galston, *Liberal Purposes: Goods, Virtues, and Diversity in the Liberal State* (New York: Cambridge Univ. Press, 1991); Elizabeth Frazer and Nicola Lacey, *The Politics of Community: A Feminist Critique of the Liberal-Communitarian Debate* (Toronto: Univ. of Toronto Press, 1993); and the communitarian quarterly *The Responsive Community.*

viation of poverty will come from the acts of government and poor people alone. But it has become clear that the dispute today over social welfare is caused by deeper differences in presuppositions. It is no longer plausible for policymakers to argue simply that a greater good for a greater number of poor individuals might be achieved by a particular policy at a certain public expense. Instead, those who are involved in policy disputes ought to return to questions about whether and why government should even be making certain laws or instituting particular programs. The question is: who should be responsible, and in what way, for the circumstances in which people live? What, in particular, is government's proper responsibility in relation to the differentiated responsibilities that belong to families, schools, churches, businesses, and the many other institutions that together compose society?[9]

9. The debate over the book by Richard J. Hernstein and Charles Murray, *The Bell Curve* (New York: Free Press, 1994), is instructive here. The authors and many of their critics assume that human beings are individual behavioral mechanisms to be measured and assessed in terms of various biologically and environmentally abstracted determinants. Hernstein and Murray try to make the case that an unrealistic ideal of social equality has misled policymakers to ignore the fact of certain genetic and racial differences among people. In the present knowledge society, individuals with higher IQs are getting better jobs and generally doing better economically, and little can be done to change that by social engineering aimed at overcoming racial and other group differences. The "only answer to the problem of group differences," the authors write in a later article, "is an energetic and uncompromising recommitment to individualism." Murray and Hernstein, "Race, Genes and I.Q. — An Apologia," *New Republic*, Oct. 31, 1994, 35.

Some of *The Bell Curve*'s critics think Hernstein and Murray are subtly (or not so subtly) encouraging citizens and governments to give up the fight to overcome racism and economic inequality. In other words, they read the book as a social Darwinist apologia for letting individuals rise or fall, live or die, on their own merits and initiatives. Hernstein and Murray say they are only facing reality. If people do not have to endure the discouragement that comes from falsely raised expectations, then different groups of individuals will be free to "take pride in their group" regardless of whether the individuals who compose it have high intelligence or some other dominant characteristic. Government should not hold out false promises that leave less intelligent people (or differently colored people, or differently talented people) feeling like losers because government efforts have not made them equal to others.

From my point of view, the uncomfortable thing about this debate is its "social scientific" abstraction of individuals from the real social and institutional contexts of human meaning; that abstraction is then followed by the further reduction of the human person by means of generalizing measurements of intelligence, genes, economic class,

Human Maturation

I am not a child-development expert, and the following discussion does not depend on great expertise in that field, even though it may require reformulation in the light of criticism offered by those who have such expertise.[10] The argument I want to make is in the realm of philosophical anthropology and is offered with the aim of trying to reorient thinking with regard to the nature and purpose of government's responsibility.

Child development, it appears to me, begins for the newborn in a completely undifferentiated social context and, in our kind of society, gradually widens out to the differentiated world of institutions and relationships that a person comes to know as an adult. Parents in a family

---

and so forth. One consequence is that by the end of their *New Republic* article, Murray and Hernstein can refer to "groups" only in a manner that artificially and indiscriminately lumps clans, communities, ethnic groups, states of origin (such as "Texans" and "Minnesotans"), and neighborhoods together as examples of "groups" (pp. 36-37). Not only is each of these a different sort of entity; all of them are quite different from families, churches, business enterprises, and other social organizations. Furthermore, nowhere do Murray and Hernstein (or most of their critics) consider seriously that human identity is defined preeminently by a divine-human relationship. It may well be true that governments ought not to build their social policies on the assumption that racial and innate intelligence differences can be overcome by social engineering. But the "only alternative" to that is certainly *not* for governments to treat people as simply autonomous individuals. Justice needs to be done to people in their different institutions and relationships as social creatures who simultaneously bear various kinds of obligation for one another. To assess these multiple communal meanings requires a different kind of social science and radically different assumptions about human nature.

Some of the debate over *The Bell Curve* can be found in the numerous critical responses in *New Republic,* Oct. 31, 1994. See also, for example, Alan Ryan, "Apocalypse Now?" *New York Review of Books,* Nov. 17, 1994, 7-11; Charles Lane, "The Tainted Sources of 'The Bell Curve,'" *New York Review of Books,* Dec. 1, 1994, 14-19; and "How Clever is Charles Murray?" *Economist,* Oct. 22, 1994.

10. This is not the place to discuss competing views of child development — physical, social, psychological, religious, and so forth — but merely to emphasize again that fundamentally different assumptions about the nature of the human creature — male and female — lead to different perceptions and analyses of the developmental process. Cf., e.g., Charles Taylor, *Sources of the Self* (Cambridge: Harvard Univ. Press, 1989); Erik H. Erikson, *Childhood and Society* (New York: W. W. Norton, 1963); Roy Clouser, *The Myth of Religious Neutrality: An Essay on the Hidden Role of Religious Belief in Theories* (Notre Dame: Univ. of Notre Dame Press, 1991); Abraham J. Heschel, *Who is Man?* (Stanford: Stanford Univ. Press, 1965).

already know and experience the differentiated social world, but the newborn begins only with the family (or part of a family or some kind of family substitute). This is not to underestimate the significance of the birth event as a differentiating movement from womb to the larger open "nest" of the home. But the birth experience — even when involving high-tech medical assistance — is a newborn's experience with his or her mother, and (one hopes) with the encouragement and involvement of the father, siblings, and an extended family. A newborn enters the world and begins to mature from within a highly undifferentiated and intimate social setting — mother, child, and immediate family. Every bodily function, every experience inside and eventually outside the home, is experienced by the infant through the mediation of the family.

This is one of the reasons, I believe, why family analogies are so often used by every differentiated institution and social experience. The school principal or the college president will say, "We are like a family here." Marian Wright Edelman wants Americans to think of themselves as a family responsible for "our" children.[11] To overcome racism and other forms of civic injustice or alienation, people will often speak of the need to reach out to all our "brothers and sisters." But when we are careful to discern the limits of analogies and metaphors, we realize that a state, a school, and even a friendly and intimate workplace are not "families." All of these are differentiated institutions, organizations, and societal relationships that presuppose a prior undifferentiated family experience of infancy and childhood, which all adults have (or should have) experienced.[12]

The first point I want to emphasize about this distinction between differentiated and undifferentiated social experience is that the legitimate process of societal differentiation does not contradict a child's initial undifferentiated family experience. To the contrary, it depends on it. Healthy societal differentiation demonstrates the peculiar truth that mature people can experience *multiple* responsibilities all at the same time as an expression

11. Marian Wright Edelman, *Families in Peril: An Agenda for Social Change* (Cambridge: Harvard Univ. Press, 1987), 33.

12. For a valuable recent update on the importance of the family — particularly the two-parent family — for children, see Barbara Dafoe Whitehead, "Dan Quayle Was Right," *Atlantic Monthly,* April 1993, 47-84. Cf. also David Blankenhorn, Steven Bayme, and Jean Bethke Elshtain, eds., *Rebuilding the Nest: A New Commitment to the American Family* (Milwaukee: Family Service America, 1990); Linda Gordon, *Pitied but Not Entitled: Single Mothers and the History of Welfare* (New York: Free Press, 1994).

of their *singular*, integrated human identity. Spouses in a marriage are always and everywhere married to one another, even when separated in space; but each is also more than a spouse. The woman who is a wife might also be a journalist, a church member, a student, and a citizen at the same time. None of those differentiated "roles" or experiences is defined in terms of the others, and none requires the undifferentiated reduction of the others to itself. Another journalist need not be married, or belong to a church, or attend school.

On the other hand, unhealthy differentiation, or, perhaps better said, antinormative resistance to social differentiation, is another story. In a differentiated society, the family whose husband and father refuses to allow the wife and mother to function in any role other than wife and mother is not thereby strengthening family unity but is violating the woman's full personhood.[13] A state that seeks to bind its citizens into a closer civic community by assuming to itself the omnicompetent authority to govern all institutions of faith, communications media, schooling, and the economy is not creating a more integrated and equal society but is violating the responsibilities that belong to people in other capacities. It is perpetuating injustice, not strengthening public justice.

This first point might be summed up as follows: the healthy (normative) differentiation of society opens the way to a multiplicity of responsibilities that are mutually compatible with, not mutually exclusive of, one another. People can hold or exercise multiple responsibilities simultaneously precisely because none of them is exhaustive; none of them demands the entire life of a person; none may lay claim to an undifferentiated, omnicompetent authority. The other side of this coin is that any differentiated institution that seeks to lay claim to an authority beyond its competence will inevitably collide and interfere with other differentiated institutions and responsibilities.

The single apparent anomaly here is the family. I have just argued that infants and young children, from birth through some later stage of

13. Stressing the importance of a strong family for children must not be played off against women's rights as if the two are incompatible. See Van Leeuwen, esp. 416-51; Jean Bethke Elshtain, *Power Trips and Other Journeys: Essays in Feminism as Civic Discourse* (Madison: Univ. of Wisconsin Press, 1990), and Elshtain, "Contesting Care" (a book review article), *American Political Science Review* 88, no. 4 (1994): 966-70; Elizabeth Fox-Genovese, *Feminism without Illusions: A Critique of Individualism* (Chapel Hill: Univ. of North Carolina Press, 1991).

maturation, experience (or should experience) all of life from within the undifferentiated context of family life. But if the family itself is but one differentiated social institution among many, and if the family may not lay claim to omnicompetent authority over all of society, then how may it function in such an all-encompassing, undifferentiated way for children?

This important question prepares the way for my second main point about child development as seen from the perspective of government's authority for civil law and public policy. The key factor that dissolves the apparent anomaly is the distinction between children and adults. The family, from the standpoint of the parents and the rest of society, *is* but one differentiated institution among many. Parents do not, and should not, have omnicompetent authority over society, or even over their own children. Parents may not, for instance, displace the state in deciding to end the life of their children, whether for reasons of crime or for some cultic exercise. In what I am calling a properly differentiated society, parents no longer rule over closed clans, or feudal estates, or *pater familial* communities in which the father was judge, jury, and executioner of all family members. If one assumes, as I believe we should, that parents ought not to have omnicompetent authority over their children, one should then see normative child rearing as the parental obligation to raise children toward maturity for life in an open, differentiated society, not for slavery or stunted growth within the confines of a closed family, autonomous plantation, or totalitarian state.

Nevertheless, within the limits of their differentiated authority, parents should be recognized by the state as having the *principal* and full mediated responsibility for rearing children from birth to the age of majority.[14] The experience of children from birth through infancy and childhood, in other words, ought to be recognized as an experience that legitimately moves from undifferentiated, integral, *family* care and mediation to participation in a complex social world with a differentiated character. To be truly human in maturity is to experience life as an integral whole even

14. On the rights of the family, see David Wagner, "The Family and the Constitution," *First Things*, Aug.–Sept. 1994, 23-28; Bruce C. Hafen, "Individualism in Family Law," in Blankenhorn, Bayme, Elshtain, 161-78; Elshtain, "The Family and Civic Life," in *Power Trips and Other Journeys*, 45-60. For more on social as well as individual rights see also Deal W. Hudson, "Human Nature, Human Rights, and the Crisis among Western Intellectuals," *Notes et Documents*, no. 38 (Sept. –Dec. 1993): 31-53, and Paul Marshall, "Two Types of Rights," *Canadian Journal of Political Science* 25, no. 4 (1992): 661-76.

though it is a complex wholeness constituted, in part, by a differentiated society. But the healthy connectedness and mutual compatibility of diverse social responsibilities becomes possible only if people can mature into a differentiated society from the early childhood experience of an undifferentiated family bond (or close family substitute).

Much more needs to be said about the unique qualities of the family — why two parents are normative; why divorce and family breakup are so devastating for children; why healthy extended-family ties can be so good; and much more. But rather than pursue a discussion of the internal life of the family, I want to keep attention focused on the public side of doing justice to families in a differentiated society.

From what has just been said it follows that public policies oriented to children ought always to be oriented toward strengthening family life and parental responsibility for children. In other words, no other differentiated institution, including the state, should be allowed to displace parental responsibility for child rearing. Governments certainly should guard the lives of all citizens, including children, from any molestation or threat to life. Thus, intrusion into highly dysfunctional homes to protect children (or spouses) from abuse is part of the proper task of government.[15] But of course from this point of view child abuse is not a legitimate part of child rearing; it actually represents parental abrogation of child-rearing responsibility. Healthy child rearing, on the other hand, involves the oversight and nurturing of children from the newborn's completely undifferentiated experience through to majority independence.

The responsibility of parenting includes the formative nurturing of children, guiding children into every conceivable realm of responsibility — responsibilities that children themselves will one day take on in a fully differentiated way when they have become mature. As children, however, they need to learn basic manners, a "mother" language (or two), right from wrong, many different skills, habits of social interchange, and so forth. However, in order for this diverse range of experience to hold together in an integral fashion for children, parents need to have the authority (without suffering any public inhibition or discrimination) to decide whether and

15. Cf. Elshtain, "The Family Crisis and State Intervention: The Construction of Child Abuse as Social Problem and Popular Rhetoric," in *Power Trips and Other Journeys*, 73-88; Mary-Lou Weisman, "When Parents are Not in the Best Interests of the Child," *Atlantic Monthly*, July 1994, 43-63.

where to attend church;[16] where to send their children to school;[17] what music and TV programs the children may listen to; what they may eat; and so much more. In other words, from out of an infant's undifferentiated experience in the family she receives the guidance that leads her ever so gradually into the interconnected meaning of the differentiated society in which she gradually becomes a responsible actor. Public policy, therefore, ought to respect an exceedingly wide range of parental responsibility over the undifferentiated experience of minor children.

The obverse side of this principle is that public policy ought *not* to allow any other differentiated institution, including the state, to act with an undifferentiated "paternal" or "maternal" authority over people. This means something distinct for children and adults. For children it means that the law ought *not* to recognize parentlike authority as belonging to anyone other than parents. And in the case of schools, where young children will be under teachers who serve *in loco parentis,* it should be the parents themselves, not governments, who have *principal* responsibility to choose those schools.

For adults, on the other hand, no single differentiated institution should be allowed to act toward employees, citizens, students, church members, and the like *as if* it had undifferentiated, parentlike authority. All tendencies toward a paternalistic or maternalistic state, in other words, are dangerous. Public policies that ask schools, for example, to function as homes, jails, job-training centers, and much more are misguided policies. And when the government itself acts as if it is responsible to help poor people by becoming their substitute spouse, parent, employer, counselor, and more, then we can be sure that something is wrong.[18]

In sum, the unique reality of child development should lead us to a special consideration of the unique character of the family in a differentiated society. The special character of child development should also

16. Cf. John E. Coons, "The Religious Rights of Children" (paper presented at the Conference on Religious Human Rights, Emory University, Atlanta, Oct. 7–9, 1994).

17. On parental rights in education, see Charles L. Glenn's essay elsewhere in this volume; John E. Coons and Stephen Sugarman, *Education by Choice: The Case for Family Control* (Berkeley: Univ. of California Press, 1978); James W. Skillen, ed., *The School-Choice Controversy: What is Constitutional?* (Grand Rapids, Mich.: Baker Books, 1993). Cf. also Barbara Dafoe Whitehead, "The Failure of Sex Education," *Atlantic Monthly,* Oct. 1994, 55-80.

18. Center for Public Justice, esp. 565-69.

lead us to a recognition of the radical difference between legitimately undifferentiated childhood experience in the family, on the one hand, and the illegitimacy of any adult exercise of undifferentiated responsibility in a differentiated society, on the other. My argument here is a normative one about what *ought* to be the case; I am not trying to describe something that exists or will happen inevitably. One's normative vision orients perception in a way that leads to judgments about healthy and unhealthy, legitimate and illegitimate social conditions and institutional responsibilities.

Adult Independence in a Differentiated Society

If what I have said about human identity, maturation, and life in a differentiated society is true, then from a political/legal point of view the healthy, proper goal for adult maturity should not be maximum individual autonomy and thus maximum freedom to be either responsible or irresponsible as each individual chooses. Rather, maturity and independence should be viewed as the successful assumption by each individual of personal responsibilities in a differentiated society. This means at least three things.

First of all, we will have to recognize that an adult is no longer a child. An adult is ready to put dependence on parents behind, leaving the relatively undifferentiated authority structure of the home to enter a diverse range of relationships, institutions, and organizations in which he or she can exercise talents and contribute services in ways that will also contribute to his or her own fulfillment.

Second, maturation into adult independence also means the assumption of obligations that do not fall to children. Adults retain the civil rights of personal protection, but now those are the rights of citizens who should be responsible for the decisions they make in a variety of institutions and relationships. Government and the courts may not treat adults as if they are children — wards or clients of an undifferentiated, paternalistic (or maternalistic) state. Government ought not to base its actions on the assumption that public laws may always trump the authority of schools, businesses, families, churches, and other organizations in a way that releases individuals from their responsibilities in those nonpolitical arenas.[19]

19. On the question of an emerging (or hardening) "culture of poverty" in the United States as it relates to the failure of individuals and various nongovernment

Finally, maturation should mean the obligation to participate fully in the civic community, which itself is one of the many differentiated realms of adult responsibility. The political community has its own obligations and privileges. Thus, for example, citizens pay taxes and perform other civic duties to help government fulfill its responsibility to uphold the law, preserve the good order of society, respond to public emergencies, and pursue fundamental reform where systemic injustice exists.

More than enough has been said already to make it evident that my argument depends on a particular set of assumptions and framework of presuppositions about the identity of human beings and their purpose in this world. People who hold contrasting assumptions will view matters quite differently. My assumptions depend on a Christian worldview, which is oriented by biblical revelation. This is not to say that everything presented in this argument comes from biblical texts. Rather, my understanding of contemporary human life is grounded in the conviction that the whole of reality is God's historically differentiating creation, that human irresponsibility and the degradation of society are due to the expression of human sinfulness in all areas of life, and that hope for renewal in personal lives and for reform in each part of society is possible because of God's redeeming work in Jesus Christ.

From a Christian point of view, one will recognize that human beings, male and female, come to know themselves, in the course of maturation, as creatures who will always remain something of a question to themselves. That is to say, human identity is not exhausted by any or all of the functions and activities of life, because humans have been created in the image of God. Self-identity and self-realization in all areas of life are tied to the knowledge of God. Human identity in its fullness, therefore, is not to be found in rationality, or sociability, or economic productivity, or genetic patterns. To be the image of God is to have an identity that is not exhausted in the family, the political community, or the church, nor in art or science.

---

institutions to fulfill their responsibilities, see Lawrence M. Mead, *Beyond Entitlement: The Social Obligations of Citizenship* (New York: Free Press, 1986); Moynihan; Ellwood, esp. 189-230; Joe Klein, "A Tale of Two Cities," *Newsweek*, Aug. 15, 1994, 57; Kay S. Hymowitz, "Real Life on the Teen Mommy Track," *Washington Post*, Nov. 13, 1994, C1; Patrick Day et al., "The Black Man in America," *New York Times Magazine*, Dec. 4, 1994, 72-110; and William Raspberry, "The Urban League Action Plan," *Washington Post*, July 17, 1994.

All of these functions and communal relationships are facets of what it means to be human, but human identity cannot be reduced to any or all of them. Altogether, these diverse dimensions of human life find their unity and fullness in a human-divine relationship that holds them together in a deeper unity, because human identity in the image of God points beyond itself to the One in whose image human beings have been created.[20]

The very fact that human creatures have come to different conclusions about their own identity shows that they are responsible creatures called to reflect, to choose, to make judgments, to draw conclusions, and to act on their convictions. Even when, in disobedience against God, human beings seek ultimate fulfillment in one or another creaturely function or earthly relationship rather than in God, they exhibit capabilities and qualities that inhere only in the image of God, not in other earthly creatures. God has given human beings real responsibility to shape life in this world, even to the point of their own destruction if their deeds are evil or misguided. Human beings shape both themselves and history; they are not merely shaped by others or by historical or genetic forces. They are not locked into a repetitive cycle of animal instincts that change little, if at all, over the generations. Humans are indeed social, familial, political, aesthetic, scientific, playful creatures, but they have an underlying, integrating wholeness about them that cannot be reduced to any one of these institutions, abilities, or characteristics.

To confess that human beings are created in the image of God is to say that being human means discovering why the center of gravity in human life cannot be found in any single human characteristic or role but only in God himself. We have been created ultimately for fellowship with God — for an eternal destiny. If life reveals its true meaning only in this light, then human responsibility entails searching for the true and limited purpose of each relationship and institution of the creation. Each is important, each offers an opportunity for the exercise of human responsibility in relation to God.

20. See Berkouwer, esp. 194-233; Dooyeweerd, 173-95.

Government's Public Welfare Responsibilities

One important institution of human society that is essential to the communal life of the image of God is the political community of citizens under government. The task of discerning *what* government's responsibilities should be is part of the entire enterprise of developing a public philosophy, an inescapable obligation for human beings called by God to mutual responsibility and to the care of creation. To recognize that human beings are in the image of God and that any human institution, including the state, is limited in its responsibility and incapable of bearing omnicompetent authority will lead us to a modest view of the state's competence and to the conviction that the government's very duty to do justice requires that it protect the diverse nongovernmental competencies of its citizens. A biblical point of view, in other words, entails both a very high view of human beings as the image of God and the firm conviction that adult responsibility in a differentiated society is essential to the existence of a just social order. The last thing government may do to fulfill its own responsibility is to treat humans as if they are nothing more than behavioral animals. Nor may government frame its laws on the basis of an assumption that human beings are free to be irresponsible and that government will always be there to pick up the pieces while allowing those irresponsibilities to continue.

If, from a biblical point of view, we argue that human maturation into adult responsibility should *not* mean maximum freedom from obligation to anyone other than oneself, then it is incumbent on us to articulate what we mean by healthy (legitimate, proper, normative) adult freedom, which carries with it responsibilities in the diverse range of institutions and relationships of a differentiated society.

At the same time, if we accept the legitimacy of the ongoing differentiation of society and the central importance of child development toward mature, responsible adulthood in God's world, it is incumbent on us to articulate an evaluation of the apparent human deformities associated with severe poverty. Who is responsible to make judgments about antinormative and unhealthy social conditions, and who is responsible to address those deformities?

One who assumes that the chief goal of human development is individual autonomy might argue that whenever an individual finds himself or herself less free than he or she would like to be because of low income, that person may legitimately appeal to the state for help. After all, according to one version of liberal political doctrine, the state is the highest expression of self-government, of individual autonomy expressed through contracts with other autonomous individuals. To look to the state for help in achieving one's freedom is precisely what one should do in following the self-liberating, self-governing process.

Appealing to the same standard of individual autonomy, however, a more conservative libertarian might reach another conclusion. Dependence on the state for support is still a form of undesirable dependency. It does not lead to individual freedom even if one rationalizes that government's action is an expression of autonomous self-government. A key problem with American society, in this view, is that dependency in many forms has displaced individual self-sufficiency. Instead, if the state is to do anything, it should quit redistributing wealth via taxes and require the poor to become self-supporting like everyone else.

If, however, one begins with the philosophy I have tried to outline above, one reaches different conclusions. People are neither individually self-sufficient nor boundlessly self-determining by means of the contractual, democratic state. Rather, they are creatures responsible for one another in a diversity of relationships and institutions, the norms of which are posited not by individual or collective will but by the Creator. The government of a state is called by God to the normative task of securing justice for all citizens and to the upholding of nonpolitical institutions and responsibilities that God has given to people who are always more than citizens.

Thus, the first responsibility of government in the face of deformity and unhealthy human development is to help call people to the full range of their diverse responsibilities. The state should not take over the care of children when children are in need but should instead encourage parents and help hold them accountable for their child-rearing obligations. The state should not assume responsibility for "parenting" all its youngest citizens in preparation for adult responsibilities and occupations, but instead should make sure that parents, educators, and employers are fulfilling such responsibilities.

In this sense, a properly ordered society is one in which government's basic function is, through law, to uphold the multiple accountability structures of society. "Standard public operating policies" of the kind I have in mind are things such as the dependency deduction for income tax; public funding for parentally chosen education; the fair and equitable enforcement of contracts; a social security system; and enforceable rules for public health and well-being such as garbage disposal, fire protection, and the swift and just punishment of criminal behavior. With regard to these general functions of seeing to the just ordering of society, government is fulfilling its welfare responsibilities when it properly recognizes and supports (and penalizes the failures of) other institutions that have responsibilities for the rearing and educating of children, for the development and offering of jobs, and so forth.[21]

But there are also circumstances in which unusual, even catastrophic, crises arise. These may be natural disasters such as earthquakes, hurricanes, or floods. They may come as a result of war, massive civil unrest, or a crime wave. Under these circumstances, most of us have no difficulty in seeing that the state is the legitimate authority to exercise emergency powers for the protection of the public commonwealth. To the extent that today's poverty crisis is the result of catastrophic and emergency deformities, then it may be time to ask whether the standard programs for protection of the public welfare are sufficient to address the need. If crime, large-scale unemployment, and completely (or mainly) failing schools reveal a form of social degeneracy that cannot be reformed by means of standard public operating policies, then emergency powers may be needed to help reorder the situation.[22]

Obviously, an emergency response by government to deformities caused by various human irresponsibilities is something quite different from flying in massive supplies of food and water to hurricane victims. People enduring a natural disaster are presumed to be capable of fulfilling ordinary responsibilities once they receive the emergency assistance. Within weeks or months, the emergency operation can be called off. But in the case of a vast social/cultural crisis in a differentiated society, it is precisely the density of criminals, or of illiterate and unemployable people, or of children without adequate homes that creates the problem. The need is not simply for a few more food stamps or new textbooks or better locks on the doors. The kind of emergency action needed in the case of cultural break-

21. See Drucker.

22. Cf. Leon R. Kass, "Am I My Foolish Brother's Keeper," *American Enterprise*, Nov.–Dec. 1994, 16-27.

down may require government's coordination, but clearly the means will have to be different from those used to address a large-scale natural disaster.

Beyond government's standard public operating policies and its preparedness to respond to emergencies, it should also seek to fulfill its calling by working diligently to reform fundamentally unjust structures in society. This is the level at which the most difficult judgments have to be made about public welfare responsibility. The needs may be urgent, but remedies require long-term change. Better schools, better job training, more responsible parents, a decrease in crime, improved health care, more extensive human support networks among families and across neighborhoods — all of these are needed in a differentiated society, but they cannot be created by government and shipped in from the outside.

Even here, however, if we begin with the idea that government's job is to support the recovery of diverse human responsibilities in a variety of institutions, seeing to it that justice is done to each of them, then some significant new pointers can be given to policymakers. Instead of simply trying directly to liberate individuals from bad circumstances by giving them public funds or other assistance, policymakers should look for ways to strengthen and assist parents, teachers, employers, and organizations such as churches that are capable of offering meaningful, direct, personal assistance. Instead of looking only at measurements of economic inequality, policymakers will need to consider measurements of "responsibility inequality" to see how people can be encouraged (and in some cases compelled) to fulfill the responsibilities that are tied to the exercise of their adult freedom.

Conclusion

The argument of this chapter is preliminary and suggestive. It emphasizes the importance of the basic assumptions and presuppositions that guide human thinking about government's task in society. Radically different views of human nature often lead to radically different views of human purpose and responsibility. That is part of the reason for our current crisis in developing sound welfare policies. Americans do not share a consensus about human identity and responsibility. Welfare policies grounded in one set of assumptions will look quite different from those grounded in another set of assumptions.

A Christian worldview perceives a creation filled with people created in the image of God, capable of being both responsible and irresponsible in a wide variety of ways. In God's creation, human beings are playing a creative role in shaping complex, differentiating societies. In those complex social orders, government's task should be to uphold public justice, to reinforce the accountability structures in which people are capable of fulfilling a diverse range of obligations. Welfare policies should be designed (1) to help people recover responsibility, (2) to require various institutions to fulfill their callings, and (3) to pursue the long-term, structural reforms that may be necessary to overcome unjust social patterns. A biblical view of human life, of the human maturation process, and of the differentiated structure of society helps to illuminate the conditions of poverty as we now find them in the United States. That same point of view indicates the need for some very significant changes in government's welfare policies.

Biblical Teaching and the Objectives of Welfare Policy in the United States[1]

John D. Mason

FEW FEDERAL POLICIES are as harshly criticized as our welfare programs. Most citizens appear to believe that long-term welfare "dependency" has reached crisis proportions, requiring reforms to impose some form of work requirement ("workfare") as a condition for receiving public assistance. A popular Clinton campaign theme in 1992, for example, was "two years and out" for those who go on welfare — after two years of receiving welfare a recipient would be required to take a job.

Many conservatives would restrict welfare even more than this. At a minimum there should be a tough form of workfare, forcing recipients to take "just any job." Radical critics would eliminate public welfare altogether, forcing the poor to rely on traditional forms of extended family support and charitable assistance.[2] Conservatives believe that the American economy offers sufficient employment opportunity for all who are willing to expend the necessary effort, and they are confident that virtually anyone, when pressed, can scrape by.

1. The arguments of this chapter have been informed by all members of the Welfare Responsibility team, with specific suggestions for improvement coming from Stanley Carlson-Thies, Lawrence Mead, and James Skillen. My colleague Stephen Smith made numerous suggestions to improve the presentation. I remain solely responsible for any remaining errors in analysis and awkwardness in presentation.

2. See, e.g., C. Murray's editorial page article, "The Coming White Underclass," *Wall Street Journal,* Oct. 23, 1993.

Liberal critics of this new conservative welfare consensus either are content with existing welfare programs or at most would allow a soft form of workfare — work encouragement and expectation, but without tough requirements. They believe that labor market prospects for lower-income workers have diminished as the economy has shifted from high-paying manufacturing jobs toward service sector jobs that pay high wages only for well-educated workers. To enforce anything resembling hard workfare in this economy would either force already discouraged poor citizens into terribly demeaning jobs or strip from them the only financial assistance available.

What ethical guidance can be brought to this important debate to help policymakers decide whether to embrace a soft or hard form of workfare, to remain with the existing system of welfare, or to seriously restrict or eliminate welfare altogether? To confront these questions, as with all difficult questions facing a democracy, it is important for each ethical community to revisit and sharpen the instruction of its ethical tradition. Having done so, it can reenter the public square of contesting ethical traditions with a renewed sense of its own optimal goals as well as a surer sense of the trade-offs it can accept.

This chapter reexamines the ethical foundations of those communities that seek contemporary guidance in the biblical (and especially pentateuchal) provisions concerning the proper treatment of the poor. This group is not confined to theologically conservative Christians and Jews. From the colonial period to the present, to understand the American sense of moral obligation for the poor, whether in the form of private charity or of public welfare, we must turn to the influences of orthodox Christianity.[3] A better understanding of the biblical provisions regarding treatment of the poor, then, not only will help us see the direction in which we, as Christians, should push welfare reform but also will give us broader insight into the constraints on welfare policy and the role that might be played by private assistance to the poor.

I will begin by sketching the underlying goals of our current welfare system. I will then turn to our primary concern, an analysis of biblical teaching concerning assistance of the poor. We will look first at the structure of the welfare system commended by the Law of Moses for early Israel and

3. See Paul Boyer, *Urban Masses & Moral Order in America, 1820–1920* (Cambridge: Harvard Univ. Press, 1978).

then assess the normative objectives of the system. The concluding section applies the guidelines drawn from the Bible to the current debate over American welfare policy. My essential argument is that assistance to the poor should have as its chief goal establishing and maintaining economically and socially secure families. According to my argument, public authority has a key role to play in achieving this goal. In an extended appendix, I critique two contemporary Christian interpreters who argue against the legitimacy of government welfare.

The Objectives of Welfare in the United States

The American welfare system is widely seen as a failure. But what are its goals? What are the basic objectives of this system as it has developed since the 1930s? When people refer to welfare, they typically have in mind three basic programs: (1) AFDC (Aid to Families with Dependent Children): cash assistance to primarily single-parent, low-income families; (2) food stamps: coupons that can be used to purchase food; (3) Medicaid: in-kind (not cash) medical assistance. Casting the net a bit wider brings in (4) SSI (Supplemental Security Income): cash assistance for the aged and disabled not adequately assisted by Social Security; (5) the EITC (earned income tax credit): a reduction in the tax poorer families owe on earned income; and (6) access to publicly subsidized housing. The broadest definition embraces all government-mediated assistance helping those who might be poor without it: Social Security (including Medicare); unemployment compensation; publicly funded education — Head Start and public schools generally; and numerous other programs.[4]

Many critics these days are concerned mainly about whether too many welfare recipients are being allowed to receive public assistance without having to work; hence the plea for "workfare." Other contested pieces of the welfare puzzle in recent years include the following: What are the legitimate rights of welfare recipients in their dealings with government agencies? Should a woman on welfare be granted increased

4. Government's various income redistribution policies and programs scatter benefits far wider than to the poor ("welfare" for the nonpoor?), both earlier in our nation's history and at present (price support subsidies to farmers, educational funding, import protection, zoning protection for suburban communities, etc).

assistance if she bears additional children? What is the appropriate level of financial assistance for the poor, and should individual states be allowed to establish different support levels? Should government aggressively identify and pursue nonsupporting parents (even teen parents?) and force them to contribute financially toward the support of their children?

It is important, however, not to be led astray by these diverse questions. Past attempts to resolve one or another narrow concern have too often yielded counterproductive results. For example, out of an earlier concern not to provide public assistance to employable males, we created incentives for some families not to form in the first place and for some marriages to be officially dissolved in an effort to gain eligibility for public assistance. If we are to evaluate properly the separate pieces of the welfare problem in a way that lessens the potential for such counterproductive reforms, we need to have a firm grasp on welfare's purpose in the social and economic order. A useful place to begin is with a number of expert assessments of the objectives of the American welfare system as it has developed since the 1930s.[5]

In an important study based on contemporaneous debates and commentaries, historian James Patterson has assessed the first significant federal commitment to welfare in the 1930s as follows:

5. For the pre-1930 period, see T. Skocpol, *Protecting Soldiers & Mothers: The Political Origins of Social Policy in the United States* (Cambridge: Harvard Univ. Press, 1992); note also her assessment, in the "Introduction," of competing explanations for the origins of a federal welfare effort. Most analysts of the system begun in the 1930s conclude that "elimination of poverty" has not been the (sole) objective of welfare policy. After all, it is argued, a nation as wealthy as the United States could eliminate poverty if this was the overriding objective. Obviously other goals must have been more important. For the best-known argument along these lines, see F. Piven and R. Cloward, *Regulating the Poor: The Functions of Public Welfare* (New York: Random House, 1971), which claims that welfare programs were created reluctantly in the face of social unrest (brought on by unemployment) and offer niggardly assistance; the objective is preventing social unrest, not eliminating poverty. W. Trattner, ed., *Social Welfare or Social Control? Some Historical Reflections on 'Regulating the Poor'* (Knoxville: Univ. of Tennessee Press, 1983), presents a historical evaluation of this thesis. A useful work in the tradition of Piven and Cloward is M. Katz, *In the Shadow of the Poorhouse: A Social History of Welfare in America* (New York: Basic Books, 1986), which proposes four objectives of American-style welfare: relief of misery, preservation of social order and discipline, regulation of the labor market, and political mobilization.

> The most obvious characteristic of the new order was its primary reliance on contributory social insurance and its concomitant distaste for welfare, a reliance reflecting the age-old distinction between the deserving and the undeserving poor. The American emphasis, moreover, was unique; other western nations developed a blend of social policies, including family allowances, health services, housing allowances, and assistance, that benefited poor and nonpoor alike and obscured the distinction between social insurance and welfare. The separation of the two policies in the United States narrowed severely the scope of welfare, segregating general assistance and categorical aid as *the* cash-relief, means-tested programs and making the stigma for those who participated all the greater.[6]

Based on Patterson's analysis, we can piece together the following outline: (1) because of a general confidence that most citizens could provide for themselves with a normal amount of effort, welfare assistance (as distinct from social insurance programs like Social Security) should be limited and should subject recipients to stigmatizing treatment; (2) nonetheless, extended economic depression had convinced most that some centralized welfare assistance was required; (3) granting the necessity of welfare, this was to be as localized as possible, with numerous concessions to individual state distinctives.

As Patterson and others have observed, the objectives of the welfare system changed during the 1960s, with a liberalization of benefits and, in limited areas (especially medical care), the creation of entitlements — all in all a "softening of attitudes toward the poor."[7] But given (failed) efforts in the 1970s during both Republican and Democratic administrations to create an assured basic income for any low-income family, and successful reforms in the 1980s reversing several of the liberalizing changes made

6. Patterson, *America's Struggle against Poverty, 1900–1980* (Cambridge: Harvard Univ. Press, 1981), 76.

7. Patterson, 171. The most prominent exponent of this view is Charles Murray in his work *Losing Ground: American Social Policy, 1950–1980* (New York: Basic Books, 1984). During the 1960s, Murray argues, welfare policy was modified to reflect a changed view of the causes of poverty: poverty had been understood to result primarily from personal failure; the new view attributed poverty primarily to the structure of the economy. Policy was revised to extend assistance from the nonemployable to all the poor, to make welfare a right rather than a reluctant and constrained provision, and to seek equal outcomes rather than provide the tools for more equal opportunity.

during the 1960s (tightening the administration of AFDC and initiating work requirements), it can plausibly be argued that a generally consistent set of American values has constrained welfare administration from the 1930s to the present.

Robert Lampman, a sage observer, has boiled down the goals of our broad social assistance system to: (1) offsetting income losses (Social Security, unemployment insurance); (2) helping people to buy the essentials of life (education, food, health care); (3) reducing income poverty (cash transfer programs such as AFDC); and (4) sharing the tax burden fairly (a "progressive" income tax, and today the earned income tax credit).[8] Note Lampman's use of verbs like offsetting, helping, and reducing — rather than anything suggesting outright eliminating — poverty.

Irwin Garfinkel suggests that the welfare system seeks to balance three conflicting basic values shared by all members of American society (including the poor): (1) a compassionate concern to help those less fortunate than ourselves; (2) a constraining concern to promote self-reliance among welfare recipients; and (3) a thrifty concern to do whatever we do as inexpensively as possible.[9] It has been cheaper, for example, to give the poor money rather than to provide the necessary programs to help them become self-reliant — and hence the third-mentioned value dominates the second. Similarly, out of a concern for thrift and self-reliance, we established categorical programs that typically denied assistance to employable males. In both these cases the outcome appears to have been some marital disruption and greater dependency upon welfare than would otherwise be the case, thereby tending to make welfare mothers less self-reliant.

In *Poor Support,* his influential book on poverty and welfare, David Ellwood argues that although Americans are willing to use government to help the poor, they have come to hate welfare programs as a means for doing so. "Welfare is a flawed method of helping people who are poor and disadvantaged. Welfare brings some of our most precious values — involving autonomy, responsibility, work, family, community, and compassion —

8. Lampman, "Goals & Purposes of Social Welfare Expenditures," in P. Sommers, ed., *Welfare Reform in America: Perspective & Prospects* (Boston: Kluwer-Nijhoff, 1982), 3-14.

9. Garfinkel, "Income Support Policy: Where We've Come From & Where We Should Be Going," Discussion Paper no. 490-78 (Institute for Research on Poverty, University of Wisconsin, Apr. 1978).

into conflict," he says.[10] Given this unhappy state of affairs we need a fundamental reconceptualization of government-mediated assistance in order to assist the poor both more effectively and in socially acceptable ways. Ellwood discerns the following underlying values in Americans' views about poverty and helping the poor: (1) people can provide for themselves if they are willing to make the necessary sacrifices (autonomy of the individual); (2) people should work hard both to provide for their families and as a mark of strong character (virtue of work); (3) the nuclear family remains the primary social and economic unit (primacy of the family); and (4) people have a desire for community — seen in everything from religion to neighborhood — which manifests itself in compassion for others (sense of community). But Ellwood views the welfare system as unnecessarily forcing these values into conflict. Offering greater financial assistance to poorer families, for example, weakens the resolve to work, and in the case of single mothers weakens the commitment to form and maintain a two-parent family. Though in his assessment of American values the family receives strong affirmation, the structure of welfare in fact has done little to reinforce the family.

Patterson's assessment of the origins of the contemporary welfare system suggests a more constricted and possibly harsher set of objectives than do the other analysts: Americans had a "distaste" for welfare and therefore sought to stigmatize it. There is another troubling observation to make here: in the lists from Garfinkel and Ellwood compassion is seen as different from a concern for work and self-reliance. But cannot one promote self-reliance and a strong work ethic out of a compassionate concern for those involved? In considering these various *lists* of objectives for American welfare, we should further wonder if part of our difficulty is that we desire welfare to satisfy too many different objectives. But what objective should dominate? What criteria can we offer policymakers to help them prioritize the objectives of welfare?

10. Ellwood, *Poor Support: Poverty in the American Family* (New York: Basic Books, 1988), 6. Note that "welfare" for Ellwood is a *specific* set of current programs, and not a generic term for government-mediated assistance programs, as in this chapter.

A Biblical Welfare System?

How can we justify turning to ancient biblical materials for criteria by which to assess and reform contemporary welfare policy?[11] Throughout the Bible, from Genesis through Revelation, the claim is made that Yahweh is the God of all creation and all peoples and that the instruction he provided to early Israel and the early Christian community is valid for all nations.[12] Christian commentators through the ages have disagreed, of course, about precisely how this material can guide us. Some argue that little ethical guidance can be found in the Pentateuch but that more helpful instruction can be found in the prophetic concern for justice and the New Testament emphasis upon love as the fullest expression of the Mosaic Law. Others accept the entire Bible as a guide, yet believe that much of the pentateuchal material is relevant primarily to the Christian community and not the broader society.

My view is that within the numerous legal and extralegal provisions designed to inform life in early Israel, God encoded ethical emphases or guidelines that form a normative foundation that is developed in the remainder of the Bible.[13] These guidelines, along with the fuller understand-

11. See, further, sections I and III of J. Mason and K. Schaefer, "The Bible, the State, & the Economy: A Framework for Analysis," *Christian Scholar's Review* 10 (Sept. 1990): 45-64. J. Hamilton, in his *Social Justice & Deuteronomy: The Case of Deuteronomy 15* (Atlanta: Scholars Press, 1992), adopts a very different hermeneutical approach. Rather than seeking to set these laws in the early centuries of Israel's life in Palestine, he emphasizes the much later date during which the texts of Scripture were compiled and edited — a time in which Israel was in exile. Accordingly he examines the texts in terms of deliberately chosen literary construction and rhetorical devices, presuming that they were designed to convince a people out of power to take these laws seriously. Even so, he comes to many of the same conclusions developed here.

12. See Gen. 18:18; 2 Kings 19:15; Job 12:23; Ps. 22:27f.; Isa. 2:2-5, 42:4ff.; Dan. 7:27; Mic. 4:1ff.; Zech. 8:20ff.; Matt. 25:32; Gal. 3:8; and Rev. 2:26, 21:24, 22:2, among many other similar citations. For analysis, see also D. Van Winkle, "The Relationship of the Nations to Yahweh & to Israel in Isaiah XL–LV," *Vetus Testamentum* 35, no. 4 (1985): 446-58, and C. Scobie, "Israel & the Nations: An Essay in Biblical Theology," *Tyndale Bulletin* 43, no. 2 (1992): 283-305, which extends the primarily Old Testament emphasis of this theme to New Testament affirmation and refinement.

13. Throughout this chapter I use interchangeably "the Mosaic Law," "the pentateuchal provisions," "the Laws of Moses," "God providing his Law through Moses" — and no doubt similar expressions. There has been a long debate, at least since Alt's argument in the 1930s, that because many of the pentateuchal provisions have counterparts in the law codes of other early Near Eastern societies, these laws must not have

ing and greater refinement provided by the totality of the Bible and informed by commentary from the Jewish and Christian faith communities over the centuries, are to be held up before all nations as a measuring rod for discerning what are just and righteous institutions and dealings.

Christopher Wright states this position in the following terms: "What God did with Israel in their land functions for us as a model or paradigm from which we draw principles and objectives for our socio-ethical endeavor in secular society."[14] He goes on,

> The purpose of redemption is ultimately to restore the perfection of God's purpose in creation, that perfection which sin and the fall have corrupted. Israel, as God's redeemed community, was to have been a "light to the nations" — not just the vehicle of God's redemption, but an illustration of it in actual historical life. Israel's socio-economic life and institutions, therefore, have a paradigmatic or exemplary function in principle. It is not that they are to be simply and slavishly imitated, but rather that they are models within a particular cultural context of principles of justice, humaneness, equality, responsibility, and so forth which are applicable, *mutatis mutandis,* to all people in subsequent cultural contexts.[15]

---

been given by God through Moses but were dictated by the ordinary circumstances of life in that region. I embrace the traditional view that in ways that may not be clear to us today God delivered through Moses at least the foundations for (Exod. 19 and 20), if not the totality of, all the legal and extralegal provisions in the Pentateuch that were to instruct early Israel. On this debate, see E. Otto, "Town & Rural Countryside in Ancient Israelite Law: Reception & Redaction in Cuneiform & Israelite Law," *Journal for the Study of the Old Testament* 57 (1993): 3-22, which argues that uniquely Israelite laws from the villages were later formally codified in urban centers in which Mesopotamian cultures were more influential, thereby giving the laws foreign glosses that were not part of the original.

14. Wright, *God's People in God's Land: Family, Land, & Property in the Old Testament* (Grand Rapids, Mich.: Eerdmans, 1990), 175-76.

15. Wright, xviii. Similarly, "[T]he law affords an insight into the contours of God's own ideal will for his people and for all mankind. . . . To do good, on such a view, is to imitate God, to do the things he would do, if he were a human being; and what these things are can be read off in some measure from the things he has done, especially his acts of love and faithfulness towards Israel in the crucial early years of her existence. . . . [F]or the Old Testament as we have it ethics is a matter of imitating the pattern of God's own actions, in salvation and in creation, because these spring from a pattern which always exists in his own mind and by which he governs the world with

Love of God and neighbor is the chief commandment for human life. But love is not abstract and contentless. Love is the fulfillment of the "Law and Prophets" (Mark 12:28-31; Rom. 13:9; Gal. 5:14). Stephen Mott explains that such a broad norm as love must be given specific content in any particular situation:

> It is the Law of God that love brings to completeness. Love is a commitment to the good of the other, but it does not in itself specify what that good is. The implementation of love must depend upon a theory of human needs and of values and of how one loves. The morality that directs the way in which one loves in the Bible is the Law of God, articulated in the Old Testament and clarified in the New.[16]

The message of the Bible is directed not only to God's people. The same principles offer guidance to all peoples and nations. God is the creator and ruler of all creatures and nations, and his people Israel were to be the "light to the nations."

What then are the guidelines found within the pentateuchal passages dealing with treatment of the poor, and how does the fullness of the Bible help us understand them? As we will see, there is a great deal of relevant material that makes it clear that some type of systematized response to poverty is commended. But is the normative response some system of "welfare," with the government-mediated income redistribution implicit therein? If so, what fundamental objective was the system designed to achieve? Or is the normative system based in private action without government mediation, whereby families and larger voluntary gatherings manifest their faith by sacrificial giving to those in need? In sharpest relief, these are the two options before us.

I conclude that the system of assistance commended in the Law of Moses most likely did involve government-mediated income redistribution, although not of the form we have constructed in the United States. At a minimum, faced with debilitating poverty within society, the Law of Moses

---

justice and mercy. Torah — in one aspect simply the law of Moses — is in another aspect the design according to which the world was created, and which makes sense of it; and by adhering to it human beings form part of God's plan, and enjoy a kind of fellowship with him." J. Barton, "Approaches to Ethics in the Old Testament," in J. Rogerson, ed., *Beginning Old Testament Study* (Philadelphia: Westminster Press, 1982), 128-30.

16. Mott, *Biblical Ethics & Social Change* (New York: Oxford Univ. Press, 1982), 49; see also 76-78, 99-100, 192ff., esp. 199.

recommends an organized system of community response beyond the person or family involved.

Occasional adversities are the stuff of life, confronting each family at one time or another: a field receives too little rain and the harvest is ruined; a factory closes with little hope of new employment within the region; a spouse or child dies; life-threatening sickness sets in. It is only during the latter decades of the twentieth century that a few people in economically advantaged parts of the world have been able to avoid the bulk of these shocks and to soften the remaining ones. Debilitating poverty has been a particularly devastating form of adversity. During such times, the extended family (occasionally joined by broader clan/neighborhood assistance when the adversity is particularly devastating) has been the primary source of comfort and assistance throughout all of world history and in all social settings. As we shall argue below, this is how it should be; God established the extended family to serve these necessary roles.

When, however, the extended or nuclear family becomes broken or dysfunctional, or when it cannot provide the needed help because the condition is too severe, assistance from the wider community becomes necessary. This is the consistent message of the entire Bible. It is taught clearly in the Law of Moses in the provisions to be considered immediately below. It is repeated systematically in the wisdom literature and by the prophets in their instructions to the princes of Israel.[17] It is there in the well-known judgment scene of Matthew 25:31ff., and in Paul's admonitions for wealthier churches to provide economic assistance to their poorer brothers and sisters (II Cor. 8). Indeed, the fundamental message of the New Testament is that each one of us, however self-sufficient we may think we are, is so unable to avoid all the adversities of life and thereby to resolve our ultimate problems on our own that we need outside assistance. We need God's provisions for us in Christ and all that he accomplished, along with the indwelling presence of the Holy Spirit; and we also need our extended family (I Tim. 5), along with the assistance of the larger community during periods of severe distress.

Let us now consider the system of assistance for the poor commended by the Law of Moses. To grasp this instruction properly we must understand something of the social and economic life of early Israel.[18] The vast majority

17. Job 29:7-12; Ps. 72; Jer. 22:15f.; Ezek. 34; Mic. 3.

18. For more detail, see my "Biblical Teaching & Assisting the Poor," *Transforma-*

of Israelites in that era lived in small villages as members of extended families of typically three generations, in what in Hebrew is called the *bet'ab* (house of the father) and what Wright calls the "household" (because potentially slaves and residential employees also were included). The patriarchal head of a *bet'ab* would serve as one of the governing elders of his Israelite village. Indeed, a number of villages would have been composed almost solely of related *bet'avoth*, or what the Hebrew refers to as a *mishpāhâ* and Gottwald calls a "protective association of extended families."[19] The presence of major trade routes running through the land suggests market-related economic activity and hence the potential for specialization in production. For the majority of the population, however, subsistence agriculture would have been the main source of economic well-being.[20]

To the extent that there was a government recognizable to us, it was composed essentially of the elders of a village's extended families, who interpreted and enforced the Law of Moses.[21] A telling passage from the

---

tion 4 (Apr./June 1987): 1-14, and "Centralization & Decentralization in Social Arrangements: Explorations into Biblical Social Ethics," *Journal of the Association of Christian Economists [U.K.]*, no. 13 (1992): 3-47. Christopher Wright treats this same material, drawing basically similar conclusions, albeit with several different emphases. See especially chapters 4 and 5 of his *God's People in God's Land.*

19. N. Gottwald, *The Tribes of Yahweh* (Maryknoll, N.Y.: Orbis Books, 1979). See also C. H. J. De Geus, *Tribes of Israel* (Amsterdam: Van Gorcum, 1979).

20. See L. Stager, "The Archaeology of the Family in Ancient Israel," *BASOR* (Bulletin of the American Schools for Oriental Research) 260 (1985): 1-35, and D. Hopkins, "Life on the Land: The Subsistence Struggles of Early Israel," *Biblical Archaeologist* 50 (1987): 178-91, for careful accounts of what life for the normal Israelite was like. For example, the eastern regions of the land in which the Israelites were concentrated (during at least the earlier years of settlement) receives limited and seasonally concentrated rainfall, so that the construction of cisterns to catch and hold the available water was an important community-based task.

21. A number of studies have established that these elders, typically gathering at the main gate of the village, provided political oversight to the community and handled disputes between villagers. See R. Wilson, "Enforcing the Covenant: The Mechanisms of Judicial Authority in Early Israel," in H. Huffman et al., eds., *The Quest for the Kingdom of God* (Winona Lake, Ind.: Eisenbrauns, 1983), 59-75; H. Boecker, *Law & the Administration of Justice in the Old Testament & Ancient East* (Minneapolis: Augsburg Publishing House, 1980); K. Whitelam, *The Just King: Monarchic Judicial Authority in Ancient Israel*, Journal for the Study of the Old Testament, Supp. Series 12 (Sheffield: JSOT Press, 1979); and J. Salmon, "Judicial Authority in Early Israel: An Historical Investigation of Old Testament Institutions" (Ph.D. diss., Princeton Theological Seminary, 1968).

Book of Job offers rich insight into the normative nature of the Israelite governing authority in the premonarchic era.

> When I went to the gate of the city and took my seat in the public square, the young men saw me and stepped aside and the old men rose to their feet; the chief men refrained from speaking and covered their mouths with their hands; the voices of the nobles were hushed, and their tongues stuck to the roof of their mouths. Whoever heard me spoke well of me, and those who saw me commended me, because I rescued the poor who cried for help, and the fatherless who had none to assist him. The man who was dying blessed me; I made the widow's heart sing. I put on righteousness as my clothing; justice was my robe and my turban. I was eyes to the blind and feet to the lame. I was a father to the needy; I took up the case of the stranger. I broke the fangs of the wicked and snatched the victims from their teeth. (29:7-17)

Job joins the other elders before the people in the "public square." In such capacity righteousness and justice are the legal norms, and these clearly required a special concern for weaker members of the community. These "judges" hardly are passive officials. Job saw himself as eyes to the blind, feet to the lame, and father to the needy. The picture is one in which the local governing authority not only issued decisions to contested claims but actively intervened to make sure that righteousness and justice characterized the community. The normative standard for all this, the standard that decreed righteousness and justice and that specified these norms in a vast number of cases, was the Law of Moses.

In its earliest history, Israel apparently had no permanent central government. Israel was to have neither king[22] nor standing army,[23] making

22. I see no other way to interpret 1 Samuel 8. An earthly kingship was not God's preference for Israel. In a review article of G. Gerbrandt's *Kingship According to the Deuteronomistic History,* David Howard argues that the Bible is pro-kingship. The king, however, must not be one "like the other nations have" (1 Sam. 8:5), but a king who would be like Moses and Joshua and lead himself and his people into submission to the standards of the Pentateuch. See D. Howard, "The Case for Kingship in Deuteronomy & the Former Prophets," *Westminster Theological Journal* 52 (1990): 101-15. For a similar argument see P. Satterthwaite, "'No King in Israel': Narrative Criticism & Judges 17–21," *Tyndale Bulletin* 44, no. 1 (1993): 75-88.

23. Joshua and Judges record a number of the military encounters caused by the movement of the Israelite tribes into an already occupied land. In the accounts the

her unique among the nations. Equally unique at the time was the instruction that those responsible for Israel's cult (the sons of Levi) were to be granted no allotment of land and were to depend upon voluntary offerings (Num. 18:8ff.), and this was accompanied by numerous admonitions to other Israelites not to forsake them (Deut. 12:19). In this way, twin dangers from the concentration of economic and political power were to be avoided, namely, (1) the use of power to selfish ends and the detriment of common Israelites, especially the poor (II Sam. 11; I Kings 21; Amos 2:6-7; 5:12); and (2) the merging of centralized political-economic power with the temple, thereby wrongly appropriating the true King's name for unrighteous ends.[24]

But despite the warning of God through Samuel (I Sam. 8), Israel succumbed to temptation to be like the surrounding nations and embraced the monarchy. Yet Israel's king was to be different from the kings of surrounding nations.[25] Exactly like the village elders, Israel's king was to be a steward of the covenant conditions of the Law of Moses (Deut. 17:14ff.) and was to establish justice and righteousness (I Kings 10:9), with special concern for the weaker members of society (Ps. 72:1-4, 12-14). He was so to protect property rights that each family could sit under its own vine and fig tree (Mic. 4:4).

The nation that received the Law of Moses was initially a scattered network of Israelite villages.[26] This socioeconomic setting serves as some-

---

leadership arose from common men (and women — Judges 4 and 5) who were not part of a continuing military hierarchy, and troops were raised popularly as needed.

24. "As Solomon enthralled Yahweh as a patron of the dynasty, so David initiated the process by which Yahweh ceased to be god of Israel and became god of the king. The liberator god had become the symbol and the patron of an oppressive oligarchy." J. McKenzie, "The Sack of Israel," in Huffman et al., 33.

25. Considering the troubles that afflicted Israel's kings, we must wonder how powerful in fact they were. For example, they could not prevent Israel's sacred documents (many of which were prepared during their watch) from saying much that was negative about the idea and practice of the kingship. In "Israel's Judicial System in the Pre-exilic Period," *Jewish Quarterly Review* 74 (1983): 229-48, R. Wilson argues that King David's power may not have extended much beyond Jerusalem.

26. Norman Gottwald, the leading scholar to use a sociological model to explain the emergence of early Israel, describes that society as "an egalitarian, extended-family, segmentary tribal society with an agricultural-pastoral economic base . . . characterized by profound resistance and opposition to the forms of political domination and social stratification that had become normative in the chief cultural and political centers of the ancient Near East." Gottwald, 389. See also DeGeus.

thing of a paradigm within a paradigm: it is a simplified social reality that allows us to see God's ethical intentions clearly. To these villages, then, God provided an extensive set of instructions about how to care for the poor in their midst.

Poorer brothers falling into poverty should be granted zero-interest loans, with cancellation of any remaining balance after six years (Exod. 22:25; Lev. 25:35ff.; Deut. 15:1ff.). Israelites committed to slavery for debt repayment were to be released after six years, assuming the debt had not been repaid earlier (Exod. 21:2ff.; Lev. 25:47ff., 39ff.; Deut. 15:12ff.). An Israelite forced to sell his land for debt repayment should have the land returned in the jubilee year (Lev. 25:8ff.) — unless, we presume, the fair market value had been raised earlier and the land repurchased.

Each of these provisions is associated in some way with indebtedness and loan repayment, and it seems likely that they were intended primarily for otherwise able-bodied extended families that would have the capacity to accumulate a surplus sufficient to meet loan obligations. Implicit within each provision, therefore, is the reality that more work than normal would be expected, in order to repay the loan or purchase back one's freedom or one's land. Even so, each provision presumes some act of community compassion: to make the zero-interest loan in the first place, to remit an outstanding loan balance or release a person from enslavement after six years, to return a family's land in the forty-ninth year.

The remaining provisions are not attached to repayment and thereby assume a stronger element of community compassion or charity. It seems likely, therefore, that they were intended primarily for weaker families or individuals. Gleanings and corners of fields were to be left ungathered and unharvested for the poor, especially the widows, orphans, and sojourners (Lev. 19:9f.; 23:22; Deut. 24:19ff.).[27] Each field was to be left fallow or unworked every seventh year, with the natural growth available to the poor (Exod. 23:10f.; Lev. 25:1ff.). The tithe in every third year should go to widows, orphans, and sojourners, in addition to the Levites (Deut. 14:28f.;

27. Deuteronomy 24:19ff. explicitly mentions grain, olives, and the vineyard. The grain harvest was conducted from April through June, with barley preceding wheat. The grape harvest ran through the summer months to October, and the olive harvest took place in late October and November. In other words, there was a continuous annual flow of gleanings from midspring through late fall for the poor who were able to go to the fields and gather them.

26:12). Work obviously was involved in gathering the gleanings and harvesting the fallow-year growth, but such effort was not as strenuous as in the provisions connected with loan repayment. It seems likely, therefore, that the third-year tithe was intended for the least able among the poor, who were not expected to work in exchange for assistance.[28]

When faced with requests for or situations demanding assistance, what level or standard of assistance should be used? The instruction attending several of the specific provisions commends "sufficiency for need" (Lev. 25:35; Deut. 14:29; 15:8). In determining what that requires in any specific situation, the theme of the entire Bible urges a generous rather than a niggardly interpretation,[29] and hence "liberal" sufficiency for need. Assistance to the poor was intended to maintain each family unit as an economically viable and contributing member of the community, such that the family would be assured that *if it worked the normal amount* and *otherwise remained a faithful member of the community,* the community would not allow economic difficulties to so debilitate the family that it could not continue to be viable and contributing.[30]

In addition to these specific provisions, more well-to-do members of society were admonished generally to care for the poor and needy by, for example, sharing feast days with widows, orphans, and sojourners (Deut. 16:11-14). This is taught explicitly in passages like Exodus 22:21ff. and Deuteronomy 15:11; 24:10ff. It is affirmed throughout the Old Testament in passages referring to the "poor and needy" (e.g., Job 29:11ff.; Ps. 72; Jer. 22:16). It is implicit in God's whole treatment of Israel, rescuing his people

28. The particular Hebrew words describing "poor" persons in early Israel (primarily *'ebyon* and *'ani,* but also *dal*) imply that the primary reason for different economic outcomes was not lack of ambition but adverse circumstances. There are other Hebrew words speaking of those who were poor due to laziness, with most English translations using "sluggards" or "idlers" in these cases. These terms *(atsel* and *remiyyah)* are found primarily in the Proverbs and not in the narratives dealing with the first several centuries of the settled Israelite nation.

29. Exod. 16:18; 22:21; Lev. 25:38; Deut. 24:18, 22; Ezek. 47:14; 2 Cor. 8:13.

30. Gottwald argues that one of the salient functions of the *mishpāhâ* was "to protect the socio-economic integrity of *beth'avoth* threatened with diminution or extinction." The *mishpāhâ* "did not intersect with and impinge upon the family . . . but it heightened and brought to prominence the centrality of the family. . . . Instead of qualifying the power and importance of the family, as a clan would necessarily do, the protective association of families maximized and guarded the integrity and viability of the member families." Gottwald, 315-16.

from slavery in Egypt and providing them a land with wells they did not dig and vineyards they did not plant, even when because of their disobedience they were undeserving (Deut. 6:10ff.; 8:7–9:6). Not surprisingly it echoes throughout the New Testament as well (Luke 16:19ff.; Gal. 6:10; I John 3:17).

I have noted several structural elements that characterized this system of assistance: an able-bodied/dependent distinction related to loan receipt, implicit work obligations, and a liberal level of assistance. But an important question remains: Was this a welfare system involving government-mediated income redistribution or a system of privately orchestrated voluntary provision? A number of commentators argue that these provisions call for voluntary compliance only and that the moral and legal power of the village elders would not have been used to enforce them.[31] The use of "motive clauses" attached to a number of these laws, whereby an appeal is made to God if the instruction is not honored, suggests to some the legal unenforceability of such laws.[32]

There can be no doubt that voluntary compliance was the ideal. Given their previous experience in Egypt, as well as the excessive and corrupt presence of the governing authority in virtually all surrounding nations of the time, the Israelite preference (and God's desire) was for a polity with the least oppressive role possible for a centralized governing authority.[33] The question, however, is whether a breach of the ideal of voluntary compliance would have been met by some attempt at moral or legal coercion by the village elders. In our reconstruction of how these provisions were lived out in practice, intervention by the elders appears very likely. If so, then we must consider ancient Israel's system to be a form of government-mediated welfare.

31. See S. Loewenstamm, "Law," in B. Mazar, ed., *The World History of the Jewish People,* vol. III: *Judges* (New Brunswick, N.J.: Rutgers Univ. Press, 1971), 246f.; and A. Phillips, "Prophecy & Law," in R. Coggins et al., eds., *Israel's Prophetic Tradition: Essays in Honour of Peter R. Ackroyd* (New York: Cambridge Univ. Press, 1982), 222.

32. "In general, the motive clauses . . . are attached to unenforceable rather than policeable laws." R. Uitti, "Israel's Underprivileged & Gemser's Motive Clause," *Society of Biblical Literature,* 1975 Seminar Papers, vol. 1 (Chicago: Palmer House, 1975), 7-13. Uitti also notes that the use of motive clauses regarding the underprivileged is but a small fraction of the total use of these clauses; he does not conclude that the presence of the motive clause therefore means such provisions are legally unenforceable; it only suggests that they may be difficult to enforce.

Consider, for example, the case of a creditor who demands interest or payment in the seventh year, or of a gleaner who is denied access to a farmer's field. The offended party could complain to the "elders at the gate," who then would be compelled to render a ruling. Most likely the initial response would be a call for the offending party to respect the law — a judicial intrusion requiring no further action. Were this response to fail, however, the elders most likely would become an administrative body and assure the poorer family of adequate assistance — in which case some type of mandatory income redistribution seems likely. Favoring this interpretation is the fact that a number of texts make reference to the "rights" or "cause" of the poor, words with unmistakable legal significance.[34] We must presume, then, that those responsible for interpreting and overseeing the enforcement of these laws would have held the community as accountable for them as for the other laws.[35]

It is this principle of government acting on behalf of the poor when the resources of extended family and clan prove insufficient that we see in the dramatic narrative of Jacob and his extended family finding relief from famine in Egypt (Gen. 37–50).[36] This narrative preceded the announcement of the Law through Moses; nevertheless it must, of course, be understood within the framework of the biblical teaching about God's designs for humankind.[37]

33. See various works by George Mendenhall, who argues there was very little (if any) state in premonarchic Israel, e.g., *The Tenth Generation* (Baltimore: Johns Hopkins Univ. Press, 1973), e.g., 28; and "The Suzerainty Treaty Structure: Thirty Years Later," in E. Firmage et al., eds., *Religion & Law: Biblical-Judaic & Islamic Perspectives* (Winona Lake, Ind.: Eisenbrauns, 1990), 85-100.

34. Exod. 23:6; Deut. 24:17; 27:19; Job 36:6; Ps. 140:12; Prov. 29:7; 31:9; Isa. 10:2; Jer. 5:28.

35. D. Patrick argues that the provisions dealing with the underprivileged grew out of actual legal proceedings and court rulings, with the result that here "we have real law governing precisely defined legal relationships." Patrick, "The Rights of the Underprivileged," *Society of Biblical Literature*, 2. D. Daube understands this social legislation similarly; see Daube, *Studies in Biblical Law* (New York: Cambridge Univ. Press, 1947), 45.

36. For a more detailed treatment of this appeal, see my "Centralization & Decentralization." The use of centralized government measures in the face of dire emergencies is not limited in the Bible to the Joseph narrative. The book of Esther records a very similar concentration of political power by one chosen of God to preserve Israel from extinction by sword.

37. "[Torah] says in the form of story what the essential character and moral

But the story seems out of character at first glance. Given the pentateuchal preference for a decentralized government structure built on a healthy network of extended families and clan responsibility, what are we to make of the highly centralized assistance mediated through the power of the Egyptian government that is recorded in Genesis 47:13-26 with what clearly seems to be the narrator's approval?[38] The key point, I believe, is that under imminent threat of widespread starvation, the normal and normative reliance upon decentralized means would become too risky and thus inadequate. Grain must be stored and then allocated in ways to prevent engrossing and to make sure that all citizens and not just a few receive subsistence. God intends that the power of the government be used to achieve just ends, which under these circumstances required government intervention to save lives — of Jacob and his family as well as their Egyptian hosts.[39]

---

obligations for any current audience might be by depicting the character and moral obligations of the normative past." G. Coats, *Genesis, with an Introduction to Narrative Literature* (Grand Rapids, Mich.: Eerdmans, 1983), 25.

38. These crucial verses have been questioned by many commentators, critical and conservative alike, as not part of the larger narrative or not intending the extreme concentration the text seems to portray, but many of these same commentators praise Joseph as a wise administrator under very difficult conditions. I refer again to my "Centralization & Decentralization" for further discussion.

39. God does not always limit himself to such natural means: recall the manna and water during the exodus from Egypt. That he allowed the use of an oppressive government structure (consider the slavery of Israel that followed) to provide physical salvation for his people in this extreme circumstance is telling. It is difficult to know whether the precise measures listed were necessary to this end, but we cannot discount this. Could it be that socioeconomic conditions would have been worse in the midst of the extreme scarcity were it not for the measures Joseph undertook? In any event, there may well have been a second crucial purpose for this strategic use of government power. As the narrator is very concerned to point out (Gen. 46:31ff.), Joseph carefully orchestrates a request before Pharaoh for Jacob and his entourage to settle in Goshen. Was this simply to be closer to Palestine (to make a quick getaway?), to encounter less economic persecution from the Egyptians, or to enjoy the fertile land of that region? Perhaps each of these, but also more: I conclude that God through Joseph (and the power of the government) was anxious to establish a "cultural space" for Israel wherein the Israelites could live out their commitment to him in as much freedom and faithfulness as possible. If Abraham's descendants were to be a blessing to all nations, they needed to be faithful to their God and his expectations for them, and cultural distance (reflecting religious values rather than ethnic distinctives) was as important as their

If we consider all of this material together, I believe we must conclude that the presence of debilitating poverty in a land is of such seriousness in God's eyes as to require a *systematized* response. As we have seen, the recommended system utilized (1) an able-bodied/dependent distinction in the *type* of assistance, not (as in the case of many American programs) as the *basis* for assistance; (2) a work requirement marked by elements of compassion; and (3) a level of assistance we may term "liberal sufficiency for need."

Was this a system of government welfare something like the one we have built? We have seen that the ideal polity for early Israel was a limited governing authority, reflecting God's preference for deconcentrated political power (accompanied by deconcentrations in property ownership and in economic life generally).[40] But we may not stop there. One of the normative roles for the deconcentrated governing authority of local village elders was to assure that the poor were assisted properly. Ideally and typically this would have been done through private initiative (Deut. 16; Job 31). The initial act of the elders when a case was appealed to them would be to encourage the private parties involved to honor the instructions of

physical salvation to serve this grand purpose. The critical passage of Genesis 45:5-8, where Joseph explains to his brothers why it was necessary for him to go to Egypt as he did, mentions two outcomes: "to preserve for you a remnant on earth and to save your lives by a great deliverance." Most commentators have seen these as two sides of the same coin. But might this statement represent the two purposes identified here for Israel by Joseph's administration: to save their lives and to assure them a cultural space?

40. See my "Centralization & Decentralization." In a sea of voluntarily structured institutions there were clear islands of compulsion to help bring about compliance to God's desires as revealed in the Law of Moses: Joshua *ordered* the men of the eastern tribes to march before the others in taking possession of the promised land (Josh. 1); David *ordered* the soldiers who had captured the plunder to share it with those who stayed behind (1 Sam. 30); Ezra, certainly a careful student of the Law, was allowed to use the state treasury (Ezra 7:20) to supplement the freewill offering (Ezra 7:16) in rebuilding the Temple, and along with the elders *ordered* all exiles to assemble subject to loss of property (Ezra 10:8); Nehemiah *ordered* those who had offended their Jewish brothers to repay them (Neh. 5:11), and he later recorded a voluntary renewing of the covenant and then *ordered* certain measures to prevent sinful practice (Neh. 13:19). In other words, amidst God's general preference for limited and decentralized government authority there was indeed a normative compulsion exercised by those who held government power, so that the community would conduct itself in ways consistent with the Law of Moses.

the law. Ultimately, however, if efforts at private resolution were insufficient, the elders would have compelled a response — albeit in as deconcentrated a way as possible. The governing authorities were not the only or even the first authorities charged to come to the aid of the needy. However, it was their task to ensure that those who did bear the responsibility fulfilled it. If we accept that all nations are to order themselves in accordance with the guidelines laid down for God's people in the Law of Moses, then we should strive for a system that brings together in a similar way public power and private responsibility.[41]

The Objectives of Israel's Welfare System

The best guide for understanding the basic objectives of Israel's welfare system, in my view, is Christopher Wright's *God's People in God's Land,*[42] a work in Old Testament property ethics. Starting with a quest to discern the normative role of property, Wright was led to the Bible's more foundational concern for the social and economic well-being of the family. A theological assessment of land and property is "inseparable from Israel's consciousness of their unique covenant relationship with Yahweh," and this

41. The Bible promises a condition of this-worldly personal and social harmony (referred to as *shalom*) for the nation that orders itself consistently with the ethical urgings embedded in the Law of Moses. To see this, examine the structure of the Mosaic covenant generally (Exod. 23:25ff.; Lev. 26:3-13; Deut. 28:1-14) as well as the promised state of harmony in the prophets (Isa. 11:6-9; Ezek. 34:23-31; Hos. 2:14-23). Mendenhall characterizes it as "a condition of peace in which every man could sit under his own fig tree and under his own grapevine (1 Kings 4:24; Mic. 4:4), doing 'what was right in his own eyes' (Judg. 17:6; 21:25; Deut. 12:8; Prov. 12:15)," in his *Tenth Generation,* pp. 26-27. See also D. Gillett, "Shalom: Content for a Slogan," *Themelios* 1 (Summer 1976): 80-84; D. Wiseman, "Law & Order in Old Testament Times," *Vox Evangelica* 7 (1973): 5-21, especially 14f. L. Kohler writes, "Community life depends entirely upon peace, that is a state of affairs in which the members of the community have their claims and needs fairly adjusted to one another. The one force which makes for this peace and preserves it is law." Kohler, *Hebrew Man* (London: SCM Press, 1956), 150-51.

42. An earlier version of this book was presented as his doctoral dissertation at Cambridge University in 1977. Parenthetical references refer to Wright's book until further notice. See also M. Schluter and R. Clements, *Reactivating the Extended Family: From Biblical Norms to Public Policy in Britain* (Cambridge: Jubilee Centre Publications, 1986).

ultimately is "earthed" in the family (p. 23). The primary family unit in mind, as we have seen, is the extended family, the *bet'ab* or "household." Based largely on Wright's work, I propose the following: as the social and economic well-being of the family was the objective of the Bible's instructions regarding property and land in general, so also was this the objective of Israel's welfare system — and so should this be the objective of the welfare system in any nation.[43]

Why is the family fundamentally important within society? There are three crucial functions that only the family can serve adequately. The family is (1) the surest setting in which to pass on the faith in Yahweh and to form a personal character that takes on God-pleasing values; (2) the surest setting wherein the individual finds any lasting sense of personal significance and meaning; and (3) the surest setting from which effective service is offered to the larger community.

God's chief concern is that we come both to acknowledge and to worship him and to live a life of obedience to him. We should expect therefore to find in the Bible social arrangements geared to this end. Wright points to "the internal role of the family as a vehicle of continuity for the faith, history, and traditions of Israel," emphasizing both the didactic function of teaching the Law (Deut. 6:7, 11:19) and the catechetical function of rehearsing cultic institutions and memorials of historical events (Exod. 12:26f.; 13:14f.; Deut. 6:20ff.; Josh. 4:6f.; 21ff.). "As a didactic force throughout succeeding generations, the family stood at the center of the twin relationships between Israel and Yahweh and between Israel and their land (as stressed in Dt. 32:47)" (pp. 81ff.).

Moral philosophy has again in recent years been occupied with the conditions most conducive for the formation of virtuous character.[44] The Bible affirms that this is done best within socially and economically secure families seeking to affirm the traditional virtues, a claim to which a growing body of contemporary evidence lends support.[45] Reflecting on his several

43. I believe my application of his work conforms with the spirit of his overall argument. That his argument does not proceed in the way I use it may reflect the fact that he came to emphasize the family somewhat indirectly, having begun his work with an investigation of property and land ethics; that origin, I think, only underscores the importance of the weight he places on the family.

44. For a leading argument, see Alasdair MacIntyre, *After Virtue* (Notre Dame: Univ. of Notre Dame Press, 1981).

45. See, e.g., J. Q. Wilson, *The Moral Sense* (New York: Free Press, 1993).

decades of work in biblical studies, George Mendenhall recently observed that the "transcendent ground of ethic in the Sinai covenant is perhaps one of the most important aspects of the biblical heritage to Western cultures." We have therein an ethic that "excludes behavior that works to the detriment of others," and that (tied by covenant) constrains otherwise harmful behavior "no matter where and in what context that individual acts."[46] A healthy society requires individuals who possess a morally upright character. This is best achieved within socially and economically secure families.

Second, the healthy family provides the surest setting, short of our relationship with God, for individuals to experience a sense of personal significance and meaning in life. This is as true for the child who, we may hope, is wrapped in love as he or she is nurtured through the maturation process, as it is for the mature adult. Wright makes this point particularly for the so-called dependent persons of the biblical era — wives, children, slaves, and resident aliens. Each of these raises difficult issues for us today because they "belonged" in some way to the head of the household. However, in each case, Wright argues, the ownership relationship was colored more by the responsibilities of the head of the household than by his rights.

> The relationship between Israel and Yahweh was vested, initially at any rate, in the socio-economic fabric of household-plus-land units. On them lay a large measure of responsibility for the fulfillment of the obligations of the relationship and for the preservation of its historical traditions. Furthermore, it was by belonging within a household, with its portion of land as the proof of its share in the people of Yahweh, that the individual Israelite shared in the privileges and protection of this relationship. (p. 88)

We may extend this claim beyond the provisions holding for early Israel, as Wright has presented them, because of our conviction that those provisions reveal the proper social basis for all of us to find the acceptance and significance and meaning that God wants us to experience in our earthly lives.

Finally, it is within the family that individuals best are groomed for offering service to the larger community. In Wright's work this is expressed well by the role of the household head as one of the governing elders of the local village:

46. Mendenhall, 97-98.

> Now it is probable, though the evidence is not very explicit, that the main qualification for eldership and the exercise of its judicial rights was the possession of landed property and family. . . . Anthony Phillips is correct in emphasizing the disastrous consequences arising for an Israelite from the dispossession of home and property. Apart from the obvious economic disabilities, it meant loss of standing and participation in a sphere of social life where the obligations of the relationship with God impinged most closely on the practical realities of society — the local administration of justice. (pp. 80-81)

The elders' participation in local administration made possible the system of a decentralized governing authority built on widely dispersed land ownership along family lines that characterized early Israel. A worthy elder originated in a family that nurtured sound character in a man and taught responsible stewardship, and these, in turn, were grounded in the Law of Moses and in the rehearsal of God's faithfulness to Israel and the family through good and lean years. Though modern societies increasingly depend on external schooling to groom leaders, it remains the case that character formation in the family is critical and that extrafamily training is most successful when the family actively supports it.

Because the family has such important functions to perform within society, it is crucial that it be protected both socially and economically. That appears to be the intent of a number of significant biblical provisions. Wright points to the normative economic supports for the family. Foundational is the jubilee claim that God is the true owner of all property (Lev. 25:23). Wright observes:

> Yahweh's ownership of the land is affirmed to ensure the security of *individual families* by preventing permanent alienation of *their land*. It is not simply a grand statement of national belief about the national territory, but the theological sanction of an *internal* economic system of land tenure. (p. 63, emphasis his)

Although he grants it is an argument from silence, Wright finds it "an impressive fact that the whole Old Testament provides not a single case of an Israelite voluntarily selling land outside his family group," and he observes that the "silence of the text is matched by the absence as yet of any inscriptional evidence from Palestine of Israelite sale and purchase of land, though there is abundant evidence of such transactions from Canaanite and surrounding societies" (p. 56). Where there was forced sale of one's land to pay debts, the jubilee institution of Leviticus 25 was provided to restore the land to the family of original ownership (pp. 123ff.).

Emphasizing the importance of each family continuing to own its own land as a source of economic well-being, the law contains numerous provisions protecting private property rights. Boundary stones marking out property lines, for instance, were not to be moved (pp. 128ff.). The eighth and tenth commandments prohibit theft and coveting — property sins, in both cases (pp. 131ff.). Theft, Wright observes,

> was not solely an attack on property, but indirectly on the fellow Israelite's person and on the stability and viability of his family. The prohibition of theft, therefore, did not imply the "sanctity of property" *per se,* but rather *the sanctity of the relationship between the Israelite household and Yahweh.* It was this relationship which could be impaired or destroyed in its material aspects by theft. In such a threat at the domestic level lay, as we have seen, a potential, intrinsic threat to the national relationship with God. (p. 136, emphases his)

Forbidding coveteousness gives the Decalogue a radical thrust, making it more than mere legislation, and seeks to prevent at its source the desire that ultimately leads to measures (legal or illegal) that would deprive a family of its economic base.[47]

The Mosaic Law provided for the family to be protected socially as well as economically. The fifth commandment, calling for honor of parents, contains within it a dual warning: failure to maintain the social foundation of the family will ultimately give rise to loss of its economic foundation. Wright notes two practices that could destroy the social stability of the family: rebellious behavior by children and adultery. The laws prescribing death "for any form of open disrespect for parental authority" had a positive intent:

> They are not relics of a harsh *patria potestas* or an arbitrary, authoritarian patriarchy. They are in fact safeguards of the *national* well-being. For

47. "[T]he biblical law of property was concerned less with the efficient use and transfer of a commercial asset than with protecting the rights of the family to the source of their economic survival, not only against outsiders but even against individual members of the family itself." R. Westbrook, *Property & the Family in Biblical Law* (Sheffield, UK: JSOT Press, 1991), 11.

> violation of parental authority — rejection of the domestic jurisdiction of the head of the household — was a crime against the stability of the nation inasmuch as it was an attack upon that on which the nation's relationship with God was grounded — the household. (p. 78)

Then, in the context of his argument that the Pentateuch affirms a generally more influential and less demeaned role for women than often thought, Wright considers the "loose woman" of Proverbs 2:

> The thread of thought . . . which runs through Prov. 2:12-22 and the related passages, is this: one who, by attention to wisdom, is saved from the "loose" woman and so maintains the integrity and strength of his own household stays within the community of the "righteous" (v. 20) and continues to enjoy its prime privilege — possession of a share in the land (v. 21). But one who gets entangled with such a woman, who has thrown off the obligations of her family and marital relationship and has thus stepped "outside" both her household and thereby also the spiritual relationship of the nation of Yahweh, is likely to end up ruining his own family and substance. In so doing he will cut himself off from the privilege of sharing in the land with the rest of God's people. Worst of all, he risks, through neglect of his family, the complete extinction of extirpation. In short, he "has no sense"; he "destroys himself" (6:32). (p. 96)

Protecting the family socially and economically, both from within and from without, was thus the intent of much of the legal and extralegal material of the Pentateuch. God's desires as revealed in these provisions also help us to understand better the burning concerns of the prophets.

> The abuses in the [socioeconomic] sphere were not merely a "symptom" of Israel's degeneracy. They constituted in themselves, in fact, a major "virus" which threatened the stability of society and *thereby also* the relationship with Yahweh. The prophets denounced them so vehemently because they saw in them an *intrinsic* threat to that relationship through the effect they were having on the units of landowning households. This familial aspect becomes explicit in such texts as Mic. 2:1-3, 8-9; 7:5-6; and Is. 5:8-10. If . . . the experience of the relationship with God was vested in the household units of Israel — just as possession of the land was vested in inalienable family inheritances — then the socio-economic forces and changes which were destroying these family land units would inevitably and "internally" destroy the nation's relationship with God as well. (p. 109)

Wright goes on to show that this same concern is carried into the New Testament, expositing particularly Ephesians 2:11–3:6 (pp. 111ff.). His general argument is that in Christ all peoples are allowed to enjoy the privileges and responsibilities of God's people. This granted, there is to be no less a concern in Christ's body, the church, for the social and economic stability of families (a "deeply practical mutual responsibility") than was true in the Old Testament: "The explicit purpose of the Exodus was the enjoyment of the rich blessing of God in his 'good land': the goal of redemption through Christ is 'for a sincere love of the brethren' (I Pet. 1:22), with all its practical implications" (p. 113).

In establishing the importance of privately assigned property, the Law of Moses intended to give to families a solid foundation. As Wright argues and I affirm strongly, the Bible prefers private property not as an end in itself, nor necessarily because of its concern for individual rights (although the Bible is indeed very concerned for the individual's rights *as well as* responsibilities), but because privately assigned property rights assure economic protection of the family better than alternative regimes of property rights assignments. The greater affirmation is the importance of the family.

> When we speak of "property rights" in the Old Testament, it is clear from the foregoing that we are not concerned with an abstract, impersonal principle, nor with an *inherent* sacrosanctity of property *per se*. A person's right to the security and integrity of his ancestral land and other property was based (1) on his relationship to Yahweh, as a member of the community of his people, of which relationship and status his land was the symbol and guarantee and (2) on the fact that his land and property were essential to the economic viability of his household, with all its social and religious significance for the individuals within it and for the national well-being before God. On the basis of the Old Testament, therefore, we cannot speak of property itself being "sacred" or of the "sanctity of property." It is the *relationships*, Godward and humanward, of which property is a function and indicator, which are alone sacred. (pp. 140-41, emphases his)

The preference for decentralized property ownership implicitly affirms not just the economic well-being of the family but also the political and economic *responsibility* of the family. It affirms, in the political sphere, the "network" of local families (the *mishpāhâ*), operating at times informally and voluntaristically, and at times formally and officially as the "elders at the gate." As noted, there was a clear preference in the Pentateuch for resolving most of Israel's problems at the village level. As Mendenhall and Gottwald, among others, have made clear, this was a radical break with the practice of the surrounding nations and therefore reveals the uniquely Yahwistic nature of Israel's formation. These preferences for early Israel offer us insight today in the way God ideally would work with any nation.

Based on the guidelines we have examined, I believe that the preferred solution to the problems of poverty in contemporary America would combine some interplay between regional government coalitions and voluntary associations such as churches and para-church organizations. Larger metropolitan regions today are organized somewhat like the network of early Israelite villages. Passing in and out of the gate in order to go to and from work in the fields of Palestine has its counterpart today in commuting throughout a metropolitan region. Indeed, metropolitan regions are coherent economic entities, and therefore should in some way be coherent political entities so that their problems (such as poverty) can be resolved at the local level rather than being foisted up to the state and national levels. The type of "federalism" held forth in the Bible has a central governing authority serving primarily as a source of informal authority to hold the various parties (private and public) at the local level responsible for accomplishing the necessary political and economic tasks of society. As the central source of authority the central government must act when those otherwise responsible fail in their responsibility. However, even in these cases the ideal form of centralized government action would be to devolve the actual resolution to as low a level as feasible, compelling the responsible institutions to fulfill their tasks, instead of displacing their functions.

The important point is the Bible's unmistakable support for the social and economic health and responsibility of the family, whatever government structures and programs may be in place. The Bible clearly presumes that the extended family is the normative basic social institution. As we have seen, the overriding objective of Israel's system of assistance was to establish and maintain economically secure families — strong nuclear families, at least, and strong extended families by preference. And so it is that in I Timothy 5 Paul instructs grandchildren to be financially responsible for their grandmothers so that the church need not assume this responsibility.

Conclusion

This chapter began not with the issue of strengthening "traditional" families[48] but rather with citizen dissatisfaction over the administration of welfare in the United States. The key concern is growing dependency and the insufficiency of the work effort of people relying on public assistance. But because a focus on single pieces of the welfare system risks generating counterproductive reforms, we turned to the larger question of what role welfare properly should play within society. We thus "backed into" our concern for the family.

Strengthening families has not been an objective of the American welfare system as it has developed; indeed, the various incentives of the system tend to erode rather than bolster families. The biblical emphasis is just the opposite. An examination of the Bible's commended system for addressing debilitating poverty makes unmistakable the social and economic importance of strong families and the necessity that "welfare" measures serve to utilize and strengthen families.

If we look around at our society today, we cannot help but notice a tight connection between debilitating poverty and weak families. In the midst of waning economic opportunity in central cities[49] and, more gener-

48. By "traditional" family I mean intact nuclear families located socially and economically within supportive extended families. American society has struggled during the second half of the twentieth century to discern how important this traditional family really is. See, e.g., S. Ruggles, "The Transformation of American Family Structure," *American Historical Review* 49 (1994): 103-28; D. Popenoe, "American Family Decline, 1960-1990: A Review & Appraisal," and responses in *Journal of Marriage & the Family* 55 (1993): 527-55; B. Whitehead, "Dan Quayle Was Right," *Atlantic Monthly*, Apr. 1993, 47ff.; D. Hamburg, "The American Family Transformed," *Society* 30 (Jan.-Feb. 1993): 60-69; J. Q. Wilson, "The Family-Values Debate," *Commentary*, Apr. 1993, 24-31. The "traditional" family norm that I have in mind is not male-dominated in any harmful way. After instructing wives to submit to their husbands, St. Paul instructs husbands to love their wives as Christ loved the church and gave himself up for her (Eph. 5:22ff.). Christ sacrificed beyond human comprehension (Isa. 52:13–53:12) for the church; he washed the feet of his disciples as an example of how faithful Christians are to treat one another — sacrificial service (John 13:1ff.). The "wife of noble character" of Proverbs 31 hardly appears to be dominated or harmfully submissive, but rather a strong partner to her husband. My desire is to establish the norm of biblical instruction and not the sin-tainted and imperfect image of that norm.

49. The long-running debate over a "spatial mismatch" between the location of

ally, for lower-skilled workers,[50] and amidst attacks on the "traditional" family from popular culture and cultural elites alike,[51] it is not surprising

---

jobs and the location of workers continues. John Kain, the Harvard economist credited with starting the debate in a May 1968 *Quarterly Journal of Economics* article, argued that inner-city residents face great difficulties obtaining and holding jobs in outlying suburban areas. His critics maintained that the reality is better understood as "race and not space." See E. Ellwood, "The Spatial Mismatch Hypothesis: Are There Teenage Jobs Missing in the Ghetto," in R. Freeman and H. Holzer, eds., *The Black Youth Employment Crisis* (Chicago: Univ. of Chicago Press, 1986); C. Jencks, *Rethinking Social Policy: Race, Poverty, & the Underclass* (Cambridge: Harvard Univ. Press, 1992), esp. ch. 4; and L. Mead, *The New Politics of Poverty* (New York: Basic Books, 1992). I find convincing Kain's recent reaffirmation of his position in a massive review of the literature: "The Spatial Mismatch Hypothesis: Three Decades Later," *Housing Policy Debate* 3, no. 2 (1992): 371-460. For even more recent confirming evidence, see H. Holzer et al., "Work, Search, & Travel among White & Black Youth," *Journal of Urban Economics* 35 (1994): 320-45; H. Holzer, "Black Employment Problems: New Evidence, Old Questions," *Journal of Policy Analysis & Management* 13 (1994): 699-722; and K. Ihlanfeldt and M. Young, "Intrametropolitan Variation in Wage Rates: The Case of Atlanta Fast-Food Restaurant Workers," *Review of Economics & Statistics* 76 (1994): 425-33. The reality of spatial mismatch makes even more foreboding the fact that levels of concentrated poverty in central city regions continue to grow, according to the 1990 census. See P. Jargowsky, "Ghetto Poverty among Blacks in the 1980s," *Journal of Policy Analysis & Management* 13 (1994): 288-310; J. Kasarda, "Inner-City Concentrated Poverty & Neighborhood Distress: 1970–1990," *Housing Policy Debate* 4, no. 3 (1993): 253-301; and G. Galster and R. Mincy, "Understanding the Changing Fortunes of Metropolitan Neighborhoods: 1980–1990," *Housing Policy Debate* 4, no. 3 (1993): 303-52. I have to agree with W. J. Wilson's emphasis on "social isolation" as the grave constricting reality of the pockets of concentrated poverty that lie in or near most central cities of the United States. See his *The Truly Disadvantaged: The Inner City, the Underclass, & Public Policy* (Chicago: Univ. of Chicago Press, 1987).

50. A debate, equally as intense as the "spatial mismatch" issue noted in the previous footnote, rages around the question of whether there is growing inequality among laborers. A consensus seems to have emerged that shifts in technology increasingly have favored better-educated workers and have hurt lower-skilled workers, thus giving rise to what some have called a "structural twist" in the labor market.

51. In addition to the dismissive attitudes of many in academia and the press, I have in mind the message of so much popular media and music: the misogynous lyrics of too many popular songs, the so-called comedy routines filled with appeals to racial and ethnic bigotry, and too much film and television fare displaying values contrary to nurturing strong traditional families. I do not intend to give nontraditional families any feelings of inadequacy; to the contrary, my goal is for far greater compassion to be extended to these family units, at the same time as measures are taken to prevent more broken families from forming.

that especially single-parent families face great difficulty in coping economically and in other ways.

It is my judgment that the social and economic environment of the second half of the twentieth century has created debilitating forms of poverty in a way that could not have occurred earlier in U.S. history when the traditional family was stronger and when unskilled workers could find remunerative jobs in the emerging industrial sector. Even today, where traditional families remain strong — one thinks of many recent immigrants to the United States from all parts of the world — economic difficulty (even within adverse central city locations) is far less likely to become debilitating. What is especially distressing about poverty today is that the nation's historically most disadvantaged citizens — subject earlier to slavery, and subsequently to subtle and not-so-subtle forms of harmful race-based treatment by the dominant white citizenry — are again the most afflicted by debilitating poverty and social dysfunction.

The welfare system sits uneasily in the midst of these developments. But when it was created in the mid-1930s, who could have foreseen the unfortunate future development of the family, the economy, and the city? Yet a lack of prophetic vision is no excuse for the system's disincentives for establishing and maintaining strong families, extended or nuclear.

Social Security for the aged is widely judged a great success for lowering the incidence of poverty in a group that otherwise is prone to high rates of poverty. As it did so, however, it lessened incentives for members of extended families to care for one another privately. As an alternative the United States could have used either a positive financial enducement (perhaps tax-based) for family members to care for their own parents or some actual requirement that the younger generations financially support their elders (perhaps through assessments on their income taxes if their elders applied for government assistance). Either of these could reflect the Bible's aggressive concern for family responsibility. Unemployment insurance, on the other hand, apart from administrative problems that create incentives for prolonged idleness for unscrupulous participants, probably strengthens the intact nuclear family.

Critics generally agree that American welfare (AFDC, food stamps, and Medicaid) has discouraged the formation and stability of traditional families. Most evaluations have focused on nuclear families and asked whether the availability of welfare assistance has encouraged families to separate (probably not an overwhelming number) or allowed unmarried couples not to marry despite having borne a child (a greater number).[52] But disincentives to extended family responsibility have not been studied adequately — which itself tells us something about the nature of the U.S. commitment to the extended family.

When Americans look at welfare, they are troubled especially by dependency and nonwork by able-bodied recipients of assistance. These are legitimate concerns in light of the ethical thrust of biblical teaching. The message of this chapter is that in our efforts to address dependency and workfare we should use as our ethical touchstone the impact of any changes upon the well-being of families. We must always evaluate whether a particular reform effort will help establish and maintain strong families or whether it contains instead incentives to weaken family formation and stability.

An attempt to strengthen families through welfare policy changes runs the risk of being overly generous with benefits and insufficiently tough with obligations. Encouraging AFDC mothers to take greater parental responsibility seems to conflict with pushing them into employment, for instance. Changing the rules so that fathers and husbands join or stay in families that continue to receive AFDC seems unfair when so many other families have to labor very hard, without government support, to barely keep afloat. But strong families are the key to overcoming debilitating poverty. That, as we have seen, is the wisdom of the Bible. So if we must err when we design and implement welfare policy, I urge that we err in the direction of providing too many, rather than too few, incentives to form and maintain families.

52. The deductive case is stronger than the empirical evidence offered to discern it. See R. Moffitt, "Incentive Effects of the U.S. Welfare System: A Review," *Journal of Economic Literature* 30 (1992): 1-61; T. P. Schultz, "Marital Status & Fertility in the United States: Welfare & Labor Market Effects," *Journal of Human Resources* 29 (1994): 637-59; I. Garfinkel and S. McLanahan, "Single Mother Families, Economic Insecurity, & Government Policy" (IRP Conference paper, May 28–30, 1992, Institute for Research on Poverty, University of Wisconsin-Madison). Regarding female-headedness, most studies find that welfare, though a contributing factor, certainly is not the most important cause. Conditions in labor markets and the general cultural climate affecting the acceptability of single parenthood within society are far more important as causes.

Appendix: The Bible and Government Welfare: A Critique of the Critics

In this appendix I respond briefly to two critics of the kind of biblical interpretation and social analysis I have proposed. Calvin Beisner, especially in his book *Prosperity & Poverty,* carefully develops the argument that biblical teaching severely limits the legitimate scope of government action to assist the poor.[53] Marvin Olasky, in *The Tragedy of American Compassion,* provides a reading of the history of American private and public welfare that supports the view that voluntary help for the poor is much to be preferred over government programs.[54]

The Bible and Public Welfare

Calvin Beisner systematically argues that there is no biblical warrant for government to assist the poor. He summarizes his argument in this fashion: "The only proper conclusion for the Christian who understands the ethical principles and the economic and historical facts is to oppose government transfer payments to the poor, to seek to have them abolished, *and then to learn and practice Biblically just and economically effective ways of helping the poor instead.*"[55]

The normative role of the government, for Beisner, is to assure a just society, with justice interpreted as "rendering impartially to each his due in conforming with the standard of rightness, whether in personal or in social relations" (p. 53). The standard of rightness for the Christian is the Decalogue, a standard so "naturally" right that, as Paul states (Rom. 2:14-15), it is written on the hearts of non-Christians. This is the standard embodied in Jesus' teaching of the Golden Rule (the summary of the Law and the Prophets) and it is the standard reflected in the natural law tradition (p. 45).

53. Beisner, *Prosperity & Poverty: The Compassionate Use of Resources in a World of Scarcity* (Westchester, Ill.: Crossway Books, 1988).

54. Olasky, *The Tragedy of American Compassion* (Wheaton, Ill.: Crossway Books, 1992).

55. Beisner, 187, emphasis his. Subsequent references to this book will be in parentheses in the text.

Beisner's normative conception of government allows no forcible income redistribution other than that related to remedial justice in compensation for a violation of one's rights (p. 51). "Distributive justice" refers to "arrangements in society by which each man obtains what his nature and his labor entitle him to, without oppression or evasion" (p. 50). Assisting the poor by forcible redistribution of income violates the right of the person being taxed to keep his or her property and it compromises the government's requirement of impartiality by making it partial to poorer individuals. Love, not government-mediated redistribution, is what leads to proper assistance to the poor. "Love not only does not violate another's rights, but also builds him up" (I Cor. 8:1b). The government can "do positive good by praising people who do good," but that is its limit (pp. 150ff.).

Beisner makes his argument forcefully and with careful attention to Scripture.[56] But it is not difficult to find critics of his "thin" conception of justice. Just as John Rawls and Robert Nozick duel on secular grounds about the meaning of justice,[57] Beisner's view has been criticized on biblical grounds by Stephen Charles Mott.[58] It was just such a dispute that prompted me to return to the Bible, and particularly to the pentateuchal passages that speak to the responsibility of the nonpoor Israelites for poverty in their midst. On that foundation I must reject Beisner's argument

56. I take seriously Beisner's humble statement that while he hopes his "book rests on accurate understanding of economic principles and sound Biblical interpretation, I know my fallibility. Thus I welcome corrections from my brothers and sisters in Christ, whether of exegesis or of economic analysis" (p. xiv). I respect his handling of Scripture, and generally agree with the way he understands the use of biblical law today: "my use of Biblical Law presupposes simply that the same moral Law that was perfectly suited to mankind's need for moral instruction four thousand years ago, is perfectly suited to mankind's need for moral instruction today. It imparts wise, important, and clear instruction for the economic activities of individuals, families, churches, societies, States, and the whole human race" (p. 228). But there is a less than humble tone too many places in the book, and Beisner is harsh in characterizing the views of fellow Christians who take the Bible as seriously as he does but who draw different implications from it.

57. Rawls, *A Theory of Justice* (Cambridge: Harvard Univ. Press, 1971); Nozick, *Anarchy, State, & Utopia* (New York: Basic Books, 1974).

58. Mott, "The Partiality of Biblical Justice," *Transformation* 10 (Jan.-Apr. 1993): 23-29, an article written in response to Beisner's "Justice & Poverty: Two Views Contrasted," pp. 16-22 in the same issue.

that there is no biblical warrant to justify government action to redistribute income.

Beisner is correct to stress that the ideal and primary responsibility for addressing poverty rests with extended families and voluntaristic responses. This is a point made over the centuries by many other Christian thinkers. Listen to the voices of two prominent European Christians, writing a century apart but in the context of societies similar to ours. First, Abraham Kuyper, Dutch Calvinist theologian and political leader:

> Government exists to administer [God's] justice on earth, and to uphold that justice. The tasks of family and society therefore lie outside government's jurisdiction. With those it is not to meddle. But as soon as there is any clash among the different spheres of life, where one sphere trespasses on or violates the domain which by divine ordinance belongs to the other, then it is the God-given duty of government to uphold justice before arbitrariness, and to withstand, by the justice of God, the physical superiority of the stronger. What it may not do is to grant such assurance of justice to one sphere and withhold it from another. . . .
>
> As for the other type of state aid — namely the distribution of money — it is certain that such intervention is not excluded in Israel's lawgiving, but there it is held to a minimum. Therefore I say that, unless you wish to undermine the position of the laboring class and destroy its natural resilience, the material assistance of the state should be confined to an absolute minimum. The continuing welfare of people and nation, including labor, lies only in powerful individual initiative.[59]

A century after Kuyper, a similar position was proposed by John Paul II, in his 1991 encyclical *Centesimus Annus:*

> [Rehearsing the themes of the 1891 encyclical *Rerum Novarum*:] The State, however, has the task of determining the juridical framework within which economic affairs are to be conducted, and thus of safeguarding the prerequisites of a free economy, which presumes a certain equality betweeen the parties, such that one party would not be so powerful as practically to reduce the other to subservience.

59. Kuyper, *The Problem of Poverty,* ed. James W. Skillen (Grand Rapids, Mich.: Baker Book House, 1991), 71f. This was an address delivered to the first Christian Social Congress in the Netherlands in 1891.

> The State must contribute to the achievement of these goals both directly and indirectly. Indirectly and according to the *principle of subsidiarity,* by creating favorable conditions for the free exercise of economic activity, which will lead to abundant opportunities for employment and sources of wealth. Directly and according to the *principle of solidarity,* by defending the weakest, by placing certain limits on the autonomy of the parties who determine working conditions, and by ensuring in every case the necessary minimum support for the unemployed worker.
>
> [Applying the themes of *Rerum Novarum* to the contemporary scene:] [E]xcesses and abuses, especially in recent years, have provoked very harsh criticisms of the Welfare State, dubbed the "Social Assistance State." Malfunctions and defects in the Social Assistance State are the result of an inadequate understanding of the tasks proper to the State. Here again the principle of subsidiarity must be respected. . . .
>
> By intervening directly and depriving society of its responsibility, the Social Assistance State leads to a loss of human energies and an inordinate increase of public agencies, which are dominated more by bureaucratic ways of thinking than by concern for serving their clients . . . it would appear that needs are best understood and satisfied by people who are closest to them and who act as neighbors to those in need.[60]

Any direct government response to the needs of the poor, therefore, should be a secondary one. Its first responsibility is to mandate extended family accountability as much as feasible (without weakening the ties of family viability). But just as necessary and important is government's secondary responsibility: to supplement the family and voluntary responses when they prove insufficient to restore poorer members of society to the healthy family viability and responsibility the Bible commends. Government must carefully find ways both to support families and to hold them responsible. The clear goal is the social and economic viability of the (extended) family.

Suppose, however, that we try to remain within the confines of Beisner's argument that the role of government is to do no more than "to render impartially to each his due in conforming with the standard of rightness" and to "do positive good by praising people who do good." What then do we do

60. John Paul II, *Centesimus Annus* (Encyclical Letter of the Supreme Pontiff on the Hundredth Anniversary of *Rerum Novarum*) (Boston: St. Paul Books, 1991), paragraphs 15 and 48.

with those numerous biblical texts cited in the main body of this chapter about the "rights" or "cause" of the poor?[61] As I noted, these words carry unmistakable legal significance and establish rights that, in Beisner's framework, must be the responsibility of the government to uphold as a matter of justice. And I have suggested the following as a description of what these rights meant in the time of early Israel: a family or individual who was working the expected amount and otherwise seeking to be a responsible member of the community would have the community's assurance that economic difficulties would not debilitate the family or individual so much that it could not continue to be a viable and contributing member of the community. Assuring such rights in this manner more than likely involved some forms of government-mediated income redistribution on a number of occasions.[62]

The Sufficiency of Private Charity

The second argument I will address is that of Marvin Olasky. He reviews the American experience of private assistance, concentrating primarily on the response to urban poverty in the nineteenth and early twentieth centuries,[63] identifies the attributes of effective charity, and offers these historical insights as the basis for reforming welfare today. Olasky chronicles

61. Two Hebrew words are used for "rights" and "cause." The predominant word is *mishpat,* which is used elsewhere to refer to the laws and judgments of God. At Psalms 140:12 (with *mishpat*), Proverbs 29:7 and 31:9, and Jeremiah 22:16, the word is *din* and means, most likely, "righteous judgment" or "legal claim." Moreover, the Hebrew words used for "poor" in these contexts (primarily *'ani* and *'ebyon*) describe Israelites who were poor due to circumstances largely beyond their control, and not to laziness, such that they were seen as deserving of community assistance. See a more detailed argument in my "Biblical Teaching & Assisting the Poor," *Transformation* 4 (Apr./June 1987): 1-14, esp. the sections "Standard for Assistance" and "Legal Status of the Provisions."

62. At p. 157, note 36, Beisner seems implicitly to grant my argument, by noting that the gleanings to which the poor have access belong not to the owner but to God — and therefore the poor have a "right" to them: a right, I presume, local governmental overseers would have protected were there a complaint.

63. Not as carefully, however, as Paul Boyer's earlier study, *Urban Masses & Moral Order in America,* which covers most of the same material. Curiously, Olasky does not cite Boyer's work. Olasky carries his story to the present, but his treatment of the recent period offers little that has not been presented more systematically by Charles Murray in *Losing Ground* and other places.

and systematizes the voluntary efforts of primarily nonemployed middle-class wives to address urban squalor and poverty, stressing particularly their willingness to "suffer with" the poor (personal involvement) — and to exercise, in the process, a form of tough love by categorizing and assisting those who were truly needy. These efforts largely were fueled by earnest Christians and Jews who were submitting themselves to regular teaching about the importance of sacrificial ministry to the poor.[64]

According to the attributes of effective assistance as practiced in nineteenth-century America, the conditions of any poor individual or family were investigated personally to determine whether they were truly deserving. Where behavioral traits contributed to the poverty, changes in these traits were made the condition for assistance. In-kind assistance was preferred to cash assistance, and dolegiving and almsgiving were discouraged because they broke down independence and undermined character. Olasky offers us a mnemonic list of seven "marks of compassion," which include (in addition to the items already mentioned) the importance of helping the poor find employment and of establishing a right relationship with God.

Although Olasky suggests that in the years prior to the 1930s assistance was wholly in the hands of private agencies and individuals, he in fact records a considerable amount of local government assistance. This must mean that in some situations, at least, public assistance may bear the marks of authentic compassion, even though Olasky is at pains to argue that bad (public) charity drives out good (private) charity. And while he rightly emphasizes the beneficial effects of a voluntary response, he also shows, but with less emphasis, that there existed a number of limitations on the adequacy of this response. He speaks at a number of places, for instance, of "compassion fatigue" in the face of overwhelming squalor and seeming hopelessness. He bemoans, particularly, the post–Civil War movement of the middle class away from the central cities, thereby breaking the spatial proximity that naturally encouraged volunteerism. The emerging reality of middle-class suburbanization strained existing charitable organi-

64. Olasky writes, "Effective help in the cities, as in the country-side, had to be personal; those who were better-off were to *suffer with* the troubled. It had to be conditional; when the recipient was responsible for his plight, he was to indicate a willingness to change. It had to honor those among the poor who did not give up; they had to be treated not as chumps but as human beings who deserved great 'respect for character'" (p. 31).

zations, forcing them to rely upon greater professionalization in both fund-raising appeals and the use of hired employees in place of volunteers.[65] Writing of the early 1930s, he notes that charitable agencies

> had their own short-term exigencies, as the better off also were affected by economic pressures, and as groups devoted to personal interaction had trouble adjusting to masses at the door. Sadly, just as the Depression increased demand — from 1929-32 — at least four hundred of the nation's private welfare agencies went under. But the problems of supply were also the result of a long-term trend toward impersonal contribution.[66]

Olasky's numerous examples of sacrificial effort and good works, as American citizens struggled amidst the growing strains of industrialization and urbanization, serve us well — as does his helpful catalogue of the nature of an effective response. Yet, despite his own agenda, his history also helps us understand why this nation started down the road to government-overseen welfare programs. Voluntary efforts, he shows, became insufficient to the need early in this century. This was due in part to what he terms growing "economic segregation," by which the nonpoor increasingly separated themselves geographically from the poor and thus lost sight of them and their plight.[67] But he points as well to another, and even more important, cause of the decline in volunteerism:

65. Olasky says, "[A]s professionals began to dominate the realm of compassion, volunteers began to depart. It is not clear whether the supply first slackened, or whether professionals worked to decrease the demand. Some cities showed simultaneous movement" (p. 146); "Agencies began to report a dearth of volunteers" (p. 147).

66. Olasky, 149-50.

67. In a society and era otherwise opposed to active government intervention, how can we explain the aggressive call at the turn of the twentieth century from the social gospel movement (and others) for government involvement, were the charitable response at all adequate? Olasky offers us useful insight: "The growth of economic segregation and mediated compassion made it easy for many of the better-off to 'measure community needs through abstractions: publicity, lectures, the photographs in annual reports. Communications innovations, like professionalization, separated the twentieth-century donor from the object of his largesse. [Donors] could exercise the obligations of stewardship at a safe remove from the problems they were helping to solve'" (p. 147). "By the 1920s, a University of Chicago sociologist who interviewed nearby suburban residents found them complacent in their isolation and hardly likely to venture into poor areas. . . . Initially, the willingness to give money grew as the desire to give time decreased" (pp. 147-48).

> [T]hroughout the nineteenth century, the rock on which compassion stood was undergoing erosion. The chief erosion was theological: the belief that sinful man, left to himself, would return to wilderness, seemed harshly pessimistic. Other erosion toward the end of the century was political and economic, as Social Darwinists and Social Universalists both assailed the idea that personal involvement could make a substantial difference. The erosion for a time did not seem crucial, but the long-term effect was severe enough to make the twentieth century not the Christian century, as celebrants in 1900 predicted, but the century of wilderness returning.[68]

If Olasky's argument here is correct, then, contrary to his implication, the all-too-reluctant entry by governments into the fight against poverty was an essential step, because the religious foundations of the earlier volunteer efforts had become seriously undermined.

As the newly dominant congressional Republicans began in early 1995 drastically to reform the welfare system, Olasky and his argument became identified with the view that private charity in the nineteenth century offered a more effective and a sufficient response compared to government-mediated assistance, and that the poor of the nation today would be served more compassionately by returning to the earlier arrangement. However, his own historical account offers contradictory evidence of the sufficiency of the earlier response. Indeed, the longer historical record shows that an effective response typically has combined private and public efforts, whether we range back to Talmudic teaching about care for the urban poor around 500 A.D., examine poverty relief in the Middle Ages and under Luther and Calvin, or look to colonial New England, which modeled its provisions consciously on biblical teaching.[69] On what basis, then, can one call today for moving to primary reliance upon private assistance, especially

68. Olasky, 220.

69. See M. Katz, *Protection of the Weak in the Talmud* (New York: Columbia Univ. Press, 1975); C. Lindberg, *Beyond Charity: Reformational Initiatives for the Poor* (Minneapolis: Fortress Press, 1993); R. Kingdon, "Calvinism & Social Welfare," *Calvin Theological Journal* 17 (1982): 212-30. Olasky himself notes of the colonial American response to poverty, "Those who made room for widows and orphans [in their homes] often received compensation for out-of-pocket expenditures from town councils or other community organizations" (p. 7). He also observes, among other examples, an orphanage in New York City in the early nineteenth century, organized through charitable efforts, receiving a "state subsidy" (p. 14).

without having in place the religious commitment that gave rise to the earlier private response? Olasky's historical survey would be far more useful than it is had he analyzed the interplay between public and private efforts, in the context of the unique U.S. cultural reality, and then offered the outlines of where and how strategic forms of government intervention can complement and improve the generally more effective private response without in the process discouraging private charity.

As to the usefulness of Olasky's analysis for us today: to the extent that spatial proximity between the poor and nonpoor no longer is what it was in the nineteenth century, to the extent that middle-class wives are not in their homes and available for volunteer activities, and to the extent that significant portions of potential volunteers are not being taught regularly in churches and synagogues to mark their lives with sacrificial giving, one wonders seriously whether the commended response of Olasky could possibly bear comparable fruit today.

Foundations of the Welfare Responsibility of the Government

Stephen Charles Mott

GOVERNMENT PROGRAMS that provide financial and other assistance to the poor are commonly looked upon with great suspicion in the United States. Laissez-faire economic thinking, although no longer dominating actual policymaking, remains a potent ideal for both politicians and citizens. Public welfare programs are viewed as morally suspect and without deep historical roots. The assumption is that government welfare provisions and the welfare state are responses to the social problems spawned by the industrial revolution. Given the size and complexity of modern society, the easy political response to the social crisis was to use government's powers of taxation to redistribute goods and services to the disadvantaged, displacing older and morally superior nongovernmental approaches to helping the poor. Such suspicions of government welfare provision can undercut public support, demoralize practitioners and recipients, and make political leaders reluctant to commit government to an antipoverty fight sufficiently extensive to cope with the real dimensions of the problem.

In this chapter I argue that the state's welfare responsibilities are thoroughly grounded in Scripture, in Christian theology, and in historical premodern practices within Western Christendom. I conclude that the laissez-faire presumption that government cannot legitimately provide welfare assistance is unsupportable.

The first section demonstrates the biblical and theological foundations for a government role in providing financial assistance to the needy. I will pay attention here to the social aspects of human nature, the nature of power, the purpose of government, and the requirements of justice. The social nature of humanity, the plight caused by sin, and the requirement of justice that the needy be protected all point to the responsibility of government to give aid to the needy, when this is not provided sufficiently by other elements of the society. Indeed this responsibility is explicitly required of rulers in the Bible.

The second section shows the extensive history of government assistance to the needy prior to the modern period. I will emphasize the legal aspects of the church's provisions for the needy in the Middle Ages, the growing control of welfare by municipal governments in the late Middle Ages, and especially the Protestant Reformers' support for the shift of responsibility from the institutional church to the state.

This chapter makes no case for any particular public policy proposal, and it focuses on only one of the normative functions of government. The direct provision of goods and services does not exhaust the government's tasks on behalf of the poor; it has a responsibility, for instance, also for just economic structures. Correspondingly, welfare is only one aspect of the deeper economic strategy of the Bible, which centers on empowerment in community. Nevertheless, the Law presumes that its provisions designed to tie people to productive power would not always be sufficient in practice, so that the needy would require the direct provision of goods.

Biblical and Theological Groundings

The Social Nature of Humanity

The theological foundations of welfare include biblical conceptions of human nature, sin, power, the purpose of government, and justice. Some understanding of human nature always lies at the base of any public policy, and its effectiveness depends upon the validity of that assumption.

According to the Judeo-Christian perspective, humanity always lives in community. Human beings by nature find in life together the security and common benefits of the good life. It is assumed in Cain's punishment and his ultimate building of a city that to be apart from community is unnatural and undesirable. The Puritan theologian William Perkins accordingly tied human happiness to living together in justice: "The common good of men stands in this, not onely that they live, but that they live well, in righteousnes and holines, and consequently in true happinesse."[1] Plato acknowledges our social nature when he attributes the creation of cities to our need for others: "We do not severally suffice for our own needs, but each of us lacks many things" (*Republic*, 369c). By nature people contribute to one another in community.

This focus on the common good has important implications for property rights and welfare. Thomas Aquinas gave expression to an ancient tradition of Christian social thought, ranging back to Augustine and Ambrose, when he argued that God has arranged the natural order so that material goods are provided for the satisfaction of human needs. A right to private property therefore must not detract from the general welfare. The duty to manage property in the interests of all takes precedence over private rights. Owners should not consider property as only their own. Whatever a person has in excess, he argued, "is owed, of natural right, to the poor for their sustenance."[2]

Government is an aspect of community and is inherent in human life. This perspective is contrary to the social contract theory at the base of liberal political philosophy, which hypothesizes that warring individuals choose to put aside their independent existence by contracting to have a society, and then formed a government to which they transferred their individual rights.

Persons, however, are neither historically nor logically antecedent to society. As social beings they are physically, emotionally, and rationally interdependent and have inherent duties of care and responsibility for one another. Authority, corporate responsibility, and collective decision making are essential to every form of human life.[3] In this sense government is not a consequence of the Fall. It exists in part so that the community can act intentionally as a whole in carrying out its responsibilities, including those of mutual care. Some decisions must be made by the central authority.[4] These include priorities of the community, such as empowerment of the

1. William Perkins, "A Treatise of the Vocations or Callings of Men," in E. Morgan, ed., *Puritan Political Ideas 1558–1794,* American Heritage Series (Indianapolis: Bobbs-Merrill, 1965), 39.

2. Thomas Aquinas, *Summa Theologiae,* 2a2ae. 66, 2, 7 in Aquinas, *Selected Political Writings,* ed. D'Entrèves (Oxford: Blackwell, 1948), 169, 171; cf. 1a2ae. 94, 5, p. 127.

3. Richard J. Mouw, *Political Evangelism* (Grand Rapids, Mich.: Eerdmans, 1973), 45.

4. John C. Bennett, *Christians and the State* (New York: Scribner's, 1958), 86.

weak, if these priorities are otherwise are not being met by other groups in the community.

The government is also a response to selfish and antisocial behaviors, which mar and inhibit our nature as God created it. Government encourages us to fulfill our responsibilities to others by assuring us that we will not stand alone if we act on the social impulse to come to the aid of the weak.[5] In this sense, the state regathers the community.

The state contributes to social cohesion in other pertinent ways. Rather than needlessly carrying out all services directly, the state encourages other institutions in the community to carry out their responsibilities, including care of the economically dependent. These institutions include family, church, nongovernmental social agencies, guilds, and unions.[6] For example, the government can encourage businesses to provide job training for low-income people in exchange for tax breaks or adjustments in zoning laws.

The depth of social need in a society, however, may be more than can be handled by nongovernmental institutions. James Luther Adams, although the leading theologian and advocate of voluntary associations, warned against an ideological commitment to the private spirit that "leaves it to people of tender conscience to cope with pervasive maladjustments by means of voluntary associations, thus relieving government, or the community as a whole, of responsibility." This can be in reality merely a giving in to the antisocial priorities of "the more intractable power groups of the local or regional community."[7] When indirect approaches are not effective in restraining harmful group activity or in maintaining vital social functions, the state must act more directly in coercing submission to patterns of justice[8] or in directly carrying out vital services. The prospect of this compulsion supports its arbitrating and molding functions.

In summary, as interdependent beings we have responsibilities in

5. Malcolm Feeley, "Coercion and Compliance: A New Look at an Old Problem," *Law and Society Review* 4 (1970): 512.

6. The state molds the process of mutual support among the groups, according to Reinhold Niebuhr, *The Nature and Destiny of Man*, vol. 2: *Human Destiny* (New York: Scribner's, 1964), 266.

7. James Luther Adams, "Freedom and Association," in Adams, *On Being Human Religiously*, ed. M. Stackhouse (Boston: Beacon, 1976), 80-81. Cf. Daniel C. Maguire, *A New American Justice: Ending the White Male Monopolies* (Garden City, N.J.: Doubleday, 1980), 25, 104.

8. Niebuhr, 266.

community for one another. When the community otherwise does not sufficiently carry them out, government action is needed. One of these priorities is care of the needy.

Intervening Power

The communal aspect of human nature provides one of the roots that the state has in human life. The other root is power.

Power is the chance to realize one's own will in communal action even against the resistance of others.[9] It is a gift from God, the creator and sustainer. Human power exists as the way we make actual our possibilities of being, which God presents as a particular gift designed for each life.[10] Power thus is essential to human life and is not the outcome of the Fall.

In the actual human condition since the Fall, sinful actions against others pervert the intentions of the Creator. The ability to act in accordance with one's created being exists in the context of persons and forces that would thwart the divine intention. The fallen use of power to impede the Creator's intentions for the lives of others is *exploitive power.* In fallen reality, fulfilling the Creator's intentions requires resisting such exploitive power.[11] The exercise of *defensive power* against the resistance of others is a necessary and legitimate means to enable us to be the creatures that we perceive God has created us to be.

Defensive power includes control of material necessities of life, which also are given by God. Significant struggles of men and women in the Bible relate to economic survival. God "gives power over" wealth and property for enjoyment (Eccles. 5:19). By contrast, there are situations where this use of defensive power (same verb as in 5:19) is lacking, and wealth and property are in the power of a stranger (Eccles. 6:2; cf. Isa. 65:22; Ps. 128:2).

The special attention that Scripture gives to the plight of the widow,

9. Max Weber, *Economy and Society: An Outline of Interpretative Sociology,* vol. 2, ed. G. Roth and C. Wittick, 4th ed. (New York: Bedminster, 1968), 926.

10. For this perspective on power in the writings of Paul Tillich and James Luther Adams, see, for example, Tillich, *Love, Power, and Justice: Ontological Analyses and Ethical Applications* (New York: Oxford Univ. Press, 1954), esp. 35-53, and Adams, "Theological Bases of Social Action," in his *Taking Time Seriously* (Glencoe, Ill.: Free Press, 1957), esp. 42, 50.

11. Paul Tillich, "The Problem of Power" (1931), in Tillich, *The Interpretation of History* (New York: Scribner's, 1936), 193.

the orphan, the poor, and the resident alien reflects its awareness of the potential for evil in powerlessness. In the center of Job's declaration of the injustices done to these groups is the statement: "The powerful possess the land" (Job 22:8, NRSV; cf. Job 35:9; Eccl. 4:1).

Exploitive power allows lust to work its will.[12] "Alas for those who devise wickedness and evil deeds upon their beds! When the morning dawns, they perform it, because it is in their power. They covet. . . . They oppress . . ." (Mic. 2:1-2, NRSV). Thus the structure of unequal power leads to exploitation.

A Christian political philosophy accordingly must be based on a realism about human nature in light of the universality of sin. Alongside the created wonder in human life exists a persistent and pernicious tendency toward evil. The social consequences of this pervasive aspect of human nature must be firmly faced.

Powerful forces prey on the weak, and human selfishness resists the full costs of the community's obligations. Individual egoism is heightened in group conflict, and sin is disguised and justified as victims are blamed for their own plight. An *intervening power* is necessary to limit exploitive power. Karl Rahner correctly sees that this use of power is justified by the sinful actions that it opposes.[13]

Intervening power is an inherent part of social living, supplementing the inadequacies of an individual's or a group's defensive power. Political and economic relief is accomplished by power. Power produces changes to guarantee basic human needs and to resist the forces that deny them. Intervening power is creative as it reestablishes the power of being by thwarting exploitive power. Intervening power restores defensive power by defeating exploitive power.

The source and model is God, who in common grace and in special grace restores the power of being by overcoming the forces that pervert the creation. God exerts power as the defender of the poor. Yahweh does "justice for the orphan and the oppressed" (Ps. 10:18, NRSV) by "break[ing] the arm [that is, power] of the wicked" (v. 15) "so that those from earth may strike terror no more" (v. 18).

12. So Aristotle stated that all people do what they wish if they have the power (*Politics,* 1312b3, cf. 1313b32).

13. Karl Rahner, "The Theology of Power," in Rahner, *Theological Investigations,* vol. 4 (Baltimore: Helicon, 1966), 395.

God's normal way of exerting power is through human creatures, who are God's lieutenants on the earth. The created being of the first man and woman possessed the power to subdue the earth as God's vicegerents bearing God's image in their power (Gen. 1:26-30).[14] This mandate is clarified as one of service and care (Gen. 2:15).[15]

Power is thus a charge from God to be used. The earth to subdue is now the world of the Fall. When human justice fails and there is "no one to intervene," God acts in direct and extraordinary ways (Isa. 59:15-18), but the proper situation is when the government and other human institutions are faithful channels of God's intervening power. Groups, which we know biblically and socially to be endemic to human life, function to make possible the fulfillment of wider obligations.

Justice determines the proper limits and applications of intervening power. Paul Tillich states that justice is but the structure of power; without it, power becomes destructive.[16] Power, on the other hand, provides fiber and grit for justice. "I put on justice," Job proclaimed. "I championed the cause of the stranger. I broke the fangs of the unrighteous, and made them drop their prey from their teeth" (Job 29:14, 16-17). In the words of Martin Luther King, Jr., "Power without love is reckless and abusive and . . . love without power is sentimental and anemic. Power at its best is love implementing the demands of justice."[17]

The need for government to exercise intervening power is understated by those who would rely primarily on the forces of economic competition. Neglect of the pervasiveness of exploitive power, which is so forcefully portrayed in Scripture, contributes to the advocacy of merely individualistic solutions to social injustice and to a mistaken faith in natural harmonies.

The market provides insufficient control of greed and allows genuine needs to remain unmet. For many, to be sure, economic needs are adequately supplied by the market. This is the market's proper and most

14. Hans Walter Wolff, *Anthropology of the Old Testament* (Philadelphia: Fortress, 1974), 163.

15. William J. Dumbrell, "Genesis 1–3, Ecology, and the Dominion of Man," *Crux* 21, no. 4 (1985): 21.

16. Paul Tillich, "Shadow and Substance: A Theory of Power" (1965), in Tillich, *Political Expectation*, ed. J. L. Adams (New York: Harper, 1971), 118.

17. Martin Luther King, *Where Do We Go from Here: Chaos or Community?* (Boston: Beacon, 1967), 37.

essential function. Needs and desires, however, are not efficiently distinguished by the market system. The market responds to wants. Whether or not these wants are genuine needs is not discerned and does not matter to its processes.[18] What is required for the welfare of the poor may not offer the most available profit, if any, to the sellers. As Marx pointed out, when people have no money in this system, their needs effectively do not exist.[19] Rights, including benefit rights, must be part of the checks and balances on the market.[20]

Where basic economic needs are not provided for, the community as a whole has a responsibility to modify the market process or to supplement it. In this the government has a final responsibility for the benefit rights of those who otherwise are left deficient (this theme is developed further in the following section, "The Purpose of the State and Social Justice"). These rights mark the areas in which people need to be empowered.

Government action to assist the poor is necessary. Biblical realism about power is incompatible with a strategy of strengthening the economic position of the wealthy in the hope of eventual benefit to the poor. It is striking that the classical prophets' indictment of social injustice came at a time when poverty increased in the midst of economic expansion.[21] The biblical materials portray a society with a high degree of conflict between the mighty and the lowly, an image that corresponds with the Bible's portrayal of human nature. The Christian view of universal depravity prevents a reliance on the benevolence of the economically powerful. Victor Hugo stated the point memorably: "There is always more misery among the lower classes than there is humanity in the higher."[22]

Because of human sinfulness, human rights cannot be fulfilled by voluntary actions alone. Jonathan Edwards defended the legal obligation of the towns in his day "to defend every one who otherwise would be an object of charity." People reduced to extreme poverty should not

18. Cf. Daniel Bell, *The Cultural Contradictions of Capitalism* (New York: Basic Books, 1976), 222-23.

19. Karl Marx, "Economic and Philosophical Manuscripts," 3.42-43, in Marx, *Early Writings*, ed. T. B. Bottomore (New York: McGraw-Hill, 1963), 192.

20. Arthur M. Okun, *Equality and Efficiency: The Big Tradeoff* (Washington, D.C.: Brookings Institution, 1975), 13-14.

21. Cf. S. C. Mott, "The Contribution of the Bible to Economic Thought," *Transformation* 4, nos. 3-4 (1987): 28.

22. Victor Hugo, *Les Misérables*, Fantine 1.2, vol. 1 (London: Dent, 1909), 10.

> be left to so precarious a source of supply as voluntary charity. . . . It is fit that there should be something sure for them to depend upon. But a voluntary charity in this corrupt world is an uncertain thing. Therefore the wisdom of the legislature did not think fit to leave those who are so reduced, upon such a precarious foundation for subsistence.[23]

Because of its view of human nature, Scripture sees a peril in the lack of (defensive) power and also in an excess of power (the occasion of exploitive power). Reinhold Niebuhr rightly argued that since social injustice is supported by the self-interest of the powerful, it cannot be overcome by appeals to reason.[24] Power is never completely under the control of reason and conscience. Justice must be politically powerful as well as rationally legitimized. Ensuring a just distribution of resources to the needy requires the supporting arm of government.

Power in the form of the intervening actions of the state thus is needed because of sin. Access to material goods essential to life, which should be part of the defensive power of each basic unit, often is insufficient, and other individuals and institutions in the community that have the responsibility to aid are reluctant to make the necessary sacrifices. Government action then is needed.

The Purpose of the State and Social Justice

We now move from analyzing power to a direct consideration of how the purpose of the state relates to its responsibilities to the needy. The objective of the state is not merely to maintain an equilibrium of power in society. Its purpose is not merely to enable other groups in the society to carry out their tasks. The state has a positive meaning of its own. The positive meaning of the state is justice. Its essence is to bear, posit, and enforce justice. "The Lord has made you king to execute justice and righteousness," Solomon was reminded (1 Kings 10:9; cf. Jer. 22:15-16). In this section we look directly at the purpose of government as it relates to care for the poor. In the next section we will discuss more fully the nature of justice.

23. Jonathan Edwards, "Christian Charity," in *Works of President Edwards,* 1817, Research and Source Work 27, vol. 5 (New York: Franklin, 1968), 428-29.

24. Reinhold Niebuhr, *Moral Man and Immoral Society,* 1932 (New York: Scribner's, 1960), xii, xiv-xv, 21.

Government's positive purpose of advancing justice is seen in the biblical materials that present the ideal monarch. Behind these materials are principles for the proper conduct of government. Since they are presenting an ideal, these principles are normative for other forms of government as they confront perennial questions of civil rule. The ideal monarch is presented in two strands of material. The first is the ideal monarch in the royal psalms.

Psalm 72, for example, reflects the following purpose for the ruler: "May he defend the cause of the poor of the people, give deliverance to the needy, and crush the oppressor" (v. 4, NRSV). This task is identified as the work of justice (vv. 1-3, 7). Justice is understood as the use of power for deliverance of the needy and oppressed.

In Psalm 72 there are oppressors of the poor, separate from the state, who need to be crushed. State power, despite its dangers, is necessary for society because of the evil of such exploiting groups ("on the side of the oppressors there was power" [Eccles. 4:1]). Without governmental power to counter the evil power of such groups, there is "no one to comfort" the oppressed (Eccles. 4:1). Whether in the hands of the monarch or the village elders (Amos 5:12, 15), the government's power is to be used for the deliverance of the economically weak.[25] Among government's tasks is the guarantee that the traditional "rights of the poor" are met (Jer. 22:15-16; cf. the next section).

The second strand presenting the ideal ruler is found in prophecies of the coming messianic ruler. For example, Isaiah 11:4 (NRSV) states, "But with righteousness he shall judge the poor, and decide with equity for the meek of the earth; he shall smite the earth with the rod of his mouth, and with the breath of his lips he shall kill the wicked."

Such an ideal ruler would take responsibility like a shepherd for the needs of the people: "He shall feed them and be their shepherd" (Ezek. 34:23). In Ezekiel 34 the failure of the shepherds, that is, the rulers, of Israel to "feed" the people is described in verse 4. The same phrases are repeated to describe God's promise of justice: "And I will make them lie down, says the Lord GOD. I will seek the lost, and I will bring back the strayed, and I will bind up the injured, and I will strengthen the weak, but the fat and the strong I will destroy. I will feed them in justice" (vv. 15-16, NRSV). This promise will be fulfilled by the anticipated Davidic ruler (vv. 23-24). Similarly, in Isaiah 32:1-8 the promised just and wise monarch is contrasted to the fool who leaves the hungry unsatisfied (v. 6).

25. Cf. also Ps. 45:4-5; 101:8; Jer. 21:12; 22:15-16.

These materials apply beyond the limits of Israel in its unique role in salvation history. Israel's monarch was a channel of God's justice (Ps. 72:1), but God's justice extends to the whole world (e.g., Ps. 9:7-9). All governments are theocratic in their proper functions of social justice and have been appointed by God for this. All legitimate rulers are instituted by God and are God's servants for human good (Rom. 13:1, 4). Romans 13 is structurally similar to Psalm 72:1 in viewing the ruler as a channel of God's authority. The cry, "Give the king thy justice, O God" (Ps. 72:1), thus is answered not only in the government provided for the Old Testament people of God.

The Old Testament materials help us to understand the nature of "the good" (v. 4) that is the purpose of the state in Romans 13. The understanding of government in Hellenistic Judaism (reflecting also the view of the Hebrew Bible), particularly in Philo of Alexandria, a contemporary of Paul, is also important in understanding the content of "the good" in v. 4. In this view of government the monarch is the shepherd and the father of the people. The ruler has the duty of caring for them. Government has many positive social functions, particularly in welfare. The ideal government distributes "in proportion to the necessary needs" of life so that there is no "excess for luxury" nor lack (Philo, *On Joseph*, 243; cf. 2 Cor. 8:13-15).

Daniel 4:27 is important for this question of the universal application of the ideal of the monarch as the protector of the weak. The Babylonian monarch is enjoined to carry out "justice and . . . mercy to the oppressed," the same kind of delivering of justice as in Psalm 72:4. Similarly in Proverbs 31:9, King Lemuel, who is to "defend the rights of the poor and needy" (NRSV), is generally considered to be a northern Arabian monarch. "The general obligation of the Israelite king to see that persons otherwise not adequately protected or provided for should enjoy fair treatment in judicial proceedings and should receive the daily necessities of life is evidently understood as the duty of all kings."[26]

The literature of the nations of the ancient Near East, as in Israel, presents the hallmark of the ideal monarch to be this "special concern for the poor and helpless"[27] in texts that share significant characteristics with

26. Meredith G. Kline, *Kingdom Prologue* (Hamilton, Mass.: Meredith G. Kline, 1983), 34, citing Dan. 4:27 in support.

27. Kline, 34. Cf. F. Charles Fensham, "Widow, Orphan, and the Poor in Ancient Near Eastern Legal and Wisdom Literature," *Journal of Near Eastern Studies* 21 (1962): 129-34.

biblical texts concerning the monarch. "The scepter of justice," used only in Psalm 45:6, occurs in Neo-Assyrian texts concerning monarchs whose pursuits of justice are commended in this way: "The king my lord has revived the one who was guilty (and) condemned to death. The one who was imprisoned for many years is released. Those who were sick for many days have got well, the hungry have been sated, the parched have been anointed, the naked have been covered with clothes."[28] Such a background helps us to understand better the justice function of the ideal monarch in Israel. It also again shows that this ideal is not restricted to Israel or the church.

Where patterned, institutionalized maldistribution exists, the first duty of government is to correct it.[29] The welfare task of the government then takes place in the context of a specific commitment of the state to the interests of oppressed classes or groups within the society. Advancing justice requires a change in the balance of power among the groups of the society. The state functions to modify the society by reducing disproportions of power by conscious shifts in the balance of power. The taxing powers are used not merely for current revenue needs but also to deconcentrate power through the redistribution of income.[30] With criteria attuned to basic needs of the people, the state watches over the justice of the distributing operations of the economy.[31] As Aristotle put it, the purpose of the state is not merely to prevent mutual harm and facilitate the exchange of goods, although these are necessary preconditions. The purpose is the good life, life that is full and sufficient (*Politics* 1280b30-35; cf. 1252b30). This life relates to proper temporal needs, rather than to materialistic accumulation (1257b43).

Looking at the biblical materials that describe normatively the duties of the ruler, we see that a basic responsibility is to deliver the needy and to shepherd them so that they receive the daily necessities of life. Such care is understood to be the duty of all rulers, "Christian" or not.

28. Letter by Adad-Shumu-usur to King Assurbanipal, ABL no. 2, 10, cited in J. P. J. Olivier, "The Sceptre of Justice and Ps. 45:7b," *Journal of Northwest Semitic Languages* 7 (1979): 50. Cf. Ezek. 34:4; Ps. 146:7-9.

29. Maguire, 92-93.

30. Niebuhr, *Human Destiny,* 266.

31. Cf. José Porfirio Miranda, *Marx and the Bible: A Critique of the Philosophy of Oppression* (Maryknoll, N.Y.: Orbis, 1974), 30.

The Requirements of Justice

Justice, we have seen, determines the application of intervening power and defines the tasks of government. To understand more completely the state's role in welfare, the nature of biblical justice must be addressed more fully.

Justice identifies what is essential in life shared together in community and indicates the proper tasks of the government in supporting the common good. The nature of justice defines the work of government so fundamentally that statements of the purpose of government must depend upon that understanding. As James Madison wrote, "Justice is the end of government. It is the end of civil society. It has ever been and ever will be pursued until it be obtained, or until liberty be lost in the pursuit."[32] Yet, while justice is widely accepted as stating the purpose of government, there is great disagreement concerning the nature of justice.[33]

Human rights, the fabric of justice, are grounded by Christian theology in the dignity bestowed on every person by God's universal love, particularly as demonstrated in creation (Gen. 9:6; Job 31:13-15) and in Christ's atonement (Rom. 5:6-10). As *rights* they reflect the respect that is due to every person. Such respect is integral to the command of universal love, corresponding to God's love (Matt. 5:43-48; 1 John 3:16; 4:10-11, 19).

In the context of the Judeo-Christian affirmation of the goodness of the material and social creation, human rights uphold human dignity by supporting the basic requirements for the material and social well-being of every person. Rights spell out permanently, for individuals and communities, the fixed duties that constitute the meaning of love in typical situations of competing claims on neighborly love, such as limited material resources. Rights extend the gaze of love from spontaneous responses to the needs of individuals to the formal structure of the interaction of the groups within which individuals are caught up.

To treat people equally, justice looks for barriers that interfere with their chances to be equal in the basic goods of society or to be participating members in the community. It takes into consideration certain handicaps that hinder pursuit of the opportunities for life in society.

The handicaps that justice considers go beyond individual physical

32. James Madison, *The Federalist,* No. 51.

33. For further biblical documentation for this section on justice, see S. C. Mott, *A Christian Perspective on Political Thought* (New York: Oxford Univ. Press, 1993), ch. 5.

disabilities and personal plights. Significant handicaps can be found in poverty or prejudice. A just society considers and protects the good life of each person. It provides equal protection to all and removes any discrimination that prevents equality of opportunity. Distributive justice describes the standard by which the advantages of living in society are assigned. Considering and protecting the good life include a substantive justice that gives special consideration to disadvantaged groups by providing essential social and economic assets that they cannot otherwise obtain.[34] Several aspects of biblical justice support this understanding of distributive justice.

The close relationship of biblical justice to love and grace[35] makes justice creatively attentive to differences in need and oriented to those who are afflicted in their social relations. Because of unequal needs, equal provision of basic rights requires justice to be partial in order to be impartial. Partiality to the weak is the most striking characteristic of biblical justice.[36] In the raging social struggles in which the poor are perennially victims of injustice, God and the followers of God take up the cause of the weak. Throughout the Bible rulers and leaders are called on to exercise justice through concern for the weak and powerless.[37]

The good life in Scripture is understood in terms of the social nature of humanity, which we discussed above. Justice is restoration to community. In deliverance, with which justice is closely associated,[38] the people are returned to the situation of life in community that God intends for them. As seen in the jubilee and formulated in Leviticus 25:35-36, the poor are described as being on the verge of falling out of the community because of their economic distress: "Their power is diminished *with you*." It is, then, in a context of communal solidarity that the dignity of the poor is upheld. The rest of the community is reminded that poor are their own flesh (Isa. 58:7) and that they too once were in need (Exod. 23:9).

The community's responsibility to its diminished members is "to make

34. Cf. William Frankena, "The Concept of Social Justice," in R. Brandt, ed., *Social Justice* (Englewood Cliffs, N.J.: Prentice-Hall, 1962), 18-21.

35. Deut. 10:18-19; Isa. 30:18; Jer. 9:24; Hos. 2:19; 10:12; 12:7; Mic. 6:8.

36. Cf. Norman H. Snaith, *The Distinctive Ideas of the Old Testament* (London: Epworth, 1944), 68, 71-72, and James H. Cone, *God of the Oppressed* (New York: Seabury, 1975), 70-71.

37. Ps. 72:1-4; Prov. 31:8-9; Isa. 1:10, 17, 23, 26; Jer. 22:2-3, 14-15; Dan. 4:27.

38. Justice is deliverance, and the ruler accordingly is required to provide deliverance from oppression (Jer. 21:12; 22:2-3; Ps. 72:4).

them strong" again, restoring them to participation in community (Lev. 25:35). The purpose of this empowerment is "that they may live *beside you* in the land." Indeed, Sodom was condemned for not carrying out this empowerment of the poor, thus showing the universality of this mandate beyond the Mosaic covenantal community (Ezek. 16:49). In Psalm 107:36 (NRSV) the hungry, who receive God's steadfast love, are able to "establish a town to live in." Once more they can be active, participating members of a community. The concern is for the person in community and what it takes to maintain the individual in that relationship. Community membership means the ability to share fully within one's capacity and potential in each essential aspect of community.[39]

Participation in community has multiple dimensions. Its spheres include political protection and decision making, social interchange and standing, economic production, education, culture, and religion. It also includes physical life itself and the food and shelter most commonly associated with welfare.

Ensuring the conditions for participation in community requires a focus on the basic needs for life in community. Achieving such justice includes provision of material essentials of life, such as food and shelter: "The LORD . . . executes justice for the orphan and the widow, and loves the strangers, providing them food and clothing" (Deut. 10:18, NRSV). According to the psalmist, the Lord "executes justice for the oppressed [and] gives food to the hungry" (Ps. 146:7, NRSV).[40] "Food and clothing" is a Hebraism for what is indispensable.[41] In an important modern statement of benefit rights, Pope John XXIII, in the encyclical *Pacem in Terris,* stated that each person has the right "to the means necessary for the proper development of life, particularly food, clothing, shelter, medical care, rest, and finally, the necessary social services."[42]

39. Rights are the privileges of membership in the communities to which we belong. Cf. Max L. Stackhouse, *Creeds, Society, and Human Rights: A Study in Three Cultures* (Grand Rapids, Mich.: Eerdmans, 1984), 5, 44, 104-5.

40. Job 24, describing the benefits that are taken away through injustice, includes food (vv. 6, 10), drink (v. 11), clothing, and shelter (vv. 7, 10). Cf. Job 22, where injustice includes the sins of omission of withholding drink from the weary and bread from the hungry (vv. 7, 23; cf. 8:6; 31:17, 19).

41. C. Spicq, *Les Épîtres Pastorales,* Études Bibliques, 4th ed. (Paris: Gabalda, 1969), 190 (on 1 Tim. 6:8).

42. Pope John XXIII, *Pacem in Terris,* 11, in C. Carlen, ed., *Papal Encyclicals,* vol. 5: *1958–1981* (n.p.: Consortium, 1981), 108.

The inclusion in biblical justice of these material essentials for life in community conflicts with the philosophy of the negative state, which does not recognize benefit rights. The freedom (or procedural) rights that are protected in the idea of the negative state are indeed crucial to justice. Biblical justice, however, also includes positive rights, which are the responsibility of the community to ensure. The ruler is not pictured as a power who is neutral and only punitive. The needs to which justice responds are civil and political, but also social and economic.

Indeed, the Law, which justice ought to enforce, contained a long list of benefit rights. Holding as security a matter essential for life was proscribed as a matter of "justice" (Deut. 24:12-13). Interest on consumptive loans was prohibited as a harmful economic activity that threatened a person's community status (Lev. 25:35-37). The Law provided land to each extended family (Lev. 25), also a matter of justice.[43] Food was the subject of several of the stipulations of the Law. The poor received food in the sabbatical year (Exod. 23:10-11) and in what was passed over in the first harvesting (Deut. 24:19-22; Lev. 19:9-10). The hungry were to be allowed immediate consumption of food in the grainfields (Deut. 23:24-25). By a transfer payment, every third year 10 percent of the harvest was put in storehouses in the towns for the poor (Deut. 14:28). Those who were without land or otherwise were unable to be self-sufficient still had rights in the land.[44] Their powerless situation was recognized, and they were given a degree of empowerment to produce from the land or to be fed from it. These rights limited the control of others over their own productive property and the profit from it.

The partiality of justice thus means that some sectors of the community bear a heavier burden for the provision of benefit rights. Benefit rights draw from a base of economic resources that is limited in extent, so that those with more than they need are called on to share with fellow citizens who have widely varying needs.

The traditional criterion of distributive justice that is most appropriate for biblical justice is distribution according to needs. When justice is set forth by biblical writers, it is the basic needs for inclusion in commu-

43. Land is the provision of justice in Num. 27:5-6. Moses brings before the Lord an appeal for "justice" (["case," NRSV] v. 5) in land inheritance.

44. Cf. Walter Rauchenbusch, *Christianity and the Social Crisis* (Boston: Pilgrim, 1907), 20.

nity that are addressed, and these concerns give direction to the economic, social, and legal ordering of the community. The government's just role thus must include nurturing and monitoring other institutions of society and supplementing them as required so that the essential conditions for fulfillment of the basic needs of all are maintained. Often this means that the state must use the system of taxation to provide directly for the food, shelter, and health needs of the poor.

To carry out the responsibilities of intervening power required of them, civil authorities must consider assistance to the weak to be one of their central tasks. The deliverance that the poor, as social beings, receive is a restoration to community, which includes the material essentials of life in community. A benefit-oriented justice directs the proper concerns of government and law.

Premodern Governmental Welfare

This interpretation of Scripture is confirmed by the long tradition of the church. It is confirmed as well by the long history of government provision of financial assistance to the needy.

Those who consider governmental welfare to be a modern invention need only be reminded of street names in many of our older towns. "Town Farm Road" once went to the residence provided by the community for the poor. In Gloucester, Massachusetts, for example, a third of the town budget in 1757 went to provisions for the poor.[45] What is new about the twentieth-century developments is not the initiation of a key government role in helping the needy but rather the centralization of funding and regulation of such help at the state and federal levels. Neither municipal nor central expressions of care for the poor would have been a surprise to earlier inhabitants of Western nations.

45. H. Wheatland et al., eds., *The Standard History of Essex County, Massachusetts* (Boston: Jewett, 1878), 141. What is important is the principle; neither the number of the poor nor the size of the total town budget was high. In 1776, the town took out a loan for this provision for the poor. John D. Babson, *History of the Town of Gloucester, Cape Ann, 1860* (Gloucester, Mass.: Peter Smith, 1972), 408.

The Historical Role of Government Welfare

From the beginning, Christians have recognized that their theology requires government care of the poor. Ancient Christians inherited this understanding not only from biblical faith but also from the Hellenistic and Roman conception of the emperor as the "head of the community" *(Pater Patriae)* with a special concern for the welfare of the weak, especially the elderly, women, and children.[46]

Byzantine and late Roman emperors had responsibilities for feeding their people. In the late Middle Ages the monarch's traditional role as guardian of the common good was appealed to as grounds for the crown's assumption of supervisory responsibilities over relief operations. From then on the central state was generally considered to have a duty to look after the poor, although even earlier there are significant examples of royal alimony.[47]

Throughout the Middle Ages the primary institution in charge of welfare was the church. For the parish level, the Fourth Lateran Council of 1215 reinforced a time-honored practice, stating that a fixed and adequate portion of the revenues of the church was to go to the care of the poor. The mandatory revenues supplemented a great variety of voluntary giving and care by individuals and groups within the church.

Ecclesiastical responsibilities were not separated from the civil, however, in the sense of a distinction of the voluntary or private from the public and legal, or of modern conceptions of the separation of church and state. The church's laws had a civil nature. They were enforced in ecclesiastical courts, in which the higher penalties were imprisonment or excommunication. The tithes for the revenues of the church were legally binding taxes.[48]

Civic life was not seen as separate from religious life. Imperial authority and the church cooperated for the unfortunate. Constantine autho-

46. Thomas Wiedemann, *Adults and Children in the Roman Empire* (New Haven: Yale Univ. Press, 1989), 39.

47. Such as under Louis IX of France in the thirteenth century. See Mìchel Mollat, *The Poor in the Middle Ages*, 1978 (New Haven: Yale Univ. Press, 1986), 19, 137, 272. Appeals for royal administrative supervision were made by Philippe de Mézières, Dom Pedro, and Geiter of Kayersberg. King Manuel of Portugal carried out such reform in 1498.

48. Brian Tierney, *Medieval Poor Law: A Sketch of Canonical Theory and Its Application in England* (Berkeley: Univ. of California Press, 1959), 3, 5, 83, 96-97.

rized the church to receive legacies for this purpose, and his successors expanded such measures. The government saw to it that the property of church and monasteries and alms were used for charitable purposes. For example, in 1324 the count ordered the monasteries of Ghent to distribute immediately all the grain in warehouses collected from the tithe.[49]

The interconnection of secular and ecclesiastical authority regarding welfare was particularly pronounced at the municipal level in the late Middle Ages. As early as the twelfth century, city officials began to establish controls over traditional charitable institutions, such as leper hospitals.[50] The number of cities grew rapidly in this period. They developed an urban consciousness and a new system of urban law. At the heart of this law was a covenant, which included a promise of mutual assistance and protection with regard to all aspects of the community's social, economic, and political life for those in the subordinated communities on which the city was founded. Included was assistance to the poor. The cities and towns were regarded as divinely instituted for such tasks.[51] Emergency situations in which church funds were insufficient provided another occasion for the expansion of secular authority.[52]

By the thirteenth century, as the city developed into a political corporation, organized citizens extended its legal powers into welfare areas that had been the preserve of the church. Hospitals were a key institution. Since the citizens had already been providing the means for such activities, they laid claims upon the right of control also. By the fourteenth century, the norm was that the jurisdiction of the church in hospitals was limited to pastoral care.

In this transition a supervisory role by elected town administrators over relief of the poor developed first. Significant secular funding came later. In cases of loans, funds did come from the monarch, the state bank, or town revenues. For the Poor Table, which was the center for distribution to the poor, funds sometimes came from town revenues. Other forms of aid in which public roles became increasingly evident included lawyers appointed for the poor and pawnbroking institutions. Relief became more

49. Carter H. Lindberg, *Beyond Charity: Reformation Initiatives for the Poor* (Minneapolis: Fortress, 1993), 52; Mollat, 19-20, 160.

50. Mollat, 100.

51. Harold J. Berman, *Law and Revolution: The Formation of the Western Legal Tradition* (Cambridge: Harvard Univ. Press, 1983), 356, 393-95; Lindberg, 53-54.

52. Mollat, 161, 272; Lindberg, 80.

regulated, with tighter designations of those eligible for help, restrictions on begging, work requirements, and residences for those who were eligible for relief.[53]

In summary, while the church was the basic institution for the financial relief of the poor in the Middle Ages, its responsibilities had a significant civil character. Certain forms of giving for the poor were mandatory and upheld by courts of law. The church's task also was increasingly more closely interconnected with central, territorial, and particularly municipal secular authorities.

The Contribution of the Protestant Reformation

The Protestant Reformation provided strong impetus to the late medieval transition to increased secular involvement in welfare relief for the poor. Martin Luther approached this subject from the vantage point of his central conception of justification by grace alone through faith. He viewed the many layers of ecclesiastical giving to the poor as an expression of seeking salvation through merit. The transfer of welfare to secular government was a means to purify the church.

For Luther, as well as for Erasmus and others, the purpose of charity was the service of one's neighbor. Giving to the poor was an integral aspect of being a Christian, not its grounds. For Ulrich Zwingli, the decision for the gospel was also a decision for the public good. In the Protestant cities this perspective was worked out in making social welfare a public duty of the entire community.[54]

The communal response to the evangelical commandment of love for the neighbor was combined with the Protestant sense of the spiritual significance of the active life. Luther proclaimed that "after the Gospel or the ministry," there is no greater virtue than that of a ruler who makes and enforces just laws. Such rule aids those who are really poor more effectively than charity. It is a virtue greater than the rightly lauded act of a prince or princess washing the feet of the poor. It makes the whole land into a kind of charitable institution.[55] As Andreas Karlstadt (later Luther's opponent but in this matter

53. Lindberg, 54-63; Mollat, 140, 144-45, 278, 290-91, 298-99.

54. Lindberg, 72, 94, 125, 143.

55. Martin Luther, "Psalm 82," in *Luther's Works,* vol. 13: *Selected Psalms,* ed. J. Pelikan (Philadelphia: Concordia, 1956), 53-54; cf. Lindberg, 109, 116.

influenced by Luther) put it, "Where one falls into poverty, everyone, and in particular the highest civil authority, should have compassion upon the poor and . . . open his hand and lend the poor brother what he needs." Karlstadt went on to appeal to "princes, officials, mayors, judges, village-mayors, and other magistrates" to examine how they could use their particular station to maintain the poor.[56] Luther assigned to the territorial state the authority that the church had previously held over socioeconomic matters.[57]

Luther shared the earlier perspective of seeing the civil community and the church community as coextensive, forming a single unit in which state and church were not easily distinguishable. "Every city should support its own poor" and supervise it, such as through a warden.[58] Luther advocated two basic models. In one the funds came from voluntary sources, particularly funds from expropriated church properties, foundations, and testaments. The municipality would provide the administration.

The other model that Luther enthusiastically supported and advocated was that of Leisnig (1523), in which the maintenance of the poor was funded by taxation. In Johann Eberlin's Protestant utopia (1521), the city's common purse was to provide what was needed for the poor beyond that which the churches supplied. And as the alternative to the priests, whom Eberlin viewed as exploiting the poor for their own gain, the authorities would have great diligence for the poor.[59]

John Calvin, for his part, had an activistic and functional view of the state — more so than most of the Christian theologians who preceded him. For him the state is a humanizing force. Because of sin it is "a means of preservation, now indeed indispensable."[60] He cited the Old Testament

56. Andreas Karlstadt, "There Should Be No Beggars among Christians" (1522), ed. C. Lindberg, in C. Lindberg, ed., *Piety, Politics, and Ethics*, G. W. Forell Festschrift, Sixteenth Century Essays & Studies 3 (Kirksville, Mo.: Sixteenth Century Journal, 1984), 161; cf. Lindberg, 120-21.

57. Lindberg, 113.

58. Martin Luther, "To the Christian Nobility of the German Nation Concerning the Reform of the Christian Estate" (1520), in *Luther's Works*, vol. 44: *The Christian in Society*, ed. J. Atkinson (Philadelphia: Fortress, 1966), 189-90; cf. Lindberg, 105.

59. Lindberg, 75, 123, 125, 128, 132; cf. W. D. J. Cargill Thompson, *The Political Thought of Martin Luther*, ed. P. Broadhead (Sussex: Harvester, 1984), 167. Many Roman Catholic cities adopted these Lutheran social innovations (Lindberg, 146).

60. As phrased by Abraham Kuyper, *Lectures on Calvinism*, Stone Foundation Lectures, 1898 (Grand Rapids, Mich.: Eerdmans, 1931), 81.

passages regarding rulers executing justice by delivering the poor and widow. The rulers are to "give aid and protection to the oppressed."[61] The purpose of government is the promotion of peace and well-being, as well as the worship of God.[62]

Harro Höpfl has demonstrated that Calvin believed that if every Christian commonwealth were to do its duty of righteousness and piety, amelioration of the world would result. The key change would be for communities to implement fully the laws already in existence. These laws included centuries-old provisions for the poor, regulations concerning just wages, schools, and hospitals, and measures to discourage luxury.[63]

The Protestant Reformation thus gave strong theological affirmation, and in their cities actual working models, of the state's responsibility to provide material support for the poor.

Conclusion

We have demonstrated that the responsibility of the government for the welfare of the poor is firmly grounded in biblical thought and in the structure of Christian theology. Because human beings are social by nature, when the community does not otherwise sufficiently provide care for the weak, collective action and authority are needed. The fallen condition of life requires an intervening power to guarantee basic human needs and to resist the forces that deny them. Government is guided in this by the principle of justice, which is attentive to differences in need and requires that some sectors of the community bear a heavier burden for the provision of benefit rights.

61. John Calvin, *Institutes of the Christian Religion,* ed. J. McNeill, Library of Christian Classics, 20-21 (Philadelphia: Westminster, 1960), 4.20.9 (p. 1496), citing Jer. 22:3 and Ps. 82:3-4. Calvin saw the Israelite state as a model for other states, since God had used the best conceivable means to lead God's people to peace and harmony. This application was distinguished from Israel's peculiar role as a type of the future rule of Christ. Gisbert Beyerhaus, *Studien zur Staatsanschauung Calvins,* Neue Studien zur Geschichte der Theologie und der Kirche 7 (Berlin: Trowitzsch, 1910), 132, 140.

62. Calvin, 4.20.9, pp. 1495-96.

63. Höpfl, *The Christian Polity of John Calvin,* Studies in the History and Theory of Politics (Cambridge: Cambridge Univ. Press, 1982), 195-96. The magistrates' power also was essential for public institutions for the relief of distress (p. 191).

This interpretation of Scripture is affirmed by the tradition of the church prior to the modern period. In the late Middle Ages the church was the institution primarily responsible for financial aid to the poor, but its role had a significant civil character. Its regulations and tithes were legally enforced, and its responsibilities were increasingly interconnected with that of the municipalities. The transition to municipal control of welfare received a significant impetus from the Protestant Reformation, which made social welfare a public duty of the entire community, replacing ecclesiastical giving to the poor, which was viewed as an attempt to gain salvation by merit. Theology and history thus provide a foundation for governmental welfare.

This demonstration does not dictate a particular public policy stance in our present situation. The materials in fact indicate a variety of relationships between the government and the civil community in carrying out this responsibility. It does, however, establish in principle the normativeness of the government's responsibility in this area.

The government's provision of goods and services to the needy may not be the most important task it can perform for them. Vital changes such as the modification of power relationships, the establishment of a new order of priorities in society, and the encouragement of new models of life and culture are not accomplished in this way. Government welfare remains, however, a continual need, and it is a permanent responsibility of human communities.

The Poverty Debate and Human Nature

Lawrence M. Mead

POVERTY is the most important issue in American social policy. In the world's richest country, 37 million Americans were poor in 1992, or 14.5 percent of the population. Within poverty, the core issue is welfare. About 14 million people currently live on Aid to Families with Dependent Children (AFDC), the most important national welfare program.[1] Many of them are dependent long-term, and this group is at the center of the nation's worst social ills, including child abuse, school failure, drug addiction, homelessness, and crime.

Controversy over poverty and its associated evils is intense, strong enough to dominate national politics at many moments. Such social issues helped elect the Republican majority to Congress in 1994. Roughly, the dispute is about whether to provide new advantages to the poor or "get tough" with them. We should not interpret the debate as a classic struggle between liberals and conservatives over the size of government. Rather, the poverty controversy has a different pattern that I call dependency politics. At issue is not so much the scale of government as whether to hold poor adults responsible for the conduct that, in many cases, makes them poor. Typically, conservatives do not seek to abandon the poor, but they do want to enforce good behavior. Liberals resist.

1. U.S. Department of Commerce, Bureau of the Census, *Poverty in the United States: 1992,* Series P-60, No. 185 (Washington, D.C.: GPO, Sept. 1993), table 1; U.S. House of Representatives, Committee on Ways and Means, *Overview of Entitlement Programs: 1993 Green Book* (Washington, D.C.: GPO, June 7, 1993), 685.

Our political culture is not honest in confronting problems involving personal behavior, and that is one reason poverty persists. Most serious poverty today results because the parents of children fail to stay together and to work. Our leaders, however, often sidestep these problems. They recommend opportunity-oriented solutions that assume that the poor are already self-reliant. We want to "liberate" or "empower" them to get ahead on their own. Such measures achieve little for the seriously poor because they commonly lack the personal organization to take advantage of opportunity. A paternalistic social policy — one that combines support with requirements that the dependent function in minimal ways — would achieve more. But such an approach is difficult to square with our beliefs that everyone can be a self-reliant individualist and that expanding freedom is the purpose of government.

Organized religion bears considerable blame for the impasse. The institutional church has stiffly resisted a more authoritative social policy. Liberal church people assign the entire responsibility for poverty to society, dismissing talk of behavioral problems as unloving, while fundamentalists would cut back government programs in the name of "traditional values." A more thoughtful — and more biblical — theology of poverty might prepare the society to confront the problem more honestly. An ideal policy would emphasize tough governmental enforcement of essential civilities such as law-abidingness and work effort, but would also assign a key role to nongovernmental organizations, including churches. They would help enforce the essential civilities, promote other virtues beyond the minimal, and build personal relationships with the needy. Such a conception is actually quite close to what Christians have understood as community.

The sections below briefly describe the current poverty problem, what research and policy experience suggest about it, the political controversy about it, the shortcomings of that debate, the role of religious beliefs in the problem, and an alternative theology and policy that would achieve more.

Poverty and Its Causes

Depending on how expansively "poverty" is defined, it embraces anywhere from 25 percent to less than 5 percent of the American population. The problem looks larger if one sets a higher poverty line, defines poverty in narrowly economic terms, as the government does, and measures the poor at a moment in time. The problem looks smaller if one sets a lower poverty line, limits the poor to people with serious personal problems, and measures poverty over time, since less than half of those who become poor stay that way for more than two years. Many Americans encounter "hard times" for a year or two, but very few belong to the "underclass."

This discussion takes a moderate position. I define poverty in income terms as the government does, but I focus on the subgroups that raise behavioral issues and thus cause the greatest political concern. These are the long-term poor, meaning those who remain poor for several years, and especially those among the long-term poor who are of working age. These groups comprise, respectively, about a half and a third of the poor measured in a single year.[2] Currently, that implies numbers of 18 and 12 million people, or 7 and 5 percent of the population.[3] Thus understood, the poor are not numerous, but their presence and problems have still been enough to preoccupy domestic policy.

Poverty is not new. Western societies have always contained destitute people, and there has always been debate over how to cope with them. But poverty was largely a local concern. In America it became prominent as a national issue only in the 1960s. Three changes largely explain this. One is that the poor are much more obtrusive to the better-off today than a generation ago. Many rural poor people, particularly blacks from the South and Hispanics from Mexico and Puerto Rico, have moved to northern cities, where they are more visible. Mentally ill people have been dismissed from mental hospitals, and the police have less authority to evict vagrants from the streets than they formerly did. For the middle class, it is one thing to read of destitute sharecroppers in Mississippi, quite another to be accosted by panhandlers on the streets of New York.

A second change is that today's poor are notably less self-reliant than yesteryear's. Serious poverty today usually arises, at least in the first instance, from the lifestyle of the poor themselves. Most often, the initial cause is that poor parents have children out of wedlock, the fathers do not support them, and the mothers go on welfare rather than work themselves. The hallmark of today's poor adults is that they seldom work consistently. In

2. Mary Jo Bane and David T. Ellwood, "Slipping into and out of Poverty: The Dynamics of Spells," *Journal of Human Resources* 21, no. 1 (1986): 12; Isabel V. Sawhill, "The Underclass: An Overview," *Public Interest,* no. 96 (1989): 4-6.

3. Bureau of the Census, *Poverty 1992,* tables 1, 3.

1959, 68 percent of the heads of poor families worked at some time in the year, but in 1992 only 49 percent did so. Over the same years, the percentage working full-year and full-time dropped from 31 to 15 percent.[4] Almost all this decline occurred by 1975; there has been little change since. As fewer of the poor have worked, more have lived off welfare and other benefit programs. AFDC grew from 4 million recipients in 1960 to nearly 14 million in 1992.[5]

Much of the work decline is due to the simple fact that rising wages pulled most of the working poor out of poverty in these years. It is natural that the remaining poor should now largely be nonworking. However, it seems that many of the remaining poor could also work. While most welfare mothers are not employed, three-quarters of other single mothers do work, over half of them full-time. The proportion of poor who are working-aged — not children or elderly — has risen since the 1960s, and is now 50 percent, yet the proportion of the employable poor who actually work has fallen.[6]

Meanwhile, work levels among the rest of the population have risen to the highest levels in history, as women and teenagers have flooded into jobs in unprecedented numbers. Table 1 on page 213 contrasts the proportions of the poor and nonpoor, in several demographic categories, who worked in 1991.

In all categories, the difference in work level between the poor and the nonpoor is enormous, particularly for full-year, full-time employment, where the multiple is four or five times. This divergence in employment trends between the bottom and the middle of society has made programs to help the working-aged poor — especially welfare programs — immensely more controversial than before.

4. U.S. Department of Commerce, Bureau of the Census, *Characteristics of the Population below the Poverty Level: 1984*, Series P-60, no. 152 (Washington, D.C.: GPO, June 1986), table 4; Bureau of the Census, *Poverty 1992*, table 19.

5. U.S. Department of Commerce, Bureau of the Census, *Statistical Abstract of the United States 1982–83* (Washington, D.C.: GPO, Dec. 1982), 340; Committee on Ways and Means, 685.

6. Bureau of the Census, *Poverty 1992*, table 3; Sheldon Danziger and Peter Gottschalk, "Work, Poverty, and the Working Poor: A Multifaceted Problem," *Monthly Labor Review* 109, no. 9 (1986): 17-21. A higher proportion of the poor are working-aged because the size of welfare families has fallen and rising Social Security payments have lifted most of the elderly and disabled out of poverty.

Table 1

	Poor	Nonpoor
Percent of individuals 15 and over who		
Worked at any time:	39.8	72.0
Full-year and full-time:	9.0	45.0
Percent of family heads who		
Worked at any time:	50.4	80.5
Full-year and full-time:	15.8	61.1
Percent of female family heads who		
Worked at any time:	42.4	76.1
Full-year and full-time:	9.5	54.5
Percent of families with two or more workers	16.8	62.6

SOURCE: U.S. Department of Commerce, Bureau of the Census, *Poverty in the United States: 1991,* Series P-60, no. 181 (Washington, DC: U.S. Government Printing Office, August 1992), xiv-xv.

A third change, perhaps the most fundamental, is that it is much tougher today than formerly to attribute poverty to forces outside the needy themselves.[7] Perhaps the poor fail to work because they are unable to. Before 1960, much of poverty could be blamed on the fact that unskilled wages were too low for many people to escape poverty even if they worked, or the fact that Jim Crow made it difficult for many nonwhites to find jobs. More recent explanations are that the poor cannot work because factory jobs have left the inner city, white-collar jobs require too much education, immigrants are taking jobs away from poor Americans, child care is lacking, welfare creates disincentives against work (because grants are reduced if earnings rise), or welfare recipients lack the skills for employment.

Unfortunately, there is little basis for any of these theories today. Due to economic growth, it is now rare for families to be poor long-term by the official standard if the adults work regular hours. Due to civil rights reforms, the nonwhite poor are seldom kept out of all employment, and the black

7. The following discussion draws on Lawrence M. Mead, *The New Politics of Poverty: The Nonworking Poor in America* (New York: Basic Books, 1992), chs. 3–8, and Mead, "Poverty: How Little We Know," *Social Service Review* 68, no. 3 (1994): 322-50.

middle class has grown. Research suggests that jobs, at least at low wages, commonly are available, at least to those seeking them at a given time. Immigrants do not appear to be crowding the poor out of jobs, welfare disincentives are weaker than supposed, and a lack of child care or skills is seldom a bar to working in some job. Each of these factors explains a small part of the work problem, but none can account for the huge difference in work levels between the poor and nonpoor.[8]

Among many commentators, the view that poverty must be due to racial bias is irrepressible. After all, most of the long-term poor are black. Perhaps white people no longer talk like racists, liberals say, but they still refuse to accept blacks as equals, and this explains the degradation of the group.[9] Yet most experts doubt that race can be the immediate cause of the current social problem. It is true that most whites resist aggressive policies to promote racial equality such as busing, affirmative action, or other preferences for blacks, but overt prejudice against blacks clearly has declined. And these favorable developments occurred in the same period when entrenched poverty appeared among inner-city blacks. Since the two directions of change are inverse, race cannot be the immediate cause of the ghetto. More plausibly, historic racism produced the disadvantage and defeatism now found among the worst-off blacks, and this, much more than any contemporary bias, now keeps them poor.[10]

This is not to deny that racism is still an evil in American life. Middle-class blacks and women seeking professional careers still face some bias, and there is discrimination against minorities seeking housing in white areas. Unequal opportunity has a good deal to do with unequal fortunes among the employed. Above all, people with more education get better jobs than those with less, and deindustrialization clearly has hurt many factory workers. But on the whole, these facts do not explain poverty. By and large, those who suffer from barriers and unequal opportunity are working people, few of whom are poor long-term, while most of the poor are

8. Some argue that all the barriers together can explain nonwork, but this assumes they are independent and additive. In fact, many of them are competitive, so simply to aggregate them would exaggerate how much we can explain. How much of poverty all barriers explain is judgmental.

9. Andrew Hacker, *Two Nations: Black and White, Separate, Hostile, Unequal* (New York: Scribners, 1992).

10. William Julius Wilson, *The Declining Significance of Race: Blacks and Changing American Institutions*, 2nd ed. (Chicago: Univ. of Chicago Press, 1980).

nonworking. Injustice due to unequal chances is not generally the cause of poverty. Perhaps it is unfair that the black poor have to live in ghettos — but this does not usually explain why they seldom work steadily.[11] Social barriers explain *inequality among workers* much better than they do *lack of all employment*, which is now the initial cause of most poverty among the working-aged.

There is no longer any "smoking gun" out in society that can explain persistent poverty well. It remains a mystery why so many poor adults become poor when the chance to live better seems available. The main explanation, I believe, must lie in the historic backgrounds of the ethnic groups most likely to be poor — blacks, Hispanics, and Native Americans. While most members of these groups have escaped poverty and welfare, a minority of each, along with many whites, have succumbed to a conviction that there is no hope for them to prosper in America. That feeling seems to arise from the difficult histories of the heavily poor groups. The memory of past denials of opportunity, as mediated through harsh family lives, seems now to keep many nonwhites poor, even though society in recent decades has become more fair.

The point of mentioning these hard facts is not to deny help to people who appear "undeserving." It is rather to urge that the nature of that help must change. When people do not help themselves, benefits and opportunity are no longer sufficient to overcome poverty. Since the late 1970s, policymakers have tacitly agreed. Social policy has gradually given up reforming society and instead focused on managing the lives of the poor. One cause no doubt is conservative political trends in the nation, but the more fundamental reason is that structural explanations of poverty have become implausible. If poverty is due mainly to behavior rather than social barriers, then behavior, rather than society, must be changed. Above all, unwed childbearing must be discouraged and work levels raised.

Programs and policies that tried to uplift the poor without questioning lifestyle have achieved little. Training and education programs where participation is voluntary attract mainly the transient poor, those likely to get out of poverty without assistance. Work incentives in welfare, which

11. Christopher Jencks and Susan E. Mayer, "Residential Segregation, Job Proximity, and Black Job Opportunities," in Laurence E. Lynn, Jr., and Michael G. H. McGeary, eds., *Inner-City Poverty in the United States* (Washington, D.C.: National Academy Press, 1990), ch. 5.

allow working recipients to keep some earnings net of any reduction in their grants, have virtually no effect on work levels. Even giving the disadvantaged government jobs does not cause them to work more steadily in regular positions afterward. No voluntary policy has reached the core of the poverty population — long-term welfare mothers and their departed spouses — because none has caused them to work more consistently.

That is why social policy has turned toward enforcing work. Since 1967, and especially since 1988, AFDC has required rising proportions of welfare mothers to participate in work programs as a condition of eligibility for aid. States are using child support laws to require more absent fathers to work to help support their families. In addition, schools have enforced standards more firmly, homeless shelters police the conduct of their residents, and law enforcement has become tougher. The evidence is that such paternalist policies, which combine support for the poor with demands for functioning, offer more hope to ameliorate poverty than just doing more for the poor — or doing less. The best answer to poverty is not to subsidize people, or to abandon them. It is to direct lives.

Mandatory work programs in welfare have shown more power to raise work effort among the dependent than any voluntary policy. Such programs increase employment noticeably, although none to date has reduced the welfare rolls by much. They increase by much more the share of recipients doing something to help themselves — either working, looking for work, or training for jobs. The key to success is that the programs achieve high participation rates, and the key to this is that they be mandatory and enforce participation stringently. Secondarily, most participants must actually work rather than go into education or training. Outsiders sometimes say the programs are "forcing" people to work, but that would be to assume that the recipients oppose working. Actually, they want to work, "workfare" helps them do it, and as a result most clients support the programs.[12]

12. Lawrence M. Mead, "The Potential for Work Enforcement: A Study of WIN," *Journal of Policy Analysis and Management* 7, no. 2 (1988): 264-88; Mead, "Should Workfare Be Mandatory? What Research Says," *Journal of Policy Analysis and Management* 9, no. 3 (1990): 400-404.

The Politics of Poverty

The change in the character of poverty has reshaped American politics.[13] Before 1960, political debate took what I call a progressive form. The leading issue was how much government should do to promote the advancement of ordinary people. Should it intervene in the economy more or less, spend more or less? Should it protect people from unemployment and assist them with various benefit programs, or should it trust the free market to provide growing wealth and opportunity? Liberals typically said the former, conservatives the latter. The crucible of this debate was the Great Depression, when the New Deal vastly enlarged the role of government in the teeth of business opposition.

The battle was a structural one, over the values and the proper organization of society. Should government insulate people from the marketplace or not? The contest largely avoided personal issues. Both sides presumed that individuals were able to advance their own self-interest, if not society's. This premise, which I call the competence assumption, was taken for granted in all American thinking, on both right and left. Those who made claims in progressive politics were presumed to be workers, or if unemployed to have a steady work history. Take care of workers, it was believed, and families and children would take care of themselves.

After 1960, however, these issues were shoved back on the agenda by the disorders of the inner city. The great question became, not how to promote advancement among workers, but how to integrate disadvantaged groups who typically did not work. The race issue was transitional. The civil rights movement, and later feminism, began as progressive movements seeking greater opportunity for functioning citizens who usually were employed. The demand was compelling, more equal opportunity was granted, and working blacks and women advanced to higher income and status. But after civil rights, attention shifted to worse-off blacks who did not apparently profit from opportunity — the jobless welfare mothers and nonworking men of the inner city. The watershed was the middle and late 1960s, when urban riots broke out and the welfare rolls doubled.

Controversy over the new disorders fell into a pattern different from

13. The following discussion draws on Mead, *New Politics,* chs. 1–2, 9–11. For a parallel interpretation, see Myron A. Levine, *Presidential Campaigns and Elections: Issues, Image, and Partisanship* (Itasca, Ill.: F. E. Peacock, 1992).

that of the progressive era, what I call dependency politics. The key dispute was no longer about collectivism or the redistribution of wealth. It was about the personal lives of the poor — their propensity to unwed parenthood, crime, and above all nonwork. Typically, liberals approached the functional problems dispassionately, saying society was responsible and we must understand the "underlying causes." Conservatives exonerated society and blamed the problems on misconduct by the poor themselves.

Poverty called competence into question as the older working-class radicalism had not. Whereas progressive politics debated social organization and took personal organization for granted, dependency politics did just the opposite. Exactly because the poor were usually not employed, they were not "deserving," and demands to change the society could not be made in their name. Poverty posed a threat of crime, dependency, and declining schools, not radicalism. Personal behavior was intensely disputed, but basic changes in social arrangements could not be proposed. Largely because of this, the Great Society period of the 1960s and 1970s did not fundamentally enlarge the welfare state. It is true that spending for health and the elderly vastly increased, but the United States never enacted the programs of guaranteed jobs or income found in some European countries. While the Great Society is blamed for a bloated welfare system, dependency grew mainly because more people eligible for welfare decided to claim it, not because new programs were enacted.

The shift of focus from class to conduct can be seen in debates about how to reform welfare, the core issue of the new era. The earliest debates, in the 1960s, were progressive in tone. Liberals wanted to extend welfare coverage from single-parent to two-parent families, while conservatives resisted, fearful of the cost and burdens on the economy. Liberals wanted to federalize welfare, conservatives to keep it local. As female-headedness rose and work levels fell among the poor, however, these issues faded and behavioral issues came to the fore. The most contentious of these was whether to require adult recipients to work in return for support. By the 1980s, the work issue was ascendant, and the landmark Family Support Act of 1988 aimed primarily to strengthen work requirements. In debates on the act, the parties easily compromised their differences over welfare costs and coverage, but bitterly divided over how strong the work expectation should be.

The change from progressive to dependency themes clearly benefited Republicans. In the decades from the New Deal through 1964, Democrats won most presidential elections by proposing that government do more to help working Americans. But from 1968 on, Republicans won most elections, in large measure, by accusing Democrats of laxity on welfare and crime. Democrats' reluctance to enforce values such as the work ethic became even more unpopular than Republican resistance to bigger government had been. Jimmy Carter in 1976 and Bill Clinton in 1992 were able to defeat the GOP because of bad economic conditions, but also because they took conservative stands on social order issues. Clinton's promise to "end welfare as we know it" anchored his appeal to a restive middle class. Concern about crime and welfare were driving forces behind the Republicans' victory in the 1994 midterm election.

Is the Change Real?

Some social critics contend that the issues in politics have not really changed. Dependency themes such as crime and welfare are just red herrings used by the right to keep issues of class or racial equality off the agenda.[14] But the disorders are not the invention of conservative publicists; they pose real threats to the society, and the voters are naturally concerned. Some fear that conservative moralism will deny all help to the needy.

But while dependency politics has helped elect Republican officeholders, it does not serve the classical antigovernment agenda of the right. Traditional conservatives, like liberals, made the competence assumption. The population must be functional before greater redistribution to the needy can be justified, but also before government can be cut back. The nonworking poor cannot deserve new benefits, but neither could they survive without government. Ronald Reagan's hopes to cut the welfare state were largely defeated because Congress, and the public, would not countenance an abandonment of the poor. Reagan's real legacy was to strengthen work requirements in welfare.

Another rejoinder is that, even if poverty is a real issue, the best solution to it is still the progressive one. Keep focused on the economics of poverty,

14. Michael B. Katz, *In the Shadow of the Poorhouse: A Social History of Welfare in America* (New York: Basic Books, 1986); Frances Fox Piven and Richard A. Cloward, *Regulating the Poor: The Functions of Public Welfare*, updated ed. (New York: Vintage, 1993).

and the behavioral problems will take care of themselves. For a liberal, that means to build up government and benefits for the poor; for a conservative, to cut them back. Each expects that if the scale of effort changes in the recommended direction, dysfunction will recede. To change how much is spent and done will somehow "send a message" to the poor. In the liberal version, if society manifests its commitment to the needy, they will be encouraged and function better. In the conservative version, if society reduces support to the "undeserving," they will have to work and marry or starve.[15] Unfortunately, there is little evidence for either position. The Great Society era saw a massive buildup of spending on poverty, the Reagan era a more limited cutting back. But neither shift solved entrenched poverty, because neither caused nonworking adults to take and hold available jobs.

Yet a further reply is that the answer is still to change the scale of government, but there must be programs specifically aimed at competence. Liberal theorists say that government must guarantee "agency" to the poor, meaning the ability to act effectively in their own interests, through education and training services focused on skills. Society must assure the "self-respect" that is essential to responsible citizenship.[16] But government lacks the capacity to provide agency, even if it wanted to. Even the most successful training and education programs have only minor effects on the abilities of their participants.[17] Even the new, paternalist social policies change the behavior of the poor much more than their skills. Overwhelmingly, the capacities of people are determined by their family and social background, and government can do very little to increase them.[18]

This is not to say that the lesser confidence of some groups in America

15. For the liberal viewpoint, see Margaret Weir et al., eds., *The Politics of Social Policy in the United States* (Princeton: Princeton Univ. Press, 1988). For the conservative view, see Charles Murray, *Losing Ground: American Social Policy, 1950–1980* (New York: Basic Books, 1984).

16. Amy Gutmann, ed., *Democracy and the Welfare State* (Princeton: Princeton Univ. Press, 1988), chs. 1–3, 5, 11.

17. Some argue that very intensive programs that intervene in the family and reach children at a young age could achieve more, but the best results are recorded by exemplary, experimental programs that could not be implemented on a large scale. See Lisbeth B. Schorr with Daniel Schorr, *Within Our Reach: Breaking the Cycle of Disadvantage* (New York: Doubleday, 1988).

18. Henry J. Aaron, *Politics and the Professors: The Great Society in Perspective* (Washington, D.C.: Brookings, 1978).

may not ultimately be society's fault. The fact that blacks and other minorities succumb to poverty much more often than whites probably is due largely to the inferior opportunity these groups suffered in times past, not only in this country but in their countries of origin in the Third World. Their historical experience simply has not ratified the confident belief in individual mastery that animates the white population, which looks back to a more fortunate history in America and Europe. For this reason, white society owes an ongoing obligation to improve conditions for nonwhites.

However, the tie between social structure and poverty now lies too far back in time for social changes to achieve much. Society may ultimately have caused today's poor adults to function poorly, but the damage is passed on largely by what they themselves do. Poverty is sustained less because society is still unfair than because of the upbringing children receive in poor families. Too often, disadvantaged adults prove to be ineffective parents. They do not prepare their children well to succeed, and the children are likely, in turn, to fail their offspring. The pattern can continue through generations, incubated in the family, even though the outside society has become more fair.

The family weakness is closely related to the work problem. Adults who do not work steadily lack the resources to succeed as parents. Poor fathers abandon their children and the mothers go on welfare largely for lack of earnings. They also lack the authority to pass on the society's values to children. Parents who do not get through school or work steadily can hardly convince their offspring to do so. If their parents are defeated by the outside world, children easily conclude that they will be, too. They then approach school or the job market without hope, expecting to fail themselves, and that fear becomes self-fulfilling.

Family problems, of course, are not unique to the poor. The quality of parenting seems to have declined among Americans of all backgrounds in recent decades. Adults have spent more time on themselves and their careers, less on homemaking and child rearing. Middle-class children suffer some of the same neglect seen among welfare children. If the poor are doing worse as parents, they may have learned it from their betters.[19] Family problems, however, are nowhere near as serious among the middle class as among the poor, and the connection to work is opposite: for most Amer-

19. Myron Magnet, *The Dream and the Nightmare: The Sixties' Legacy to the Underclass* (New York: William Morrow, 1993).

icans, the main strain on the family is too much parental employment; for the poor, it is too little.

The claim that injustice explains dysfunction sounds plausible. Like other people, the poor project their despair onto the society. They, or their advocates, claim that if people were better treated, they would behave better. But unfortunately, when problems are personal, they are typically rooted in early life and thus resistant to later suasions. Justice cannot undo history. While social unfairness in the past may have broken the black family, gestures of social commitment in the present cannot restore it. Forms of compensation for blacks such as aggressive school busing or affirmative action might be worthwhile, despite white resistance, if they could improve functioning. But they cannot reverse the damage that weak families do to children before they ever reach school. There was less despair among poor blacks under Jim Crow than there is today. For though society was less just in that era, families were stronger.

This is not to say that society should do nothing, only that what it does must be more complex than a reflex of conscience. The cure for alienation cannot be simply to do more for the needy, or to do less. Rather, it lies in restoring the poor family and, more broadly, the health of relationships among the worst-off. That is a task for the new, more authoritative social policies, and for nongovernmental communities such as churches, and not for social reform.

Dependency Issues

Thus, the issues raised by dependency politics must be appreciated in their own terms, not forced into a progressive mold. The main question in social politics cannot be whether society is committed to the poor, or too committed, but how to respond to the personal dysfunctions that today mainly give rise to the social problem. And that question in fact dominates politics.

Dependency politics arises in the first instance from claims to disadvantage. Popular upset exists over the disorders of the ghetto, but advocates say the poor face special problems in supporting themselves and getting ahead. Equal opportunity is achieved in theory but not in practice, it is said, due to a lack of jobs, covert bias against minorities, lack of child care, and so on. Fix these problems, and the disorders will abate. Claims by better-off minorities and feminists typically take this same form, alleging various denials of fairness that disadvantage the group in question. Conservatives claim in response that there is opportunity, and that if the claimants cannot seize it that is their fault. Both sides scrutinize the life of poor families and job-seekers, looking for facts to support their positions. Is it really true that they *cannot* work and avoid welfare and crime?

Thus, the immediate issue is empirical, not about principles. Few in social politics ever dispute the basic idea of equal opportunity as a framework for justice. Conservatives do not say that the poor, minorities, or women are not entitled to an equal chance to win jobs or other preferment on the basis of merit. Liberals do not say that claimant groups are entitled to reward or advancement without merit or effort, or that final economic outcomes should be equal. The issue is not what kind of society we should have, but whether that society is achieved in practice. Whether society is "really" fair, not what fairness should mean, is now the great question that divides American leaders and voters.[20]

It is often said that the current social debate is about "values," but this was much more true of the progressive era. During the New Deal, the prestige of Communism was at its height, and the possibility of a collectivist, nonmarket society in America was seriously discussed. Federal decisions to manage the economy and provide mass benefit programs such as Social Security decisively changed America. So did the Great Society equal opportunity reforms, which prohibited using race and gender as bases for allocating preferred education and careers. In dependency politics, in contrast, values per se are not at issue, only the realization of values. No one disputes that the work ethic and obedience to the law are good things. There is no evidence that the poor themselves question these values. Rather, for mysterious reasons, they have difficulty living by them. The issue, rather, is whether they should have to conform, given the conditions they face.

Philosophers speak of a conflict between the values of freedom and equality in America, between the principles of allowing everyone to get ahead on his or her own and imposing more equal outcomes.[21] That is the

20. Sidney Verba and Gary R. Orren, *Equality in America: The View from the Top* (Cambridge: Harvard Univ. Press, 1985); James R. Kluegel and Eliot R. Smith, *Beliefs About Inequality: Americans' Views of What Is and What Ought to Be* (New York: Aldine de Gruyter, 1986).

21. Vernon Louis Parrington, *Main Currents in American Thought,* vols. 1–2 (New York: Harcourt Brace Jovanovich, 1954); H. Mark Roelofs, *Ideology and Myth in American Politics: A Critique of a National Political Mind* (Boston: Little, Brown, 1976).

issue between John Rawls, the best-known philosopher of the welfare state, and his opponents.[22] But this is to frame the social question in outdated, progressive terms. Actually, those claiming disadvantage dispute the practical fairness of society, not its principles. "The equality debate in America . . . is not over whether anyone really deserves to be at the bottom or whether the losers are always worthy of help from government, but over whether those currently at the bottom are the ones who deserve to be there, and thus whether government should assist them."[23] To this debate, John Rawls and his critics are virtually irrelevant.

One might think that research could settle whether opportunity exists for the poor, but it does not. The evidence reviewed above does suggest that there are seldom prohibitive barriers to poor adults who seek to escape welfare and need. But each barrier theory has just enough truth to it for proponents to claim that it contains the answer to poverty. And research conclusions speak of the average case. Poor people in some particular situation may still be trapped. Government surveys do not suggest that child care is scarce or costly for the nation generally, but advocates still say that care is unavailable in their neighborhoods.

The real differences are in deeper-lying beliefs about who the poor are as people. On the surface, experts and politicians may debate whether opportunity is available to the poor, but where they really divide is over how poor adults should or could *respond* to their situation. One of these issues is personal responsibility. Conservatives seek to hold the poor accountable for their problems, while liberals blame the problems on adverse living conditions and say that society is responsible.

In the progressive era, the left said that government, not workers, was accountable for impersonal economic outcomes such as unemployment. Present-day liberals use the same logic to explain away the personal problems that, today, more often cause poverty. They posit a more diffuse social determinism that I call sociologism. They say, for example, that a teenager who grows up in a depressed neighborhood with bad schools will inevitably become pregnant or get into crime. Conservatives say it is not inevitable; people must be held responsible at least for personal probity, if not for economic success. However tough life is, the poor, like

22. John Rawls, *A Theory of Justice* (Cambridge: Harvard Univ. Press, 1971); Robert Nozick, *Anarchy, State, and Utopia* (New York: Basic Books, 1974).

23. Verba and Orren, 83.

the Hebrews in the desert, should be expected to obey the Ten Commandments.

These positions need not be opposites. The capable citizen is not an abstraction but is formed by the society, especially by the family, the school, and the local community.[24] People who function well learn personal responsibility from these influences, just as many poor people seem not to learn it. Similarly, outside pressure is not a substitute for moral beliefs but one of the reasons children internalize values in the first place. The authoritative social policy that is emerging makes use of institutional and community pressures precisely to enforce norms. It avoids the traditional battle over whether the poor deserve any help at all. Yet politically, social influence and individual responsibility typically are cast as opposites. Those who would exempt the poor from personal accountability speak of social causes while their opponents resist.

Positions on responsibility tend to hinge on a yet more fundamental issue — competence. Whatever situation the poor face, does one think that they have the capacity to cope with life on their own? Conservatives say yes, while liberals doubt, and today this may be the deepest difference between them. One side sees the poor as uncivil exploiters of society, the other as victims of diffuse injustices. This difference is the reason conservatives are willing to enforce personal responsibility while liberals are not. The conservatives sound more hostile to the poor than liberals, who say they are "overwhelmed by the environment" and thus "beneath moral choice."[25] But the right is also more respectful of the needy as moral equals. Conservatives treat poor adults as moral agents, while liberals condescend.

Related to competence is the question of what motivates behavior. Are the poor rational maximizers, who respond to incentives and act according to economic interest? Or do they respond more to noneconomic suasions, such as destructive peer group pressures? Here the division is not so much between conservatives and liberals as between optimists and pessimists. Optimists think simple incentives or constraints, such as welfare or low wages, explain nonwork and poverty; change the payoffs and poverty will decline. Pessimists see the personality of the poor as more damaged and less self-reliant.

24. Michael J. Sandel, *Liberalism and the Limits of Justice* (Cambridge: Cambridge Univ. Press, 1982).

25. Michael Harrington, *The Other America: Poverty in the United States*, rev. ed. (Baltimore: Penguin Books, 1971), 144, 171.

The question of human nature is so important for one's theories and prescriptions about poverty that experts have been forced to address it. By nature and training, most of them are technicians, not philosophers. Yet several have recently written general statements of what they take to be the personality of the poor. David Ellwood is a liberal economist who is protective of the poor but sees them as rationally motivated.[26] William Julius Wilson is also liberal but more pessimistic about competence than Ellwood.[27] Charles Murray is a conservative who regards the poor as competent, but as open to amoral behavior if government intervenes unwisely.[28] Kevin Hopkins is another conservative who doubts both the rationality and morality of the poor.[29] The following table summarizes the differences:

		Morality is	
		Orthodox	Doubtful
Motivation is	Rational	Ellwood	Murray
	Nonrational	Wilson	Hopkins

Policy positions largely follow from these understandings. Conservatives, who think the poor could be responsible but are not, are the readiest to enforce values; they recommend repressing disorder and reforming or curbing welfare to discourage dependency. Liberals, who think the poor are moral but overwhelmed, prefer to address the "underlying causes" of poverty. They want to expand opportunity and fend off punitive social pressures such as racism. Those who are optimistic about motivation, whether liberal or conservative, base policy on incentives. Ellwood blames nonwork largely on low wages for the unskilled, and would take steps to

26. David T. Ellwood, "Understanding Dependency: Choices, Confidence, or Culture?" study prepared for the U.S. Department of Health and Human Services (Waltham, Mass.: Brandeis Univ., Center for Human Resources, Nov. 1987).

27. William Julius Wilson, "The American Underclass: Inner-City Ghettos and the Norms of Citizenship," the Godkin Lecture, delivered at the Kennedy School of Government, Harvard University, Cambridge, Mass., April 26, 1988.

28. Charles Murray, *In Pursuit: Of Happiness and Good Government* (New York: Simon and Schuster, 1988).

29. Kevin R. Hopkins et al., *Welfare Dependency: Behavior, Culture, and Public Policy,* study prepared for the U.S. Department of Health and Human Services (Alexandria, Va.: Hudson Institute, Sept. 1987).

"make work pay"; Murray blames it on disincentives created by government and would abolish welfare. The pessimists talk of sterner measures. Wilson calls for restructuring urban economies to integrate the ghetto, while Hopkins doubts that any policy has the power to overcome poverty culture. The views of most players in the poverty debate vary along these dimensions.[30]

I believe that conservatives have the best of the barriers debate, that opportunity in the United States usually is sufficient to get out of poverty and off welfare. But liberals have the more plausible view of poverty psychology. Even if observers can see opportunity, the seriously poor do feel overwhelmed by their situation. They believe in orthodox values such as the work ethic but feel unable to live by them in practice. That suggests that the trend away from social reform and toward managing personal behavior is justified. If barriers created by government or society do not explain poverty, then government need not intervene in society very much more or less than it does. At the same time, the poor need help to succeed within this structure.

The nature of that help must combine support with expectations. Government must offer opportunity but also enforce standards for good behavior. That points toward the policies of law and order, tougher schools, and welfare work requirements that are already developing. If one lacks personal organization, the way forward is obligation, not freedom. Those who would live well in a free society must first be bound.

Deficiencies of the Debate

Unfortunately, American political culture makes it difficult to discuss authoritative policies openly, let alone establish them. We are good at debating whether government should do "more" or "less" for people, an issue that no longer has much relevance to poverty. We are much more loath to discuss reshaping the lives of the poor. For to do this requires some admission that the psychology of poverty is different from that of the middle class. The idea that some people need guidance to live is heresy to a political order

30. My own interpretation is akin to Wilson's, except that I think the main structural cause of poverty is a permissive social policy that does not enforce work and other mores, rather than deindustrialization. We differ, that is, about the opportunity structure more than about the nature of the poor. See Mead, *New Politics,* ch. 7.

deeply committed to the competence assumption. Liberals find it prohibitive to admit that the needy might require anything other than benefits and protections from government, while to conservatives the idea that people need something other than the freedom to get ahead sounds like Big Brother.

For this reason, over the last thirty years, antipoverty policymakers have restlessly searched for voluntary solutions to the work problem. Only when it was clear that opportunity, incentives, and optional programs alone would not raise work levels were tougher measures proposed. When welfare work requirements were first discussed in Congress in the 1960s and 1970s, liberals opposed them as coercive. Many conservatives preferred to promote work simply by cutting welfare eligibility, so that fewer employable poor could get on the rolls in the first place. The policy of enforcing work within welfare went ahead out of necessity, but without either side openly embracing the idea of obligation as a dimension of social policy.[31]

In the 1980s, liberal resistance abated slowly in the face of positive evaluations of workfare programs, and these studies justified the Family Support Act. Most conservatives came to favor work enforcement, if only because it was politically impossible to trim welfare eligibility very much. But on the right as well as the left, it was still fashionable to concoct incentives-based solutions to poverty that assumed competence rather than producing it. Jack Kemp, a leading Republican, speaks of "empowering" the poor through enterprise zones, in which taxes and regulations on employers are reduced in return for their locating in the inner city. Liberals speak of giving poor youth "individual development accounts" to finance further education or training.[32] There is no evidence that such devices would achieve much, but they appeal to the deep-seated wish to believe that today's needy are just like other people.

There is also a tendency for political leaders and planners to prosecute old progressive disputes at the expense of clear thinking about poverty. One argues for a certain policy, not because it really fits the social problem, but because it suits one's general position about the role and scale of government. One defines poverty psychology so as to suit that prescription. Thus,

31. Lawrence M. Mead, *Beyond Entitlement: The Social Obligations of Citizenship* (New York: Free Press, 1986), chs. 8–10.

32. Robert Haveman, *Starting Even: An Equal Opportunity Program to Combat the Nation's New Poverty* (New York: Simon and Schuster, 1988), 168-71.

the planners of the Great Society wanted Washington to take control of welfare from state and local governments, which they saw as reactionary and racist toward the poor. To justify this, they construed the poor as huddled victims of invidious local practices, such as oppressive welfare or segregated schools, that only federal mandates could overcome.[33]

Some conservatives, for their part, want to structure social programs around "mediating structures" — churches, religious schools, neighborhood associations, and other voluntary organizations. These bodies would receive public funds to provide social benefits or services, so that they become intermediaries between government and the dependent. Proponents justify this by painting federal programs as intrusive and the poor as lost souls who need help from small, personalized institutions rather than government bureaucracy.[34]

These arguments may be valid as general constitutional prescriptions, but typically they do not rest on any deep inquiry about the nature and needs of the poor. Dependency issues should be debated in their own terms, not as adjuncts of these older issues. They should be settled on the basis of evidence about poverty psychology. From this policy conclusions should follow, rather than the other way around.

Religious Attitudes

One reason we hesitate to confront the personal face of poverty, I believe, is the influence of organized religion. I refer not to the laity but to professional church leaders, particularly seminary faculty and the official representatives of denominations who testify in Congressional hearings. These figures would be surprised to hear that they have political influence, but among elites they have probably been the strongest force resisting a more authoritative social policy.

In congressional hearings about welfare and poverty, church spokespersons have typically raised the most liberal voices. Representatives

33. Sar A. Levitan, *The Great Society's Poor Law: A New Approach to Poverty* (Baltimore: Johns Hopkins Press, 1969), 59-60.

34. Peter L. Berger and Richard John Neuhaus, *To Empower People: The Role of Mediating Structures in Public Policy* (Washington, D.C.: American Enterprise Institute, 1977).

of virtually all denominations, Catholic as well as Protestant, have called for vastly increased spending for the poor with few if any demands made on them in return. On their argument, welfare should be expanded in coverage and benefits so that all Americans are guaranteed an income, regardless of employment or employability. To do this is nothing more than justice to the victims of American capitalism and racism. Society must affirm the personhood of the needy without questioning lifestyle, because "the poor are a special charge of God." The rich cannot resist, because all wealth is God's, to be used for the benefit of the community. To raise any objection is unworthy of a largely Christian nation.[35]

In hearings on welfare reform in the 1960s and 1970s, liberal church witnesses demanded that expanded benefits be entitlements, given on the basis of need alone. They strongly resisted the rising sentiment in Congress for work requirements, which they interpreted as judgmental and oppressive. The initial, though not the final, draft of the Catholic Bishops' pastoral letter on the U.S. economy bitterly denounced "workfare" as "a particularly objectionable requirement." Work was part of the answer to poverty, the bishops said, but government could not impose it. We must see the poor not as miscreants, they advised, but "as brothers and sisters who, precisely because they are in need, have special claims on us."[36] The new paternalist social policies are well justified on the merits, yet they have faced unrelenting resistance from the institutional church.

Most professional church people take strongly liberal positions on the key personality issues in poverty. They see the poor not as morally responsible for their situation, but as innocent victims of social injustice. The entire burden of alleviating their condition falls on society. Certainly one reason for this stance is the primacy given to poverty in the Gospels, at least as liberal theologians interpret them. Jesus makes loving treatment of the needy the touchstone of the good individual and the just society. He predicts that at the end of the age, "the last will be first, and the first last" (Matt. 20:16). He foretells that God will judge even those who do not know him according to whether they gave the hungry food or the naked clothing (Matt. 25:31-46).

35. Mead, *Beyond Entitlement,* 212-14.

36. National Catholic Conference, "Catholic Social Teaching and the U.S. Economy: First Draft — Bishops' Pastoral," *Origins: NC Documentary Service,* vol. 14, nos. 22-23, pp. 366-67.

Liberal interpreters take this loving treatment to mean simple, unjudging solicitude — just giving the needy what they want. Jesus does sometimes suggest as much (Matt. 5:42). It is easy to agree because of the sympathetic image that the poor present in nearly all the Gospel stories. They sincerely seek betterment, admit their own shortcomings, and ask for assistance rather than demanding it as a right. In current terminology, they are "easy to help." Such an image was no doubt valid for most of the needy in Jesus' time. It was a primitive age, which afforded ordinary people vastly less wealth, opportunity, and security than our own. Many people became destitute because of plague, famine, war, or other disasters that had no connection to personal "deservingness."

That image is much less plausible, however, in a modern, affluent society, remote from war, where hardship is cushioned by a welfare state. Church leaders who cling to the biblical face of poverty simply cannot reckon with the difficulty of uplifting most of today's seriously poor, few of whom are easy to help. Those religious who actually work with the needy know this. Remarked one monk serving the homeless, "In the Scriptures, Christ raised people from the dead. We don't have in the Scriptures people who refused to be raised from the dead. But that's what we're dealing with some of the time."[37]

A related attitude is suspicion of the "law," meaning not only governmental or religious strictures but general societal expectations such as the work ethic. The liberal church interprets Jesus as having liberated his followers from the law, so it is improper for society to impose any standards on the needy. One should not "judge" others, lest one be judged (Luke 6:37). The sense that sin must be admitted and reproved has lapsed. Again, the Bible gives grounds for this view. In the liberal interpretation, Israel was a legalistic society that had forgotten that the essence of goodness was not to follow rules, but to love God and one's neighbor.

The New Testament call for liberation, however, does not occur in a vacuum. It is not directed against public expectations as such. The Gospel takes for granted the entire structure of norms that Israel inherited from the Old Testament. Jesus says that he comes to fulfill the law, not to overthrow it (Matt. 5:7-19). He teaches that people should relate to each other, and to God, out of love rather than legalism. But the law is still necessary in a fallen society. St. Paul did not hesitate to "command" church members "living in idleness"

37. "Catholic Order Helps the Homeless," *New York Times,* Jan. 20, 1991, p. 24.

to "earn their own living" (2 Thess. 3:10-12). For a Christian, the law does not "save" spiritually, but it remains a valid statement of God's will. Only those who have struggled to fulfill it really know that they need God's grace, and are ready to receive it. In Paul's words, "the law was our custodian until Christ came, that we might be justified by faith" (Gal. 3:24). One can reach the New Testament only by travelling through the Old.

Modern-day America, furthermore, is hardly as regimented as ancient Israel. We are law- and lawyer-ridden, but law in the moral sense of a public code of behavior has sadly declined. That itself is one cause of the social problem. Today's Americans, and especially the poor, need to accept the law as "right" and as "fine gold" (Ps. 19:8, 10).

Of course, not all church leaders are liberals. Like other elites, they are polarized, more than the laity. The leaders of fundamentalist denominations are much less indulgent toward the poor than the mainline religious establishment. They call for a restoration of "Judeo-Christian values," meaning not only the work ethic and law-abidingness but the traditional male-headed family. Until recently, this perspective had little influence on national social policy, but more influence at the local level.

The religious right, however, shares with the left a remarkable suspicion of government. To Christians of either persuasion, the social or religious community is supposed to be small and intimate, attuned to the innermost needs of its members. Bureaucratic programs, with their faceless staffs and impersonal routines, are seen as insensitive and even destructive. This attitude easily lends support to the liberal feeling that the poor are victims, or to the conservative view that government is a corrupter. Each side gives secular authority little role in the ordering of society.

These antigovernment attitudes, too, have a scriptural root. The politics of the Bible is predemocratic, so it contains few direct lessons for our own time.[38] What does emerge clearly is pessimism about the political enterprise. Both the Old and New Testaments present government as an important calling, and they dignify it by exalted standards. But they also suggest that, by these standards, government usually fails. Jesus and the prophets denounced most of the rulers they knew as oppressors. In New Testament times, Palestine was ruled by Rome, making government seem even more distant and arbitrary.

38. However, much of the prophetic, moralistic style of American politics derives indirectly from the Bible. See H. Mark Roelofs, "The Prophetic President: Charisma in the American Political Tradition," *Polity* 25, no. 1 (1992): 1-20.

But we now know that the great age of political development was to come. The ideas of law and democracy invented by Greece and Rome became the basis for a Western political culture in which government is not arbitrary but a means of popular self-government. It is now imaginable, as it seldom is in the Bible, that government can claim exalted purposes, that an entire society can use it to serve God's will.

A New Theology of Poverty

Of these traditional church attitudes, the most helpful for overcoming poverty is the emphasis on local community. We are used to thinking of poverty as a lack of money, but the needy may be poorest in terms of secure ties to others. They lack not so much economic resources as "social capital," or other people whom they can call upon according to need.[39] Merely to give the poor money or some other impersonal resource is not sufficient. As Edward Wynne has written, "Healthy human beings are not the product of costly bureaucratic systems, but of engagement, caring, persistent attention, and — most importantly — of demanding relationships."[40] Again, the individual capable of autonomy is in fact formed by his or her family and community.

The biblical tradition perceives that the true solution to poverty is to integrate the outcast into a community at a personal level.[41] Ties with specific people can affirm the individual as no bureaucratic policy can. And such ties, by their nature, are reciprocal. Those who receive must also give. Personal ties help people in ways consistent with dignity, as bureaucratic entitlement programs often do not. Modern societies that minimize social problems, such as Japan and Switzerland, do so by resisting the isolation of the poor, by involving them intensely in relationships with mainstream people at the local level.[42]

39. James S. Coleman, "Parental Involvement in Education" (Chicago: Univ. of Chicago, Department of Sociology, February 6, 1990); Robert D. Putnam, "The Prosperous Community: Social Capital and Public Life," *American Prospect,* no. 13 (1993): 35-42.

40. Edward A. Wynne, *Social Security: A Reciprocity System under Pressure* (Boulder, Colo.: Westview, 1980), 138.

41. Paul Marshall, *Thine Is the Kingdom: A Biblical Perspective on the Nature of Government and Politics Today,* reprint ed. (Vancouver, B.C.: Regent College Bookstore, 1993), 106.

42. David H. Bayley, "Learning About Crime — The Japanese Experience," *Public*

The paternalist social policy that is emerging is built on such relationships. An effective work program motivates its participants as much (or more) by the ties they develop to other clients and staff as by economic incentives to work. People get a job to impress their friends in the program — and not to let them down. Churches can involve the poor in a community that is at once limitlessly giving and intensely demanding. Because of such ties, a strong church such as the Mormons can be much more effective than government in overcoming poverty. Even in the ghetto, where civil society has virtually collapsed, some black churches report successes at motivating men to face up to their responsibilities to wives and children.[43]

Other churchly attitudes are less helpful. Liberal church people must reassess their images of who the poor are and what government should do for them. They must give up the sentimental view that the poor are innocents who have nothing to do with their predicament. Fortunately, there is one story in the Gospels that suggests how Jesus might respond to poor people of a less "deserving" type. At the Pool of Bethesda, he meets a cripple who has lain there helpless for thirty-eight years. The man complains that no one will help him get into the pool, which was believed to cure infirmities. This tendency to project one's problems onto the environment is typical of the culture of poverty.

Jesus does not do what the cripple hopes he will. Rather, Jesus asks whether he wants to be healed. And, when the man goes on complaining, he demands, "Rise, take up your pallet, and walk." The man abruptly does as he is told, and finds he is cured. Later, Jesus accosts him again and says, "See, you are well! Sin no more, that nothing worse befall you." The man goes away grateful, saying that Jesus has healed him (John 5:2-15). This approach to dependency is certainly not the unjudging solicitude recommended by the liberal church. Jesus questions the will of the poor person himself. He does not flinch to make demands. That is what people require when they refuse to accept responsibility for themselves. In the circumstances, it was the loving response.

Equally, in helping today's poor, the law cannot be seen as an enemy.

Interest, no. 44 (1976): 55-68; Ralph Segalman, "Welfare and Dependency in Switzerland," *Public Interest,* no. 82 (1986): 106-21.

43. Tucker Carlson, "Holy Dolers: The Secular Lessons of Mormon Charity," *Policy Review,* no. 59 (1992): 25-31; Tucker, "That Old-Time Religion: Why Black Men Are Returning to Church," *Policy Review,* no. 61 (1992): 13-17.

Clear expectations about good behavior are essential if one is to live an orderly life and maintain relationships. To meet the just demands of others is also an essential basis of self-respect. The poor must be honored with the same essential expectations that society makes of the better-off. They, like other people, must be bound before they can be freed.

The need to set and enforce standards is something that local religious who serve the poor seem to understand better than their leaders. Policy analysts find that Catholic parochial schools are, on average, much better than the public schools at educating poor children. A major reason is that they enforce order and learning standards much more firmly.[44] Other religious charitable operations are also highly structured. In a Catholic homeless shelter near New York, for example, residents must refrain from violence and put in time in the kitchen or working on the grounds. According to one friar on the staff, "charity" is all to the good, "[b]ut we have to talk about these men's dignity. They are children of God and they have an obligation to better themselves."[45]

Further, the church community cannot enforce standards alone. Government plays an indispensable role. True, large-scale bureaucracy cannot relate to the poor in a personal way. But precisely because the community that can do this is small, it must depend on the political regime to promote order and industry in the larger society. Again, there is some scriptural support. Although the image of government in the Bible is generally severe, Jesus does say that we should "[r]ender to Caesar the things that are Caesar's" (Mark 12:17). The Gospels actually portray Roman officials quite sympathetically as guardians of public order.

Public authorities play a necessary, if fallen, part in God's design. Believers should obey them, Paul says, as "instituted by God" (Rom. 13:1-7). In medieval society, secular rulers were supposed to share with the church the responsibility of leading society toward salvation. Even under a constitution that separates church and state, as in America, government seeks ends of order and prosperity that even church people must support.

44. James S. Coleman et al., *High School Achievement: Public, Catholic and Private Schools Compared* (New York: Basic Books, 1982).

45. Joseph Berger, "Homeless Men Rekindle Hope at Friars' Mountainside Refuge," *New York Times,* Dec. 28, 1985, pp. 25-26.

The Welfare Community

These scattered traditions suggest a complex vision of a more inclusive nation. The solution to poverty today is not primarily giving the needy good things. It is integrating them into a society that gives and receives expectations at several levels. There must be intimate communities, including churches, that involve the poor with other people at a face-to-face level, both giving and receiving support. There must also be a set of public rights and norms, prevailing throughout the society, that can be taken for granted by the smaller communities.

Belonging at an individual level is local and particular, as it must be, but citizenship is national and impersonal. A person builds "social capital" through constructive relationships with his or her family and the people he or she knows personally. At the same time, a person associates with other citizens in more impersonal arenas — politics and the workplace. On a personal level, one is a relative, neighbor, and friend. At this level, people may expect a lot of each other in terms of time, effort, or money, but the demands occur among people who know each other well enough to permit this.

On a public level, most people are not well acquainted. But there can still be a community if a common civility permits strangers to trust one another as citizens and workers. In America, one receives the rights to "life, liberty, and the pursuit of happiness," plus certain government benefits such as Social Security, in return for working, obeying the law, and paying taxes. These rights and obligations — partly defined by social programs — constitute an operational definition of citizenship. To achieve equality in America, as most Americans understand that, does not require leveling private incomes. It means, rather, that people are alike in their public identities, that they claim the same rights and discharge the same essential obligations.[46] To become incorporated in community, therefore, the poor must become our neighbors, but also our fellow citizens.

Such a vision is not far from the society we see in the Book of Acts. The early church grew up as small communities in several eastern cities under the aegis of Rome. The empire, of course, sometimes persecuted the church, but in most times it was indifferent to religion, as the American

46. Mead, *Beyond Entitlement*, 6-7, 233-46.

government is today.[47] The regime sheltered local institutions that, though formally private, helped govern the society. The current welfare state has a surprisingly similar structure. National policies are decided in Washington, but detailed administration is mostly delegated to local governments, which in turn contract many services to nonprofit bodies, including churches. These institutions help administer both the benefits and the obligations that give content to American citizenship.

Government-funded organizations are particularly important in the districts most afflicted by poverty. In the inner city, and also in some depressed rural areas, the private institutions that once held the community together have weakened as working families have departed. Only working adults have much to contribute to their local church, club, or chamber of commerce. The most important organizations still functioning today are often contractors drawing public funds to carry out various service programs — some churches and synagogues, community action agencies, nonprofit housing and development bodies, charitable missions, and so on.

Governing the Society

Governing through this system is not entirely a governmental affair. Society enforces some critical civilities with coercive sanctions. People are fined or imprisoned if they commit crime, fail to pay taxes, serve in the military if drafted, and so on. Such penalties today are always imposed through public authority, that is, through law. Sanctions that infringe rights are not legitimate unless imposed through democratic decision and implemented through a judicial process that protects individual rights.

But in less formal ways, nongovernmental institutions also help uphold public norms, as well as further expectations that we do not enforce with law. Churches and synagogues extol decency toward others, private schools promote learning, while the market economy rewards success in serving the customer. Through such channels, unofficial pressures spur people to display virtue and excellence far above the minimum that is enforced through public authority.

What norms should be governmentally enforced is a political question

47. Things changed, of course, after A.D. 313, when Christianity became the official religion of the empire.

with no determinate answer. The Constitution limits the ends for which government may coerce people, but these strictures settle surprisingly little. The Supreme Court has allowed the federal and state governments to regulate the economy for virtually any purpose. It has also allowed legislatures to attach virtually any conditions to social benefits, provided the recipients enter the programs voluntarily. Thus, work or other obligations tied to welfare have faced no serious constitutional challenge.[48] The disputes the requirements raise are entirely political, rooted in the profound differences over responsibility and competence discussed above.

My own view is that government should directly enforce the civilities most essential to public order. It must repress lawbreaking, draft soldiers, and so on. With slightly less urgency, it should enforce the obligations that Americans must discharge to be regarded as equals in the public realm. To achieve equal citizenship is America's innermost purpose. Political participation is part of equal citizenship, but few feel that voting should be mandatory. The case is otherwise with employment. People regard working as essential to their social standing, so to assure employment by those not working is the major domestic imperative American government faces.[49]

While market pressures suffice to enforce work for most people, government must do so for adults on welfare or other benefits, as necessity may not lead them to work on their own. Local governments also enforce attendance in school. It is reasonable that these social obligations should be enforced, in part, through social programs. Government may justly deny support to adults who do not work if employable, or who fail to keep their children in school. In upholding obligations this way, government does not literally force compliance; it merely denies support to people who do not comply. However, a parallel to legal sanctions is clear, and the Supreme Court has insisted that denials of benefits observe due process.[50]

It is in enforcing these social competences that public and private institutions cooperate most closely. Private educators join with public ones in forming the citizens of the next generation, while nonprofit agencies, including churches, serve as contractors to social service and welfare agencies. When benefits are denied to enforce work or other obligations, the

48. Mead, *Beyond Entitlement,* 170-71.

49. Judith N. Shklar, *American Citizenship: The Quest for Inclusion* (Cambridge: Harvard Univ. Press, 1991).

50. *Goldberg v. Kelly,* 397 U.S. 254 (1970).

sanction is formally at the hands of public agencies operating under due process. But it is often nonprofit contractors who certify to government that clients have not attended required activities, looked for work, or stayed in school. This formalizes some of the enforcement role that such institutions always played unofficially.

There are dangers in having nongovernmental bodies wield such authority. One of the evils of welfare before 1960 was that the treatment of recipients was highly discretionary, varying sharply from place to place. Local social workers often had the power to deny benefits or make invidious demands of the dependent purely on their own authority. The welfare rights movement forced the elimination of much of this discretion, although states retain control of welfare benefit levels. The growing role of contractors in enforcing welfare obligations might risk a return to the *ancien régime.* The new authoritative policies depend on caregivers' communication of demands to the poor at a face-to-face level, and many caregivers will be employees of entities outside government. The fear that private organizations not subject to democratic controls might deny rights or benefits accounts for much of the resistance to "mediating structures."

The current welfare obligations, however, mainly reflect policies enacted by Congress and state legislatures. The authority is coming from democratic decisions, not administrators, although some discretion in implementation is unavoidable. Social policy is becoming more law-based, even as the execution of policy relies more on contractors and less on traditional public administration. In this situation, to delegate part of the enforcement role to nonprofit bodies seems reasonable, provided that the ultimate power to deny support rests with public agencies.

By these means, the two levels of the good society — local community and national citizenship — may cooperate closely. The same institutions that give meaning to life at a private level have, in many cases, become servants of the state in carrying out public programs. This collaboration, while worrisome to some, could help promote a more Christian social order — one that would make real demands on the poor as well as support the vulnerable. Society must accept that combination if, in dealing with poverty, it is to be "wise as serpents and innocent as doves" (Mt. 10:16).

Leading the Culture

Religious thinking about poverty should not challenge these arrangements radically, since they reflect necessity, but rather should understand their inner logic and push it forward. The great advantage of the emerging policy is that it fits the actual needs of the poor, whereas the standard attitudes of American politics do not. If the church reconstructed its own thinking in parallel ways, it could lead the nation toward agreement on the key identity issues that underlie dependency politics.

A realistic theology of poverty, like an effective social policy, must transcend the opposites of the conventional political mind. Federal programs and "mediating structures" are not set against each other. Rather, both play a role in a single conception. More important, the opposite images of the poor are transcended. They are seen as neither victims nor victimizers, but as members of a community, who may be both saints and sinners. Viewed psychologically, the great strength of the Christian tradition is its ability to embrace shortcoming and yet summon people to virtue. Somehow, through faith, the believer who admits weakness and feels accepted is able to move on to self-reliance; "for when I am weak," as Paul said, "then I am strong" (2 Cor. 12:10).

The ability to accept both strength and weakness is one hallmark of individual and social maturity. One reason the identity issues in dependency politics are so distressing is that competent people are threatened by incompetence, and the incompetent by strength. Most people attain self-mastery only through self-denial, and remain subject to temptation. They shudder to think what a disordered life would mean. When they confront dysfunction in the poor, they evade it as too terrible to admit.

The conservative style is to repress weakness by denying that the poor really have to be as disordered as they are; if they would only behave better, all would be well. The liberal mode is to admit dysfunction, but only in the other. Those who condescend to the needy project onto them the weakness they would rather not admit in themselves. Conversely, the poor are threatened by the mastery of the better-off, for if they controlled their lives in the same manner, they would become responsible for personal problems that they now foist on the society. Thus poor blacks talk of "the man" and project the competence they deny in themselves onto "whitey."

In a meritocratic, postreform society, these identities of competent and incompetent have become the chief stratification, eclipsing older class differences. Experts and commentators type some people as "privileged" and others as "disadvantaged" on the basis of personal style, without any knowledge of their economic circumstances. People are termed "rich" if they have an upstanding, reliable manner, and "poor" if they do not. No structural reform of the society could alter these identities. For in our current politics, personality, not income or class, is the defining quality about a person. The great divide in society lies not between the rich and less rich, but between those who can and those who cannot assume responsibility for themselves.

The biblical tradition overrides that division by summoning every individual to be both weak and strong, poor and rich. The believer is humble — penitent, vulnerable, meek — before God, yet called to realize God's will in the world. It is those who "wait upon the Lord" who "shall renew their strength" (Isa. 40:21). Those who fully accept their own fears are most able to deal with the poor honestly, without using them for personal purposes. They can accept dependents as fellow sinners, yet also demand that they take command of their lives for their own good and God's, without a need to condescend. One reason why nuns, priests, and monks appear to do well working with the disadvantaged may be that they have come to terms with their own vulnerabilities more than most caregivers. Thus they can accept weakness, and yet go on to expect effort and excellence.

The deepest meaning of community is that the projections that the rich and poor direct at each other should be withdrawn. The strong must claim their own weakness, rather than attribute it to the poor; and the weak must claim their strength, rather than attribute it to the rich.[51] That implies that the elite must lay down some of the responsibilities it has assumed for the poor through government, and the poor must pick them up. Requirements in welfare such as work may sound oppressive, but their purpose is only to shift some of the onus for poverty from government to the dependent. The burden of overcoming poverty is then shared. By making some demands on the recipients, society declares that it cannot do without their efforts, and so treats them more as equals. It becomes imaginable that, some day, the rich should depend on the poor in more important ways. Then, at least at the level of identity, they would be rich and poor no longer.

51. Paul Tournier, *The Strong and the Weak,* trans. Edwin Hudson (Philadelphia: Westminster Press, 1963).

The poverty debate is really about identity. The church can speak to that issue as no other institution does. By speaking boldly and honestly, church leaders have as much power as anyone to lead the nation toward a more realistic social policy, and thus toward a renewed national community.

Opposite Sexes or Neighboring Sexes? The Importance of Gender in the Welfare Responsibility Debate

Mary Stewart Van Leeuwen

IN HER 1947 essay on women titled "The Human-Not-Quite-Human," Dorothy Sayers wondered why women and men were referred to as "opposite sexes" rather than "neighboring sexes."[1] The issue to which Sayers referred was whether women and men are essentially more alike than different, and whether their apparent differences in behavior are inherent or changeable. This "nature versus nurture" debate regarding the origin of male-female behavioral differences was constantly aired during the first wave of Western feminism, which began in the last half of the nineteenth century and continued through the women's suffrage movement of the early twentieth century.[2] The debate was resurrected during the current wave of feminism, which began in the 1960s, and has shown no evidence of dying away.

But in fact the nature/nurture question can never be definitively resolved, at least not by an appeal to science. We cannot randomly assign people to be male or female at birth, nor (despite the now standard social scientific distinction between "sex" and "gender") can we disentangle bio-

1. In Dorothy L. Sayers, *Unpopular Opinions* (1947). Reprinted in Sayers, *Are Women Human?* (Grand Rapids, Mich.: Eerdmans, 1971), 37-47.

2. See, e.g., Olive Banks, *Faces of Feminism: A Study of Feminism as a Social Movement* (New York: St. Martin's Press, 1981); Nancy Cott, *The Grounding of Modern Feminism* (New Haven: Yale Univ. Press, 1987); and Aileen S. Kraditor, *The Ideas of the Woman Suffrage Movement, 1890–1920* (Garden City, N.Y.: Doubleday-Anchor, 1971).

logical sex from the social forces and expectations associated with it. Thus, essential conditions for inferring cause and effect — the manipulation of an independent variable and the control of extraneous variables — cannot be met, and this means that "all data on sex differences, no matter what research method is used, are correlational data; [thus] it is more accurate to speak of *sex-related* differences than of *sex-caused* differences."[3]

However, despite these methodological barriers people continue to argue about the relative importance of nature, nurture, social necessity, and free choice for the roles assigned to men and women. A major reason for doing so is that any conclusions reached will necessarily have profound implications for social policy and the distribution of welfare resources. Thus if we conclude that infants (other things being equal) thrive best under the primary care of their biological mothers, then family supports might better take the form of tax credits or family allowances rather than tax deductions for day care. Moreover, a policy that requires welfare recipients to work as a condition of receiving aid would then exempt mothers of children below a certain age, but not fathers.

If we further conclude that adults are not simply "interchangeable parts" within the family — that is, if (other things being equal) children of both sexes need stable role models of both sexes for optimal cognitive, social, and gender-identity development, then this suggests further policies: ones that make divorce less easy, that discourage single parenthood, that sanction only heterosexual marriages, and that encourage absent fathers — not just their financial resources — to return to their partners and children. And if women, by reason of biology, experience, or both, are more domestically oriented than men, then policies that make it easy for wives and mothers to move in and out of the waged workforce at various stages of the life cycle without creating extreme economic vulnerability will be preferable to "sex-blind" policies that assume interchangeable career paths for women and men.

3. Hilary Lips, *Sex and Gender: An Introduction*, 2nd ed. (Mountain View, Calif.: Mayfield, 1993), 77. The only way to disentangle the effects of heredity from environment is to hold the one constant while allowing the other to vary, as happens in the case of identical twins who are raised in separate environments. However, while such "natural experiments" have shed light on the overall heritability of character traits as diverse as cancer-proneness and depression, they can tell us nothing about the degree to which behavioral differences between males and females originate in biology or elsewhere, for the simple reason that identical twins must be of the same sex.

It is tempting to assume (as popular rhetoric does) that feminists all line up neatly to the left in these issues and defenders of the so-called traditional family (more accurately labeled the modern family) to the right. It is often further assumed that Catholics and evangelicals fall almost invariably into the traditionalist camp, and that mainstream Protestants support an almost unlimited (and state-supported) diversity of family forms. But the picture is more complex than this, and part of the task of this chapter is to show how. To do so I will compare three approaches to family ethics and its associated policies: the approach of defenders of the (so-called) traditional family, the approach of mainstream feminists, and the approach of feminist object-relations theorists. Then I will turn to some considerations of theological anthropology, the area of inquiry that explores what it means to be human in light of a biblical worldview. Lastly, I will suggest some directions for welfare policy reform and policy implementation in light of the first two parts of the chapter.

Three Approaches to Gender and Family Ethics

The Changing Face of Traditionalism

Historically, traditionalist views have included a wide range of perspectives on the economic, social, and moral responsibility of the state to its citizens, but they have all shared a belief about essential differences in women's and men's "natures," or at least about the social desirability of a gendered division of labor regardless of any actual similarities or differences between men and women.[4] Thus the "traditional" family was taken to be one in which women were responsible for the tasks of "social reproduction" within the domestic realm — that is, the preparation of food, the maintenance of clothing and household, the physical and emotional care of family members throughout the life cycle — while men were to engage in public-realm

4. For a more detailed treatment of these issues, and an introduction to the pertinent literature, see Susan Cohen and Mary Fainsod Katzenstein, "The War over the Family is Not over the Family," in Sanford M. Dornbusch and Myra H. Strober, eds., *Feminism, Children and the New Families* (New York: Guilford, 1988), 25-46. See also Kenneth Clatterbaugh, *Contemporary Perspectives on Masculinity: Men, Women, and Politics in Modern Society* (Boulder, Colo.: Westview Press, 1990), esp. ch. 2.

employment in order to finance the social reproduction needs of the family.[5] Built into this definition was a presumption of husbandly headship and wifely dependence, a presumption that, despite its cultural romanticization, was certainly not egalitarian — theologically, legally, or economically.[6]

Traditionalists from the New Right have insisted for decades on religiously and/or biologically based differences in women's and men's vocations.[7] More recently, those of a neoconservative bent have conceded the need for gender-neutral (but not affirmative-action-supporting) laws to equalize educational and job opportunities for men and women, while still holding that it would be better for society if wives, and more especially mothers of young children, largely opted for domesticity rather than paid employment.[8] However, while new rightists and neoconservatives claim to be supporting the "traditional" family, the implicit dichotomies they assume between public and private, waged workplace and home, breadwinning father and domesticated mother (which they promote as unchanging and/or desirable norms of family life) are, in the long sweep of history, anything but "traditional." They are adaptations that occurred largely in response to the nineteenth-century industrial revolution and the urbanization trends that accompanied it. Prior to that time, and notwithstanding the norm of patriarchal family authority, gender roles overlapped considerably, and the traditional family was one in which workplace, dwelling place, and child-rearing space typically coexisted for both men and women. In such a subsistence agricultural and craft-based society large families are an economic asset, all family members past early childhood contribute to

5. Barbara Laslett and Johanna Brenner, "Gender and Social Reproduction: Historical Perspectives," *Annual Review of Sociology* 15 (1989): 381-401.

6. See Susan Moller Okin, *Justice, Gender, and the Family* (New York: Basic Books, 1989).

7. For example, Jerry Falwell, *Listen, America* (New York: Doubleday, 1980); George Gilder, *Men and Marriage* (Gretna, La.: Pelican, 1987); Phyllis Schlafly, *The Power of the Positive Woman* (New York: Jove, 1978); *The Power of the Christian Woman* (Cincinnati: Stanford, 1981).

8. See, e.g., Brigitte Berger and Peter L. Berger, *The War Over the Family: Capturing the Middle Ground* (New York: Anchor Doubleday, 1983), and Katherine Kersten, "What Do Women Want? A Conservative Feminist Manifesto," *Policy Review* (Spring 1991), reprinted in Paul T. Jersild and Dale A. Johnson, eds., *Moral Issues and Christian Perspective*, 5th ed. (Fort Worth: Harcourt, Brace, Jovanovich, 1993), 111-27.

household subsistence, and children of both sexes have more equal exposure to adult role models of both sexes.[9]

All of this changed as Victorian ideology adapted to an increasingly urban, industrial economy by invoking a social norm that assigned wage earning almost entirely to men and domestic duties almost entirely to women (aided, where wealth permitted, by working-class servants of both sexes). This extreme gendering of the public/domestic dichotomy — variously called "the doctrine of separate spheres," "the cult of domesticity," and "the cult of true womanhood" — became a staple of nineteenth-century social thought in both Europe and America.[10]

Although this doctrine more or less followed the course of the industrial revolution on both sides of the Atlantic, it took some time to be fully developed. Until protective labor legislation ruled otherwise, women and children worked under often appalling conditions in mills and factories, sometimes together with their husbands and fathers, who were designated as family foremen in an attempt to replicate in the industrial setting the patriarchally driven family work group of preindustrial times. Against such conditions feminists, trade unionists, philanthropists, and clergy joined forces to lobby for child labor laws, protective legislation regarding women's waged work, and the male head-of-household "family wage."[11] The result was the so-called traditional but actually quite modern family, whose emergence was motivated at least in part by an increasingly widespread concern for the safety of women and children, especially those living in cities and other industrial areas.

The doctrine of separate spheres thus allocated to women the behavioral tasks of nurturing husbands and children and maintaining the home. Their parallel ethical task, in the common parlance of the day, was to be "angels of the home" — that is, to be moral and spiritual examples

9. See, e.g., Carl Degler, *At Odds: Women and the Family in America from the Revolution to the Present* (New York: Oxford, 1980), and Barbara Leslie Epstein, *The Politics of Domesticity: Women, Evangelism and Temperance in Nineteenth Century America* (Middletown, Conn.: Wesleyan Univ. Press, 1981).

10. On the development of the "separate spheres" doctrine in America, see Degler. For a religiously buttressed defense of the doctrine by a prominent, turn-of-the-century Dutch Calvinist, see Abraham Kuyper, *De Eerepositie der Vrouw (The Woman's Place of Honor)* (Kampen: J. H. Kok, 1932), trans. Irene Brouwer Konyndyk, Calvin College, Grand Rapids, Mich., 1990.

11. Eli Zaretsky, *Capitalism, the Family and Personal Life,* 2nd ed. (New York: Harper and Row, 1986).

to other family members, but especially to husbands, whose work in the competitive, rough-and-tumble public realm ever threatened to debase them. In their role as angels of the home, women were now generally considered to be the moral superiors of men (provided, of course, that they actually *did* stay at home and not try to join men in the public realm) — an intriguing reversal of the centuries-old assumption that, for biological and/or religious reasons, women were men's moral inferiors.[12]

Historians who call this separate-spheres doctrine "cultic" usually do so in order to pass negative judgment on it: they see the "cult of true womanhood" as a thinly disguised ideological tool for both restricting the scope of women's activities and degrading their economic power in the family relative to earlier times. But this conclusion is simplistic, for in bequeathing women a superior morality as angels of the home, many apologists for the separate-spheres doctrine intended not only to protect children from inappropriate factory labor, but also to elevate women's status, both materially and psychologically. Materially, by confining women's attentions to the home, they released them from the heavy labor required by both farming and industrial settings. And psychologically, in the words of historian Carl Degler,

> within the home women did gain a new recognition and in the process broke the ancient hierarchy that had assigned superiority to men in all spheres of activity. Domesticity, in short, was an alternative to patriarchy, both in intention and in fact. By asserting a companionate [as opposed to a servile] role for women, it implicitly denied patriarchy.[13]

However, even the best-motivated social policies are subject to the law of unintended consequences. Despite the rhetoric about companionate marriage, the growing isolation and economic marginalization of urban women in the home increased the risk of unchecked domestic violence — physical, sexual, and emotional — on the part of husbands inclined to it. The "angel of the home" doctrine made it difficult for women to protest or expose such abuse since the doctrine implied at worst that an abused woman had failed to be sufficiently "angelic," and at best that it was women's duty to bear such suffering in noble (and ennobling) silence.[14]

12. See, e.g., Rosemary Radford Ruether, *Sexism and God-Talk: Towards a Feminist Theology* (Boston: Beacon Press, 1983), esp. ch. 4.

13. Degler, 28.

14. See, e.g., Elizabeth Pleck, *Domestic Tyranny: The Making of American Social*

Moreover, by the 1960s the doctrine of separate spheres had so dichotomized men's and women's activities — at least in the urban middle class — that a second wave of feminism arose in protest against it. In *The Feminine Mystique* (a book whose 1963 publication is often cited as the event that launched second-wave feminism in America) journalist Betty Friedan documented the "problem that had no name" — that is, the plight of isolated homemakers whose education and talents were being underutilized as they floundered in a sea of compulsory domesticity. Her liberal-feminist solution was not to eliminate, but at least to degender, the public/domestic dichotomy through legislative and educational reforms that would permit women to enter the public realms of the academy, the marketplace, and the political forum on an equal footing with men.[15]

Since that time, many items on the liberal feminist agenda have borne legislative fruit — for example, the Equal Employment Opportunity Act and the Title IX Educational Amendment Act of 1972, the Equal Credit Opportunity Act of 1974, the Pregnancy Disability Act of 1978, and the Family and Medical Leave Act of 1993. Since the 1960s, it has been liberal feminists who have campaigned to get women into public office; who have worked to change laws and customs that limited women's access to certain schools, organizations, and occupations; who have mounted campaigns against gender stereotyping in the media; and who have promoted changes in schools to give women students more equitable opportunities in classroom and athletic activities. "It is doubtful," writes philosopher Rosemarie Tong, "that without liberal feminists' efforts, so many women could have achieved their newfound professional and occupational stature."[16]

For all its accomplishments, however, liberal feminism has been faulted for its narrow focus on a middle-class white women's agenda.[17] For

---

Policy against Family Violence from Colonial Times to the Present (New York: Oxford Univ. Press, 1987).

15. Betty Friedan, *The Feminine Mystique* (New York: Norton, 1963).

16. Rosemarie Tong, *Feminist Thought: A Comprehensive Introduction* (Boulder, Colo.: Westview Press, 1989), 38.

17. See, e.g., bell hooks, *Talking Back: Thinking Feminist, Thinking Black* (Boston: South End Press, 1989); Alison M. Jaggar, *Feminist Politics and Human Nature* (Totowa, N.J.: Rowman and Allenheld, 1983); Rosemarie Tong, *Feminist Thought: A Comprehensive Introduction* (Boulder, Colo.: Westview Press, 1989); and Mary Stewart Van Leeuwen, Annelies Knoppers, Margaret L. Koch, Douglas J. Schuurman, and Helen M. Sterk, *After*

example, it is simply not true that all women — even all married women — were floundering in domesticity prior to the 1960s. Many working-class women from all ethnic groups did not even have the choice to be bored in suburbia: their subsistence and that of their dependents required them to be in the waged workforce in whatever jobs they could get. Social histories of this period indicate that working-class women had many of the same attitudes to waged employment as their male peers: pride in being breadwinners on whom other family members could depend and enjoyment of the camaraderie of adult workmates, but often, at the same time, resentment and frustration over low wages and limited job mobility.[18] Moreover, women with families generally had to cope with the additional burden of the "double day" or "second shift": they went home from the office, shop, or factory to a round of domestic duties from which gender ideology exempted their husbands and other male family members. Then, as now, the degendering of the domestic/public dichotomy was far from complete, because the movement of women from home to waged workforce was rarely balanced by men's corresponding assumption of more child care and other domestic responsibilities associated with social reproduction.[19]

Eden: Facing the Challenge of Gender Reconciliation (Grand Rapids, Mich.: Eerdmans, 1993), esp. chs. 4, 14.

18. See, e.g., Barbara Mayer Wertheimer, *We Were There: The Story of Working Women in America* (New York: Pantheon, 1977).

19. Arlie Hochschild, *The Second Shift: Working Parents and the Revolution at Home* (New York: Viking, 1989). See also Van Leeuwen et al., esp. chs. 15 and 16. Numerous "time-budget" studies (of how family members spend their time) show that domestic labor is gendered both by the *type* of tasks done and the *time* spent on them. On average, married men in America spend 11 to 15 hours a week on domestic tasks, whereas women spend 33 to 55 hours, and these figures show little variation by social class or by degree of participation in the waged workforce. Moreover, men typically do quite different domestic tasks than women. Women on average do the more daily tasks that cannot be put off — household upkeep and ensuring that children are clean, fed, and regular about doing homework and chores. Men, by contrast, do the more occasional household tasks (e.g., outdoor, house exterior, and car maintenance), whose scheduling is also more flexible. With regard to child care, they tend to do the less mundane tasks of playing with the children, reading to them, going on outings, and encouraging sports participation. While these are averages to which there are obviously individual exceptions, the above-described pattern is quite consistent across a variety of time-budget studies. See, e.g., Lesley Doyal, "Waged Work and Women's Well-Being," *Women's Studies International Forum* 13 (1990): 587-604; Rosemary Deem, *All Work and*

Over the past thirty years, feminist activism and scholarship (of the kind summarized above) have combined with the rigors of a changing economy to turn many "pure" traditionalists into "new" traditionalists with regard to gender relations. Many people, including many self-styled religious conservatives, say in effect "I'm not a feminist, but . . ." and then go on to endorse a surprising number of items from the (mostly) liberal-feminist agenda. Classic liberal feminism, like liberal political theory generally, emphasizes the universality of human rationality, autonomy, and abstract standards of justice. It also maintains a separation of public from private life, and holds that reforms in law, custom, and education are sufficient to bring women into the civil and economic mainstream of modern life. Thus, when a person says "I'm not a feminist, but I believe in equal pay for equal work," or "but I believe women should be allowed to run for public office," or "but I believe that government interference in private life should be minimized" — then that person (protestations to the contrary) is more or less a supporter of liberal feminism.[20] And self-styled traditionalists, while adhering to a rhetoric of changeless norms regarding the shape of family and gender roles, are becoming more and more like liberal feminists in their actual practice.[21]

No Play? The Sociology of Women and Leisure (Milton Keynes, U.K.: Open Univ. Press, 1986); and Meg Luxton, *More Than a Labour of Love: Three Generations of Women's Work in the Home* (Toronto: The Women's Press, 1980).

20. There are, of course, also selective alliances between new traditionalists and radical feminists, particularly on the issues of pornography and sexual abuse. See, e.g., Wendy Kaminer, "Feminists Against the First Amendment," *Atlantic Monthly,* Nov. 1992, 111-18. In addition, the emergent communitarian movement in the U.S. seeks to balance the traditional liberal emphasis on individual rights with a renewed concern for social responsibility and civic virtue, within a commitment to gender egalitarianism and gender role flexibility. See, e.g., Jean Bethke Elshtain, "Feminism, Family, and Community," *Dissent* 30, no. 1 (1983): 103-10; "Feminism, Community, and Freedom," *Dissent* 30, no. 2 (1983): 247-55; and Amitai Etzioni, *Public Policy in a New Key* (New Brunswick, N.J.: Transaction, 1992).

21. Thus, turn-of-the-century fundamentalist Christians decried birth control and women's suffrage as antibiblical, while today's profamily Christian conservatives, claiming to be equally and "unchangingly" biblical, urge women in their audiences to exercise their civic and moral duty by voting (for select candidates, of course) and give them instruction on the use of birth control within marriage. See Janet Wilson James, ed., *Women in American Religion* (Philadelphia: Univ. of Pennsylvania Press, 1980), and Ruth A. Tucker, *Women in the Maze: Questions and Answers on Biblical Equality*

A recent example of this shift can be seen in an article on family values written by UCLA management professor James Q. Wilson. "Most Americans," he asserted, "understand the difference between a traditional family and an oppressive one; they want the former but not the latter."[22] He went on to explain that what most Americans (himself included) mean by the phrase "traditional family values" is "not male supremacy, spouse abuse, or docile wives, but the over-riding importance of two-parent families that make child care their central responsibility."[23] But however much one may agree with Wilson's definition of traditional family values, it is certainly not what the phrase meant up until recently. The fact that traditionalists have continued to move away from the separate-spheres doctrine, and toward an increasing acceptance of functional gender equality, is largely the result of three decades of feminist activism that "new traditionalists" like Wilson routinely fail to acknowledge.

The Changing Face of Mainstream Feminism

This tension between the rhetoric of gender role essentialism and the practice of progressively less-gendered roles has its counterpart among mainstream feminists in the growing contrast between "feminine" and "feminist" ethics.[24] Feminist ethics is centrally concerned with the *empowerment* of women: it thus focuses on the elimination of patriarchal domination and the attainment of justice for women in both the public and private spheres of life. Its activism has embraced not only the liberal feminist agenda of extending women's civil, educational, and reproductive rights, but also causes initiated by radical feminists, such as the exposure and elimination

---

(Downers Grove, Ill.: InterVarsity Press, 1992). Sociologist Judith Stacey, who has studied the growing gap between evangelicals' rhetoric about male headship and their actual tolerance of a variety of postmodern family forms, refers to the residual theology of male headship as "patriarchy of the last gasp." See her *Brave New Families: Stories of Domestic Upheaval in Late Twentieth Century America* (New York: Basic Books, 1990).

22. James Q. Wilson, "The Family-Values Debate," *Commentary* 95, no. 4 (1993): 31.

23. Wilson, 31.

24. See Betty Sichel, "Different Strains and Strands: Feminist Contributions to Ethical Theory," *Newsletter on Feminism* 90, no. 2 (1991): 90, and Rosemarie Tong, *Feminine and Feminist Ethics* (Belmont, Calif.: Wadsworth, 1993).

of male violence toward women and the censorship of hard pornography. Feminine ethics, by contrast, is more concerned with the *preservation, elevation,* and *appreciation* of what is held to be women's unique moral voice, with its focus on care, compassion, and mutuality, regardless of what this might mean for gender justice in its narrowest sense.[25]

Feminine ethics draws on a stream of theory and research that began in the early 1980s, documenting what have come to be known as women's and/or maternal ways of thinking, interacting, and making moral choices. With regard to thinking, the writers in this tradition challenged the artificial separation of reason from emotion and from personal and ideological commitments, and demonstrated the extent to which women, more than men, allow all of these to function simultaneously in their cognitive activities.[26] With regard to social interaction, they documented the ways women aim for cooperation and the preservation of human networks, while men more often strive to maintain hierarchies marked by interpersonal competition.[27] And with regard to morality, they rejected the mainstream (largely male) ethical assumption that adequate moral decisions are always based on abstract, universal principles, and never on commitments to actual people such as one's children, other kin, and friends.[28]

25. The tension between feminine and feminist ethics is not unique to Second Wave feminism but was a regular point of debate among nineteenth-century (First Wave) feminists as well. See, e.g., Kraditor, *The Ideas of the Woman Suffrage Movement.* However, in contemporary feminist theory there is a growing acknowledgment that feminine ethics needs to be qualified by feminist ethical concerns, and vice versa (see in particular Tong, *Feminine and Feminist Ethics*). As a terminological note, those who emphasize feminist ethics are also sometimes called "political feminists" and those who emphasize feminine ethics are sometimes labeled "social" or "cultural" feminists.

26. For example, Mary Field Belenky et al., *Women's Ways of Knowing: The Development of Self, Voice and Mind* (New York: Basic Books, 1986); Evelyn Fox Keller, *Reflections on Gender and Science* (New Haven: Yale Univ. Press, 1985); Sandra Harding, *Whose Science, Whose Knowledge? Thinking from Women's Lives* (Ithaca, N.Y.: Cornell Univ. Press, 1991); Jane Duran, *Towards a Feminist Epistemology* (Savage, Md.: Rowman and Littlefield, 1991).

27. For example, Joyce Treblicot, ed., *Mothering: Essays in Feminist Theory* (Totowa, N.J.: Rowman and Allenheld, 1983); Nel Noddings, *Caring: A Feminine Approach to Ethics and Moral Education* (Berkeley: Univ. of California Press, 1984); Sara Ruddick, *Maternal Thinking: Towards a Politics of Peace* (New York: Ballantine, 1989); Deborah Tannen, *You Just Don't Understand: Women and Men in Conversation* (New York: William Morrow, 1990).

28. For example, Carol Gilligan, *In a Different Voice: Psychological Theory and*

But despite these differences between feminist and feminine ethicists, both groups have participated in a recent shift of rhetoric regarding the family. From the early 1960s until the late 1970s, feminists concentrated on exposing the degree to which traditional (that is, modern) family life collaborated with legal, economic, religious, and cultural constraints to keep women from exercising the autonomy and self-development accorded to men. Recently, however, a consensus has begun to develop across the feminist spectrum regarding the developmental needs of children. Family disruption and reconfiguration are now less frequently defended as triumphs for the cause of diversity, and there is a growing recognition that, other things being equal, children do best in economically secure households with a dependable constellation of adults.[29] Indeed, a 1988 review of the relevant literature observed the following:

> Most feminists and conservatives would agree on a "bottom line" of childrearing — that infants and young children need constant, committed devotion from a stable cast of adults. Nor does there appear to be an irremediable polarization over how such basic children's needs are to be met. The right prefers the full-time presence of the biological mother but is not implacably opposed to at least a limited array of alternative arrangements. Some feminists are deeply opposed to the institution of full-time motherhood under conditions of patriarchy. Others . . . celebrate the possibility of the reconsecration of mothering in a domestic setting that may or may not involve shared parenting. Some feminist theories appear to prefer dual, heterosexual parenting; others reject or do not require such arrangements.[30]

Women's Development (Cambridge: Harvard Univ. Press, 1982); Barbara H. Andolsen, Christine E. Gudorf, and Mary D. Pellauer, eds., *Women's Consciousness, Women's Conscience: A Reader in Feminist Ethics* (San Francisco: Harper and Row, 1985); Diana Teitjens Meyers, Kenneth Kipnis, and Cornelius F. Murphy, Jr., eds., *Kindred Matters: Rethinking the Philosophy of the Family* (Ithaca, N.Y.: Cornell Univ. Press, 1993).

29. See, e.g., Lenore Weitzman, *The Divorce Revolution: The Unexpected Social and Economic Consequences for Women and Children in America* (New York: The Free Press, 1985); Cohen and Katzenstein; Susan E. Krantz, "Divorce and Children," in Dornbusch and Strober, *Feminism, Children and the New Families;* Judith S. Wallerstein and Sandra Blakeslee, *Second Chances: Men, Women and Children in a Decade after Divorce* (New York: Ticknor and Fields, 1989).

30. Cohen and Katzenstein, 36-37.

Thus the salient issue is not so much whether motherhood should be evacuated in the interests of women's development[31] but rather whether a diversity of family forms should be endorsed. Where do feminists stand on this issue? Whether they are more concerned about feminist or feminine ethics, most appear to be strong supporters of a diversification of family types. On this account, although it is agreed that children need economically stable households with a reliable cast of adults, it is assumed that moral and public policy support should be extended not just to married heterosexual parents, but to any stable household unit, including single fathers and mothers, parent/grandparent households, homosexual couples with adoptive or biological children, and single parents of whatever sexual orientation who rely on the supplementary help of friends in order to rear their children.

To feminist ethicists, societal acceptance of a diversity of family forms would necessarily weaken male dominance — physical, sexual, and economic — within the domestic arena. And to feminine ethicists, the same pluralization would affirm and give space to women's nurturing capacities without requiring them to compromise with the less nurturant, more abstract, and competitive style of a male partner.[32] Thus, writes sociologist Judith Stacey, "In the postmodern period a truly democratic kinship order, one that does not favor authority, heterosexuality, a particular division of labor, or a single household or parenting arrangement [becomes] thinkable for the first time in history."[33] Psychologist Diane Ehrensaft agrees:

> It is imperative that mothering, the daily acts, concerns, and sensibilities that go into the nurturance and rearing of a child, does not become obsolete, but that society makes room for mothering to extend to any combination of adults — women and men, women and women, or men

31. See, e.g., Jeffner Allen, "Motherhood: The Annihilation of Women," in Treblicot, 315-30.

32. See, e.g., Adrienne Rich, *Of Woman Born: Motherhood as Experience and Institution* (New York: Norton, 1976). It should also be noted that some feminists are dubious about the turn to feminine ethics because its "re-essentialization" of gendered virtues could provide an excuse for hegemonic males to assign *all* caretaking — domestic and public — to women as a labor of love based on their (now self-professed) inherent nurturing capacities. For a further discussion of this debate, see Van Leeuwen et al., chs. 12, 13.

33. Stacey, 258.

and men — who are committed to raising a child together. In other words, it is time for mothering to become a genderless affair.[34]

Object-Relations Theory: Defending Heterosexual Coparenting

There is, however, one set of feminist voices that would hesitate to endorse such a wide variety of family forms, insisting instead on the necessity for strong involvement of both father figures and mother figures in child rearing. But far from trying to resurrect the so-called traditional family, with its doctrine of separate spheres, feminist object-relations theorists argue that both male misogyny and the female impulse to overinvest in nurturing are rooted in the very gendering of the public/domestic split that most feminists have worked to eradicate, and therefore that any policy that discourages heterosexual coparenting may in fact undercut the feminist agenda by increasing male misogyny and the marginalization of women from public life.[35]

The problem, according to these feminists working in the depth-psychological tradition, begins in early infancy when children are highly bonded to a primary caretaker, who (in societies with a highly gendered division of labor) is usually a woman. That little girls thus have a same-sex caretaker and primary love-object while little boys do not becomes significant around the age of three, when children of both sexes acquire "gender constancy" — that is, the recognition that being male or female is a permanent state of nature. This is less immediately problematic for girls, who proceed to learn their expected gender roles by doing what they would do

34. Diane Ehrensaft, *Parenting Together: Men and Women Sharing the Care of Their Children* (Urbana, Ill.: Univ. of Illinois Press, 1987), xi. See also Barrie Thorne, "Feminism and the Family: Two Decades of Thought," in Barrie Thorne and Marilyn Yalom, eds., *Rethinking the Family: Some Feminist Questions* (Boston: Northeastern Univ. Press, 1992).

35. See, e.g., Dorothy Dinnerstein, *The Mermaid and the Minotaur: Sexual Arrangements and Human Malaise* (New York: Harper Colophon, 1977); Nancy Chodorow, *The Reproduction of Mothering: Psychoanalysis and the Sociology of Gender* (Berkeley: Univ. of California Press, 1978); Lillian Rubin, *Intimate Strangers: Men and Women Together* (New York: Harper and Row, 1983); Myriam Miedzian, *Boys Will Be Boys: Breaking the Link Between Masculinity and Violence* (New York: Doubleday, 1991).

anyway — namely, copy what their mother does. But boys are placed in something of a quandary: they are expected to disidentify with the most powerful and admired person in their small world, and instead to become like the parent whom they rarely see — namely, their father.

Feminist object-relations theorists hold that this asymmetrical pattern of parenting is at the root of both the "reproduction of mothering" and the "reproduction of misogyny." Little girls, strongly bonded to their mothers and not required to disidentify with them just when their gender identity is being consolidated, tend to grow up with more permeable ego boundaries and a greater desire to stay connected to specific others, including children of their own. And, feminine ethics notwithstanding, this is not an unmixed blessing, for it may result in the underdevelopment of more abstract civic virtues (such as the ability to set aside particular kin loyalties in order to apply universal norms of justice when appropriate), which liberal feminists for the past two centuries have been insisting it is women's right and duty to exercise.

Boys, on the other hand, are forced to figure out what it means to be culturally masculine in the virtual absence of a same-sex caretaker. As a result, they are apt to conclude that becoming a man means becoming as unlike women as possible. As they grow older, they may escalate this exercise in compensatory masculinity, at worst scorning and abusing women while engaging in other antisocial acts singly or with other males, at best distancing themselves from whatever they see as "women's work," including the hands-on caretaking of their own children, thus helping to reproduce the cycle of feminized parenting and male misogyny in the next generation.[36]

If this object-relations account is substantially correct, then some empirically testable hypotheses follow. First, other things being equal, misogynist attitudes and hypermasculine behavior should be greatest in families and cultures where the caretaking of young children is most assiduously avoided by (or denied to) men. By contrast, low levels of misogyny and hypermasculinity — among younger and older males alike — will be like-

36. It is not inconsistent with this object-relations analysis for men to alternate scorn of women with their veneration (as, e.g., in cultures where women are categorized as either "madonnas" or "whores"). Either strategy marginalizes women and keeps them from being seen as fellow human beings with whom one can share activity in both domestic and public realms.

liest in families and cultures where there is active, nurturant, and authoritative (as opposed to authoritarian) father involvement in childcare. Empirical research in both Western and non-Western settings supports both of these hypotheses.[37] Moreover, another body of research shows a positive correlation between father presence and daughters' development of achievement, postponement of adolescent sexual activity, and formation of more stable adult marriages.[38]

Such research findings, combined with the clinical experience of object-relations feminists, lead most of them to be strong supporters of het-

37. See, e.g., Marvin E. Wolfgang, Leonard Savitz, and Norman Johnson, eds., *The Sociology of Crime and Delinquency* (New York: Wiley, 1962); Margaret K. Bacon, Irvin L. Child, and Herbert Barry, "A Cross-Cultural Study of the Correlates of Crime," *Journal of Abnormal and Social Psychology* 66, no. 4 (1963): 291-300; Beatrice B. Whiting and John W. M. Whiting, *Children of Six Cultures* (Cambridge: Harvard Univ. Press, 1975); Michael Lamb, ed., *The Role of the Father in Child Development* (New York: Wiley, 1981); Nancy Eisenberg, ed., *The Development of Prosocial Behavior* (New York: Academic Press, 1982); Kyle Pruett, *The Nurturing Father* (New York: Warner, 1987); Miedzian; Wilson. A comprehensive review of the relevant literature can also be found in David Blankenhorn, *Fatherless America: Confronting Our Most Urgent Social Problem* (New York: Basic Books, 1994).

38. See, e.g., Patricia Draper and Henry Harpending, "Father Absence and Reproductive Strategy: An Evolutionary Perspective," *Journal of Anthropological Research* 38, no. 3 (1982): 255-73, and Mary Stewart Van Leeuwen, *Gender and Grace: Love, Work and Parenting in a Changing World* (Downers Grove, IL: InterVarsity Press, 1990), esp. ch. 8. It should be noted that observed relationships between family type and child behavioral outcomes are necessarily based on correlational studies, not experimental ones, which can isolate causal connections. Just as we cannot randomly assign children to be male or female at birth, so too we cannot randomly assign infants to be reared in families that differ by socioeconomic class and parental configuration, in order to compare outcomes. However, the next-best approximation to an experimental design is a longitudinal study, whereby randomly *selected* groups of children already living in assorted family configurations are followed from birth to maturity, with various measures of development, stress, and adjustment taken at regular intervals. Although not extensive (since longitudinal studies are difficult and expensive to conduct), the relevant literature in this area also supports the thesis that, on average, two-parent, heterosexual families produce better outcomes for children of both sexes, regardless of socioeconomic class, than families in which stable fathers (or father surrogates) are absent. See, e.g., Sheppard Kellam et al., "Family Structure and the Mental Health of Children," *Archives of General Psychiatry* 34 (1977): 1012-22, and "The Long-Term Evolution of the Family Structure of Teenage and Older Mothers," *Journal of Marriage and the Family* 44 (1982): 539-44. For a brief overview of correlational and longitudinal studies in this area, see also Wilson.

erosexual coparenting — that is, the generally equal distribution of hands-on childcare between fathers and mothers. As might be expected, however, their conclusions have not gone unchallenged by those who endorse an unlimited diversity of family forms. For example, psychologist Joseph Pleck claims that the root problem is not the absence of fathers, but the traditional practice of imposing rigid gender roles on boys and girls. Thus, he concludes, if cultural ideals about what is appropriately "masculine" were to become more flexible, boys raised by women would not need to act hypermasculine to prove their manhood, as it would be acceptable for "real men" to be empathic, caring, and emotionally connected.[39]

Feminist object-relations theorists would certainly not disagree that rigidly gender-stereotyped roles contribute to misogyny and other forms of exaggerated masculinity. However, as clinician Myriam Miedzian points out, the anthropological, psychological, and sociological data suggest that it is largely the lack of paternal involvement that produces rigid, dichotomous, and hierarchical notions of gender roles in the first place. "It may be," she writes, "that male involvement in nurturant fathering is a condition of more fluid sex roles and decreased [male] violence."[40] Future research may increasingly support this conjecture as the effects of pluralized family forms filter down to the next generation.

But what exactly is it about involved fathering that lessens the risk of male violence and other forms of hypermasculinity in sons, including a rigidly traditionalist view of appropriate sex roles? It must be said at the outset that this is still something of a mystery, as is the way that involved fathering operates to reduce the risk of prematurely active sexuality and low achievement motivation in daughters. This should not surprise us much, since until recently "parenting" was effectively equated with "mothering" and studies on the nature and dynamics of fathering were almost unknown. Nonetheless, a preliminary reading of the literature suggests that nurturant, authoritative father presence operates in two complementary ways to promote these outcomes.

Negatively, involved fatherly presence acts as a check on boys' aggressiveness as they grow older, something that mothers cannot do as easily, however well motivated they may be. Indeed, for some educational activists in the African-American community, the rationale behind the movement

39. Joseph Pleck, *The Myth of Masculinity* (Cambridge, Mass.: M.I.T. Press, 1983).
40. Miedzian, 87-88.

for Afrocentric schools is not just the conviction that their children need pride-instilling exposure to an Afrocentric curriculum, but the belief that boys especially need to experience this in single-sex classrooms. Supporters of this movement, both men and women, assert that at least for now young black males (especially those from single-mother homes) need single-sex settings in which black male teachers provide firm discipline and model the virtues of learning and self-restraint, in order to forestall the hyper-masculine behaviors that have helped make murder the leading cause of death for young black males over ten years of age, placed more young black men in prison than in college, and contributed to casual attitudes about parenting responsibilities. The school principal of one such school in Detroit observed that African-American single mothers "tend to raise their girls and love their boys."[41] In other words, they often find it easier to be firm with their daughters than with their sons, in part because they themselves have experienced the hazards and temptations of growing up female — but not male. On this account, adult men may contribute to the socialization of young males simply by being able to see through them more readily and by being willing to confront and redirect hypermasculine "acting out" before it reaches epidemic proportions.

Even more important, however, are the positive effects that involved fathers can have on children of both sexes. By reassuring both sons and daughters that they are valued and loved as unique individuals, and by raising them in a fashion that is nurturant as well as appropriately authoritative, fathers can implicitly certify their children "masculine enough" and "feminine enough" to get on with the more important business of being human. In other words, nurturant fathering helps relieve children of the anxiety of "proving themselves" adequately masculine or feminine (boys by engaging in truculent and misogynist activities, girls by becoming prematurely and too indiscriminately sexual), and can thus free their energies for the acquisition of more adaptive — and less rigidly gender-stereotyped — relational and work skills. Psychiatrist Frank Pittman has been especially perceptive about this second, positive aspect of fathering, especially in relation to boys' development. From his experience of three decades as a counselor to men struggling with identity issues, he writes:

41. Karen Houppert, "Establish Afrocentric, All-Male Academies," *Utne Reader*, no. 61 (1994): 85.

> Most boys nowadays are growing up with fathers who spend little, if any, time with them. Ironically, when the boy most needs to practice being a man, his father is off somewhere playing at being a boy. . . . Instead of real-life fathers, boys grow up with myths of fathers, while mothers, whatever their significance out there in the world, reign supreme at home and in the life of the boy. If fathers have run out on mothers, in any of the many ways men use to escape women, then boys can't imagine that their masculinity is sufficient until they too run away from women and join the world of men. . . . Boys who don't have fathers they know and love don't know how much masculinity is enough.
>
> Fathers have the authority to let boys relax the requirements of the masculine model: If our fathers accept us, then that declares us masculine enough to join the company of men. In effect, boys then have their diplomas in masculinity and can go on to develop other skills. . . . A boy may spend his entire life seeking that acceptance, the love and approval of his father, and with it a reprieve from masculine striving. If boys can't get acceptance from their fathers, then they are dependent on the company of other men to overwhelm the father's rejecting voices or the echoing sounds of paternal silence.[42]

One might legitimately ask at this point if mothers are not equally important in this process of certifying children "masculine enough" and "feminine enough." Indeed, they are; still, it is not mother absence from families, but father absence (physical and/or psychological) that has been the greater problem in our society since the industrial revolution. And the bottom line appears to be this: children of both sexes need interaction with nurturant, authoritative adult role models of both sexes in order to develop a secure gender identity, which then (paradoxically) allows them to relate to each other primarily as human beings, rather than as reduced, gender-role caricatures.[43]

42. Frank Pittman, "Beyond the B.S. and the Drumbeating: Staggering Through Life as a Man," *Psychology Today* 25, no. 1 (1992): 82-83.

43. Marian Wright Edelman's best-selling little book *The Measure of Our Success: A Letter to My Children and Yours* (New York: HarperCollins, 1992) implicitly endorses this goal for gender relations when she lists, as Lesson 7 for her sons, "Remember that your wife is not your mother or your maid, but your partner and friend." She then goes on to recall that, even in the segregated setting of the 1940s and 50s in which she was raised as the daughter of a black Baptist pastor, her parents expected their sons and daughters both to achieve in the public realm and be competent task sharers in all areas of domestic life, and modeled these expectations in their own lives (pp. 46-50).

Feminist object-relations theory does not require that such role models always and only be the child's biological parents — but it strongly suggests that there are limits to the diversity of family forms that can be encouraged around a core norm of heterosexual, egalitarian coparenting.

Some Considerations from Theological Anthropology

So far we have seen that self-styled family traditionalists are becoming functionally more flexible and egalitarian in their view of gender roles and relations. At the same time feminists, acknowledging the need of children for stable homes, are becoming more supportive of intact families. Many feminists want the definition of what constitutes a "family" to be broadened to include any adult or combination of adults committed to bringing a child to maturity. However, one group of feminists — those in the depth-psychological tradition known as object-relations theory — have made a strong case for the normativity of the two-parent, heterosexual coparenting family, on the grounds that it is the one most likely to promote egalitarian gender attitudes, reliable male parental involvement, and a self-image for females that goes beyond reproduction and mothering to active responsibility in the economic and civic realms.

Does this mean that some common ground can be found regarding the minimal shape of family life and the kind of public policies that should support it? And what, if anything, can theological anthropology contribute to answering this question? I come to the latter question as a Calvinist layperson working in the neo-Reformational tradition, one that, long before the advent of both feminist and postmodern philosophy of science, rejected the Enlightenment assumption that the power of human reason makes it possible to generate totally "objective" and "value-free" knowledge. On the contrary, this tradition asserts that every person, whether knowingly or not, works from the basis of a worldview — that is, from a rock-bottom set of faith assumptions about the nature of reality. It also holds that our worldviews — whether they are at root Christian, Marxist, naturalist, pantheist, or something else — are not (Enlightenment thinking to the contrary) confirmed or disconfirmed by reason, scholarship, or science. Rather, worldviews are the spiritual frameworks within which we *build* not just our scholarly and scientific theories, but also our visions of work, society, and the meaning of even our smallest everyday decisions and actions.

When refracted through a Reformed lens, the concept of a Christian worldview receives another important twist — namely, an insistence on the simultaneous working out of the themes of creation, sin, and redemption in all areas of life. Reformed creation theology supports the conviction that women and men of all ages, abilities, classes, and ethnicities are equally made in God's image and equally called "to diligently develop and use their God-given gifts for the good of home, church, and society."[44] For when we look at that great passage from the creation account in Genesis 1:26-28 — the passage containing what Reformed theologians often call the "cultural mandate" to humankind — we do not find God saying to the first female, "Be fruitful and multiply," and to the first male, "Subdue the earth." On the contrary, *both* are called to both accountable dominion and accountable sociability and fruitfulness: "And God blessed *them* and said to *them*, 'Be fruitful and multiply, and fill the earth and subdue it. . . .'" There is no warrant here for rigidly gendered spheres or activities, nor (in either of the creation accounts) for male domination. Both women and men, made in the image of God, are called to unfold the potential of creation in all areas of life, to engage in good, stewardly, and God-honoring activities *together*, whether those activities take place close to the hearth, within the worship setting, or elsewhere in the social and natural world.

Now if we could simply stop with a creation theology of work, worship, and gender relations we probably would not have to struggle over the relationship of gender to public policy. But the biblical drama only begins with the act of creation. And it is only after both members of the primal pair foolishly assert their independence from God in Act Two — the fall — that the cosmic love story of mutuality and equality goes awry. The results for gender relations include the degeneration of the male's legitimate, accountable dominion into self-seeking domination, first of the woman, then (in the next generation's murder of Abel by Cain) of other men. For the woman, legitimate, creational sociability degenerates into social enmeshment: "Your desire shall be to your husband," God warns in Genesis 3:16,

44. Statement of Faith of Christians for Biblical Equality, 380 Lafayette Road South, Suite 122, St. Paul, MN 55107. For good introductions to Reformed creation theology and its application to intellectual and social life, see Brian J. Walsh and J. Richard Middleton, *The Transforming Vision: Shaping a Christian World View* (Downers Grove, Ill.: InterVarsity Press, 1984), and Albert M. Wolters, *Creation Regained: Biblical Basics for a Reformational World View* (Grand Rapids, Mich.: Eerdmans, 1985).

"and he shall rule over you." The woman's flaw complementary to the man's domination is thus the temptation to cling to relationships even when they are creationally warped by abuse and injustice.[45]

In spite of all this, God's cultural and social mandates continue. Men and women still jointly image God, however distorted that image may be, and thus are called to do cultural work that has God's blessing, including the crafting and recrafting of human roles and relationships that make for a just and orderly society at varying points in history. Then in the third, redemptive act of the biblical drama God takes on human flesh in order to show even more clearly what is needed to sow the seeds of kingdom justice, righteousness, and peace.

Although Jesus preached no sermons specifically on gender relations, his actions toward women clearly stood as a challenge to the patriarchal attitudes and practices of his day. Particularly noteworthy is his refusal, on several occasions, to endorse the prevailing assumption that women's status depended almost entirely on their childbearing and domestic functions.[46] At the same time, Jesus' refusal to be the "military messiah" that many had hoped for, his disregard for material security, and his refusal to play by the rules of the religious establishment of the day all undermine stereotypical notions (then and now) of the successful male. Additionally, Paul's sermon on love in I Corinthians 13, his sermon on the whole armor of God in Ephesians 6, and his list of the fruits of the spirit in Galatians 5 show no hint of a rigidly gendered division of traits: together they describe essential character traits of every Christian, female or male.

None of this means that a gendered division of labor is always wrong; for example, in the previous section I have defended the idea that there is at least a modest complementarity in the way that mothers and fathers function to help children to secure and then transcend their gender identities. What this brief biblical theology of gender relations does affirm is this: whatever roles we embrace as women or men, single or married, are secondary (and flexibly subordinate) to the shared creational calling to "fill

45. See Judith Plaskow, *Sex, Sin, and Grace: Women's Experience and the Theologies of Reinhold Niebuhr and Paul Tillich* (Lanham, Md.: University Press of America, 1980), and Van Leeuwen, esp. ch. 2.

46. For example, Luke 10:28-42 and 11:27-28; Matt. 12:46-50. See also Elisabeth Schüssler Fiorenza, *In Memory of Her: A Feminist Theological Reconstruction of Christian Origins* (New York: Crossroads, 1984).

the earth and subdue it," and the shared redemptive calling to work toward the restoration of God's kingdom *shalom*. In light of the biblical drama, women and men are indeed "neighboring sexes," not "opposite sexes."

Implications for Welfare Reform

America's welfare crisis takes somewhat different forms among different classes of people. Among the chronically poor, the interlocking problems include low levels of education, a high incidence of single motherhood, low rates of male employment and family support, and the stress of living in increasingly violent neighborhoods. Among working- and middle-class families, the increasing need for two wage earners means that even in two-parent families, children are less at risk of being underfathered than of simply being underparented. American children as a whole appear to be faring worse than their own parents did as children, as evidenced by falling test scores and rising rates of childhood and adolescent homicide, suicide, and behavioral and learning disorders.[47]

47. Nicholas Zill and Charlotte Schoenborn, "Developmental, Learning and Emotional Problems: Health of Our Nation's Children, United States, 1988," National Center for Health Statistics, DHHS Publication PHS-91-1250. That these problems are no longer limited to the so-called underclass of society is anecdotally affirmed by William H. Willimon, the chaplain of Duke University, in his recent article, "Reaching and Teaching the Abandoned Generation," *Christian Century* 110, no. 29 (1993): 1016-19. Citing (especially male) students' preoccupation with professionalism and power, the consequences of escalating alcohol abuse, and the gap between the rhetoric of pluralism and students' inability to bridge racial barriers, Willimon concludes that university faculty and administrators have mistakenly abandoned their function as moral (not just intellectual) mentors to young people on the assumption that college-age students are already adults who need only be encouraged to think and make decisions for themselves. "But," asserts Willimon, "students are not adults. At best a student is . . . a 'novice adult.' Few students are capable of 'making their own decisions' or 'thinking for themselves.' Leaving them to themselves, with no skills for discernment, meager personal experience, and a narrow worldview, they become the willing victims of the most totalitarian form of government ever devised — namely, submission to their peers, obeisance to people just like them." This, Willimon observes, "is not freedom." Rather, it risks deteriorating into a late-adolescent version of *Lord of the Flies*. Similar concerns are voiced by Christina Hoff Sommers (a feminist philosopher at Clark University) in her article "How to Teach Right and Wrong: A Blueprint for Moral Education in a Pluralistic Age," *Christianity Today* 37, no. 15 (1993): 33-37.

In all these cases, gender is a significant variable, for how we respond to the problems of each group will depend, among other things, on how we believe gender, work, and parenting should go together. I have already shown that the gulf between self-styled traditionalists and some feminists is not as great as the rhetoric of each group would suggest, especially with regard to the issues of gender equality and the developmental needs of children. Consequently, I suggest that welfare policy might be built around the following common goal: "How can we put children first without putting women last or putting men on the sidelines?"

The three parts of this question must be kept together, for although there is a broad consensus on the urgency of attending to children's needs in America, self-styled traditionalists may still be tempted to address those needs by resurrecting the doctrine of separate spheres and restoring male patriarchy within the family, albeit in a kinder, gentler form. This solution is both theologically and psychologically suspect, for it assumes that men are somehow more "naturally" made for achievement in the public realm (and little else) while women are "naturally" made for domesticity (and little else). But even Sigmund Freud recognized that two essential needs for human happiness were love and work, which is simply a secularized expression of the biblical truth that all of us — women and men alike — are created for both responsible sociability and responsible dominion. We are not doing a favor to men, women, or children if we reinvent welfare policies that assume (even were the economy to allow families to manage on a single wage) that child care is exclusively women's mandate and breadwinning is exclusively men's.

At the same time, we cannot (as some feminists and some self-serving males assert) meet children's developmental and women's achievement/affiliative needs by declaring male family involvement strictly optional. Let it be admitted at the outset that sometimes divorce and/or single parenthood is the lesser of two evils, especially when there is a history of chronic abuse or irresponsibility on the part of a partner. Let it also be said — repeatedly — that many single parents do a magnificent job of parenting under very challenging circumstances. At present, given the residual strength of the separate-spheres doctrine, such single parents are mostly mothers. But single-parent fathers are increasingly common, and their efforts at responsible parenting need to be recognized and supported precisely because they are in the minority and are often considered inherently incapable of hands-on nurturing.

Moreover, with adequate support from sources as diverse as school, youth groups, family members, and healthy peers, children in single-parent homes can show a gratifying resistance to at-risk behaviors such as substance abuse, precocious sexual activity, and antisocial behavior.[48] But none of this obviates the fact that, other things being equal, children of both sexes best develop a balanced sense of "love and work" if they grow up in stable households with nurturant, authoritative (as opposed to authoritarian) adult role models of both sexes. Without either lapsing into a reendorsement of patriarchy or being moralistic and neglectful toward single-parent families, we need to craft our welfare policies and our supporting institutions around this "core" norm.

My chapter concludes with specific policy recommendations of two sorts. Negatively, we need policies aimed at reversing parental irresponsibility by both males and females and at improving the basic health and safety of children. Positively, we need policies that make it easier for parents already motivated by a sense of responsibility to support their children and each other in ways that do not require a regression to the separate-spheres doctrine.[49]

Reversing Parental Irresponsibility and Improving Child Health and Safety

By 1993, the overall rate of out-of-wedlock births in America had reached a level of almost 30 percent; among African-Americans, it had reached 66 percent. Moreover, the poverty rate of children whose parents neither get married nor finish high school is a staggering 79 percent — as opposed to 8 percent for those whose parents do both. At present, the cost of Aid for Families with Dependent Children (AFDC) is $13 billion a year. Now it is quite true that there are Americans expressing great indignation over the cost of AFDC who do not bat an eyelash over the $300 billion need to bail

48. See, e.g., Peter L. Benson and Eugene C. Roehlkepartain, *Youth in Single-Parent Families: Risk and Resiliency* (Minneapolis: Search Institute, 1993).

49. Many of the policy recommendations that follow are drawn from the Communitarian Network's Capitol Hill Teach-In on the Future of the Family (Washington, D.C., November 1993), at which a variety of academics, policy specialists, and bipartisan legislators advanced policy strategies "to enable parents to be parents."

out fiscally irresponsible savings and loan institutions. Nor do many of these same people agonize over the fact that 53 percent of the federal tax intake goes to entitlement spending, 14 percent to service the national debt, and 10 percent to military spending, leaving a mere 23 percent for discretionary spending on all other programs — research, social, educational, and cultural.

In spite of this evidence for the warped nature of America's national priorities, many people continue to treat welfare reform as the most important and urgent of the nation's economic priorities — even though, in Marian Wright Edelman's words, "welfare queens can't hold a candle to corporate kings in raiding the public purse."[50] Nevertheless, welfare reform *is* important — not so much because of its present cost in dollars, but because of the disincentives toward waged work and marriage that characterize the present system and the chronic marginalization of children and adults from the economic and societal mainstream that results. One policy reform that would begin to change this incentive structure while still providing a safety net for children and single parents is the national child support assurance proposal.[51]

This "assured benefits" proposal has both a structural and an ethical parallel with the survivors' benefit component of Social Security that was introduced in 1930. Prior to that time, three-fourths of the welfare caseload consisted of widows with children; now only 2 percent are in this category, in part because of the "preventive social security" of survivors' benefits. Structurally, the child support assurance parallels survivors' benefits in that it has prior financial contributions as an eligibility requirement. (In this respect it is quite unlike the current AFDC program.) Ethically, the parallel is as follows: just as we require dead parents to have helped provide for their surviving family members' support by contributing to Social Security while alive and working, so we should require absent but alive parents (90 percent of whom are male at this point) to contribute to the ongoing support of their children.

At present, some $35 to 50 billion *should* be forthcoming in child support by absent parents; in fact, only about $11 million is being paid, and only about 40 percent of single-parent children receive any support at all from the absent parent. That a third of all collections are done (badly, at present) on an interstate basis also underscores the need for such a program to be

50. Edelman, 91.

51. The following summary draws on the work of Columbia University's Irwin Garfinkel, as presented at the Teach-In on the Future of the Family.

national in character. The program would include the following components: (1) routine establishment of paternity at birth as an eligibility requirement for any future benefits; (2) I.R.S.-based collection of support payments from absent parents via a 17 percent payroll tax (which means that the obligation is pegged to income, and thus does not disproportionately penalize absent parents who have low income or who lose jobs); (3) at the same time (as with widows' Social Security benefits) receipt of benefits not conditional on reduced participation in the workforce by the custodial parent; and (4) for families whose absent parent's contributions fall below a set minimum (e.g., $2000 per year for one child, $3000 for two, etc.) a backup federally funded "safety net" to bring payments up to the minimum, disbursed through the Social Security Administration and funded by savings from AFDC and a slight increase in the Social Security payroll tax.

Note that while providing income security, the assured benefit proposal does so in a way that changes behavioral incentives. Whereas welfare at present discourages waged work and stable, two-parent households, the assured benefit program serves as a disincentive for divorce or desertion on the part of either parent, complements rather than replaces work income by both parents, and requires prior financial contributions through work (or through community service for the chronically jobless) as a condition of eligibility. It is also a scheme that has been shown to work in other industrialized nations, such as Sweden, as a means for promoting parental responsibility while not penalizing waged work on the part of either parent.

Needless to say, for such a scheme to work equally well in America, parallel reforms are needed to ensure that children have basic health coverage regardless of the level of their parents' participation in the waged workforce. Every dollar invested in preventive health care for mothers and infants (for example, through prenatal care and child immunization) saves over three dollars later on. In addition, every dollar invested in quality preschool programs saves almost five dollars later on. And it costs more than twice as much to place a child in foster care as to provide family preservation services — for example, through family centers patterned after the old settlement house model (which helped immigrants of an earlier time cope with the stress of adjusting to a new culture) or through joint public-private ventures, which channel tax dollars to family services provided by religious and other nonprofit organizations.[52]

52. Edelman, 92. Also needed is the reform of insurance regulations and welfare

But even improvements in basic health care, preschool education, and family support services will do little for children's chances of life success (especially in inner cities, but increasingly also in the suburbs) if we are unwilling to get serious about gun control. It is a strange irony that many conservatives who preach about the need to encourage personal responsibility among the poor are equally adamant about keeping semiautomatic rifles freely circulating and having fewer requirements for owning and using firearms than for possessing and driving a car. As a result, some 135,000 children bring guns to school each day, close to half a million violent crimes occur in and around schools each year, and some inner-city children live in such a constant climate of violence that they show the same symptoms of post-traumatic stress disorder as Vietnam combat veterans.[53] Needless to say, none of this is conducive to optimal child development or to cultivating either the capacity or the motivation to assume productive adult roles.

Positive Supports for Parenting

Despite the high publicity profile given to welfare recipients, most poor families include at least one parent in the waged workforce, and pay a high percentage of their income for housing alone. Some are in single-earner, others in double-earner, households, but in either case, they need the support for parenting that would result from three areas of policy reform — namely, the institution of child allowances, the removal of tax penalties on married couples, and the provision of greater employment benefits for part-time workers.

With regard to the first of these, we should first note that forty years ago, dependent tax exemptions offset 40 percent of families' taxable income.

---

policies surrounding mental health services. At present, neither of these allows for the funding of treatment based on a family-systems approach, but only on the basis of individually identified problems (e.g., categorization of individuals according to the American Psychiatric Association's Diagnostic and Statistical Manual). And yet marriage and family therapy — which treats the family as a unit for both diagnosis and cure of mental problems in the officially identified patient — has been shown to be cost-effective in terms of preventing more severe problems later on.

53. Edelman, 87.

Today, those same exemptions offset only 11 percent of taxable income, and even a child tax credit of $1000 per child would not restore the tax advantage that families enjoyed forty years ago.[54] In addition, the working poor usually do not have sufficient income to be taxable, and thus do not benefit from the dependent exemption. The net result is that, in our current welfare/tax system, most benefits go to those in the lowest and the highest socioeconomic strata, with no adequate safety net for the working poor in between. Moreover, under the present system, if a typical welfare recipient marries a typical minimum-wage worker, their joint income falls by an average of 30 percent — hardly an incentive to get married and/or to stay working. A universal child allowance — for example, in the form of a $1000 tax benefit for each child — would go some way toward rectifying these disparities and disincentives. At present, sixty-three nations worldwide provide some kind of family allowance to workers and their children; it is high time America became the sixty-fourth.[55]

In the second place, we need to revise the present policy of taxing marital cooperation — that is, taxing married couples at a higher rate than singles. In addition to providing an incentive to live together without benefit of marriage, the present policy takes needed income from those who are struggling to be responsible parents. The present policy is based on the reasonable assumption that two can live together more cheaply than apart, and yet it is puzzling that the resulting higher tax rates are applied *only* to married couples, and not to apartment mates, cohabiting couples, carpoolers, or office sharers, most of whom are not burdened with the task of raising children together.

Finally, we need to improve the pay and fringe benefits of part-time

54. If the dependent tax exemption had been adjusted over the years for inflation, it would now be a standard $8650, instead of the present $2000 — or, alternately, it would be the equivalent of a $1400 tax credit. These figures are based on a presentation by C. Eugene Steuerle, of the Urban Institute, at the Teach-In on the Future of the Family.

55. One possibility for financing such an allowance is to stop the deduction of mortgage interest payments from taxable income, except perhaps for the first house purchased. Under the present system, anyone who can muster the down payment for a house can continue to use home equity loans as a source of cheap, revolving credit indefinitely, because of this mortgage interest deduction. This amounts to billions of potential tax dollars annually, and gives no support to the working poor, who cannot usually afford to finance home ownership anyway.

workers, who constitute 18 percent of the labor force at any given time and two-thirds of whom are women.[56] It is worth noting that, prior to 1970, most part-time employment was assumed voluntarily — often by women concerned to preserve time and energy for family. Today, most part-time work is involuntary — that is, it is employer-driven, not employee-driven — including most of the new jobs created in the current economic recovery. Part-time workers on average earn only 62 percent of the hourly wage of full-time workers, and in only 28 percent of institutions do part-time workers receive any medical and life insurance benefits. Unemployment insurance is extended only to those working more than thirty-five hours a week, and part-time workers pay Social Security taxes on a higher proportion of their wages than full-time workers.

In most of the industrialized world it is simply illegal to discriminate against part-time workers in the ways just mentioned, especially since (given that the majority of part-time workers are women) it amounts to the practice of indirect sex discrimination. Hourly wages are the same for full-time and part-time workers, the same benefits are provided to part-time workers on a prorated basis, and if part-time workers are used at all, it is due either to worker request or to the scheduling needs of the company. Part-time workers thus cannot be used as a way to cut corners on wages and benefits, as is becoming increasingly the case in the United States.[57] Given the increasing percentage of workers of both sexes who are employed part-time, reforms such as those mentioned above would allow a household to earn an adequate "family wage" without forcing its parents to be chronically absent from the home front.

Concluding Comments

In the long run, society cannot function unless most of its members act responsibly because they believe it is right to do so, and not solely because of external incentives or sanctions. Nevertheless, to the extent that it is the

56. These and the following figures are based on the work of Eileen Appelbaum of the Economic Policy Institute, as presented at the Teach-In on the Future of the Family.

57. For example, Australia, Scandinavia, and the U.K. have legislation prohibiting differential treatment of part-time workers, whereas Canada, like the U.S., does not.

function of government to enable people to undertake their responsibilities in various spheres, policy reforms such as those just mentioned are necessary, if not sufficient, conditions for the conduct of responsible parenting. In addition, we need public-private cooperation in the setting up of many more programs for marriage and parent training, among both adults and school-aged children.[58]

Among waged-working parents — whether in two- or one-parent families — an urgent need is simply to make more time for parenting amid the demands of economic survival. Thus family-leave policies — not just for the care of newborns, but of older children and other dependents — need to become more generous and more standardized; this is another area in which America lags shamefully behind other industrialized nations. Moreover, these same leave policies should take seriously the need of infants for a bonding period of several months with one or (preferably) both parents, but also the well-established finding that *after* the first year of life, infants placed in quality day-care settings are not at risk for insecure attachment or other problems in the early school years.[59] Flextime work hours and, where feasible, the option of telecommuting to allow some waged work to be done at home would also help parents (and, indeed, all citizens) toward the goal of "putting children first." It is high time we began to regard children as a national resource for whom all citizens share responsibility, and not as just an individual indulgence and/or burden for those who choose to bear them.

Finally, without being either moralistic or heavy-handed, we need to support policies that make family breakup less likely to occur in the first place. In the past, the economic dependence of women and the social stigma associated with divorce kept a lot of marriages together to the advantage of children but to the detriment of women, and sometimes men. Such sanctions no longer work, nor do I think most of us would want to return to a heavy reliance on them. (Recall that it was the children of those

58. The Philadelphia-based program and elementary school curriculum known as Education for Parenting, developed originally by Quakers for nonsectarian use, but based on their commitment to nonviolence, is one excellent example. For further information, they can be contacted at 31 West Coulter Street, Philadelphia, Penn. 19144.

59. In fact, these risks are not even present in the first year of life, provided that infants spend twenty hours or less per week in day-care settings. See Jay Belsky, "The 'Effects' of Day Care Reconsidered," *Early Childhood Research Quarterly* 3 (1988): 235-72, and Tiffany Field, *Infancy* (Cambridge: Harvard Univ. Press, 1990).

more-stable 1950s marriages who divorced with increasing abandon during the 1960s and 70s, so family life cannot have been that perfect back then!) We are now dealing with women and men who more and more take gender equality — economic, political, and psychological — as a given. They rightly perceive that marriage must be more like a successful friendship than a relationship of complementary dependencies within an unquestioned framework of patriarchal authority.

In all of this churches, mosques, and synagogues need to affirm the norm of egalitarian, two-parent families while dealing realistically and compassionately with those who depart from it. Such a view, writes practical theologian Don Browning, "recognizes that the family crisis is caused both by cultural changes and by social-systemic developments in areas of work, economics, childcare and gender inequality." Furthermore, he and a colleague write,

> this view recognizes, along with the conservative voices, that unfettered individualism and its drive for adult fulfillment at the expense of children presents a real threat to the family. But [it also] sees the drive toward individualism as partially good. It supports, for example, the push towards more equality for women. Aspects of individualism can be included with integrity in those interpretations of Christian love which see it as commanding a strenuous equal regard for both self and other. This view tries to hold individual fulfillment and regard for the other, be it spouse or children or both, in rigorous balance.[60]

Clearly, in a pluralistic society, neither church nor state can force such a view on people. But to the extent that such a view reflects creation norms, the operation of which are to everyone's benefit, our modeling of those norms will command not only respect but also, in the long run, emulation.

60. Don S. Browning and Ian Evison, "The Family Debate: A Middle Way," *Christian Century* 110, no. 21 (1993): 712-16.

III. SOCIAL COMPLEXITY AND DIVERSE RESPONSIBILITIES

Rights Talk and Welfare Policy

Paul Marshall

THE UNITED STATES has been labeled the "land of rights," unique in its "prodigality in bestowing the rights label," in its obsession with litigation, and in its infestation of lawyers. Hence it is ironic that this is the Western country that, more than any other, conducts its debates on welfare policy and, indeed, economic policy in general, without any developed or widespread notion of "welfare rights."[1] I will suggest that, despite drawbacks, this lacuna is a fortunate one and that it would now be counterproductive to introduce such a notion. Any approach to welfare reform should heed experiences elsewhere, which have usually led to restrictions being placed on the scope of "economic rights." If, nevertheless, some notion of welfare rights is introduced, it should be a general one that highlights aspirations and the importance of state action rather than a specific one that mandates particular individual guarantees.

Meanings of Rights

Perhaps the most common contemporary way, worldwide, of addressing normative political issues is the language of rights and human rights.[2] Issues

1. These characterizations are from Mary Ann Glendon's *Rights Talk: The Impoverishment of Political Discourse* (New York: Basic Books, 1991), x and ch. 1.

2. See Paul Marshall, "Two Types of Rights," *Canadian Journal of Political Science* 25, no. 4 (1992): 661-76.

as diverse as race, abortion, international trade, political freedoms, court procedure, and medical practice are addressed in terms of rights and, more specifically, human rights. This is true in theoretical reflection and political struggles, whether domestic, international, or transnational. Apart from the widespread use of rights language in policy and law, views of human rights are central to many modern theories of politics. They occur in lectures and journals as much as in courts and demonstrations.

The stress on human rights is strengthened by the claim that they are *universal,* as in the United Nations' *Universal Declaration of Human Rights.* On a slightly less exalted plane, they are often regarded as *fundamental.* In the 1966 *International Covenants on Human Rights* they are described as "the foundation of freedom, justice, and peace in the world." More prosaically, they have been described as "trumps," as basic elements that, when rightfully claimed, override other considerations such as propriety, efficiency, and communal solidarity.[3]

This is reflected in modern international standards and the international law of human rights. The operative principle here is that states commit themselves by treaty to treat their own citizens in a protective way. The legal power of the treaty helps to shape domestic law and makes possible international review and repercussions if a state violates its commitment. In general we can say that human rights are given a higher, if not indeed the highest, status compared to other normative elements within politics.

The rights protected by international law usually include "civil and political" rights. These typically involve freedom from discrimination; rights to life, liberty, and security of the person; freedom from torture; freedom of movement; the right to a nationality and to property; freedom of religion, opinion, and expression; and the right to take part in the government of one's country. The rights on this list are supported by most human-rights advocates. But many charters now often include another group, usually referred to as "economic, social, and cultural" rights. These include the right to social security; the right to work; the right to a standard of living adequate for well-being; and the right to education.

3. While a view of rights as "trumps" was articulated most clearly by Ronald Dworkin, the idea rests on a broad tendency in modern jurisprudence. See the survey in H. Gillman, "The Evolution of the Rights Trump in the American Constitutional Tradition" (paper presented at the Annual Meeting of the American Political Science Association, Washington, D.C., Sept. 1991).

Because of this multiplication of meanings, human rights suffer from major conceptual and definitional problems.[4] While this is true of many concepts in public policy, the problem is particularly acute in the sphere of rights. A vague concept of "rights" pervades the modern, and especially the American, consciousness. In some instances it reflects a commitment to some precise and articulate view of rights per se, as distinct from a developed view of duties, responsibilities, prudence, ethics, or charity. However, in many more cases it has simply become a common word with which to express our general concerns and hopes. Someone who claims that "everyone has a right to decent housing" might mean that this is a consequence of some specific inherent human right, or they may even mean that a proper interpretation of the law requires it. But they are more likely to mean nothing more than that people *should have* decent housing, and that it would be just and fair for the rest of us to try to make sure such housing is available. Hence the term "rights" often loses any specific content and becomes a general term of approval or disapproval, commendation or criticism.

Intertwined with these variations is a distinction that one might expect to be rarely, if ever, confused. This is the distinction between "innate human rights" and "legal human rights."[5] "Innate human rights" (alternatively described as "natural rights," "inherent rights," or "moral rights") are thought to be a particular type of claim, somehow intrinsic to human beings, that entitles people to protection by or provision from others, especially states. "Legal human rights" are guarantees contained in positive law and capable of sustaining a legal appeal. This distinction is hardly a subtle one, yet it is often confused. Occasionally these two are treated as identical, but more common is the assumption, often inarticulate, that the two necessarily have some close connection. This usually occurs through a melding of vocabulary where, for example, certain claimed items, usually acknowledged as absent in current positive law, are articulated as inherent rights with the overall purpose of justifying their establishment as legal

4. One of the striking features of many treatments of economic and welfare rights is that despite their precision over aspects of social policy, the authors never really ask what they mean by a right. A good example of this is Ellen Frankel Paul, Fred D. Miller, Jr., and Jeffrey Paul, eds., *Economic Rights* (New York: Cambridge Univ. Press, 1992), the "Introduction" of which claims that "it is difficult to think of any moral or political theory which does not implicitly or explicitly incorporate some theory of economic rights" (p. vii).

5. This discussion is adapted from my "Two Types of Rights."

human rights. In President Bill Clinton's claims that access to health care is a right, the two meanings of rights are melded since the defense of the former is assumed to be a justification of the latter.

Hence the expression "rights" is used in three broad senses:

- to express a belief that human beings have a general responsibility to deal kindly and justly with one another;
- to refer to legislation or constitutional enactments giving legal guarantees, or to the need for such legislation;
- to express a precise view that human beings (and perhaps other things within the world) have "innate" or "inherent" rights (this is a view distinct from, and often at odds with, views of natural law and utilitarianism).

The first of these views is shared by almost everyone with any concern for justice. The second has to do with the question of what, if any, rights legislation should be created. The third is a more precise ethical "rights view," usually involving a concept of inherent rights, and it is on this type of view that I will now concentrate.

The Problem of Inherent Rights

The nature of an ethical rights view can be illustrated by some questions that I ask students. Imagine that you freely make an agreement with a close friend that for money you will accept responsibility for one week to care for their child, walk their dog, water their plants, and paint their bathroom. I then ask, Do you have a responsibility to care for the child? Yes, the students say. Walk the dog? Yes. Water the plants? Yes. Paint the bathroom? Yes. So we are agreed that we have a responsibility to do these things. Then I ask, Does the child have a right to be cared for by you? The class invariably will answer yes. Does the dog have a right to be walked by you? Here we lose some, but most of the class still comes through with a yes. Do the plants have a right to be watered by you? Here we lose most of them, although a few diehard ecological types still answer in the affirmative. Finally, if I ask whether the bathroom has a right to be painted, then — so far — we lose everybody. The consensus is that we have a responsibility to do all these things, but that we do not necessarily think at the same time that others have a right to something. *Inherent rights are not simply the obverse of duties or responsibilities.* Rather, the conception constitutes a particular way of approaching moral and legal questions. *The inherent rights conception begins not with an assertion of duty but with an assertion of a subjective moral power, and attempts to construct a view of duty, morality, obligation, and legality on the basis of this supposed moral power.*[6]

The notion of an "inherent right" (phrased at the time as a "natural right"), as distinct from justice, duty, or natural law, appeared first in discussions among medieval canon lawyers debating whether Adam or Jesus had any property rights.[7] In the modern age this view is usually regarded as necessarily benign, but it actually can have dire consequences. Not only have innate or natural rights been used to justify something other than legal human rights, but they have also appeared in *opposition* to what are widely regarded as proper legal human rights. This can be illustrated starkly by the debates on slavery in Spain in the early part of the sixteenth century.[8]

The Spaniards, rather than trying to catch slaves, usually attempted to trade for already enslaved people on the coast of Africa. This activity could, in principle at least, be justified if one could show that it was possible for people to have become slaves on legitimate grounds. Those who held to the type of natural rights views propagated by Gerson held that rights were like property, indeed that a prepolitical right to property was the very epitome of a right. People owned their rights and could dispose of them.

6. This point is too often neglected by Christians, and others, who try to draw out a notion of rights from the biblical injunctions to care for our neighbor. See my "Rights," in the *New Dictionary of Ethics and Pastoral Theology* (Leicester, Eng.: Intervarsity Press, forthcoming).

7. On this history see R. Tuck, *Natural Rights Theories: Their Origin and Development* (Cambridge: Cambridge Univ. Press, 1979); A. S. McGrade, "Ockham and the Birth of Individual Rights," in B. Tierney and P. Linehan, eds., *Authority and Power: Studies in Medieval Law and Government* (Cambridge: Cambridge Univ. Press, 1980), 149-65; and B. Tierney, "Villey, Ockham and the Origins of Individual Rights," in J. Witte and F. S. Alexander, eds., *The Weightier Matters of the Law: Essays on Law and Religion* (Atlanta: Scholars Press, 1988), 1-32.

8. See Tuck, 48-50. For background see Thomas F. O'Meara, "Spanish Theologians and Native Americans in the Years After Columbus" (paper delivered at the Kellogg Institute, University of Notre Dame, October 31, 1991), and Lewis Hanke, *Aristotle and the American Indians: A Study in Race Prejudice in the Modern World* (Bloomington: Indiana Univ. Press, 1959). See also Paul Marshall, *Human Rights Theories in Christian Perspective* (Toronto: Institute for Christian Studies, 1983).

As rights were thought to inhere in the human person rather than in the civil order, then a person could legitimately sell them, forfeit them, or give them away. Thus, people could alienate all their rights and become slaves, people without rights, in a legitimate way. Hence certain people could justly be slaves, and trade in such slaves would be acceptable. These were slim grounds, but grounds they were, and they were used. Indeed, they were similar to the grounds that Hobbes later used to justify political absolutism in a situation where, purportedly, an entire people, in order to receive protection, had traded away its rights in a social contract. Indeed, natural rights views have a broad correlation with political absolutism.

The most notable exception to the early modern association of natural rights doctrines and authoritarian views of government is in the work of John Locke. But Locke defended positive legal rights only by circumscribing and limiting the scope of natural rights. The strategy he followed was similar to that of the Dominicans in the Spanish slavery debates: he stressed the limits of human freedom by asserting that we are only stewards of what is properly God's, and he affirmed that man's liberty did not extend to his being able to destroy himself, since he was God's property.[9] In Locke the limitations on government stemmed from the original *limitation on* people's *own rights* in the state of nature. What people did not have themselves they could not transfer to government. Government could not rightfully do to people what people had no right to do to themselves.[10]

This brief historical excursus suggests that inherent human rights need have little to do with a justification of legal human rights; indeed, they can even lead to the opposite. There is no simple way of crossing the boundary between the "moral" or "natural" and the legal. An assertion of a moral right to welfare, even if believed, may not take us very far in understanding what type of government action, if any, should be taken. Consequently, if we are concerned to develop good welfare policies, *the*

9. Locke, *Two Treatises of Government*, bk. 2, ch. 2, par. 6; bk. 2, ch. 4, par. 23.

10. In his *The Political Thought of John Locke* (Cambridge: Cambridge Univ. Press, 1969), John Dunn pointed out that Locke's resistance theory was an extension of his rejection of suicide. Richard Ashcraft develops a similar theme in relation to property in his *Revolutionary Politics and Locke's 'Two Treatises of Government'* (Princeton: Princeton Univ. Press, 1987), 258f. Perhaps the limitation on natural freedom in Locke stems, in turn, from God's right over human beings, and so the foundation of political freedom remains a form of natural right.

nature of rights themselves indicates that we need to consider not only a doctrine of inherent rights but the proper nature of political and social relations.

Rights as Relations

Clearly, the inherent-rights view is only one possible view of the value, and the need for respect and protection, of humans, and it is quite parochial. Most people in history who have argued for love, respect, and the welfare of others have *not* done so on the basis that those others had inherent rights. One reason they did not do so is connected with the nature of an inherent right and with human relations. When we deal with a right we cannot just deal with A's right in abstraction, but we must also involve A's right to B, and when we do so, we involve the C who should respect this right, and perhaps the D who should enforce it. *A statement of right necessarily specifies a particular type of relation between A, B, C, and D.* It is difficult to see how what is in fact a *relation between* several persons and things in differing circumstances could be found as inherent in one of them or even in each of them considered distinctly.[11] A right is always a *relationship between more than one* and so cannot be *inherent* within one.

Hence, historically, we find that the discussion of rights has originated within political relations and has developed as the political order itself has developed. Actual law has played a considerable role in shaping rights, not only in the sense that for rights to mean much in practice they have to find expression in law, but also in the sense that theorizing about rights has often been a response to, and has taken place within, developments in law.[12]

If rights exist in political settings and cannot be understood as inherent in particular individuals, then an assertion of inherent rights in fact truncates a relation by treating it as an individual characteristic. The content of the relationship then becomes provided by supposed individual attributes such as autonomy, agency, and interests. The result is a depiction of communities as collections of individuals, and communal relations as

11. See the comments in L. W. Sumner, *The Moral Foundation of Rights* (Oxford: Clarendon Press, 1987), 126.

12. See Paul Marshall, "Dooyeweerd's Empirical Theory of Rights," in C. T. McIntire, ed., *The Legacy of Herman Dooyeweerd* (Lanham, Md.: University Press of America, 1985), 124f., and my "Two Types of Rights."

intercourse between rights-bearing individuals. The question of what it is good to do tends to be subsumed under questions of what someone has a right to do. The question of what others owe to us gives content to the question of what we might owe each other. For these reasons Kierkegaard regarded a concern for rights, even rights for all, as evocative of self-love. Simone Weil thought rights had "a commercial flavor; essentially evocative of legal claims and arguments. Rights are always asserted in a tone of contention. . . ."[13] Mary Ann Glendon maintains that not so much rights themselves but a near-exclusive fixation on them has hobbled American politics and poisoned its social relations. The overweening emphasis on the theme of rights has produced "its exaggerated absoluteness, its hyper-individualism, its insularity, and its silence with respect to personal, civic, and collective responsibilities."[14] This, in turn, makes it

> extremely difficult for us to develop an adequate conceptual apparatus for taking into account the sorts of groups within which human character, competence, and capacity for citizenship are formed. . . . For individual freedom and the general welfare alike depend on the condition of the fine texture of civil society — on a fragile ecology for which we have no name.[15]

The Debate over Economic and Welfare Rights

The expression "economic rights" is usually used to refer to two types of items. One is protection of economic activities from invasion by government. This usually goes under the general rubric of "property rights" and has a long history in the United States, including the Fifth Amendment's strictures against taking property without just compensation. The other type is legal guarantees of government provision of economic goods and services such as housing, health care, or income. Such guarantees are often called "welfare rights."

13. See Meirlys Owens, "The Notion of Human Rights: A Reconsideration," *American Philosophical Quarterly* 6 (1969): 244.

14. Glendon, x.

15. Glendon, 109-10. Similar themes occur in the attempts to import the notion of rights into ecological discussions. See Paul Marshall, "Does the Creation Have Rights?" *Studies in Christian Ethics* 6, no. 2 (1993): 31-49.

There is clearly something attractive about considering welfare provisions as rights. To do so treats them with the utmost gravity and recognizes that they are central concerns of the political community. It articulates them in the foundational language of, particularly, American politics, and it articulates them as fundamental claims rather than charitable options. Though they are often treated as if they were of very recent vintage and, consequently, an intrusion on the rights front, they are quite an old idea.[16] As early as 1758 Montesquieu argued in his survey of laws of the world that the state "owes all the citizens an assured sustenance, nourishment, suitable clothing, and a kind of life which is not contrary to health," while the French Constitution of 1791 required a system of free public education and public assistance.[17] Bismarck is credited with establishing a basic social security system in Germany at the end of the nineteenth century. Since 1919 the International Labor Organization has formulated international labor standards and developed conventions on forced labor, freedom of association, elimination of discrimination in employment, safe conditions of employment, and social security.

The *Charter* of the United Nations commits its members to "higher standards of living, full employment, and conditions of economic and social progress," while the 1948 *Universal Declaration of Human Rights* claims that "Everyone has the right to a standard of living adequate for the health and well-being of himself and his family" (Article 25[1]). More substantial recognition came in the United Nations' *Covenants,* which are binding on their signatories. The *Covenant on Economic, Social and Cultural Rights* calls member states to "recognise the right of everyone to an adequate standard of living for himself and his family, including adequate food, clothing and housing, and to the continuous improvement of living conditions" (Article 11[1]). The European *Social Charter* of 1961 similarly commits its members to an extensive list of social and economic rights, while now over half of national constitutions worldwide commit their governments to some such rights.[18]

16. A useful survey is given in Sally Morphet, "Economic, Social and Cultural Rights: The Development of Governments' Views," in Ralph Beddard and Dilys M. Hill, eds., *Economic, Social and Cultural Rights: Progress and Achievement* (London: MacMillan, 1992), 74-92.

17. Montesquieu, *The Spirit of the Laws,* pt. 4, ch. 29 (Cambridge: Cambridge Univ. Press, 1989), 455.

18. For an outline of OECD country provisions, see "The Protection of Social and Economic Rights: A Comparative Study," Staff Paper, Constitutional Law and Policy Division, Ministry of the Attorney General, Government of Ontario, Sept. 19, 1991.

Since the development of welfare states began a half-century ago, the notion of welfare has become inextricably interwoven with the notion of rights. This is for three reasons:

- Those states wealthy enough to contemplate universal welfare arrangements are those in the West which are strongly influenced by liberalism and in which rights have been the dominant mode of political rhetoric.
- The growth of welfare states took place since the Second World War (in tandem with Keynesianism), at a time when rights became the justifying rationale for the victorious Allied cause and when the formation of rights in positive law (both international and municipal) was proceeding apace.
- The principal idea of the welfare state (that a social safety net should be both universal and guaranteed) is itself akin to a rights idea.

Concerned about mushrooming welfare or economic rights conceptions, several commentators, notably Maurice Cranston, have argued that whereas civil and political rights are "universal," "paramount," and "categorical," economic rights (in the present case, "welfare rights") are none of these and are simply in a different "logical category."[19] The argument of paramountcy is that political rights are of immediate and overwhelming importance, whereas some famous economic rights, such as the right to periodic holidays with pay (Article 24 of the U.N. *Declaration*), may well be desirable but are hardly a *sine qua non* of a just political order. The other arguments cluster around the contention that a government can fulfill genuine political rights at any time simply by doing nothing, which is why such rights are often called "negative rights," as distinct from "positive rights," which would require some type of positive action.[20] Hence a government has no excuse for not fulfilling political rights immediately. It can afford to do so since it costs nothing, and the state can in principle do

19. Maurice Cranston, *What are Human Rights?* (New York: Basic Books, 1962), 54, ch. 3. For a summary of these discussions, see Jack Donnelly, *Universal Human Rights in Theory and Practice* (Ithaca, N.Y.: Cornell Univ. Press, 1989), 31ff.

20. This vocabulary of rights uses a view of positivity and negativity derived from Isaiah Berlin's famous distinction of "positive" and "negative" liberties in his "Two Concepts of Liberty," in his *Four Essays on Liberty* (New York: Oxford Univ. Press, 1969), 118-72.

it wherever it has power. Such rights are not subject to the limits of scarcity. As Charles Fried puts it, "If I am left alone, the commodity I obtain does not seem to be a scarce or limited one. How can we run out of people not harming each other, not lying to each other, leaving each other alone?"[21]

One final argument is that whereas political rights are *limits,* economic rights are *ideals.* Limits must be *obeyed,* whereas ideals must be *aimed for,* and lumping these two very different categories together can undercut political rights. If an economic right is believed to be a genuine right and it is also acknowledged that it cannot be fulfilled immediately, or perhaps even in the future, then we have admitted that a state legitimately need not immediately fulfil its rights obligations. If this is so, then states can, and many do, use it to justify all their violations of rights, including detention without trial or restrictions on speech and religion. Such states use their economic programs to assert that they do promote human rights even though they deny political and civil rights. The effect of "affirmations of so-called human rights which are not human rights at all is to push *all* talk of human rights out of the clear realm of the morally compelling onto the twilight world of utopian aspiration."[22]

Those who defend economic rights (that is, welfare rights) mobilize a series of counterarguments.[23] They argue that economic rights can be of paramount importance: holidays with pay may not be the most fortunate example, but the right to food is. Surely nothing can be more vital than access to food, since without it other rights disappear very quickly. On the general question of costs, maintaining laws costs money for police, lawyers, and prisons. Political rights of participation also cost money: democracy is expensive since it requires elections, parliaments, and publicity. Furthermore, protecting rights from attack by others in the society also requires resources. A government may not itself restrict your speech, but this may be of little help if your neighbors consistently do so and the government either will not or

21. Quoted in Raymond Plant, "A Defence of Welfare Rights," in Beddard and Hill, 30. Plant also adds that the necessity to deal with scarcity means that utilitarian and consequentialist arguments must come into play and that this undermines the whole structure of a rights-based discourse (cf. p. 31).

22. Maurice Cranston, "Human Rights: Real and Supposed," in D. D. Raphael, ed., *Political Theory and the Rights of Man* (London: MacMillan, 1967), 52.

23. See, e.g., Susan Miller Okin, "Liberty and Welfare: Some Issues in Human Rights Theory," in J. R. Pennock and J. W. Chapman, eds., *Human Rights* (New York: New York Univ. Press, 1981), 230-56.

cannot do anything about it. Consequently economic rights proponents maintain that questions of scarcity and costs arise here also.

If we focus less on the bare notion of a right and instead consider rights in terms of political and social relations and the theory of the state, we can separate the distinction of positive and negative rights from the distinction of political and economic rights. Not all political rights are negative, and not all economic rights (such as rights to property) are positive. We could then use a threefold division: (1) negative rights, (2) positive political rights, and (3) positive economic rights.

(1) Negative rights, such as rights to free speech, freedom of religion, freedom of property, freedom from arbitrary detention, and so forth, are rights that require forbearance from government: they require governments not to do anything. These rights can always be met since they are not dependent on scarce resources, and so they can be categorical and universal. An exception could be a situation where a government cannot control its own minions, such as unauthorized death squads in the police or military. In such a situation the government factually could not fulfill the requirement of even a negative right. But, while this is true, in this circumstance the government is *failing to be a government.* It is not merely that it is derelict in some area within its sovereignty, but that the area has begun actually to lie beyond its sovereignty: it is an area where it cannot in fact govern, an area beyond its factual jurisdiction. The situation described is a collapse of government per se. In this sense, negative rights cannot always be fulfilled. But this would be an amazingly stringent condition — that rights would be guaranteed even if there were no functioning government. What we can say is that *if there is a government capable of governing, then negative rights can be met.* This is a universality not shared by the other forms of rights.

(2) Positive political rights are rights of a political kind, such as a right to vote, or to a fair trial, or to be defended from enemies, that require specific government actions and resources. Hence a well-intentioned government may be unable to meet such requirements, and so such rights are not as universal or categorical as negative rights: rather, they suffer in principle from the same limitations due to scarcity as do positive economic rights. However, these rights are specifically related to the task of government. Even those who think that some economic rights, such as a right to eat, may be more important than some political rights, such as a right to vote, believe that it is specifically a government concern to be involved with criminal justice or democratic procedure. In this sense there is agreement

that these are particularly government functions and that governments have a responsibility to carry them out at some point. Consequently, though positive political rights have something in common with positive economic rights, they are more intimately tied to the peculiar task of the state.

(3) Positive economic rights, such as a guaranteed annual income, guaranteed access to health care, or the general panoply of guaranteed welfare provisions, suffer from the same problems as positive political rights in that they involve a commitment of scarce resources and so are difficult, and in some cases impossible, to guarantee. They have the additional problem that, unlike positive political rights, they refer to needs that can in principle be met by bodies other than government. Consequently their relation to government has a contingency not shared by the other forms of rights.

Hence we can say that negative rights refer to necessary features of just government, positive political rights refer to policies that are necessarily governmental in character, and positive economic rights refer to policies that governments may pursue.[24]

We need not resolve here the semantic question of whether all economic rights should be called rights. But what is clear from this survey of arguments is that welfare rights are necessarily matters of public policy that need to be moderated depending on the resources available. They do not trump other political considerations, but must be developed within the context of such considerations.

Welfare and the Problem of Rights

We noted above that there is something attractive about treating welfare provisions as rights in that it recognizes that they are not simply charitable options but central concerns of the political community. However, as we have also seen, a rights focus has several drawbacks. It tends to blend the political idea that rights should be fundamental political commitments beyond the reach of day-to-day policymaking with the philosophic idea described above that rights are individual moral possessions. This individualist blending has several adverse consequences:

24. I have sought to address some of these questions in my *Human Rights Theories in Christian Perspective* and in "Innate Rights and Just Relations," *Koers* 56, no. 2 (1991): 139-49.

- Rights are, in the West, usually treated as *individual* moral possessions, which then encourages targeting welfare at "individuals." This works to the detriment of recognizing and reinforcing the multiple communal relations in which people live.
- Rights are usually understood as *guarantees* that must be fulfilled, regardless of the responsibility of the rights bearer. However, in the case of welfare provisions the question of personal and other responsibility can be paramount. In this situation a rights infatuation can ignore and erode responsibility.
- Rights are usually understood to be *universal.* They apply equally to all within a jurisdiction. However, welfare needs vary dramatically: what is suitable in one setting may actually be destructive in another. A rights focus undercuts adaptability.
- Rights are moral claims calling for *government* guarantees; they focus on persons in their relation to government. But if this relation is stressed to the neglect of other relations, then the responsibility of others in society is eroded.
- Rights are *inflexible.* This is their virtue: they put abrogation beyond the reach, or beyond the easy reach, of executives and legislatures — something that is absolutely vital when dealing with torture and massacre. But in the shifting and bewilderingly complex world of social welfare, such inflexibility will be inordinately costly and even crippling.

These objections arise from a simple analysis of the nature of a *right as such* rather than from a study of rights-based welfare policy. But they are strikingly parallel to the problems in current policy noted in other chapters in this volume. Lawrence Mead, for instance, points to problems of programs and policies that do not "question lifestyle." He stresses the need to "direct lives," to focus on the "health of relationships," and to find a way forward that involves "obligation."[25] Bob Goudzwaard emphasizes "community life," "strong social ties," and "living subjects within a society of differentiated responsibilities."[26] A common theme is the need for *responsibility,* including *personal* responsibility for one's own situation and also *communal* responsibility in other sectors of society, notably the so-

25. Lawrence Mead, "The Poverty Debate and Human Nature."

26. Bob Goudzwaard, "Who Cares? Poverty and the Dynamics of Responsibility: An Outsider's Contribution to the American Debate on Poverty and Welfare."

called mediating structures, such as families, schools, churches, businesses, and voluntary associations. The project essay *A New Vision for Welfare Reform* is remarkable for its stress on a "responsibility crisis" and the need for "multiple responsibilities," and for its claim that "government's primary aim should be to call people and institutions to their own responsibilities."[27] Human beings are to be seen as "interdependent, mutually responsible creatures, never self-sufficient individuals."[28]

This ethos of responsibility is the opposite of a rights ethos. Rights call for guarantees that, *ceteris paribus,* are independent of whether those who have the rights use them responsibly. The exercise of their rights is necessarily their own affair, their own sovereign area of decision, an area beyond executive or legislative control — indeed, an area beyond the prerogative of the state itself. Consequently any call for societal responsibility will be in tension with a call for welfare rights.

Welfare Rights as Aspirations

Despite the problems we have noted, there is still a great stress worldwide on the notion of welfare rights.[29] But because of problems such as these, the push for welfare guarantees has been sharply relativized and contextualized. The notion of rights that actually seems to operate in most jurisdictions is not a harder, justiciable, and enforceable demand for rights guarantees, nor a stress on inherent rights, but rather a softer sense reflecting a view of welfare rights as ideals, in which rights are seen as exhortations to governments to take the issue with the utmost seriousness.[30]

For example, the United Nations can investigate states' conduct under the terms of the *International Covenant on Civil and Political Rights.* But the *International Covenant on Economic, Social and Cultural Rights* only requires participating states to report on their own activities.[31] The covenant on

27. Center for Public Justice, *A New Vision for Welfare Reform: An Essay in Draft* (Washington, D.C.: Center for Public Justice, 1994), reprinted in the Appendix to this volume, 565ff.

28. Center for Public Justice, 562.

29. See appendix II to this chapter.

30. This also seems to be the case in the U.S. state constitutions that contain welfare rights and provisions. See appendix I to this chapter.

31. The 1993 United Nations conference on human rights in Vienna called for a

political rights was formulated as a *standard* of conduct; the covenant on social and economic rights was formulated as a *goal* of policy. The economic covenant obliges a signatory, in Article 2(1), to fulfill its obligations "to the maximum of its available resources, with a view to achieving progressively the full realisation of the rights recognised in the present Covenant by all appropriate means." It is also careful to recognize some social factors, especially the family, that are fundamental to a consideration of rights. Article 10(1) says, "[T]he widest possible protection and assistance should be accorded to the family, which is the natural and fundamental group unit of society, particularly for its establishment and while it is responsible for the care and education of dependent children." Article 13(3) says, "[T]he States Parties to the present Covenant undertake to have respect for the liberty of parents . . . to choose for their children schools, other than those established by the public authorities . . . and to ensure the religious and moral education of their children in conformity with their own convictions." Even with these restrictions, this covenant was more or less moribund for most of its first legal decade. One U.N. official described the organization's attention to socioeconomic rights as characterized by "hypocrisy and longwindedness."[32]

Similarly, in the European treaties the *Social Charter* was kept separate from the *European Covenant on Human Rights* itself. The charter also describes the family "as a fundamental unit of society," which has the right to "appropriate social, legal and economic protection" (pt. 1, art. 16).[33] And, despite

---

strengthening of the Committee on Social, Economic and Cultural Rights (formed in 1985) and for "perhaps adding an optional protocol [similar to the one for the *Covenant on Civil and Political Rights* — PM] to the existing *Covenant* that would make allowance for an individual complaints procedure." See Johan van der Vyver, "The World Conference on Human Rights," unpublished report, Vienna, June 1993, p. 33.

32. Quoted in Philip Alston, "Out of the Abyss: The Challenges Confronting the New U.N. Committee on Economic, Social and Cultural Rights," *Human Rights Quarterly* 9, no. 3 (1987): 379. See also David P. Forsythe, *The Internationalization of Human Rights* (Lexington, Mass.: Lexington Books, 1991), 69.

33. In this respect it is important to note the influence of Christian Democratic views on the development of the charters. John Humphrey, who produced the first draft of the Universal Declaration of Human Rights, noted "it seemed at times that the chief protagonists in the conference room were the Roman Catholics and the Communists, with the latter a poor second." John P. Humphrey, *Human Rights and the United Nations: A Great Adventure* (Dobbs Ferry, N.Y.: Transnational Publishers, 1984), 32, summarized in Morphet, 77. On the European developments see Joan Lockwood O'Donovan's ex-

being the most developed international system of economic guarantees, it has what David Forsythe calls "a certain vagueness" in its standards. He adds that "it is not . . . clear how those standards have affected national public policy."[34]

Many national constitutions are also careful to restrict and focus their economic rights.[35] Spain, Ireland, India, Malta, Pakistan, and Bangladesh expressly specify that their economic guarantees are statements of principle and are not justiciable. Others note that their provisions are to be limited by available fiscal resources.[36] The rights are seen as ideals, as "aspirations," or as "programmatic." Almost no jurisdiction is willing to give economic guarantees the kind of status that it extends to political rights.[37]

Closing

Mary Ann Glendon has described current American rights talk as conspicuous in "its starkness and simplicity, its prodigality in bestowing the rights label, its legalistic character, its exaggerated absoluteness, its hyperindividualism, its insularity, and its silence with respect to personal, civic, and collective responsibilities." It produces a "near-aphasia concerning responsibilities . . . without assuming . . . corresponding personal and civic obligations." It gives "excessive homage to individual independence and self sufficiency," and concentrates on the "individual and the state at the expense of the intermediate groups of civil society."[38] It is no accident that these are some of the traits that we noticed with rights language and conceptions in general. The prob-

---

cellent "Subsidiarity and Political Authority in Theological Perspective," *Studies in Christian Ethics* 6, no. 1 (1993): 17-34.

34. Forsythe, 42.

35. This is also the case with respect to the welfare provisions contained in U.S. state constitutions. See appendix I to this chapter.

36. Turkey, El Salvador, Gabon, Pakistan, India, Jordan. See "The Protection of Social and Economic Rights." Alan Wolfe has some worthwhile comments to make on the distinction between, and the advantages and disadvantages of, absolute and conditional welfare rights, in his "The Rights to Welfare and the Obligation to Society," *Responsive Community* 1, no. 2 (1991): 12-22.

37. But the 1986 "Limburg Principles" insist that no states have "the right to defer indefinitely efforts to ensure full realisation." See Julia Hausermann, "The Realisation and Implementation of Economic, Social and Cultural Rights," in Beddard and Hill, 52.

38. Glendon, x-xi, 14.

lems of using rights notions to deal with welfare may be enough on their own, but they are likely to be doubly difficult in the current American ethos. The concept of rights as ideals, or of "programmatic" rights, is unfamiliar in the United States, so that any economic rights would likely be interpreted and pursued with all of America's customary litigious gusto.[39] The drawbacks of welfare as a right in other, less rights-focused jurisdictions are likely to be sharply exacerbated in the United States. For these reasons Americans would be wise to avoid a rights focus in their welfare policy.

This reticence with respect to a more hard-edged view of rights of course says nothing per se about the importance of welfare as a priority in public policy.[40] But such policy could well learn from the international documents, especially the European, which are both restrained in the extravagance of their formulation and respectful of the life of society in their application.

Appendix I: Provisions in Constitutions of States of the United States that Relate to Social Assistance[41]

Alabama	"[I]t shall be the duty of the legislature to require the several counties of this state to make adequate provision for maintenance of the poor" (art. IV, sec. 88).
Alaska	"The legislature shall provide for public welfare' (art. VII, sec. 5).
California	The legislature and the people "shall have power to provide for the administration of the relief of hardship and destitution, whether resulting from unemployment or from other cause . . ." (art. XVI, sec. 11).
Georgia	Authorizes local governments to contract with public entities for the care of the indigent sick (art. IV, sec. 3, par. 1).
Illinois	"[The Constitution is ordained, among other reasons, to] eliminate poverty and inequality; assure legal, social and

39. Mary Ann Glendon, "Rights and Responsibilities Viewed from Afar: The Case of Welfare Rights," *Responsive Community* 4, no. 2 (1994): 39.

40. In this respect it is interesting to note that *A New Vision for Welfare Reform* calls for "government support of a free education for every child" (575). This can be regarded as a type of economic welfare right.

41. Adapted from "The Protection of Social and Economic Rights."

	economic justice; [and] provide opportunity for the fullest development of the individual" (Preamble).
Indiana	Authorizes county boards to establish farms to house those who "have claims upon the . . . aid of society" (art. IX, sec. 3).
Kansas	"The . . . counties of the state shall provide . . . for those inhabitants who . . . may have claims upon the aid of society" (art. VII, sec. 4).
Louisiana	Authorizes the legislature to establish welfare and unemployment compensation as well as public health measures (art. XII, sec. 8).
Mississippi	Authorizes a board of supervisors to provide homes to those who have claims upon the aid of society (art. XIV, sec. 262).
Missouri	"[T]he general assembly shall establish a department of public health and welfare . . ." (art. IV, sec. 37).
Montana	"The legislature shall provide such economic assistance and social and rehabilitative services as may be necessary for those inhabitants who, by reason of age, infirmities, or misfortune may have need for the aid of society" (art. XII, sec. 3[3]).
New Mexico	Authorizes state and local governments to make provisions relating to the care of sick and indigent persons (art. IX, sec. 14).
New York	"The aid, care and support of the needy are public concerns and shall be provided by the state and by such of its subdivisions, and in such manner and by such means, as the legislature may from time to time determine" (art. XVII, sec. 1).
North Carolina	"Beneficent provision for the poor, the unfortunate, and the orphan is one of the first duties of a civilized and a Christian state. Therefore the General Assembly shall provide for and define the duties of a board of public welfare" (art. XI, sec. 4).
Oklahoma	"The legislature and people are authorized to provide by appropriate legislation for the relief and care of needy, aged persons who are unable to provide for themselves, and other needy persons who, on account of immature age, physical infirmity, disability, or other cause, are unable to provide or care for themselves" (art. XXV, sec. 1).
Texas	Authorizes the payment of assistance to the needy (art. III, sec. 51a).

Wyoming	Requires the legislature to provide for "the health and morality of the people" (art. VII, sec. 20).

Appendix II: Number of Constitutional Economic Guarantees Worldwide[42]

More than one-half of the constitutions of the countries of the world contain express provisions regarding social and economic rights or principles. The kinds of rights protected include:

- Social assistance: more than fifty-five constitutions refer to a right or state duty with respect to social assistance.
- Minimum standard of living: more than thirty constitutions refer to the right to a minimum standard of living, either as a guaranteed minimum right or as a duty of the state to progressively raise the standard of living; the right to food is guaranteed in twelve constitutions and the right to clothing is referred to in at least six; there are also constitutions in which the preamble or directive principles of state policy set out general state objectives to achieve an equitable distribution of wealth or to manage the economy to secure maximum welfare and to provide adequate means of livelihood.
- Health care: over fifty-five constitutions refer to a right or state duty with respect to health care.
- Housing: more than thirty constitutions enshrine a right or state duty with respect to housing.
- Employment: more than sixty constitutions refer to the right to work, either as a right per se inhering in the individual or as an aim of state policy.
- Education: more than seventy constitutions ensure the right to education, usually referring to it as the right to free education.
- Environment: the right to a clean and healthy environment is enshrined in at least twenty-five constitutions.

42. The primary source for this information is A. P. Blaustein and G. H. Flanz, eds., *Constitutions of Countries of the World* (1990). I have adapted it from "The Protection of Social and Economic Rights."

- Culture: well over thirty constitutions refer to a right to culture or to a state duty to promote culture.
- Protection of the family: at least twenty-five constitutions refer to a state duty to provide special protection to the family, which may include maternity leave, day care, or youth employment restrictions.

The Antipoverty Dynamic of Religion: Lessons from Guatemala for U.S. Welfare Policy

Anne Motley Hallum

PRESIDENT BILL CLINTON campaigned on a promise to end "welfare as we know it." But the proposal his welfare reform task force produced, while an improvement over the current stagnant policy, appears to be a classic example of treating the symptoms of poverty more than the causes. The four goals identified by the task force are: improved child support, primarily through aggressive collection of payments from noncustodial parents; more money for education for those in poverty; a time limit of two years for receipt of welfare benefits, after which the recipient must find work or work in public service employment; and, finally, making work pay through a larger earned income tax credit.[1] All of these goals may be laudable as the stopgap measures that they are. But, just as with previous policies, the focus is delivering a certain amount of aid (dollars or job training or manufactured service jobs). They do not address one of the deeper causes for endemic poverty: the decline of a sense of individual and community responsibility.

But the reality is that the national government is not the best agent for instilling a sense of community or responsibility. The massive government bureaucracy can issue mandates and sanctions if individuals do not meet certain responsibilities, but it is inherently too far removed to change fundamental attitudes of the poor and their neighbors. Ironically, however,

1. Rick Santorum, "Welfare as We've Always Known It," *Washington Post National Weekly Edition,* Dec. 20-26, 1993, p. 25.

the government has handicapped the very institutions that may be best equipped for tackling the root problems of poverty: religious bodies. Because of the common interpretation of the establishment clause of the First Amendment, government policymakers largely avoid utilizing religious entities as instruments for implementing welfare policies. However, as Stephen Carter and other constitutional scholars have argued, this avoidance stems from the mistaken and ahistorical view that the establishment clause was meant to protect the policy world from religious influences, when the clause is more correctly interpreted as a protection of religion from the state.[2]

Religious institutions can be sources for personal empowerment and feelings of efficacy among the poor. They can also instill deep-seated attitudes of caring and responsibility for other members of the family and the community. Nonreligious neighborhood organizations to help the poor can also be effective at turning lives around. But the points to be made here are (1) that thousands of *religious* bodies are already in place with valuable resources for overcoming poverty, and (2) that religion has a unique transformative power for individuals, and conceivably for societies, that could be encouraged by the government in a neutral manner. Instead, in many cases the government places obstacles in the way of religious involvement.

This chapter will make a case for religious programs as essential antipoverty tools by examining welfare policy in Guatemala, a nation that is very unlike the United States, but that nevertheless has some important policy lessons for us. Research included a review of pertinent social science literature as well as my own fieldwork and interviewing in Guatemala from 1990 through 1994. Two questions are key: What are some of the secrets of successful approaches to alleviating poverty? and Can they be widely replicated? My overriding theme is that government welfare policy should enlist religious groups in combatting poverty, because they offer to the poor something indispensable that government cannot provide. Most U.S. welfare programs and proposals for welfare reform take aim at the symptoms of poverty; this chapter will demonstrate how a decentralized approach via the vast network of religious bodies can strike at causes.

2. Stephen L. Carter, *The Culture of Disbelief: How American Law and Politics Trivialize Religious Devotion* (New York: Basic Books, 1993), 107-15.

Protestants and Government Welfare "Policy" in Guatemala

The Central American nation of Guatemala has approximately 11 million people, 46 percent of whom are under the age of fifteen years. The per capita gross national product is only about $920, and less than 60 percent of the population have access even to safe drinking water. In 1989, the U.N. Human Development Report classified 71 percent of the country's population as living in "absolute poverty."[3] Furthermore, the Guatemalan government only began inching toward democracy in 1985 with the election of President Cerezo, and the country has been torn apart by a vicious civil war that is only winding down in the 1990s after more than thirty years of fighting.

Obviously, the *scopes* of the problem of poverty in Guatemala and in the United States are not comparable, but the poverty suffered by families and neighborhoods in the United States can be just as cruel and often seems just as intractable as in Guatemala. In Guatemala, poverty is greater and the resources to reduce it substantially are clearly insufficient. On the other hand, there is a dynamism that deserves close examination — some people and communities are moving from great poverty to a better life.

The governmental response to poverty in Guatemala in recent decades has been quite simple: encourage nongovernmental charitable organizations to take on the job. Most charitable organizations in recent decades have been Protestant religious bodies. For instance, the government's National Reconstruction Committee maintains contracts for development projects with nongovernmental organizations (NGOs) in an attempt to coordinate various charitable projects. Of 150 such projects that were on file in this office in 1992, 135 were with Protestant organizations.[4] These contractual projects are usually administered by volunteers at the village and neighborhood level and often have foreign mission funding.[5] The

3. U.N. Development Program, *Human Development Report 1993* (New York, 1993), 159, 171.

4. Roy Peterson, director of external relations, Summer Institute of Linguistics, interview with author, Guatemala City, Guatemala, Nov. 2, 1993.

5. Inter-Hemispheric Education Resource Center, *Directory and Analysis: Private Organizations with U.S. Connections — Guatemala* (Albuquerque, N.M., 1988), describes 155 NGOs working in Guatemala, many of which are religious, and includes their size, funding sources, and descriptions of their service projects. My own nongovernmental organization working in Guatemala, the Alliance for International Re-

projects range from the building of schools and clinics to the development of tree nurseries and potable water systems and the stimulation of microbusinesses. Such projects, of course, are *in addition to* the supportive work of thousands of individual congregations ministering to their members.

The presence of numerous active Protestant organizations that the government could utilize is a fairly recent development. In the late 1970s and 1980s, a sudden surge in the number of U.S. Protestant groups throughout Latin America occurred because many U.S. mission boards chose to emphasize the region during those decades. It is no coincidence that the time period of greatest growth of these churches was also a period of evangelical resurgence within the United States. Although it is extremely difficult to measure the extent of Protestant conversion in Guatemala, one frequently cited estimate is that over 25 percent of the population is now Protestant, with no sign of slowing down.[6] Another estimate, referring to all of Latin America, claims that the number of evangelicals doubled to fifty million during the 1980s.[7] A major reason for the wildfire spread of Protestantism, even in the absence of foreign missionaries, is the activism of church members and the ease of forming new churches. Unlike the hierarchical demands of Catholicism, or the seminary requirements for pastors in some mainline Protestant denominations, most evangelical congregations only require their pastor to communicate the "gift of the Spirit." This is a highly flexible, localized system, appropriate for a society in which a majority of the people are poor and illiterate.

---

forestation, Inc., based at Stetson University, is not identified as a Protestant organization and is not funded by an official mission board, although much of its funding comes from U.S. church members. It is likely that the unofficial support from religious groups in the U.S. is substantial although impossible to document accurately.

6. David Stoll, *Is Latin America Turning Protestant? The Politics of Evangelical Growth* (Berkeley: Univ. of California Press, 1990), 9. A competing estimate of evangelical growth in Guatemala puts the figure at over 2.5 million, or about 30 percent of the population; see Resource Center, 8; Brook Larmer, "Guatemala: Evangelical Spurt Meets Spiritual Needs and Political Goals," *Christian Science Monitor,* March 9, 1989. However, Stoll, while confirming the spectacular growth of evangelicalism, also notes how questionable the estimates are (p. 125).

7. Laura Nuzzi O'Shaughnessy, "Onward Christian Soldiers: The Case of Protestantism in Central America," in Emile Sahliyeh, ed., *Religious Resurgence and Politics in the Contemporary World* (Albany: State Univ. of New York Press, 1990), 104.

Guatemalan political leaders have tapped into the pervasive network of religious resources wherever they can because the financial base of the government is simply inadequate to provide aid to poor communities. Governmental weakness is due to a variety of long-standing factors, discussion of which is beyond the scope of this chapter. Our purpose is not to analyze causes for the government's financial straits, but to examine the effectiveness of its chosen response (or nonresponse).

Before we proceed, we must assert that the government's treatment of poverty in Guatemala is unsatisfactory. To find signs of a more hopeful future for the country at this point, one must look behind the discouraging aggregate data to the success stories of individual families and communities. Thus, the approach to alleviating poverty emphasized in this chapter is a micro-level approach rather than a macro-level approach of economic and political policymaking. Yet as Cecilia Loreto Mariz has written in a recent book about religion and poverty in Brazil,

> [A]lthough more limited in their consequences than larger political measures, the everyday attempts to improve living conditions by small groups of the poor and their families are equally important. The everyday struggles of the poor may not only solve an immediate need, allowing a particular population to survive, but may also foster cultural transformations, producing a long-standing and *less reversible change* in the population.[8]

The growth of active religious organizations, which the Guatemalan government has used to its advantage, has long-term implications for cultural and economic change often beyond what the government, or anyone else for that matter, can envision. Let us examine *how* religious involvement is having an impact on the lives of Guatemalans in poverty.

The Nature of Religious Change and the Antipoverty Value of Religion

The rate of Protestant conversion throughout Latin America has become so rapid that it has attracted the attention of social scientists, who have

8. Cecilia Loreto Mariz, *Coping with Poverty: Pentecostals and Christian Base Communities in Brazil* (Philadelphia: Temple Univ. Press, 1994), 4 (emphasis added).

begun to analyze the causes and potential societal consequences of this phenomenon. Initially, scholarly observers tended to dismiss the conversion from Catholicism to Protestantism as an irrational, temporary escape from desperate poverty toward promises of salvation, complete with manipulation by mission entrepreneurs from the United States. It was argued that true conversion was not taking place since people were simply repeating what the Protestant missionaries wished to hear in order to receive the surplus food and medicines many missionaries hand out. This was undoubtedly true to some extent.[9] However, the size of the Protestant movement in Latin America, the rapidity of its growth, and the apparent depth of commitment of its members have compelled closer analysis.[10] It is now acknowledged that most Protestants, or "evangelicals" as they are called in Central America, are not temporary members; instead they generally change their lifestyles, attend church several nights a week, evangelize to their friends and family, and may become pastors themselves in a new neighborhood church.

In the passage quoted above, Mariz hypothesizes that deep-seated cultural change can eventually occur through these everyday struggles and triumphs. Religion is a central part of such empowering transformations, directly contradicting Marx's familiar depiction of religion as an "opiate of the masses" that supports the status quo powers. In an essay reviewing ten social science books that all address the societal impact of religion, Daniel Levine summarizes their similar conclusion:

> [Religion has] a tremendous *consolidating* power. I refer to the peculiar ability of religious metaphors, places, and rituals to sum up and intensify

9. Sara Diamond, *Spiritual Warfare: The Politics of the Christian Right* (Boston: South End Press, 1989). Diamond delivers a highly polemical attack on missionaries as preying on the desperation and naïveté of the poor. See also Christian Lalive D'Epinay, *Haven to the Masses: A Study of the Pentecostal Movement in Chile* (London: Lutterworth Press, 1969). Epinay is a pioneer in researching Protestantism in Latin America; however, his focus on escapism is condescending and misses the pragmatic, rational aspects of Protestant conversion that more recent studies are addressing. See also Larmer.

10. Edward L. Cleary and Hannah Stewart-Gambino, eds., *Conflict and Competition: The Latin American Church in a Changing Environment* (Boulder, Colo.: Lynne Rienner, 1992); Virginia Garrard-Burnett and David Stoll, eds., *Rethinking Protestantism in Latin America* (Philadelphia: Temple Univ. Press, 1993); David Martin, *Tongues of Fire: The Explosion of Protestantism in Latin America* (London: Blackwell, 1990); Mariz; Stoll.

> experience. They do this by joining everyday events to a sense of supernatural intervention and by reinforcing religious ideas with material resources and a net of repeated human interactions. This is what religious organizations and rituals *do,* and this is why they are so powerful at unifying behavior across social levels and in different arenas and walks of life.[11]

In less academic language, the "tremendous *consolidating* power" of religion in a "net of repeated human interactions" could also be termed "community building." All of the authors Levine reviews took the micro-level approach in their research and analysis, agreeing that examining politics and religion and social programs from the macro-level had missed the more subtle and deep-seated changes that occurred "from below." They demonstrate how "the search for meaning and control goes on in the spaces available in everyday life," and they concur that religion "can provide a seedbed for new kinds of leadership and solidarities."[12] The crucial points relative to welfare policy are that religious gatherings are recognized sources for fostering leadership, building communities, and transforming lives.

What have researchers learned about *how* religious involvement improves the living standards of Guatemalans? Before looking at the research, it is important to note the difficulty of demonstrating definitively the economic consequences of religion because of the presence of numerous influencing variables. For instance, evangelical conversion occurs most frequently among people who are extremely poor, and a greater proportion of members are women than men, and older rather than younger. Thus, they tend to face more economic problems at the outset, and it is difficult to pinpoint the economic ramifications of religion. On the other hand, a positive influencing variable that can be assumed but not measured is that people who convert are particularly open to change and innovation in general, and this initial attitude helps them raise their standard of living. These are points to keep in mind as we examine the anthropological research. However, several studies in Latin America do indicate that evangelicals, at the very least, appear to succeed in coping with poverty well enough not to worsen their economic situation, and many do improve it.[13]

11. Daniel H. Levine, "Religion and Politics in Comparative and Historical Perspective," *Comparative Politics* 19, no. 1 (1986): 97 (emphasis in original).

12. Levine, 106.

13. Mariz, 36, 41.

One early study by Bruce R. Roberts found that low-income Protestants in Guatemala City learned habits of household budgeting and also provided mutual assistance to brothers and sisters in need: "Should a Protestant in one of the neighborhoods need help to improve or repair his house, install drainage, or obtain a loan, other members of his congregation join together to give help. If a Protestant is out of a job or wants to change his work, other members of his congregation help him find work."[14] I discovered a similar attitude when visiting the slums and dumps of Guatemala City with the Protestant pastor who directed a church project for the *Areas Marginales* (marginal areas). We visited small bakeries and neighborhood stores that had received seed money from the churches, as well as an oasis in the slums of numerous concrete-block homes that members had joined together to build.

This supportive characteristic of many of the urban Protestant churches has also been identified in remote areas of the countryside. A recent study of Mayan women in a rural area of Guatemala where many of the men had been killed in political violence discovered a similar church community:

> The nightly services allow women a safe haven to participate in communal activities. . . . [T]hey provide pleasurable diversion with the clapping, shouting, and praying. Church members also help each other, work together to build houses, plant and harvest corn. *Cultos* [services] provide a place and space within which to rebuild a sense of trust and community. . . . The women talk about their suffering and sorrows, and they look for ways in which they can work together to change their situation.[15]

The evangelical churches are the central institutions of this Mayan village and provide the women with "a mechanism to recapture control over their lives."[16]

A fascinating study of evangelical conversion in Colombia also focused on the role of women. Elizabeth Brusco found that women take the lead in the conversion process and then urge their husbands to join the church in an effort to lead them away from drinking and other aspects of

14. Bryan R. Roberts, "Protestant Groups and Coping with Urban Life in Guatemala," *American Journal of Sociology* 6 (1968): 766.

15. Linda Green, "Shifting Affiliations: Mayan Widows and *Evangelicos* in Guatemala," in Garrard-Burnett and Stoll, 173.

16. Green, 162.

machismo.[17] Similarly, a study of religious communities in Brazil noted that, despite common images of wifely submission, female Pentecostal church members had found increased authority and confidence at home through their familiarity with biblical references.[18] My interviews both in Guatemala City and in villages repeatedly confirmed this pattern. In the village of Pastores, for instance, I met an evangelical preacher who proudly pointed to his wife when I asked why he became an evangelical. "She brought me to the church so I would give up drinking," he said. The key to Protestant conversion is not the televangelists nor the mass crusades; it occurs most frequently at the household level and for pragmatic reasons.

The strict lifestyle stressed by the Protestant churches dovetails with the emphasis on saving. Mariz identifies ways in which saving is encouraged among Pentecostals, which is the fastest-growing segment of Protestantism. Most obviously, Mariz notes that asceticism becomes an important saving strategy since consumption of alcohol is eliminated, as well as purchase of anything viewed as "vanities."[19] Separate studies by Virginia G. Burnett, Paul R. Turner, and Sheldon Annis confirm that rural Pentecostals in Guatemala are able to save money as they abstain from alcohol and from the traditional festivals.[20]

A second reason for increased saving among Pentecostals is a religious interpretation of the gospel as explicitly valuing the ability to save. By offering a belief system centered on God's providence for each person, Protestantism looks to a more hopeful future — an automatic incentive to set aside money for a better day. Thus, a changed lifestyle, a reinforcing belief system, and a supportive community allow many Protestant families to reallocate their resources. Interestingly, I spoke with employers in Guatemala who indicated that the good *reputation* of the evangelicals was also helping them economically. One prominent businessman was unrestrained in voicing his opinion:

17. Stoll, 318-19.

18. John Burdick, "Rethinking the Study of Social Movements: The Case of Christian Base Communities in Urban Brazil," in Arturo Escobar and Sonia Alvarez, eds., *The Making of Social Movements in Latin America: Identity, Strategy and Democracy* (Boulder, Colo.: Westview Press, 1992), 177-78.

19. Mariz, 130.

20. Sheldon Annis, *God and Production in a Guatemala Town* (Austin: Univ. of Texas Press, 1987); Virginia G. Burnett, "A History of Protestantism in Guatemala" (Ph.D. diss., Tulane University, 1986); Paul R. Turner, "Religious Conversion and Community Development," *Journal for the Scientific Study of Religion* 18, no. 3 (1979): 252-60.

> I have seventy employees, and I can tell you the evangelicals are more productive, more trustworthy, the better employees. The first thing the evangelicals do is have an impact on alcoholism, and that's the biggest problem in this country! You can go to any hospital and that's why the majority of the people are there. Around these evangelicals, prosperity begins to bloom.[21]

Anthropologist Sheldon Annis has conducted the most detailed study of religion and micro-level change in Guatemala in his book *God and Production in a Guatemalan Town.*[22] Annis combines participant observation with survey research uncovering the family economies of residents of San Antonio Aguas Calientes, Guatemala. Although his original research was about migratory labor and land distribution, Annis learned that the factor most predictive of which families would be upwardly mobile was Protestantism. This was not because the evangelicals worked harder than Catholics, but because they were highly motivated to *save* — even pennies a day — to improve their lives in a material way that would parallel their spiritual rebirth. The most common phrase heard among the many evangelicals in the town was *"del suelo al cielo,"* or "from the dirt floor to the sky; from rags to riches." Annis recounts several *suelo al cielo* stories, as evangelicals were able to save money because they gave up alcohol, luxuries, and costly traditional festivals. He found that overall, average Catholic wealth was only .81 of the average Protestant wealth, and that Protestants were more than twice as likely as Catholics to own a vehicle. Furthermore, Protestants showed more future-orientation than Catholics, as the Protestant children were more likely to go to school and Protestants were more likely to work in upwardly mobile occupations leading to small business ownership (e.g., in tailoring, tourism, transportation). The Catholic families in the town tended to work in subsistence farming, primarily planting corn. However, even when they too remained in agriculture, the Protestants used more advanced farming techniques, planted high-yielding commodities, and did better than Catholics by almost every measure of agricultural productivity.[23] Annis found similar patterns in comparing textile entre-

21. Dennis Wheeler, director of PAVA service organization and owner of Dona Luisa Restaurant, interview with author, Antigua, Guatemala, January 25, 1993.

22. Annis, esp. chs. 5, 6.

23. Annis, 102-5. David Clawson, "Religious Allegiance and Economic Development in Rural Latin America," *Journal of Interamerican Studies and World Affairs* 26, no.

preneurship between Catholic and Protestant women — the evangelical women were more successful at making money from the sale of their weavings.[24]

Annis's research avoids being normative — he documents and analyzes the economic structure of the town as a scholar. If anything, he regrets the cultural changes that Protestantism is reinforcing. However, Annis concludes that macro-level forces such as the civil war, the agro-export economy, and the influx of tourism are inevitably disrupting the cultural stability of traditional Catholicism and subsistence farming. Protestantism is not the cause of these massive changes occurring in most Latin American nations. Instead, a large part of its appeal at the micro-level is that it is a practical theology that gives the people a tool for adapting and even prevailing in the midst of changes going on around them. For our purposes, the key point of Annis's study is that *religion* was the decisive variable that explained why some families were able to improve their economic situation and future prospects and some were not.

Let me summarize the primary reasons religious organizations can be so useful in combatting poverty. Most obviously, mission organizations with foreign funding often contain development and service components. I have already noted the 135 contractual arrangements the Guatemalan government has with Protestant organizations for such projects as building schools, medical clinics, and potable water systems and developing microbusinesses. This same approach is practiced by the U.S. government. The U.S. Agency for International Development (AID) for decades has depended on existing religious networks to distribute foreign aid. AID has found that organizations such as Catholic Relief Services, World Vision, and Central American Mission have efficient and extensive networks with access even to remote villages.[25]

---

4 (1984): 499-524, has very similar findings from his study of a village in central Mexico (similar in culture to that of Guatemala), that literacy, agricultural innovation, and productivity are higher among Protestants than Catholics.

24. Annis, 132-37.

25. J. Bruce Nichols, *The Uneasy Alliance: Religion, Refugee Work, and U.S. Foreign Policy* (New York: Oxford Univ. Press, 1988). Nichols's book is a fascinating study of the church/state dilemma for U.S. government officials in distributing foreign aid and efforts to find a "humanitarian zone of cooperation" (p. 99), while avoiding government support for proselytizing.

However, it is important not to overstate the significance of the foreign missionary aid the Guatemalan churches receive. The Protestant churches in particular are now entering a phase of being wholly Guatemalan, even though U.S. mission efforts provided their original impetus and support. For instance, the superintendent for the *Asambleas de Dios en Guatemala,* the largest Pentecostal denomination in the country, was adamant regarding the lack of a connection between his church and the U.S. Assemblies of God Foreign Missions. He was very proud of the fact that the church was growing from the ground up rather than from the top down. Indeed, most Protestant churches throughout Latin America now are led by Latin Americans.[26] The evangelical churches seek and find independence from the founding mission agencies as soon as they are able — just as they value individual responsibility and independence for their members.

Thus, the established Pentecostal churches as a rule do not receive much external aid, nor do they provide institutional charity for their members. Members do not expect material assistance from the church organization; however, in emergencies, members do expect and receive material assistance from other *individual* members of the church community. They also receive emotional and spiritual support. The evangelical family with whom I resided would frequently visit and pray with families that were experiencing economic hardship. Years earlier, my family had depended on their "brothers and sisters in the faith" during their own struggles with alcoholism and efforts to buy a house. Now they were more than willing to reciprocate.[27]

The primary approach of the churches in alleviating poverty is not to provide welfare, but to encourage change in individual behavior in the context of a spiritual community. Churches expect members to adopt ascetic, disciplined lifestyles, including abstaining from sexual promiscuity and from alcohol. But members do not struggle alone in the quest for a changed material and spiritual life. They participate in church fellowship, often nightly services with spirited singing and socializing that replace the now unacceptable practices. It is in the community

26. Juan Everildo Velasquez, general superintendent, interview with author, Guatemala City, Guatemala, July 8, 1990; see also David Stoll, "Introduction: Rethinking Protestantism in Latin America," in Garrard-Burnett and Stoll, 4.

27. Mariz, 84.

setting that members learn the theology that God has a plan for their future and that with faith and disciplined lives they can help bring that plan into fruition. Furthermore, they have role models all around them of people who have worked hard and received the blessings of God. It is a crucial point that these role models are their peers, with similar backgrounds of oppression and hardship. Thus, the churches teach attitudinal and behavioral change in the setting of a close-knit group of "brothers" and "sisters" going through the same process — a powerful combination.

Catholics and Protestants: Contrasting Models

The Roman Catholic Church has a long history in Guatemala and an impressive tradition of serving the poor. As just one example, Catholic Relief Services has served for decades as a channel for distributing U.S. government food assistance and donations from the U.S. Catholic Church to local organizations.[28] However, the Catholic Church is also bureaucratic, understaffed, and generally weaker in Latin America than many people realize. For example, over two-thirds of the clergy of the Guatemalan Catholic Church are foreigners. The bishop of the diocese of Solola wearily stated in an interview that he had only fifty-two priests for a population of nine hundred thousand, and ten of the priests were American missionaries. He acknowledged that the Catholic Church neglected its pastoral duties because of the shortage of clergy and also because of complacency.[29] This neglect is one reason why only approximately 15 percent of avowed Catholics even attend Mass regularly.[30] The significance of the comparisons given in the preceding section between Catholics and Protestants is that the Catholics were generally *not* active members of any religious community, whereas the Protestants were. However, it is not that Catholics have not

28. Resource Center, 27.

29. Bishop Edurardo Fuentes, interview with author, Panajachel, Guatemala, July 7, 1990.

30. John Hall, professor of mission, Nazarene Seminario, interview with author, San José, Costa Rica, July 8, 1993. Researchers consistently note the lack of active practice by the majority of Catholics, especially as compared to the Protestants. See one of the few examples of *quantitative* research, conducted by Brian Froehle, "The Catholic Church and Politics in Venezuela," in Cleary and Stewart-Gambino, 119.

desired active involvement in a religious community, but that the church leaders needed to sustain strong parishes simply have not been available.

In the late 1960s and 1970s, the Catholic Church in Latin America endorsed aspects of "liberation theology," which emphasized the task of undertaking systemic political and social change on behalf of the poor. The primary tool of liberation theology was the establishment of Christian base communities (*comunidades eclesiais de base,* or CEBs) in which small groups of Catholics would meet to discuss the Scripture as it related to tangible ways to alleviate poverty and injustice. At first, the Vatican strongly supported liberation theology, partly because it eased the staffing problem in Latin America — CEBs could be organized by lay "delegates of the word," who still required training, but not to the extent of priests or nuns. Catholic Christian base communities have external funding for service projects, and like the Protestants, they stress that the work of building schools, streets, clinics, and like projects should be done by the poor themselves. As one member of a CEB explained, "assistance is just this: You make and give to the other, then they do not participate in anything. They just receive, they thank you and it is finished. . . . Doing things for people does not help them improve, but doing things with people helps them improve."[31] The material aid delivered through CEBs emphasizes community responsibility for community projects.

The social science literature examining liberation theology in Latin America is now extensive, and it documents examples of how the poor have been mobilized in many areas.[32] Christian base communities continue to meet and work throughout the region, but their numbers do not compare with the proliferation of evangelical congregations. Because the CEBs might appear to be similar in their approach to development to the Protestant programs, it is important to analyze briefly why the latter groups are so much more widespread and growing far faster.

This is a complex comparison deserving in-depth examination, but

31. Mariz, 88.

32. Among the best political science works in English on liberation theology are Daniel H. Levine, *Popular Voices in Latin American Catholicism* (Princeton: Princeton Univ. Press, 1992); Scott Mainwaring and Alexander Wilde, eds., *The Progressive Church in Latin America* (Notre Dame: Univ. of Notre Dame Press, 1983); and John R. Pottenger, *The Political Theory of Liberation Theology: Toward a Reconvergence of Social Values and Social Science* (Albany: State Univ. of New York Press, 1986).

only some summary points can be made here.[33] First, the Vatican has backed away from its earlier enthusiasm for liberation theology because of the controversial, revolutionary implications of *systemic* change. In fact, the Catholic hierarchy has aggressively appointed new bishops in Latin America who oppose liberation theology, which is an obvious reason for the stagnation of the nascent movement.[34] But more factors are operating here than structural persecution, because the CEBs that remain in Latin America are still small and weak, on average, when compared to the Protestant churches.

In contrast to liberation theology, one appeal of Protestantism is that it calls for change at the individual and family level rather than for direct economic or political change. Feelings of political inefficacy are common among the poor, but conceivably anyone with the right inspiration and supporting community can make changes in his or her personal life. Furthermore, the intellectualism of liberation theology narrows its appeal and effect. For instance, a study of a CEB in Brazil notes the presence of newsletters, books, and discussion guides often written in social science vocabulary. The people liberation theology is trying to reach are often alienated by this intellectualism. As one less than literate woman said when she dropped out of a CEB, "[T]here in the groups, they only like people who can respond prettily, according to what's written there in their books. They no longer value faith, just reading."[35] A historian of the Latin American churches succinctly explained to me the distinction between the two models: he observed that the Christian base communities were important because their priority was to uplift the poor. "But," he continued, "the evangelical churches are even more empowering. They don't just take the side of the poor, they *are* the poor."[36] It should not be surprising, therefore, that the members of these churches know the most effective ways to comfort, discipline, assist, and motivate their members.

33. See Burdick; Mariz; Penny Lernoux, *People of God: The Struggle for World Catholicism* (New York: Viking Press, 1989); and Stoll, "Introduction," in Garrard-Burnett and Stoll, 4-7.

34. "Christian base communities after Santo Domingo — an interview with theologian Pablo Richard," *Latinamerica Press,* June 3, 1993, p. 5.

35. Burdick, 174.

36. Gary Campbell, director of Centro Ecumenico Antonio Valdivieso, interview with author, Managua, Nicaragua, Nov. 8, 1993.

The authentic grass-roots approach of the Protestants (especially the Pentecostals) does not mean that there are no macro-level political and economic consequences. If a movement is widespread and if individual lives are transformed, change will reverberate to the level of the economy and politics. This is the argument that sociologist Max Weber made in *The Protestant Ethic and the Spirit of Capitalism.*[37] Weber attempted to show that although religions could be nonrational and emotional at their core, they can contain elements of rationalism in a material sense that match capitalist attitudes and lead to improved living conditions. To Weber, Protestantism was a particularly "rationalized" religion with a particular moral ethic. The familiar phrase "Protestant work ethic" inaccurately implies that Protestants work harder than Catholics or others, when Weber's more significant distinction is the Protestant emphasis on *saving* money for investment in the future.

Weber, of course, was examining particular cultures that were far different from Latin America and whose capitalist bent was due to numerous variables in addition to Protestantism. The Protestantism in Guatemala appears to be more community oriented than the Protestantism Weber examined. An intensive survey of democratic values in Guatemala found that

> various "non-Catholic" Christian groups, largely Protestant fundamentalist, exhibit significantly (.001) higher communal participation than do Catholics. We also found that those with no religion had the lowest level of participation. . . . Apparently, these new groups do help stimulate local level participation.[38]

It is far too early in the Latin American experience with widespread Protestantism to predict the ultimate consequences of political-economic change; we can only say that macro-level changes are likely if the movement continues to expand.

It is also difficult to make predictions regarding the future direction of the Catholic Church in Latin America, which has been challenged to its

37. Max Weber, *The Protestant Ethic and the Spirit of Capitalism,* trans. Talcott Parsons (New York: Scribner, 1958).

38. Mitchell A. Seligson and Joel M. Jutkowitz, *Guatemalan Values and the Prospects for Democratic Development* (Development Associates, Univ. of Pittsburgh, and Asociacion de Investigacion y Estudios Sociales [ASIES], Mar. 1994), 91.

core by the Protestant movement. The traditional reliance on trained bishops, priests, and nuns has meant neglected parishes and largely empty cathedrals. Thus, several of the comparisons in this chapter are less about Catholics versus Protestants than about nonreligious versus religious groupings. Nor have the CEBs of liberation theology been an altogether effective response to Protestantism by the Catholic Church, as we have seen. A third Catholic approach has been the recent phenomenon of Charismatic Catholic churches, which emulate the emotional style of Pentecostal services but with Catholic theology. The Vatican has expressed ambivalence about the Charismatic Catholics, trying to maintain the essence of Catholic teachings within the popular services. Meanwhile, the Protestant churches grow by leaps and bounds, guided by their own members rather than by an external hierarchy.

Conclusion and Implications

Despite many positive and enduring aspects of the Protestant movement in Latin America, until recently most social scientists have ignored the movement or focused on the negative examples of missionaries who practiced extreme exploitation and manipulation.[39] Now, however, researchers are taking a closer look at the phenomenon of massive Protestant conversions and are taking a micro-level approach, seeking to understand the motives of the people themselves. They are recognizing that a movement that numbers in the tens of millions cannot be based solely on manipulation or bribery or threats, but is at its core the outcome of deliberate *choices* to join a community. Researchers are now analyzing why the poorest of the poor are so drawn to the storefront churches and what they are finding. We have seen that a remarkable consensus is emerging regarding pragmatic reasons and beneficial results for the poor in terms of coping with, and in some instances, overcoming poverty.

In terms of the base of welfare policy, when we compare these findings with studies of poverty in the United States we see two highly contrasting patterns of response to poverty. In the United States, there is an entrenched,

39. See n. 9, above. See also Stoll, *Is Latin America Turning Protestant?* esp. ch. 1, in which he presents a critical analysis of the intellectual bias of researchers favoring liberation theology over Protestantism.

sophisticated government welfare system, yet there is also long-term dependency and hopelessness among a significant number of the poor. Here we are not talking about the majority of the poor in the United States, who have fallen on hard times for a year or two, but about the 5 to 7 percent of the population who are persistently poor. This is a growing segment of the poor who survive on government aid but who are not able or are not motivated to improve their lives. In the United States, thousands of churches are active on behalf of the poor, but they are, by design, largely excluded from the government-run system of assisting the poor. For instance, some of the more innovative welfare programs are increasingly implemented through contracts between the government and local, private organizations that administer the programs. But, ironically, churches are often ruled out as competitors for such contracts simply on the basis of their religious commitment. Instead of being drawn upon as effective, distinctive resources in welfare policy, the churches have been marginalized.[40]

In Guatemala, government provides essentially no welfare assistance, nor does it seriously address basic issues of economic opportunity for its population as the U.S. government has tried to do for U.S. citizens. On the other hand, the Guatemalan government works with religious groups and encourages them to be engaged in charitable work and to proliferate throughout the country. The antipoverty fight in this extremely poor country is carried on by nongovernmental organizations, principally religious ones, which have great latitude to provide direct services to the poor. Even more important than any church-run assistance programs is the fact that active church membership fosters the deep-seated changes in habits and attitudes that are essential for economic improvement in a developing society. Social science research is confirming the distinctive contribution religious participation makes in bettering the lives of the poor in Latin America.

Thus, when religious organizations are excluded by U.S. policymakers, our society is losing a vital resource for addressing chronic causes of poverty. In an eloquent book about mistakes in government welfare policy and about life in a Chicago ghetto, Nicholas Lemann describes in detail why poverty can be so enslaving. His book reminds us that being poor in America is as devastating as it is anywhere in the world, and it reminds us of the moral urgency to address poverty with a new vision. Lemann writes,

40. Carter, 108-23.

> The ghettos bear the accumulated weight of all the bad in our country's racial history, and they are now among the worst places to live in the world. Programs for middle-class blacks — affirmative action and minority set-asides — are never going to set the country aflame with a sense of righteous purpose. Neither will family allowances or an increase in the Earned Income Tax Credit. . . . The more clearly we can be made to see that and to understand the causes of the situation, the less likely it is that we will let it stand.[41]

Lemann recommends an intensive, personal strategy for reaching those trapped in the ghettos and is optimistic about the eventual ability of such one-on-one programs to succeed. For instance, programs offering counseling about sex at the level of the local high school can reduce teenage pregnancy rates. Programs that send caring social workers into the homes of expectant mothers to provide prenatal care can result in healthier babies. The Yale University Child Study Center has a program offering personalized school involvement in the lives of students and their parents, and has raised the achievement scores of the most impoverished elementary school students.[42] "Family First," a Chicago program, is one of hundreds of family-preservation efforts across the country. It offers help in getting food and clothes, counseling, parenting classes, and constant access to a social worker who will teach recipients how to manage a household.[43] These are examples of micro-level government responses aimed at changing behavior and instilling a more future-oriented attitude. They have far more potential for turning lives around than the traditional policy of simply distributing welfare benefits.

The above-mentioned programs are all effective, but as we seek to "understand the causes of the situation," as Lemann urges us to do, we can see the additional benefits religious programs offer. Such programs confront the roots of poverty found in destructive behavior, lack of community, and attitudes of hopelessness. Churches have had dramatic results in improving the lives of the poor because of what they offer: a supportive community of friends and role models who were also poor; an acceptance of responsibility for one's family; a confident belief in God's plan for each person's future. In the developing nation of Guatemala, many desperately

41. Nicholas Lemann, *The Promised Land: The Great Black Migration and How It Changed America* (New York: Knopf, 1991), 353.

42. Lemann, 350.

poor people are finding in the churches a means for rising out of poverty despite the long odds against them. The same dynamic should be released in the United States. Policymakers should enlist religious organizations in addressing our own welfare crisis because of the distinctive and essential contribution religion can make in redirecting the lives of the long-term poor.

Family Issues in Welfare Reform: Developmental Pathways as a Theoretical Framework for Understanding Generational Cycles of Poverty

Cynthia Jones Neal

POOR CHILDREN, the National Commission on Children has reminded us,

> have the most health problems and the least access to [health] care. They are growing up in families that experience the most stress, yet receive the least social support. They are at the highest risk for educational failure, and they often attend the worst schools. They are in the greatest danger of following paths that jeopardize their futures, yet they enjoy the fewest legitimate job opportunities.[1]

Poverty directly harms all who suffer from insufficient food, housing that does not protect, schools that do not educate, and inadequate access to necessary health care. But poverty also has an indirect, yet equally important, negative effect on the development of young children. This indirect and often invisible effect operates within their own homes. It occurs in their relationships with their own parents. Inadequate or distorted parenting can harm children more seriously than any lack of material necessities and with consequences less easily overcome.

If welfare reform is adequately to address the real needs of the poor, it must take into account the effect that poverty can have on the way poor

1. National Commission on Children, *Opening the Doors to America's Children* (Washington, D.C.: National Commission on Children, 1990), 36.

parents relate to their children and how the distorted parenting that often results can persist into the next generation. In turn, if we are to intervene successfully in the cycle of poverty, we must understand its pernicious and potentially deadly impact on the growing self-concept of the child — his or her view of the self and of all subsequent relationships. Policies seeking to increase welfare responsibility are flawed and will ultimately fail if they ignore the developmental pathways that shape conceptions of the self, views of relationships, and notions of a person's role in society. In this chapter I will propose a developmental perspective to facilitate our understanding of generational cycles of poverty and I will suggest policies that promote welfare responsibility.

An Ecological Model for Understanding Development

When one looks at the multifaceted nature of the generational cycle of poverty, the question naturally arises: at what point can we enter the cycle and begin the analysis without interrupting the flow that maintains the overall context necessary for our understanding? If we represent the generational cycle as a circle, then wherever we break into it we begin with incomplete information. Anything examined at that break in the circle can be fully understood only by knowledge of the entire circle. Each narrative within the cycle, whether it is that of the current children or the parents and their developmental history, must be understood contextually.

One way to begin the process of understanding developmentally the generational cycle of poverty is to utilize the ecological model proposed by Urie Bronfenbrenner. He proposes that development can best be conceptualized as a series of "nested structures, each inside the next, like a set of Russian dolls," with each structure affecting the rest of the nested structures. The immediate setting, the microsystem, contains the developing person, and includes the home, the classroom, the laboratory, and so on. The second structure, the mesosystem, comprises the interconnections between immediate settings or microsystems (for example, how communication between home and school affects the child's ability to learn). The third structure, the exosystem, includes those events that may not contain the developing person but affect him or her (for example, parental employment or human services departments' decisions about foster care placement). The fourth structure, the macrosystem, contains the "blueprint for the organization of the society" (for example, the federal government's budget priorities or state laws concerning marriage and schooling).[2]

Bronfenbrenner proposes that a dyadic relationship within the microsystem forms the building block for development. Specifically, the optimal condition for learning and motivation occurs within the infant-caregiver relationship. He maintains that reciprocity, the balance of power, and the quality of the affective relationship are important variables of the dyadic relationship. These aspects of the home, and specifically of the dyad, prepare the developing person for competence and responsibility, both social and psychological, in other settings and in other relationships.

It is readily apparent that all four systems must be examined when working through the complicated issues concerning welfare. Welfare reform proponents have been dealing with poverty and welfare at the level of the exosystem. However, when poverty is treated only at this level, it is very tempting to design policy in a way that ignores the realities of specific lives in their particular contexts, ignoring, for instance, the all-important microsystem of the developing child.

In this chapter, by contrast, I will be working primarily at the level of the microsystem, examining family life in context and the effects that external factors have on a family's capacity to nurture and take responsibility for its children. It is my conviction that welfare policies that focus only on the upper levels (e.g., the ecosystem or the macrosystem) without consideration of the microsystem processes that shape a child's mental representations of self and the self in relation to the external world may yield short-term benefits at best.

Personal Narratives of Poverty

Too often welfare policy is debated by government officials and university academics who have no idea of the extreme pressures faced each day by those living in poverty. Many poor parents face and fight obstacles that would paralyze those of us who discuss and write about the problems of the poor. Typically their lives are not just made difficult by the scarcity of finances but are hampered as well by inadequate or unavailable child care,

2. Bronfenbrenner, *The Ecology of Human Development* (Cambridge: Harvard Univ. Press, 1979), 3-4.

unreliable or unavailable transportation, or a low-wage employer's inability to provide health insurance. The poor have faces and stories. They are not merely statistics to be analyzed and manipulated.

My talks with Kathy Jones (not her real name), a social worker who has been on and off welfare herself, have made me painfully aware of the unjust set of choices that she has had to face. She was forced to choose between finding a job and accepting welfare assistance in the form of a monthly check and medical benefits for her four children (one of whom has asthma). Her preference is to work. But this is a costly choice: it means the loss of medical benefits, total dependence on an often unreliable public transportation system, an enervating search for affordable yet quality child care, and the insecurities of a bottom-rank job. Yet opting to receive welfare has its own high costs: it damages her self-esteem and makes her subject to demeaning treatment at the welfare office — being regarded as "some scum bag off the streets," in her words. The price of welfare is her sense of competence and worth, her status as a contributing member of society. Whichever choice she makes, she is left with a sense of despair. If she chooses welfare, the despair that accompanies her feelings of inadequacy and incompetence is validated by the treatment the welfare workers give her. For those workers, too, are barely making it; they are underpaid and overworked and suffer similarly from a sense of being devalued. Their own self-esteem and their personal resources are limited. Here is a separate part of the welfare crisis that requires attention.

If Kathy chooses the work track, thereby losing both benefits and security, she must still deal with despair because every day, moment by moment, she is fully aware that she is barely making it. At any point, one bill or emergency will put her over the edge. Such despair and loss of self-esteem inevitably leaves a parent psychologically unavailable to his or her children. Whichever option is chosen, there is enormous stress on the family. Neither choice is really a viable choice.

Kathy is employed as a social worker in Chicago's public housing projects. She investigates poor families' problems and attempts to track down resources to meet their needs. Working full-time in this high-stress job nets her a total of only $17,000 per year. On this salary she must raise four children, two of them teenagers. The irony must not escape us!

Poor families are stressed families. One way to deal with the stress of poverty is to try to escape psychologically if physical escape is not possible. For many, especially in the housing projects, drugs are the way out, a whole approach to life and part of the neighborhood culture. Addicts are constantly searching for the high they experienced the first time. Their search to relive that first high, or at least to escape their circumstances, all too often means further damage to their children, children already handicapped by poverty.

Exhaustion, depression, and despair are constant companions of many of the families that evade the drug culture. These parents often do not have the emotional resources to parent in a way that is sensitive and appropriate for their children's needs. Entire groups of children have grown up without the emotional availability and sensitive responsiveness that is so essential for the formation of an image of the self as a worthwhile person. We are seeing this generation grow up and produce more children and more violence.

The poorest neighborhoods also have the worst schools. According to Kathy, who attended inner-city schools herself and whose four children do the same, "The teachers don't care anymore. They are exhausted, underpaid, overworked, and no longer hold to the ideals with which they began their careers."

Alex Kotlowitz has written movingly of such problems of inner-city public schools. Even the committed teachers become discouraged when faced with the constant trials of inner-city education. Of one he writes, "while she hadn't lost her enthusiasm for teaching, she had become a bit leery of investing as much energy and time as she once did." He goes on,

> Ms. Barone tired of the large classes, which at one point swelled to as many as thirty-four students — they now numbered around twenty-five — and of the funding cutbacks. And she worried so much about her children, many of whom came in tired or sad or distracted, that she eventually developed an ulcerated colon.
>
> The relentless violence of the neighborhood also wore her down. The parking lot behind the school had been the site of numerous gang battles. When the powerful sounds of .357 Magnums and sawed-off shotguns echoed off the school walls, the streetwise students slid off their chairs and huddled under their desks. . . . Ms. Barone, along with other teachers, placed the back of her chair against a pillar so that there would be a solid object between herself and the window.[3]

3. Alex Kotlowitz, *There Are No Children Here* (New York: Doubleday Anchor, 1991), 66-67.

Kotlowitz goes on to describe how Ms. Barone feared even the walk between her car and the school, for the dangers were ever present. She dared not wear jewelry and carried a cheap plastic handbag.

Of course not all inner-city teachers face such unremitting violence and despair. But Ms. Barone's experience is not uncommon. There are other problems. Too many principals no longer serve as advocates for their teachers or students; they lack both incentive and reward for doing so. Kathy grieves that many of the children in the inner city are going to schools that give them the same negative messages they receive from their homes. Moreover, such children too often are simply passed on from one grade to another without having gained reading or math skills.

I asked Kathy, "What do you think is going on with the increase in teenage pregnancy? Why is it that younger and younger kids are getting pregnant? Some say that it is a calculated act on these girls' part." She responded quickly:

> You bet. How would you feel if you were sitting in a classroom where you can't read or do simple math problems? You feel stupid and don't want the other girls to think you are stupid. You need to understand. Your group is the most important part of your life. You already feel bad about yourself. What is the one thing you can do? The same thing your mama did! You can have a baby who's gonna love you. And you know how to go down and get on the system and begin receiving that check. Now which one do you think is gonna make you feel like something? Remember, you're only 14 or 15 years old. Staying in that school not knowing how to read or do math, feeling stupid, or go have a baby and be a woman?

Not surprisingly, when these children give birth to their children while living with their own mothers, they often become enmeshed in more complicated familial conflicts. And whether they live alone after leaving their parents' home or move in with girlfriends or boyfriends who are also still mere children themselves, their babies start getting shuttled between home and outside caregivers.

Perhaps the stories of three other young and poor mothers will add to our understanding of the complex cycle of poverty and its burdens:

> **First young mother:** Right now I'm at the stage where everything is piling, bills and all little things. Little things are things that do it. I can't find a baby-sitter right now 'cos I can't pay her — I try to go

get help from welfare and they tell me I make too much money. They can't go to daycare 'cos there's no space — they can only go Monday and Friday but I need the other days too and now I work all day Friday, Saturday, Sunday, Monday — so they went to my sister and she keeps them and sometimes I didn't see my kids from Thursday to Monday — but now that don't work no more and it's one thing after another going on in my life. I gotta find a way to work, to go to school, I gotta go to the Laundromat, I try to get food — now my car broke down . . . no matter how hard you try you're always going to be two steps behind because whoever the force is, never wants you to succeed.[4]

Second young mother: I don't want to be on ADC but I had to get back so I could get caught up on my rent and get Medicaid for my baby . . . so I was working 40 hours and since I got back on ADC I had to cut back to 15-20 hours a week — I hate being on ADC, they make you feel so belittled I hate that! I hate going to the office and I hate dealing with the social worker and dealing with every worker that has something to say about my life. . . . Sometimes they make you think that they're the one giving you this money and they're not — it's the government and they make me pay taxes so I'm the one giving the money back to myself. . . . [Sometimes] I just sit in the bathroom with the door shut and locked so [my daughter] can't open it. . . . She can beat on the door but I don't care — I have to deal with her and then she screams and howls when I run up and grab her and I start crying. . . .[5]

Third young mother: Things that may have kept Des from being at the point he's at now maybe could have been prevented if I could afford proper child care. . . . I mean it's a drug area, where dope is sold. His great-aunt drinks beer, she smokes weed. There's people running in and out all the time. I mean the area is just a criminal area — it's poverty and that's where Des had to go because I could not afford the child care I would want him in. . . . Well, he goes to

4. Valerie Polakow, *Lives on the Edge: Single Mothers and Their Children in the Other America* (Chicago: Univ. of Chicago Press, 1993), 64.

5. Polakow, 68.

> the sitter from 7:45 in the morning and then he goes to school at 12:30 and then he gets out of school at 3:30 and then back to the sitter at 4:00 and then I get off work at 4:30 and catch the bus and get to him about 5:00 and then we catch the bus again and then we get home about 6:00, I see Des for bedtime . . . and then we start another day.[6]

These vignettes from Valerie Polakow's book on poor single mothers clearly illustrate the precarious nature of these women's lives. If the buses are late, hours are changed, a child becomes ill, or the schools have extended time off, then their schedule unravels, causing their tightly controlled systems to collapse. But the pain of the mothers' lives is only part of the story. We must listen to these narratives not just from their point of view but also from that of their children. What must it be like to grow up in a home that is full of so much stress and despair and so many transitions?

Let me emphasize strongly, as I analyze the inadequate parenting that results in children having a low view of themselves and establishing distorted relationships with others, that I do not believe that all poor parents are "bad" parents. However, I do suggest that it is extremely difficult to be available to and supportive of a growing child when one is walking such a thin line between hope and despair.

This, indeed, is the cycle of poverty. Each new generation, raised by parents facing debilitating circumstances and lacking a solid foundation for parenting well, in turn finds itself lacking the emotional and social tools necessary to nurture its own offspring. John Bowlby warns that "of the many types of psychological disturbances resulting from maternal deprivation, the effects on one's ability to nurture and parent are potentially the most serious."[7] I would add that *both* maternal and paternal deprivation affect one's ability to nurture and parent responsibly. Children need both parents to nurture and care for them. Unfortunately it is the case that very many children in our country are growing up without fathers. All four stories just related are of families lacking fathers. The absence of these fathers is a direct loss for the children and results in greater stress for the mothers and limited income for the family unit that has been abandoned.

6. Polakow, 71, 73.

7. John Bowlby, "Attachment and Loss: Retrospect and Prospect," *American Journal of Orthopsychiatry* 52 (1982): 675.

Developmental Pathways

The poor women's stories show the tragic reality of parenting when there is little vision or hope. Children raised in such circumstances of deep poverty and despair are poorly equipped to raise their own children well. It is in attempting to understand the cycle of poverty at this level that developmental psychology has much to teach us about the connections between poverty, welfare use, and responsibility.

The ability to take appropriate responsibility for one's self and family requires a conception of the self as competent and able to nurture. Developmental theory maintains that these conceptions of self and expectations about the external world's response to the self originate in the child's early attachment relationship. The child's inner representation of this relationship organizes and guides his or her behavior, shaping subsequent developmental pathways. Developmental research demonstrates how these early views of the self and the self's relationship to the caregiver predict later positive or negative adjustment.

Utilizing the developmental pathways conception as a framework for understanding personality, Bowlby contends that all individuals have a range of possible pathways on which to travel. And yet, as one pathway is taken, the number of pathways then available diminishes and opportunities for new directions decrease. Thus the attachment relationship formed between the parent and child has a powerful and formative effect on the child's journey toward adulthood.

> A principal variable in the development of each individual personality is, I believe, the pathway along which his attachment behavior comes to be organized and further that that pathway is determined in high degree by the way his parent-figures treat him, not only during his infancy but throughout his childhood and adolescence as well. A principal means by which such experiences influence personality development is held to be through their effects on *how a person construes the world about him and on how he expects persons to whom he might become attached to behave,* both of which are derivatives of the representational models of his parents that he has built up during his childhood.[8]

8. John Bowlby, *A Secure Base: Parent-Child Attachment and Healthy Human Development* (New York: Basic Books, 1988), 65 (emphasis added).

In effect, the views a person holds of the self and of other significant relationships (that is, inner representations or, in Bowlby's term, the internal working model) are conceived in the early attachment relationship of parent and child. Moreover, this inner representation guides the person's expectations of society at large and his or her role in it. It is clear, then, that careful attention must be paid to the effects of parental despair and mistakes on this early attachment relationship. If our means of helping people trapped in poverty are to be improved, it is vital that we come to understand how developmental pathways are formed and how they are distorted when the family unit is distorted by poverty and a lack of hope.

According to attachment theory, the early "dance" between the infant and the caregiver — what is also known as the "emotional dialogue" of the parent/child dyad — lays the foundation for the quality of the attachment relationship that will have so much influence on the development of the self and a person's relationships with others.

The Critical Role of the Early Emotional Dialogue

Research indicates that an important ingredient of positive development is a healthy emotional dialogue between infant and caregiver. The converse appears also to be true. Negative or dysfunctional development results from failures in these early interactions.

Edward Tronick describes the affective communication system that exists between infants and their caregivers. Two different scenarios illustrate the concept:

> Imagine two infant-mother pairs playing the game of peek-a-boo. In the first, the infant abruptly turns away from his mother as the game reaches its "peek" [sic] of intensity and begins to suck on his thumb and stare into space with a dull facial expression. The mother stops playing and sits back watching her infant. After a few seconds the infant turns back to her with an interested and inviting expression. The mother moves closer, smiles, and says in a high-pitched, exaggerated voice, "Oh, now you're back!" He smiles in response and vocalizes. As they finish crowing together, the infant reinserts his thumb and looks away. The mother again waits. After a few seconds the infant turns back to her, and they greet each other with big smiles.

> Imagine a second similar situation except that after this infant turns away, she does not look back at her mother. The mother waits but then leans over into the infant's line of vision while clicking her tongue to attract her attention. The infant, however, ignores the mother and continues to look away. Undaunted, the mother persists and moves her head closer to the infant. The infant grimaces and fusses while she pushes at the mother's face. Within seconds she turns even further away from her mother and continues to suck on her thumb.[9]

Here are two emotional dialogues with two different outcomes. Both mothers overstep during the dance, miscalculating the intensity of their role and leaving the child in need of a break from the interaction. These missteps are called interactive failures and are entirely normal. They are merely errors that need repair. Fortunately, infants as young as six months old are equipped with various coping strategies to deal with such a lack of synchrony. So we see, in both scenes, that the infant looks away and begins sucking the thumb. This is a coping strategy that allows them to calm down and regulate their emotional state. Quite a remarkable feat for such a small child! Both mothers have the opportunity to monitor their infant's communication and to wait for the child to indicate readiness to continue the interaction. Initially, both mothers do respect their infant's needs. However, the second mother eventually intrudes upon her infant's retreat, forcing her attention upon the child. The child withdraws further, even at one point pushing the mother away.

These infants have experienced very different consequences in their interaction with their mothers. The first infant has learned that when he needs space to calm down from an emotionally arousing interaction, his caregiver respects that space and waits for him to indicate readiness to continue. The child has also learned that he has the power to elicit communication from his mother. This leaves him in a positive affective state. As such positive experiences accumulate, the child learns that he is cared for and valued and that he is able to elicit from his caregivers needed resources. The second child does not have the same positive experience as the first. This infant leaves the experience in a negative affective state, hitting

9. Edward Tronick, "Emotions and Emotional Communication in Infants," *American Psychologist* (special issue: "Children and Their Development: Knowledge Base, Research Agenda, and Social Policy Application") 34 (1989): 112.

at her mom, attempting to avert all interaction. The accumulation of these kinds of interactions will *not* give this child the sense that she is cared for and valued, and she certainly will not learn that her messages are respected.

We might consider a third type of interaction. Here the infant attempts to engage the caregiver in an interaction, either through crying or smiling, through fussing or happy vocalization, and is unable to elicit either a positive or a negative response. The circumstance might be an infant whose mother is depressed or addicted and who responds only sporadically to her child. The interactions occur so infrequently and inconsistently that they are not so much a response to the child as an intrusion into the child's space. A history of either repeated attempts by the child that are rebuffed or inconsistent but intrusive summons for interaction by the parent may result in a child lacking a sense of efficacy, deeply doubtful of his or her ability to gain needed care, and harboring a view of the self as lacking any value or worth.

Infants demonstrate as early as six months of age certain preferred coping strategies for the purpose of regulating their emotional state when there is a mismatch between their expectations for the interaction and the reality of the interaction.[10] When there is such a mismatch, so that the infant must utilize some coping strategy, there are positive benefits for the infant who is able successfully to repair the disjunction. Successful repair increases the infant's sense of efficacy and competence. Further, as the infant accumulates a history of successful repair, she or he develops a pattern of coping strategies to be brought to interactions with adults other than the early caregiver.

Obviously these coping strategies are limited and immature and there is continued need for the caregiver to take primary responsibility for the regulatory role, at least as far as being able to sense and respond to the child's cues. Emotional development is subject to disregulation when the parent is unable to play this important role. When the interactive failures persist without repair — when the dyad suffers a consistent inability to "dance" effectively — those strategies for disengagement or withdrawal from interaction can become defensive. And just as positive interaction with parents equips a child for healthy relationships with peers and with other

10. Edward Tronick and Andrew Gianino, "Interactive Mismatch and Repair: Challenges to the Coping Infant," *Zero to Three: Bulletin of the National Center for Clinical Infant Programs* 6, no. 3 (1986).

adults, so also does the repetition of a harmful "dance" predispose the child to dysfunctional relationships. The need continually to resort to defensive coping behaviors in the dyadic relationship can harden into a pattern of disengaged and withdrawn behaviors that are employed in all relationships, regardless of the circumstances.

This early "dance" with the caregiver is a precursor or foundation for the quality of the attachment relationship. The numerous transitions from home to outside care settings experienced by many infants born into poverty, the poor quality of the child care many poor families must tolerate, and the suboptimal parenting often provided by stressed parents who themselves labor with a low self-image certainly place these infants at high risk for developing disengaged, defensive coping mechanisms. This, in turn, compromises the emerging attachment relationship.

The Attachment Relationship

The quality of the emotional "dance" is directly reflected in the quality of the attachment relationship that is developed as the caregiver's major role evolves into the regulation of internal security. Internal security or insecurity is the outcome of the accumulated experiences during the first year of life with the parent: responsive versus nonresponsive or rejecting, sensitive versus insensitive. Does the child view the parent as a secure base from whom to explore and to whom she or he can return when stressed or fearful? In addition to providing a sense of self-efficacy, internal locus of control, and curiosity, the attachment relationship provides the foundation for the experience of all other intimate relationships. This includes the process of meeting dependency needs, the ability to nurture others, and the manner of dealing with loss and separation.[11]

Bowlby defines attachment behavior

> as any form of behavior that results in a person attaining or maintaining proximity to some other clearly identified individual who is conceived as better able to cope with the world. It is most obvious whenever the person is frightened, fatigued, or sick, and is assuaged by comforting and caregiving. At other times the behavior is less in evidence. Nevertheless

11. John Bowlby, *Attachment*, 2nd ed. (New York: Basic Books, 1982).

> for a person to know that an attachment figure is available and responsive gives him a strong and pervasive feeling of security, and so encourages him to value and continue the relationship. . . . The biological function attributed to it is that of protection. To remain within easy access of a familiar individual known to be ready and willing to come to our aid in an emergency is clearly a good insurance policy — whatever our age.[12]

The knowledge that the attachment figure is available and responsive provides the infant with a sense of security. The caregiver serves as a "secure base" from which to explore but to which the infant can return when frightened or stressed.

Studies examining attachment relationships have identified three classifications to describe the quality of the relationship.[13] Children classified as securely attached easily demonstrate their belief that the caregiver serves as a secure base. They easily separate to explore novel surroundings, seeking and finding comfort and reassurance when stressed or frightened. Those classified as ambivalent or avoidant demonstrate the opposite. Children described with an ambivalent attachment find it difficult to separate from their caregivers and when frightened or stressed have difficulty finding needed comfort from them. Children classified as avoidant in their attachment relationship manifest active avoidance of their caregiver in most situations, including stressful ones.[14]

Antecedent parental behaviors have been shown to correlate significantly with attachment classification. These studies show that infants classified as avoidant have mothers who were not only insensitive to infant signals in a variety of contexts during the first half of the first year but also behaviorally and verbally communicated dislike of physical contact with

12. John Bowlby, *A Secure Base,* 26-27.

13. Building on Bowlby's notion of attachment, Mary Ainsworth and her colleagues developed the methodology most often utilized in studies of attachment. See M. Ainsworth, M. Blehar, E. Waters, and S. Wall, *Patterns of Attachment: A Psychological Study of the Strange Situation* (Hillsdale, N.J.: Erlbaum, 1978).

14. The methodology utilized in this research is such that the classifications identified are not merely samples of caregiver-child behavior. Rather than a set of behaviors that the child exhibits when stressed, this particular research design captures the child's view of the parent with regard to security and protection. For an excellent compilation of studies examining various components of attachment, see Inge Bretherton and Everett Waters, "Growing Points of Attachment Theory and Research," *Monographs of the Society for Research in Child Development* 50, nos. 1-2, serial no. 209 (1985).

their infants. Furthermore, the emotional expressiveness of these mothers was generally dispirited or flat. In the case of infants classified as resistant, parents did not reject physical contact but rather provided inconsistent care and responsiveness. The predominant parental behavior related to a secure attachment classification is sensitivity to infant signals during the first six months of life and a warm and affectionate relationship with the infant.

It is noteworthy that fathers are not so often mentioned in this research. Unfortunately, mothers have typically taken primary responsibility for nurturing the children in our society. Early developmental research merely accepted this as a given rather than question the assumption that mothers are inherently the only "natural" caregiver. However, in more recent studies examining attachment relationships between fathers and their infants, we find similar classifications as those found with mother-child dyads, showing that fathers as well as mothers are capable of nurturing and developing high-quality affective relationships with their children[15] — and also just as capable of distorting their infant's developing sense of self.

Although the attachment system proposed by Bowlby does not become organized until the second half of the first year, the quality of the early emotional communication system — the emotional dialogue between infant and caregiver — sets the stage for the child's view of the attachment relationship, signaling whether or not the caregiver is available and responsive and thereby able to serve as a secure base.

In sum, research examining the importance of the early attachment relationship suggests that a reciprocal interaction within a warm interpersonal relationship that endures over time leads to the development of a secure attachment. In other words, from a warm, nurturing, and responsive "dance" between the parent and the infant emerges a securely attached child, a child prepared for more extensive exploratory behavior, possessing more tolerance for frustration, developing an increased internal locus of control, and having greater motivation to attend to and learn from the caregiver.[16] Ellen Skinner states that

> one of the effects of interactions with a sensitive caregiver is an increased awareness of the effects one's actions exert on the environment; through

15. Kyle Pruett, *The Nurturing Father* (New York: Warner, 1987).

16. Urie Bronfenbrenner, "Is Early Intervention Effective?" in M. Guttenlag and E. L. Struenig, eds., *Handbook of Evaluation Research,* vol. 2 (Beverly Hills: Sage, 1975).

> prolonged experience, the child develops a generalized sense of the self as an effective agent. This sense of control in turn provides the motivational basis for sustained engagement with both the social and nonsocial environment even under conditions of difficulty, ambiguity, or novelty.[17]

Mastery motivation, increased attention span, positive affect, persistence in problem solving, curiosity, and sociability are among the preschool behaviors found in infants classified as secure. Insecure children, classified as resistant, are more easily frustrated, whiny, and negative when solving problems than either secure or avoidant children. Furthermore, these children display more dependent behaviors. Children classified as avoidant tend to show more hostile behavior to peers and are less likely to seek help when faced with a difficult task or when physically hurt.

In analyzing both the antecedent parental behaviors and subsequent preschool behaviors of the children of families suffering the stress and despair of poverty, we see that many poor parents have few emotional resources to provide the necessary warmth and affective behaviors essential for their children's healthy emotional development. This should not surprise us. Remember Kathy's concerns about the prevalence of drugs in the homes of many of the poor families with which she works. An additional concern is the teenage mothers and fathers who are children themselves, with dependency needs not yet met. Such young parents often lack the necessary emotional resources; even worse, fathers typically are absent in the case of teenage pregnancies, so that the mother and child are further stressed. Indeed, single mothers of any age are faced with great challenges, as the earlier stories showed: ". . . no matter how hard you try you're always going to be two steps behind because whoever the force is, never wants you to succeed," or "I just sit in the bathroom with the door shut and locked so she can't open it. . . . She can beat on the door but I don't care. . . ." A secure attachment can be compromised when parents are stressed by poverty and all the problems associated with it. This in turn sets the stage for a child's growing sense of the self as unloved and incompetent.

17. Ellen Skinner, "The Origins of Young Children's Perceived Control: Mother Contingent and Sensitive Behavior," *International Journal of Behavioral Development* 9 (1986): 360.

The Internal Working Model

Understanding how the quality of the early infant-parent dance lays the foundation for the quality of the attachment relationship provides us now with the tools to understand the "birth of the self." One's inner representation, or the *internal working model,* of the self is birthed from the attachment relationship. *Who I am as a person cannot be understood without reference to my early attachment relationships.* Bowlby describes the "internal working model" as a mental representation of the self and the self in relation to the external world. In essence, conceptions of the self and expectations of the world's response to the self (responsive versus rejecting) are derived initially from the child's view of the attachment relationship. On the basis of this initial view the child organizes the information from the attachment relationship into a subsequent view of the self as one who is able to elicit needed care (or not) and as one who is valued and therefore valuable (or not). Where both parents are available to a child, the opportunity for a secure attachment with at least one of them is increased; a secure attachment relationship with one of the parents may override some of the negative effects of an insecure relationship with the other parent. Obviously, a secure relationship with both parents is the optimal condition, leading to more positive generalized expectations and view of the self.

If the parent rejects or ridicules the child's needs, the child develops a representation of the self as not worthy of love, without value, and without the necessary tools to gain that which one needs from the environment. Conversely, if the caregiver is responsive, sensitive to the child's cues, and available to meet the child's needs, the child develops a representation of the self as a person loved and worthy of support, a person able to elicit the care needed.

As the child matures through the first year of life, the child begins to see the self as separate from the caregiver. If a child is required to develop detached coping skills during that first year due to the disregulation caused by the parent's inability to read and respond sensitively to infant cues, these coping skills become defensive and ultimately maladaptive as the child matures into adulthood. According to Bowlby, through the use of these detached coping skills the child "is effectively excluding any sensory inflow that would elicit his attachment behavior and thus avoiding any risk at being rebuffed and becoming distressed and disorganized; in addition he is avoiding any risk of eliciting hostile behavior from his mother."[18]

For children being raised in environments filled with poverty, drugs, and violence, certain behaviors can have early survival benefits. Alex Kotlowitz writes of just such an environment when he records the daily life of two boys being raised in a Chicago public housing project. When he first approached the mother about the idea of writing the story of two of her boys, she consented. But she also corrected Kotlowitz's idea of childhood in the projects: "But you know, there are no children here. They've seen too much to be children." Kotlowitz confirms her wisdom as he writes about her sons:

> [A]s Lafeyette and Pharaoh played on the jungle gym in mid afternoon, shooting broke out. A young girl jumping rope crumpled to the ground. Lafeyette ran into his building, dragging behind him one of the triplets. Pharaoh, then seven, panicked. He ran blindly until he bumped into one of the huge green trash containers that dot the landscape. He pulled himself up and over, landing in a foot of garbage. Porkchop [his cousin] followed. For half an hour, the two huddled in the foul-smelling meat scraps and empty pizza boxes, waiting for the shooting to stop, arguing about when they should make a break for their respective homes. Finally, the shooting subsided and they climbed out, smelling like dirty dishes. They watched as paramedics attended to the girl, who luckily had been shot only in the leg. Her frightened mother, who had fainted, was being revived. It was at the point that Pharaoh first told his mother, "I didn't wanna know what was happening."[19]

In such circumstances it can become too painful to know, too painful to feel. This seven-year-old boy has already developed certain survival skills, not just for physical safety but also for emotional safety. Violent episodes, unfortunately, are a common occurrence in the lives of poor children. It is deplorable that in one of the wealthiest countries in the world, thousands of seven-year-old children have to dodge bullets nearly daily. Moreover, their parents, themselves raised in the projects, have also "seen too much" at too early an age. Before they became parents, when

18. John Bowlby, *Loss: Sadness and Depression* (New York: Basic Books, 1980), 73.
19. Kotlowitz, 40.

they were but children, they developed a detached, hardened representation of themselves and the world in which they live. It would be difficult for any of us to see so much and yet let ourselves feel deeply. As Mary Stewart Van Leeuwen once reminded me, "It's hard to raise a child in a concentration camp."

Developmental History's Impact on Nurturant and Responsible Behavior

When these children grow up and become parents, they are likely to have difficulty understanding and responding to their child's cues that communicate the need for love and intimacy. Conceivably they may distrust affection shown or demands made by their child, perhaps even projecting ill will upon them. Therefore if we desire to assist families that are distressed economically and psychologically, we must recognize the importance of the parents' developmental history and its effect on their ability to nurture and care for their own young.

Our developmental history bequeaths to us either positive or negative psychological resources. We are typically completely unaware of this heritage. But these "ghosts in the nursery" are vitally important.

> In every nursery there are ghosts. They are the visitors from the remembered past of the parents; the uninvited guests at the christening. . . . [In some families, the] intruders from the past have taken up residence in the nursery, claiming tradition and rights of ownership. They have been present at the christening for two or more generations. While no one has issued an invitation, the ghosts take up residence and conduct the rehearsal of the family tragedy from a tattered script.

These researchers go on to report:

> In our Infant Mental Health Program we have seen many of these families and their babies. The baby is already in peril by the time we meet him, showing the early signs of emotional starvation, or grave symptoms, or developmental impairment. In each of these cases, the baby has become a silent partner in a family tragedy. The baby in these families is burdened by the oppressive past of his parents from the moment he enters the

> world. The parent, it seems, is condemned to repeat the tragedy of his childhood with his own baby in terrible and exacting detail.[20]

Alice Miller has expressed the same idea more lyrically: "You can drive the devil out of your garden but you will find him again in the garden of your son."[21] In other words, while you may deny the "ghosts" and repress your troubled past, you will nevertheless visit your past upon your child, in essence passing the distorted developmental torch to the next generation, unless awareness and change intervene. I believe it is something like this process to which the Scriptures refer when we are told that the "sins of the fathers" are passed on to succeeding generations.

It is critical that we understand this process if we hope to break the generational cycle of poverty. When parents are emotionally unavailable or inconsistently responsive, due perhaps to their own defensive adaptations and negative self-concepts, their children develop coping mechanisms that become defenses against the world. The child constructs a model of the self as unlovable and incompetent and the expectation that the caregiver and eventually all others are unable or unwilling to meet her needs. As the child grows and then becomes a parent, she carries with her these "ghosts," which she visits upon her own child, thus perpetuating the cycle.

Recent research demonstrates that the quality of the attachment relationships of adults with their own parents is highly correlated to the quality of their attachments to their own children.[22] J. Belsky found that parents' developmental histories have the most profound effect on their ability to parent their children well. The effect is both direct — shaping the parents' psychological resources — and indirect — shaping their ability to obtain appropriate sources of support from others, from a spouse, from friends, or from coworkers.[23]

20. S. Fraiberg, E. Adelson, and V. Shapiro, "Ghost in the Nursery," *Journal of the American Academy of Child Psychiatry* 14 (1975): 387-88.

21. Alice Miller, *The Drama of the Gifted Child: The Search for the True Self* (New York: Basic Books, 1981), 27.

22. M. H. Ricks, "The Social Transmission of Parental Behavior: Attachment Across Generations," *Monographs of the Society for Research in Child Development* 50, nos. 1-2, serial no. 209 (1985).

23. J. Belsky, "The Determinants of Parenting: A Process Model," *Child Development* 55 (1984): 83-96.

The internal working model is a dynamic system. However, its characteristics are very deeply rooted in the quality of those critical early relationships in life. Of course, one's representation of the self is continually being modified through interpretation of one's present circumstances. But our tendency is to interpret personal events and interactions in the light of past events and interactions. We selectively attend to those phenomena most familiar or only slightly novel. This makes the reorganization of one's self-representation very difficult. Change is not impossible, but there can be no doubt that a person's conception of his or her self is highly resistant to change. This is why it is crucial that intervention with families at risk begin early and encompass a range of assistance and training opportunities.

Interventions to Break the Cycle of Poverty

If we utilize the theoretical concept of developmental pathways as a way of framing appropriate interventions at the microsystem level, then the important issues of generational cycles of poverty and welfare reform may be more adequately addressed. I have argued for one particular way of understanding why we see such variation between people in their ability to act responsibly toward themselves, their children, and the wider society. I have suggested as well a way of understanding how parents pass on the burden of poverty to their children. What remains is the challenge of proposing ways to help parents in need so that the vicious intergenerational cycle of poverty can be ended.

People who have succeeded in escaping entrapment in poverty typically are animated by a vision of a better future for themselves and their children. That vision drives them to overcome, rather than give in to, the challenges that threaten to overwhelm them. But having such a positive vision for oneself and for the future of one's family requires internal healing of the "ghosts" from one's troubled past. We all need others to believe in us. Thus effective interventions into the cycle of poverty must begin with the parents' inner representation. Changes here will necessarily have consequences for the inner representations of the children in the family. Reorganization of one's self-concept from a negative image to one of value and competence is possible only if psychological resources are brought into play along with material improvements. As the person begins to gain a healthier view of the self, she or he will be able to see more options and choices. In other words, the ability to see new options and to choose a different path for the future depends on one's view of one's self.

Parental training that fosters the reorganization of negative self-concepts into competent and nurturing inner representations is necessary if parents are to take appropriate responsibility for their families. Parents who themselves were raised in dysfunctional and chaotic homes often need massive nurturance and support before they are able to respond appropriately to their children with warmth and affection. This need is not limited to poor families, of course. Wealth does not automatically produce warm and nurturing relationships within the family. However, it remains the case that poor families often have limited access to the resources that would help them overcome their "ghosts" and adopt a better parenting style with their children.

While effective intervention into the developmental process and into the inner recesses of parents' self-conceptions is difficult, it is not impossible. The Harvard Family Research Project has analyzed a number of successful government-sponsored programs to improve the effectiveness of parenting. Programs such as Connecticut's Parent Education and Support Centers, the Family Support Centers in Maryland, Early Childhood Family Education in Minnesota, and Parents as Teachers in Missouri have all proven to be helpful to disadvantaged families.[24]

Research I have conducted with Rafael Diaz shows that even parents with very poor self-concepts and parenting styles can effectively be helped.[25] The mothers we studied had all been ordered by the courts to participate in a therapeutic preschool due to abuse and neglect of their children. All of them were highly "at risk," as measured by being young, being poor, having many children, and having low levels of education. These mothers rarely used praise and encouragement in teaching their children; they relied primarily on commands and were intrusive and insensitive or else unaware of their children's abilities to perform the tasks. According to the cognitive

24. B. Hausman and H. Weiss, "State-Sponsored Family Support and Education: The Rationale for School-based Services," Harvard Family Research Project (1987); H. Weiss, "State Family Support and Education Programs: Lessons from the Pioneers," *American Journal of Orthopsychiatry* 59, no. 1 (1989): 32-48.

25. Cynthia Neal and Rafael Diaz, "Teaching for Self-Regulation: A Comparison of Low and High Risk Mothers," presented at the biennial meeting of the Society for Research in Child Development, Kansas City, Mo., 1989.

development literature, such inadequacies are typical of poor parents, though less so of middle-class parents. It is striking that these negative interactional patterns characterized the mothers under study even though the intent of the preschool was to counteract them, and some of the mothers had been participating in the program for as long as a year. It was apparent that additional and intensive training was necessary if high-risk parents were to become able to teach and interact with their children more effectively. From these findings, then, I designed a program that succeeded in helping parents who were in similar situations as these mothers to become better early teachers of their children.[26]

Parents and their three-year-old children were randomly assigned to the intervention group or to a waiting-list control group. The intervention group took part in three group discussion sessions, meeting once a week for three weeks. These three sessions were used to instruct the parent in several teaching skills: the use of praise and encouragement, effective verbal teaching strategies such as the use of questions and explanations, and a particular quality of teaching described as "scaffolding" (defined below). In addition, each parent was individually videotaped during a teaching interaction with his or her child after each group discussion session. The instructor viewed the videotape with the parent and gave explicit feedback concerning the differences between optimal and observed parental behavior.

The intervention and control groups differed in their amount of improvement on all teaching dimensions. Parents receiving the intervention instruction dramatically improved the quality of their teaching by increasing their use of praise and encouragement, positive affective tone, high-quality verbal teaching, and the ability to scaffold. Scaffolding refers to a quality of teaching consisting of the ability to read the child's cues during the teaching interaction and to adjust the level of support as the child's ability to perform independently becomes evident. These parents also decreased their use of commands and increased their use of explanations. By contrast, parents in the control group showed no improvement at all in their ability to teach their children appropriately.

The magnitude of the improvement for the intervention group indi-

26. Cynthia Neal, "Within the Zone of Proximal Development: High-risk Parents' Scaffolding and Their Children's Performance" (paper presented to the Society for Research in Child Development, Seattle, Wash., 1991).

cates that, although these parents were already participating in a program that provided much-needed support, in order for them to become effective agents in their own children's development they needed additional tools. The preschool program gave the parents child-raising assistance, served them as an advocate with other programs and authorities, and provided them with connections to other community resources. What they needed, in addition to these forms of support, however, was direct training in specific aspects of parenting. Such assistance enabled these parents to develop the ability to respond appropriately to their children's behavioral cues. Significantly, the children of the parents receiving the intervention markedly increased their active engagement with their parent.

Several aspects of this intervention program worked together to encourage the parents to improve their role as their children's early teacher. The group format gave parents the opportunity to discuss their worries and concerns in a safe setting with peers with similar-aged children and similar personal problems. By making possible individualized visual feedback, the use of videotaping helped bring home to parents the lessons about the most effective ways to interact with their children. Further, in interactions with the parents the instructor carefully modeled the desired teaching behaviors, demonstrating warm affect, appropriate verbal teaching, and scaffolding.

The parents involved in this intervention program were a captive audience; they were at the preschool due to court orders. And certainly the observed results would not have been forthcoming without the context of the therapeutic preschool. However, I am convinced that these factors do not explain away the intervention's successes. The key was the specific character of the parenting assistance coupled with the strong desire of these at-risk parents to become better parents. Such a desire provides a solid foundation for programs to support and to educate parents. Fortunately, most parents deeply desire to care well for their children; exceptions would be parents so addicted to drugs or other destructive behavior that they have abdicated their parental role.

But effective parent education requires more than well-designed programs and parents who desire to raise their children more effectively. The context of the parent and child cannot be ignored. Too often inner-city life is essentially a "war zone." As long as gangs control public housing, drug use dominates neighborhoods, and schools neither effectively teach nor even ensure the safety of their pupils, the best parent education programs can hardly inspire and enable parents to become very effective in fulfilling their responsibility to help their children to maturity. For a parent to become able sensitively to respond to a child's cues requires the adult to shed many defensive coping strategies. However, if the family resides in a "war zone," it may be neither possible nor wise for the parent — or the child — to adopt a more open posture. As the young boy, Pharaoh, told his mother, "I didn't wanna know what was happening." Only in this way could he survive emotionally.

Beyond Interventions

Many American families face barriers that inhibit their ability to exercise their appropriate responsibilities. Thomas Corbett notes that "[i]t is often said that the test of a society's compassion is how it treats its most vulnerable members — the old and the young."[27] America has done much to lower the poverty rate of the elderly. But the same cannot be said in the case of the young. More children are born poor today than thirty years ago. The current figure is over 14 million children in poverty. More and more children enter life already burdened, before they have even taken their first step. These children and those responsible for raising them must have appropriate support and services if the growth of childhood poverty is to be reversed. Intervention programs to improve parenting are important, but they cannot stand alone. The problem of inadequate cognitive development of the children of poor families helps us see the need for broader solutions than only interventions with parents.

It should be no surprise that children from economically disadvantaged homes are disproportionately represented in special education placements and grade retention. Many poor parents find it difficult to negotiate successfully with the public school system on behalf of their children and to work with their children to promote their learning. Economic disadvantage, of course, does not dictate poor family functioning or disengagement from the children's education. Many poor families do remarkable jobs raising their children in extremely challenging conditions. However, often the parents of poor families have themselves been inadequately educated,

27. Thomas Corbett, "Child Poverty and Welfare Reform: Progress or Paralysis?" *Focus* (Institute for Research on Poverty) 15, no. 1 (Spring 1993): 2.

due to incompetent or overextended teachers, resource-poor schools, or the failure of their parents to instill vision and motivation. Parents with such a heritage may have been left without the ability or impulse to promote the cognitive development of their own children.

There is solid evidence that poor families tend not to promote cognitive development.[28] Middle-class mothers typically are less controlling and disapproving and give greater attention to their children than do lower-class mothers. In problem-solving situations, middle-class mothers are more likely to give their children nonspecific suggestions and guidance in the form of questions, and they are more likely to praise their children for what they are doing right than to blame them for errors. Lower-class mothers are more likely to intrude physically on their children and to give negative feedback.[29] Lower-class parents are more likely to use an imperative control style with their children, utilizing less complex communication patterns and providing fewer explanations to their children.

Such findings help us understand why lower-class children tend to be less successful than middle-class children in school environments. As R. D. Hess and V. C. Shipman summarize the evidence,

> the cognitive environment of the culturally disadvantaged child is one in which behavior is controlled by imperatives rather than by attention to the individual characteristics of a specific situation, and one in which behavior is neither mediated by verbal cues which offer opportunities for using language as a tool for labeling, ordering, and manipulating stimuli in the environment, nor mediated by teaching that relates events to one another and the present to the future. The meaning of deprivation would thus seem to be a deprivation of meaning in the early cognitive relationships between mother and child.[30]

28. L. Beckwith and S. E. Cohen, "Home Environment and Cognitive Competence in Preterm Children During the First 5 Years," in A. W. Gottfried, ed., *Home Environment and Early Cognitive Development: Longitudinal Research* (Orlando: Academic Press, 1984); R. H. Bradley and B. M. Caldwell, "Home Observation for Measure of the Environment: A Validation Study of Screening Efficiency," *American Journal of Mental Deficiency* 81 (1977): 417-25.

29. H. L. Bee, L. F. VanEgeren, A. P. Streissguth, B. A. Nyman, and M. S. Leckie, "Social Class Differences in Maternal Teaching Strategies and Speech Patterns," *Developmental Psychology* 1 (1969): 726-34.

30. R. D. Hess and V. C. Shipman, "Maternal Influences Upon Early Learning:

In my own research, I discovered that high-risk mothers taught their children using many commands, few questions, and little praise. Low-risk mothers, by contrast, lavishly praised and encouraged their children, used many conceptual questions, and talked much about plans and activities. According to the research, the strongest predictor of children's improvement was praise and encouragement. Such praise and encouragement was more likely the higher the mother's socioeconomic status (SES), as measured by level of education achieved, the number of people in the household who work, and the occupations of the employed.

But why is higher socioeconomic status related so strongly to more effective interaction between mothers and their children? I believe it is because praise and encouragement of a child require not only time and skill but also emotional availability and emotional energy. It cannot be a surprise that the stress of poverty contributes to maternal depression and that it drains away emotional energy. It is not the case that impoverished mothers are inherently "bad teachers"; rather, the enervating conditions of poverty deplete the reservoir of energy that successful teaching requires.

Home environments that promote cognitive development are characterized by these factors: warmth, responsiveness, praise and encouragement, verbal rationales, frequent explanations, and the use of questions instead of only commands. The research literature further suggests the importance of appropriate stimulation, sufficient play equipment, encouragement for academic achievement, and conversations that attach meaning to experiences.[31]

Economic poverty does not preclude parents from enriching their children's lives with good parenting. But it remains the case that families living in impoverished conditions are less likely to be able to provide their children with these parental and environmental factors that promote cognitive development. Poor children, then, may be doubly handicapped. If they live in inner cities, the schools to which they must go are likely to be

---

The Cognitive Environments of Urban, Pre-school Children," in R. D. Hess and R. M. Bear, eds., *Early Education: Current Theory, Research, and Action* (Chicago: Aldine, 1968), 103. See also C. P. Deutsch and M. Deutsch, "Brief Reflections on the Theory of Early Childhood Enrichment Programs," in the same volume.

31. R. H. Bradley and B. M. Caldwell, "174 Children: A Study of the Relationship Between Home Environment and Cognitive Development During the First 5 Years," in Gottfried.

deficient in resources and ineffective as learning institutions. But their home environments, too, are likely to be deficient in those qualities and resources that promote children's learning. In sum, in too many instances both the schools and the parents fail the children.

The Importance of Hope

A stronger and more effective government commitment to the poor and better-designed intervention programs for parents would provide resources and skills that are desperately needed by many impoverished families. Parents need good schooling when they are growing up, but as adults they need to be able to find and fill economic opportunities if they are to be able to assume financial responsibility for their children. Low-cost housing, safe neighborhoods, and access to needed medical and mental-health care are all important as well if poor families are to thrive. But a societal commitment to providing such policies and programs would have an additional and essential effect: hope would begin to grow in families and neighborhoods in crisis.

Hope is intangible, but it is indispensable if the cycle of poverty is to be broken. Kathy, my social-work informant, will make it, because she wants a better life for her children and is determined to achieve it no matter what the barriers are. Families that succeed despite desperate odds have caught a vision that the future can be better, and they work ceaselessly to achieve it. Vision: is it not this that motivates us? We are seized by a vision for the future, a plan that offers opportunities to use our gifts and talents in some meaningful way. With a vision come hope, courage, and energy. Breaking the cycle of poverty will have to begin at this level.

But how do poor parents and families capture a vision? What does it take for them to become animated by the possibilities of a transformed future rather than trapped by the harsh realities of their present circumstances? Kathy's story and the stories of the other three women illustrate the struggle of poor parents to capture a new vision for themselves and for their children. What made the difference for these women? Why are they so intent upon terminating the cycle of poverty and creating a different pathway for their children? Kathy says that it often just takes one other person who believes in you, someone "who encourages small steps toward becoming responsible, helping you to see yourself differently." Valerie

Polakow, writing about teen mothers who are seeking to advance beyond their current circumstances, notes, "We see how the small interventions that these teenagers did receive — a sensitive preschool teacher, a teen-parent center, a public health nurse, a brief encounter with a caring social worker — were critical events in their lives."[32] Someone has stepped into the cycle of poverty and by doing so has helped to create a new developmental pathway upon which these families may journey.

Such encouragements and small interventions are not enough by themselves, I am convinced. They must be bolstered by government action that enables full progress to be made toward responsibility. Parents energized to go forward must find opportunities for advance.

Polakow claims that "the language of public assistance views such interventions only from a cost-benefit instrumental perspective, and evaluates them in terms of later economic payoffs." But, she urges,

> [P]erhaps it is not only a redistribution of resources that is necessary but a redistribution of sensibilities, a different way of seeing. We need to see that poor teenage mothers' lives and those of their young children *matter*. Poverty discourse has failed to give equal meaning to their dailiness, to *their* experiences on *our* horizons.[33]

Here is a key to lasting welfare reform: we must understand that *poor teenage mothers' lives and those of their young children matter*. Indeed, all poor families should matter to us. It should matter that too many homes are headed by single women. It should matter that fathers so often leave and take no responsibility for their children. It should matter that even those who have caught a new vision lead lives precariously on the edge. Truly it is a tragedy when the proponents of welfare reform fail to hear and respond to the cries of the poor.

In this chapter I have argued that policies seeking to increase welfare responsibility will fail if they ignore the developmental pathways that shape conceptions of the self, views of relationships, and convictions about one's place in society. If our examination of welfare begins with the stories of those suffering the despair and low self-image of poverty, we will better understand the challenging developmental pathways along which the poor journey.

32. Polakow, 78.
33. Polakow, 78.

If we listen to recipients who are working to make it off public assistance, we will hear stories of mentors or support persons who have entered their lives, believed in them, and helped them to shape a new vision for themselves and their families. Unfortunately, we will also hear stories of the many barriers that confront these struggling families: violent neighborhoods, unsafe schools, poor health care.

If we take these stories seriously, we will work at all levels of the multifaceted problem of poor people and poor communities. We will work to resolve problems at the levels of the exosystem and macrosystem. But we will also work to bring healing to the microsystem: the family. Many parents who are trapped in the intergenerational cycle of poverty were raised without the necessary parental warmth and responsiveness. They have now carried these "ghosts" into their own nurseries. Mentoring these parents, providing instruction and modeling for nurturing interactions with their children, and serving as advocates for them at the government level is a simple but essential first step in helping these families gain the ability to take appropriate responsibility for their children. We must begin by hearing and responding to *their* experiences.

If the analysis of this chapter is correct, then a wise and just welfare policy will go beyond merely changing the current AFDC program. Reform must go beyond enriching benefits or adding obligations. Reform must go beyond the provision of transitional support while women and men find work and get established in the labor force. Welfare reformers must recognize that intervention at the level of the microsystem, the family, is often necessary. To break the cycle of poverty, sensitive and appropriate parent education assistance must be added to the resources and requirements designed to move parents to independence. If we can work with poor parents in this comprehensive way, then they will become able to nurture and take responsibility for their children.

Rural Poverty: Christian Charity and Social Justice Responses

Mary P. Van Hook

ALTHOUGH THE MEDIA tend to focus on the problems of urban America, especially the inner cities, an equally damaging if less obvious poverty is present in the rural areas of this country. Rural poverty accounts for a substantial part of the poverty in the United States (as well as in other countries in the world) and has important implications for social policy generally. This is a poverty with many facets, reflecting the diversity of rural areas — boarded-up storefronts of dying small towns; impoverished families living amidst the natural beauty of Appalachia; generation after generation debilitated by poverty in the rural South; struggling migrant families; Native American reservations barren of jobs and hope and inundated with problems of alcoholism; and small clusters of rundown houses or mobile homes in rural areas set away from more prosperous farms and houses.

Incorporating rural issues into the discussion about fighting poverty has been difficult due to the complexity of rural poverty and the diversity of rural areas. But it is also due to the tendency of policymakers, who mainly have an urban orientation, to ignore some of the specific needs of rural areas or erroneously to equate rural with agricultural policies. This chapter seeks to introduce the rural dimension into the poverty debate by means of an analysis of the nature of rural poverty and a discussion of some of the central issues involved in addressing rural poverty.

A particular concern in this chapter is the relative value of the social-justice approach as compared to the Christian-charity approach to poverty, as well as the implications of rural impoverishment for the broader national debate about poverty and welfare reform. A careful analysis of rural poverty not only supplies information about this important phenomenon but also challenges some of the stereotypical views of poverty in America. As such, it forces us to adopt a broad, rather than a narrow and personalistic, conception of welfare responsibility. Understanding rural poverty is impossible without assessing the competing structural and individual explanations for poverty, which in turn forces us to confront the alternative approaches of charity and social justice and to engage the larger questions about how poverty in America can most fruitfully be addressed.

Christian-Charity and Social-Justice Approaches to Poverty

Biblical teaching and the Christian tradition express a strong concern for the plight of the impoverished. Christians have differed, however, in their interpretations of the biblical mandate to be good neighbors to the needy. Two broad traditions have developed within the Christian community: the Christian-charity approach and the social-justice perspective. Both are rooted in Scripture and seek to be faithful to biblical understandings of society, state, church, and individuals. Both traditions have influenced the responses of church and state toward poverty as a social issue and toward persons who are poor.[1]

Christian charity brings to mind responses like church appeals for food for Thanksgiving baskets, adopt-a-family efforts at Christmas, fund-raising benefits to help a family struggling with the loss of its house by fire or with a major medical bill, or, on a global scale, grain collections for starving persons in other parts of the world. These efforts represent helping responses to specific crises and are not designed to change the basic social structure of the local or global community. This familiar approach is derived from scriptural mandates to care for the poor and the widowed. The early Christians further viewed charity as a means of obeying God and thus of demonstrating salvation. While caring for the poor was viewed as

1. I have found two books especially helpful in considering these issues: R. Sider, ed., *Evangelicals and Development: Toward a Theology of Social Change* (Philadelphia: Westminster Press, 1982); and M. Paget-Wilkes, *Poverty, Revolution and the Church* (Exeter, Eng.: Paternoster Press, 1981).

important, the church did not seek to change the social structures that created and maintained poverty. Currently, the impetus for charity arises from a view that Christians should be good stewards of the gifts God has given them. Such stewardship includes a responsibility to help others as special needs arise.

The social-justice perspective goes beyond this personal and crisis-oriented response to examine the structures of society to determine whether social or economic systems provide adequately for the essential needs of all members of the community (both locally and globally). If basic needs are not adequately met, the social-justice approach dictates making structural changes such as the redistribution of wealth through modification of the pattern of wages or the ownership of land. The prophets of the Old Testament continually called for social justice and indicated that knowledge of God must be manifested in a concern for the poor and oppressed. Their words were addressed not only to individuals but to the kings as leaders of nations and creators of government policies, and to the community as a whole. The prophets reminded the community that God's justice required not only right treatment of the in-group but also right treatment of aliens within the community. For the prophets, knowing God and doing justice were synonymous. The Scriptures also address social structures specifically through, for example, land redistribution during the year of jubilee. Jesus affirms his identification with the poor through his lifestyle, his statements ("As you did it not to one of the least of these, you did it not to me"), and his fury at the money changers who were using the place of worship to exploit the poor.

Historically, it was Luther's shift in the understanding of the basis of salvation that opened the way for a new emphasis on alleviating the sources of poverty. More recently, the stark inequalities of the contemporary world, especially in what we used to call the "Third-World" nations, have forced churches to consider again the issue of social justice. Evangelicals have found it difficult to affirm social-justice strategies to address poverty because such efforts have tended to be identified with the social gospel. Yet evangelical meetings and statements such as the Lausanne Congress on World Evangelism (1974), the Consultation on the Theology of Development (1980), and the Consultation on the Church in Response to Human Need (1983) have all supported a social-justice approach. Such initiatives have pointed out the need to demonstrate Christ's victory through social change in this world that will help honor and restore the image of God in man. From this perspective, one cannot honor important aspects of the image of God without redressing gross inequality.

Neither of these approaches is sufficient in itself. That is an important conclusion that a careful analysis of rural poverty will teach us. As we come to grips with the varied dimensions of all poverty by examining the specific characteristics of rural poverty in America, we will be driven to go beyond the Christian-charity and social-justice approaches to a perspective oriented to transformation and the building of genuine community.

Rural Poverty

What is the nature of rural poverty? Whom does it affect? What causes and perpetuates poverty in rural areas? Only after we can answer these questions will we be able to assess the respective merits of the Christian-charity and the social-justice approaches and to formulate an appropriate response to rural poverty.

For some people, poverty represents a short chapter in their lives, occasioned by the loss of a job, a severe illness, or some other catastrophe. Once the job is found, the medical bills paid, or some other immediate need is met, they are able to move on to other chapters in their lives. But poverty can also be a persistent phenomenon in which persons are just managing to stay afloat while economic disaster lurks as an ongoing and ever-present possibility. While both types of poverty are important and can be very painful for the people involved, we will emphasize persistent poverty in this discussion because it poses the most difficult problem to solve and because it can even be transmitted from one generation to the next.

It is an abstraction to talk about "rural poverty" as a general phenomenon, for this requires us to collapse together widely differing areas and conditions. Nevertheless, studies of a variety of rural locations all point to a common theme: rural areas tend to have limited opportunity structures — the means by which people can advance and move out of poverty. These limited opportunities tend to increase rural poverty generally and they have important implications for addressing rural poverty. These structures affect persons differently depending on gender, racial background, and previous family experiences with poverty. As we discuss the nature of rural poverty and review the types of persons at risk, we will examine how limitations in opportunity structures contribute to these patterns of poverty.

Historical Trends in Rural Poverty

Poverty in rural America is not a static reality but one that changes all the time. In an important recent study, the Task Force on Rural Poverty of the Rural Sociological Society has identified three distinct phases of rural poverty in the United States since World War II:[2]

- *Phase 1. 1945–1960.* This was an era of growth in urban America but economic decline in rural areas. The result was a significant out-migration from rural areas to urban areas with their greater economic opportunity. Rural areas became places of persistent poverty from which the fortunate few escaped to reap the benefits of economic growth in urban areas.
- *Phase 2. 1960s–late 1970s.* This was a time of growth and revitalization in rural areas. There was talk of a rural renaissance and general optimism about the future of rural America. The manufacturing and service sectors grew in rural areas, and with them the population expanded.
- *Phase 3. 1980s–1990s.* This most recent period represents a return to the pessimistic outlook of the immediate postwar decades. The farm crisis and ongoing economic restructuring have resulted in the decline of adequately paying jobs and in extensive farm and small-business failures. There was a downturn generally of agriculture, mining, energy, forestry, and manufacturing, leading to increased unemployment and underemployment, many business failures, deepening fiscal problems for local governments, and a renewal of out-migration.

Concerted efforts have been made during this recent period to improve rural economies through industrial development, but the results have been mixed. Some communities had benefited from the location of manufacturing plants in rural areas during the 1960s and 70s, but this security

2. The Task Force's report has been published as *Persistent Poverty in Rural America* (Boulder, Colo.: Westview Press, 1993). Other especially important studies of rural poverty are Janet Fitchen, *Endangered Spaces, Enduring Places: Change, Identity, and Survival in Rural America* (Boulder, Colo.: Westview Press, 1991); C. Flora and J. Christianson, *Rural Policies for the 1990's* (Boulder, Colo.: Westview Press, 1991); Ann Tickamyer and Cynthia Duncan, "Poverty and Opportunity Structure in Rural America," *Annual Review of Sociology* 16, no. 1 (1990): 67-86; and Leon Ginsberg, ed., *Social Work in Rural Communities*, 2nd ed. (Alexandria, Va.: Council on Social Work Education, 1994).

also ended with the upheavals created by recent economic restructuring. Many "new poor" have joined the chronically poor in remote, depressed areas. The appearance of these "new poor" has made it clear that rural poverty will persist as long as there are few job opportunities and existing employment remains unstable and poorly paid.

The seriousness of the problem of rural poverty these days is marked by the 16.3 percent rate of poverty across rural America, compared to 12.7 percent in the rest of America for the same year (1990). The rural poverty rate is an average figure, covering both areas with limited poverty and those with extensive poverty. Currently communities located outside metropolitan areas have one-fifth of the nation's population but one-third of the poor. Poverty is a major problem especially in the South, in the Ozarks and Appalachia, and on American Indian reservations. Income inequalities between the rich and the poor are greater in rural than in metropolitan areas.

Rural Population Groups at Risk of Poverty

A number of distinct groups of rural residents are especially prone to poverty. A review of these groups and of the reasons for their greater risk of poverty will deepen our understanding of the factors that lead to poverty in rural America.

Children

In 1990 nearly 23 percent of children living in rural areas were poor; in the South the rate reached 28.7 percent. This meant that more than 3.4 million children in nonmetropolitan areas were poor that year. Poverty rates for children have been increasing significantly since the early 1980s. Childhood poverty is especially concentrated in certain rural areas. According to the 1980 census, in twenty-eight counties across the nation, all of them rural, half of the children lived in poverty. Twenty-one of the counties were in the Mississippi Delta, two were in Appalachia, three covered the Dakota reservations of South Dakota, and two were in Texas, along the Mexican border. Rural children are also at great risk for long-term poverty.[3]

3. In addition to the sources listed above, see Arloc Sherman, *Falling by the Wayside: Children in Rural America* (Washington, D.C.: Children's Defense Fund, 1992).

The poverty risks of children are, of course, intricately linked with the economic status of their families. Increased poverty rates for children have been associated especially with the declining employment opportunities and low wages of adult rural workers, as well as with changes in family composition, in which more children are living in one-parent families. However, although the proportion of single-parent families has been increasing in rural areas, increased rural childhood poverty cannot be attributed primarily to changes in family structure, for poor rural children still typically are living with both parents.

The negative features of much employment in rural areas contribute substantially to the problem of poverty for rural children and their families. In 1987, 65 percent of poor rural families had at least one working member, but employment was not enough to keep these families above the poverty line. In the period from 1979 to 1988, real rural wages fell by 7 percent (in contrast to a 2 percent increase in urban areas) and wages for young families fell even faster. These low wage rates meant that in 1990, 22 percent of men and 43 percent of women who worked full-time did not earn over the poverty rate for a family of three.

Because of declining wage rates, the poverty rate for rural families with at least one worker rose by one-third (from 8 percent to 10.7 percent) during the years 1979 to 1988, and the poverty rate of working families increased faster than that of rural families generally. As a result of low wage scales in rural areas, even having two wage earners in a family is not a guarantee of avoiding poverty: for example, nearly 10 percent of young rural families (adults between 18 and 29 years of age) with two wage earners were living below the poverty level. The rate of increase in poverty rates for rural families with a father present was similar to that of rural families generally.

Negative community attitudes also play a role in perpetuating poverty for many rural children. Poor children are subject to social stereotyping and social distancing from others in the community. Teachers have lower expectations of poor children, tracking them into lower achievement levels. Poor children tend to drop out of school earlier, diminishing their chances for economic success (the dropout rates of rural poor children are nearly three times as high as for other children). The difficulties are compounded by the scarcity of educational funds generally in rural communities, while costs tend to be higher due to small school sizes and heavy demands for transportation. Because public schools are funded primarily through local taxes, poor rural communities have extremely limited means to provide an adequate education for their children. Children living in poor families are also more vulnerable to other disruptions, as evidenced by increased numbers of children in shelter care placements.

In addition to their direct impact on poor children, these harmful economic and social conditions may also hamper them indirectly, by increasing the stresses within their families and by negatively affecting their parents and the relationship between parents and children.[4]

Women and Families Headed by Women

Women and families dependent on them tend to be poorer primarily because women generally receive lower wages and have fewer job opportunities than men in rural areas. Rural women are less likely to be participating in the paid labor force, have higher rates of involuntary part-time employment, and earn less than their metropolitan counterparts. Although rural women are increasingly part of the paid labor force, this change has not been reflected in a decline in the level of poverty for women.[5]

The current economic restructuring in rural areas has further disadvantaged women because the kinds of jobs that are becoming increasingly prevalent are the ones in which women typically make the least money. The gender wage gaps in common employment categories, based on full-time, full-year employment, are as follows: manufacturing, 0.61; retail, 0.59; finance and insurance, 0.49; and services, 0.63. The economic position of rural women is relatively weak in general also because of their traditionally large role in the nonwage activities of the community. Rural families and communities have long depended on the contributions of women (including income-producing activities on farms and small businesses), yet these economic contributions do not appear in the official statistics. Women's activities have often been part of the informal economy, efforts to make

4. See Cynthia Jones Neal's important chapter in this volume, "Family Issues in Welfare Reform: Developmental Pathways as a Theoretical Framework for Understanding Generational Cycles of Poverty."

5. In addition to the general studies listed above, see E. Martinez-Brawley and N. Durbin, "Women in the Rural Occupation Structure: The Poverty Connection," *Human Services in the Rural Environment* 10, no. 4/vol. 11, no. 1 (1987): 19-39.

limited family dollars stretch, and unpaid work on the farm and in family businesses. These necessary activities limit women's ability to participate in the paid labor sector and their eligibility for various social insurance programs. Lack of available and affordable child care in rural areas also helps keep women in poverty.

Although living in a single-parent household plays a less important role in the poverty of rural children than it does in the case of urban children, as indicated previously, this is a growing problem in rural areas. Currently 39 percent of rural poor households are headed by women. Children living in rural female-headed households are approximately three times more likely to be poor than children living in two-parent families. Not only are these children more likely to be poor, but many of them occupy the ranks of the very poor — one-third of rural children living in female-headed families are living at one-half the poverty line. Rural single-parent households headed by women are described by one author as facing a triple vulnerability to poverty: they are more likely to be poor than urban single-parent families, more likely to be in deep poverty (less than 75 percent of the poverty line), and more likely to stay poor for a long time (80 percent for at least three years).[6] The rate and depth of poverty for rural single-parent families has grown worse in recent years. It remains the case, however, that single-parent composition is not the primary factor in the poverty of children and families in rural areas.

The Elderly

Poverty among the elderly in rural areas is more of a problem than is typical in metropolitan areas due to the higher proportion of elderly persons in rural areas and the increased risk factors of the rural elderly. Rural elderly persons tend to be older (more are above seventy-five years of age), to be less educated, and to be less likely to enjoy adequate retirement income. Fortunately there has been a reduction in the risk of poverty for the rural elderly in recent years due to increased benefits in programs such as Social Security and SSI. The out-migration of young people from rural areas has, however, reduced the general support system for the rural elderly.

6. Janet Fitchen, "Rural Poverty and Rural Social Work," in Ginsberg, 99-117.

Minority Groups

While the vast majority (73 percent) of the rural poor are white, racial and ethnic minorities bear the brunt of economic hardship in rural areas. Poverty rates for rural African-Americans and Hispanics are at least double that of rural whites, and higher than or at least equal to the rates for members of these groups living in the inner cities. The rate of poverty for rural Native American young people (38 percent) is double that of their urban cohorts (18 percent), and more than half of the children living on many rural reservations live in poverty.

Several factors contribute to these higher rates of poverty for minority groups.[7] First, many tend to live in areas that have traditionally been poverty-stricken. Consequently there are few employment opportunities, and the available work pays such low wages that persons employed in full-time, full-year jobs cannot raise their families out of poverty. Among persons holding full-time, full-year jobs in rural areas, 26 percent of rural American Indians, 25 percent of African-Americans, and 28 percent of Mexican-Americans did not earn enough to raise their families above the poverty level. These figures do not include the many who are unable to find full-time work. Nearly one-half of rural American Indians, African-Americans, and Mexican-Americans are underemployed and are able to provide at best marginally adequate incomes for their families.

Members of minority groups are further disadvantaged by their lack of educational preparation for the current job market due to inadequate community education and training resources. Underemployed and lacking training, they are often unequipped with the skills needed for the contemporary job market.

Discrimination and rigid social structures in some areas have further contributed to the poverty of minority groups by constricting essential opportunities. Discriminatory attitudes can create powerful messages regarding educational expectations for minority children and create barriers that prevent persons who might be qualified from obtaining important opportunities. As exemplified by the recent Iowa farm crisis, when economic problems occur in rural areas, minority groups can be the most vulnerable to losing their jobs and facing poverty. Minority group members

7. See, in addition to the general studies listed above, Gene Summer, "Minorities in Rural Society," in Ginsberg, 119-29.

who have moved into rural communities to take poorly paid jobs in the food-processing industry not only must contend with low wages but are also often isolated from the main social support systems in the communities.

The civil rights movement, unfortunately, had little positive effect on poverty-striken rural blacks because, in expanding opportunity, it benefited primarily those best positioned to take advantage of new chances. Moreover, economic development in the South has occurred primarily in the urban areas. The growth in the incidence of female-headed families among rural minorities has further increased the risk of poverty. In 1960, 27 percent of poor black families in rural areas were headed by women, while in 1980 this proportion had reached 59 percent.

Structural Dimensions of Rural Poverty

Working nonminority families comprise the majority of the rural poor. A number of factors contribute to the poverty risk of these working families as well as make poverty more likely for other members of rural communities. These factors have important implications for antipoverty policymaking.[8]

Economic Growth Trends

Economic growth in rural areas has tended to be skewed toward low-tech, low-skilled, and low-paying jobs. Historically, rural areas have competed for jobs on the basis of their low wages, low taxes, and subsidies to relocating businesses. Such policies result in poorly paying jobs that fail to raise people out of poverty. Efforts to entice outside companies to come to rural areas on this basis have brought companies lacking any loyalty to the community. As the U.S. economy has become increasingly integrated into the global economy, these companies are now frequently shifting such jobs to developing countries.[9] Since small communities tend to depend on one or two industries, they have little economic flexibility when these firms leave. Stable

8. See especially Tickamyer and Duncan.

9. See Max Stackhouse, "Beneath and beyond the State: Social, Global, and Religious Changes That Shape Welfare Reform," 20-47 in this volume.

jobs in manufacturing have tended to be replaced by piecework employment or jobs in the service industry, which typically are low-paying, frequently part-time, and usually without benefits. Service jobs are not very abundant in small communities in any case, and as rural communities decline in size, even fewer service jobs are needed. At the same time, as farms become more commercialized and larger, they increasingly bypass local economic systems, eroding the towns' commercial bases and contributing to the shrinkage of local service opportunities.

The branch manufacturing plants established in rural areas by urban companies have tended to be low-technology. These branch offices have biased the occupational structure of rural areas toward lower-skilled manual workers, driving rural workers with technical and managerial skills to seek jobs in more prosperous urban areas. Entry-level positions tend to be poorly paying and lacking certainty of upward mobility. Local rural branches of a company have limited influence on headquarters' policy and tend to need few people of advanced standing in their own operations. Given such dynamics, the ratio of complex to routine operations in rural areas has remained stagnant despite the increase in skills and complexity demanded by urban companies.

Employers in rural areas frequently need not compete hard for workers. People can be reluctant to leave the local area because of family connections or attachment to the local way of life. Thus they may choose to remain despite the limited opportunities for advancement. Furthermore, persons from poor families in rural areas may feel insecure about their ability to cope in other settings. Unionization is also very limited in rural communities.

The small size of many rural businesses makes it difficult for them to pay adequate wages or benefits. Even in relatively prosperous rural communities, most jobs in small local businesses start at the minimum wage and do not offer medical or other benefits. As a result rural workers frequently lack medical insurance or are insured only for catastrophes. As branches of larger companies move into rural areas, they create jobs, but only at low wages (the so-called Wal-Mart phenomenon). It is true that the small companies displaced by these branches typically also paid poorly, but the owners of these companies were part of the community leadership structure and thus helped maintain the viability of the rural communities.

Social Support Systems

The main source of poverty in rural areas is the constricted earning potential of the local economies. But rural families are harmed as well by the tearing of the rural social support system caused by the nature of rural poverty, particular features of the rural environment, and the characteristics of the social service programs that serve the needy. Rural residents in general are harmed by access and quality problems in medical services, education, transportation, and general community services. Two-parent working-poor families are often ineligible for help despite living in poverty. Rural states frequently pay very low benefits under the AFDC program. The average poor rural family lives in a state with a maximum AFDC benefit in January 1991 of just $311 a month for a family of three with no other income — just 35 percent of the federal poverty level. The benefits received by rural families are less than two-thirds what urban families receive.

The safety net is further weakened by the distances people may have to travel to receive help and by transportation difficulties, by social stigmas placed on the needy, by a lack of community support for social programs, and by ignorance of available help. Moreover, in rural areas coverage of the other social programs on which the poor rely is incomplete. Only half of poor rural children received Medicaid in 1987, for example. Unemployment benefits tend to be lower, do not match the long unemployment periods, and fail to cover many in rural areas. Rural states tend not to supplement federal SSI payments. Housing subsidies are lower in rural areas. The recent expansion of the earned income tax credit program, on the other hand, will be helpful to rural families because it obviates transportation difficulties and offers help for families with working parents.

A vital assistance role has long been played in rural areas by an informal support system comprising the extended family, churches, friendships, and community groups. This support system has been under stress recently due to the out-migration of young people and others possessed of the economic and educational resources to allow departure; the need for women to begin working outside the home, making them less available for meeting the myriad of family and community needs; and the necessity of many to commute long hours to other communities for work.[10]

10. See my "Family Response to the Farm Crisis: A Study in Coping," *Social Work* 35, no. 5 (1990): 425-33, and Fitchen.

Poor families tend to be outside the social support systems that undergird the more prosperous families of their communities, decreasing the resources available to the poor. Many rural poor live in communities where poverty is pervasive, so that community resources are very limited.

Fighting Rural Poverty: Possible Solutions

Given this portrait of rural poverty, what are the viable strategies to overcome it? What are the respective merits of the social-justice and the Christian-charity approaches as guides in the fight against rural poverty?

The human-capital theory of poverty suggests one major strategy to deal with the problem of the poor in rural America. The approach here is to improve the quality of persons in rural areas — to increase education levels and job skills. Evidence for the value of this strategy is mixed. In support of this approach is the fact that many young people in rural areas are not gaining the skills they will need for an increasingly technical world. Rural youth generally are taking fewer math and science classes, tend to have lower educational expectations for themselves, and score lower on the SAT than do urban youth. Many rural adults lack the skills needed for contemporary jobs and fall further behind during periods of underemployment or unemployment.

But rural communities are constantly confronted with the problem of the "brain drain" — the phenomenon that bright and educated rural young people leave their communities due to the lack of economic opportunities. Rural areas too often educate their young people only to lose them. There is also less financial benefit from educational investment in rural youth than in urban youth. Without the presence of jobs requiring advanced skills, communities may easily overeducate their youth. Yet rural communities need persons who can attract the high-skill jobs that pay enough to maintain families above the poverty line.

Evidence from analyses of training programs supports the need to link education and training with efforts to provide new employment opportunities. Thirteen weeks after participation in one federal job-training program, a third of participants in rural areas were still unemployed, and of those with jobs, half were earning less than $5.00 per hour. Job-preparedness efforts need to be coupled with the expansion of employment opportunity. Any welfare reform initiative that emphasizes a time limit on benefits with the goal of moving recipients into employment must address the weak employment situation in rural areas and should be paired with expanded efforts at community economic development. The need for rural economic development on a community level as well as an individual basis has been stressed consistently in conferences and reports dealing with rural economic affairs from many disciplines and perspectives.

The problem of rural poverty, it is clear, is multifaceted and cannot be viewed solely in terms of a lack of preparedness, personal failings, or lack of effort of the individual involved. Strategies that address only ways to help persons become more individually responsible and/or capable, or that are prompted by concern for individuals at particularly difficult times in their lives, fail to comprehend and address the structural barriers present for many enmeshed in rural poverty.

For Christians as well as for society as a whole, rural poverty raises a profound moral issue. Do we regard social benefits to be rights or entitlements, or only charitable benefits forthcoming or not at the initiative of the better-off? The American welfare system is designed to make the receipt of benefits as unattractive as possible in order to discourage people from depending on the welfare system — the so-called least benefits principle.[11] And while members of rural communities and churches have often been very generous to persons in time of crisis, there has been a tendency to view people who are poor — especially those for whom the problem is an ongoing one — as failing somehow or other. During the recent farm crisis many farmers and rural businesspeople experienced demeaning treatment by church leaders when they sought help. People not threatened by poverty too easily presume that impoverishment is due to individual failings and not at all a consequence of features of the economic structure.

But as we have seen above, the basic source of growing rural poverty is the economic system present in these areas — especially the low wage scale and limited economic opportunities. These negative factors are compounded by social stigma; isolation; differential opportunities due to race, gender, and family background; and the absence of adequate basic community supports such as transportation, health services, and high-quality educational programs.

The Christian-charity approach is effective in addressing emergencies

11. See the discussion in John Mason's chapter in this volume, "Biblical Teaching and the Objectives of Welfare Policy in the United States," 145-84.

that threaten a person or family with impoverishment. But the social-justice approach appears to address more adequately the nature of persistent poverty in rural areas. Poverty and welfare these days are often discussed in terms of a crisis of responsibility. Unfortunately, responsibility is too often understood in merely individualistic terms, such as whether parents are being adequately responsible for their children. Certainly individual and family responsibility are very important, and all efforts that enable and encourage people to assume their appropriate responsibilities should be supported. *A New Vision for Welfare Reform*[12] rightly stresses the need for multiple sectors of society to be involved in a recovery of responsibility. Other chapters in this volume address constitutional and legal barriers preventing religious community organizations from playing their full roles as partners in promoting responsible action and in coming to the aid of the poor.

A solely individual focus wrongly neglects issues of responsibility at a societal and community level. Rural poverty raises critical questions about the nature of our responsibility as members of a society in which persons can work very hard and yet remain poor and in which women and minorities face constricted economic opportunities. Questions of societal responsibility pose very different issues about what kinds of responses to poverty are legitimate and even mandated. Adopting a societal approach does not produce easy answers about how to solve the complex problem of ongoing poverty in rural or urban areas. However, it does suggest a direction and, equally important, a mindset.

Specifying the best way to expand rural economic opportunites in an era of global economic competition is daunting. Neither economic experts nor gatherings of policymakers from the developed countries of the world seem able to go much further than to acknowledge the need and to recommend that solutions be found. But the problem of constricted rural economic opportunities cannot be evaded. We cannot help but question the nature of Christian responsibility when community leaders in rural areas, including those who espouse a Christian commitment, owe their prosperity to wage scales for their employees that are so low that even two people working full-time cannot maintain a family above the poverty line. There may be no rural equivalent to the scandal of Chrysler executives

12. Center for Public Justice, *A New Vision for Welfare Reform: An Essay in Draft* (Washington, D.C.: Center for Public Justice, 1994), reprinted in the Appendix to this volume.

reaping incomes in excess of $9 million while planning for many of their employees to lose their jobs, but rural income differentials pose their own extremely serious moral challenge.

A social-justice response to rural poverty advocates a particular governmental responsibility in the fight against poverty. In this perspective, government is to serve as a social agent for communal responsibility. The social-justice approach rejects the least benefits approach to social welfare, which creates programs that fail to meet the important needs of poor persons and that stigmatize persons receiving social benefits. The social-justice approach rejects the deficit reduction strategy by which local, state, and national political leaders turn first to social programs to find expenditure cuts. The social-justice approach does not blindly support all welfare programs, but it does question the fear of employing government as an agent of justice for the poor.

The social-justice approach also guides us to prefer particular social programs. Given the essential social role of the family and the growing threats to its integrity, it is important to endorse programs that support, rather than punish, two-parent families (e.g., the earned income tax credit program). Programs that enable poor families to have the necessary resources to improve their situation should be favored. Examples include policies that permit assets to be accumulated in order to pursue schooling or to buy tools; Iowa's current program designed to enable poor families to develop the resource base needed to escape poverty; expanded access to reliable transportation; and the increased availability of affordable, quality child care.

Designing adequate programs is a complex issue. Inadequate policies may have the consequence of miring people even deeper in poverty or adding to the stresses that contribute to family breakups. Simply expanding jobs is insufficient, if the wages are too low to support a family and adequate supplemental supports such as tax credits, health care benefits, or low-cost child care are not available. Programs that enable people to develop adequate job skills should be paired with initiatives to address the social factors and educational failures that contribute to the skill deficits and with support for community development strategies. Health care reforms to make insurance accessible to the many who are self-employed or whose employers cannot afford to offer the benefit are important, but they should be coupled with reforms that enable rural areas to attract and retain the needed medical professionals and facilities. The increased poverty risks faced by women and by members of minority groups suggest the need rigorously to evaluate the range of policies in terms of their impact on groups that have traditionally suffered discrimination.

The particular interpretation of rural poverty I have developed here should also guide our understanding of community-based programs. The essential need of affordable day care for low-income working families in rural areas is a case in point. An examination of the industrial/employment pattern in rural areas makes it clear that recent economic development has been built according to a low-wage strategy, with wages inadequate to meet the needs of family members, and that women and minority group members have been particularly disadvantaged in the rural wage scale. The challenge of paying for appropriate day care is thus more than an individual issue. This raises an important question: should public support for day care be regarded primarily as assistance to individual families or instead as a form of public utility that upholds the economic activities of the community? The former approach views the family as the beneficiary of the community's charity; the latter views the low-paying companies, and the local economy as a whole, as the primary beneficiary of the service. When I moved to a rural southern town many years ago, the local director of the county employment office suggested that I should pay my child care worker an extremely low wage. When I protested, she claimed that the public provided subsidized housing and food stamps to supplement the wages of employees such as my child care worker. But if so, then the social-justice approach forces us to ask who is really being subsidized by social welfare programs: the individuals who sustain the local economy through their low wages or the community and its employers who benefit from the low wage scale?

I have suggested several ways in which the social-justice perspective should guide our approach to rural poverty. But there remains an important place for the personalized and individualized assistance advocated by the Christian-charity tradition. People will always have crises that require the support of the local and larger communities. Rallying together as a church and as a community not only benefits the person involved but also helps maintain the sense of community that is so important in this impersonal and alienating modern world.

There is growing concern about the decline of community in rural areas generally. It has led to a fraying of the natural sources of support — the neighborhood, the extended family, churches, and other social groups

— that have helped to rear children, provide assistance in emergencies, and supply a sense of order and mutual care for members of the community. As more and more families need to send both parents to employment out of the home and even out of the local community, this vital communal sense and the social network have become tattered. Both poor families and those enjoying greater financial security are negatively affected by the weakening of community. As a central institution in rural areas, the church faces the challenge to work to retain and build the sense and reality of a supportive community. The challenge of rebuilding a sense of community can help to transcend both the potentially impersonal nature of the social-justice approach and the potentially demeaning and patronizing nature of the Christian-charity approach to fighting poverty. For community represents a thick web of interconnections, and it is just this that is missing in a fragmented and selfish world that easily justifies the devaluation of persons through the operations of the economic and social order.

A Biblical Challenge to Analysis and Action

The Bible includes an important parable that illumines the issue of poverty in both rural and urban areas: the parable Jesus told of the laborers in a vineyard (Matt. 20:1-16). Some workers toiled all day; others waited for hours and were hired only near the end of the workday. When all who had labored received at the end of the day the same wages, those who had worked the whole day bitterly protested. But the owner of the vineyard reminded them that they had willingly gone to work for the wage they had been paid. And Jesus added that "the last will be first, and the first will be last."

The force of this parable was hammered home for me during a recent trip to Zimbabwe, when I watched men wait for days on end for the opportunity to work for a day. The parable reminds us that both sets of workers had limited control over the time during which they could work, and it emphasizes our need to lead lives based on a sense of grace rather than entitlement. Through grace alone we are given the family background, the citizenship rights, and the economic, intellectual, and personal resources that allow us to supply the needs of our families and also to reach out to others in greater need. The social-justice perspective reminds us that we are challenged and indeed privileged not only to give a caring "handout" from our bounty but also to seek social solutions that create a genuine sharing of the resources of society with our fellow creatures. According to this perspective, serving the poor is a matter of enabling the poor to obtain what is rightfully theirs, recognizing the rights that poor people have because they, too, are created beings with a God-given inheritance that has been distorted by unjust social structures and the harmful actions of individuals and groups.

The focus of this chapter has been poverty in rural areas. Yet the issue of individual versus structural causes of poverty and the different merits of the social-justice versus the Christianity-charity approaches certainly transcend the specific topic of rural poverty. Our examination of rural poverty should help us to go beyond the stereotypes of poverty, which link improverishment to single-parent, nonworking, minority families and which stress a purported lack of personal responsibility. Poverty can be the product of deeply embedded structural conditions as well as personal factors, and it gathers into its ranks two-parent families and families with dual full-time workers.

This examination of rural poverty should challenge us to look for similar structural factors in urban settings. How must we interpret the poverty consequences of the deindustrialization that has stripped many urban areas of well-paying but low-skill factory jobs? When businesses relocate from inner cities to suburbs, what are the consequences for city residents who desire to work? How can working parents maintain their employment when taking the child to a doctor means a six-hour wait in an emergency room? What is the impact on inner-city African-American families when black males find it difficult to obtain adequately paying legal employment? What is the poverty effect of the enormous differences in school quality between inner-city and suburban public schools? What structure must social programs have in order not only to enforce accountability from recipients but also to ensure that the recipients have the personal, social, and economic resources needed to meet their responsibilities? What does it take to reestablish in urban areas the sense and reality of real community?

If we are to respond adequately to questions such as these, we should begin with the challenge of *A New Vision for Welfare Reform:* rightly addressing poverty and welfare reform requires complex interventions involving the partnership of various sectors of society as well as a moral commitment to work toward a just society in which the creational dignity of all persons is valued.

Doing Analysis as Service along "The Way": The Social Policy Analysis of the Center for Public Justice[1]

John Hiemstra

CHRISTIAN ANALYSES of social policy are frequently indistinguishable from secular studies. Apart from biblical quotations or strong appeals to morality, Christian analyses of poverty tend to mirror the polarized options found in mainstream society: the poor are responsible for their own situation versus the poor are determined by and victims of their situation; poverty is due to lack of a wealth creation versus poverty results from a faulty distribution of wealth; poverty will be solved through fuller freedom for markets versus poverty will be overcome by increased state interference in the economy.

The Center for Public Justice (the Center), in sharp contrast, uses a refreshing "foundational approach" to poverty analysis in its project from which this book stems. The strength of the Center's approach comes from digging to the foundations of the polarities in contemporary poverty analysis. The Center uncovers the structural factors and deeper religious motives that shape American responses to the question: who should do what about poverty and when?

In this chapter I examine the Center's approach to social policy in its welfare project, and in particular analyze the Center's argument about

1. Thanks to Gerald Vandezande, Jake Kuiken, John Van Dyk, Heather Looy, David Long, Harry VanBelle, Bob Bruinsma, Alyce Oosterhuis, David Peters-Woods, Harry Kits, Stephanie Baker Collins, David Koyzis, Paul Marshall, Stanley Carlson-Thies, Harry Groenewold, and Vaden House for commenting on an earlier version of this chapter.

poverty and welfare, *A New Vision for Welfare Reform: An Essay in Draft*.[2] In addition to the strengths of the Center's foundational approach, I identify a tendency toward intellectualism in its work.[3] I close with some suggestions on how we might move away from intellectualism in our analyses and toward a type of analysis that is more serviceable to our communal walk along the way of Christ.

The Center's "Welfare Responsibility" Project

The Center begins its analysis of welfare reform by asking why the "Great Society" welfare policies have failed. Furthermore, why has this failure generated such widespread critique and a general lack of consensus on what should be done today? The welfare policy debate remains hot and unresolved, the Center argues, because it "is caught on the horns of dilemmas fostered by a faulty vision of human responsibility."[4] The welfare policy debate is trapped between the untenable positions of "pragmatic liberalism and pragmatic conservatism."[5] These positions assume fundamental differences on the role of the state and specifically its responsibility to alleviate poverty.

In order to tackle this dilemma, the Center undertakes a "foundational analysis." The Center's understanding of this type of analysis is indebted to the ideas of the Protestant wing of the Dutch Christian democratic movement. Of particular importance are the ideas of Guillaume Groen Van Prinsterer (1801–1876), Abraham Kuyper (1837–1920), and Herman Dooyeweerd (1894–1977).[6] This movement argued that social and political

2. Center for Public Justice, *A New Vision for Welfare Reform: An Essay in Draft* (Washington, D.C.: Center for Public Justice, 1994), reprinted in the Appendix to this volume.

3. Critique of the tendency toward intellectualism in the Center's approach is also, in a sense, a critique of my own policy research and teaching, which also has tended in that direction.

4. Center for Public Justice, *A New Vision*, 578.

5. "The Center for Public Justice" introductory brochure, 1992–1993. This polarization is referred to in the welfare project also as a tension between individualism and collectivism, individual freedom and social determinism, and a market versus a structuralist approach. See Stanley W. Carlson-Thies, "The Crisis of American Welfare: Issues, Theses, Resources," Center for Public Justice, Jan. 1993.

6. For an introduction to these ideas see James W. Skillen and Rockne M. McCarthy, eds., *Political Order and the Plural Structure of Society* (Atlanta: Scholars Press, 1991).

life are directly founded in the creative and redemptive word of God. Redemption in Christ liberates all of life from sin, although this liberation will not be complete until Christ returns.

Several consequences of this view of life have shaped the Center's approach to politics. First, politics is seen as a legitimate avenue for serving God and neighbor. The proper way to serve in politics becomes not apologetics or evangelism but explicitly *political* action. Furthermore, Christian political action cannot stop with acts of charity but must, in the words of Abraham Kuyper, also perform an "architectonic critique of human society."[7] The founders of the Center for Public Justice appropriated this legacy by creating an institution to conduct "a quality program of high intellectual integrity to advance the best possible public service through civic education and public policy research."[8]

Foundational analysis has been central to the Center's welfare policy project. This means that the Center's research has gone "beneath disputes over program details and statistics to the underlying assumptions that shape interpretations of poverty and the policies designed to assist the needy." It is at this "deeper level" that the Center wants to expose the core problems behind the dilemmas in the welfare policy debates.[9] In an introduction to the project, the Center's Executive Director, James Skillen, says that this "deeper level" concerns matters of "basic public philosophy," including "the religious and moral roots of the American welfare crisis." It was at this level that he hopes the project "might be able to make a distinctive, if not entirely original, contribution to thinking about social welfare."[10]

The Center does not discuss its approach in the project literature. However, a helpful explanation of this type of foundational approach is given by Bob Goudzwaard in *Capitalism and Progress.* He suggests that societal problems should be analyzed at two "depth levels." The first level

7. See Abraham Kuyper, *The Problem of Poverty,* ed. James W. Skillen (1891; Grand Rapids, Mich.: Baker, 1991), 51.

8. "The Center for Public Justice" brochure. The Center's emphasis became more theoretical when its board decided, due to difficulties in membership recruitment, to shift focus from seeking to form a popular Christian political movement (the Association for Public Justice). See APJ Executive Director James W. Skillen's letter to the APJ membership, Jan. 25, 1994.

9. James W. Skillen, "An Introduction to the Social Welfare Project," Nov. 1992, pp. 3, 4, 6.

10. Skillen, "An Introduction," 6-7.

is "the present structures of society." The second, and deeper, level is "the central religious motives that direct a culture and its society."[11] The depth levels of structures and religious motives are not separate entities that relate externally, but are complementary ways of analyzing the complete picture. A focus on religious motives is only one way of analyzing an integral social and political reality.[12]

The design of the Center's project clearly shows that it intends to do a foundational critique. The central question for the project was: "How ought Christian leaders to understand the relation between human rights and responsibilities in diverse institutions and communities, each of which entails its own form of moral obligation and accountability?"[13] The project was to produce "a public philosophy of human responsibility that is at once both individual and corporate." The Center would develop its public philosophy from "a justice viewpoint grounded in biblical assumptions about human nature and responsibility." The Center believes that this public philosophy will "yield more penetrating insights and motivate a more dynamic, flexible, and challenging approach to problems such as public welfare."[14] It would provide "understanding" to policymakers, leaders, government, churches, universities, and ordinary people and in this way stimulate all to responsible action in their respective tasks.

11. Bob Goudzwaard, *Capitalism and Progress: A Diagnosis of Western Society* (Toronto: Wedge, and Grand Rapids, Mich.: Eerdmans, 1979), xix-xxv. A version of this model adapted for use by a policy organization is John A. Olthuis, "Peeling an Onion: Reflections on CJL's Energy Project," *Catalyst* (Citizens for Public Justice, Toronto), Spring 1978, pp. 22-30. The model is applied in Murray MacAdam, Nancy Friday, John Hiemstra, and Mark Vander Vennen, *Changing Course: A Study Guide for Canadian Social Analysis* (Toronto: Citizens for Public Justice, 1987).

12. The religious integrality of all social things is evident from Goudzwaard's comment that "three basic biblical rules . . . together explain man's relation to God and to his theoretical and practical pursuits." They are: people are always serving god(s) in their lives; every person is transformed into an image of his or her god; and mankind creates and forms a structure of society in its own image. See his "Our Gods have Failed Us," in his *Aid for the Overdeveloped West* (Toronto: Wedge, 1975), 14-15.

13. Skillen, "An Introduction," 1.

14. "The Center for Public Justice" brochure. The Center has been working with a theory of "multiple accountability structures in society" for many years, but the idea of applying it to welfare policy came as Skillen reviewed books on social policy by Charles Murray and Michael Novak. See Skillen, "An Introduction," 7. For the reviews, see Skillen, "A Consensus in Need of a Philosophy," *This World,* no. 21 (1988): 136-39, and his "In Search of Something that Works," *Christianity Today,* June 14, 1985, pp. 26-29.

The Center's emphasis on doing foundational analysis does not mean it ignores the need for practical inner-city service or social work. Rather, it believes poverty must be tackled at a multitude of levels simultaneously. Skillen writes, "Multiple institutions shape our lives in so many closely intertwined ways. For Christians to face the urban crisis, therefore, we need a biblical perspective of work, politics, investment, education, the stewardship of resources, and much more."[15]

To carry out its foundational analysis of welfare policy, the Center designed a three-year research project. A "core team," comprising primarily university scholars, was appointed to help guide the project and to contribute to "research and writing."[16] The Center wanted this team "to make possible an approach that will be both richly diverse and well balanced. Members of the team," it announced, "represent a large number of human networks concerned with Christian social, economic, and political responsibilities."[17] Core team members were commissioned to write papers on a variety of topics that would enrich the discussions and help develop the Center's ideas. Other papers were invited from a variety of additional contributors, the majority of whom were also academics.[18] Most of these papers are included in the present book, which is the final major product of the project.

The centerpiece of the Center's welfare project is *A New Vision for Welfare Reform* (hereafter referred to as *A New Vision;* parenthetical page references are to this essay, as reprinted in the Appendix). Written by Stanley W. Carlson-Thies, the project director, and James W. Skillen, a draft of *A New Vision* appeared in print in 1994 and was to be rewritten in 1995. The essay was described as a "vision" that would make a scholarly contribution to the welfare policy discussions. The Center hoped the essay would "encourage creative thinking, intense debate, further scholarship, and innovative policy making" (551).

A major conference was held in May 1994 with the intention of bringing together "critical thinkers and creative reformers."[19] The conference was designed to encourage and assist participants to engage the four

15. James W. Skillen, "Agony in the City," *Moody,* Jan. 1990, pp. 24-25. See also his "Justice for Your Urban Neighbors-in-Law," *Banner,* March 30, 1994, pp. 8-10.

16. Skillen, "An Introduction," 7.

17. "Core Team Chosen for Social Welfare Project," *Public Justice Report,* Jan.–Feb. 1993, p. 6.

18. The papers' authors are listed at the end of *A New Vision for Welfare Reform.*

19. "Core Team Chosen," 6.

theses developed in *A New Vision.* At the last minute, a number of practicing politicians and policy advisors were invited to speak at the conference. A few of the conference attenders were people affected by social welfare policies. Discussions at the conference ranged from the theory of the *New Vision* essay to practical issues of poverty and welfare policy.

Foundational Analysis in *A New Vision for Welfare Reform*

In this section, I examine how *A New Vision* contributes a foundational analysis of the welfare crisis, critiquing its empirical analysis and its alternative theoretical account of welfare responsibility. I will note several strengths and weaknesses of the argument.

A New Vision points out a number of deep causes of the American welfare policy dilemma. It correctly suggests that the "poverty crisis cannot be assessed narrowly as an income crisis of poor people" and that "citizens should not expect the solution to come solely from the assistance programs of federal and state governments" (554). The Center is on the right track to note that these issues should not be explored "in the abstract" as intellectual historians might do; they must be engaged by policy-minded citizens concerned with the pressing social crises of our day.[20] *A New Vision* does in fact avoid doing an "intellectual history" of welfare policy.

The Center's Empirical Analysis

A New Vision is divided into four parts. Its empirical analysis of the American situation and political culture appears in part one, "Welfare Policy in a Bind" (555-59). The authors note that this part is not intended to "provide an extensive critique of existing and proposed welfare policies."[21] Instead, they briefly note three signs of America's welfare policy dilemma: the practical

20. Skillen, "An Introduction," 6-7.

21. Center for Public Justice, *A New Vision,* 551-52. For the project's initial work on welfare policy literature, which identified five major theoretical approaches to welfare policy failure, see Carlson-Thies, "Crisis of American Welfare"; "Common Reading List" (1993); "Essential Reading on Poverty and Welfare," in Center for Public Justice, *A New Vision;* and "Welfare Responsibility: Surveying the Territory," *Public Justice Report,* Mar.–Apr. 1993, 4-5.

failures of the social policies, the crisis of legitimacy around government action on welfare, and the impasse in the current efforts at policy reform (555-56). Then they make the bold and un-American admission that "our political culture itself is part of the crisis" (554). They explore this claim by developing a succinct five-point list of "problematic assumptions and patterns" in American public life that contribute to the current welfare dilemma. These points criticize "sacred cows" such as the belief that society is composed of autonomous, free, and self-determining individuals, that the economic marketplace is the primary realm for realizing both the individual and public good, and that government's main task is to promote economic growth.

While this list is useful and even daring, it reflects weaknesses in the Center's method of analysis. First, the way the five assumptions are formulated suggests a far too analytical role for faith in human life and so fails to capture adequately the *dynamic* of religious motives in American society. This occurs, for example, in *A New Vision*'s account of America's "growing scepticism," fading "hope for the future," and loss of "confidence in government's ability to do anything about the worst forms of poverty" (553). While these are extremely powerful phenomena, they are not first and foremost due to a lack of "accurate understanding" of life or to "problematic assumptions" (554). Rather, they are symptoms of a society that trusts in an enslaving idol rather than the liberating God of the Bible. Idolatrous trust in economic growth, science, and technology now breathes life into many societal assumptions and practices. The Center's account of these assumptions suggests they motivate us directly as propositional statements. Instead, the Center's analysis should give an account of the fuller religious dynamic shaping American society, a dynamic that is not, first of all, analytical in character.[22]

A second weakness is that the essay's empirical analysis does not evaluate *actual* societal structures. Central to the Center's "foundational approach" is the need to account for the role of actual structures in human society. But part one of *A New Vision* gives only a brief propositionalized account of structures rather than an actual analysis of social structures. It focuses on faulty assumptions behind structures rather than on how the current structural state of affairs relates to poverty. In order for analysis to be

22. See Bob Goudzwaard, "Socioeconomic Life: A Way of Confession," in his *Aid for the Overdeveloped West,* 23-30, and Harry A. Van Belle, "Some Things Every Christian Psychologist Should Think About (Maybe)," July 3, 1986.

serviceable to healing, it must start with an examination of actual operating societal structures. This weakness is magnified later, when the Center uses its assumption-based account of structures to construct its alternative theories.

A third way the Center's analysis weakens its "foundational approach" is that it does not pay adequate attention to empirical *context.*[23] Contexts are important, Richard Mouw and Sander Griffioen argue in *Pluralisms and Horizons,* because they are "the ways in which different cultural groups do in fact combine directional visions and associational practices into unique *configurations.*"[24] Directional (religious) visions of life do not occur in the abstract, nor do associational (structural) practices. For example, American family patterns in the 1990s are different from those in Ethiopia today, and also from those in America in 1860. The role that family breakdown in America plays in poverty needs to be analyzed in light of the current context, that is, how family beliefs and structures are dynamically combined today. *A New Vision for Welfare Reform* leaves largely unaddressed this context that shapes American society, "welfare programs," and the current "design and size of government."

The Center's Theoretical Contribution

The Center's alternative theories are developed in the last three parts of *A New Vision.* The logic of these parts is noted in the initial project description:

> [The Center] is convinced that another point of view — a justice viewpoint grounded in biblical assumptions about human nature and responsibility — will yield more penetrating insights and motivate a more dynamic, flexible, and challenging approach to problems such as public welfare.[25]

23. The Center, however, has done more of this type of work on education policies. See James W. Skillen, "Educational Freedom with Justice," in Skillen, ed., *The School Choice Controversy: What is Constitutional?* (Grand Rapids, Mich.: Baker, 1993), 67-85, and Rockne M. McCarthy, James W. Skillen, and William Harper, *Disestablishment a Second Time: Genuine Pluralism for American Schools* (Grand Rapids, Mich.: Eerdmans, 1982).

24. Mouw and Griffioen, *Pluralisms and Horizons* (Grand Rapids, Mich.: Eerdmans, 1993), 153. See further all of chapter seven.

25. "The Center for Public Justice" brochure.

This logic suggests that a proper understanding of "biblical assumptions" will yield "penetrating insights" and produce a helpful, practical "approach to problems such as public welfare."

Part two of the essay, "In Search of a Better Worldview," develops this logic by outlining a five-point list of biblical assumptions (559-65) as the Center's alternative to the false assumptions noted in part one. Part three, "A Responsibility Crisis," uses these biblical assumptions to show the need for, and to develop the outline of, a theory of "multiple accountability structures in society." The fourth part, "To Do Justice," further develops this social theory into a discussion of the justice role of the state. *A New Vision* clearly intends these theories to "lead to creative innovations in policy making" (552).

In these thetical parts of the argument, the Center makes important contributions. Its five-point list of contrasting assumptions points out important aspects of a biblical direction for social policy. The idea of the "manifold character of human responsibility" sheds helpful "new light" on the poverty and welfare crisis (565). As *A New Vision* states:

> In a highly differentiated and interdependent society . . . the only answer to human degradation is to seek the recovery of responsibility on all fronts simultaneously. The approach we have suggested here demands recognition of the multiplicity of human vocations so that no single aim or purpose in society is allowed to overwhelm others. . . . A government that ignores some of its own duties, or that tries to take on obligations that do not belong to it, will not be acting to fulfil its vocation to do justice to a richly differentiated society. (569)

This helpful insight may help break the impasse of current programs that leave so many people trapped in poverty.

The Center's approach to formulating its theory, however, raises several problems related to those noted above. First, the Center formulates its biblical beliefs as a list of abstract propositions. Although not so stated, this implies that biblical faith functions in life like rational propositions. Admittedly, analysis of faith can serve to clarify or deepen features of its content. But just and righteous living is neither inspired nor guided by faith *propositions.* People do not make better parents, nor governments make better policies, if they start from an intellectual articulation of biblical assumptions. Religious assumptions need to be grasped in the heart, not just rationally apprehended, in order to inspire obedient living, politics, or theory. Yet *A New Vision* implies that a correct list of assumptions will inspire good theory making and moral action.

Second, the Center's biblical theory of the "manifold character of human responsibility" tends to treat poor people abstractly. This is ironic since the Center criticizes those who blame poverty on the "situation" or on the "poor themselves" for treating the problem of poverty "far too narrowly and abstractly as a lack of income" (565). The Center does not want to solve poverty simply by making a cash injection, but by calling a wide variety of institutions and offices to their own distinct responsibilities (566-67). When the Center applies this theory in an example, however, it slips into a new form of abstraction. *A New Vision* suggests that if people, families, or schools live with the legacy of "slavery and legal discrimination" or in a broken-down neighborhood, they still have responsibilities "that are not transferable and that may not be discounted" (568-69). This treats poor people in difficult circumstances in an abstracted way. A variety of things may happen *around* people (e.g., crime, neighborhood breakdown, lack of services) or directly *to* them (e.g., sickness, divorce, mental illness) that might reduce the scope of their agency. Some rights and responsibilities may have to be temporarily or sometimes permanently reduced, transferred, or discounted. If theory is to avoid treating people abstractly, it must be more than an expression of good assumptions.[26]

Third, *A New Vision*'s account of the role of the state (569-78) is simultaneously fruitful and problematic. To begin with, the Center argues that its theory of "multiple accountability structures in society" leads to a "particular understanding of government's responsibility in and for society." Social diversity "cannot exist apart from a framework of public law and order that gives each its due, making it possible for all to thrive simultaneously in the same territory" (570). A strength of the Center's social

26. Perhaps this is part of the tendency in the Kuyperian tradition to see science primarily as an "expression" of principles. See N. P. Wolterstorff, *The Project of a Christian University in a Postmodern Culture* (Amsterdam: Free Univ. Press, 1988), 18. For a more contextual articulation of a theory of "multiple, simultaneous vocations," see "Charter of Social Rights and Responsibilities," Citizens for Public Justice, Toronto, undated. Also see the Citizens for Public Justice listing of "10 criteria for economic policy making" in Gerald Vandezande, *Christians in the Crisis: Toward Responsible Citizenship* (Toronto: Anglican Book Centre, 1983), 63-64, and six "cornerstones for socio-economic policy" in a brief to the Ontario prebudget consultation, "Working Together for Justice," Citizens for Public Justice, Toronto, 1993.

theory is the recognition that the state is "essential."[27] *A New Vision* elaborates this political philosophy by arguing that

> government's attempts to overcome or ameliorate poverty should take the *primary* course of trying to strengthen the accountability structures that constitute the warp and woof of society. Why should we not see welfare policies as having the aim of restoring people and institutions to their diverse responsibilities in a healthy society, rather than aiming directly and abstractly to lift the income of poor people above a certain poverty line? . . . We believe that government's primary aim should be to call people and institutions to their own responsibilities. (569)

In doing this, a government needs to be careful not to ignore "some of its own duties," but also not "to take on obligations that do not belong to it" (569).

While the Center's theories of societal responsibilities and the state's role are logically constructed from its list of biblical assumptions, these theories do not fit back into real life easily. This is evident, for example, in the Center's formulation of the *ways* a government carries out its role in society. The Center identifies three "modes" in which governments act: by upholding a just social order, by assisting with relief in emergencies, and by acting to bring about fundamental reforms where patterns of injustice exist.[28] This formulation is helpful in that it stresses the need for the state to act forcefully against poverty. The weakness, however, is that it is not, in fact, defining *modes* of state action, but rather describing ideal-typical *situations* to which a state responds — "a just social order" (570-72), "an emergency" case (572-73), or a situation dominated by "patterns of injustice" (573-78). In the first two cases, the essay argues, the state may presume "the basic soundness of both the people and the institutions" (572), while in the third case this cannot be assumed. This formulation seems necessary in order to make the essay's theoretical solutions applicable to the multidimensional social problems the Center wants to help solve.

One problem with this formulation is that life never comes in discrete

27. The Center's idea of a "framework of public law and order" suggests that the state helps to integrate society. It is not clear whether this means that the state integrates different social entities, enables them to integrate, supplements their integration, or repairs their faulty integration.

28. Center for Public Justice, *A New Vision,* 570ff. This threefold formulation was already used in Skillen, "An Introduction," 4-6.

packages. Governments face unique and changing situations that simultaneously contain all types of health and brokenness. "Normal" suburban life cannot be addressed apart from its intrinsic connection to the "emergency" situations in inner cities. More important, "basically sound" suburban life itself contains deep distortions, while "basically unsound" inner-city life has strong and healthy features and participants. Government needs to develop policies to deal with the diverse blends of justice and oppression within distinct situations.

A second problem with the formulation is that the Center does not address how, or in which ways, a government actually carries out its task in these situations. Government primarily acts in society by (1) gathering information and using it to persuade, (2) taxing and spending money, (3) issuing authoritative laws and regulations, and (4) developing a state agency to directly provide a good.[29] These are the *ways* a government can create a "framework of public law and order that gives each its due, making it possible for all to thrive simultaneously in the same territory" (570).

Another way to formulate government's role among the "multiple accountability structures in society" would be to think of it as always embedded within actual social situations. In each situation, the government discerns whether public justice exists, that is, whether people or social institutions are colliding, are unwilling to carry out their distinctive tasks, have had their tasks improperly absorbed by others, are disabled by lack of resources, are demanding excessive resources, are oppressing others, or are suffering oppression. Government should then respond by revising the public legal framework so that the real, presently existing diversity of people, communities, and institutions are justly reintegrated within the society. Government needs to ascertain whether, and in which ways, it ought to respond by using its distinct and limited powers to admonish, enable, regulate, require, or provide. It might decide to call certain people and institutions back to their tasks, or ensure they can access the resources needed to fulfill their callings, or step in and fulfill a social function that no one else is able or willing to meet. Over time, as a government discerns changes in society, it might decide to address the problems in new ways.[30]

29. See Leslie A. Pal, *Public Policy Analysis,* 2nd ed. (Scarborough, Ont.: Nelson, 1992), 138-70, and Christopher C. Hood, *The Tools of Government* (London: MacMillan, 1983).

30. Kuyper changed his mind on the role of the state in school policy and social

Analyzing the Center's Approach

The Center's "foundational approach" to social analysis makes a distinctive Christian contribution to our understanding of social policy. It draws attention to the interplay between everyday practices and policy, the deeper social structures, and the religious vision of the people. Yet the questions I have raised about the Center's empirical analysis and theory making do signal problems in the way that it implemented this approach. In this section, I explore the character of these problems.

Theory and Practice?

Does the Center's approach produce analysis and theory that are too abstract and thus too far removed from practice? *A New Vision* intends to do theory, and I affirm that theory, to be true to its nature, must involve abstraction.[31] Theory about social life and welfare policy will not serve policymaking better if it is forced to become something other than theory.

Has the Center done too much theory in its project? As a policy organization the Center chose to contribute to the poverty debate primarily by doing theory.[32] But was this too much theory? The Center determined that

---

policy because of changed circumstances. In the 1880s he said government should not directly fund schools, but switched by 1914 to insist on government funding. His reasoning is in *Anti-revolutionaire Staatkunde* 2 (1916–17): 461. He also warned against dependency on the state in his 1891 speech, reprinted as *The Problem of Poverty,* 62. But later he recognized that the state would have to play a larger role in social life. See Kuyper, *Wat Nu?* (Kampen: Kok, 1918). On adjusting policies see also Bob Goudzwaard, "Economische Politiek," in W. P. Berghuis, ed., *Anti-Revolutionair Bestek* (Aalten: Uitgeversmaatschappij de Graafschap, 1964), 248-315.

31. Hendrik Hart, "The Idea of the Inner Reformation of the Sciences," in Paul A. Marshall and Robert E. Vander Vennen, eds., *Social Science in Christian Perspective* (Lanham, Md.: UPA, 1988), 25. Also see Hart, "The Articulation of a Belief: A Link between Rationality and Commitment," in Hendrik Hart, Johan Vander Hoeven, and Nicholas Wolterstorff, eds., *Rationality in the Calvinian Tradition* (Lanham, Md.: UPA, 1983), 221; and Roy A. Clouser, *The Myth of Religious Neutrality: An Essay on the Hidden Role of Religious Belief in Theories* (Notre Dame: Univ. of Notre Dame Press, 1991), 51-73.

32. Skillen has done some helpful work on "the act of theorizing and the act of political duty," but more is needed on what it means to combine these tasks in a policy institute. See his "Towards a Comprehensive Science of Politics," *Philosophia Reformata* (1988): 57.

the context and character of the problem required this much theory. In principle, I think there are situations in which a heavily theoretical approach can make a valuable contribution to understanding a policy problem.

Has the Center's approach inappropriately emphasized either theory or practice at the expense of the other? For example, theory is often seen as superior to action because it is presumed to offer truer insight into human and nonhuman nature. Theory is expected to provide normative direction for practice. Conversely, when practice is seen as superior, it is assumed to offer the means of changing the world while theory simply talks about inapplicable ideas.

The Center's approach does not move in either of these directions. In fact, Skillen argues in another place that theory does not reveal norms or give privileged insight into God's will for life.[33] He notes, "Political scientists [along with everyone else] surely have a role to play, a contribution to make, in helping us to gain a true insight into political reality, and if their theory is true, it will help us all grasp more clearly what exists both in its deformity and in its relative goodness."[34] The Center strongly supports street-level social work and the recovery of moral responsibility in every area of life. It simply maintains that its own contribution will be theoretical.[35] Furthermore, at another point Skillen rejects the theory-and-practice dilemma. He argues that "the act of theorizing and the act of political duty are two different kinds of *acts.*" But neither activity is superior, and both need to be done in response to God's norms.[36]

Faith and Theory?

The Center takes faith seriously in its analysis and theory making. Its approach reflects the view that faith and learning should not be linked externally. Rather, Christian beliefs ought to control theorizing internally.[37]

33. Skillen, "Comprehensive Science of Politics," 55f.

34. Skillen, "Comprehensive Science of Politics," 56.

35. Skillen, "Agony in the City," and Skillen, "Justice for Urban Neighbors."

36. Skillen, "Comprehensive Science of Politics," 55f. (my emphasis). See Hendrik Hart, "Theory and Praxis: A Response," in *Justice in the International Economic Order* (Grand Rapids: Calvin College, 1980), 99-103.

37. For an elaboration of this point, see Hart, "The Idea of the Inner Reformation of the Sciences," and Clouser.

The social and political theories in *A New Vision for Welfare Reform* are not recycled secular theories with biblical "goals" or "limits" attached externally. Rather, the Center works to develop social and political theories, or reform them, with biblical principles internally illuminating these activities.

Faith and Practice?

In *Until Justice and Peace Embrace,* Nicholas Wolterstorff raises the question whether faith ought to guide the selection of practices we choose for theorizing. He argues that the tradition within which the Center works has tended to see the end of theorizing to be the "construction of nomological theory," where this theory-creation is guided by Christian faith. While Wolterstorff "substantially" agrees with this view, he wants more done about the "direction governance" of theory. "Christian conviction" should also shape the "*direction* in which scholars turn their inquiries; it determines the *governing interest* of their theorizing."[38] He wants "theorizing that places itself in the service of the cause of justice"; scholars, he argues, "will have to weigh the importance of occupying that great edifice of culture against the importance of entering into some project of social reform. And always they will have to do this weighing in the light of their total, concrete situation."[39]

Skillen responds to Wolterstorff's challenge by stating that, in light of his role as executive director of the Center, his "sympathies are strongly with Wolterstorff here."[40] Indeed, the Center's welfare project is dedicated to bringing justice to the poor. In another article, Skillen clarifies his position:

> Yes, Christian political scientists ought to direct their theorizing in ways that will aid the wider community of citizens (including themselves as citizens) to do justice. But this simply says that all theory grows from and reflects back on life in its fullness, and that theoreticians are more than scientists or philosophers; they are human beings with many additional responsibilities before God.[41]

38. Wolterstorff, *Until Justice and Peace Embrace,* 166.

39. Wolterstorff, *Until Justice and Peace Embrace,* 164, 172.

40. Skillen, "Politics and Justice and Peace," *Reformed Journal,* Dec. 1984, pp. 17-22.

41. Skillen, "Comprehensive Science of Politics," 57.

This statement implies that the activity of theory somehow operates side-by-side with other activities.

Intellectualism?

The above exploration suggests that the Center's approach to analysis does not treat faith, theory, and practice as "three distinct and separate orders of reality or three separate modes of life."[42] However, the Center does tend to intellectualize these human ways of functioning in its social and political analysis. This is so even though the authors of *A New Vision* want their analysis to "lead to creative innovations in policy making" (552).

By "intellectualism" I mean the tendency to address and resolve real-life problems as though they are primarily logical problems. When the Center does its foundational analysis, it tends to reduce concrete problems concerning structures and beliefs to propositional accounts of these realities. The Center proposes a list of biblical assumptions as an alternative to what it identifies as the reigning assumptions, but it does so in the form of propositions that respond in logical fashion to the initial list. These propositions are elaborated into a social and political theory that again logically responds to the initial statement of the problem. This approach is problematic because, while it produces solutions that logically solve the abstract account of problems in the essay, the solutions are too narrowly logical to adequately solve the original, multidimensional welfare problems.

This approach is problematic because it produces abstract results that are too unidimensional to adequately illuminate the complexity and multidimensionality of real-life predicaments.

Doing Theory as Participation in "The Way"

The Center's foundational analysis of the structural and religious depth-dimensions of welfare problems offers helpful ways to address social prob-

42. See John Van Dyk's general argument that Western Christianity is plagued by an understanding of these three as separate entities that need to be related in a hierarchical fashion: "The Relation Between Faith and Action: An Introduction," *Pro Rege* 10, no. 4 (1982): 2-7.

lems. In this section, I want to suggest some ways this type of foundational analysis might become less intellectualistic and more serviceable to concrete policymaking.

Theory and "The Way"

Theory may deal with elements of faith in propositions, but it should not theorize about problems as though people are motivated by faith propositions. This is true whether we analyze obedient or disobedient faiths. Faith does not speak through concepts but directly to our hearts (Prov. 4:23; Mark 7:21; Matt. 12:34). José Míguez Bonino makes this point, when he argues that the word of God does not come to us as

> a *conceptual communication* but as a creative event, a history-making pronouncement. Its truth does not consist in some correspondence to an idea but in its efficacy in carrying out God's promise or fulfilling his judgement. Correspondingly, what is required of Israel is not an *ethical inference* but an obedient participation — whether in action or suffering — in God's active righteousness and mercy. Faith is always a concrete obedience.[43]

For Bonino, the life of faith is "walking" with God in the light of his word. In a similar way, John Van Dyk warns of the tendency of the church to intellectualize doctrine. "Christian doctrine," he points out, "*is* the Gospel, consisting of *both* the message of salvation *and* a new way of life. Doctrine is therefore directed beyond knowing to a change of heart and a change in life. Doctrine is 'The Way,' a single unbroken response to the Word."[44]

From these observations we can conclude that faith, theory, and practice should be seen as aspects of one integral walk along "The Way." They are internally linked in life because they are facets of our participation in "The Way."

43. José Míguez Bonino, *Doing Theology in a Revolutionary Situation* (Philadelphia: Fortress Press, 1975), 89 (my emphasis).

44. Van Dyk, 6.

Faith Inspires All Action

Herman Dooyeweerd, a prominent figure in the Center's tradition, notes that it is a mistake to think theory can guide our lives.[45] When a worldview community moves into a new historical situation, he argues, it is forced to discern and develop new cultural responses. A community's religious worldview guides its response to this situation. Dooyeweerd offers two strikingly relevant examples. First, Abraham Kuyper's "radical Christian view of science [theory]" was not born "from a philosophical or systematic tendency but rather in the midst of a concrete situation of life." A new situation "stimulated young Neo-Calvinism to a consideration of its religious calling in the realm of science."

Second, early Christians living in the Roman Empire initially did not participate in politics and viewed it as negative. But "when the possibility of exercising influence in these realms had been created," he suggests, the worldview of early Christians led them to develop a "positive view" of the task of Christians in politics.[46]

Dooyeweerd's view of both policymaking and theorizing as religious activities done in response to new situations sheds light on the Center's project. *A New Vision* was intended to offer a "vision," a "viewpoint," or a "distinctive outlook on reality." But rather than speak to the heart or directly invite participation in what God is doing for the poor, the essay speaks in propositions and unsituated theory. This weakens the truth and power behind the Center's idea of "multiple accountability structures in society" because this notion is not first of all an intellectual idea but a religiously inspired principle.[47] To effectively encourage new policy developments, *A New Vision* needs to speak more directly from its underlying beliefs.

45. Herman Dooyeweerd, *A New Critique of Theoretical Thought*, vol. 1 (n.p.: Presbyterian and Reformed Publishing, 1969), 158, 164.

46. Dooyeweerd, 157, 158. See a parallel argument by Bob Goudzwaard in his *Aid for the Overdeveloped West*, 14-15.

47. Bob Goudzwaard, "Tweemaal Publieke Gerechtigheid," *Beweging* 55, no. 4 (1991): 63-66.

Theory Is Not a Tool

Theory is too often viewed as a tool that can be guided by our worldview. Calvin Seerveld dissents, arguing that theory is the analytical unfolding *of* our worldview. Theory is "schooled memory."[48] Theory is an activity we engage in to deepen our integral, religiously fired worldviews.[49] Policymakers see, identify, and analyze concrete, multidimensional policy problems through their worldviews. Worldviews also inspire the shape of new policy proposals.[50]

Theory can deepen our understanding of the functions of things, the character of entities, and the nature of events and processes. This contribution of theory comes as a schooling of our larger biblical vision of justice for the poor; solidarity with the needy; reconciliation between social, economic, and racial groups; and willingness to sacrifice, suffer, and take up our cross to end oppression.[51] This all occurs as part of our walk along "The Way," which, as *A New Vision* emphasizes, is rooted in the renewal of all creation through the sacrifice of Jesus Christ (564). Theory needs to function as a deepening of policymakers' worldviews or it will fail to contribute to the making of wise policies.

Theory and Context

Doing theory in "The Way" of Jesus must be based on a careful reading of the context. Walking the way of Christ is practical, relevant, and concrete. In his massive political party program for the Netherlands, Abraham Kuyper argues that his theory was developed not for some "imaginary world," but for the "real world." He argues that political theorizing must take on

48. Calvin Seerveld, "Philosophy as Schooled Memory," *Anakainosis* 5, no. 1 (1982): 1-6.

49. On the systematics of belief, worldview, and experience, see James H. Olthuis, "On Worldviews," in Paul A. Marshall, Sander Griffioen, and Richard J. Mouw, eds., *Stained Glass: Worldviews and Social Science* (Lanham, Md.: UPA, 1989), 26-40.

50. I make these arguments in more detail in "The Role of Worldviews in the Politics of Accommodation: A Case Study of Dutch Broadcasting Policy (1919–1930)" (Ph.D. diss., University of Calgary, 1992).

51. For good examples of theory-deepened vision, see Kuyper, *The Problem of Poverty,* 37, 38, 45-46, 60, 62, and 77.

the present world in all its diversity, deformity, and plurality in order to be valid theory.[52] This was Kuyper's answer to the Enlightenment theorists' claim to offer universal and abstract principles for reforming any situation.

Theory and policy analysis are not only influenced by our faiths, but also by our "reading" of our context. Analyzing policy problems, setting policy goals, and determining appropriate policy instruments are all activities that depend on a careful exegesis of context. Policy analysis — with its strong empirical side — must be directly rooted in the actual policy problems for a proper judgment of what should be done and in which way.

Theory and the Structures-for Reality

Understanding a context is also important for our analysis of social structures. Our experience in creation, when viewed in the light of Scripture, provides the data for understanding the "structures-for" our social lives. This argument is developed by James H. Olthuis in an article on Dooyeweerd's philosophy. To begin with, Olthuis argues that creation does not "have" meaning but "is" meaning. Thus, we need to distinguish, though not separate, God's word or "law" and "that which is subject to the law." "The law-order is the structure-for the structure-of creation," Olthuis argues, and "the structures-for are realized in the structures-of. The structures-of are incarnations of the structures-for." Without each other, neither has meaning.

The significance of this view for doing social and political theory is that "[O]ne only discovers the structures-for (law) through and in the structures-of (facticity subject to the law). . . . [O]ne goes to work empirically investigating experience in order through observed regularities to gain clearer insight into the transcendental order holding for reality."[53] To

52. Kuyper, *Ons Program,* 2nd ed. without appendices (Amsterdam: J. H. Kruyt, 1880), 474. Also, commenting on the Dutch character of his major theological work, *Principles of Sacred Theology,* Kuyper says, "Being an enemy to abstractions, and a lover of the concreteness of representation, the author could not do anything else than write from the environment in which he lives." Kuyper, *Principles* (1st ed., 1898; Grand Rapids, Mich.: Eerdmans, 1954), ix.

53. James H. Olthuis, "The Reality of Societal Structures," Institute for Christian Studies, Toronto, undated, 3, 4, 5, 10.

theorize well about social and political structures, we must necessarily examine current, historical, empirical society in light of the Bible. Theory, like all knowledge, is dependent on this experience of reality for its material. Reality provides this material because the "structures-of" things, people, events, and processes reveal the "structures-for" life. Olthuis cautions, however, that our theory should not be equated with the structures-for but must be seen only as our limited and sinful account of these structures-for.[54]

Theory and Sin

A New Vision notes the problem that sin and unbelief may distort our choices in shaping theory. But another problem that may occur is that sin enters our analysis through our distorted social experience. Wolterstorff mentions this problem as a "strategic" concern at the end of an essay on "Theory and Praxis." He says, "[I]t seems to me imperative that in our practice of scholarship we do our best to break out of the bondage of our situation as relatively well-to-do members of the First World in order to be able to hear the cries of the deprived and oppressed of humanity."[55] He suggests that we must "listen to those who because of their social background or goals or sympathies see the situation differently than we do." We also need to listen to "the prophetic word of the Bible, that great unmasker of self-deceit." Perhaps these paths join, he concludes, because "by listening to the cries of the oppressed and deprived we are enabled genuinely to hear the word of the prophets" and of Jesus.[56]

I think Wolterstorff is correct in highlighting this problem. Listening helps our understanding of problems to be more insightful and thus more serviceable. I would add that we need to listen to the Bible not only to discern suffering and oppression but also to discern in a sin-torn world the "structures-for" human social, economic, and political life. Reforming wel-

54. Our accounts are our limited creaturely and sin-stained responses to God's structures for life. For an example of tentativeness in our knowledge of "structures-for," see Citizens for Public Justice, Toronto, "Guidelines for Christian Political Service," part I, B.

55. Wolterstorff, *Until Justice and Peace Embrace*, 173.

56. Wolterstorff, *Until Justice and Peace Embrace*, 176.

fare policy and recharging multiple societal responsibilities require an understanding of what the "structures-for" are and how they relate to the problems and experiences of the poor.

Theory and Dialogue

Dialogue is a central aim of the Center's welfare project. However, when we suggest that theory is, at least in part, an extrapolation of biblical assumptions, we in practice reduce the possibility of learning from others. Too often the Christian community has made theory the exclusive preserve of professionals.[57] But if theory really is about the structures-for reality, as Olthuis argues, then full-time theorists need to dialogue with a wide variety of people, including the poor.

The fact that theory is not a one-way street proceeding from professional scholars to everyone else was driven home to me some time ago in a political philosophy class. An aboriginal-Canadian student asked the professor if he could write his paper on aboriginal political philosophy. He was told flatly that no such thing existed. The student responded that while there had been no specialists in political theory among his people, they had thought about the nature of life, the character of knowing, the structure of relationships, and so on. There was a "theory," although it had not yet been articulated by scholars. I think that while such ideas may not be systematized, they can be useful windows on the structures-for reality that theorists need to learn from.[58]

57. This is also true of the tradition in which the Center works. Dooyeweerd suggests that while everyone engages in worldview thought, only "philosophic thinkers" engage in theoretical thought (p. 128). Roy Clouser's distinction between "common sense" and "scientific and philosophic" theory, while helpful, has to do with levels of abstraction and different methods of proof and is often understood to require professionalized theory. See Clouser, 51-73.

58. Paul Marshall's admonition to be careful about liberation theology's call to listen to the poor is in order only if one assumes that "scientific tools" are neutral and do not influence listening. But if we listen, aware of scientific bias and with the Bible open, then the "experience of the poor" is a welcome and critical element for developing theory and policy making. See Marshall, *Thine is the Kingdom: A Biblical Perspective on the Nature of Government and Politics Today* (rpt. ed.; Vancouver, B.C. : Regent College Bookstore, 1993), 73-75.

Thus, the Center's welfare project needs to see the poor not only as participants in activating our mutual responsibilities in multiple vocations but as dialogue partners in our theorizing about these vocations. Furthermore, as the Center suggests, Christians must also dialogue with others who may not be Christian. Gerald Vandezande articulates this positively: "We must be receptive to the diversity of experience and insight of all who struggle for equity and fairness, including those who do not confess Jesus but in whose lives the Spirit is also moving to accomplish God's purposes in history."[59]

Conclusion

The questions I have raised in this chapter are intended to serve as ways to make social and political analysis and theory more serviceable to the coming of justice in everyday life. I have noted strengths and weaknesses in the Center's analysis of social policy. My intention is to nudge Christian policy analysts away from detached intellectualism and on to greater political and theoretical service. Christian policy- and theory-making, including my own, need increasingly to become activities done along the liberating "Way" of Jesus.

59. Gerald Vandezande, *Let Justice Flow! Taking Healing Steps in a Wounded World* (Toronto: CJL Foundation, 1994), 19. See also Mouw and Griffioen, *Pluralisms and Horizons,* and Richard J. Mouw, *Distorted Truth: What Every Christian Needs to Know About the Battle for the Mind* (San Francisco: Harper & Row, 1989).

IV. TOWARD LASTING REFORM

Free Schools and the Revival of Urban Communities

Charles L. Glenn

"PUBLIC" SCHOOLING, in its inner-city form, has come to have the same negative connotation as "public" housing, and for much the same reason: its clientele is correctly perceived as predominantly black and Hispanic, without other schooling options, and unlikely to negotiate the challenges of contemporary life successfully. Even worse, the urban public schools attended by millions of America's poorest children are increasingly seen not only to be failing to provide a sufficiently effective education, but to be contributing to the disasters of inner-city life.

However, these same linkages also operate in reverse. The central contention of this chapter is that a new form of relationship between inner-city families and schools not only will improve the efficacy of schooling, but also can play an important role in restoring healthy community life. I will suggest that the restructured relationship will help to provide a context of mutual responsibility within which more adults in these distressed neighborhoods will begin to live productive lives and to function effectively as parents, workers, and citizens.

Pathologies of Urban Life

Our discussion must start with the fact that God's grace abounds in the inner city and not with the *dis*grace that is also abundantly present. To describe the life of poor people in American society in terms of pathologies alone, as so many commentators do, is not only to do them an injustice, but also to exclude from our understanding of the situation the reason why we have a right to be hopeful.

Anthropologist Reginald Clark's close study of poor black families in Chicago whose children were doing well in high school found that *things they did* made a significant difference.

> The family's main contribution to a child's success in school is made through parents' dispositions and interpersonal relationships with the child in the household. . . . [A] family's ability to equip its young members with survival and "success" knowledge is determined by the parents' (and other older family members') own upbringing, the parents' past relationships and experiences in community institutions, the parents' current support networks, social relationships and other circumstances outside the home, and, most centrally, the parents' current social relationships in the home, and their satisfaction with themselves and with home conditions.[1]

Furthermore, the life of inner-city churches — often far more intense than that of the churches of the middle class — and the deep, sustaining spiritual convictions of many individuals are clear signs, to the believer, that "where sin increased, grace increased all the more" (Rom. 5:20).

According to Clark, successful students were guided by particular "sacred and secular moral orientations" and were upheld by their parents' disinclination to allow their children to see themselves as passive victims of a racist and exploitative system. These successful (though impoverished) inner-city parents were taking charge of their own lives and those of their children.

Thus the central policy question, surely, is how to build on the strengths that already exist among poor people, rather than to continue to treat the needy as helpless victims. To follow the biblical message, it is to learn how to recognize the signs of grace and to prepare for it by removing the barriers that human sinfulness (and not that of poor people alone) has put in the way. This sinfulness is evident both in personal irresponsibility and in structural arrangements that systematically devalue those whom God values highly. There is enough guilt to go around, and then some.

1. R. M. Clark, *Family Life and School Achievement: Why Poor Black Children Succeed or Fail* (Chicago: Univ. of Chicago Press, 1983), 1.

To adopt a strategy of building on the signs of grace in the inner city does not call for a naïve optimism about the "goodness" of the poor; indeed, it is precisely by understanding them (and ourselves) as sinners in need of redemption that we can make an accurate estimate of how costly and difficult that redemption will be. Costly and difficult, but by no means impossible.

The evidence of the pathology of urban life — high unemployment, crime and violence, inadequate schooling, the collapse of family life — is all too familiar, whether recited by conservatives or liberals. This weakening of social organization cannot be attributed to worsening economic conditions. Indeed, William Julius Wilson's argument in *The Truly Disadvantaged* is that inner-city social disorder owes much to the *improving* situation of those African-Americans who succeed in getting a foot on the ladder of opportunity.[2] Therefore its remedy will not be found in traditional measures to stimulate the economy. A dynamic economy is greatly to be desired, but it will not of itself address the root problems of America's underclass. Nor will job-training programs or work requirements for public assistance, as useful as those might be, replace well-functioning families. Some adults may develop, through a sort of conversion, the habits of purposeful action that sustain a useful life, but for most of us those habits are learned when we are children, partly in school but building on what we had already learned in our families. Unfortunately, as a former pastor in Brooklyn has written, "by any material measure, the people of that community are better off now than they were thirty years ago. And yet the conclusion is irresistible that they are, all in all, worse off. . . . We might reasonably ask whether, in all of human history, we can find an instance of a large population group in which the institution of the family simply disappeared."[3]

The weakening of the family has far-reaching consequences. But why is the mess that some people make of their family lives a fit concern for social policy? One reason is that children are better off in families that are functioning well, with two biological parents who are making a reasonable success of marriage. In this instance, as in many others, research has recently

2. William Julius Wilson, *The Truly Disadvantaged* (Chicago: Univ. of Chicago Press, 1987).

3. R. J. Neuhaus, *America against Itself: Moral Vision and the Public Order* (Notre Dame: Univ. of Notre Dame Press, 1992), 79, 83.

been confirming what everyone except researchers already knew. As one welfare expert has summarized this evidence, "The vast majority of children who are raised entirely in a two-parent home will never be poor during childhood. By contrast, the vast majority of children who spend time in a single-parent home will experience poverty."[4]

The same point can be put even more bluntly: "family structure is by far the best predictor of child poverty."[5] Important as the level of schooling attained is for the escape from poverty or economic marginality, parents' marital status turns out to be even more significant.

> The conclusion that the best antipoverty program for children is a stable, intact family holds even for families with modest levels of educational attainment. For married high school graduates with children, the 1991 poverty rate was 7 percent, versus more than 41 percent for families headed by female high school graduates. For married high school dropouts with children, the poverty rate was 25 percent, versus more than 62 percent for families headed by female high school dropouts.[6]

Some experts minimize the impact of family structure on the poverty rate, insisting that "breakup changes the economic circumstances of parents only if they are employed. . . . Lack of earnings, not breakup, explains virtually all of the increase in poverty in the 1980s."[7] But the family structure issue is not primarily one of marriage breakup through divorce or desertion but rather of young women having children before they have acquired work qualifications or work experience; even if they do obtain employment, it is unlikely to lift them and their children above the poverty line.

The negative effects of family disorder on children are not limited to economic hardship. A national survey published in 1991 found that both children and parents from two-parent families were more positive on a

4. E. C. Kamarck and W. A. Galston, "A Progressive Family Policy for the 1990s," in W. Marshall and M. Schram, eds., *Mandate for Change* (New York: Berkley Books, 1993), 157, citing David T. Ellwood.

5. S. J. South and S. E. Tolnay, "Relative Well-Being among Children and the Elderly: The Effects of Age Group Size and Family Structure," *The Sociological Quarterly* 33 (1992): 115-33.

6. Kamarck and Galston, 159.

7. L. M. Mead, *The New Politics of Poverty: The Nonworking Poor in America* (New York: Basic Books, 1992), 55.

whole range of factors than were those from single-parent families.[8] The absence of a parent (usually the father) is "often accompanied by psychological consequences, which include higher than average levels of youth suicide, low intellectual and educational performance, and higher than average rates of mental illness, violence, and drug use."[9] An important qualification of this finding is that suicide rates do not appear to be higher among teenagers whose fathers have died; it is family breakup that has the devastating effect.[10]

Family structure in neighborhoods also appears to be a more powerful predictor of crime than either the race or the income level of the residents.[11] "Neighborhood standards may be set by mothers," James Q. Wilson points out, "but they are enforced by fathers, or at least by adult males. Neighborhoods without fathers are neighborhoods without men able and willing to confront errant youth. . . ."[12] And youth who are not confronted have little chance of mending their ways.

Schools and the Crisis of Family Life

A related reason for a policy concern with families is that the success of children in school (and thus, in a credential-driven economy, in much of life) is directly, though not inevitably, related to the nature of their family life. This is not to say that we can do nothing directly to improve the efficacy of urban schooling. For example, an increased commitment of funding would make it possible to provide caring — not custodial — adults to supervise and interact with children twelve hours a day or more during the school year and during summers as well. An effective strategy would require the option of residential programs for some, and it would require outreach to families in their homes (routine in Europe but almost unknown in

8. National Commission on Children, *Speaking of Kids: A National Survey of Children and Parents* (Washington, D.C.: National Commission on Children, 1991).

9. Kamarck and Galston, 162.

10. J. S. Wodarski and P. Harris, "Adolescent Suicide: A Review of Influences and the Means for Prevention," *Social Work* 32, no. 6 (1987): 477-84.

11. D. A. Smith and G. R. Jarjoura, "Social Structure and Criminal Victimization," *Journal of Research in Crime and Delinquency* 25 (1988): 27-52.

12. Cited by D. Blankenhorn, "Fatherless America" (Minneapolis: Center for the American Experiment, 1993), 1.

American education). In short, it would require "comprehensive and intensive services" provided by staff "with the time and skill to establish relationships based on mutual respect and trust."[13]

When the idea of "urban boarding schools" was first raised, it seemed an insult to the adequacy of inner-city parents. Now many of those parents are themselves crying out for help, for anything to give their children a safe environment within which to grow. Public policy should no longer ignore what parents tell us by putting their children in nonpublic schools that they cannot well afford.

To enable public and nonpublic schools to provide a truly supportive environment for children with severe physical, social, emotional, and other disabilities, and to do so for at least twice as many hours a year as schools now operate, would require a very substantial additional investment. However, even a massive investment of resources would not produce the desired results without a change in the dynamic of the relationship between family and school. It is not enough that schools start doing certain things differently; they must become different kinds of institutions in relation to the families that they serve.

Linkages between school and home in the inner city tend to founder on passivity on the one side and an immovable bureaucratic and professional culture on the other. The poor are not alone in keeping at a distance from public schools as they function in large school systems. Herbert Gans notes that most "middle Americans" practice "*organizational avoidance.* They seek mainly intimate and informal relations and groups, and try to avoid all but the essential contacts with formal organizations, not only the national ones of the 'larger society' but also local ones."[14]

It is very appropriate that some inner-city public schools have begun to provide parent centers, staffed with outreach workers and providing educational and support services for the parents of pupils.[15] It is also appropriate that many schools must now consult with parent representa-

13. L. B. Schorr with D. Schorr, *Within Our Reach* (New York: Doubleday, 1988), xxii.

14. H. J. Gans, *Middle American Individualism* (New York: Oxford Univ. Press, 1991), 43.

15. My colleague, professor Vivian Johnson, is conducting a nationwide study of such parent centers in urban schools for the National Research Center on Families, Communities, Schools and Children's Learning.

tives as they make certain kinds of decisions. The well-known structural reforms in Chicago offer the most notable example of mandatory involvement of parents in decision making.[16]

But simply spending more money and devising ingenious new programs will not do the trick, unless we change the internal dynamic of the school in its relationship with the surrounding environment. The relationship of schools with families has an impact that goes beyond what children experience in school; it either increases the alienation of inner-city life or helps to build healthy community. It either strengthens the role of families or further marginalizes them. And strong families, more than any other factor, enable schools to be effective in their educational mission.

James Coleman puts the research results in characteristically direct terms: "Schools are successful primarily for children from strong family backgrounds. Schools are singularly unsuccessful for children from weak or disorganized families."[17] After all, "the family is the institution in which children have their earliest education, their earliest experiences in the learning of languages, the nurturance of cognitive, emotional, and motor competencies, the maintenance of interpersonal relationships, the internalization of values, and the assignment of meaning to the world."[18]

In view of the significance of education within the family, it is not surprising that studies by researchers at Princeton and Johns Hopkins concluded that growing up in a single-parent family tended to depress a pupil's academic achievement and attendance. One interesting finding was that, as a family broke up, parents became less involved in the education of their children; another was that what parents *do* cannot explain the entire difference in academic achievement, since "the *strength of the attachment* between parents and child" had a direct impact on school success.[19]

Intermediate-level pupils from single-parent families have been found to be more disruptive and less academically successful than their classmates

16. G. A. Hess, *School Restructuring, Chicago Style* (Newbury Park, Calif.: Corwin Press, 1991).

17. J. Coleman, "The Family, the Community, and the Future of Education," in B. Weston, ed., *Education and the American Family: A Research Synthesis* (New York: New York Univ. Press, 1989), 169.

18. L. A. Cremin, *Popular Education and Its Discontents* (New York: Harper & Row, 1990), 53.

19. N. M. Astore and S. S. McLanahan, "Family Structure, Parental Practices and High School Completion," *American Sociological Review* 56 (1991): 309-20.

from two-parent families, holding race and class constant.[20] A study of third graders found that those whose parents had divorced were judged by their teachers as more maladjusted and less successful in schoolwork than children from intact families.[21]

Coleman suggests that much of the decline in student achievement can be traced to breakdown in the nuclear family. "Parents became much less able to raise children in a stable, orderly fashion."[22] As Sara Lawrence Lightfoot put it, "the family teaches what matters most."[23] If the family fails to teach those things, the efforts of teachers are immeasurably more difficult, and perhaps ultimately in vain.

This does not mean that only middle-class families, or indeed only two-parent families, can provide the essential preparation and support. Reginald Clark observed that the Chicago parents in his study who were doing a successful job of raising their children in extremely difficult circumstances "do not believe the school should provide all or even most of the academic training and support for the child. . . . They are likely to say that 'The world don't owe you anything; you owe something to yourself.' "[24]

Since "families are the strongest factor in the development and maintenance of human competence," it seems likely that "the solution to the problem of children who [do] not benefit from schooling [does] not lie in devoting more resources to schools, but in doing something about the way the parents treat the child at home."[25] If there is any measure within the reach of public policy that can help parents to function more effectively, both in the home and in relation to the formal schooling of their children, it would be at least as important as any of the school reforms to which we devote so much effort.

20. D. R. Featherstone, B. P. Cundick, and L. C. Jensen, "Differences in School Behavior and Achievement Between Children From Intact, Reconstituted, and Single-Parent Families," *Adolescence* 27 (1992): 1-11.

21. Hoyt, et al., "Anxiety and Depression in Young Children of Divorce," *Journal of Clinical Child Psychology* 19 (1990): 26-32.

22. Quoted in B. J. Christensen, "America's Academic Dilemma: The Family and the Schools," *The Family in America* 2, no. 6 (1988): 2.

23. S. L. Lawrence, "Families as Educators," in D. Bell, ed., *Shades of Brown: New Perspectives on School Desegregation* (New York: Teachers College Press, 1980), 8.

24. Clark, 122-23.

25. M. Eastman, *Family: The Vital Factor* (North Blackburn, Australia: Collins-Dove, 1989), xvi.

However, it is one thing to agree that public policy for education should seek to support families, and quite another to urge that schools take on the support of families as a major aspect of their mission. There are two primary dangers inherent in such an assignment of responsibility. The first is that it could further weaken the capacity of schools to carry out their primary function of providing instruction in those academic skills that are essential to a modern economy and society; school staff are already too distracted by the conflicting demands placed on them. The second is that there is an inherent danger in encouraging government to use schools as an instrument of social policy, particularly when that entails seeking to influence the attitudes and beliefs of pupils.[26]

Giving Parents the Opportunity to Be Responsible

Despite these cautions, there are compelling reasons for those who set educational policy to think seriously about the consequences for the health of families of the way that schools are organized and relate to their environment.

It is not enough to talk in school about the importance of families, if the educational system is so organized as to deny parents the opportunity to make significant decisions. The present system of assignment of pupils to schools in the United States is almost unique among the nations with universal schooling in its refusal to acknowledge the right of parents to choose schools for their children. This is a right spelled out explicitly in the major international covenants protecting human rights.[27] For example, the *Universal Declaration of Human Rights* (1948) states that "parents have a prior right to choose the kind of education that shall be given to their children." The nations signing the *International Covenant on Economic, Social and Cultural Rights* (1966) agreed "to have respect for the liberty of parents . . . to choose for their children schools, other than those established by public authorities, which conform to such minimum educational standards as may be laid down or approved by the State and to ensure the

26. Charles L. Glenn, *The Myth of the Common School* (Amherst: Univ. of Massachusetts Press, 1988).

27. The passages that follow are taken from the very useful collection entitled *Liberté d'enseignement. Les textes* (Geneva: Organisation internationale pour le développement de la liberté d'enseignement, n.d.).

religious and moral education of their children in conformity with their own convictions."

John Coons has argued eloquently that American education frustrates parents in exercising this right and duty:

> From top to bottom its structure effectively frustrates the choices of parent and child which the law protects in every other realm of life. Parents choose shoes, food, games, hours and every other important feature of a child's life. In education this liberty is not only opposed but squelched. Ordinary families with all their rich variety in culture and values are forced to accept the form, content and ideology of a politically dictated education. Public schools, as presently organized, chill the traffic in ideas that is generated by free family choices in every other area of life. Though they vest in the mantle of freedom and diversity, in fact they flout this deepest purpose of the First Amendment.[28]

Some assert that government should make the decisions about the education of children because some parents — and poor parents in general — are incapable of doing so and indeed simply do not care.[29] Of course there are some inadequate and irresponsible parents, of every social class, and society must have ways of intervening to protect individual children from situations of clearly established abuse and neglect, including that of their need for an education. But research by the Center on Families, Communities, Schools and Children's Learning shows that urban parents of all racial/ethnic groups are keenly interested in making school choices for their children and use a variety of means of obtaining information and reaching conclusions about which schools would best meet their needs.[30] Policy for the great majority should not be guided by the need to deal with exceptional cases.

Children are not well served by policies that treat their parents as incapable of responsible decision making. The message conveyed by a system in which parents are expected to be passive is that responsible choice, the expression of character or virtue, is exercised *for,* not *by,* the individual.

28. J. Coons, "Intellectual Liberty and the Schools," *Notre Dame Journal of Law, Ethics and Public Policy* 2 (1985): 515.

29. A. Thernstrom, "Is Choice a Necessity?" *The Public Interest,* no. 101 (1990).

30. C. Glenn, K. McLaughlin, and L. Salganik, *Parent Information for School Choice: The Case of Massachusetts* (Boston: Center on Families, Communities, Schools and Children's Learning, 1993).

This lesson encourages personal irresponsibility. An opportunity is thereby lost to engage parents and their children together in making decisions whose consequences are immediately apparent to both.

There is a growing recognition, among liberals as well as conservatives, that an answer to persistent poverty and social disorganization will have to be found in a change in the attitudes and behavior of the poor themselves as well as in the circumstances that surround and affect them. Thus Marian Wright Edelman of the Children's Defense Fund told an interviewer, "What scares me is that today people don't have the sense that they can struggle and change things."[31] New government programs to bring the "underclass" or "truly disadvantaged" into the social mainstream, absent that conviction among the intended beneficiaries, seem certain to produce results as meager as those of the programs that went before.

How can the persistently poor develop the *competence* — "not only intelligence, but foresight, energy, discipline, and the ability to sacrifice for the future"[32] — that would enable them to escape from poverty? Do schools have a part to play in helping in the development of this competence, of what could equally well be called, in Aristotle's sense, the habit of virtuous action? I believe that they do, in several ways.

Schools are complex phenomena, producing effects that go far beyond the manifest content of classroom instruction. The two effects that will concern us here are those on pupils through the internal life of the school, and those on parents and communities through the manner in which the school functions in relation to them.

Inner-city schools have had their mission defined for them by opinion makers steeped in the liberal belief that the poor are simply victims of circumstances, without ultimate responsibility for their own actions, who must not be "blamed" or expected to find their own solutions. As a result, the staff of these schools have tended to operate with low expectations and to concentrate, with pupils, on various forms of remedial education, and with their parents, on an attempt to minimize "interference." The operative assumption is that both parents and pupils can be defined adequately by what they lack of the qualities that would make them worthy of real respect. Kenneth Clark's recollection of the schools he attended in Harlem, in the 1930s, presents a very different picture:

31. Quoted in Mead, *New Politics,* 164.
32. Mead, *New Politics,* 19.

> [T]he teachers were concerned with holding *all* of us to high standards, because they were convinced *all* of us were educable. We had not yet come to that particular breakdown in the public education of minorities which is due to . . . the sloppy, sentimental good intentions of certain educators, who *reduce* learning standards for low-status youngsters, because they believe . . . it is impossible for them to learn as much as suburban children. . . . But when I was going to public school we had teachers who did not consider themselves . . . rationalizers of educational inequities. They were asked to teach reading, arithmetic, grammar, and they *did*.[33]

The prevalent attitude today, by contrast, has developed as part of a larger unwillingness to base social policy on solid convictions about responsibility. It is not that educators became more judgmental toward the poor; to the contrary, they have become systematically *non*judgmental, in the sense of adopting an attitude of not expecting anything in particular from those whom they regard as society's victims. Circumstances or structures are the cause of the problems, in this view. To the adherents of this liberal perspective, as Wilson points out, any talk of cultural factors — about choices and approaches to life — seems merely a sophisticated way to blame people already victimized again and again by society.[34]

But the extensive research carried out over the past two decades on effective schools shows to the contrary that choices and approaches, that is, cultural factors, make all the difference for poor children and their families. Social disorganization and other factors that inhibit the educational success of children from poor families can be counteracted by schools with the appropriate inner structures.[35] Schools *can* make a difference. Children and youth whose lives outside of school are characterized by disorder and lack of purpose can be helped to become achievers in school and also in life, when purposeful order is the rule inside the school's door.

That is the message of successful inner-city schools like Holy Angels school in Chicago, which provides what appears to be an unusually success-

33. Interview with Nat Hentoff (1982), quoted in L. M. Mead, *Beyond Entitlement* (New York: Free Press, 1986), 248-49.

34. Wilson, 14.

35. See, e.g., M. Rutter et al., *Fifteen Thousand Hours: Secondary Schools and Their Effects on Children* (Cambridge: Harvard Univ. Press, 1979), and P. Mortimore et al., *School Matters* (Berkeley: Univ. of California Press, 1988).

ful education to thirteen hundred black children,[36] and the celebrated Westside (Chicago) Preparatory School, founded by Marva Collins. What these and other all-black schools of demonstrated effectiveness have in common is a determination to maintain high expectations and to provide a disciplined though supportive environment for learning. The same was true of the experimental all-male class set up at Matthew Henson Elementary School in Baltimore during the 1990–1991 school year, with very encouraging results; though all the boys, and their teacher, were black, the emphasis was not on inculcating an "Afrocentric consciousness" but on mentoring, encouragement, and academic and social discipline.[37]

Families can also make a difference, as Reginald Clark illustrated in his moving account of poor black families in Chicago whose daily interactions with their children provided support and structure that led to success in school. "[I]t is the family members' *beliefs, activities,* and overall *cultural style,*" he found, "not the family units' composition or social status, that produces the requisite mental structures for effective and desirable behavior during classroom lessons."[38]

It remains true, however, that education is most likely to be effective when schools and families function in a mutually supportive fashion. Unfortunately, the linkages between families and schools have grown weaker in all sectors of society, leading to frequent complaints by teachers that their efforts are no longer supported adequately by the home. More than half of those surveyed in a recent poll, for example, responded that "strengthening parents' role in their children's education" should be the highest priority for public education policy.[39]

Coleman has argued that there is a general decline in parents' ability and willingness, in a postindustrial society, to provide a consistent structure of expectations and attitudes that will lead to success in school. Even parents whose "human capital" — educational level and income — has grown have a diminished "social capital" of legitimacy in the exercise of authority in relation to their children and of willingness simply to *pay attention* to their

36. P. H. Shields, "Holy Angels: Pocket of Excellence," *Journal of Negro Education* 58, no. 2 (1989).

37. D. Viadero, "Baltimore Class Tests Theory of Providing 'Positive Role Model' for Young Black Boys," *Education Week,* Feb. 13, 1991.

38. Clark, 1-2.

39. J. Richardson, "Teachers in Poll Seek Greater Federal Push for Parent Involvement," *Education Week,* May 19, 1993, 10.

children. The decline of residential communities and of the institutions of face-to-face socialization have placed a burden on schools that they cannot adequately bear. It is poor children who are most vulnerable to the effects of this loss, and who most urgently need the creation of new institutions beyond the nuclear family within which they can find both emotional safety and encouragement.[40]

Support cannot be provided effectively by bureaucratically structured institutions like human service agencies and public schools as now constituted. The authors of the influential book *Reinventing Government* suggested a way of classifying the functions that are now largely monopolized by government according to which of three "sectors" is best able to carry them out. Government itself, they write, is best at "policy management, regulation, ensuring equity, preventing discrimination or exploitation, ensuring continuity and stability of services, and ensuring social cohesion." Business is best at innovating and adapting to rapid change. It is what they call the "third sector" of voluntary, nonprofit organizations that is "best at performing tasks that generate little or no profit, demand compassion and commitment to individuals, require extensive trust on the part of customers or clients, needs hands-on, personal attention . . . and involve the enforcement of moral codes and individual responsibility for behavior."[41]

The strengths of "third sector" organizations are very much those called for by Coleman, who has similarly argued that schools outside the public sector that are freely chosen for their religious or pedagogical character are better able to set and enforce expectations that lead to achievement, especially for poor and vulnerable children, than are public schools enrolling pupils on the basis of residence. "Family background makes much less difference for achievement in Catholic schools than in public schools. This greater homogeneity of achievement in the Catholic sector (as well as the lesser racial and ethnic segregation of the Catholic sector) suggests that the ideal of the common school is more nearly met in the Catholic schools than in the public schools."[42]

40. J. S. Coleman, "Families and Schools," *Educational Researcher* 16, no. 6 (1987): 32-38.

41. D. Osborne and T. Gaebler, *Reinventing Government* (Reading, Mass.: Addison-Wesley, 1992), 45-46.

42. J. S. Coleman, "Quality and Equality in American Education: Public and Catholic Schools" (1981), reprinted in *Equality and Achievement in Education* (Boulder: Westview Press, 1990), 247.

This leads to his conclusion that "the strict separation of church and state, as practiced in America, has been harmful to the least advantaged and particularly harmful to children in the black community."[43] It is important that it become more feasible for new kinds of schools to be established that are based on shared beliefs about education and the formation of character, whether these have a religious basis or not, and whether the schools are operated by government or by "third sector" organizations. Such schools would, as Coleman suggests, provide a far more intensive and extensive environment for children than is possible for public schools as now constituted and staffed.

Schools characterized by a shared sense of purpose, a sort of educational covenant — schools that have been freely chosen by families — can help in turn to develop in families a sense of the significance of their own efforts. Schools can help families to act more effectively by operating as though what families — whatever their social class — do is significant. Poor parents, perhaps more than others, need to be given opportunities to make important decisions about the well-being of their children, within a framework of policy that ensures that, so far as possible, no educationally bad choices are made.[44]

A policy supporting parent choice of schools is one way in which government not only can validate the decision making of parents but also can make room within the educational system for differing views of what education is all about. Normative judgments are the essential stuff of successful family life and of successful education. They cannot be avoided. Neither should they be imposed by the state. That is why only a system of schooling based on family choice of schools would permit the uninhibited expression of particular angles on the truth within schools that have been freely chosen.

Unfortunately, among the loudest voices proclaiming the collapse of the family are those of educators and human service professionals who see this as an occasion for further expanding the role of their institutions. They should instead be asking to what extent these institutions — public schooling, public housing, the welfare system — have contributed to the loss of functions that has deprived family life of much of its traditional significance for family members.

43. Coleman, "Families and Schools."

44. Charles Glenn, "Letting Poor Parents Act Responsibly," *The Journal of Family and Culture* 2, no. 3 (1986).

The school can play an important role in restoring meaning to family life, and thus to helping families function more effectively, but only if we learn to think differently about the school's mission and indeed about what sort of institution it is. We must not continue to conceive of the school as an agent of government, serving the purposes of the wider society according to the principle that educational bureaucrats know best what is good for children, and of parents as a supporting cast whose collaboration is sought so long as they subordinate themselves to the professional definition of what is needful.

Of course there is a continuing role for professional expertise as well as for a societal concern for the schooling of each of its citizens, though the growing popularity of home schooling among parents who are themselves highly educated within the formal system suggests that the credibility of both educators and society at large has weakened considerably. What is needed to restore the appropriate balance is not an abdication on the part of teachers to the unassisted judgments of parents, but a more profound concept of the nature of educational expertise and how it should be put to work. Teachers who have reflected deeply about the common purposes of education and how they can best be pursued for pupils who are infinitely diverse will have no difficulty persuading parents to trust them to work in the best interests of their children. Teachers of this quality will have no need to drape themselves in the mantle of professional omniscience, nor to mystify the learning process so that parents can have no part in it.

Teachers who are truly educated themselves are essential, but such teachers will need to work — indeed, will consent to work only — in schools that are communities for learning rather than branch offices of a government bureaucracy.

School Autonomy and Effective Education

Bureaucracy is a necessary feature of life in a complex society, but it performs certain functions badly. Any social activity that requires initiative and the frequent exercise of judgment cannot be done well if it is constrained by bureaucratic rules intended to ensure fairness and impartiality through detailed prescription of the procedures to be followed under all circumstances. Teaching is a nonbureaucratic art, and bureaucratic regulation within large school systems has done profound damage to the ability and even the willingness of teachers to respond to individual needs and strengths. "The freer schools are from external control — the more autonomous, the less subject to bureaucratic constraints — the more likely they are to have effective organizations."[45]

The bureaucratic control of urban schooling does damage not only to what occurs in the classroom but also to the relationship between schools and the families they are intended to serve and to parents' ability to gain experience with association in the interest of their children. Tocqueville warned a century and a half ago:

> [W]hat political power could ever carry on the vast multitude of lesser undertakings which associations daily enable American citizens to control? . . . The more government takes the place of associations, the more will individuals lose the idea of forming associations and need the government to come to their help. That is a vicious circle of cause and effect. . . . The morals and intelligence of a democratic people would be in as much danger as its commerce and industry if ever a government wholly usurped the place of private associations. Feelings and ideas are renewed, the heart enlarged, and the understanding developed only by the reciprocal action of men one upon another.[46]

I was in a position to observe the great extension of government action in inner-city neighborhoods and its effect on the institutions that had long served a vital social role of maintaining "the morals and intelligence," the ability to work together and to confront and solve problems, of the people who lived in those areas. From 1961 to early 1966 I was a community organizer and minister in Boston's Roxbury section, from 1966 through 1968 I was the national Episcopal Church's staff member responsible for helping local church-related efforts to participate in the War on Poverty, from 1968 through 1970 (while earning my degree in educational administration) I was a community representative in Boston's Model Cities program, and in 1970 I became the education coordinator for Model Cities programs statewide, and then the state's official responsible for urban education for the next twenty years.

45. J. E. Chubb and T. M. Moe, *Politics, Markets and America's Schools* (Washington, D.C.: The Brookings Institution, 1990), 19, 187.

46. A. de Tocqueville, *Democracy in America*, ed. J. P. Mayer, trans. George Lawrence (New York: Harper & Row, 1988), 515.

One irony about the government efforts in which I participated is that they were launched with the intention of building on elements of community action that already existed, and with a mandate to include "the maximum feasible participation of the poor." In 1967 I conducted a study for the National Council of Churches of how "maximum feasible participation" was functioning in two hundred poor areas across the country, and found that it had generally had a profoundly distorting effect on the existing community structures. An army of "poverty hustlers" had come into existence, employing confrontational tactics to obtain large amounts of government and charitable funding for programs that produced very few lasting benefits. In the process, many neighborhood-based institutions that could not or would not adapt themselves to the new order were discredited if not swept away.

Part of the difficulty was that those who set policy for and administered the new government programs had very little respect for the ways in which the poor were already organizing their lives: through storefront churches and other institutions whose focus was on mutual support in the difficulties of life at the bottom, rather than on radical political change. The men and women exercising leadership in these organizations created by the poor themselves were usually morally conservative and cautious toward the structures of power; they were considered "Uncle Toms" and "Aunt Sallies" by the "poverty warriors."

> So the poverty professionals were always on the lookout for the bad-acting dudes who were the "real leaders," the "natural leaders," the "charismatic figures" in the ghetto jungle. . . . From the beginning the poverty program was aimed at helping ghetto people rise up against their oppressors. . . . It was no accident that Huey Newton and Bobby Seale drew up the ten-point program of the Black Panther Party one night in the offices of the North Oakland Poverty Center.[47]

An illustration of this almost comically perverse process of misrepresentation was perpetrated by the Boston Model Cities Program, which decided that parents in my racially mixed neighborhood should be "organized,"

47. From T. Wolfe's amusing *Radical Chic & Mau-mauing the Flak Catchers* (New York: Farrar, Straus and Giroux, 1970), 122, which captures the spirit of the times very well. J. L. Pressman and A. Wildavsky, *Implementation* (Berkeley: Univ. of California Press, 1973), gives a good account of the failure of an attempt at comprehensive renewal of Oakland.

and hired two young women with impeccable radical credentials to do the job. Since I represented the area on the citywide antipoverty board, they came to me for suggestions about what issues would most effectively dramatize the need for fundamental change. I suggested that they begin by helping the existing parent association of a local school to organize the upcoming spaghetti supper to raise funds for the school, as a way of becoming known and trusted by the active parents. They rejected the idea scornfully: those parents were precisely the compromising flunkies who must be swept away. Instead, the professional organizers put up posters all over the neighborhood announcing a rally to attack "educational genocide" against black pupils in the same, racially integrated, school. I was the only parent who attended their rally, but the traditional parent association's efforts to draw minority parents into school activities were severely hindered by the resulting climate of suspicion, and it soon disbanded. The would-be community organizers (themselves white) denounced the servile spirit of the black community for their failure to "heighten contradictions," and soon moved on.

Community Schools and the Revival of Civil Society

What we have been learning over these past decades of repeated failure to reverse the degradation of our inner cities is the importance and value of the ways in which people seek to manage their own lives. Sociologist Amitai Etzioni describes the importance of the institutions that, in the inner city, have largely been lost:

> Social institutions — the family, the school, neighborhoods, voluntary associations — serve to countervail excessive individualism, to sustain mutuality and civility in three ways:
>
> 1. They stand between the individual and the government, protecting each from the other.
>
> 2. They set patterns and make arrangements that discharge at least some of the tasks that otherwise are loaded on the government or overwhelm individuals.
>
> 3. They "educate" individuals. They introduce and reinforce a mentality that sustains individuals' mutual and civil commitments.[48]

48. A. Etzioni, *An Immodest Agenda* (New York: McGraw-Hill, 1984), 94.

The loss of these institutions produces a downward spiral, since they depend on each other for support. As community institutions are no longer capable of performing their socializing and supportive functions, individuals no longer develop the commitments and the social skills that in turn sustain institutions.

Bureaucratic organizations, as Tocqueville pointed out, cannot replace the social organizations that people create for themselves. This is not to suggest that government has no role, but that it should not be seeking to do what can better be done by nongovernmental organizations. This leaves government free to *govern*, to set the general rules that assure fairness and that protect the common interest. As *Reinventing Government* puts it, "governments . . . may no longer produce services, but they are still responsible for making sure needs are met. When governments abdicate this steering responsibility, disaster often follows. The massive deinstitutionalization of mental patients . . . was a perfect example."[49]

Government, which operates for the society as a whole, must articulate clear expectations and create procedural safeguards, and beyond that direct its efforts to encouraging a vigorous civil society, which is "the space of uncoerced human association and also the set of relational networks — formed for the sake of family, faith, interest, and ideology — that fill this space."[50] This is the sphere of life that has largely been squeezed out of inner-city residential areas.

The social integration of the inner-city welfare and working poor is an important object of public policy. It depends on the health of the social institutions with which they interact on a daily basis. Healthy institutions — schools, churches, associations of all kinds — will also help maintain the social-class mix whose loss, as Wilson has pointed out, is having such devastating effects. Inner-city areas are losing the stable working-class and lower-middle-class families whose leadership and resources are essential to those institutions. Improvement in the lives of the poor will therefore depend on making the areas where they live communities that can sustain social institutions. This will require, as Wilson puts it, "a massive effort to restabilize institutions and create a social and economic milieu necessary to sustain such institutions."[51]

49. Osborne and Gaebler, 73.

50. M. Walzer, "The Idea of Civil Society," *Dissent* 38 (1991): 293.

51. Wilson, 158.

There is ample evidence that inner-city parents are deeply concerned about the schooling of their children, and that this concern extends to both the quality of academic work and the climate and character of the school. They are more dissatisfied with the schools to which their children are assigned than are other parents, and more supportive of school-choice measures, including vouchers.[52] When given the opportunity, they are inclined to make use of alternative schools. Hundreds of community-based schools can be found in inner cities, though they lead a precarious existence in the absence of any form of public support. John Witte's careful evaluation of the voucher program in Milwaukee makes clear that, while by no means performing miracles, the nongovernment schools taking part are functioning reasonably well and involving parents far more intensively than did the public schools that their children previously attended.[53]

Discussion of how to create effective urban schools has, until recently, largely overlooked the quiet growth of alternatives to public schooling through initiatives in minority communities. While there was national debate over the decision by Detroit school authorities to create three schools designated for black pupils, the simultaneous creation of three "interfaith" schools serving the same population received little attention.[54]

The most widespread form by far of schools organized by minority communities is supplemental schools serving the children and grandchildren of immigrants. There were 4,893 "ethnic schools" identified in an American survey in the late 1970s, "maintained, by and large, by ethnic communities that are competently English-speaking" but for whom "language maintenance is viewed as a moral necessity." J. A. Fishman points out that the primary focus of these schools is not on foreign-born children who do not speak English, but on children born in this country whose first language is English but whose parents — themselves well acculturated — wish to maintain their ethnic connections. "The entry of Chicano, Puerto Rican and Native American children into such schools is a sign of their 'Americanization.'"[55]

52. Glenn, McLaughlin, and Salganik.

53. J. F. Witte, A. B. Bailey, and C. A. Thorn, "Third-year Report, Milwaukee Parental Choice Program," University of Wisconsin-Madison, Department of Political Science, and The Robert LaFollette Institute of Public Affairs, Dec. 1993.

54. See *Education Week*, Sept. 4, 1991.

55. J. A. Fishman, *Language and Ethnicity in Minority Sociolinguistic Perspective* (Clevedon, Avon, Eng.: Multilingual Matters, 1989), 454, 458.

The primary concerns expressed by ethnically self-conscious parents tend to be the values, the behaviors, and the religious beliefs and practices that they desire to be manifested in the education of their children. American experience demonstrates that immigrant groups can preserve their ethnic churches and associations, and through them express and pass on at least some elements of their traditions and values for several generations after abandoning the use of their original language. Turkish, Moroccan, and Pakistani parents in Western Europe who stress the teaching of Islam over that of their mother tongue exhibit a sound grasp of which elements of identity have power to resist acculturation. Establishing and maintaining a supplemental Koran school — so often deplored by ethnic elites and mainstream educators — may thus be perceived as the most important element of maintaining religious practice:

> For parents seeking legitimacy in relation to their children, it is invested with a role which they have not — or which they believe they have not — been able to play; it is up to the mosque to transmit the heritage which they believe is lost or in danger, at best, of disappearing, [and] to revive the values that are believed to be on deposit, to apply them literally in the first instance and then to bequeath them. Under this perspective, the need for a Koran school is the first need; it precedes and serves as the basis for the demand for places of prayer.[56]

The strategy is exactly that followed by Catholic immigrants to American cities a century ago, building their parochial schools before their churches. Similarly today, when the supplemental instruction organized by an ethnic community does not seem adequate to counter the effects of mandatory state schooling on their children's values and loyalties, immigrant parents may begin to demand separate full-time schools that place their own goals for education above or alongside those of the host society.

For example, some Asian immigrants in England have been arguing for the right to receive government support for separate schools based on Islam, parallel to the support given to Catholic and Protestant schools.[57]

56. D. El yazami, *Présence Musulmane et immigration, L'Immigration dans l'histoire nationale* (Paris: CEFISEM, 1988), 74.

57. J. Rex, "The Urban Sociology of Religion and Islam in Birmingham," in T. Gerholm and Y. G. Lithman, eds., *The New Islamic Presence in Western Europe* (London: Mansell, 1988), 213.

The leader of the group sponsoring the Islamia School pointed out that it was "mixed racially and has 23 nationalities"; the goal was not ethnic or linguistic preservation but religious expression.

Efforts to start such alternative schools are motivated by a growing conviction that no accommodation to Muslim beliefs and values is "feasible or indeed desirable within the existing system and in order to provide a true Islamic education for their children, it is necessary to provide Muslim [publicly funded] schools." As a government commission was told,

> a major worry for Muslim parents is the fact that their children soon begin to adopt English standards and ideas. . . . Islam is not something which can be learnt and adhered to overnight. It must be lived, breathed and fostered until it cannot be separated from life itself. Most Muslims acknowledge that Britain is a fair place to live, and in many ways they have come to depend upon it for their livelihood, but it is hard to judge how possible it is to live as a Muslim within the society as a whole.[58]

As of the 1994–95 school year, no Islamic schools had been granted public funds, but it was widely anticipated that the situation would change in the near future, given the commitment of the Conservative government to support parental choice of schools. The government's policy document, *Choice and Diversity: A New Framework for Schools* (July 1992), signaled this direction by including a provision to allow schools to "opt in" to the publicly funded system. This is expected to result eventually in public funding for Muslim as well as ultra-Orthodox Jewish and evangelical Christian schools, which have not been able to benefit from the arrangements under which more mainstream religious schools have long been supported by the government.[59]

The Dutch education system is based on a constitutional guarantee of

58. *Education for All: The Report of the Committee of Inquiry into the Education of Children from Ethnic Minority Groups* (the "Swann Report") (London: HMSO, 1985), 504.

59. Controversy broke out again in February 1995, with the rejection of an application for "voluntary aided status" (which is enjoyed by hundreds of Anglican and Roman Catholic and some Jewish schools) from an Islamic girls school in Bradford. The government insisted it had nothing against Islamic schools as such but that this school had management and structural deficiencies. Muslim leaders complained of a continuing pattern of unfair treatment. See N. Pyke, "Muslims Vow to Try Again," *Times Educational Supplement* (London), Feb. 24, 1995, p. 11.

the freedom to establish and obtain public funding for any school that is able to attract a sufficient number of pupils and meets other government requirements. However, authorities for some years did not encourage the use of this freedom for the operation of schools by ethnic and linguistic minority groups.[60] While recognizing that each group had a right "to live and give shape to their own identity," the government insisted that "in general there is no difference between minorities and the rest of the population."[61]

An earlier draft of the government policy had stressed that "if minorities mostly or exclusively call on values and/or interests that differ from those of the host society and set themselves apart from this society, that will lead to isolation. Members of the group can then be held back from actually orienting themselves to the surrounding society, at the cost of their chances within the society."[62] Although there was no question of the *right* of Hindu and Muslim groups to set up schools and — if enough parents selected these schools — to receive full public funding, local authorities were not eager to give their approval. The resistance reflected in large part the opposition of many Labor Party leaders — in control of the government of most cities, where immigrants are concentrated — to nonpublic schooling in general and to the teaching of religion within the framework of formal schooling. Despite the resistance of authorities, however, a publicly funded Islamic school was able to get off the ground with a hundred pupils in late 1988, and others have followed.

The worry of those supporting the Islamic (and Hindu) schools is with the *values* of Dutch society and thus of Dutch schools, and they seek to provide an alternative schooling that is more consistent with the beliefs of immigrant parents, while equipping pupils to participate fully in the Dutch economy. These communities are seeking to reinforce their ability to socialize their children in values with which they are comfortable, to protect and isolate them in some respects from the acids of modernity. The call for Hindu and Islamic schools is not related to ethnic nationalism or to a "myth of return," but to the universal desire of parents to have a major

60. H. B. Entzinger, *Het minderhedenbeleid* (Meppel, Netherlands: Boom, 1984), 116.

61. "Regeringsnota over het minderhedenbeleid," Tweede Kamer (The Hague), zitting 1982–83.

62. "Ontwerp-minderhedennota" (The Hague: Ministerie van Binnenlandse Zaken, 1981).

say in the raising of their children. The "positive scenario" for these schools is that

> this institutional segregation must lead later to societal integration. Through separate establishment schools can strengthen the cultural distinctiveness and self-worth of pupils. The schools make pupils conscious of their culture and their position in The Netherlands. . . . As their identity is strengthened, they will be better able — as individuals and as a group — to protect themselves from domination and discrimination. More [Islamic] schools should therefore be established. Self-organization can contribute to a considerable extent to the maintenance of culture and to better school achievement.[63]

The new schools in the Netherlands are *Islamic* rather than Turkish or Moroccan. Even though all the pupils might turn out to be of one ethnic origin, Dutch educational policy would not allow a school to be established on that basis. Religion, by contrast, is a privileged basis for school selection, since it enjoys protection as a right of conscience.[64]

The rejection of mainstream education has been emphatic in certain African-American circles in the United States, where it is asserted that the extreme social distress of the black underclass is directly related to public schooling. In the words of one advocate, "the educational system and socialization process devised by this dominant culture has proven to be dysfunctional and genocidal to the African American community."[65]

A study in 1991 identified 284 "independent neighborhood schools," most of which enrolled predominantly or exclusively black pupils. Altogether this represented more than 50,000 students, compared with some 6.7 million black pupils attending public schools. The largest number of black pupils outside the public system — some 220,000 — are in Catholic schools, including schools in the South founded long ago to serve the

63. J. Teunissen, "Basisscholen op islamitische en hindoeïstische grondslag," *Migrantenstudies* 6, no. 2 (1990): 54.

64. J. Rath, K. Groenendijk, and R. Penninx, "Nederland en de islam. Een programma van onderzoek," *Migrantenstudies* 8, no. 1 (1992): 32.

65. N. Warfield-Coppock, "The Rites of Passage Movement: A Resurgence of African-Centered Practices for Socializing African American Youth," *Journal of Negro Education* 61, no. 4 (1992): 471.

children of freed slaves, and schools in northern urban neighborhoods abandoned by white ethnic Catholics. Upwardly mobile black families living in these areas frequently choose a Catholic school as "a functional alternative . . . for quality suburban schools"; 53 percent of the black pupils in heavily minority Catholic schools, one study found, were not Catholics.[66] Considerable interest has been shown recently in indications that these schools may be particularly effective in educating pupils who would otherwise be at risk of academic and social failure.[67]

Muslim education in the United States has developed completely outside the publicly supported sector, making perhaps its first appearance in the unorthodox form of the "Black Muslim" schools started by Elijah Muhammad's movement in Detroit and Chicago in the early 1930s. Since the mid-1970s, thirty-eight of the schools associated with this movement have become orthodox Muslim schools known as Sister Clara Muhammad Schools, with much less stress on rejection of the majority society (and race) and much more on Islamic teaching.[68]

The Council of Independent Black Institutions represents about thirty schools across the United States that subscribe to various aspects of an Afrocentric curriculum, including the "Nguzo Saba," or "Seven Principles of Blackness," formulated by Karenga in the 1960s. The purpose of this approach has been described by one principal as "to improve the self-esteem, self-worth and self-confidence of the [black] child so he will have the coping skills necessary to merge into the broader pluralistic society and to deal with racism and some of the things he will confront as a Black man."[69]

The emphasis of these schools is not on educating children to live apart from American society (as might be the goal of Hasidic or Amish

66. J. G. Cibulka, T. J. O'Brien, and D. Zewe, *Inner-City Private Elementary Schools: A Study* (Milwaukee: Marquette Univ. Press, 1982), 47.

67. P. L. Benson et al., *Catholic High Schools: Their Impact on Low-income Students* (Washington, D.C.: National Catholic Education Association, 1986); J. S. Coleman and T. Hoffer, *Public and Private High Schools: The Impact of Communities* (New York: Basic Books, 1987).

68. H. M. Rashid and Z. Muhammad, "The Sister Clara Muhammad Schools: Pioneers in the Development of Islamic Education in America," *Journal of Negro Education* 61, no. 2 (1992): 178-85.

69. K. Holt, quoted in K. Lomotey, "Independent Black Institutions: African-Centered Education Models," *Journal of Negro Education* 61, no. 4 (1992): 461.

schooling), but to equip them to contend successfully with the pressures of life in the society as a person of color. Parents of children in black independent schools interviewed in one survey "indicated that they utilized the schools to 'buy time' for their children in settings that allowed them to develop as free as possible from the limitations imposed by racism."[70]

Although "Afrocentric transformation" — defined as struggling "to define social reality with Africa at the center" of consciousness — may be the goal of some of the founders of black independent schools, it appears that the motivation of parents in paying tuition and sending their children has more to do with concerns about the deficiencies of public schooling. A survey of black parents with children in thirty-six independent schools in the Washington, D.C., area found that "lack of Afrocentric curriculum" ranked twenty-first out of twenty-four factors in their rejection of public schools, while "lack of discipline" and "poor standards" ranked first and second.[71] There are some indications, indeed, that pupils in black independent schools *do* achieve above national norms.[72] Most black independent schools focus more on academic achievement and a supportive environment than on recovering an African heritage, though it is the latter agenda that has inspired policy debate and efforts to create racially separate public schools.

A number of Protestant schools have been started by black churches in Los Angeles, Kansas City, Detroit, Milwaukee, Boston, and other cities. In these schools, the emphasis is much less on Afrocentric elements and much more on the failure of public schools to provide the moral and religious instruction that the parents who choose these schools want for their children. It is thus not the "Eurocentric" nature of public schools so much as their pervasive secularism and moral incoherence that give impetus to these schools.

Government itself should not lend its authority to one or another of these perspectives. An Afrocentric *public* school is as inappropriate as would be a Catholic or a Baptist *public* school. The government should be respect-

70. M. J. Shujaa, "Afrocentric Transformation and Parental Choice in African American Independent Schools," *Journal of Negro Education* 61, no. 2 (1992): 154.

71. F. C. Jones-Wilson, N. L. Arnez, and C. A. Asbury, "Why Not Public Schools?" *Journal of Negro Education* 61, no. 2 (1992): 131.

72. J. D. Ratteray, "Independent Neighborhood Schools: A Framework for the Education of African Americans," *Journal of Negro Education* 61, no. 2 (1992): 143-46.

ful toward all perspectives to the extent that they merit respect, but partial toward none — not even the secularism or "indifferentism" that characterizes too many public schools. Achieving this balance is of course a matter of enormous difficulty, which cannot be discussed here.

Since schooling based on clearly defined perspectives is likely to be more efficacious than schooling that must scrupulously preserve its neutrality, there is a strong case for encouraging alternatives outside the present public system. The desire of some educators and some parents for an Afrocentric curriculum, for example, could most appropriately be accommodated through providing funding to whatever school the parents freely select for their children, rather than through abandoning the perspectival neutrality of the common public school.

To the extent that some Latino parents wish to entrust their children to schools in which Spanish is a language of instruction and there is a strong emphasis on the cultures of Latin America, a scrupulous concern for liberty suggests that they should be able to choose nontransitional bilingual education without forfeiting the right to free education for their children. So long as government makes education compulsory, it must be free; but education that does not correspond to what parents consider fitting for their children is in no sense free. The parent must pay either the cost of tuition or the cost of a violated conscience. As legal scholar John Coons has argued,

> The right to form families and to determine the scope of their children's practical liberty is for most men and women the primary occasion for choice and responsibility. One does not have to be rich or well placed to experience the family. The opportunity over a span of fifteen or twenty years to attempt the transmission of one's deepest values to a beloved child provides a unique arena for the creative impulse. Here is the communication of ideas in its most elemental mode. Parental expression, for all its invisibility to the media, is an activity with profound First Amendment implications.[73]

There is indeed no principled reason *not* to respect the right of parents to make decisions about the schooling their children will receive, and to allow the public funds for education to follow those choices, within a

73. Coons, 511.

framework of policy that assures the adequacy of schools eligible for funding and that protects the interests of minority, poor, and otherwise vulnerable children. There is a fundamental difference between what government may legitimately teach in its own schools and what it may allow parents to choose for their children, without forfeiting a free education; the first is an establishment question, the second a question of the free exercise of conscience.

Who is making the argument for deliberately separate schools? This goes to the issue of legitimacy. Is it appropriate for the politicians and government officials of the host society to decide, on behalf of racial- or language-minority children, that they are better off if schooled separately from the majority, in order to preserve their home language and ethnic identity? Surely not! Nor are progressive academics or well-assimilated ethnic elites qualified to make that decision.

No, the only ones who can legitimately — and effectively — decide whether minority-language children and youth will maintain and develop the culture and perhaps the language of their ancestors are those children and youth themselves, along with their parents acting on their behalf. Many minority-group parents may choose and indeed make great sacrifices to assure that their children receive a separate education in the interest of continuity with the parents' own identity, beliefs, and values. There is growing evidence, in Western Europe and in other Western democracies, that "countermodernization" is in full career in reaction to the high price exacted by modernity on personal satisfactions and family life, and that one of the forms it takes is the desire by parents — especially those culturally on the margins of society — to exercise more control over the education of their children.

These parents appear determined not to accept the entire package that contemporary society offers, but to enable their children to pick and choose those elements of tradition and of modernity that will represent their own act of cultural creativity. Who can say that they are wrong? On the other hand, it is not the function of government to maintain minority cultures, any more than it is its proper role to impose the majority culture through a monopoly system of compulsory schooling.

Summing Up

If it is an important goal of social policy to reduce the alienation and marginalization of minority communities and to create opportunities for inner-city families to function effectively in support of their children, a good place to start would be with the institutions that these communities themselves create and sustain. Despite the process of middle-class exodus described by Wilson in *The Truly Disadvantaged,* there continue to be thousands of functioning social institutions in America's inner cities, and these are continually developing new leadership through their complex organizational life. Churches are of course the most common, but as we have seen, schools are not far behind when circumstances permit.

Churches are relatively inexpensive institutions to operate, especially if (as is common in the inner city) the pastor earns most of his or her income from a secular occupation. Schools are far more expensive, since they require the presence of teachers and others all day, every day; to be effective in an inner-city environment, they also need to provide a variety of support services and extended-day programs that add to the expense. It is not surprising that inner-city independent schools exist from hand to mouth, and many fail to survive despite the devotion of those who teach and send their children.

What is required is a shift in public policy that would provide support to those nongovernment schools that provide an effective education to poor children, and that would do so in a manner that strengthens the latent ability of parents and others to "take care of business." Why not establish policies that make schools more like the associations that people organize for themselves?

J. S. Coleman and T. Hoffer have suggested, along these lines, that "policies which would bring about expansion of choice should contain provisions that encourage the growth of social structures that can provide the social capital important to a school. Policies . . . that would facilitate the creation of schools by institutions in which parents of prospective students are already involved exemplify this."[74] Schools started by inner-city churches, by neighborhood associations, by organizations based on a common homeland (the Trinidad and Tobago Association or the League of Haitian Families) could provide a reason for cooperation over time and an

74. Coleman and Hoffer, 243.

opportunity to develop trust and the habit of being trustworthy. It is in the nature of schools that they are *daily* and thus promote continued involvement; the educational process is face-to-face and lends itself to developing habits of cooperation.

This is not the place to describe the framework of public policies that would provide a balance between school-level autonomy and the common needs of the society, between free initiative and public accountability.[75] But here are key elements of an appropriate framework:

- Inclusion of all schools and all parents, with effective parent information and counseling about the choices available.
- A simple process of starting new public and nonpublic schools, as in the charter school provisions included in recent American education reform legislation and in the new Russian education statute.
- Start-up loans available to new school associations that can demonstrate commitment from the parents of a sufficient number of prospective pupils.
- Protections for teachers so that they may enjoy the benefits now offered by union membership without the associated rigidities of seniority, negotiated terms of work, etc.
- Definition of expected outcomes and a process for periodic assessment of how much each school has benefited its pupils, with consequences for performance too far below that of comparable schools.

The most appropriate vehicle for creating new schools and for holding schools accountable to society as well as to parents is what is commonly referred to as a school "charter." In order to obtain public funding, those planning or operating schools would be required to define, in a legally binding document, what the character and mission of the school is, how it will operate, and how it will be accountable for results. The charter should serve three important functions: (1) as an occasion for those directly concerned with the individual school to become clear about the mission of the school and how it will function in carrying out that mission, (2) as an instrument for accountability to be used by government on behalf of society

75. See Charles Glenn, "Controlled Choice in Massachusetts Public Schools," *The Public Interest,* no. 103 (1991), and J. E. Coons and S. D. Sugarman, *Scholarships for Children* (Berkeley: Institute of Governmental Studies Press, 1992).

to assure that each school is making an appropriate contribution to the schooling of citizens, and (3) as a barrier to arbitrary, officious, or untimely interference by government in the operation of a school. The charter is thus intended as a guarantee of both independence and accountability.

Use of charters not only would provide a method for the recognition and appropriate regulation of nongovernment schools, but also could be adapted to allow public schools to become more authentically self-directing than do the various "school-based management" schemes. It is for this reason that American education reformers have been promoting the same idea vigorously, and it has now been incorporated into the laws of half a dozen states, including Massachusetts, California, Georgia, and Minnesota.[76]

Self-governing schools, with charters that make learning objectives explicit and that are accountable to parents, could function as communities for learning in which teachers, parents, and pupils share an animating sense of purpose. Schools flourish only on the basis of free choice by those who work in them and by those who entrust children to them, since, as Coleman points out, "the conception of a child assigned by the state to a particular school is a conception that was viable when the school was an outgrowth of a homogeneous community. It is not viable for most schools today."[77] The authentic contemporary form of Horace Mann's "common school" is a school that has been chosen by parents and teachers who are committed to working together.

This is not to suggest that the "disconnected poor," the "underclass," or the "truly disadvantaged" are poised and ready to create and operate their own institutions through a spontaneous process worthy of a Frank Capra film. Such a romantic notion ignores the profound impact of social disorganization and the mistrust and fear that prevail in many inner-city neighborhoods. It is to insist, however, that a start be made in reviving urban communities by making it much easier for parents, teachers, and community institutions like churches to establish and maintain schools that

76. As part of the federally funded activities of the National Research Center on Families, Communities, Schools and Children's Learning, we are making a comparative analysis of the various provisions for charter schools in state laws and reform proposals. The preliminary report is Abby R. Weiss, "Variations on a Trend in Public Education," *New Schools, New Communities* 11, no. 1 (1994): 10-20.

77. Coleman, "The Family, the Community," 181.

will not only respond to the needs of children but also serve to develop new habits of cooperation and problem solving among adults.

It may be that the most difficult challenge would be to persuade the social policy establishment, with its deeply rooted opposition to "vouchers" for schooling, to accept public funding for schools that are not under direct government control. Over the past several years the liberal *Boston Globe* has carried several very positive articles about newly established inner-city Catholic middle schools — Nativity Prep for boys and Mother Caroline Academy for girls — that by all accounts are doing a remarkable job with pupils who have not been well served by the public schools. Characteristically, however, the paper continues its unwavering opposition to any public support for such schools.

There are two parts to the revival of urban communities, as there are to making a garden. One is pulling out the weeds, reducing social disorder; the other is creating a fertile soil for the growth of the associational life that sustains social order.

Inner-city public schools do not now generally play a positive role in this garden making. On the one hand, they are perceived (not always fairly) as places of disorder, unable to bring their weeds under control, while on the other they offer a harsh and sterile soil for the growth of cooperation and mutual trust. Schools typically function in a bureaucratic fashion, which increases the alienation of poor parents and children. Public schools do not belong to the communities that they serve; families are *members* of inner-city churches, but they are *clients* of inner-city public schools — all the difference in the world.

Schools that truly belong to the parents who send their children provide settings of unparalleled intensity for development of the habits of responsible activity on the part of adults and children alike. Accepting the promotion of such schools as an appropriate goal of public policy would be consistent with other "reinventing government" measures such as tenant management and ownership of housing developments. It would by no means be a magic remedy for the ills caused by social disorder and weakened families, but it would create the framework within which healing could begin.

Overcoming Poverty: The Role of Religiously Based Nonprofit Organizations[1]

Stephen V. Monsma

THE POOR are indeed still with us. Thirty-four million Americans — 15 percent of the population — live below the official poverty line.[2] The figures are even worse for certain groupings within the general population. Of the children below eighteen years of age, 21 percent, or one in five, live in poverty. An appalling 47 percent of African-American children below eighteen years of age are poor; 40 percent of Hispanic children are poor.

Less certain are the causes of poverty. Some locate the primary cause in conditions and circumstances outside the poor themselves, such as racial or gender discrimination, bad schools, and shifts in the job market. Others locate the primary cause of poverty in attitudes and behaviors of the poor themselves, such as unrealistic expectations, noncompletion of school, drug abuse, and a failure to take responsibility for their own decisions. I will not attempt to resolve that issue in this chapter. Both types of factors no doubt play an important role.

1. I would like to thank Pepperdine University for a university research grant and a sabbatical leave during the 1993–94 academic year and Calvin College's Center for Christian Scholarship for an appointment as a visiting scholar during the 1993–94 academic year. This chapter was made possible by their assistance. Some brief sections of this chapter were first published in my "The Mixing of Church and State: Religious Nonprofit Organizations and Public Money," Calvin Center for Christian Scholarship pamphlet, no. 1 (1994).

2. This statistic and the following ones are from U.S. Bureau of the Census, *Statistical Abstract of the United States: 1994* (Washington, D.C.: GPO, 1994), 475-76.

The extent to which poverty arises from circumstances outside the poor or from their own self-limiting attitudes and behaviors should not qualify the love and concern Christians should demonstrate toward the poor. The poor are image bearers of God and as such possess a human worth and dignity that should command our love, concern, and respect. Further, self-defeating attitudes and behaviors often find their origins in conditions over which a poor person has had no control, such as abuse and neglect as a young child; the insecurity of an unstable, single-parent family while growing up; or an environment steeped in drugs, sex, and violence. Only God knows the horrors some children experience. "There but for the grace of God go I" is the appropriate response.

If the Christian community, which is part of a broader political community, is to live out love and concern for the poor, it must take into account both the structural aspects and the attitudinal and behavioral components of poverty. To do otherwise would be to ignore basic facts and ultimately misserve the poor themselves.

The typical liberal response to poverty of putting more money into the hands of the poor by way of direct subsidies and grants and trying to change societywide structures such as discriminatory practices or economic dislocations is flawed. This approach does not take into account the self-limiting attitudes and behaviors of the poor themselves. But the typical conservative response of simply cutting back on, or even eliminating, whole antipoverty programs is equally flawed, since it deals only indirectly with attitudes and behaviors and not at all with social and economic barriers. Michael Novak is surely on the right path when he writes:

> What we are seeking is a *new way.* Between the excessive individual laissez-faire and the excessive collectivism of social democracy, there remains to be discovered a new "third way" — a welfare *society* whose pivot is less the state than the civil society; and in which the state's method of operation is *indirect* by way of strengthening civil society, rather than direct by way of repressing it.[3]

I believe three basic principles or approaches need to be incorporated into any attempts to deal with poverty in the United States, if we are to rise

3. Michael Novak, "The Crisis of the Welfare State," *Crisis,* July–Aug. 1993, 6. Emphases in the original.

above the standard liberal and conservative remedies and begin to realize a new "third way." One is to insist that the poor who receive help incur certain obligations. On the basis of public justice the poor have a right to expect — and even demand — certain supports and help from the broader society, but society has a right to demand that in turn the poor live up to certain obligations. As Lawrence Mead has been writing for some time, help for the poor must be a reciprocal relationship, not a one-way street.[4] For example, it is entirely appropriate to require that recipients of AFDC funds, as a condition of receiving their grants, attend certain job-search or basic-education classes, or, if they are minors, live with their parents and complete high school.

A second basic element of any antipoverty program must be a strong preventive component. Those who complete high school and do not have children out of wedlock are unlikely to be poor. Thus programs to strengthen the family and other supportive networks and to encourage young people to complete high school and to develop responsible sexual attitudes and practices should be high on any list of antipoverty programs. In the long run — and even in the not-so-long run — the largest gains in fighting poverty are probably to be found here and in other preventive programs.

The third crucial aspect of an effective antipoverty program is working with the poor on a personal, individual level to solve problems and supply the help needed. Sometimes the problems and needs may be physical in nature, such as child care or transportation to enable one to take advantage of available employment opportunities. But often the needs are psychological in nature, such as encouragement when one suffers a bad day, or peer pressure to supply motivations that otherwise would be lacking.

Large, centralized public bureaucracies are poorly suited to achieve all three of these facets of an effective antipoverty program. Large bureaucracies do some things well. When the task is getting out large numbers of checks to eligible recipients by a set date bureaucracies can perform marvelously. They use ID numbers, computerized lists, uniform rules, and standardized forms in order to determine eligibility, process the paperwork, and clear up any glitches that develop.

The very nature of modern bureaucracies that makes them effective for some tasks, however, leaves them without the flexibility and creativity

4. See Lawrence Mead, *Beyond Entitlement: The Social Obligations of Citizenship* (New York: Free Press, 1986).

needed for other tasks. Bureaucracy, by its very nature, lacks the adaptability needed to relate to persons as individuals and to make decisions based on individual circumstances. Equally important, large government bureaucracies are not structured to build on and make the best use of support structures that may be present in poor persons' environments. Modern bureaucracies tend to ignore family structures, neighborhood and church groups, and informal networks of friends. Instead, they usually supplant them, creating their own centralized, standardized structures. The nature of modern bureaucracies means they are singularly ineffective at encouraging a youngster to stay in school, or upholding a young father struggling to support his family with a low-paying, menial job, or working with a young single mother with such low self-esteem that she is a pushover for any irresponsible man who comes along offering a little attention. When dealing with the problems typically related to poverty, what is needed is a more personalized, individualized approach that takes advantage of already existing structures and strengths in a person's environment. New approaches to solving the problem of poverty and new structures to carry out those approaches are needed.

This is where the nonprofit sector, and especially religiously based nonprofit institutions and agencies, has the potential to play an important role. What government with its large centralized bureaucracies is ill suited to do, nonprofit organizations are well suited to do. They have the flexibility, the community and neighborhood roots, and often the religious and moral authority needed to relate personally to those in need and to work with existing structures, building on them instead of supplanting them.

Marvin Olasky has made the point that prior to the twentieth century society's primary antipoverty tool consisted of private, nonprofit — usually religiously based — agencies and institutions.[5] He makes a strong case that they were able to tailor help to the needs of specific individuals and to combine compassion with the expectation of changed behavior in a way that today's large government agencies cannot do. In today's highly mobile, urbanized, and often anonymous society it is impossible simply to return to such a system, yet I am convinced that it is possible to capture many of the advantages of the nineteenth-century approach to poverty by developing a partnership between government and the nonprofit sector. Nonprofit

5. Marvin Olasky, *The Tragedy of American Compassion* (Washington, D.C.: Regnery Gateway, 1992).

agencies — rooted in churches, synagogues, temples, mosques, neighborhoods, and ethnic communities — constitute a resource in fighting poverty whose potential is not being fully tapped. A partnership between them and government constitutes a "third way" with great potential for overcoming much of today's persistent poverty and social distress.

In this chapter I first consider more fully the nature of nonprofit organizations and why they — and especially religiously based nonprofit organizations — have an enormous potential to play a vital role in the struggle to overcome poverty. The next two sections consider several key legal principles developed by the Supreme Court that keep religious nonprofits from realizing their full potential in a government-nonprofit partnership. The final section suggests a new principle that would enable religious nonprofits to be full partners with government in helping the poor overcome poverty.

The Nonprofit Sector

Four characteristics of the nonprofit sector are important to note in order to understand its potential for preventing and overcoming poverty. The first is the sheer number and pervasiveness of nonprofit associations. All the evidence indicates that they constitute one of the fastest growing, most dynamic sectors in society. There were approximately 1.4 million nonprofit associations in the United States in 1992, up 27 percent from 1977.[6] Their total income was estimated in 1990 to be $316 billion — a 336 percent increase from their total income of $94 billion in 1977.[7] Over 11 percent of the American workforce, or 16 million persons, works in the nonprofit sector.[8] In education, 24 percent of all elementary and secondary schools are private, nonprofit schools, enrolling 11 percent of all students.[9] The

6. Virginia Ann Hodgkinson, Murray S. Weitzman, Christopher M. Toppe, and Stephen M. Noga, *Nonprofit Almanac, 1992–1993* (San Francisco: Jossey-Bass, 1992), 16, 23. On the size and significance of the nonprofit sector also see Gabriel Rudney, "The Scope and Dimensions of Nonprofit Activity," in Walter W. Powell, ed., *The Nonprofit Sector* (New Haven: Yale Univ. Press, 1987), 55-64.

7. Hodgkinson et al., 26-27.

8. Hodgkinson et al., 28-29.

9. Lester M. Salamon, *America's Nonprofit Sector* (New York: The Foundation Center, 1992), 76, 73.

social service field is dominated by nonprofit agencies. Some 74 percent of all social service revenues go to nonprofit agencies, and nonprofits employ 58 percent of the workers in the social service field.[10] Michael O'Neill has noted, "Nonprofits employ more civilians than the federal government and the fifty state governments combined. The yearly budget of the American nonprofit sector exceeds the budgets of all but seven nations in the world."[11]

A second key characteristic of the nonprofit sector is that it is often used by the various governments of the United States — national, state, and local — to accomplish their public policy objectives. Governments often fund the programs and activities of nonprofit organizations rather than create their own offices to provide services directly. Lester Salamon has concluded that "government has tended to turn to nonprofit providers to help deliver publicly funded services — in health, education, and social services. . . . Although government provides most of the funds in many of the key social welfare fields, private institutions deliver most of the services."[12] Nonprofit organizations receive approximately 31 percent of their income from government sources, and in the social service field that figure climbs to 42 percent.[13]

This pattern of government achieving public policy objectives by funding private, nonprofit organizations and of private, nonprofit organizations looking to government as a major source of funds has led various observers to coin terms such as the "third sector," the "third America," and "third party government" to refer to the nonprofit sector.[14] All of these terms suggest the need to think of more than just a public sector and a private sector. There is a third reality not accounted for by the public-private bifurcation. The nonprofit sector is neither wholly private nor wholly public, but instead is marked by nonpublic institutions and agencies that perform public services and sometimes receive large amounts of government funding.

10. Salamon, *America's Nonprofit Sector,* 82-83.

11. Michael O'Neill, *The Third America: The Emergence of the Nonprofit Sector in the United States* (San Francisco: Jossey-Bass, 1989), 1-2.

12. Salamon, *America's Nonprofit Sector,* 105.

13. Salamon, *America's Nonprofit Sector,* 26-27.

14. See David Osborne and Ted Gaebler, *Reinventing Government* (New York: Penguin Books, 1992); O'Neill; Lester M. Salamon, "Rethinking Public Management: Third-Party Government and the Changing Forms of Government Action," *Public Policy,* 29 (1981): 255-75.

A third key characteristic of the nonprofit sector is that many nonprofit institutions and agencies have strong religious roots. Historically, religiously motivated and religiously based organizations have played a vital role in many areas of public service.[15] Typically, religiously based nonprofit organizations have led the way in seeking to meet social needs. Secular nonprofit organizations and government then followed suit. Michael O'Neill, in a chapter revealingly entitled "Religion: Godmother of the Nonprofit Sector," concludes the following:

> Religion is a large and important part of the nonprofit sector and has given birth to many other nonprofit institutions: health, education, social service, international assistance, advocacy, mutual assistance, and even some cultural and grantmaking organizations. Directly and indirectly, religion has been the major formative influence on America's independent sector.[16]

The twin facts that the nonprofit sector receives large amounts of government funds and that many nonprofit organizations have a religious nature produce the surprising result that many religiously based organizations receive large amounts of government funds, just as their secular counterparts do. As Steven Smith and Michael Lipsky note, "Even sectarian organizations receive substantial amounts of government funding. Catholic Charities U.S.A. estimates that 44 percent of affiliate agency revenues in fiscal year 1988 were from government."[17]

In addition to the large number of nonprofit agencies, their receipt of public funds, and the religious nature of many of them, it is helpful to note, in the fourth place, the evidence that many of them are doing an exceptionally effective job in their endeavors, especially in working with persons from disadvantaged backgrounds. The evidence continues to accumulate that Catholic inner-city schools are doing a better job of teaching young people than are their public-school counterparts.[18] "The achieve-

15. For excellent historical summaries see O'Neill, ch. 2, and Peter Dobkin Hall, "A Historical Overview of the Private Nonprofit Sector," in Powell, 3-26.

16. O'Neill, 20.

17. Steven Rathgeb Smith and Michael Lipsky, *Nonprofits for Hire: The Welfare State in the Age of Contracting* (Cambridge: Harvard Univ. Press, 1993), 8-9.

18. See James S. Coleman, Thomas Hoffer, and Sally Kilgore, *High School Achievement: Public, Catholic, and Private Schools Compared* (New York: Basic Books, 1982);

ment growth benefits of Catholic school attendance are especially strong for students who are in one way or another disadvantaged: lower socio-economic status, black, or Hispanic," according to James Coleman and Thomas Hoffer.[19] John Chubb and Terry Moe report: "Private schools serving poorer children seem to be doing a better and more equal job of promoting academic achievement than public schools serving comparable children."[20]

Another striking instance of success is a Michigan program that helps abused and neglected children. Rather than removing the children from their homes and placing them in foster care, this program works intensively with the parents, identifying and helping to find solutions to the problems that have overwhelmed them. Thus far the program has achieved greater success at less cost than the traditional approach. The director reports that a key to its success is the state's practice of contracting with private child service agencies to run the program instead of relying on state employees. Many of the private, nonprofit agencies taking part in this program are religious in nature.[21]

Referring to a church-based program offering support to recovering drug addicts, one Louisiana judge has declared, "I very much desperately need some place to send drug offenders. The church programs work better than any other programs."[22] Although few systematic studies have been done outside K-12 education, countless instances of success stories of religiously based social service programs could be cited.

The reasons for the success nonprofits have often experienced in dealing with seemingly intractable social problems is, I suspect, threefold. One reason is their greater flexibility. Government agencies are typically

---

James S. Coleman and Thomas Hoffer, *Public and Private High Schools* (New York: Basic Books, 1987); and John E. Chubb and Terry M. Moe, "Politics, Markets, and Equality in Schools" (paper given at the annual meeting of the American Political Science Association, Sept. 1992).

19. Coleman and Hoffer, 196.

20. Chubb and Moe, 27.

21. Cilia W. Dugger, "New York Studies Detroit Model on Avoiding Foster Care," *New York Times,* July 27, 1991, pp. 25, 27; Harold Gazan, deputy director for child and family services, Michigan Department of Social Service, interview with author, Mar. 5, 1994.

22. Judge Bob Downing, quoted in American Alliance for Rights and Responsibilities, *Re: Rights and Responsibilities* (Nov. 1994), 3.

very large, with rigid civil service rules governing hiring, firing, promotion, work schedules, and work assignments. Civil service employees increasingly are unionized, and union contracts further reduce the flexibility of state agencies. In addition, any attempt at new approaches carries with it serious, statewide consequences and potential political embarrassments. Meanwhile, nonprofits are not under civil service rules, and typically are not unionized. Because they are small, they can be used to demonstrate two or three different approaches simultaneously in different parts of the state or even in the same community.

A second advantage nonprofits have is a sense of dedication or commitment to a cause that is hard to maintain in large government bureaucracies. Many persons work in nonprofit agencies for less money than they could earn either in similar public agencies or in for-profit organizations. They put in longer hours for less pay because they care about people and approach their work as a mission. This is especially true in religiously based nonprofits. Down through the centuries many deeply religious persons have sought to live out the biblical injunction to feed the hungry and care for the needy by dedicating their lives to religiously based schools, hospitals, hospices, shelters for battered women, homeless shelters, and countless other agencies of mercy and caring.

A third advantage of religiously based nonprofits is their ability to speak the language of morality and of religious or ethnic solidarity. Nonprofit organizations based on shared religious or ethnic traditions can call upon vital resources in their attempts to change human behavior that no government agency could ever have at its disposal.

David Osborne and Ted Gaebler, in their best-selling book *Reinventing Government,* tied all three of these characteristics of the nonprofit sector together with these words:

> The third sector tends to be best at performing tasks that generate little or no profit, demand compassion and commitment to individuals, require extensive trust on the part of customers or clients, need hands-on, personal attention . . . and involve the enforcement of moral codes and individual responsibility for behavior.[23]

Judging from these arguments and evidence, it would appear that a government-nonprofit partnership is an obvious choice in overcoming

23. Osborne and Gaebler, 46; cf. 346.

poverty. All that is needed, it would seem, is a deepening and widening of a pattern that is already in existence. Unfortunately, all is not well. Due to certain legal interpretations, there are significant limitations and restrictions on the use of religiously based nonprofit organizations to fight poverty. Until these interpretations are modified, religiously based nonprofit organizations will not be able to play the full role they are potentially capable of playing in preventing and overcoming poverty, to the detriment of the nonprofits, the poor, and society.

Three Key Legal Principles

The Supreme Court, in dozens of decisions stretching over fifty years, has established three basic principles relevant to a consideration of public funds and the role of religiously based nonprofit organizations. It is necessary to understand these principles to understand the existing barriers that confront the nonprofit sector in meeting the needs of the poor.

The first principle is that of *no aid to religion.* In a crucial 1947 decision, *Everson v. Board of Education,* the Supreme Court ruled that no government aid may be given in support of religion, either to one religious group or to religion generally. In an often quoted passage, Justice Hugo Black, writing for the Court majority, stated, "The 'establishment of religion' clause of the First Amendment means at least this: Neither a state nor the Federal Government can set up a church. Neither can pass laws which aid one religion, *aid all religions,* or prefer one religion over another."[24] A few sentences later Black added, "In the words of Jefferson, the clause against establishment of religion by law was intended to erect 'a wall of separation between church and State.'"[25] With those words the Supreme Court adopted the legal doctrine of no aid to religion. It is under this principle that the Court has disallowed almost all forms of aid to nonpublic, religiously based K-12 schools. Allowing aid would, it has ruled, "foster an impermissible degree of entanglement [of church and state],"[26] "have the impermissible effect of advancing religion,"[27] and lead to "the symbolic union of church and state."[28]

24. *Everson v. Board of Education,* 330 U.S. at 15 (1947). Emphasis added.
25. *Everson v. Board of Education,* at 16.
26. *Lemon v. Kurtzman,* 403 U.S. at 615 (1971).
27. *Meek v. Pittenger,* 421 U.S. at 366 (1975).
28. *Grand Rapids School District v. Ball,* 473 U.S. at 390 (1985).

This leads to a second key principle established by the *Everson* decision. Somewhat surprisingly, the Supreme Court held that, in spite of the no-aid doctrine it articulated, New Jersey could pay for the transportation of children to religiously based elementary and secondary schools. This leads to an obvious question. How did Justice Black square the giving of aid for the transportation of children to religiously based schools with his own just-enunciated no-aid doctrine? He did so by articulating a second legal principle: *the sacred/secular distinction.* Black held that the sacred and secular facets of an organization can be distinguished and that public funds may flow to the secular, but not to the sacred, facet. He began by distinguishing between programs that would contribute "money to the schools" or would "support them," on the one hand, and programs, such as the one being challenged in that case, in which money flowed only to activities "indisputably marked off from the religious function" of schools, on the other hand.[29] He held that bus transportation was clearly separable from the religious mission of the schools. Thus it could be supported by public funds.

A third legal doctrine the Supreme Court has developed is the *"pervasively sectarian" standard.* An organization is "pervasively sectarian" if its religious and secular aspects are so closely intertwined that any public funds going to it would inevitably aid religion. No public funds may go to pervasively sectarian organizations, even if those funds are designed to support only the purportedly secular programs of those organizations. Justice Lewis Powell, writing for the Court in one case, described the standard in these words: "Aid normally may be thought to have a primary effect of advancing religion when it flows to an institution in which religion is so pervasive that a substantial portion of its functions are subsumed in the religious mission."[30] He then went on to point out that the college whose receipt of government funds was being challenged was not marked by a pervasively religious nature such as this and therefore could receive public funds.

Less clear, however, are the exact characteristics of a "pervasively sectarian" organization. How religious can a nonprofit association be and still not be tagged "pervasively sectarian"? No one knows. There is some evidence that factors such as hiring persons in keeping with the organization's religious orientation, having certain required religious exercises, and

29. *Everson v. Board of Education,* at 18.
30. *Hunt v. McNair,* 413 U.S. at 743 (1973).

seeking to influence the religious views of those being served are factors that could stamp an organization as being pervasively sectarian.[31] Many observers, however, would agree with Justice Harry Blackmun in his description of the "pervasively sectarian" standard as "a vaguely defined work of art."[32] This legal principle is important because the Supreme Court has largely relied on it to deny public funding to religiously based elementary and secondary schools. The Court, however, has thus far never held any religious nonprofit association other than a K-12 school to be pervasively sectarian.

In summary, the basis on which the Supreme Court has reached its decisions in the area of public funds and nonprofit organizations is first of all a strict no-aid-to-religion doctrine. Once this doctrine is accepted, the only way government can use its financial resources to support religiously based nonprofit organizations that have the potential to play key roles in combating poverty is to posit a dichotomy between the religious and the secular tasks being performed by religious organizations, and then argue that the public funds are going only to support the secular tasks. However, such action is constitutionally acceptable, according to the Supreme Court, only if the agency does not fall into the ill-defined camp of a pervasively sectarian organization.

Problems in Achieving a Government-Nonprofit Partnership

The three key legal principles just considered lead to two major problems that work to thwart a full partnership between government and religious nonprofit associations. The first problem is that one of the most effective poverty prevention agents in existence — private, religiously based secondary and elementary schools — has been excluded from public funding schemes. While families are the first line of defense against poverty, they need the support of the schools their children attend to back up their messages of self-reliance and duty and to model the lesson that effort and work pay off. And surely when families are not conveying the right message

31. See the Supreme Court's plurality opinion in *Roemer v. Maryland Public Works Board*, 426 U.S. at 755-59 (1976).

32. *Bowen v. Kendrick*, 487 U.S. at 631 (1987).

to their children — when the first line of defense against poverty has broken down — then schools, as the second line of defense, are essential as a source of stability, inspiration, and skills. As noted earlier, persuasive evidence continues to mount indicating that nonpublic schools, and Catholic schools in particular, are doing a more effective job of educating children from high-poverty areas than are the public schools. The differences are often not minor or marginal, but substantial. For example, a *Newsday* reporter has written of a Catholic school located in the Bronx, "in one of the nation's poorest urban communities," that

> [d]espite the surrounding threats of violence and their own humble beginnings, students at St. Angela's — like many of the archdiocese's inner-city schools — do remarkably well. Test scores for St. Angela's 489 students show a pattern of exceeding state standards for reading, writing and especially math.[33]

It is in this area of K-12 education that the evidence documenting the excellent job being done by religious nonprofits is the most systematic and complete; and, ironically, it is in this area that the Supreme Court has explicitly said that nonprofits must get by without the financial support of the broader society.[34] As a result, one of the most effective means of preventing poverty — one that performs a crucial public service — has been significantly weakened, with especially devastating results in high-poverty areas where effective programs are desperately needed. Catholic and other religiously based nonpublic schools have been left to make do and struggle as best they can. If they could be fully utilized in a nonprofit-government partnership, their impact could be enormous.

A second problem created by the legal principles described in the previous section is that many of the religious nonprofit agencies and institutions that receive public funds must do so under conditions that pose a

33. Thomas Maier, "Learning in Fortress Bronx," *Newsday,* May 17, 1993, 17. Additional examples can be found in Jean Merl, "Inner-City Students Find Success at Catholic Schools," *Los Angeles Times,* March 31, 1992, sec. A, pp. 1, 18-19; Susan Chira, "Where Children Learn How to Learn: Inner-City Pupils in Catholic Schools," *New York Times,* Nov. 20, 1991, sec. A, p. 14; and Bret Schundler, "The Simple Logic of School Choice," *New York Times,* Oct. 28, 1993, sec. A, p. 15.

34. The most persuasive systematic studies are the three studies cited in footnote 18, above.

threat to their religious autonomy. The concept of religious autonomy simply says that religious communities and associations must be free to live out their religiously rooted beliefs. The problem is that under current conditions the autonomy of religious nonprofits receiving public money is at risk.

During the past forty years, four Supreme Court decisions made use of the legal principles discussed earlier to approve the distribution of public funds to religiously based nonprofit organizations. Three of the four cases challenged programs of financial aid to religiously based colleges and universities. In all three cases the Supreme Court maintained its no-aid-to-religion position, while nevertheless approving aid programs to these religious institutions by means of the sacred/secular distinction and the pervasively sectarian standard.

The aid programs under challenge were approved because the Supreme Court was willing to accept the separability of the secular and sacred aspects of education at religiously based colleges and therefore could assert that the public aid was in support of the secular programs but not the religious mission of the colleges. By making a sharp distinction between the religious and the secular elements in a college education and then funding only the secular elements, government can distribute funds to a religious college without supporting religion. That, at least, is the legal theory. In one of the cases, the Court observed that the challenged program of aid "was carefully drafted to ensure that the federally subsidized facilities would be devoted to the secular and not the religious function of the recipient institutions."[35] Another decision noted that "the secular and sectarian activities of the colleges were easily separated."[36] This decision also quoted approvingly a lower court's finding that "the colleges perform 'essentially secular educational functions' that are distinct and separable from religious activity."[37] Also crucial to the Court's reasoning in these three cases was its conclusion that the colleges and universities receiving government funds were not pervasively sectarian. It was this nonpervasively sectarian nature that, the Supreme Court judged, enabled the institutions' religious and secular facets to be clearly separated so that the religious aspects would not receive public funds.

35. *Tilton v. Richardson,* 403 U.S. at 679 (1971).
36. *Roemer v. Maryland Public Works Board,* at 764.
37. *Roemer v. Maryland Public Works Board,* at 762.

A fourth Supreme Court decision dealing with public funds for religiously based nonprofit associations is *Bowen v. Kendrick.* In this case the Court considered whether or not Congress could constitutionally grant funds to religiously based agencies under the Adolescent Family Life Act (AFLA), a federal government program that authorizes grants to public and private nonprofit agencies that provide services relating to teenage sexuality and pregnancies. The act specifically called for the involvement of religious nonprofit organizations. As the Supreme Court itself described the conclusion of the lower court: "As written, the AFLA makes it possible for religiously affiliated grantees to teach adolescents on issues that can be considered 'fundamental elements of religious doctrine.'"[38] The Supreme Court held that on its face AFLA is constitutional and remanded the case to the lower courts to determine whether or not as actually carried out it met constitutional standards.

This decision was rooted firmly in the sacred/secular distinction and the pervasively sectarian standard. The Supreme Court concluded AFLA was fulfilling a primarily secular, not a religious, purpose and that it had not been demonstrated that the agencies receiving public funds were pervasively sectarian (thereby permitting a separation between the religious and the secular). At one point Chief Justice William Rehnquist, writing for the Court majority, said that "nothing in our prior cases warrants the presumption adopted by the District Court that religiously affiliated AFLA grantees are not capable of carrying out their functions under the AFLA in a lawful, *secular manner.*"[39] Later the Court went on to say:

> The facially neutral projects authorized by the AFLA — including pregnancy testing, adoption counseling and referral services, prenatal and postnatal care, educational services, residential care, child care, consumer education, etc., — are not themselves "specifically religious activities," and they are not converted into such activities by the fact that they are carried out by organizations with religious affiliations.[40]

However, the Court suggested that if it could be shown that the agencies receiving funds were pervasively sectarian, similar to religious secondary and elementary schools, they would not be eligible for aid.[41]

38. *Bowen v. Kendrick,* at 598.
39. *Bowen v. Kendrick,* at 612. Emphasis added.
40. *Bowen v. Kendrick,* at 613.
41. *Bowen v. Kendrick,* at 621.

This review of recent Supreme Court decisions reveals serious threats to the autonomy of religiously based nonprofits that accept public funds. First, religious nonprofit associations' freedom to live out their religious beliefs in the programs they run is at risk; second, their ability to define their boundaries — to determine who is and is not a member — is threatened.

The heart of the first problem lies in the fact that the sacred/secular dichotomy is, for many religious nonprofits, a false dichotomy that in practice simply does not exist. Michael Scanlon, the president of Franciscan University, has eloquently expressed the intertwined nature of religion and learning in a Catholic college or university:

> A Catholic college is not just a college that focuses primarily on academics or sports and adds something Catholic, such as a chaplain or a few theology courses. To the contrary, if it doesn't partake of the nature of Jesus as the Way, the Truth, and the Life, we shouldn't call it *Christian.* If it isn't committed to seeking Christ's truth, the way of the Gospel, the way of the disciples, and life in the Holy Spirit, then we shouldn't call it *Christian.* Additionally, if it is not under the lordship of Jesus Christ and submitted to the authority of the Catholic Church, we shouldn't call it Catholic.[42]

However, if Franciscan University, Yeshiva University, or Wheaton College in Illinois seeks to integrate Catholic, Jewish, or evangelical Protestant beliefs into the fabric of the institution and not ghettoize them in the form of "a chaplain or a few theology courses," the Supreme Court's entire sacred/secular distinction comes crashing down. Then such institutions are in danger of being judged pervasively sectarian and losing their eligibility for government funds. It is hard to disagree with Justice Blackmun when he wrote in a dissenting opinion in *Bowen v. Kendrick:* "To presume that AFLA counselors from religious organizations can put their beliefs aside when counseling an adolescent on matters that are part of religious doctrine is simply unrealistic."[43] To require a religiously based agency to set aside its religious convictions as it seeks to guide adolescents to develop a responsible approach to sexuality, when they barely have a solid self-concept and live in the midst of a society that glorifies sexual excess, is fatally to

42. Michael Scanlon, "Keeping Colleges Catholic," *Crisis,* Oct. 1993, 34.

43. From Justice Blackmun's dissent in *Bowen v. Kendrick,* at 636.

damage the message of the agency and to force it to deny its defining beliefs. The agency's religious autonomy is violated when the government says that the price of receiving public funds is to accept restrictions on living out and practicing its religious beliefs.

Some highly troubling cases demonstrate that concerns about the freedom of religious nonprofits to operate on the basis of their religious beliefs are not merely hypothetical. In 1988 a Catholic foster care agency was forced by the courts to provide contraceptives to two teenage girls that New York City had placed with it.[44] In another case a conservative Protestant adoption agency was told by the California courts that it could not favor fellow conservative Protestants in placing children in adoptive homes.[45] Cases such as these have led law professor Carl Esbeck to conclude: "A position advocating operational autonomy for a religious agency is considerably undercut when the agency is supported by government funds."[46]

The second problem current legal principles pose for the autonomy of religiously based nonprofit organizations concerns their ability to define their own boundaries, that is, to determine who is and is not a member of the group. A religious group that is not allowed to define who is and is not a member of the group almost ceases to exist as a distinct entity. Sometimes the Supreme Court and individual justices have recognized this. Justice William Brennan in a concurring opinion once wrote:

> Determining that certain activities are in furtherance of an organization's religious mission, and that only those committed to that mission should conduct them, is thus a means by which a religious community defines itself. Solicitude for a church's ability to do so reflects the idea that furtherance of the autonomy of religious organizations often furthers individual religious freedom as well.[47]

44. See *Arneth v. Gross,* 699 F.Supp. 450 (S.D.N.Y. 1988), and the account of this incident in Carl H. Esbeck, "Government Regulation of Religiously Based Social Services: The First Amendment Considerations," *Hastings Constitutional Law Quarterly* 19 (1992): 405.

45. See *Scott v. Family Ministries,* 135 Cal. Rptr. 430 (1976), and the account of this incident in Esbeck, 400-402.

46. Esbeck, 402.

47. *Corporation of the Presiding Bishop v. Amos,* 483 U.S. at 342 (1987).

However, the Supreme Court has never clarified whether or not a religious nonprofit that receives public funds may choose to hire only persons in agreement with that nonprofit's religious beliefs.

In a plurality opinion, the Supreme Court once suggested that the nonuse of religion as a criterion for hiring faculty tended to confirm that a religious college or university was not pervasively sectarian and thus might be eligible for public funds. The opinion spoke of the absence of a "hiring bias" and efforts "to stack its faculty with members of a particular religious group."[48] In another case, in which public funds for religiously based K-12 schools were disallowed, the Court cited as evidence of the schools' pervasively sectarian nature and thus their ineligibility for government money the fact that they "have faculties and student bodies composed largely of adherents of the particular denomination, and give preference in attendance to children belonging to the denomination."[49]

Do these decisions mean the Supreme Court would insist that religious nonprofit agencies receiving public money not make hiring decisions on religious grounds? Could a Jewish agency receiving public funds to resettle Jewish refugees from abroad be required to hire Muslim counselors, or could an evangelical Protestant college be required to hire thoroughgoing secularists as faculty members, or could a mainline Protestant family-planning agency be required to hire traditional Catholics? The answers to these questions are uncertain. What is certain is that if the answers are "yes," then the ability of religious associations to define themselves — and thereby their existence as distinct religious entities — would be destroyed.

That this concern is not purely hypothetical is revealed by a 1989 federal district court decision that ruled a publicly funded domestic violence shelter run by the Salvation Army in Pascagoula, Mississippi, could not fire a domestic abuse counselor who had turned out to be a witch — a devotee of the ancient, pagan religion of Wicca.[50] The district court ruled that since the Salvation Army — an evangelical Protestant church — was receiving substantial public funds in support of the position and its domestic violence center, it had no legal right to dismiss a counselor based on her religious beliefs. The judge ruled that

48. *Roemer v. Maryland Public Works Board,* at 757.

49. *Grand Rapids School District v. Ball,* at 384, n. 6.

50. See *Dodge v. Salvation Army,* 1989 WL 53857 (S.D. Miss.), and Joseph L. Conn, "Bewitched," *Church and State* 42 (June 1989): 124-26.

> [b]ased on the facts in the present case, the effect of the government substantially, if not exclusively, funding a position such as the Victims' Assistance Coordinator and then allowing the Salvation Army to choose the person to fill or maintain the position based on religious preference clearly has the effect of advancing religion and is unconstitutional.[51]

The Salvation Army settled the case out of court instead of appealing it to a higher court. Thus this decision ought not to be interpreted as established law in this area, but it surely stands as a warning sign of a danger inherent in current legal reasoning. The assumption underlying the court's ruling was that if a religious nonprofit receives public money, to all intents and purposes it loses its religious autonomy and becomes indistinguishable from a government agency.[52] Such an assumption rejects the concept of autonomy for religious institutions protected by legal and constitutional bulwarks.

When religious organizations engage in activities of compassion and help to the needy, they are seeking to live out their religiously based sense of compassion, and for many sincere believers this has intertwined physical, emotional, and spiritual dimensions. But in accordance with current legal doctrine, religious nonprofit agencies may now receive public money only on the basis of a sacred/secular dichotomy. The money they receive may be used only to fund secular activities. But this places the religious agencies in an untenable position.

If counseling and helping the needy is a purely secular activity, there can be no justification for an agency to give preference in hiring persons who agree with the religious basis of the agency. Practicing a religious preference in hiring would then be pure discrimination, as odious as racial discrimination. But if there are spiritual dimensions to counseling and helping the needy, then a religious organization's requirement of a religious orientation in its employees is a reasonable, bona fide demand. Religiously based nonprofit organizations are in a terrible dilemma. As religious agencies, many sincerely believe that it is defensible, even essential, that the persons they hire to work with the poor should share the religious commitments of the organization. Yet to be eligible to receive government

51. *Dodge v. Salvation Army,* at 3.

52. This, in fact, is the exact conclusion lower courts have on occasion reached. See *Scott v. Family Ministries* and *Arneth v. Gross.*

money, they must pretend that those they hire are engaged in secular tasks, tasks for which religion is irrelevant. But if they engage in that pretense, they lose their only legitimate reason to hire only persons who share the agency's religious commitment.

In short, religious nonprofit organizations that receive public funds run risks in their ability to embody their religious beliefs in the programs they run and in their ability to define their boundaries by hiring only persons in religious agreement with them. That is where current legal doctrine leads. This does not necessarily mean that all religious agencies receiving public funds today are in actual practice experiencing a loss of their religious autonomy. Many appear to be able to receive large amounts of public funds and still maintain much of their religious autonomy.[53] The key point is that the logic of current legal doctrine places them in a highly vulnerable position. The long-run tendencies and pressures are in the direction of weakening and undermining the religious autonomy of nonprofits that receive public funding.

When religiously based nonprofit organizations lose their religious autonomy and are forced in greater or lesser degree to violate or ignore their religiously rooted beliefs, or when they can no longer define who they are by hiring staff members in agreement with their religious beliefs and commitments, their effectiveness as an important source of help to the poor is reduced, perhaps drastically reduced. For, paradoxical as it may sound, the ability of religiously based nonprofit organizations to be of temporal, this-worldly help in combating poverty is to a significant degree dependent on their ability to maintain a spiritual, otherworldly identity.

Four factors are important here. First, it is often the religious identity of a religious organization that enables it to attract staff members of dedication and devotion, people who see their work for the organization as a mission, as a means of living out their faith. Second, it is the religious elements in religious organizations' programs that often give needy persons the discipline and the ideals that have been lacking in their lives. From Saint Francis of Assisi to present-day participants in Alcoholics Anonymous, religious ideals and beliefs have inspired changes in behavior. To the extent

53. This is one conclusion I reach in a broad study of religiously based child and family service agencies, international aid and relief agencies, and colleges and universities. See my forthcoming *When Sacred and Secular Mix: Religious Nonprofit Organizations and Public Money.*

that these must be violated or suppressed as a condition for receiving public funds, religious agencies are rendered less effective.

A third key advantage of religiously based nonprofits that can be lost under present legal principles is the rich pluralism of religious traditions and programs they represent. As they are forced to conform more and more to a general secular standard, they start to look more and more alike, and more and more like government agencies. Mark Chopko has made the point this way:

> Religious organizations, as well as private nonreligious organizations, should resist the temptation of looking like the government simply because a governmental program is involved. Government should, for the good of the governed, strive to encourage a variety of approaches to the provision of similar services. . . . The delivery of . . . basic public goods should reflect the diverse array of organizations, religious and nonreligious, that serve our community. The Religion Clauses [of the First Amendment] were not intended to make our pluralistic people uniform, but to accommodate our pluralism fairly.[54]

A fourth consequence of current legal theories governing public funding of religious nonprofit organizations is the depressing effect they have on participation in public funding programs by religious service agencies. Not only are K-12 schools almost totally excluded from public funding, but many agencies have made a self-conscious choice not to participate in public funding programs out of fear of government interference with their religious mission. The head of a successful church-sponsored homeless program in Los Angeles once told me his organization would never dream of pursuing government funds since doing so would limit the spiritual emphasis of the program. He was convinced that the entire program would suffer if the religious dimension was removed. It is impossible to estimate how many religiously based antipoverty programs have chosen to struggle along with limited programs rather than expanding their programs with the help of public funds, due to fear of having to compromise their religious missions.

Earlier I suggested that the key strengths religiously based nonprofits bring to the struggle against poverty are their flexibility, their sense of

54. Mark E. Chopko, "Religious Access to Public Programs and Governmental Funding," *George Washington Law Review* 60 (1992): 669-70.

dedication and commitment, and their ability to speak in terms of religious norms and religious and ethnic solidarity. The legal principles and court decisions discussed in this section have a debilitating effect on all three of these strengths. The poor are the ultimate losers.

Positive Neutrality: A Possible Answer

A new standard for guiding the flow of public money to religiously based nonprofits is clearly needed. Criteria such as no aid to religion, the sacred/secular dichotomy, and the pervasively sectarian standard are harmful, as we have seen.

The standard I have termed "positive neutrality" is far superior to current legal principles. If it were adopted, a powerful force for combating poverty would be unleashed in the form of expanded efforts by thousands of religiously based nonprofit agencies and institutions. Positive neutrality holds that the First Amendment religious-freedom language should be interpreted so as to assure the neutrality of government toward persons and groups of all faiths and those of none.[55] Government should not specifically help or hinder any particular religion or religion in general, but neither should it promote secular belief systems in general. I refer to this standard as *positive* neutrality because it recognizes that if true neutrality is to be achieved, government will sometimes have to take certain positive steps that recognize, accommodate, or support religion. It also has a positive aspect in that it represents the positive effort of government to fulfill the norm of public justice. By adopting a position of neutrality toward persons and groups of all religious faiths and of none, government is promoting a just order in society. It is protecting the freedom and autonomy of persons and groups of all faiths and of no religious faith. The key to governmental neutrality is that government should not recognize, accommodate, or support any particular religion over any other, nor should it support either religious or secular worldviews and organizations over the other.

Under positive neutrality the current no-aid-to-religion dogma would be replaced by the principle of public money being allowed to go to fund the

55. I originally developed the concept of positive neutrality in my book *Positive Neutrality: Letting Religious Freedom Ring* (Westport, Conn.: Greenwood, 1993), esp. ch. 5.

programs and activities of religiously based nonprofits that are of a temporal benefit to society, *as long as* public funds are available to support similar or parallel programs of all religious traditions without favoritism and similar or parallel programs of a secular nature, whether sponsored by secular nonprofits or by government itself. In this manner governmental neutrality would be implemented within the framework of certain positive steps. Programs of certain religious traditions would not be favored over any others, and neither would either secular or religious programs in general be favored.

Under present Supreme Court jurisprudence public policy is anything but neutral. The Supreme Court assumes that by excluding religion from the public life of the nation and from public support, neutrality is achieved. But if public life is purified of all religious elements while secular elements are left free to flourish, and if public funds can flow to all sorts of secular organizations but similar organizations of a religious nature must either forego such funds or become like their secular counterparts, neutrality is not the result. A. James Richley has said it well:

> [B]anishment of religion does not represent neutrality between religion and secularism; conduct of public institutions without any acknowledgment of religion *is* secularism. . . . A society that excludes religion totally from its public life, that seems to regard religion as something against which public life must be protected, is bound to foster the impression that religion is either irrelevant or harmful.[56]

Positive neutrality would replace the old no-aid-to-religion standard and the sacred/secular and pervasively-sectarian distinctions. Under it, public money would be allowed to flow to programs whether or not they have religious aspects to them. In order to assure that a genuine neutrality is maintained and that government lives up to its responsibility to protect society from agencies — whether religious or secular — that would undermine or defraud society, nonprofit organizations would have to meet four basic conditions in order to be eligible for public funds. First, the programs or activities would have to be of temporal, this-world benefit to society; second, funding would need to be available equally to both secular and religious organizations with similar or parallel programs; third, the nonprofits could not teach hatred or intolerance or in other ways attack the

56. A. James Richley, *Religion in American Public Life* (Washington, D.C.: Brookings, 1985), 165. Emphasis in the original.

fabric of society; and fourth, the nonprofits would have to submit to minimal, nonintrusive review or accountability standards.

Under the first of these four conditions public money could not go to fund activities and programs that are primarily otherworldly in nature, that is, those that are oriented toward religious worship or affirmation and celebration of core religious beliefs. The benefits of such programs and activities are primarily otherworldly, in the sense of relating to either life after death or the inner religious self. Thus such activities as worship services, the construction of chapels, or proselytizing classes could not be funded under positive neutrality. Yet religious nonprofits and their programs with temporal benefits for society would be free to integrate religious concepts and themes into those programs, for example, by hiring only persons in agreement with their religious orientation. This condition is clearly distinguishable from the current sacred/secular bifurcation that says only supposedly secular activities and programs of religious nonprofits can be funded. Under positive neutrality, programs that have strong religious aspects woven into them would still be eligible for public funds. The crucial factor would be whether the activity or program produces this-worldly benefits for society, not some artificial separation between "secular" and "sacred" program components.

A second condition positive neutrality sets for the dispensing of public funds to religious nonprofit associations is that funds are to be made available without discrimination to all nonprofit organizations offering similar or parallel services, regardless of whether they are religiously based or secular and no matter what their religious tradition. This does not mean that the government cannot make distinctions in dispensing funds based on factors such as past successes or failures, size of agencies, and targeted service areas. Nor does it mean government funding must be withheld if only certain religious traditions actually have associations providing a certain service, or if only religious or only secular associations are offering a certain service. What it does mean is that government funding may not discriminate on the basis of associations' religious or secular nature or on the basis of their particular religious tradition. This condition — given the necessarily secular nature of government agencies — also means that if government itself is providing the same service that religious nonprofit associations are providing, then public funding should be made available in support of those religious nonprofit services. The key goal is neutrality or evenhandedness. Neither religious associations as a whole nor secular associations as a whole (including government agencies) nor religious associations of certain traditions are to be advantaged or disadvantaged.

A third limitation on the use of public funds by religious nonprofits is that public funds could not go to nonprofit organizations that teach hatred or intolerance or in other ways work to destroy the social fabric fundamental to civil society. Here religious groups would not be singled out for special limitations or conditions, but all nonprofits — secular and religious alike — would have an obligation to be supportive of the basic norms and rules of the game that unite the American people as a nation. Government has a responsibility to uphold a public order marked by justice for all; it also has a responsibility not to invade the rightful autonomy of private associations, whether religious or secular in nature. Both responsibilities must be given their due. Thus some careful distinctions are important in order that this third limitation not be misused.

A just public order is held together in part by a common commitment to certain norms and rules of the game. In free, democratic societies these revolve around such concepts as the worth and dignity of all persons, the rule of law, the right to privacy, and freedom of expression. Along with such rights go certain obligations, such as refraining from engaging in, and refraining from urging others to engage in, unlawful acts (except in certain extreme situations when the law itself seems to be violating fundamental norms so that civil disobedience becomes an acceptable option). Also, a sense of civility and tolerance is important. Tolerance and civility do not mean persons cannot disagree with and strenuously argue against others and their opinions and actions; they do mean that one does not read others out of society or out of the human race. Within Christianity there is the old adage of "hating the sin but loving the sinner." Something of this nature is relevant in the social realm more broadly, where all have the right to "hate" the opinions and practices of others — we are free to speak, argue, and demonstrate against them — but all should "love" the persons and groups that are seeking to advance the opinions and practices we "hate." Public justice means all persons are given the civic space or freedom to be what they are meant to be. This, in turn, means that others in society are not purposely to seek to provoke or antagonize them, or oppose them by unlawful or violent means. This is civility and tolerance.

The nonprofit groups — whether religious or secular — that under positive neutrality would be excluded from receiving government funds are those that reject the rule of law, teach religious or racial hatred and bigotry, or in other ways go against the basic norms that make possible a just order in society. Under its terms, groups such as the Ku Klux Klan or various neo-Nazi groups would not be eligible for aid. There will be some hard cases here. Among religious groups, for example, some might argue that the Nation of Islam — given the anti-Semitic, antiwhite rhetoric of some of its leaders — should not be eligible to participate in government funding. Others would argue that it should be eligible. With any standard, however, there will always be borderline cases, and their existence does not mean the standard itself is inadequate or inappropriate.

A fourth limitation on the nonprofits eligible to receive government funds is that they must be willing to submit to certain limited reviews or licensing standards, as long as these are directed at assuring that the services or programs for which public funds are received are in fact being provided, and that the health and safety of the program participants are not being endangered. In making such demands government would again simply be living up to its responsibility to maintain a just public order in society. Licensing standards and other government reviews should not be based on the religious beliefs and practices of the nonprofit organizations. Again, religious and secular nonprofits would be treated in the same manner. Again, therefore, neutrality would be maintained.

Positive Neutrality and Vouchers

Under positive neutrality public money could go in a number of forms to religiously based nonprofits actively working to prevent or overcome poverty. But I believe that vouchers offer the best method for publicly funding religious nonprofits because they would maximize desirable results and minimize undesirable side effects. Food stamps constitute a precedent in using what in effect are vouchers in the area of antipoverty programs. Food stamps are made available to low-income persons and families, who can then take them to whatever grocery store they wish and receive food for them. Then the merchant turns the food stamps in to the government and receives the cash they represent. The same approach has also been used widely in higher education, from the post–World War II "G.I. bill" to Pell grants and basic education opportunity grants today. Qualifying students can go to the college or university of their choice — public or private, secular or religious — and the college or university is reimbursed by the government.

Vouchers have been widely discussed in the case of K-12 education, and would be the preferred way to make public funds available to religiously based schools.[57] They could even be tailored to favor low-income families and their children, by relating the monetary value of a voucher to family income. This same form of aid could be applied to other areas, such as job training, rent subsidies, basic-education skills, drug treatment, and other support and training programs.

Taking this approach rather than other forms of funneling public money to nonprofits has at least four advantages. One is that governmental intrusion into the activities and programs of nonprofits would be minimized. One danger in using public dollars to fund nonprofit programs is that with the dollars may go unnecessary controls that have the effect of making the nonprofit organizations look very much like their governmental counterparts. When this happens, much of the diversity, flexibility, and creativity that make nonprofits attractive as public policy agents is destroyed. As seen earlier, especially in the case of religiously based nonprofits, there is a great danger of heavy-handed attempts to squeeze out or mold the religiously based practices of the agencies. By having the recipients of assistance choose which nonprofits will receive how much public money by "voting with their feet," the problem of interference in the life of the nonprofits by insensitive courts or government bureaucrats is minimized.

Similarly, a second advantage flowing from the same characteristic of vouchers is that they take government completely out of deciding which religious groups would receive how much money and how much money religiously based nonprofits as a whole would receive as compared to secular nonprofits as a whole. Again, the users of the nonprofit organizations' services would decide by their individual free-market-type decisions. This would help assure that the goal of religious neutrality is achieved.

A third advantage of vouchers over other forms of public aid is that they empower those in society who typically have the least power — the poor and near-poor. Purchasing power is put in the hands of the disadvantaged of society, thereby helping to assure that government agencies and nonprofit organizations alike will be more responsive to their needs and problems. Monopolies inherently are unresponsive — whether they exist

57. See, e.g., John E. Chubb and Terry M. Moe, *Politics, Markets, and America's Schools* (Washington, D.C.: Brookings, 1990).

under communism in Eastern Europe, in American antipoverty programs, or in central-city public schools.

A fourth advantage of vouchers is they avoid some of the strict separationist dogma found in past Supreme Court decisions, thereby making it more likely that the Supreme Court will find them constitutional. The Supreme Court has already approved tax credits for parents whose children have incurred educational expenses — including expenses at religiously based schools — and has approved state support for a blind student training to be a church worker at a Bible college. In the former case, Chief Justice William Rehnquist, writing for the Court majority, said: "Most importantly, the deduction is available for educational expenses incurred by all parents, including those whose children attend public schools and those whose children attend non-sectarian private schools or sectarian private schools."[58] In the case of the blind student attending a Bible college, Justice Thurgood Marshall declared for a unanimous Court that one of the key factors in the case was that Washington state's "program is 'made available generally without regard to the sectarian-nonsectarian, or public-nonpublic nature of the institution benefited,' and is in no way skewed towards religion."[59] With precedents such as these it appears that vouchers that could be used at private or public and religiously based or secular agencies alike would have a good chance of winning the approval of the Supreme Court.

Poverty is a deeply entrenched, seemingly intractable problem. Wars on poverty appear more likely to be lost than won. In such a situation public policy needs to take maximum advantage of whatever tools and means have proven to be effective or hold the promise of being effective. Unfortunately, the current doctrines governing the flow of public money to religiously based nonprofit agencies and institutions have worked to prevent the full use of what would be one of the most effective tools to prevent and overcome poverty. Changing those doctrines and adopting the standard of positive neutrality would do much to unleash new and powerful forces in the age-old battle against the forces that hold people in the grip of poverty.

58. *Mueller v. Allen,* 463 U.S. at 396 (1983).

59. See *Witters v. Washington Department of Services for the Blind,* 474 U.S. at 487-88 (1986). The quotation is from *Committee for Public Education v. Nyquist,* 413 U.S. at 782-83, n. 38 (1973).

Correcting the Welfare Tragedy: Toward a New Model for Church/State Partnership

Ronald J. Sider and Heidi Rolland

IF THE United States is to move toward better alternatives to the current welfare system,[1] we must understand the complex causes of the poverty that the welfare system seeks to alleviate. Too often the diverse, complex, interrelated causes have been reduced to a simplistic either/or explanation. Some have seen poverty to be largely the result of wrong personal choices (influenced, to be sure, by the larger culture) about sex, drugs, school, family, and work. Others have explained poverty largely to be the result of overarching socioeconomic structures that, willy-nilly, determine the fate of people. Only if we see that both personal choices (and cultural and spiritual factors behind those choices) and societal structures are essential causes of poverty will we be able to design better alternatives to the current welfare tragedy.

This chapter focuses on long-term rather than short-term poverty. Short-term poverty often results from personal misfortunes or crises: loss of employment, loss of a spouse, disability or major illness, the birth of a child, loss of or increase in the cost of housing. Major family events such as these account for more than half of all child poverty.[2] For a short time the people affected may require welfare to get by, but they use it as a

1. "Welfare" in this chapter generally refers to two programs: Aid to Families with Dependent Children (AFDC) and General Assistance.

2. William H. Scarbrough, "Who Are the Poor? A Demographic Perspective," in Judith A. Chafel, ed., *Child Poverty and Public Policy* (Washington, D.C.: Urban Institute Press, 1993), 79.

temporary, transitional aid — needed only until that new job is found, health is recovered, or family stability is restored.

Duration of welfare assistance, in terms of both length and number of spells, is one way to distinguish short- from long-term poverty. The majority of welfare recipients cycle on and off benefits. Almost three-fourths of welfare recipients will leave welfare within two years, although all but about a third of recipients will return. Of those on the system at any given point in time, 65 percent will receive welfare in spells for a cumulative total of eight or more years. Only 8.5 percent, however, will receive welfare *continuously* for eight or more years. Over time, these long-term users make up about a third of the total number of welfare users. For many in this minority of poor people who remain on welfare for extended periods of time, welfare has become a way of life. Because they remain on welfare while others move off the system, they make up the bulk of the AFDC caseload and budget at any given time.[3]

Obviously the line between short-term and long-term poverty is not entirely clear-cut.[4] But there are major differences between the problems of the recipient who needs assistance only for a brief time and the problems of the person who, although otherwise able to work, becomes dependent on welfare. The problem of long-term welfare use has increasingly captured the attention of welfare reformers. The overall percentage of poor people in the United States (currently around 14.5 percent) has not changed significantly in the last fifteen years, and the number of people on welfare continuously for more than five years has actually declined in the 1990s. However, the number of *women* dependent on welfare for the major part of their income for a long period of time more than tripled between 1979 and 1989.[5]

3. U.S. House of Representatives, Committee on Ways and Means, *Overview of Entitlement Programs: 1993 Green Book* (Washington, D.C.: GPO, 1993), 714-16.

4. It would be a mistake to make short-term poverty synonymous with the *deserving* poor and long-term synonymous with *undeserving*. This does not adequately recognize either the extent to which nonpoor people are protected from the economic effects of their "undeserving" behaviors nor the structural factors that contribute to faulty decision making by the entrenched poor. This chapter takes long-term dependency and its accompanying cluster of negative socioeconomic factors as its focus not because these poor people are fundamentally, morally different from mainstream Americans, but because their problems need special examination.

5. *1993 Green Book*, 699, 721.

A statistically typical portrait of long-term poverty and welfare dependency is a single black mother, in her early twenties, most likely never married, whose children are under age five.[6] She probably did not work in the last two years, though nearly one-fourth of those entering the welfare system who did work in the previous two years nevertheless will be on welfare for ten years or more. She likely does not have a high school degree (over half of welfare recipients without a high school diploma will be on AFDC ten years or more).[7] Her AFDC benefits and food stamps make up most of her income, which is still below the poverty level.[8] Contrary to popular opinion, the "welfare mother" does not have more children than the average American household.[9] Also defying the stereotype, the mother of persistently poor children most likely lives in the rural South, not in a northern ghetto.[10] However, cities do have the highest concentrations of poverty, with over a third of the poor living in central-city areas.[11] This portrait is not, of course, universal. Welfare recipients exhibit great demographic variety and fall along a continuum of dependency, spending an average total time of 6.6 years on welfare.[12]

The Causes of Long-Term Poverty

Long-term poverty has many complex causes — social, economic, political, cultural, and personal. The broad structural causes of poverty must not be

6. The Urban Institute, "What Can Be Expected From Welfare Reform?" *Policy and Research Report,* Fall 1994, 12. While long-term recipients are more likely to be black, about the same numbers of white and black caretakers receive AFDC (*1993 Green Book,* 705, 718).

7. *1993 Green Book,* 718-20.

8. In 1990, the combined benefits of antipoverty programs left 88.6 percent of female-headed families in poverty. See Sheldon H. Danziger and Daniel H. Weinberg, "The Historical Record: Trends in Family Income, Inequality and Poverty," in Sheldon H. Danziger, Gary D. Sandefur, and Daniel H. Weinberg, eds., *Confronting Poverty: Prescriptions for Change* (Cambridge: Harvard Univ. Press, 1994).

9. Lee Seglem, *State Legislatures* (May 1993), 24. The family size of AFDC households has actually decreased in the last two decades.

10. Scarbrough, 79.

11. Michael G. H. McGeary and Laurence E. Lynn, Jr., eds., *Urban Change and Poverty* (Washington, D.C.: National Academy Press, 1988), 17.

12. Congressional Research Service, "Clinton Welfare Reform Proposal: Issue Summary," *CRS Report for Congress* (Feb. 4, 1994), 2.

ignored. Macro socioeconomic changes over the last twenty years have contributed significantly to urban poverty.[13] Vast numbers of the middle class, both white and black, have migrated out of the cities, accompanied by the better-paying jobs. At the same time, immigrants and laborers have migrated into the cities in large numbers, creating a surplus of low-skilled labor. Developments in technology and the globalization of the market have resulted in a loss of higher-paying jobs in industry and other blue-collar fields, while other well-paying jobs have carried increasingly higher educational requirements.[14] The real wages of low-skill jobs have dropped significantly, resulting in an increase in the number of the employed poor. The rate of unemployment has risen, particularly for low-wage workers.[15] There are fewer low-skill entry-level jobs that can support a family above the poverty level, and few of those that are still available are located close to where most poor people live.[16] These factors have contributed to growing income inequality, with the poorest families hurt disproportionately by the economic changes of the last two decades.[17] Traditional avenues of upward mobility for the poor have significantly narrowed.

Racism, both past and present, also contributes to poverty today. Blacks and other minorities have been disproportionately affected by all of the macroeconomic changes described above.[18] Due to affirmative action

13. Although slightly more poor people live in rural areas than in central cities, most of the discussion focuses on the urban poor, for a number of reasons: public attention and welfare reform policy tend to focus on this group; more information is available about them; and while rural poverty is persistent, it is not accompanied by the same intense complex of other social problems usually associated with "dependency."

14. Suzanne M. Bianchi, "Children of Poverty: Why Are They Poor?" in Chafel, 97; John D. Kasarda, "Jobs, Migration, and Emerging Urban Mismatches," in McGeary and Lynn.

15. Sar A. Levitan and Isaac Shapiro, *Working But Poor* (Baltimore: Johns Hopkins Univ. Press, 1987); David T. Ellwood, *Poor Support* (New York: Basic Books, 1988), 99.

16. Marian Wright Edelman, *Families in Peril* (Cambridge: Harvard Univ. Press, 1987), 74; Reynolds Farley, "The Common Destiny of Blacks and Whites," in Herbert Hill and James E. Jones, Jr., eds., *Race in America: The Struggle for Equality* (Madison: Univ. of Wisconsin Press, 1993), 199.

17. Robert H. Haveman and John Karl Scholz, "The Clinton Welfare Reform Plan: Will it End *Poverty* as We Know It?" *Focus* (Institute for Research on Poverty) 16 (Winter 1994–95): 3-4.

18. William Julius Wilson, *The Truly Disadvantaged* (Chicago: Univ. of Chicago Press, 1987), 11; Farley, 199-203.

and other civil rights gains, much *overt* discrimination in employment, housing, and services has been eliminated. But subtle discrimination continues to affect minorities' economic opportunities. Blacks are still less likely than whites to be hired or promoted.[19] Over the 1980s, blacks' wages decreased relative to whites', increasing the wage inequality between black and white workers; black males earn only three-fourths of what white males do.[20] Blacks are disproportionately affected by layoffs and relocations.[21] Black workers travel farther than whites to reach their jobs.[22] Hispanics are not far ahead of blacks on most economic indicators.[23]

Closely associated with the problems of economic restructuring and the ongoing impact of racism is the deterioration of the inner cities, where one-third of the poor live. Changing demographics, particularly the steady out-migration of middle- and working-class families from ghetto neighborhoods, led to a phenomenal 182 percent increase in concentrated poverty (areas where at least forty percent of the people are poor) in major cities between 1970 and 1980.[24] The poor people who are left cannot or do not sustain the community institutions — churches, stores, schools, recreational facilities — that are essential to their social and economic well-being. Inner-city neighborhoods also suffer from the neglect of broader civic institutions — banks, public schools, the criminal justice system, sanitation, public transportation — which tends to further isolate them in their poverty. Failing schools, high crime rates, the lack of family services such as child care, and the unavailability of financing all serve to reinforce and perpetuate poverty.

The welfare system itself has also helped generate long-term poverty

19. The Urban Institute, "Auditing to Enforce Civil Rights Laws," *Policy and Research Report* 22, no. 2 (1992): 5; Jerome Culp and Bruce H. Dunson, "Brothers of a Different Color: A Preliminary Look at Employer Treatment of White and Black Youth," in Richard B. Freeman and Harry J. Holzer, eds., *The Black Youth Employment Crisis* (Chicago: Univ. of Chicago Press, 1986), 250.

20. Farley, 207; The Urban Institute, "Growing Inequality in America's Income Distribution," *Policy and Research Report* 21, no. 1 (1991): 2, 7.

21. Ronald Takaki, "A Tale of Two Decades: Race and Class in the 1880s and the 1980s," in Hill and Jones, 407.

22. David T. Ellwood, "The Spatial Mismatch Hypothesis: Are There Teenage Jobs Missing in the Ghetto?" in Freeman and Holzer, 148; Kasarda, 189.

23. Farley, 203, 222-25.

24. Wilson, 46, 56-57.

and dependency.[25] Robert Rector has described welfare's failed logic in these memorable words: "The mother has a contract with the government. She will continue to receive her 'paycheck' as long as she fulfills two conditions: 1) she does not work; and 2) she does not marry an employed male. I call this the incentive system made in hell."[26] Empirical evidence confirms that welfare benefits correlate with fewer hours spent in work, school, and job training.[27] Women whose mothers were highly dependent on welfare are four to five times as likely to become highly dependent on welfare themselves, suggesting that welfare dependency perpetuates itself.[28] Welfare restrictions against two-parent families probably also encourage breakups and inhibit some marriages.[29] But welfare also reinforces poverty for many because the "paycheck" it gives is not sufficient to meet families' needs or to support their efforts at self-improvement. Median combined AFDC and food stamp benefits are 70 percent below the poverty threshold; decreases in welfare benefits caused an estimated 2.9 million people to fall into poverty from 1979 to 1983.[30] Paradoxically, welfare seems to offer enough of an incentive to influence behavior negatively, but only enough support to help a recipient barely survive.

25. See, e.g., Charles Murray, *Losing Ground: American Social Policy, 1950–1980* (New York: Basic Books, 1984); Marvin Olasky, *The Tragedy of American Compassion* (Washington, D.C.: Regnery Gateway, 1992); Michael Novak et al., *The New Consensus on Family and Welfare* (Washington, D.C.: American Enterprise Institute for Public Policy Research, 1987); Robert Rector, "Requiem for the War on Poverty," *Policy Review,* Summer 1992.

26. Rector, 40.

27. Richard B. Freeman, "Who Escapes? The Relation of Churchgoing and Other Background Factors to the Socioeconomic Performance of Black Male Youths from Inner-City Poverty Tracts," in Freeman and Holzer, 374; Robert Lerman, "Do Welfare Programs Affect the Schooling and Work Patterns of Young Black Men?" in Freeman and Holzer, 436; Stewart M. Butler, "Guidelines for State Welfare Reform" (testimony at a hearing held by the Illinois House Republican Policy Committee in Chicago, Sept. 24, 1991), 2.

28. *1993 Green Book,* 723.

29. Family Research Council, "The Two-Parent Family: Policy Ideas for Strengthening Marriage," *Family Policy,* Apr. 1992, 4-5. However, there is no evidence for a link between welfare and teenage pregnancy or additional childbearing, according to Ellwood, 57-61, and Bianchi, 116-17.

30. *1993 Green Book,* 657-58; U.S. House of Representatives, Committee on Ways and Means, Subcommittee on Human Resources, *Sources of the Increases in Poverty, Work Effort, and Income Distribution Data* (Jan. 26, 1993), 113.

This discussion of the structural causes of contemporary poverty clearly shows the inadequacy of any simplistic, individualistic, and "spiritualized" view that the problem is merely a matter of wrongheaded, sinful personal choices. Nevertheless, mistaken choices (which are also always related to and partly shaped by social and cultural factors) are a significant part of the problem.

Nowhere is that clearer than in the correlation between poverty and the breakdown of the family. Stable two-parent families are becoming less and less common. Marriages and births to married couples have dropped sharply since the mid-1960s, while divorces have more than doubled. Families torn by divorce or separation are more vulnerable to poverty than two-parent homes; never-married mothers are even more at risk. Currently about one-third of all births are to unwed mothers; among blacks, the figure is 68 percent. Over half of the children born to unwed mothers — for blacks, two-thirds — can expect to be poor. Single mothers mean absent fathers. Nine out of ten AFDC homes lack a father; more than half the time this is because the mother was never married. Only about a third of unwed fathers provide regular support and contact with their children; only one in six mothers on AFDC receives child support payments. Overall, divorce, separation, and unwed parenthood are associated with three-quarters of all requests for AFDC.[31]

Single parenthood produces self-reinforcing social decay. Lack of a spouse is associated with significant economic, emotional, and physical disadvantages for single parents, all of which often translate into poverty.[32] In an article entitled "Dan Quayle Was Right," Barbara Dafoe Whitehead has summarized the host of harmful effects of single parenthood on children:

> Children in single-parent families are six times as likely to be poor. They are also likely to stay poor longer. Twenty-two percent of children in one-parent families will experience poverty during childhood for seven years or more, as compared with only two percent of children in two-parent families. . . . Children in single-parent families are two to three times as likely as children in two-parent families to have emotional and

31. Congressional Research Service, "Recent Statistics on Poverty in the United States: 1992," *CRS Report for Congress* (Oct. 28, 1993), 4; *1993 Green Book,* 698, 714, 718, 725; Charles Murray, "The Coming White Underclass," *Wall Street Journal,* Oct. 29, 1993; "Novel Idea in Welfare Plan: Helping Children by Helping Their Fathers," *New York Times,* Mar. 30, 1994, sec. B, p. 6.

> behavioral problems. They are also more likely to drop out of high school, to get pregnant as teenagers, to abuse drugs, and to be in trouble with the law. . . . Many children from disrupted families have a harder time achieving intimacy in a relationship, forming a stable marriage, or even holding a steady job.[33]

Daughters raised by single mothers are significantly more likely to marry young, have children young, or become single parents themselves, passing their disadvantages on to yet another generation.[34]

Part of the problem behind the sharp rise in single parenthood is that the extended family, once a crucial source of social support, is no longer either as valued or available for help.[35] The breakdown of marriage and family is also related to joblessness and to changes in the labor market, which contribute to increased mobility and other stresses on the family. William Julius Wilson attributes the high numbers of single black mothers to a "shrinking male marriageable pool" of employed young black men. A strong correlation exists between unemployment and family instability.[36] However, while structural changes have obviously contributed to the tragic decline of the American family, this decline certainly cannot be explained by socioeconomic data alone. Personal choices grounded in changing ethical norms have undeniably been factors.[37]

32. Robert H. Coombs, "Marital Status and Personal Well-Being: A Literature Review," *Family Relations,* Jan. 1991.

33. *Atlantic Monthly,* Apr. 1993, 47.

34. Sara McLanahan, Irwin Garfinkel, and Dorothy Watson, "Family Structure, Poverty, and the Underclass," in McGeary and Lynn, 125-26.

35. H. Malcolm Newton, *Can the Black Family Be Saved?* (Monterey, Calif.: African-American Evangelical Press, 1988), 94.

36. Wilson, 105. Male unemployment has risen relative to female unemployment; see Farley, 209.

37. The widespread "sexual revolution" of the 1960s and 70s prepared the way for the explosion of single motherhood in the 1980s. The prevalence of out-of-wedlock births was not limited to poor blacks; in fact, white illegitimacy has increased at over twice the rate for blacks (Farley, 214). Mainstream American culture is still ambivalent about marriage and unwilling to commit to lifelong covenants. "Media messages have minimized marriage, implying it is an outdated institution, an 'uncool' survivor of a simpler society. 'Be my girl,' the current cinema hero says, but rarely, 'my wife,'" according to Coombs, 101. This ambivalence arises within a framework of pervasive ethical relativism.

The set of personal behaviors that contribute to poverty and long-term welfare dependency is not limited to irresponsible choices regarding sex and marriage. Wrong personal decisions about drugs, alcohol, school attendance, and work can also lead to poverty.[38] While for many poor people dependence on welfare may seem to be the only viable option, some deliberately abuse the system. Other welfare recipients perpetuate their poverty through lack of motivation, failure to plan for the future, and a careless attitude toward private (and public) property. Many urban youth neglect or mistreat the community institutions that would help them escape poverty, such as schools, churches, or local businesses. Much of urban crime is directed against other poor people, suggesting that the experience of poverty may fuel a downward spiral of destructive behavior. The most extreme case is that of poor ghetto youth who live, in Cornel West's terms, "a life of horrifying meaninglessness, hopelessness, and (most important) lovelessness."[39] Such a "culture of poverty" is extremely difficult to overcome.[40]

Again, it would be foolish to view these choices as if they had no relationship to broader societal conditions such as inadequate urban schools, fewer job opportunities in the inner city, and changing ethical norms in the larger society. But persons are not mere social pawns programmed with deterministic precision by societal structures. The welfare system may present incentives for negative behavior, but it does not force anyone to pursue them. Some people, even in the worst urban ghettos, make productive choices that help them break free from poverty. Every person is created in God's image and is summoned by the Creator to responsible freedom.

A problem as complex and entrenched as long-term poverty can be

38. Freeman, 354-58. Freeman's study found that young black men not in school spend only 10 percent of their time on what mainstream Americans would call productive behaviors.

39. Cornel West, *Race Matters* (Boston: Beacon Press, 1993), 14. Wilson's *The Truly Disadvantaged* gives a comprehensive discussion of the culture of poverty or "underclass."

40. Here the contribution of America's rampant materialism to the experience of poverty should not be overlooked. See Jennifer L. Hochschild, "The Politics of the Estranged Poor," *Ethics*, Apr. 1991, 569-70, and West, 16-17. Advertising bombards well-off and poor alike with messages to seek gratification, love leisure, and expect service and satisfaction as a right: "Your way, right away," "Alive with pleasure," "Gotta have it." The attitudes, which spell dependency for the poor, define "the good life" for the wealthy.

overcome only by a wholistic approach that combines inner spiritual transformation and external changes, at both the micro and macro levels. If poverty were caused entirely by structural inequities, it could be redressed entirely through rigorous socioeconomic policies. If poverty were wholly a matter of individual choices within a cultural framework, the solution would lie solely in behavioral incentives and spiritual and moral education. But *both* external, structural causes and inner, personal causes help create poverty, and they are intertwined. A wholistic approach is needed to restore life to poor people as well as to their larger social context. Poor people need help with their external circumstances; they also (as do we all) need to be transformed in their inner person. Any one-sided policy will be inadequate and will probably serve to exacerbate the other aspects of the problem. Change must take place on multiple levels in order to make a lasting impact on poverty.

Toward a Wholistic Solution for Long-Term Poverty

The central argument of this chapter is that the best way — perhaps the only way — fundamentally to change the tragic reality of long-term welfare dependency is for our society, including policymakers, to realize that *spiritual* transformation must be a central component of the fight against poverty, and to reshape assistance efforts accordingly. This does not mean that if reformers shift the emphasis to spiritual regeneration they can then forget about structural changes. Both are needed. But it does mean that unless policies take into account the importance of the inward transformation of belief and character, nothing else will work properly. A host of explicitly faith-centered agencies are already facilitating successful long-term change in people's lives in inner cities. What is needed is a wholistic approach based on a new model of partnership between religious organizations, government, and other institutions in society.

Until recently, such a proposal would have seemed to have little prospect of acceptance among policy elites and government decision makers. But the mounting evidence of the disastrous failure of decades of government programs and the depth of the current crisis are permitting new questions to be asked. Stephen Carter's *The Culture of Disbelief*[41] and

41. Carter, *The Culture of Disbelief: How American Law and Politics Trivialize Religious Devotion* (New York: Basic Books, 1993).

President Clinton's extensive promotion of its call to allow religion to return to the center of the public square underline the change that is occurring.

How effectively could religious programs affect the behavior and circumstances of long-term welfare recipients? Precise research data are not available to answer that question adequately, in part because of a bias in much of academia against religious belief as a variable in social research. Dr. David Larson worked for ten years as a research psychiatrist at the National Institute of Mental Health. In numerous publications, he has described the lack of research on the impact of religion on people's well-being.[42]

The research that has been done confirms that people with religious faith are less likely to engage in behaviors associated with poverty — divorce, single parenthood, drug abuse, alcoholism, quitting school. Larson shows that in the cases where the impact of religious faith has been scientifically measured, the results are extremely positive. In one review of the research, active religious commitment (prayer, church attendance, etc.) was found to have a positive impact in 92 percent of the cases.[43] Religious faith decreases the likelihood of divorce; even attending church only once a month makes a person more than twice as likely to stay married as a person who attends once a year or less.[44] Junior high and high school youth who attend religious services at least once a month are about half as likely to participate in socially destructive behaviors such as alcohol and drug use, sexual activity, truancy, and misdemeanors.[45] Noted crime analyst James Q.

42. For example, see David B. Larson et al., "Systematic Analysis of Research on Religious Variables in Four Major Psychiatric Journals, 1978–1982," *American Journal of Psychiatry,* Mar. 1986, 329-34. Similarly, a survey of articles published in the *Review of Religious Research* reveals only two articles relating religion to socioeconomic well-being over the past five years.

43. David B. Larson et al., "The Anti-Tenure Factor in Religious Research in Clinical Epidemiology and Aging" and "Neglect and Misuse of the R Word, Systematic Reviews of Religious Measures in Health, Mental Health, and Aging," in Jeffrey S. Levin, ed., *Religion in Aging and Health* (Thousand Oaks, Calif.: Sage Publications, 1994); Larson et al., "Associations between Dimensions of Religious Commitment and Mental Health Reported in the *American Journal of Psychiatry* and the *Archives of General Psychology:* 1978–1989," *American Journal of Psychiatry* 4 (1992): 557-59.

44. David B. Larson and Susan S. Larson, "Is Divorce Hazardous to Your Health?" *Physician,* June 1990; also George Rekers, ed., *Family Building* (Ventura, Calif.: Regal Books, 1985), 130.

45. Search Institute, "The Faith Factor," *Source* 8 (1992), 1.

Wilson has claimed a correlation between periods of revival and reduction of crime in American history.[46]

An important study by Richard B. Freeman, a Harvard economist, showed that church involvement is the single most important factor in enabling inner-city black males to escape the destructive cycle of the ghetto. Church attendance proved a better predictor of who would escape poverty, drugs, and crime than any other variable — including income, sports, and family structure. Freeman's study indicated that churchgoing youth were more likely to use their time in socially productive, rather than destructive, ways.[47] This research suggests that religious commitment has a profound impact on people's whole lives, not just on their sense of spiritual satisfaction.

Studies also confirm, but have yet to examine comprehensively, the crucial role of churches in families' struggles against poverty and dependency. In general, churchgoers are more likely to give aid to the poor: 63 percent of church attenders (versus 44 percent of nonattenders) volunteer to help the needy; almost half of evangelical Christians are engaged in some social ministry.[48] Churches also often contribute direct financial support. The black church, in particular, has long been a cornerstone of the black community, "a major survival component" for struggling families.[49] Two-thirds of black respondents in a national survey said they received some level of support from church members.[50] Churches both relieve poverty and prevent it as they serve as employment networks, buffers against crises, and distributors of goods and services, and as they teach the values and behaviors that translate into economic well-being.

There is also growing evidence that faith-based nonprofit social agencies, such as drug and alcohol treatment programs, are more successful than secular ones. An independent study showed that Teen Challenge, the world's

46. James Q. Wilson, "Crime and American Culture," *Public Interest,* Winter 1983, 22. See also Charles Colson, *Kingdoms in Conflict* (Grand Rapids, Mich.: Zondervan, 1987), ch. 16.

47. Freeman, 354.

48. George Barna, *What Americans Believe* (Ventura, Calif.: Regal Books, 1991), 226; Ronald J. Sider, *One-Sided Christianity? Uniting the Church to Heal a Lost and Broken World* (Grand Rapids, Mich.: Zondervan, 1993), 117.

49. Newton, 92.

50. Robert Joseph Taylor and Linda M. Chatters, "Church Members as a Source of Informal Social Support," *Review of Religious Research,* Dec. 1988, 196.

largest residential drug rehabilitation program, has a 95 percent success rate for heroin users and 83 percent success rate for alcoholics, a substantially higher success rate than most.[51] Dr. Catherine Hess, former director of New York City's first methadone program for drug addicts, studied Christian drug rehabilitation programs that emphasized prayer, conversion, and the power of the Holy Spirit. She concluded that Teen Challenge was and is "probably the most effective rehabilitation program I have ever seen anywhere." Dr. Hess identified the religious component as the one aspect that produced the high success rate.[52]

The importance of religious faith in the solution of social problems is beginning to be acknowledged by leaders at both the grassroots and the national level. Many involved in social reform agree with Irene Johnson, president of the LeClaire Courts Resident Management Corporation in Chicago: "At heart, the fundamental axis of real transformation and growth is spiritual in nature."[53] Public officials are increasingly coming to share the conclusion of Anna Kondratas, formerly the assistant secretary for community planning and development at the U.S. Department of Housing and Urban Development: "In my experience, religious social service organizations often seemed to have the highest success rates because they recognized the spiritual dimension to rehabilitation that public programs did not take into account."[54]

Biblical faith helps to explain why Christian social programs combining prayer and conversion with counseling and material assistance work better than secular programs. People are not isolated bodily machines. A person is a body-soul unity made for community with God and neighbor.

51. LeRoy Gruner, "Heroin, Hashish, and Hallelujah: The Search for Meaning," *Review of Religious Research,* Dec. 1984, 177. Compare this with the finding of a federal study that only one percent of low-income drug addicts and alcoholics receiving disability benefits recover from their addictions or find work: "Few on Welfare Said to Defeat Addiction," *New York Times,* Nov. 16, 1994.

52. David Manuel, "Teen Challenge: Conquering Drugs," *Saturday Evening Post,* Dec. 1987. The distinctly Christian character of Teen Challenge contributed to another sociologist's conclusion that "the religious approach is not only a viable treatment modality but in some instances is the only approach that works" (Gruner, 177).

53. Quoted in Anna Kondratas, "Welfare Policy: Is There Common Ground?" *Hudson Briefing Paper* (Washington, D.C.: Hudson Institute, Aug. 1993), 6.

54. Anna Kondratas, now a senior fellow at the Hudson Institute, telephone interview with the authors, Mar. 28, 1994.

A rebellious relationship with God leads to tragic consequences at every level of our physical and social experience. A renewed, reconciled relationship with God contributes to better physical and emotional health, more productive choices, and improved relationships with others. It is not surprising (at least to Christians) that drug recovery programs that include prayer, conversion, supernatural empowerment by the Holy Spirit, and the embrace of a loving community of sisters and brothers are more successful than secular ones. This approach works because it is grounded in a biblical view of persons. Marxist strategies for creating new societies and even new persons through comprehensive structural change have visibly failed in our time — but so have American policies that try to solve social problems while ignoring humanity's spiritual dimension.

This is not to endorse the notion that the only way to change persons is by individual conversion. We are social beings. The structures of society influence us profoundly. Better education, housing, and job opportunities make a significant difference in people's well-being. Christian mission should be an integrated mix of evangelism, material assistance, and social transformation. Cultivating individual morality and responsibility should take place alongside pursuing social morality and responsibility — influencing culture, lobbying for just public policies, confronting racism. But by themselves, structural change and material aid cannot get to the root of the problem. Nowhere is that clearer than in our ravaged cities, where welfare programs cannot touch the pervasive sense of hopelessness and despair.

Nor does asserting that private organizations are the most effective agents for correcting social problems mean that the government has no responsibility for relieving and preventing poverty. The government has a role that only it can play, and that Christians should insist that it does play. Government is responsible for ordering society at the macro level in accordance with justice; for maintaining the infrastructure that supports social, economic, and political well-being; and for ensuring law and order. In addition, government must ensure that its policies do not encourage racism, family dissolution, unemployment, or other catalysts of poverty. Discussing the broader roles of government and church is outside the scope of this chapter, but we assume that Christians should be passionately concerned about justice in every way.[55]

55. For further discussion of a Christian philosophy of government responsibility and of the vital importance of structural justice, see these works by Ronald Sider: "To

God calls people of faith to extend themselves to help those who are disadvantaged. Christians are in a special position in society to bring real assistance and change to poor people. Religious institutions have been deeply involved in welfare throughout American history. Before government transfer programs were established, Christians and other religious people aided the nation's poor in great numbers and with a high degree of effectiveness.[56] Today, in spite of the greater availability of government aid, many religious people still are involved in social ministries. Currently, 58 percent of Christians report donating time or money to help needy people in their area.[57] Ninety million volunteers (almost half of all adults) and nine hundred thousand nonprofit organizations, many of them religiously based, help provide vital services for the poor and the general public — medical care, education, food, shelter, clothing, job training, drug rehabilitation, and child care.[58] Is it not time to try a new solution that builds on the strengths of our nation's religious communities?

Toward a New Partnership between Government and Religious Institutions

Since private faith-based programs have demonstrated a high potential for success in correcting social problems, welfare reformers should rethink the government's relationship to religious institutions that provide services to the needy. Government should not displace nongovernmental efforts to help the poor. (Nor, of course, should government abandon all responsibility to empower the poor.) Nor should government support for private-sector efforts discriminate against faith-based groups. What is needed is a new *partnership* between government and religious (and nonreligious) service groups. Are there ways for government to channel funds to effective faith-based programs that have a clear public (or "secular") purpose in a

---

Be Servant Advocates," *ESA Advocate,* Sept. 1988; "Towards a Political Philosophy," *ESA Advocate,* Oct. 1988; "The Limits of Politics," *ESA Advocate,* Nov.–Dec. 1988; and *Rich Christians in an Age of Hunger,* 3rd ed. (Dallas: Word Publishing, 1990).

56. Olasky.

57. Barna, 224.

58. "What Should We Do About the Poor?" (editorial), *First Things,* Apr. 1992, 9.

fashion that is consistent with the First Amendment? It is unjust and counterproductive for government to invest its social spending predominantly in secular public programs that are by nature less effective.[59]

Several possible policies could preserve our historic separation of church and state, and thus the independence of both, and still enable funding to go where it is most effective. Generous tax credits for certain kinds of donations might be one way. Government contracts with private faith-based organizations is another.

Perhaps it is time to think carefully, as well, about expanding the use of vouchers to allow government money to be used in the most effective programs, including those operated by religious organizations. Recent federal legislation that allows states to give families vouchers to purchase child care explicitly states that nothing "shall preclude the use of such certificates for sectarian child care services freely chosen by the parent."[60] This represents an important acknowledgment by the federal government that it should treat all qualified child-care service providers equally. The voucher system is also used to support Section 8 housing for low-income families. For years, the government has been giving the equivalent of vouchers to lower-income college students in the form of Pell grants. The individual students who receive the grants can use them in a secular, a Christian, or a Jewish university — in any accredited institution they choose. Since every eligible person receives the grants and is free to use them in any accredited school, the government in no way supports one religion over another, or secularism over religion.

59. Government social programs are often less effective than nongovernmental ones. For example, a 1984 study of fifty-seven county agencies in California found that contracting out social services to private organizations generally improved the quality of service and effectiveness of care. See Stephen Moore, "Privatization Lessons for Washington, Part II: Improving Human Services," *Heritage Foundation Backgrounder,* Sept. 28, 1988, 2. Moreover, private welfare efforts are significantly more cost-effective. Savings from privatization of welfare services range from 20 percent to 60 percent, according to John Hilke, "Cost Savings from Privatization: A Compilation of Study Findings," Mackinac Center for Public Policy (Midland, Mich.), 12. As one illustration, New York City's privately operated welfare-to-work program, America Works, claims a 68 percent success rate in helping clients leave welfare, saving the government $17,700 per year for each former recipient — and producing an annual revenue of $2 million. See Jay Mathews, "Taking Welfare Private," *Newsweek,* June 29, 1992.

60. The Child Care and Development Block Grant Act of 1990, Public Law No. 508, section 658P(2).

Might it not work to use this same voucher mechanism to deal with a broader variety of human needs? The vouchers could be in the form of government checks made out to specific qualifying individuals, who would then be free to use them at any approved agency, either religious or secular, as payment for specified services. Drug addicts, for instance, might be given vouchers to be used at any drug rehabilitation program that meets certain basic criteria of safety and success. This proposal does not call for the government to write checks to churches and synagogues; vouchers could be redeemed only at private nonprofit agencies with their own legal charter. Public money would come to faith-based agencies through vouchers brought by clients who freely choose them instead of a secular alternative. Furthermore, government money would not be used to fund private agencies' programs of Bible study, worship, spiritual formation, or religious education.

At the same time, government regulations should not discourage the religious components that are central to the programs' effectiveness. If Spirit-filled, conversion-oriented addiction recovery programs work twice as well as the local government-run program, so be it. And if a new Buddhist program proves even better, that too should be fine with the government. Individuals seeking help could take their vouchers to the most successful programs. Indeed, one important service that government could provide would be to conduct objective evaluations of all approved programs and to require that agencies post their success rates.

Could we not also give vouchers to people with a legitimate need for government support for job training? counseling? medical care? And what about the basic cash payments for welfare recipients? Might there be a way to allow faith-based programs to compete with the government bureaucracy in overseeing welfare grants?

Unfortunately, the courts have sometimes interpreted the First Amendment in a way that restricts the participation of faith-based groups in government-funded social programs or that demands that such groups deemphasize the spiritual emphasis that makes them successful. For example, agencies accepting some types of public funds may not display *any* religious symbols in their buildings or literature.[61] Such an extremist in-

61. Carl H. Esbeck, "Government Regulation of Religiously Based Social Services: The First Amendment Considerations," *Hastings Constitutional Law Quarterly* 19 (1992): 375.

terpretation of church/state separation has been supported, as Stephen Carter's *The Culture of Disbelief* shows, by a general bias against religion in the public arena. Growing public acknowledgment of the important role of religion must be accompanied by a new, constitutionally valid church-state partnership.

The basic test for constitutionality was established in the U.S. Supreme Court case of *Lemon v. Kurtzman* (1971). According to this test, a government program that benefits religion can be constitutionally acceptable if it meets the following criteria: "First, the statute must have a secular legislative purpose; second, its principal or primary effect must be one that neither advances nor inhibits religion; finally, the statute must not foster 'an excessive government entanglement with religion.'"[62]

In *Bowen v. Kendrick* (1988), the Court applied this test to the 1981 Adolescent Family Life Act, which was designed to prevent teen pregnancies. The act made funding available to religious agencies, acknowledging that "such problems are best approached through a variety of integrated and essential services provided to adolescents and their families by other family members, religious and charitable organizations, voluntary associations, and other groups in the private sector." In its decision, the Supreme Court determined that such public funding may be provided to religiously affiliated or inspired social programs only if they are not "pervasively sectarian" and if they can demonstrate that the government-funded activities do not primarily advance religion. In addition, the distribution of funds must be neutral with respect to religious affiliation: any program that benefits Christian organizations must be similarly available to Buddhists, Muslims, Jews, and atheists.[63]

In other cases, the Court has ruled that state aid to individuals could be used toward social services at even pervasively sectarian organizations, if recipients freely choose to receive services at the religious agency.[64] While child care is still a particularly sensitive issue, the courts have tended to give more license to public funding of religious child-care centers in connection

62. Esbeck, "Government Regulation of Religiously Based Social Services," 356.

63. Dean M. Kelley, "Public Funding of Social Services Related to Religious Bodies" (American Jewish Committee, 1990), 12ff.

64. *Mueller v. Allen* (1983); *Witters v. Washington Department of Services for the Blind* (1986); *Zobrest v. Catalina Foothills School District* (1993). See Carl H. Esbeck, "A Restatement of the Supreme Court's Law of Religious Freedom: Coherence, Conflict, or Chaos?" *Notre Dame Law Review* 70, no. 3 (1995): 581-650.

with the use of vouchers that allow the parents to choose the provider.[65] These recent court decisions seem to support a move toward increased church-state cooperation. "On the ascendancy is the argument that to secularize religious social ministries in order that they might participate in government programs on an equal basis with their secular counterparts is a 'penalty' the Establishment Clause does not demand."[66]

A number of legal questions remain to be resolved. First, in accepting public aid, religious organizations fall subject to potentially intrusive state regulations, although in some cases these regulations have been found to violate the free exercise clause. A second troublesome point is the extent to which religious nonprofits may make employment decisions on the basis of religion. Also, the courts have yet to define clearly what constitutes a "pervasively sectarian" institution, and they have not established clear guidelines to distinguish religious from secular activity. Many Christian agencies stress prayer, worship, evangelism, and discipling as central to the success of their social programs. They will feel threatened, rather than relieved, by the observation of Justice Blackmun that "the risk of advancing religion at public expense . . . is much greater when the religious organization is directly engaged in pedagogy, with the express intent of shaping belief and changing behavior, than where it is neutrally dispensing medication, food or shelter."[67] Wholistic, faith-based ministries to the poor may need to challenge this judicial view of what constitutes "neutral" activities.

Rethinking and modifying church-state practices of the last few decades carries significant risks as well as possibilities. In seeking a closer partnership with government, religious agencies must resist the temptation to become secularized or embroiled in political affairs. Dean Kelley, director of religious liberty for the National Council of Churches, warns religious agencies of the potential adverse consequences of accepting federal aid:

> *Tax money is political money;* you don't often use it to undercut the existing political structure. . . . Religious bodies and their agencies are not likely to offer a critical and countervailing witness to government and the whole society if they are "wired in" to the existing structure of government operations in the most binding way imaginable — by shar-

65. Kelley, 21.
66. Esbeck, "Government Regulation of Religiously Based Social Services," 352.
67. Kelley, 19.

ing the lifeblood of government, tax money. This tends to make religious bodies part of the *problem* rather than part of the *solution.* . . . Furthermore, religious bodies that have founded helping institutions to make tangible their concern for the needy often find those institutions drifting away to become more and more like their "secular counterparts."[68]

A successful partnership between church and state depends on both institutions remaining true to their best nature. Where this is not possible, the religious organization should refrain from accepting public funds rather than compromise its beliefs and undermine its effectiveness and integrity.[69] Since restrictions and regulations vary from state to state, programs should be flexible and locally grounded. Citizens, legislatures, and the courts must search for and test creative ways to allow nonprofit faith-based organizations to become more deeply involved in offering a variety of social services. Needed are new models and practices that will permit religious social agencies to use government funds while preserving their religious character and avoiding the unconstitutional mixing of church and state.

In recent years, government has increasingly sought to take advantage of the greater efficiency of both for-profit and nonprofit private agencies. Cities now contract over half of their human services funding to private organizations.[70] Government and private sector antipoverty efforts are linked in numerous ways, particularly on the local level, showing that "'public' and 'private' are not antonyms; they are two distinct but related ways of expressing the social nature of human beings."[71] Peter Drucker has recently proposed "a public policy that establishes the nonprofits as the country's first line of attack."[72] Good public policy will welcome religious nonprofits as key players in a new, more wholistic approach.

68. Kelley, 26-27 (italics in original).

69. For example, CityTeam in San Jose, California, turned down government funding to expand its highly successful substance abuse rehabilitation program because the aid carried the stipulation that CityTeam drop religious requirements for participants (Olasky, 214-15). A positive example is the compromise reached by Circle Urban Ministries and the city of Chicago, in which Circle continues to give evangelism a central place in its city-funded emergency housing program, but does not require church attendance and does not use government funds to pay for the evangelistic activity.

70. Moore, 2.

71. Novak et al., 108.

72. Quoted in Andrew C. Little, "The Future of Social Welfare May Be Just Down the Street," *Viewpoint on Public Issues,* Mackinac Center for Public Policy (Sept. 7, 1992).

This vision is not radical. It is economically realistic and historically grounded. It fits with the increasing practice of privatization. It comports with the desire of the ascendent congressional Republicans to rely more on society and less on government. It is, moreover, "consistent not only with the Clinton administration's welfare reform philosophy but also with another major theme of the administration, namely, 'reinventing government' to make it more flexible and responsive and to leverage public resources with private ones to solve social problems."[73] The task of crafting constitutionally valid public-private cooperation open to religious participation will not be easy, and the road will not be short — or without pitfalls. But this is an essential initiative.

Elements of a New Partnership to Empower the Poor through Welfare Reform

Examples that point the way toward a new model of private-public partnership are available, and they show good results. One public-private cooperative venture is Project HOMES in Fairfax County, Virginia. The Department of Housing provides housing certificates for homeless low-income families; the Department of Human Development identifies clients, coordinates the program, and trains volunteers; churches and community organizations sponsor client families, making long-term commitments to financial and social support. In four years, over 70 churches have assisted over 150 families to achieve stable housing and economic self-sufficiency.[74] Another example is a child-care voucher program in Hennepin County, Minnesota, that replaced a system of assigning low-income families to county-subsidized centers. Families were allowed to choose their own private child-care centers, including religious ones. Because of the program, the average monthly cost of child care dropped, the number of centers increased, and more families were able to find child care.[75]

The State of Michigan, like a number of other states, has taken advan-

73. Kondratas, 9.

74. Project HOMES Newsletter (Winter 1993–94); *Building on Faith: Models of Church-Sponsored Affordable Housing Programs in the Washington, D.C. Area* (Washington, D.C.: The Churches' Conference on Shelter and Housing, 1989).

75. Moore, 8.

tage of the federal government's encouragement of state experimentation with welfare reform. Some of Michigan's reforms seem to represent first steps toward a productive public/private partnership. Following a strategy of "Privatize, Eliminate, Retain, or Modify," Michigan has begun a process of evaluating state government to see what might be handled with greater quality or cost efficiency by the private sector. This approach to government has been integrated with Michigan's overall welfare reform program, "To Strengthen Michigan Families," which stresses education, employment, and community-based services. One of the components of this program, Families First, provides intensive services to preserve families at risk of having a child removed from the home, with an 80 percent success rate. In order to lower costs and improve the caseworker-to-family ratio, the state's Department of Social Services contracts all Family First services to private agencies, many of them religiously based. Contracts with private foster-care agencies — again, including religiously affiliated agencies — provide another "privatization success story," with higher-quality care delivered at a lower cost.[76]

In 1991, responding to budgetary pressures, Michigan eliminated the General Assistance program, which provided cash assistance to childless adults, many of whom were homeless. To help the 83,000 GA recipients adjust to the loss, the state expanded its emergency assistance program and contracted with the Salvation Army to coordinate the increase in services for the homeless. State funding for some 120 shelters throughout Michigan flows through the Salvation Army. The Salvation Army and the shelters it works with offer a myriad of other services. In these state-subsidized shelters, *privately* funded spiritual counseling, worship services, and Bible studies take place, without conflicting with Michigan law. The contract is temporary, but the Salvation Army expects the partnership to continue and to evolve as the state moves toward long-term solutions and a "seamless continuum of services" for the homeless.[77]

76. "To Strengthen Michigan Families," booklet printed by the Michigan Department of Social Services; Mark G. Michaelsen, "Privatized Child Foster Care Works for Michigan," *Viewpoint on Public Issues,* Mackinac Center for Public Policy (Aug. 2, 1993); telephone interviews with Stephanie Comai-Page, Michigan Department of Social Services, and Chere Calloway, privatization director, Michigan Department of Management and Budget.

77. Based on a telephone interview with Gary Bayer, Salvation Army's housing services coordinator; see also Lawrence W. Reed, "Michigan's Welfare Abolitionist," *Policy*

These stories show that new church-state partnerships *are* in the realm of the possible. What is needed is to go a step further and to extend what has been accomplished in places like Michigan and through programs such as Project HOMES. Can this basic approach be expanded to apply to a comprehensive program for welfare cash-grant recipients?

A Possible Model

We offer the basic outline of a model countywide welfare program constructed on what we believe are biblical principles about persons and society, current trends in welfare reform, successful examples of social outreach, and dreams of the future shape of social ministries. We propose here a program run by Christians. We would of course insist that any state that agreed to fund such a program would also offer to work in the same way with similar programs run by Muslims, secularists, or other groups.

1. The coordinating center for the program would be a Christian nonprofit organization, legally independent from but closely related to area churches. The Christian nonprofit would administer the program, train volunteers, coordinate services, keep case records, and serve as the liaison with government. The network of churches associated with the program would provide volunteers and funding for explicitly religious activities such as Bible studies, worship, and evangelism.

2. Participation in the program would be voluntary. Welfare recipients would enter the program with an understanding of its religious character and would have the option of a secular private or government-run alternative. However, no one could be denied entrance into the program based on their religious affiliation.

3. Funding would combine a variety of sources, public and private. Government funding would come largely via vouchers issued to welfare recipients. These vouchers would cover all the cash payments and other services now provided by public welfare programs.

Review, Fall 1993. A study of the impact of the discontinuation of General Assistance found that "the quality of life generally declined for former GA recipients," suggesting that these compensatory efforts have not been wholly sufficient to meet the need. See Sandra K. Danziger and Sherrie A. Kossoudji, "What Happened to General Assistance Recipients in Michigan?" *Focus* (Institute for Research on Poverty) 16 (Winter 1994–95): 32.

4. The welfare department would refer people to the program. Program participants would receive their cash grant and other services only as they participated cooperatively in the program; they would be free at any time to leave and return to a state-operated program. Eventually, the coordinating center could take over the task of screening and processing new welfare applicants, determining eligibility based on government guidelines.

5. The program would develop a comprehensive, integrated mix of services designed to meet the needs of the whole person: a medical clinic; marriage and family counseling services; child care; housing (with the long-term goal of home ownership); GED preparation; job training (in cooperation with local businesses, which would help design the program and guarantee job placements); and a legal clinic. Emergency needs would be met through a food pantry, utility bill assistance, and other services.

6. A wholistic philosophy would undergird all programs. All staff would be trained to deal with each person as a unique, responsible, valuable person, created in the image of God, who needs to have right relationships with God, neighbor, self, and the earth in order to be a whole person. Therefore, conversations about "spiritual" questions would be natural for the doctor or the job-skills trainer, although intensive conversations on such matters would normally be referred to volunteer spiritual counselors or the participant's volunteer sponsoring family (see the next point). But every staff person would know and act in the knowledge that a right relationship with God and the transformed character and ethical principles that personal faith brings are just as essential as new job skills.

7. Each participating family or individual would be "adopted," or sponsored, by a church family, which would agree to develop a long-term relationship, including weekly contact, support and friendship, and help with needs that arise. Regular visits by sponsoring families in the participants' homes and vice versa would be normal. Sponsoring families would receive training from the program, including training in cross-cultural communication and racial reconciliation, as appropriate. Participants would be invited, though not required or in any way coerced, to attend a church. If a welfare recipient is already a Christian, the sponsoring family would seek to nurture and strengthen that faith. If the welfare recipient is not a Christian, the sponsoring family would share its faith in natural, sensitive, nonmanipulative ways.

8. A quality Christian school, preferably funded through state education vouchers, should be available to all children of participating families.

The children would also be welcomed and included in the supporting churches' youth groups and children's programs.

9. The program would include job training programs in cooperation with the business community. The program would develop commitments for jobs for those who complete the training. The program might also run its own small businesses, training participants to become entrepreneurs themselves.

10. All participants would work, volunteer, attend school, or receive job or skills training from the time of their entrance into the program. Activities would include parenting, life skills, and home economics training; volunteer work at nonprofit agencies; or apprenticeships in local businesses. The program's child-care center would free single mothers to study or work, as well as give them a place to work or volunteer. Training would emphasize character development, community and family values, and personal fulfillment in work.

11. Every participant would be involved in a weekly small group led by a trained person (funded by the church network) who would teach biblical ethical values related to family, work, sex, parenting, etc. The small group would also give participants an opportunity to discuss relevant community issues, share personal concerns, and receive prayer.

12. Staff would include a social worker trained in family counseling. Fathers and mothers on welfare would be encouraged to go through the program together, without being penalized for having both parents present. Where family brokenness is a factor, obstacles to marital reconciliation would be addressed. Teenage mothers would be encouraged to live with their parents or a church family. Seniors in the churches would be recruited to serve as "adoptive" grandparents and to work in the child-care center, thus emphasizing the importance of extended family ties.

13. The network of churches would sponsor regular religious rallies, inviting program staff, participants, sponsoring families, church members, and others from the community. These rallies would articulate a wholistic Christian faith that cares for the whole person and would call everyone to personal faith, discipleship, biblical family life, and active volunteering in service programs.

14. The churches would fund a subunit of the program devoted to policy questions, which would study employment, housing, and demographic trends in the community, analyze government policies for their impact on the program and the people it serves, keep informed of new

insights in community development, represent the program to the state, and evaluate the program's effectiveness.

Many communities already have implemented pieces of this model. But two framework components are missing: the availability of sufficient government funds to make a comprehensive mix of services possible, and the flexibility to allow religious organizations to contribute to the public welfare effort. Our model for a cooperative welfare program could infuse the current counterproductive welfare enterprise with the expertise, efficiency, and commitment of the private sector's most able advocates for the poor — the religious community. By allowing spiritual transformation to play a central role in the fight against poverty, the tragic cycle of welfare dependency might be broken.

Our proposal makes several assumptions. The first is that such a wholistic approach, which nurtures spiritual transformation just as emphatically as it offers medical care and job training, will be far more successful than present programs in producing long-term change and will result in far more people escaping the welfare trap. The second is that there would really be enough committed Christians to make the program possible. Both assumptions might be wrong. But surely a serious five-year experiment in at least one or two daring counties somewhere in the country would be worthwhile.

Social Service Agencies and Religious Freedom: Regulation, Funding, and the First Amendment

Julia K. Stronks

A New Vision for Welfare Reform[1] argues that government welfare policies should be reformed so that they move people to fulfill the diverse responsibilities of a healthy life. It assumes, however, that this change can take hold only if we acknowledge that social reality consists of more than only individuals and government. People live their lives as members of a wide range of social institutions: families, churches, schools, companies, charitable and cultural nonprofits, recreational groups, and more. One of government's key responsibilities, the essay claims, is to uphold a good social order so that people and institutions can fulfill their diverse callings. This means that any government welfare reform must take into account the role that nongovernmental organizations play in helping people to fulfill their own diverse responsibilities in life. Churches, soup kitchens, homeless shelters, child-care centers, domestic-violence safe houses, and federal, state, and city agencies that serve low-income citizens in a variety of ways must all be considered to be part of our social fabric.

This chapter considers how contemporary jurisprudence on the religion clauses of the First Amendment to the United States Constitution is problematic for the integrity of religious nongovernmental institutions that are subject to regulation or accept government funds. The First Amendment

1. Center for Public Justice, *A New Vision for Welfare Reform: An Essay in Draft* (Washington, D.C.: Center for Public Justice, 1994), reprinted in the Appendix to this volume.

provides that "Congress shall make no law respecting an establishment of religion, or prohibiting the free exercise thereof. . . ." These few words have produced tremendous disagreement regarding the appropriate relationship between government and institutions that define themselves as "religious."

In general, when a citizen or a group invokes the *free exercise* clause, courts decide first whether or not a religion exists, and second, whether or not the state has a compelling interest to override the religious activity or belief. A compelling interest is said to exist when the state's goal is very important and there is no less restrictive way for the state to achieve the goal.

The *establishment clause* issues usually involve groups or people who believe they have been harmed by government's support of someone else's religion. The basic test for violation of this clause was set forth by the U.S. Supreme Court in *Lemon v. Kurtzman* in 1971 as follows:

- The statute must have a secular legislative purpose: did legislators have a nonreligious, secular purpose in mind or were they motivated by religious, sectarian goals?
- The statute's principal or primary effect must be one that neither advances nor inhibits religion: does it have a secular effect, meaning is it neutral in regard to religion, neither helping nor hindering it?
- The statute must not foster an excessive government entanglement with religion: does the statute require such extensive administrative oversight by government as to amount to a continuing relationship between the church and government?[2]

These broad principles for interpreting the two religion clauses are themselves a matter of continuing jurisprudential controversy. The complications only increase when the principles are applied to specific cases. For example, if government requires churches and church-related agencies to comply with licensing procedures and other regulations, is it necessarily violating the free exercise clause? Does that clause require government to keep its hands off religious institutions, or is there a way in which government could require compliance with certain obligations without interfering with the self-identity of an institution? The establishment clause, on the other hand, presents other difficult questions. If government funds social service agencies, may it or must it differentiate between religious and non-

2. *Lemon v. Kurtzman*, 403 U.S. 602 (1971).

religious agencies? Would government be violating the prohibition against "establishing" religion if it reforms welfare to include religious agencies as key deliverers of social services to the needy?

As the following analysis will show, the answers to these questions are not clear in contemporary jurisprudence. One key reason is that the courts employ a distinction between "religious" and "secular" activities that is at odds with the way some faiths understand reality. In some cases, judges assume that the distinction between the sacred and the secular activity of a religious institution is self-evident. In other cases, judges acknowledge that "religion" is not simply an added factor that an organization can embrace or reject at will. Instead, it constitutes the manner or direction in which all of the activities are carried out. If they lack an accurate and consistent understanding of religious activities and institutions, judicial decisions are inconsistent.

The issue of what the First Amendment requires when government touches religious institutions is the substance of continuing litigation at every level of our judicial system. It is a critical matter for these institutions, but essential as well for government as it seeks to devise more effective ways to assist needy people in our society. In this chapter I will examine two distinct and controverted areas of First Amendment jurisprudence: government's licensing and regulatory impact on religious social services, and the complications that accompany public funding of religious social services. The cases in the former instance fall under the "free exercise clause" of the First Amendment; the cases in the latter instance are "establishment" cases. However, just as the two clauses cannot be understood except in relation to each other, we will see that these two kinds of cases raise similar issues and reveal some common confusions.

Licensing Requirements and Regulation

Agencies that provide social services to citizens of the United States are subject to a wide variety of governmental regulatory laws. Employment practices are regulated by civil rights laws and labor laws; health and safety standards protect employees and consumers; tax codes determine which agencies must contribute to the public coffers; and zoning ordinances determine where the agencies may set up shop. But may government regulate religious charitable organizations in the same manner that it regulates other charitable groups? Or should a religious nonprofit organization providing social services be exempt from regulatory law by virtue of its religious character? Should the law distinguish between the "religious" activity of a religious organization and its "secular" activity? Can such a line be meaningfully drawn, and on what grounds could such a distinction be made?

The history of jurisprudence concerning religious freedom in this country makes it clear that these are not easy questions for the courts. The United States Supreme Court has handed down few cases applying the religious liberty provisions of the Constitution to the relationship between government and religious institutions other than schools, and the school cases that do exist have been called inconsistent and incomprehensible even by the justices themselves.[3]

I will discuss several cases involving the principle of religious liberty as it applies to government regulation of religious groups providing social services. We will see that conflicting outcomes are the result of inconsistent court specification of the character of religion and differing court views of how religion may direct or define the activity of an organization.

A Decade of Conflict: Forest Hills Early Learning Center v. Grace Baptist Church and the State of Virginia

Since 1948 the state of Virginia, like many other states, has required all child-care center operators to obtain licenses and to comply with specific health and safety regulations. For years the standards were fairly limited in scope. Until the 1970s, virtually none of the litigation involving child-care centers raised the free exercise argument that sectarian centers must be exempt from regulation or the establishment argument that the Constitution forbids such an exemption.

Throughout the 1970s, however, women entered the workforce in larger numbers, and more and more children began to be brought up in single-parent homes. The public desire for safe, regulated child care increased, and states responded by setting detailed and mandatory standards concerning not only the health and safety aspects of centers but also discipline of the children, parental involvement or control over the centers, and sometimes even the centers' curricular programs.

3. See Justice Antonin Scalia's dissent in *Edwards v. Aguillard,* 107 S. Ct. 2573 (1987).

In 1976, the Virginia Department of Welfare passed comprehensive child-care regulations. Many churches responded with the argument that their religious beliefs would permit them to accept neither licensing nor regulations. Licensing usurped the authority of God over the church, they claimed, and regulations interfered with a task — child care — that was an integral part of the church's religious ministry. In response, the Virginia legislature passed an exception to the regulations, saying that any child-care operation offered by a religious institution would be exempt from both the licensing requirement and all but the most basic safety and health regulations.

When the exemption was passed, nonsectarian child-care centers sued the state, claiming that the statute violated the establishment clause.[4] The nonsectarian centers claimed that they were at a disadvantage in competing with sectarian centers because their religious counterparts did not have to make the expensive modifications necessitated by the state regulations. The nonsectarian centers were required to comply with extensive state regulation in the areas of licensing, programs, insurance, financial resources and management, staff qualifications, and internal administration. The sectarian centers, by contrast, were subject only to minimal health and safety regulations and suffered almost no sanction if they failed even to comply with these minimum requirements. According to the nonsectarian centers, the state's exemption of the sectarian centers from virtually all regulation constituted, in effect, state support of religion and thus the constitutionally proscribed establishment of religion.

This case was litigated from 1979 through 1989. Initially the lowest federal court held that, as a matter of law, the statutory exemption was constitutional because the First Amendment permits, and may even require, that the religious freedom of sectarian centers be protected. Religious freedom, in the court's view, meant that the state must keep its hands off the religious institutions.

On appeal, however, the Fourth Circuit Court of Appeals held that there could be no general prohibition of the regulation of religious institutions or their activities. If the Forest Hills Early Learning Center wanted

4. *Forest Hills Early Learning Center v. Grace Baptist Church and the State of Virginia,* 487 F.Supp. 1378 (E.D.Va.1979), reversed and remanded, 642 F.2d 448; 540 F.Supp. 1046, affirmed in part, vacated in part and remanded, 728 F.2d 230; 661 F.Supp. 300, reversed 846 F.2d 260; rehearing denied, cert. denied 109 S.Ct. 837 (1989).

to justify its exemption on free-exercise grounds, it had to show that the exempt activities themselves were sufficiently "central" to the organization's faith identity. The Court said that the fact that an activity was a "good work" of a religious institution did not make it a "religious" activity. Core religious practices like prayer, worship, and ritual were entitled to protection, but if an organization sought a religious-liberty exemption from licensing and general regulations, it would have to show that the organization's own core religious identity was damaged by the licensing process and the regulations. The Court added that, once this initial hurdle was overcome, the state would still have the chance to deny a religious exemption based on a compelling state interest in regulation and licensing.

The circuit court sent the case back down to the district court for findings regarding the distinction between the "religious" and the "secular" activities of the sectarian child-care centers. In response, the district court's 1987 decision rephrased the issue as a question of

> whether and to what extent free exercise rights expressed in exempt activities would be burdened by the application of the state's minimum standards for licensed child care centers to church-run centers and, if so, whether that burden is nevertheless justified by a compelling state interest.[5]

The court's attempt to draw a line between religious and secular activities was summarized in a single paragraph:

> Regarding the issue of whether the operation of child care centers by class members is a part of their respective ministries, this Court concludes that *while the class members may characterize this activity as a part of their ministries, the Court is not bound to accept this characterization.* Applying the tests set forth by the Fourth Circuit, the Court concludes that the operation of child care centers by these sectarian institutions *is a secular, and not religious, activity.* Therefore, the operation of such centers is not entitled per se to free exercise protection. The operation of a child care center is not an "active expression" of the churches' particular beliefs regarding their ministering to their children but is merely incident to such "active expression."[6]

5. 661 F. Supp. 300 (E.D.Va. 1987).
6. 661 F. Supp. 300, 309 (E.D.Va. 1987)(emphasis added).

The court's analysis rested on the observation that some religious child-care agencies did not object to state licensing regulation, which was "probative" of whether or not child-care centers were an expression of "centrally held religious beliefs." Furthermore, because the church child-care centers only began to be developed in the 1970s, it was likely that their existence was a response to the growing number of women in the workforce — a "secular," not a "religious," response, in the court's view.

However, the court then proceeded to cover all bases. It said that even if the operation of a child-care center *was* a religious activity, the compelling state interest in protecting the health and safety of children justified the licensing requirement. Moreover, the licensing request was the least restrictive means of protecting this interest. For example, the information requested by the state on its one-page financial disclosure form "represents a minimal intrusion into the financial affairs of one secular activity conducted by a church — its child care center — while serving the purpose of assuring a center's financial ability to comply with the standards."[7] Because the intrusion was limited, and the state concern significant, religious interests must bow to the government.

The court then applied the same reasoning to the question of the legitimacy of state regulation of the operation of the religious child-care centers. The churches objected that the minimum curricular standards would permit the state to impose program content requirements that reflected a "secular humanism philosophy" incompatible with their religious beliefs. Without discussing any possible conflict between secular humanism and the churches' belief systems, the court simply concluded that the curricular requirements did not regulate substantive content; in its view, the requirements, in "encouraging [the] centers to provide a broad range of activities, without directing the content or substance of such activities,"[8] simply promoted the physical and mental development of the children. The churches disagreed, on the grounds that the requirement to promote a "positive self-concept" and to include rhythm, music, and dancing in the daily activities of their programs could conflict with their vision of dancing as sinful and man as depraved. In response, the court simply asserted that there was no basis to conclude that the state would interpret its regulations in such a way as to conflict with the programs of the church-run institutions.

7. 661 F. Supp. at 330.
8. 661 F. Supp. at 330.

Finally, the state also required that the child-care centers refrain from corporal punishment. The churches argued that they should be in charge of meting out discipline in accord with their own teachings. The court said that

> [b]ecause the operation of a child care center is a secular activity even when conducted by a church, the state may require a church-affiliated child care center to refrain from corporal punishment. Even if the activity were religious, the state had a compelling state interest in protecting young children in care away from home from physical and emotional harm.
>
> Where religious practices risk or endanger the health and well-being of members of society, the state may regulate such practices to avoid the adverse health consequences.[9]

It is clear from this analysis that the court and the churches were talking past each other, and that the court's solution did not address the actual conflict between the parties. The churches argued that if something is religious it ought to be beyond the reach of government. The state appeared to stress the reality that religious activity is not just internal belief, but has a real, social presence, and went on to argue that government is obliged to be involved with the social realities of the activity, even if the activity is religious in character. The court's response was to claim that the activity itself was not really religious. Apparently a church-run center taking care of children in accordance with its interpretation of Scripture is not engaged in a religious activity!

The court did not stop there. Instead it held that even if it conceded the religiosity of the activity, the state's compelling interest superseded any First Amendment protection of religion. But this is a dangererous line of argumentation. If the state can regulate without limit in the name of protecting the "health" and the "well-being" of society by resorting to the compelling-interest doctrine, then it can easily substitute its own vision of the good society for that of any given religion or faith community. But it is precisely this majoritarian regulation of faith commitments that the First Amendment was designed to protect against. Religious organizations do not have carte blanche in dealing with the children in their care, but when

9. 661 F. Supp at 311.

a court first claims that child care is not religious in nature and then claims that even if the care is religious the state's compelling interest trumps any religious protection, then regulation is a foregone conclusion.

However, even without such a resort to the compelling-interest doctrine in order to override a religious claim, the jurisprudence concerning the regulation of religious activity is confused and damaging. Here is the crux of the problem. Courts and legislatures *will* regulate the activity of religious organizations, and not all such regulation is illegitimate. The critical question is how to determine what type of activity should be within the regulatory jurisdiction of the government. If the courts approach this question with a scheme in which religious activity is shielded from regulation but secular activity is not, then the definitions of "religious" and "secular" are critical.

The *Forest Hills* child-care case illustrates the difficulties courts face when they determine for themselves which activities are religious and which are not. This difficulty was only made worse by developments at the level of the U.S. Supreme Court. One year after the district court in *Forest Hills* held the licensing and regulatory provisions to be applicable to religious child-care centers despite the legislated exemption, the Supreme Court handed down an employment case that upheld as constitutional a federal statute that gave religious institutions an exemption from civil rights employment laws.

Amos: *Protecting Religious Activity*

In the 1987 case, *Corporation of the Presiding Bishop of the Church of Jesus Christ of Latter-Day Saints v. Amos,*[10] the crux was the Supreme Court's recognition that the attempt to draw a sharp line between the "religious" and the "secular" activities of a church-related institution could *damage* the self-definition of the religious organization. Applying the *Lemon* establishment-clause test, the Court found that it was a legitimate legislative purpose "to alleviate significant governmental interference with the ability of religious organizations to define and carry out their religious missions."[11]

The intent of the Court was to promote religious liberty by protecting

10. 483 U.S. 327, 107 S.Ct. 2862, 97 L.Ed.2d 273 (1987).

11. *Amos,* 107 S.Ct. at 2868.

religious groups from laws that force them to conform their behavior. The Court also wanted to protect any religious group from having to defend its beliefs and practices in issue-by-issue free-exercise litigation before "a judge [who may] not understand its religious tenets and sense of mission."[12] The upshot of *Amos* was that if states or the federal government wanted to make special allowances for religious institutions, they could. The scope of those allowances was up to the legislatures.

The *Amos* case was handed down just as the federal district court was setting forth its condemnation of the Virginia exemption for religious child-care centers. Within weeks the Virginia case was appealed once again to the Fourth Circuit court, asking the appellate judges to use *Amos* to rule the exemption of religious child-care centers to be constitutional. In a two-page decision, the circuit court did exactly that. Ten years after the litigation had begun, the church-run child-care centers were free from government regulation.

Since the decisions of *Amos* and *Forest Hills,* numerous federal courts have upheld state laws that exempt from regulation child-care agencies integrally related to a church. Courts do this easily, without analysis.[13] However, important issues relating to the identity of religious institutions remain unresolved. First, what constitutes a "religious" organization? In the case of child-care agencies, the legislation and jurisprudence concerns centers run by churches. There has been little legal action concerning centers that are not church-operated but that regard themselves as religious and thus exempt from most regulation. This does not mean, however, that such cases will not develop. In the area of employment rights the nature of

12. *Amos,* at 2868. The Court said that legislative exemptions for religious institutions would *lessen* the risk of entanglement between church and state because the free exercise litigation that would occur absent the exemption would result in ongoing government involvement in religious affairs. "This would both chill and interfere with religious groups, enmeshing judges in intrusive and sometimes futile attempts to understand the contours, sincerity, and centrality of the religious beliefs of others." *Forest Hills* at 846, F.2d at 264.

13. For example, in *Forte v. Coler,* 725 F.Supp. 488 (M.D.Fla. 1989), the court granted summary judgment in favor of religious child-care centers, holding without discussion that "[although church-related facilities] still must comply with minimum local health, sanitation, and safety ordinances and Florida's personnel screening requirements, they are not subject to the broad ranging regulations other child care facilities must conform to." *Forte* at 490.

"religious institutions" has been litigated for years, and courts still fluctuate between being willing to create this definition themselves and allowing the institutions to define their own "religiosity."[14]

There is an important further question: does the judicial determination that the establishment clause of the First Amendment does not *prohibit* states from exempting religious institutions from generally applicable law mean that the courts will now *require* states to grant exemptions if the legislators are not inclined to do so voluntarily? Apparently it all depends. Given the concern in *Amos* that issue-by-issue litigation would entangle the courts in "religion" and threaten the self-identity of religious institutions, it seems reasonable to expect that the courts would require states to grant a general "religious" exemption to individuals and groups claiming that state laws cause them to violate their faith. In the past the courts have done exactly that, using the standard of "compelling state interest" as the criterion for deciding if state regulation of religious activity is legitimate. However, the validity of this standard has been rendered uncertain by the United States Supreme Court.

Smith: *Threat to Religious Liberty?*

In the highly publicized and criticized 1990 case known as *Employment Division, Dept. of Human Resources of Oregon v. Smith,*[15] the Supreme Court determined that in some instances the compelling-state-interest standard was inappropriate when an individual or group asserted a claim based solely on the free-exercise clause of the First Amendment. According to Justice Antonin Scalia's opinion, the right of religious free exercise does not relieve an individual of the obligation to comply with a valid and neutral law of general applicability just because he or she thinks the law constricts activity that a religion requires. Restrictions on religious activity need be only "reasonable" in order to be constitutionally sound; the state need not show a "compelling" interest in order legitimately to override a claim based on religion.[16] With this new standard to guide them, federal courts deciding

14. See J. Stronks, "Defining Religion: the Courts, Neutrality and Statutory Interpretation" (Ph.D. diss., University of Maryland, 1995).

15. 485 U.S. 660, 108 S.Ct. 1444, 99 L.Ed.2d 753 (1990).

16. Two Native American men had claimed that an Equal Employment Opportunities Commission decision denying their plea for unemployment insurance discriminated

cases concerning regulation of religious social service agencies backed away from the "hands-off" position taken by the Supreme Court in *Amos.*

A clear instance of this reversal is the decision of the Third Circuit appeals court in a case involving boarding houses operated by the Salvation Army *(Salvation Army v. New Jersey Department of Community Affairs).*[17] A Rooming and Boarding House Act had been enacted by the state of New Jersey in response to public outcry regarding the unsafe conditions of boarding houses. The legislation regulated the physical safety of the residents, but it also instituted a bill of rights for people living in the rooms, emphasizing the privacy and freedom of the residents. The voluntary rehabilitation centers run by the Salvation Army were subject to this new legislation.

The Army's centers were designed to renew and rehabilitate homeless and socially troubled men through spiritual teaching, counseling, and work therapy. Rehabilitation included mandatory "work therapy" in the Salvation Army's thrift stores. This work, for which the residents received a gratuity but no salary, helped to fund the centers but also served as a means of helping the residents take a place in society. Residents of the centers were required to engage in "spiritual activities," including religious services and spiritual counseling. Because of the communal nature of the rehabilitative process, visitation was restricted and socialization during meals and other activities was regulated. Residents, however, were free to leave the program at any time.

When the legislation was adopted, the Salvation Army asked for an exemption from the law's provisions related to the physical safety of resi-

---

against them on the basis of their religion. The EEOC denied the claim because the men were fired from their jobs for ingesting peyote, a hallucinogenic cactus, during religious ceremonies. Because the men were fired from their jobs for participating in wrongful conduct, they were precluded from collecting unemployment insurance. The Court held that the law prohibiting drugs was valid and thus the state was justified in refusing compensation. In determining whether or not the legislation was "valid," the Court asked not whether the state's interest was "compelling" but whether it was "reasonable." Furthermore, the Court acknowledged that leaving accommodation of religious expression to the legislative, political process could place minority religions at a disadvantage. As long as the law was "neutral," not distinguishing between religions, it was legal. Calling this the unavoidable consequence of democratic government, the Court stated that it was preferable to a system in which each conscience is a law unto itself.

17. 919 F.2d 183 (3rd Cir. 1990).

dents. The Army justified its request on the ground that the centers were neither "secular" nor "social," but rather central to the religious mission of the Salvation Army. The court, however, relying on the Supreme Court's recent *Smith* ruling, found that because the act was not directed toward religious activity, and thus was "neutral" toward religion, the regulation could not be successfully challenged on free-exercise grounds. The court would not require the state to grant exemptions for religious organizations.[18] Interpreted in accordance with *Smith,* the religion clauses of the First Amendment apparently do not protect religious agencies from state regulation.

The Free-Exercise Minefield

The cases in this section illustrate two problems. First, jurisprudence concerning what constitutes a "legitimate concern" of government is confused and contradictory. One purpose of the First Amendment is to protect the minority when its faith conflicts with the majority's faith or perspective. To limit the protection accorded to religion when the state's interest is compelling, and then to define "compelling" in such broad terms as protecting the "health, safety, and welfare" of society, is to weaken the First Amendment's protection of religion. Moreover, given the importance of the First Amendment's dictates regarding religion and the pivotal role of any standard of a "compelling" state interest or "reasonable" legislation, it would appear that a set of national standards or understandings is crucial. If these matters are left to state legislators, there will be no uniformity or continuity. If they are left to the judges, again there will be neither uniformity nor continuity. Precisely because there is so much judicial and legislative con-

18. *Salvation Army* was not a child-care case, but if child-care cases prior to *Salvation Army* and *Smith* are examined, the position judges will take in the future seems clear. Even before *Smith,* judges found in favor of the state when sectarian child-care centers challenged state regulations that interfered with them. The courts used the compelling-state-interest standard to justify the regulation. See, e.g., *North Valley Baptist Church v. McMahon,* 696 F. Supp. 518 (E.D. Cal. 1988). Post-*Smith,* the test moves from "compelling interest" to the lower threshold of the "reasonableness" of the state's concern. In 1994, Congress passed the Religious Freedom Restoration Act, which purports to restore the compelling-interest test to cases of this type. Litigation testing the constitutionality of this act is sure to follow.

troversy concerning these critical matters, the time is ripe for an extended public discussion about how far the state's authority should run when it touches on other institutions in society.

Second, these cases suggest that when church groups or religious institutions argue that the First Amendment requires that the government keep "hands off" in every important respect, they undercut themselves. A "hands-off" position has little support, either from the public in general or from the religious communities. Most churches and church-related agencies are willing to comply with state standards regarding the physical safety of their buildings and similar matters. At the same time, most churches and church-related agencies object to state interference when it comes to programmatic matters. Rather than pursue an untenable attack on all government regulation, we should work to distinguish between legitimate and improper regulation, between rules governing physical safety and health and rules that damage the integrity and intent of programs. Is there a principled way by which to differentiate between the two? That is the critical question in this troubled and developing area where government action touches the prime constitutional guarantee of religious liberty.

Funding Private Social Service Agencies

The uncertain distinction between "religious" and "secular" activity that complicates licensing and regulatory affairs complicates in a similar way jurisprudence concerning whether government funding of institutions with a religious connection can pass constitutional muster.

Traditionally, many of the welfare services provided in this country were supplied by private and voluntary groups, rather than by government. Churches and church-related institutions were historically at the forefront of "social work" and charitable action. However, throughout the twentieth century government has become increasingly involved in the social services arena. Yet because private agencies were so well established as service providers, the government's new interest in social service was often implemented in the form of assisting private agencies that were already operating. Because so many of the welfare or charitable agencies had a religious tie, the government thereby opened itself to the charge that in financially backing religious charities it was violating the First Amendment's prohibition against establishing religion. Interestingly enough, while the parallel issue of government aid to religious schools has spawned a tremendous amount of federal and state litigation, government assistance to religious social welfare agencies has been litigated with vigor only over the past ten years.

In this section I will analyze the jurisprudence that defines the limits of government aid to religious social service agencies. Among the important questions are these: What is the difference between a religious organization and a charitable one? Is there a constitutionally significant difference between government funding of a soup kitchen operated by a church and government funding of a soup kitchen run by people who happen to believe that God wants them to help the poor? What about a group that believes it has a moral duty to feed the poor but is not tied together by a common faith? How do the courts draw these distinctions, and what are the implications of their decisions?

Bowen: *Another Decade of Conflict*

The constitutional dilemmas raised by government funding of religious social service agencies came to the forefront upon the adoption by Congress of the Adolescent Family Life Act (AFLA) in 1981.[19] Congress passed the legislation in response to what it recognized as the "severe adverse health, social and economic consequences" that often follow pregnancy and childbirth among unmarried adolescents.[20] The act has several purposes:

- to promote self-discipline and other prudent approaches to the problem of adolescent premarital sexual relations;
- to promote adoption as an alternative for adolescent parents;
- to establish new approaches to the delivery of care services for pregnant teenagers;
- to support research concerning social causes and consequences of teenage premarital sexual involvement.

Recipients of government grants under the act are to provide care services for pregnant teens and also to provide prevention services, which may include:

19. Public Law 97-35, Stat. 578, 42 U.S.C. §§300z et seq.
20. 42 U.S.C. §300z(a)(5) (1982 ed., Supp. IV).

> pregnancy testing, maternity counseling, adoption counseling and referral services, prenatal and postnatal health care, nutritional information, counseling, child care, mental health services, educational services relating to family life and problems associated with adolescent premarital sexual relations.[21]

In adopting the AFLA, Congress explicitly acknowledged that certain social problems are so complex that government action alone is insufficient. Such problems need to be addressed "through a variety of integrated and essential services provided to adolescents and their families by other family members, *religious and charitable organizations,* voluntary associations, and other groups in the private sector as well as services provided by publicly sponsored initiatives."[22] This language is reminiscent of passages in *A New Vision for Welfare Reform.*[23] In the AFLA, Congress explicitly acknowledged the vital role that nongovernmental organizations play in the social fabric of our society.

Under the act, grant money has gone to private and public hospitals, private and public health care agencies, private community centers, private and public educational agencies, and charitable organizations. Many of the private agencies have formal ties to churches, and many others consider themselves to be religious whether or not they are formally owned by a church.

In 1984, a lawsuit was filed by a group of taxpayers, the American Jewish Congress, the American Civil Liberties Union, and three Methodist ministers, with the claim that the AFLA was unconstitutional because it violated the establishment clause of the First Amendment.[24] The district court found the AFLA to be unconstitutional because "religion" was integrated into the goals of the act and because religious organizations directly received money. The court applied the three-part *Lemon* test to decide whether the act required an impermissible government establishment of religion. It concluded that the AFLA had the valid secular purpose of "prevent[ing] social and economic injury" caused by teenage pregnancy, but that it also had the illegitimate direct effect of advancing religion

21. 42 U.S.C. §300z.
22. §300z(a)(8)(B) (emphasis added).
23. Center for Public Justice, e.g., 576ff.
24. *Bowen v. Kendrick,* 657 F.Supp. 1547, reversed and remanded 108 S.Ct. 2562 (1988).

because it expressly required grant applicants to describe how they would involve religious organizations in the provision of services.

When the case was appealed, the United States Supreme Court found that there was nothing necessarily religious about education or counseling services, even if those services were provided by a church-owned agency. Applying the *Lemon* test in its turn, the Court rejected the idea that religious institutions are unable to fulfill their functions in a "secular" manner. It agreed with the lower court that because the reduction of social and economic problems was the primary purpose of the act, the legislative purpose was secular. But the Supreme Court went on to find that no "impermissible effect" was created simply because Congress recognized the role religious organizations play in solving "secular problems." The Court distinguished between institutions that are "pervasively sectarian" and those that are merely religious, saying that only aid to organizations that could not separate their religious teaching from their services was unconstitutional.

The Court further found that although the government would have to monitor the agencies to ensure compliance with the constitutional proscription on advancing religion with the assistance of government, the third prong of the *Lemon* test was not violated because there was no excessive entanglement. There was no reason to assume that the religious organizations that received grants would be "pervasively sectarian" in the same way that, for example, parochial schools are.

Bowen *in Practice: Continued Confusion*

In *Bowen*, the Supreme Court held that the government may fund social service agencies with religious ties as long as those agencies are not pervasively sectarian. However, after a decade of litigation that continues today, answers to two important questions remain uncertain. First, what does it mean to judge that an institution is "pervasively sectarian"? Second, how may a religious institution receive government funding to help it carry out its charitable mission while retaining the autonomy it needs to preserve its religious character? The litigation spawned by *Bowen* clearly shows that the decision left unresolved the critical issues involved in government funding of religious social service agencies.

Just three years after the Supreme Court handed down its decision on the funding of religious social service institutions, a group of plaintiffs again represented by Kendrick sued Louis Sullivan, the then-secretary of the Department of Health and Human Services, on the grounds that federal funds under the AFLA were impermissibly flowing to "pervasively sectarian" organizations like A Woman's Choice, Catholic social services, and others.

The new suit *(Kendrick v. Sullivan)*[25] began in federal district court with a plea for a summary judgment on the issue of the sectarian nature of these organizations. After examining more than 1750 documents offered in support of the defendants' claims that, while their organizations were religious, they were not "pervasively" so, the court concluded that summary judgment was not appropriate and that the organizations would have to defend themselves in a series of trials to determine how sectarian each of them was.

Although the court did not give specific guidance to the judges who would be presiding over those trials, its approach to the difficult issue of the nature of religion is enlightening. The court held that the pervasively sectarian standard was a factual issue that could be determined based on the individual situations of each institution considered separately. It cautioned that the judges should limit their trials to whether a grantee's secular purposes and religious mission were inextricably intertwined, emphasizing that it would not be enough to show that the recipient of a challenged grant is affiliated with a religious institution or that it is religiously inspired. Instead the judges must ask whether the institution's religion is so pervasive that a substantial portion of the institution's functions are subsumed under its religious mission. However, the interpretive issues are much more difficult than the federal district court's instructions imply. The evidence that defendants must resort to in order to show their lack of pervasive sectarianism will be difficult to evaluate in the federal court's terms by the judges when they must make their factual rulings in the cases.

The plaintiffs in the post-*Bowen* litigation have argued that the religious missions of the religious social service organizations wholly shape the services that the organizations tender to their clients. In support of this position they argue that the religious organizations have policies that prohibit deviation from religious doctrine or that require employees to abide

25. 766 F.Supp. 1180 (D.D.C. 1991).

by religious principles. Religious leaders sit on the boards of directors of the organizations, and many of the organizations discriminate on the basis of religion in their hiring decisions.

In response, the defendants have had to argue that even if all of this is true, the organizations are not pervasively sectarian because they have created separate divisions to carry out the services for which they receive AFLA funding. These separate divisions provide "secular services"; any religious references have been excised from the literature, and staff have been instructed to keep their "personal convictions" (religious, political, prejudiced, or social) to themselves.[26]

How are judges to resolve this dispute? One problem is confusion over concepts such as "morality," "values," "religion," "spirituality," and "sectarian."[27] These concepts are all involved in the legal disputes about the religious nature of the publications produced by the religious service organizations. The Supreme Court's implicit position in *Bowen* is that institutions can have a religious grounding and do moral or good deeds, and yet not do the deeds in an impermissibly religious ("pervasively sectarian") way. Is this correct? Is morality different from religion? In what way? In deciding these cases, will the fact finder have to determine whether or not there is a moral, value-neutral — in no way religious — way to teach about sexuality?

The second problem is that the characteristics that are supposed to be used to distinguish between an institution that is only "religious" and one that is impermissibly "pervasively sectarian" are, at best, elusive. A Minnesota district court in 1990 compiled a list of the factors that justices of the United States Supreme Court have employed at one time or another to determine whether or not a religious school is pervasively sectarian. These factors include such things as whether the institution was owned and operated by members of a religious order or had on its premises religious symbols, whether members of the religious order wore clerical garb, whether prayer was a regular feature of the institution's activities, and whether religious considerations affected hiring decisions.[28]

26. 766 F.Supp. at 1184-91.

27. For criticism of the Supreme Court's use of the word "religious" interchangeably with "sectarian," see Richard Baer, "The Supreme Court's Discriminatory Use of the Term 'Sectarian,'" *Journal of Law & Politics* 6 (1990): 449-68.

28. *Minnesota Federation of Teachers v. Nelson,* 740 F.Supp. 694 (D. Minn. 1990).

The problem is that the conception of religion implicit in this list is severely limited. The list presumes religion to be constituted by rituals, prayer, and proselytizing. But there are faiths, and dimensions of all religions, that do not comport with this typology. Some faiths hold that all of life is religious, so that the absence of clerical garb has nothing to do with the actual religiosity of the organization. The distinction between religious and nonreligious practices so blithely made by the courts is foreign to every faith community that perceives life to be an integral whole.

In a supreme irony, the *Bowen* cases, which arose from the effort of Congress and the Supreme Court to clear the way for religious groups to offer their services more widely in the public square, have had the effect of requiring the religious institutions to hide their light under a bushel basket. In order to defend themselves, they are forced to argue that the services they provide are religiously neutral. For some of the organizations, compliance with the courts' guidelines is not problematic. They have little difficulty purging "God talk," prayer, and references to morality from their soup kitchens and other services. They argue that while their motivation to feed the poor may be spiritual, the acts themselves are secular. Other organizations believe that the requirement of making such a distinction violates their religious identity. Regarding life to be an integrated whole, they believe that their faith defines their actions. Excising God talk does not excise faith.

There are other serious problems as well. If religious organizations accept the courts' encouragement to draw a sharp line between the supposedly "religious" and "secular" parts of their work, they encourage the pre-*Amos* interpretation that permits states to regulate all "nonreligious" aspects of their work. Further, it is not even clear that the strategy of dividing the religious from the secular will work in the long run. Most courts follow the approach of the district court in *Forest Hills,* stating that they are not bound by the self-definition of an institution. This may be to the benefit of a religious organization, but it may not be. In the Minnesota case that generated the list of "sectarianism" criteria, for instance, even though college catalogs claimed that "there can be no division between sacred and secular subjects" and that "considering education in the light of Christ, there can be no division between sacred and secular subjects," the court found some of the institutions not to be pervasively sectarian.[29] On

29. 740 F.Supp at 718, 719.

the other hand, courts do not allow religious elementary schools to receive public funds just because they have excised God from parts of their curriculum.[30]

It is also possible that when the post-*Bowen* cases are appealed to the Supreme Court, the Court will separate social service agencies into different categories. The Court could decide that religious agencies distributing physical services are not pervasively sectarian, but those distributing advice are. This would make predicting the outcome of religious-freedom jurisprudence easier, but it would not solve the core substantive conflicts that are illustrated by these cases.

The First Amendment and Religious Social Service Agencies: A Legacy of Confusion

The cases in this analysis show that there is a series of major problems in the application of the religion clauses of the First Amendment to religious social service agencies. First, the courts are working with an assumption that traps them. Most judges assume that the "religious" is separable from the "secular" and that the dividing line can be discerned by looking for such activities as prayer, proselytizing, and worship. If these activities are excised from the institution or separated from the services the institution offers to the public, then religion has been safely set aside. But the reality is that religious expression is *unavoidably* a matter not only of personal devotion but also of the public and institutional realms. The rearing and schooling of children is a matter not just of religion but of family law and education legislation. Eating and drinking as part of religious ceremonies involves the Food and Drug Administration. The hiring and firing of employees is a matter of federal and state labor law.

Courts cannot escape this reality. The Supreme Court recognized this when it held in *Amos* that a church's religious identity and status as a religious community enfolded even the employees of its "nonreligious" endeavors, such as a gymnasium. What is required is clear and hard thinking about the nature of religion. Is it to the benefit of religious institutions to encourage some conception of a division between "religious" and "secular," or does the very effort to define such a division damage the integrity of

30. *Lemon v. Kurtzman.*

religious institutions' identity? Further, is it in fact possible to achieve "neutrality" by excising "religious" elements? Does not neutrality consist rather in government dealing in an evenhanded way with both religious and nonreligious programs and institutions?

The second problem relates to the parameters of the First Amendment. Does the First Amendment *require* state protection of the religious, or does it merely *permit* such protection? And is it the responsibility of the courts, or the legislatures, to make this determination? In either instance, the *Forest Hills, Amos, Smith,* and *Bowen* cases suggest that religious institutions are between a rock and a hard place. The good news is that sometimes the government may grant religious institutions exemptions from onerous laws that apply to other institutions. The bad news is that the government apparently is not in every case bound by the Constitution to extend such an exemption. If a legislature exercises its right not to grant an exemption, an institution cannot use its religious identity as a shield from regulation if a compelling state interest is at stake — or, judging from *Smith,* if the state law is valid, is neutral, and has general applicability.

A third problem is that, even if a legislature grants religious-freedom exemptions, institutions, in order to invoke this right, must be able to establish that they truly are religious. Prior to *Amos,* this had to be done by illustrating that there was no difference between the secular and religious activities of the institution. Jurisprudence currently presumes that it is virtually impossible to distinguish between the two. There is again both good news and bad news. The good news is that such a presumption gives religious institutions the benefit of the doubt in the case of freedom from regulation. The bad news is that religious institutions are ineligible for government funding of their services unless they are able to draw a line between religious and secular activities.

Actually, the matter is more complicated than this. The judicial division between religious and secular on which *Amos* cast doubt was reinvigorated by *Bowen* in the guise of the pervasive-sectarianism standard. If the courts recognize the difficulty of separating religious activity from secular activity, it is hard for religious institutions to claim that they are not pervasively sectarian. On the other hand, if the courts say that it is possible to separate the religious from the secular, the religious institutions weaken their case for exemptions from state regulation.

These opposite dangers result in a tightrope walk for organizations that define themselves by faith commitments. They may legally establish their religious identity and receive an exemption from regulation — but become ineligible for government funds. Or they may downplay their religious identity and lose their exemption — but gain funding. Many organizations perceive this trade-off to be coercive and thus in violation of both the free-exercise clause and the establishment clause. Other organizations accept the trade-off on the grounds that one or the other, either freedom or a share of government funds, is more important. However, it does not seem constitutionally legitimate for religious groups to be confronted with the trade-off at all. And in practical terms, in the aftermath of *Smith* it seems likely that religious groups lacking legislative clout or public favor will lose out on both freedom and funding.

Surely there must be a better way. It must be possible for religious social service agencies simultaneously to maintain their religious identities, be shielded from improper state regulation, and participate in government programs that fund social service providers.

What Do We Do Now?

The rules and standards set by the *Bowen* and *Amos* cases are confusing, but within the confusion created by the courts lie important opportunities for religious institutions to contribute to the development of First Amendment jurisprudence. The Supreme Court seems to want very much to continue the tradition of involving religious institutions in the provision of social welfare services. In fact, the Court's decision in *Bowen* could easily have been affected by *amicus curiae* briefs submitted by governors and attorneys general of states, suggesting that the "partnership" between government and churches in sheltering the homeless, tending the sick, and counseling the bereaved was one of the most effective ways in which to address our nation's social problems.

Another aspect of the court decisions is also promising. In the line of Supreme Court cases concerning public funding of religious educational institutions, it appears that one reason why sectarian colleges, but not sectarian elementary or secondary schools, have been held eligible for public money is that college-aged students are less religiously impressionable than are younger students. The *Bowen* Court could have followed this reasoning and decided that the young age of the teenagers addressed by the AFLA programs rendered religious social service agencies providing services funded by the act to be inherently pervasively sectarian. The Court chose not to take this tack, and thereby created the opportunity to utilize the religious/secular distinction to categorize the various activities of an organization rather than the organization as a whole.

This is, of course, a tricky and even a suspect distinction. Some judges have interpreted the significance of the sectarian school cases to be that if young children are involved, any connection between a church and another institution renders the latter impermissibly pervasively sectarian. If the same principle is applied in the case of social service agencies, then child-care centers, homeless shelters serving families, youth programs, and so forth would all fail the sectarianism test. Other judges, however, focus on the type of service that is offered. In the school cases, funding for services or goods that are selected by public institutions is acceptable, but funding for supplies chosen by religious institutions — even maps for geography classes — is not. Applied to the realm of social services, funding for food distribution might be allowable, but funding for services that involve intensive work with clients concerning life choices or that have a large advice-giving component might be unacceptable.

In my view, a very important initiative for religious organizations is to determine where and when government involvement is legitimate. What is the difference between the regulation of physical safety and other varieties of regulation? If we can offer a principled way to draw such distinctions and a principled argument about what kinds of government regulation are appropriate, we will build a foundation of credibility for our arguments for the protection of religious free exercise. One key place to start is by reexamining what we mean by a "religious" institution or activity. Is religion an additive quality that can be removed by excising references to God or hiding Bibles? Or does religion define the entire character of the institution?

The Supreme Court justices themselves have termed the types of distinctions drawn by the religious-freedom cases both incoherent and inconsistent. This means that the Supreme Court may be susceptible to new arguments regarding the application of the religion clauses of the First Amendment to the field of religious social service agencies. It is vital for advocates of religious service in the public square to determine how we can make a constructive contribution to the current morass of jurisprudence concerning these issues.

Balancing Care and Cure: The Place of Health Care Reform in the Welfare Reform Debate[1]

Clarke E. Cochran

WELFARE REFORM must not be done in isolation from health care reform. So I shall argue. The two policy arenas are intimately connected. The Social Security system includes Medicare. Medicaid is a form of in-kind public assistance, and its financing, eligibility, and administrative structures are linked to AFDC and other "welfare" programs. Other federal and state programs (community health centers, health professional training, indigent care laws) target the same poor people as welfare programs.

The health status of the aged and the poor lags behind the rest of the population, placing them in greater need for health care, which they would have great difficulty affording in the absence of public programs. Poor health contributes to poverty, and poverty makes health deterioration more likely. Inadequate pre- and postnatal care damage the learning ability and physical capabilities of poor children in ways that diminish future income-earning potential. Chronic and acute conditions limit the ability of the poor to work. Finally, eligibility rules for Medicaid and other public health care programs contribute to the work disincentives of welfare: parents possess a powerful incentive to keep their income below the "notch" at which

1. Thanks for early suggestions and for responses to requests for information belong to Siegrun Fox Freyss, Grace Simmons, Robin Hoover, David Caes, Grant Savage, and David Swartz. The following persons were kind enough to read early drafts and provide valuable criticism: Stanley Carlson-Thies, Cyndi Simpson, Delina Barrera, Ted Dotts, Bill Brandon, and David Cochran.

eligibility for Medicaid ends. If private health insurance at the level of Medicaid were available to all low-income single mothers, their AFDC participation would drop as much as 25 percent![2] A parent lacking private health insurance who made her children ineligible for Medicaid would be acting *irresponsibly.* Therefore, effective welfare reform must be accompanied by effective health care reform.

The existence of a health care crisis should be clear, although the recent decline in health care inflation has suggested to some policymakers that health care reform might not be urgent. However, the *Christian* answer to whether there is a health care crisis need not track public perception or congressional rhetoric. Lack of access to decent health care is, according to Christian principles, an assault on human dignity. The growing number of persons, particularly the poor, without health insurance confirms this daily assault. Moreover, technological imperatives driving the health care system not only contribute to the rising cost of health care (placing it out of reach for many), but also offend the Christian sense of human limits.

Between 35 and 40 million Americans, many of them unemployed or working in marginal jobs, or the dependents of workers, have no health insurance at any given time. Fifty million lack coverage for some period of each year. Although some of these are young and relatively healthy individuals who have chosen not to purchase health insurance, the large majority of them are women, children, and working families below or near the poverty level, who are unable to afford insurance or are uninsurable because of existing medical conditions. Despite the historic focus of social welfare policy on children, reflecting the consensus that children's health care deserves greater attention, and despite recent program expansions, Medicaid still does not cover all poor children, and many children lack access to basic health care services.[3] Moreover, state limitations on Medicaid coverage and low reimbursement

2. Robert Mofitt and Barbara L. Wolfe, "Medicaid, Welfare Dependency, and Work: Is There a Causal Link?" *Heath Care Financing Review* 15 (1993): 123-33.

3. A good introduction to the access problem is Irene Fraser, "Health Policy and Access to Care," in Theodor J. Litman and Leonard S. Robins, eds., *Health Policy and Politics*, 2nd ed. (Albany, N.Y.: Delmar, 1991), 302-19. See also Alice Sardell, "Child Health Policy in the U.S.: The Paradox of Consensus"; and Lawrence D. Brown, "The Medically Uninsured: Problem, Policies, and Politics," both in Lawrence D. Brown, ed., *Health Policy and the Disadvantaged* (Durham, N.C.: Duke Univ. Press, 1991), 17-53 and 169-83, respectively. Recent data on the uninsured may be found in D. Chollet, "Employer-Based Health Insurance in a Changing Work Force," *Health Affairs* 13, no. 1 (1994): 315-26.

rates often severely restrict the medical services and physician choice available to those who do qualify. Special access problems face rural residents and retirees whose previous employers have reneged on health coverage promises.

It would be an exaggeration to say that such persons lack any access to health care. If a person is sick enough, an emergency room somewhere is legally required to provide stabilization care. The real problem of the uninsured is that such care is often difficult to get, comes at the wrong time, and is far more costly to society than regular preventive or maintenance health care. Health care for the uninsured is "too little, too late." Moreover, recent research indicates that the uninsured receive less care than insured persons with the same diagnoses even when they do make it into hospitals or other health care institutions.[4] Race enters into this equation, as it almost always does in American social policy. Blacks and other minorities are disproportionately uninsured, and they receive fewer beneficial procedures even when they have coverage.[5]

Christian Faith and Health Care

Jesus' ministry includes dedication to healing. John's disciples ask how they are to know that Jesus is the one who is to come. He answers, "Go back and tell John what you hear and see; the blind see again, and the lame walk; lepers are cleansed, and the deaf hear, and the dead are raised to life, and the Good News is proclaimed to the poor" (Matt. 11:2-6). Attitudes toward sickness and death lie close to the heart of the Christian paradox that "[h]e who wishes to save his life shall lose it, but whoever loses his life for my sake will save it" (Luke 9:24). On one side of the paradox lies the truth that sickness and death are not part of God's plan for humanity but enter human life as consequences of sin (Gen. 3:16-23). From this perspective, illness and death are enemies of the fullness of life. Thus, Jesus announces a new abundant life (John 10:10), the kingdom of God, by healing the sick and

4. Henry J. Aaron, *Serious and Unstable Condition: Financing America's Health Care* (Washington: Brookings, 1991), 77.

5. See Mitchell F. Rice and Mylon Winn, "Black Health Care and the American Health System: A Political Perspective," in Litman and Robins, 320-34, and Jan E. Mutchler and Jeffry A. Burr, "Racial Differences in Health and Health Care Services Utilization in Later Life: The Effect of Socioeconomic Status," *Journal of Health and Social Behavior* 32 (1991): 342-56.

raising the dead. In the end, Jesus confronts his greatest enemy on the cross, accepts death, and defeats it in resurrection (1 Cor. 15:25ff.; Rom. 6:9; 2 Tim. 1:10; Phil. 2:5ff.).

The other side of the paradox, however, is that sickness and death are forever parts of *this* life. They must be accepted, even embraced, as a condition of entry into the kingdom. The disciples of Jesus must "take up their crosses" (Matt. 16:24) daily to follow him. Physical death and death to self are the only doors to eternal life.

This paradox of life and death contains complex implications for health care itself and for health policy reform. Christians follow the example of Jesus the healer. They regard sickness, suffering, and death as inimical to God's will and, therefore, struggle to oppose them. Christian hospitals, nursing homes, and clinics, as well as prayer for healing, are essential to (indeed, constitutive of) the church. Regarding death as a great enemy carries over into serious reservations about, indeed often firm opposition to, the taking of life in war, abortion, and capital punishment.

Yet Christians cannot regard illness and death as the *ultimate* enemies. Both are part of (fallen) life; pain and suffering do have meaning; death comes to all. The greatest enemy is spiritual sickness and death; this must indeed be resisted and fought ferociously. There are, however, limits even to admirable and valiant efforts to stave off physical death. These limits testify to the higher spiritual values of justice, human dignity, and freedom, as well as to the most difficult step of all Christian discipleship — to give up the struggle to control one's life on one's own terms, turning it completely over to God. In the last analysis, death must be embraced, not resisted.

It is because of such limits that *rationing* is an inescapable dimension of health care. Health cannot be the ultimate goal. Death cannot be eternally delayed. Rationing (the setting of boundaries) is not an unfortunate though unavoidable consequence of high costs. Rather, it is bound up with human finitude and the necessity of both physical death and the death to self that is at the heart of the kingdom.

Such truths as these briefly sketched must, for purposes of public policy, find their way into the language of public justice. They are not private directives to individual believers. The kingdom of God transforms the world, and its principles carry public weight. They should become part of the public discourse of Christian citizens in a liberal democratic system.

In this chapter I first shall attempt to describe the shape that health care reform should take from a Christian perspective. I shall do so by making a series of claims about justice and health care in terms of three basic principles: meeting the needs of citizens, protecting vulnerable members of society, and maintaining human dignity. I shall explore how these principles affect the responsibilities for health care that lodge in individuals and families, in voluntary associations, and in government. This view of health policy reform fits into the categories of responsibility outlined in *A New Vision for Welfare Reform.*[6] Health care access for all members of society, especially for preventive and basic medical treatment, is a fundamental part of the "good ordering of society" as a matter of justice. Providing health insurance for major illness and injury fulfills the social responsibility for "emergency relief" and the philosophical and biblical value of protecting the most vulnerable persons.

Whatever the shape of health care reform at the national level, *Christian* health care providers have three *special responsibilities:* to restore an ethic of care that challenges the dominant ethic of cure, to describe differentiated responsibilities for health care, and to embody *agape* by serving and advocating for the marginalized within the interstices of large health care structures. Christian policy advocates and health care providers must be particularly energetic in the transformation of American health care.

Health Care and Justice

Jesus' healing of poor and rich alike (blind beggars and children of public officials) points to the equal dignity of all persons. This dignity finds embodiment in terms of political theory in the liberal commitment to equal respect. Simply by virtue of existence as a child of God, created in his image, each person merits care and concern and a fair share of the world's goods. Each deserves as well the respect and recognition of fellow citizens and the civil and human rights that embody that respect.

Another principle of surpassing importance is the obligation to protect the vulnerable.[7] Just as we recognize the profound human obligation

6. Center for Public Justice, *A New Vision for Welfare Reform: An Essay in Draft* (Washington, D.C.: Center for Public Justice, 1994), reprinted in the Appendix.

7. See Robert E. Goodin, *Protecting the Vulnerable: A Re-analysis of Our Social Responsibilities* (Chicago: Univ. of Chicago Press, 1985), and *Reasons for Welfare: The Political Theory of the Welfare State* (Princeton: Princeton Univ. Press, 1988).

of parents to care for their children, because these children are vulnerable to harm, not only in general, but particularly from parents themselves, just so we recognize that illness makes persons vulnerable to a wide variety of dangers, including loss of dignity, bankruptcy, and unemployment. Those closest to the ill, but also the society whose culture creates or maintains certain vulnerabilities, thereby have obligations to protect the ill and those liable to illness (preventive care).

Finally, the fact of membership in society, in families, and in voluntary associations creates obligations to meet the essential needs of members.[8] Not to meet the needs of a member in one of these communities or associations is to place that person in the category of a second-class member. It is, in effect, to remove him or her from full and equal status in the community. The drive toward universal inclusivity in Christian faith makes this idea of the needs of members particularly appealing. A notion of justice as a web of mutual obligations and rights is particularly fruitful for Christian thinking about welfare and health care reform since it is central to both biblical theology and secular political theory. Government's obligation to meet needs extends first of all to its citizens. The obligation of Christian institutions extends more widely. The practical import of this principle will be explored below.

The three considerations briefly discussed above come together to ground a conception of public justice in health care. They suggest principles to guide the just distribution of care and the risks associated with receiving and providing care.

Any concept of justice must be linked to some form of equality. Equal health is impossible; access to health care based on merit or wealth is intolerable on Christian principles. Providing identical health care to each would be nonsensical, since individuals have vastly different needs for care. Need-based justice remains, namely distributing health resources in proportion to the need for such resources. Why, however, should *health care* be regarded as a fundamental human need? And what principles can prevent the infinite expansion of health care needs? These two questions lie at the heart of a genuine theory of public justice in health care and must be

8. Michael Walzer, *Spheres of Justice: A Defense of Pluralism and Equality* (New York: Basic Books, 1983), ch. 3. See also J. Donald Moon, "Social Democracy, Liberalism, and the Welfare State" (paper presented at the 1990 Annual Meeting of the American Political Science Association, San Francisco).

answered before the shape of health care reform can be determined from Christian principles. What follows attempts *briefly* to sketch answers.

Health is a universal human good, that is, something that is sought for itself as well as for what it contributes to human well-being. *Health care*, on the other hand, emerges as a fundamental need, that is, a basic claim on social resources, only in societies that both highly value health and have sufficient knowledge and techniques effectively to treat accident and illness and sufficient financial resources to make such treatments available to all. Only in such societies can distribution of health care on the basis of need be called a fundamental demand of justice.[9] In these societies, including all advanced democracies such as the United States, the basic equality of all citizens as first-class members demands that none arbitrarily be denied access to universally and highly valued goods. Such denial would damage dignity, testify to qualified membership equality, and make persons vulnerable to other forms of discrimination (or reflect existing unjust vulnerabilities). The aim of health care justice is not simply equality before the law or equal opportunity, nor is the goal equal material conditions for all, but rather the kind of social or moral equality that preserves the essential status of equal citizenship for all members of society.

Liberal democratic societies echo Christian anthropology in presuming that all citizens possess an equal human dignity. To deny some citizens access to the essential means to protect that dignity would be to deny them full citizenship and full humanity. This would clearly be the case with the right to vote or rights of speech and assembly. But it is equally so with other fundamental needs (food and health care, for example) that society has the means to provide.

Another way to think of this is in terms of self-respect.[10] In American society self-respect depends not on certain welfare rights or equality of condition, but rather on independence. That is, to be self-respecting in America means to stand on one's own feet and to make one's own living to the greatest extent possible. Social conditions, such as access to education and the existence of job training and of jobs, facilitate such independence. Self-respect also depends on a health care system that provides preventive

9. This argument owes much to Walzer, ch. 3, and to Mickey Kaus, who draws heavily on Walzer, in his *The End of Equality* (New York: Basic Books, 1992), chs. 3, 6.

10. See Moon, "Moral Basis of the Democratic Welfare State," in Amy Gutmann, ed., *Democracy and the Welfare State* (Princeton: Princeton Univ. Press, 1988).

and rehabilitative care so that persons can maintain or regain independence. In fact, the *political* key to selling health care reform is to place it in the context of a kind of social insurance, similar to Social Security, that is designed to allow individuals to maintain their independence and dignity in the face of illness and accident.[11]

Yet there is also a danger in defining health care as a need, for needs are infinitely expansive, threatening other social goods. From the Christian perspective, viewing health care as a *need* may place too much emphasis on bodily integrity and avoidance of death. Moreover, too great a focus on the bodily needs of the *individual patient* keeps such persons on the "ragged edge" of health care, with always one more possible treatment, with an endless need for acute, curative health care, leading to the phenomenon described by Daniel Callahan as "twice cured, once dead."[12] Thus, there must be a set of theoretical principles that specify limits to the provision of health care. Other principles would describe the basic minimum of health care to which every citizen must have access.

One such limiting principle is that, although health is a universal good, it is good as a *means*, not as an ultimate end. The cliche "when you have your health, you have everything" is of course not true. Good health does facilitate learning, positive human relations, service to neighbor, and other goods. Yet, as wonderful as health is, it is only one of the human goods that make other valuable goods more readily attainable. Because this limitation is intrinsic to health itself, there always exists a ground for hedging the claims of health (and health care, which is itself a subordinate means). The need for health, if it be conceived as an ultimate end, becomes a limitless demand that trumps the claims for resources made by education, Christian ministry, communications, friendship, and other goods. Indeed, sin itself can find an entry here, in the form of a prideful demand that "everything" be done for the sick person. Part of our health care crisis reflects the displacement of values onto *means* that are appropriate only to *ends*. This is why rationing has become an unspeakable term: health and

11. There may be some lessons here in how Social Security was transformed from a marginal and unpopular program to a central and popular part of the American welfare state. See Edward D. Berkowitz, *America's Welfare State: From Roosevelt to Reagan* (Baltimore: Johns Hopkins Univ. Press, 1991), 46-47.

12. Callahan, *What Kind of Life? The Limits of Medical Progress* (New York: Simon & Schuster, 1990), 101ff.

health care are viewed as infinite in capacity. If, however, health and health care are necessarily limited, then decisions about the appropriateness of care in various circumstances and under varying conditions are clearly required and legitimate.

Care over Cure: A Christian Perspective on Health Care

Ethicist Daniel Callahan has focused on the need to accept death at the end of a normal life and from that acceptance to recognize and enforce limits on the proliferation of medical technology.[13] Technology is indeed the chief culprit in health care inflation. Health care is a victim of its own success, a success that subtly allows the prideful notion that elimination of death might be possible with enough scientific and medical progress. Continual progress in curing diseases and repairing injuries has inflated public and professional expectations concerning health care, created overconsumption of marginally beneficial treatments, and produced inappropriate levels of curative treatments for terminal illnesses. Successful technologies promote "service intensity": over time individual patients begin to receive a higher number of services, services that carry high price tags. The aging of the population, technological progress, and inflated expectations have caused all cost-containment strategies to fail. Only if we can rein in health care technology can we reduce costs and meet the public justice requirement to extend basic care to all citizens.[14]

To rein in technology, Callahan argues, we must learn to emphasize *care* over cure. Caring is what we owe to each other as citizens; it is what binds people together. What aged and terminally ill persons need most but often find hardest to obtain is care, in the form of help with the activities of daily living, relief from painful symptoms, and company in times of loneliness and fear.

13. Callahan.

14. Callahan, esp. chs. 1–4. Callahan is not alone in seeing technology and service intensity (combined with an aging population and fee-for-service medicine) as the primary health care inflation culprits. See Aaron, 48-53, and Kenneth E. Thorpe, "Health Care Cost Containment: Reflections and Future Directions," in Anthony R. Kovner, ed., *Health Care Delivery in the United States*, 4th ed. (New York: Springer, 1990), 270-96. The need to restrain cost is not simply a matter of economic efficiency; it is also a matter of justice. Dollars expended in the health care sector become unavailable for meeting fundamental human needs in other sectors, including welfare reform.

Health care provided to all on the basis of need would be defined by three goals: (1) the meeting of bodily needs for a full life span (seventy to eighty years) and the avoidance of premature death; (2) the meeting of cognitive and emotional needs — that is, a psychologically stable mental and emotional state; and (3) the meeting of functional needs for daily living.[15] Emphasis on care also entails limits on health care research directed at additional curative technologies.

The weakest persons (the most vulnerable) have the primary claims for care. The goals of curing all conditions and of extending life indefinitely do not fit this model. This perspective recognizes that aging, sickness, decline, and death are part of the human condition, but recognizes as well our need to care for one another in the midst of these conditions. Because of its recognition of limits and its stress on the real, human needs of persons, care over cure is a fully Christian position in health care reform. Families, friendships, congregations, and stable communities will be intimately involved in providing such care. It is not merely a governmental responsibility, but a shared trust.

A Christian emphasis on health *care* would mark a return to the origin of religious hospitals in the United States, which were founded to provide comfort care for persons too poor to receive medical attention at home. These hospitals carried on the care tradition established by monasteries and other religious institutions from earlier times. At a time when medicine could do little curing, the religious institutions filled a significant gap in the health system. Religious hospitals, as well as nonprofit health institutions generally, also provided for physicians and patients a refuge from the corporate practice of medicine.[16]

By the 1950s and 1960s, however, the religious hospital (as hospitals generally) had been transformed into the "doctor's workshop," and advanced curative techniques dominated the workshop. These techniques were, of course, both expensive and lucrative, so charity and nursing care

15. Callahan, chs. 5–6.

16. On these points and those in the next paragraph, see Paul Starr, *The Social Transformation of American Medicine: The Rise of a Sovereign Profession and the Making of a Vast Industry* (New York: Basic Books, 1982), esp. ch. 4; Michael O'Neill, *The Third America: The Emergence of the Non-Profit Sector in the United States* (San Francisco: Jossey-Bass, 1989), chs. 2, 4; and Theodore R. Marmor, Mark Schlesinger, and Richard W. Smithey, "Nonprofit Organizations and Health Care," in Walter W. Powell, ed., *The Nonprofit Sector: A Research Handbook* (New Haven: Yale Univ. Press, 1987), 221-39.

were displaced. The American culture of individual initiative and self-reliance, of political and social fragmentation and mobility, also helped to move the American health care system in profound ways toward aggressive medical intervention, focus on the individual patient, and sophisticated, technological cures.[17]

By the 1990s, hospitals (religious or secular, public or private) had begun fully to enter the corporate, bureaucratic world of mergers, managed care, and ownership of clinics and physicians' practices. Hospitals of different origins and legal structures converged in organization and culture.[18] Moreover, as government took on greater responsibility for providing access to medical services for all citizens, the distinctive role of religious institutions in providing charity coverage began to seem less important and less needed.

If all of this is true, or becoming true, it suggests that the original mission of the major religious health care institutions has been fulfilled and that it is time to move on, to become again an alternative to the dominant medical system. There are many ways in which Christian health care can and should be different from the dominant culture. I shall focus on only two ways: (1) a different quality to Christian health care delivery, and (2) a Christian-influenced culture shift in the entire delivery system.

The necessity of a different quality to health care delivered by Christians is suggested by a provocative series of short essays on "What Makes Health Care Christian?"[19] Among the answers given to this question by Christian health professionals associated with the Christian Community Health Fellowship were these: focus on service, instead of control; be skeptical of the god of medicine; focus on the whole person, including the

17. Starr, 255, 278, 287, 289; Lynn Payer, *Medicine and Culture: Varieties of Treatment in the United States, England, West Germany, and France* (New York: Penguin Books, 1988).

18. There is controversy in the scholarly community on this point, and research is fairly recent on the question of whether there are major differences in the values and the quality of patient care among public hospitals, nonprofit hospitals, and proprietary hospitals. See Bradford H. Gray, "Nonprofit Hospitals and the For-Profit Challenge," *Bulletin of the New York Academy of Medicine* 66 (1990): 366-74, and Rogers Hollingsworth and Ellen Jane Hollingsworth, "A Comparison of Non-Profit, For-Profit and Public Hospitals in the United States, 1935 to the Present," PONPO Working Paper, no. 113, Program on Non-Profit Organizations, Yale University, 1986.

19. *Health and Development* 13, nos. 3-4 (1993).

spiritual; provide care as a ministry and with prayer; emphasize the needs of the poor; and exhibit the qualities of love, justice, grace, partnership, reconciliation, and attentive presence.

The second point is that Christian health professionals and policy advocates should attempt to shift the culture of medicine in the direction of care. The curative powers of modern medicine must be regarded as a gift from God, but all gifts carry the danger of misuse. One misuse is the tendency to seek cure at all costs, distorting the relationship between life and other values. Another is the tendency, once cure is no longer possible, to give up on and to warehouse (or to euthanize!) those who have begun the often lengthy process of dying. A Christian emphasis stresses sustenance for the chronically ill and the dying at home and in the presence of loved ones.[20] In the present system, once cure is abandoned, the ill are often left highly vulnerable to abuse and to the loss of human dignity. To stress that the incurable are also fellow citizens and children of God, to lavish care on them in their distress, and to help them to live and die in dignity is to place the health care accent where it belongs.

Doubting the god of "research and development" will make the Christian health reform advocate something of a "health care Luddite." It is difficult to go into the medical schools, the research laboratories, and the acute care hospitals and to challenge the gods in the machines. Yet that must be done. Technology run amok bears a major responsibility for the crisis we are in. Moreover, none of the major health reform proposals that have caught public attention challenges the infinite growth of health technology or the misplaced faith in its ultimate curative powers. Many explicitly call for increased research and development. Indeed, health professionals take it as a point of pride that America is the world leader in medical technology; indeed, that medical technology is one of our few export leaders!

The difficulty of the strategy I advocate, from the perspective of many in the Christian community, is that it raises the specter of rationing, ultimately of euthanasia or assisted suicide for the old, the ill, and the "useless." I cannot here outline a total treatment of health care rationing. However,

20. For thoughtful discussions, see Shigeaki Hinohara, "Sir William Osler's Philosophy on Death," *Annals of Internal Medicine* 118 (1993): 638-42; Sidney H. Wanzer et al., "The Physician's Responsibility toward Hopelessly Ill Patients: A Second Look," *New England Journal of Medicine* 320 (1989): 844-49.

two points are essential. First, *all* health care systems contain rationing, whether the decisions are so labeled or not. In our current system, for instance, rationing takes place according to income, insurance status, health status, limits on Medicare and Medicaid coverage and reimbursements, managed-care mechanisms, and willingness to wait in line. Rationing, indeed, is inevitable, unless a society is willing to permit the resources devoted to health care to grow without limit.

But there is also a positive justification for rationing, as strange as this may sound. Rationing, after all, is the making of choices about the utilization of resources for health care. Is not the making of wise choices exactly the critical first step in the reform of our health care system? If discussion is not to remain at the level of mere slogans, the debate about rationing must not be framed as care versus denial of care, but in terms of what kinds of care are appropriate for what kinds of conditions in which stages of life. My spotlight on care over cure is designed precisely to say that all life is precious, precious enough to deserve loving, dedicated attention regardless of a person's age or condition or distance from death. But death is not the greatest enemy. Christians must redouble efforts to provide care for all persons, abandoning none, but we need not make such "care" the all-out, high-technology assault on sickness and death that currently characterizes the American medical establishment.[21] Christian hospitals, health professionals, and health institutions have a responsibility to teach society about the importance of letting go and of dying well, about the limits of medicine, and about the ethical rationing of health technology.

Doing so may require fundamental institutional reform and a new relationship between such institutions and churches, families, and government. For example (and most radically), if a Christian hospital (even a profitable one) is not fundamentally different from a secular hospital, perhaps its trustees should sell it to the highest for-profit bidder and use the resulting capital to fund community clinics and hospices staffed by Christian nurses and physician assistants, who could be close enough to the people they serve to find ways both to get them the care they need and to dissuade them from overusing inappropriate services.[22]

21. Sophisticated discussions of rationing may be found in Norman R. Daniels, *Just Health Care* (Cambridge: Cambridge Univ. Press, 1985); Callahan; and Robert H. Blank, *Rationing Medicine* (New York: Columbia Univ. Press, 1988). The literature is vast.

22. My thinking in this respect has been stimulated by Robin Hoover, a doctoral

Differentiated Responsibilities

There are at least four major loci of health care responsibility: individuals and their immediate families and friends, the health care professions, private associations (only religious bodies and businesses will be discussed here, although others might have responsibilities from time to time), and governments (at three levels: local, state, and federal). Owing to the shape of the modern health care system, responsibilities cannot be neatly divided but must be shared. In particular, justice in health care policy requires that *risk* be shared. Usually, when considering distributive justice, concern is for fairness in allocation of tangible or intangible goods. In health care policy, however, we distribute not only medical procedures, drugs, and the tangible and intangible manifestations of care, but also the risk of the financial burden associated with major illness or accident. Modern medicine is inseparable from the financial resources and mechanisms needed to pay its bills.

The ability of individuals to take responsibility for their health care depends on the knowledge and skills possessed and communicated by the health professions, which charge for their services. Businesses have taken it upon themselves to offer health insurance to employees. Nonprofit and religious hospitals depend on federal Medicare and Medicaid funds. And on it goes. Access to health care especially revolves around risk and the ways in which insurance schemes attempt to transfer risk. Absent insurance, sick persons and their families are responsible for health and financial risks; health professionals are responsible for treatment and for the risks of nonpayment. With insurance, the risks are spread to other individuals in the insurance pool and to the managers of the insurance funds. But these risks can be transferred in various ways to government and to health professionals (e.g., managed care).[23] "Risk transfer" suggests divided and conflicted

---

student in the department of political science at Texas Tech University. An example is the transformation of St. Mary's Hospital in Minneapolis into seven small neighborhood clinics. See *National Catholic Reporter,* July 30, 1993, 6-7.

23. On the importance of risk and risk transfer, see Susan Feigenbaum, "Risk Bearing in Health Care Finance," and Donald R. Cohodes, "The Loss of Innocence: Health Care Under Siege," both in Carl J. Schramm, ed., *Health Care and Its Costs: Can the U.S. Afford Adequate Health Care?* (New York: Norton, 1987), 87-94 and 105-44, respectively; James R. Knickman and Kenneth E. Thorpe, "Financing for Health Care," in Kovner, 240-69.

responsibilities. Principles of membership, protection of the vulnerable, human dignity, and public justice, however, lead Christians to think in terms of health care as a system of *shared responsibility for risk.*[24]

Individuals and families have the primary responsibility for preventive care in the form of good health habits (nutrition, exercise, moderation in alcohol consumption, and the like).[25] They have the responsibility as well to become reasonably informed of health threats and their avoidance and to avail themselves of the care provided by others in a timely fashion. It would seem proper as well for individuals and families to treat their own minor conditions (headaches, scrapes, minor burns). Being good stewards of limited health care resources, individuals and families should not waste them on either self-limiting problems or costly, futile treatments to stave off death. Public and private health insurance that imposes modest and reasonable copayments places individuals and families in a risk-sharing scheme that may save resources in the long run. Yet discussion of individual responsibility must be carefully nuanced, lest it become another round of "blaming the victim."

Health professionals bear the responsibility for using their knowledge and skills for the good of individual patients and for the well-being of the community. They have special responsibilities to treat the vulnerable and to respect the human dignity of those in their charge. Though they have the right to make a decent living from their skills, they have the responsibility to recognize that these skills are precious community-supported resources that are not to be sold to the highest bidder, nor squandered in futile curative attempts. Managed care plans in which providers bear some risk are ways of encouraging properly limited use of scarce financial resources.

Employers must respect the dignity of their workers; they should treat them not as interchangeable, replaceable parts, but as human beings with lives outside the confines of the employment situation. Therefore,

24. The Catholic principle of subsidiarity is one way to think about this sharing. Health care needs should be the responsibility of the lowest level of society able to bear the burden. Government programs and church assistance *help* individuals and families meet their responsibilities, but do not *take over* their legitimate obligations (e.g., good health habits, long-term care, and assisting loved ones in dying). Developing the idea of subsidiarity, however, would take us too far afield.

25. See Willard G. Manning et al., *The Costs of Poor Health Habits* (Cambridge: Harvard Univ. Press, 1991).

in the context of American employment-based insurance, health insurance provision falls within their responsibilities; it is a way for them to share a degree of financial risk with their employees.[26] A safe working environment is also a primary responsibility of employers. Larger employers may also fulfill their responsibility to promote good health by providing nutritious cafeteria meals, exercise areas, and health and safety education.

The special responsibilities of churches are addressed in detail below. These responsibilities are especially to promote an ethic of care, to advocate for human dignity, and to mediate between the individual and large medical bureaucracies, both private and public. Because many of these activities will not and cannot be compensated by public or private health insurance schemes, religious bodies come to bear part of the risk for the shape of the total health care scheme.

Governments, finally, have primary responsibility for maintaining the equal membership of all citizens. This means ensuring (either directly or, whenever possible, indirectly) that the essential health care needs of *all* citizens are met. This responsibility may be fulfilled not only by direct provision of health care or direct financing of health care (although these are important mechanisms through which government shares in the risks assumed by other members of society), but also through public health measures (clean air and water, pure foods and drugs, safe streets and workplaces, health education). Government also has primary responsibility for the common good of the entire society, which calls for stewardship of all public resources, making sure that one sector (health) does not impose inordinate demands on the common good and unacceptable costs on other sectors. Ultimately, this task implies some form of social rationing of resources provided to the health care system.

The responsibilities briefly described overlap and intertwine, as for example in occupational safety and in financing of health insurance. Responsibilities may also conflict, as with sex education in families and in

26. Justice, strictly speaking, does not demand that employers provide health insurance. Some reform proposals indeed argue that they should not, a position that would make clear to workers that employer contributions to health insurance are almost always paid by workers themselves in the form of lower wages. In the short run, however, continued employer contributions are a way of cushioning the shock of redistributed health care costs.

public health campaigns. But the outline above surveys the general lay of the land regarding risk and responsibility with respect to the sectors of society. This sectorial perspective, however, is not the only way to think about justly differentiated responsibilities.

One may also consider the types of conditions that call for medical attention and the types of treatments that are applied to them. Three specific distinctions, based on health conditions and treatments, could be employed to clarify the scope of responsibilities in need-based health care premised on a standard of normal human functioning: therapeutic/nontherapeutic procedures; routine measures/extraordinary measures; and terminal/nonterminal conditions. These distinctions specify extremes, and public justice would allocate points between the extremes to the several social sectors. The three sets of extremes then would intersect the four loci of responsibility for health care: individuals, providers, groups (e.g., religious organizations and employers), and government. Certain needs are so basic to life, social solidarity, and human dignity that only social responsibility exercised through government and providing equal rights to health care can satisfy justice. Other needs seem less basic, leaving room for inequalities related to wealth and individual preference. In some of these areas the churches have a positive responsibility, rooted in gospel faith, to provide services to those unable to afford them. To describe these intersections would demand more space than is available here.[27]

Long-term care for elderly or other persons with chronic, debilitating, but not immediately life-threatening conditions presents special problems, which will grow as the population ages. At present the responsibility for such care falls primarily on families, but the Medicaid system and parts of Medicare have introduced federal responsibility. In addition, local government and voluntary agencies operate many recreation and supportive services that intersect with the health care needs of such persons. Moreover, church-related nursing homes and other facilities for the aged are an important part of the mix. It seems clear that health care reform must include some resources for long-term care. However, it will be vital for both financial and caregiving reasons not to monetize the present

27. I have tried to do so in a preliminary way in "Justice and Health Care Policy II," *Public Justice Report* 10 (Jan. 1987), reprinted in *Health and Development* 8 (Summer 1988): 31-33.

largely informal system of long-term care.[28] For families and friends to care for loved ones in sickness and in dying is a profound imitation of Christ.

In summary, given limited social resources for health care, justice requires that a minimum level of care be provided equally to all. Specification of this level of care must not be haphazard. Decisions must be made through public debate and discussion of principles of justice, of allocation criteria, and of competing demands for resources (income support, criminal justice, defense). Cost containment in health care is itself a matter of justice, for overspending on health robs resources from other social needs.

As social wealth and medical practice change, levels of coverage expand or contract, though contraction is politically and psychologically more difficult than expansion. Individual responsibility and institutional charity provide care beyond the minimal governmental level. It may reasonably be decided that some levels of care (for example, ICU care for terminal cases with no prospect of improvement) may not be made available by charity or even by individual payment.

Agape: A Special Servanthood Role

The special responsibility of the church in health care reform (and in welfare reform generally) is to minister sacrificial love to the marginalized, whether they are marginal by their own decisions or by the decisions of others, and to challenge curative and technological imperialism. The church must be attentive to the needs of those who fall between the cracks of bureaucratic systems (public or private) or whose needs are not part of the dominant ethos of the culture of medicine. This includes those who are missed by public or private insurance and those who, although possessing insurance, lack the intellectual or emotional resources to navigate the health care system.[29]

In addition to working *within* the health system to reorient it toward

28. On the financial dangers, see Hilda Richardson, "Long-term Care," in Kovner, 179ff.

29. See Parker J. Palmer, *The Company of Strangers: Christians and the Renewal of America's Public Life* (New York: Crossroad, 1981); on the importance of underutilization by the poor of public services and possible remedies, see Marsha Guffey, "Reasons and Remedies for Underutilization of Services Provided by the Public Bureaucracy," dissertation prospectus, department of political science, Texas Tech University, March 1994.

care, Christians have an obligation to work for change in the interstices of the system and in places where it does not reach. One role of Christian faith in welfare and health care reform is to witness to prophetic hope, based on the discipline of suffering and death. Therefore, the "care ethic" described above is not a cop-out in which Christian health care institutions abandon the difficult frontiers of medicine for safe, hospitable environments. Rather, Christian providers need to seek out the internal frontiers of our society where health care is difficult to deliver, such as the public health domain, the storefront clinics in run-down neighborhoods, and the rural clinics needed by migrants and other poor farmworkers. The place for Christians is not primarily in large, bureaucratic structures, but in free clinics, health education, outreach to addicts, and advocacy for the alienated and marginalized.

Christians should become experimenters in health care, just as the original Christian hospitals and nursing homes were experiments. Different forms of service delivery should be tried — for example, linking child-care and nursing home facilities, or developing AIDS ministries, long-term addiction rehabilitation facilities, and homes for crack babies. Christians with the vocation of health care should search out the needs that are not being met within the present system and discover ways to meet them, using the financial resources of present Christian health care institutions. Experimental groups need entrepreneurial leadership and start-up funds. Volunteer efforts need staff coordination. Churches are the logical source of resources, and church-affiliated hospitals control sizable chunks of money.[30]

One unmet need in the future will be the health of noncitizens, aliens who are legally or illegally resident in the United States. Governments properly have the responsibility to provide health care access for all *citizens.* Their obligations toward noncitizens are less clear. Health care professionals have an ethical obligation to provide emergency care to all *persons.* The gap to be filled by the services of Christian organizations may be the nonemergency but therapeutic and preventive care for noncitizens.

30. Once again, I am indebted to Robin Hoover. See also Steven Rathgeb Smith, "The Changing Politics of Need" (paper presented at the 1993 Annual Meeting of the American Political Science Association, Washington, D.C.). I do not minimize the difficulty of this project. Christian health care institutions and providers are wedded closely to the Constantinian temptation of power in the dominant acute care system. Chaplain Ted Dotts of Lubbock's Methodist Hospital has made this point strongly.

Another major unmet need in the future will be mediation between the poor and the health care system. Health insurance for all does not mean that all will use the insurance. Today thousands of children go unimmunized despite the availability of free shots. Some of the problem lies on the side of persons whose irresponsibility interferes with their health and the health of their children. Sometimes this irresponsibility can be traced to addictions, sometimes to ignorance, sometimes to indifference. Whatever the reason, there will always be need for outreach to these persons, for attempts to bring them into the system, and for ministry to their brokenness. There will never be enough health professionals to meet all health care needs, especially preventive, psychosocial, and spiritual needs. Therefore, churches and volunteer workers have an essential role to play in outreach, health education, and spiritual care.[31]

Yet some responsibility for the unmet needs of the poor lies with a medical system that fails the poor in many ways even when it offers them care. According to David Caes of the Christian Community Health Fellowship, which works to develop care in the interstices of the system, money is often the easiest problem to solve.[32] The difficulty is that the system is really designed for patients and providers with middle-class cultural values and expectations. Those without that culture have trouble navigating the system to reach the care they need. Lack of knowledge, bad experiences with previous providers, dehumanizing waits, and time-management issues lead them to refuse to deal with the existing system.[33] Therefore, community clinics, parish nurses, and other forms of Christian health outreach will be needed even after health care reform.

31. Grace Tazelaar, "Increasing Access to Health Care with Lay Health Personnel," *Health and Development* 13, no. 4 (1993): 3-9.

32. Telephone conversation, Dec. 1993.

33. Cultural and linguistic barriers also reinforce miscommunication between physician and patient, leading to frustration on both sides. Moreover, the acculturation of physicians leads them to be more authoritarian with poor than with middle-class patients and to attribute irresponsibility to them. See Robert Ebert, "The Changing Role of the Physician," in Schramm, 145-84, esp. 164-65; also Dan Morgan, "Even Medicaid Misses Many," *Washington Post National Weekly Edition*, Feb. 21–27, 1994, p. 12.

Conclusion

Christian health care institutions have a special responsibility to ensure that the poor and marginal have access to care beyond the government minimum. They also have a duty to demand that government meet its responsibilities and to serve those who fall between bureaucratic cracks in the public system. The connections between health care and welfare reform again become apparent. Welfare reform cannot be successful if those who are to be moved off welfare are unable to afford or to find health care for themselves and their children. Either the attraction of Medicaid will keep them attached to the welfare system or the lack of insurance will lead to sickness and health care expenses that drive people back into poverty.

Christian concern for the poor means that advocacy for access to government-guaranteed minimum health care should be part of the agenda of lobby and public interest groups, though the form it takes (single-payer, managed competition, health vouchers) is a matter for legitimate debate. At the same time, Christian doctors and hospitals must give preference to the poor rather than the well heeled or the well insured, when government has failed in its responsibilities.

A further implication of the perspective outlined here is that Christians have to examine their own allocation of resources. More sacrificial giving by individuals, for example, will be necessary if hospitals, clinics, and the like are to meet new responsibilities. Another implication is that considerable study and moral-theological reflection are needed about discontinuing treatment, deciding what high levels of care will be rationed and on what criteria, and specifying extraordinary levels of care that may be justly allocated according to the market.

All of these questions inevitably confront the meaning of death. Modern health care flirts with idolatry and the desire for earthly immortality. Death indeed must be conquered to gain eternal life, but the lesson of the cross is that death is defeated only when it is accepted. The paradox of the kingdom is that success in the struggle with death comes only through weakness. Christians care for the sick not because they hope to defeat death thereby (for Christ has already conquered), but because they love the sick person and seek to relieve suffering and to join in solidarity in the struggle toward acceptance of earthly mortality. Modern health care *can* be a great assistance in this Christian encounter with mortality. Yet this same health system contains a strong dynamic toward the denial of death, focusing on the cure of all illness, the isolation of the sick and dying in institutions, and the infinite prolongation of earthly life. The Christian health policy advocate must clearly separate compassion and justice from policies and structures promising illusory immortality.

Conclusion

Reforming Welfare and Redirecting Government

Stanley W. Carlson-Thies

WHAT CAUSES deep, persistent poverty and social collapse? What kind of assistance actually helps families and communities to overcome such a crisis? These profound questions underlie the often simplistic and dispiriting squabbles of America's welfare debate. A short-term income problem can beset nearly anyone for a host of reasons; with the help of family, friends, the church, a charity, or government assistance, people overcome this challenge. However, for a significant part of the population served by the American welfare system, the problem of poverty appears to be more complex and recalcitrant. It is persistent, less a barrier to surmount than an undertow that holds fast; it is not only a personal or family matter, but spans generations and encompasses neighborhoods; it is not so much a matter of too little money but of too many dysfunctional patterns. Tragically, this kind of poverty appears to be growing in both scope and depth. And it is growing despite a wide array of social welfare programs and extensive spending on antipoverty efforts.

The response of politicians, policy experts, and the public to persistent poverty and urban decay has been divided. To some, the growing problem proves that welfare is not effective enough; to their critics, it proves, to the contrary, that welfare is counterproductive. The first group claims that our current welfare provisions must be inadequate: if people remain mired in poverty, it must be because government's programs do not sufficiently help them to overcome their poverty.[1] Their opponents take precisely the op-

1. See, e.g., Sheldon H. Danziger and Daniel H. Weinberg, eds., *Fighting Poverty:*

posite position: welfare itself, they claim, perpetuates and deepens poverty, because it entices people to make self-defeating choices.[2]

How can welfare be both the cure for poverty and its cause? This total polarization of positions constitutes a crisis at the foundations of welfare policy and the welfare reform debate. If offering welfare assistance to people induces bad choices and dependency, then it should be withheld for the sake of those it would misdirect. Yet, welfare or not, people sometimes run into problems that outstrip their capabilities and resources; that is why welfare exists in the first place. We are confronted here with an intolerable conundrum. Human beings are not creatures who never need assistance, so it is imperative that help be available when problems arise. But whose help, and what if making help available induces people to make bad choices?

The chapters in this book help us to see that this conundrum is not only tragic but mistaken. Each chapter has its own particular focus and message about poverty or welfare; each has its own flavor, strengths, and weaknesses. But together they have a joint message. In this concluding chapter I will concentrate not on their arguments taken separately but on the guidance they give us about poverty and welfare when we consider them together. I believe there is the hopeful message here that we need not be paralyzed by the polarization of the welfare debate. We need not be trapped between two unreal options: either that welfare itself is the problem, so that the less of it there is the better off the poor will be, or that welfare itself is the solution to the problems of deep poverty, so that the more of it there is the better off the poor will be.

With varying degrees of clarity, and touching on the issue in many different ways, the chapters all reject the premise that welfare must be either the problem or the solution. They reject as well the underlying idea

---

What Works and What Doesn't (Cambridge: Harvard Univ. Press, 1986), and Sheldon H. Danziger, Gary D. Sandefur, and Daniel H. Weinberg, eds., *Confronting Poverty: Prescriptions for Change* (Cambridge: Harvard Univ. Press, 1994).

2. Robert Rector puts the case memorably: welfare offers single mothers a "paycheck" as long as they fulfill two conditions: not to work and not to marry an employed man. Welfare thus encourages and underwrites the very conditions that perpetuate poverty. See Rector, "Combatting Family Disintegration, Crime, and Dependence: Welfare Reform and Beyond," *Heritage Foundation Backgrounder,* no. 983 (1994): 7-8. The classic argument is Charles Murray, *Losing Ground: American Social Policy, 1950–1980* (New York: Basic Books, 1984).

that poverty can be interpreted as either an individual or a structural problem. They reject the idea that the poor can be absolved of their own responsibilities as well as the idea that blaming the poor is an adequate alternative. And they reject the argument that reforming welfare will suffice. The message of this book instead is this: if we seek to make welfare effective for those enmeshed in deep poverty and social distress, then it is imperative that we go beyond reforming welfare policy. Welfare policy itself must be reformed, not narrowly to fix blame and compel the poor to become responsible, but so that the poor take up the varied responsibilities of a healthy life. To understand poverty, we must transcend the individual versus structural dilemma to come to a more realistic and dynamic approach.

Deep Poverty: A Multifaceted Crisis

> *What scares me is that today people don't have the sense that they can struggle and change things. In the sixties, in Mississippi . . . [w]e always had the feeling that there was something we could do, and that there was hope. We felt in control of our lives.*
>
> — Marian Wright Edelman, Children's Defense Fund[3]

Are people poor because of their own flaws and mistaken choices or because the environment surrounding them keeps them poor? Should we locate the cause of poverty in the character and characteristics of the poor themselves or in the processes and practices of the society within which the poor must make their way? The choice of explanation is a critical one, for the response to poverty must be very different depending on whether the source of poverty is individual failure or structural injustice. But the analyses of this book help us to see that this is a false polarity, an inadequate way to approach the causes of poverty and the plight of the poor.

Consider the overtly "structuralist" analysis of rural poverty offered by Mary Van Hook. She insists that rural poverty — and by extension, urban poverty — not be misunderstood in individualistic terms as "solely"

3. Quoted in Lawrence M. Mead, *The New Politics of Poverty: The Nonworking Poor in America* (New York: Basic Books, 1992), 164.

a matter of "a lack of preparedness, personal failings, or lack of effort of the individual involved." Against such a view she notes, for instance, that most poor rural families include at least one worker, and that while rural families headed by a single mother are much more likely than two-parent rural families to be poor, most poor rural children live in intact families. She concludes that the main cause of rural poverty is the rural economic system, "especially the low wage scale and limited economic opportunities."

Yet Van Hook's own analysis shows that a purely structural or external explanation is itself inadequate. Consider the rural "brain drain": bright, educated rural youth tend to leave their communities due to limited economic opportunity. But that is just one side of the picture, according to her own account, for companies that can offer challenging and well-paying jobs are reluctant to locate in rural areas because of the low quality of the rural labor pool. Thus, as she points out, programs designed to improve the skills of rural workers must be "paired with initiatives to address the social factors and educational failures that contribute to the skill deficits and with support for community [economic] development strategies." As Van Hook says, rural poverty is "multifaceted." Rural poverty has both an individual and a structural side, and these two dimensions interact. Neither the person nor the context may be left out if we are to understand poverty.

Lawrence Mead, by contrast, seeks to understand poverty better by uncovering a more accurate view of human nature. Structuralist explanations of hard-core poverty, he insists, do not hold up under close examination. The poor may face many challenges: racism, low-end jobs that do not pay well, a poor education and inadequate skills, difficulties in securing child care. But none of these factors suffices to explain the most persistent kinds of urban poverty, Mead insists; the central cause is that the poor do not work, not that there is no opportunity to work. "There is," he says, "no longer any 'smoking gun' out in society that can explain persistent poverty well." It is not plausible to locate the source of the problems of the long-term poor outside of them, in the structure of society.

Yet it appears from Mead's analysis that we will be mistaken if we only look inwardly at the poor themselves to understand long-term poverty. He does insist that there is sufficient opportunity for the poor "usually" to leave poverty and the welfare rolls, but he goes on to argue that while opportunity may be visible to observers, the "seriously poor" in reality "feel overwhelmed by their situation." What they see is not opportunity within reach but barriers impossible to surmount. These barriers are not mirages, but real obstacles. They are internal, but for the persistently poor to overcome them, intervention from the outside is necessary. To understand deep poverty, then, it turns out to be insufficient to consider the poor in isolation. "[S]ocial influence and individual responsibility," Mead observes, "typically are cast as opposites," but this is an untenable polarity. To help the poor who are hobbled by defeatism, "[g]overnment must offer opportunity but also enforce standards for good behavior." Poverty, on Mead's account, may be neither externalized as a product of some feature of the environment nor reduced to a wholly internal and individual matter.

A further dimension of entrenched poverty, a dynamic element, is suggested by Anne Hallum's study of Guatemala. Her chapter is an exploration not of how people become poor, but rather of how they sometimes overcome poverty. In Guatemala, she shows, government welfare programs have little to do with it. The key factor instead is the transformative power of religion as it realigns people into economically fruitful ways of life. The components are simple: a new, biblical understanding of the self, family, neighbors, hope, and the destination of life, and a mutually supportive religious community. Such elements can lead persons, families, and communities to adopt new patterns of work, saving, and consumption, and to take a different stance within their environment and a different orientation toward its barriers and opportunities. Hallum does not suggest that, since an inner, religious transformation is a critical ingredient for Guatemalan economic development, then either personal skills or economic opportunity and the absence of violence are unimportant. But her account reminds us that we must not reduce the problem of persistent poverty to a static equation between a certain amount of human capital on one side and a particular quantity of economic opportunities on the other. The poor are human actors, not merely economic factors. A religious dynamic may unleash economic change; a religious transformation may be essential to overcome poverty that has become a way of life.

There is also a dynamic social dimension to entrenched poverty. At the level of neighborhoods, William Julius Wilson's classic study, *The Truly Disadvantaged,* traces the decline of poor but socially functional inner-city neighborhoods into chaotic and violent zones of concentrated poverty.[4] At

4. Wilson, *The Truly Disadvantaged: The Inner City, the Underclass, and Public Policy,* paperback ed. (Chicago: Univ. of Chicago Press, 1990).

the family level, many of the chapters in this book note the spreading negative consequences of family breakdown and nonformation in contemporary America. Single-parent families are much more likely to be poor. Their children are much more likely to do poorly in school or to drop out. Such behaviors make it highly likely that, in their turn, the children will be poor when they become adults themselves.

Mary Stewart Van Leeuwen shows how family dysfunction can reproduce itself, tearing the social fabric. Children ought to have two parents: that is the starting point. When fathers leave, or have never been present since conception, then boys tend to develop an aggressive hypermasculinity that may be manifested in predatory sex, violence, and general antisocial behavior; girls tend toward a hyperfemininity that makes early sex and childbearing likely. Such behavioral patterns have immediate negative consequences that make poverty likely. But they also make it difficult for these young men and women to establish healthy marriages and families. That difficulty, in turn, increases the likelihood that the same negative patterns will be reproduced in their children, the next generation.

Fortunately, these destructive cycles can be broken. Teachers and other caring adults may partially substitute for missing parents or somewhat compensate for inadequate fathering or mothering, as Van Leeuwen suggests. But by the same token, if these other sources of nurture and guidance are also missing, then the collapse of nuclear families helps to bring down extended families and whole neighborhoods.[5] In such circumstances, children are not raised to the manifold responsibilities of adult life, and their families and neighborhoods become not a foundation for success but a hindrance to it.

To understand deep poverty, then, we must transcend the polarity between individual and structural approaches. We must go beyond static evaluations of personal deficiencies or environmental barriers. We must see that the urban and rural crises of deep and persistent poverty are not merely economic phenomena.

What framework should we then use? Bob Goudzwaard proposes a creative alternative to conventional approaches in his chapter. An adequate analysis must "start with the concept of living subjects within a society of differentiated responsibilities," he urges. The poor are actors, not mere

5. See Elijah Anderson's emphasis on the importance of "old heads" as role models for the young in his *StreetWise: Race, Class, and Change in an Urban Community*, paperback ed. (Chicago: Univ. of Chicago Press, 1992), esp. 69ff.

objects of external impulses, and their environment comprises persons and institutions that may be acting justly or unjustly. This nonmechanical view of the person-in-society leads us to consider poverty from the perspective of the poor person and along three distinct dimensions: (1) the opportunities open to a person (the "opportunity structure"); (2) the person's internal orientation — his or her attitudes and motivation (the "internal motivation structure"); and (3) the person's capacity to utilize opportunities ("the external motivational structure"). This last dimension encompasses not only the person's resources (e.g., skills) but also the quality of the social resources (Is child care available? Is the neighborhood essentially a battlefield?). It is only when we consider the interplay of these three dimensions that we can understand poverty, Goudzwaard maintains.

Goudzwaard's framework forces us to acknowledge the complexity of poverty and the diversity of the poor population. Statistically, the poor consist of all family units falling below a poverty threshold calculated on the basis of family size and the estimated costs of living at a minimal level. But such a definition conceals at least as much as it reveals. Long-term or persistent poverty, as a number of chapters point out, is a qualitatively different problem than short-term economic need. Goudzwaard's framework shows that there are also important distinctions beyond this one.[6] Persons may be poor because they refuse to pursue employment, even though they are able to work and jobs are available — as conservatives typically argue. On the other hand, the poverty may be due to the absence of economic opportunity, as liberals usually assume. But there are also other possibilities. Poor people may lack both employment and employability, or they may lack both the skills required for work and a desire to gain those skills. They may desire to work but be hindered by dangerous conditions in the neighborhood or a lack of transportation.

As Goudzwaard emphasizes, if we are to provide genuine assistance, it is vital that we understand a person's or family's particular pattern of poverty. Requiring employment when the problem is the absence of

6. Cf. the important but incompletely realized effort to "disaggregate the poor" in Michael Novak et al., *The New Consensus on Family and Welfare: A Community of Self-Reliance* (Washington, D.C.: American Enterprise Institute for Public Policy Research and Milwaukee: Marquette Univ., 1987), and especially the illuminating distinctions proposed by Thomas Corbett in his "Child Poverty and Welfare Reform: Progress or Paralysis?" *Focus* (Institute for Research on Poverty) 15, no. 1 (1993): 1-17.

economic opportunity will provide no solution to poverty, but it is an equally mistaken and unjust strategy to supply cash assistance to a poor person who is equipped to work, who could find work, but who declines to take this step toward self-sufficiency. An appropriate helping response — effective welfare — must begin by acknowledging that the poor are actors and not mere victims, and that they are surrounded by other accountable persons and institutions, not mere "structures."

Welfare: Restoration to Multiple Responsibilities

We stubbornly persist in creating social programs we know will fail because we cannot come to grips with our real problem — private irresponsibility.

— Richard Neely, *Tragedies of Our Own Making*[7]

The great flaw of the American welfare system, according to its strongest critics these days, is that it does not hold people accountable for their mistakes. By subsidizing bad choices, it encourages the behavior that makes people poor, that perpetuates their poverty, and that makes them dependent on welfare. To stem the growth of poverty and to reform welfare, blame must be reattached to bad choices. Some critics argue that the welfare system must enforce personal responsibility; others go further, arguing that welfare itself must be ended because government assistance shields the poor from the prodding to good behavior they would otherwise receive from the market or private charities.

The arguments in this book point in another direction, however. The chapters assume that government legitimately has a welfare role and that overcoming the responsibility deficit requires more than a focus on "personal responsibility" and fixing blame. But why should government be involved? And what should be the goal of its welfare policies?

Government must fight poverty, Stephen Mott says, because it has a God-given vocation to vindicate the rights of the needy. A biblical understanding of humans as sinful creatures compels us to acknowledge that the

7. Richard Neely, *Tragedies of Our Own Making: How Private Choices Have Created Public Bankruptcy* (Urbana: Univ. of Illinois Press, 1994), 40.

poor and powerless cannot be assured of their due by either the market or voluntary generosity. They require the protection of government's strong arm and sustenance from government if it can be secured in no other way. Government's "positive meaning," Mott affirms, is "justice," which is "the use of power for deliverance of the needy and oppressed." The Bible explicitly gives government a responsibility to take care of the poor; Psalm 72, for instance, tells us that the godly king defends the poor, delivers the needy, and crushes the oppressor. Thus, long before the New Deal and Great Society, and long before the industrial revolution with its "social question," Christians believed that government has a God-given task to aid the poor.

But what is the nature of that task? Mott declines to specify; his goal is to show that there is no biblical warrant for "the laissez-faire presumption that government cannot legitimately provide welfare assistance." Unfortunately, however, the terms of his argument may mislead us unless we proceed with care. His focus is the direct tie between government and people who are poor due to oppression. And while he notes some of the vast changes over time in economic, social, and political systems, he does not probe the consequences of these developments for the contours of government's antipoverty responsibility. The impression left is that the normative welfare task of government is to give to the poor whatever they may lack, just as Ezekiel's ideal ruler takes care of the people the way a shepherd cares for his sheep. But such an interpretation of government's task mistakenly suggests that all poverty is due to unjust treatment of the poor and that government has a monopoly on coming to the aid of the poor.

Focusing on the details of God's pattern for how Israel's authorities were to care for the poor in order to identify the principles that should guide all governments, John Mason points us in a different direction. He agrees that the Bible teaches that when there is deep need that cannot be met voluntarily, government must come to the aid of the poor. Political authority in early Israel was decentralized and limited, yet it had "a special concern for the weaker members of the community" and "actively intervened to make sure that righteousness and justice characterized the community." Uplifting the poor is a matter of justice; the needy must be helped, whether or not the wealthy have been moved in their hearts to open their purses.

However, according to the biblical pattern, governments coming to the aid of the poor are not to be simple dispensers of benefits, Mason argues. Government's mode of action is to strengthen the people in the exercise of their responsibilities. The "welfare" system outlined in the Pentateuch is extensive, he shows, and the standard for help was liberal rather than stingy. But only those unable to help themselves were given benefits; those able to help themselves were aided by such means as zero-interest loans or the opportunity to glean in the fields so that they could provide for their own needs. The central intention of the biblical welfare provisions, Mason argues, was to strengthen the extended family as the social organization that both nurtured its members into economically appropriate habits and choices and came first to the aid of any members requiring assistance.

Indeed, the cry of the poor must be heard. Government is one of God's instruments to vindicate the cause of the poor. But a poor person's claim to help may not be understood as a claim to unilateral receipt of public benefits. Giving the people bread and circuses is the Roman imperial ideal, not the biblical way.

Such an intepretation of the government's normative welfare obligation is reinforced by Paul Marshall's analysis of the notion of welfare rights. In Western, and especially American, society we wave the flag of rights whenever we want to emphasize the great importance that a need be met. If the Bible declares that the cry of the poor must be heard and that government is an instrument to vindicate the cause of the poor, we feel impelled to proclaim that the poor have a right to assistance by government. But the "rights" perspective and strategy is mistaken, Marshall insists, in the case of welfare; indeed, he insists, it is not helpful to the poor themselves. The welfare-rights idea mistakenly leads us to direct welfare assistance to individuals, neglecting their social setting and its resources. The idea of a welfare right counterproductively suggests that the poor have no responsibilities of their own to fight poverty and that welfare needs are identical, so that government should adopt a universalistic rather than differentiated approach. The welfare-rights view harmfully narrows our focus to government's responsibility, diverting our attention from the responsibilities of other institutions. "[T]reating welfare provisions as rights" is valuable to the extent that it acknowledges "that they are not simply charitable options but central concerns of the political community," Marshall affirms. But the "rights ethos" is the opposite of the "ethos of responsibility" that is needed if the problem of entrenched poverty is fruitfully to be addressed.

Government has a welfare obligation, we must conclude, but its welfare task is not to be construed as the construction of a narrow economic link between government and poor persons, a channel through which government sends benefits to helpless individuals. But if this is true, what then is the appropriate goal and what are the appropriate contours of welfare policy?

To understand the purpose of welfare, James Skillen urges, we must begin by rightly understanding human nature. What should a human life be like? What is a good outcome of the process of maturation from childhood into adulthood? If human maturation is a progressive liberation from restraints, then the aim of government policy must be to foster freedom for all of its citizens. In the case of the poor, whose liberty is constrained by inadequate resources, government should supply the material base the poor need in order to be able to enjoy a broader range of possibilities. But in biblical perspective, Skillen argues, human maturation does not mean progressive release from obligation but instead the increasing ability to fulfill the manifold responsibilities of life. The mature person is the one who is able to labor reliably and creatively, to participate with insight in civic affairs, to join with others to improve the neighborhood and serve the poor, to discern the purposes of God and follow them faithfully, to enter into deep friendships and perhaps into marriage, to faithfully guide children to maturity.

What then is the purpose of welfare? Government must not, Skillen emphasizes, attempt to take over from the poor their own responsibilities; it must not try to become "their substitute spouse, parent, employer, counselor, and more." Government instead should "strengthen and assist parents, teachers, employers, and organizations such as churches" that can offer assistance to the poor in ways that directly address their difficulties with finding or holding jobs, raising their children or cleaving to a spouse, completing schooling or kicking an addiction. And government should encourage and, if need be, compel, people "to fulfill [these] responsibilities that are tied to the exercise of their adult freedom." It should neither ignore unfilled responsibilities by simply offering the poor money and other benefits nor offer itself as a substitute for the people and institutions that have neglected their own responsibilities; instead it should "support the recovery of diverse human responsibilities in a variety of institutions."

It is such an understanding of welfare that underlies Mead's advocacy of workfare and other "paternalist policies," which offer support to the poor simultaneously with "demands for functioning." Considered from this perspective, a work requirement is neither society's way of punishing the poor for their poverty, as liberal critics tend to believe, nor government's way of making welfare distasteful to recipients, as many conservatives seem to hope. Work is not a punishment, but rather one of the responsibilities of mature adults; making it obligatory emphasizes the reciprocal character of assistance[8] and helps push the deeply discouraged over their barriers. Thus Mead can conclude that "The best answer to poverty is not to subsidize people, or to abandon them. It is to direct lives."

Jean Bethke Elshtain's condemnation of "welfare as we know it" is driven by the same perspective on welfare. Welfare, especially the AFDC program, seeks to protect children, the innocent victims of poverty, by ensuring that their mothers — it is almost always just the mother, alone — have money to care for them. But is money what the children need? Of course children require food, housing, clothing, and more. But as Elshtain notes in a poignant passage, it can only be a rhetorical ploy to ask children whether they would rather have generous welfare subsidies or a loving mother and father. Of course children want parents, both of them. Money, as necessary as it is, cannot substitute for a child's parents. To the extent that AFDC has contributed to the epidemic of family collapse and nonformation, it has harmed children, whatever its intent and design. Welfare cannot replace what a child loses when the father skips out of his parenting responsibility or the mother and father decide not to keep the whole family together. At a minimum, "welfare as it should be" will be a carefully reconstructed policy that no longer supports parental neglect of child-rearing responsibilities.[9]

If parenting is important, then moving recipients into employment cannot be the exclusive goal of welfare reform, notwithstanding the importance of promoting self-sufficiency. All AFDC mothers have a parenting responsibility as well as an economic obligation. Absent fathers also have a neglected parenting responsibility to take up, which consists of more than contributing child-support payments, as vital as that is. A good welfare policy will not only promote family formation and cohesion but also encourage the fulfillment of the varied responsibilities of parents to their children.

8. See Mead's earlier book, *Beyond Entitlement: The Social Obligations of Citizenship* (New York: Free Press, 1986).

9. Elshtain ends her chapter with John McKnight's recommendation that the weight of the welfare bureaucracy and the high-minded plans of welfare do-gooders alike be removed from the necks of the poor. The money designated to be spent on behalf of the poor should just go to the poor, for governments do best at "transfer[ring] resources that enable people to act on their own behalf," she quotes McKnight as holding. But the bulk of her chapter, as we have just seen, emphasizes that some of the key problems of our current welfare and poverty complex have little to do with transferable resources. Family disintegration is neither caused by poverty nor redressed by welfare checks.

The parenting deficit of welfare families often extends beyond the absence of the father, Cynthia Jones Neal's chapter reminds us. To become mature adults, children should have good parenting, but they are often raised poorly in poor families, even when two parents are present. Mothers (fathers, too) may be heavily stressed by the challenges of life on the bottom of society, with little emotional energy for nurturing the children; moreover, they may well have been inadequately nurtured themselves as children. Raised to be defensive rather than open, pushy rather than encouraging, they too often reproduce the same negative characteristics in their own children, however much they may love them. Distorted life patterns are passed on from generation to generation.

Of course inadequate parenting, including father absence, is a plague at all levels of contemporary American society. Poor parenting is not a simple product of low income, despite all the extra stresses that poverty entails; if it were, then Neal could not report successful parenting interventions with mothers who are dependent on welfare. On the other hand, to call attention to poor parenting by impoverished parents is not to indulge in blaming the victims of poverty. The intention is just the opposite, as Neal's chapter makes clear. Poor parenting is not only a plague on the children but a key mechanism by which poverty is transmitted from one generation to the next. If persistent poverty is to be overcome, then parental irresponsibility — broken and unformed families but also dysfunctional parenting styles — must be confronted and changed. Neither enriched benefits for mothers and children nor assurance of child-support payments from absent fathers will cure this aspect of poverty; all that will suffice is a replacement of bad parenting by good parenting.

But then a better welfare policy will not merely promote work and seek to halt family fragmentation but will encourage better parenting and the restoration of families. As John Hiemstra notes, it may sometimes be the case that a person's or family's "rights and responsibilities . . . have to be temporarily or . . . permanently reduced, transferred, or discounted." Nevertheless, the purpose of welfare must be to assist the needy to move, to the farthest extent possible, to the fulfillment of the varied responsibilities of a healthy life. "[G]overnment's primary aim should be to call people and institutions to their own responsibilities," as *A New Vision for Welfare Reform* says.[10]

10. Center for Public Justice, *A New Vision for Welfare Reform: An Essay in Draft* (Washington, D.C.: Center for Public Justice, 1994), reprinted in the Appendix, 569 herein.

Welfare and Civil Society

Governments know how to create new jobs, but they don't know how to motivate people to want to work, to be decent people, to take care of themselves. They don't know that people have to be changed. To do that takes faith in God.

— quoted in *Politics of the Spirit: Religion and Multiethnicity in Los Angeles*[11]

The deep poverty and social decay that spread through inner-city America and corrode regions of rural America constitute a crisis that cannot be undone by the most lavish supply of funds, training programs, or professionalized services. Families are weak or absent; too often people lack not only a range of skills but also hope for the future; neighborhoods have lost their cohesiveness, their ability to uphold their residents. The "delicate social fabric has unravelled over the past generation," to use the words of Glenn Loury. Misguided welfare policies that encourage mistaken personal choices like out-of-wedlock childbearing "have, in effect, pulled on the loose threads of the social fabric and facilitated this unravelling." But "reversing those policies — pushing on the loose thread — will not re-weave the social fabric." "Restoring social order," Loury concludes, "will require rather more of us than that."[12] But what then is required, and from whom is it required?

We cannot get much guidance to answer these critical questions from the usual American ways of thinking about welfare, Mary Ann Glendon points out. Conservatism and liberalism fix our attention on "individuals, the state, and the market — leaving out all the intermediate institutions of civil society." But in reality "families, neighborhoods, schools, religious and workplace associations, and other communities of memory and mutual aid" are key institutions for both welfare and well-being, she insists. These

11. The passage is from a seminar held at Zoe Christian Fellowship, South Central Los Angeles, July 1993; quoted in John B. Orr, Donald E. Miller, Wade Clark Roof, and J. Gordon Melton, *Politics of the Spirit: Religion and Multiethnicity in Los Angeles* (the preliminary report of the Religion and Civic Order Project at the University of California, Santa Barbara, and the University of Southern California) ([Los Angeles]: Univ. of Southern California[?], 1994), 7.

12. Glenn C. Loury, "Three Fallacies in the Welfare Reform Debate," op-ed prepared for *New York Newsday,* Feb. 20, 1995.

"fragile social structures" are what we might call seedbeds of democracy and compassion: here is where are nurtured the attitudes of respect and compassion for others that lead citizens to support government policies to aid the needy. But civil society has also two other important connections with welfare, Glendon's chapter suggests. These social institutions are the places where people become "prepared to take significant responsibility for themselves and their own dependents." Second, Glendon hints, these social institutions, especially the religious ones, may have a special role in delivering assistance, because these groups "have proved time and again their capacity to deliver education, health care, and other social services more efficiently, effectively, and humanely than the state."

The chapters in this volume support a strong government role in assisting the needy. However, an equally strong emphasis is placed on the vital importance of the institutions of civil society in upholding well-being and helping the poor. What then should be the special role of non-governmental institutions in welfare, and how should they be related to government's own tasks? What should government do to ensure that the institutions of civil society nurture and fulfill responsibility?

The Christian community has a special obligation to care for the poor, beyond any services the government provides, Clarke Cochran argues. He advocates that the entire health care system be redesigned to deliver appropriate care and evoke responsible action, and that the dominant naturalistic goal of "cure" be replaced by the Christian ethic of "care." Yet however successful the reforms, there will always be gaps in coverage and people who are marginalized. Here is the special field for Christian service, Cochran argues. Christians should be garrisoning the "internal frontiers of our society" to ensure that health care is available to those least likely to receive it. Christians should be operating clinics for the addicted and homeless, staffing outreach services to broken or irresponsible people who stay away from care providers, serving legal and illegal immigrants. "Christian health care institutions," he says, "have a special responsibility to ensure that the poor and marginal have access to care beyond the government minimum . . . [and to] serve those who fall between bureaucratic cracks in the public system." The special task of Christian health care providers is to "minister sacrificial love to the marginalized, whether they are marginal by their own decisions or by the decisions of others."

Sacrificial love, a "special servanthood role," in Cochran's language, doubtless is a key calling of Christians individually and corporately. But there is also a special role for Christians, for those with religious faith, not only on society's outposts but also in the very *center* of society's efforts to come to the aid of the needy. Recall Cynthia Jones Neal's study of how self-defeating concepts and behaviors are passed on from one generation to the next. To break this cycle she recommends specialized parenting programs and also changes in the family's environment — improvements to schools, a reduction of neighborhood violence, and so on. She also points to one other critical factor: "hope." This is an "intangible" factor, she notes, "but it is indispensable if the cycle of poverty is to be broken. . . . Families that succeed despite desperate odds have caught a vision that the future can be better, and they work ceaselessly to achieve it." But if we deal with hope and vision, with changes in a person's and family's stance in the world, are we not in the realm of religious transformation? If so, then a religious dynamic needs to be at the heart of the helping relationship, and not only in the gaps of bureaucratic programs.

Well-functioning lives and societies do not just happen, Max Stackhouse reminds us; these are "supernatural, not natural" outcomes. They are the result of religions that emphasize productive effort, dedication to learning, commitment to neighbors, and other personal and social virtues. When life is shaped instead in dysfunctional patterns, then lasting and deep change requires that people and communities adopt a new perspective and be converted to different patterns. According to Stackhouse, this means that the Christian vision must be at the center of the helping enterprise. The various institutions that offer help ought to be *simultaneously* serving "the direct spiritual, social, and material needs of the people," for it is when material help is coupled with, or embedded in, a religious message that people can be "invited to a conversion of heart and a discernment of vocation." The church, then, "ought to be about the task of rebuilding the tissues of civil society on a firm religious foundation." Models of such religious/cultural outreach and renewal can be found in many places, Stackhouse points out.[13] "Where effective, they generate human confidence and develop social competence. They draw isolated persons into responsible families and creative economic opportunities. They alter habituated patterns of living that disrupt families and lead to criminality." It is this kind

13. Many evangelical inner-city ministries are organized in the flourishing Christian Community Development Association, headquartered at the Lawndale Christian Development Corporation, Chicago.

of help, directed not only at "exterior formation" but also "interior conversion," that should be at the center of the effort to help people trapped by poverty.

Religious change as the key to overcoming deeply rooted poverty and social disarray is strongly emphasized in the chapters by Stephen Monsma and by Ron Sider and Heidi Rolland. Distressed people and neighborhoods can best be helped by assistance programs run by churches or other religious congregations or by independent religious nonprofit organizations. Monsma argues that such programs can be more flexible and adaptable than government welfare programs. Their workers are more likely to be dedicated to the mission of helping the needy. Most important of all, religious groups and programs are able to "speak the language of morality" in working with the needy. They can speak to a person's sense of responsibility and invite the person into a community of compassion and discipline. This is important because, in biblical perspective, as Sider and Rolland point out, people are not merely bodily creatures but have a spiritual dimension and are "made for community with God and neighbor." It should be no surprise, then, that addiction recovery programs that include "prayer, conversion, supernatural empowerment by the Holy Spirit, and the embrace of a loving community of sisters and brothers are more successful than secular ones."

There should be, then, in the language of several of the chapters, a "new partnership" between government and religious social services. Or, put in another way, government, rather than persisting in creating its own bureaucratic and secular programs to help the poor, should clear the way for and support those social groups that can render help in the personal and moral or religious form that is the most efficacious when people's lives are broken.

In fact, as a number of chapters note, the various levels of government — federal, state, and local — already do often turn to nongovernmental groups, including religious ones, to carry out social programs.[14] Nevertheless, this is a deeply troubled relationship, not a partnership. Thanks to the peculiar fashion in which government's obligation to be religiously neutral has been interpreted in the United States, both the current relationship and any expanded one are fraught with problems.

14. For good overviews see Lester M. Salamon, *America's Nonprofit Sector: A Primer* (New York: The Foundation Center, 1992), and Michael O'Neill, *The Third America: The Emergence of the Nonprofit Sector in the United States* (San Francisco: Jossey-Bass, 1989).

The chief problems are carefully analyzed in the Monsma and Stronks chapters. The First Amendment's strictures about religion have been interpreted to mean that government must not give aid to religion. Thus in order to be able to receive government funds, a religious ministry must segment its operations into "religious" and "secular" parts, with only the latter being eligible for funds. This division may not suffice, however: the courts may deem the organization to be "pervasively sectarian" and thus wholly excluded from participating with secular nonprofits in government programs. Ironically, as Julia Stronks points out, the courts' designation is almost accurate: many if not most religious care providers are, in fact, pervasively *religious;* religion provides their dynamic, rationale, and pattern. If they are forced artificially to split themselves into religious and secular parts as the condition for receiving government funds, then their integrity as religious organizations is jeopardized, as Monsma emphasizes, for they will be less able to define and implement their mission in distinctively religious terms, and may be unable to hire and fire staff in accordance with religious standards.

American courts have historically been strongly committed, in principle, to protecting religious liberty. Thus social ministries, if they wrap themselves wholly in the mantle of religion, can generally hire and fire in accordance with religious criteria and carry out their missions in thoroughly religious fashion. If they do so, of course, they are ineligible to participate in government programs, or, better said, government will discriminate against them, solely because of their integral faith, when it decides which organizations are eligible to receive government funds. Moreover, keeping distant from government programs provides no guarantee of the freedom to serve others in accordance with religious convictions. Stronks points out the difficulties that surround the issues of licensing and regulation, and she emphasizes that, since the *Smith* case, it remains uncertain whether government may trump a religious agency's freedom to operate in some particular way by claiming that a law or regulation is reasonable and not targeted against religious groups.

Despite such difficulties, there exists one proven mechanism by which religiously inspired institutions can participate in public programs along with secular nongovernmental agencies: vouchers. Monsma points out several important reasons to consider the more extensive use of vouchers as a channel for government funds to support religious helping services: this method is likely to pass constitutional muster; it minimizes government intrusion into the programs receiving the funds; and by removing the funding decision from government it both empowers the needy by enabling them to choose which service to utilize and eliminates the danger of government seeking to favor any particular secular or religious group over another.[15]

For these reasons, Sider and Rolland propose the adoption of vouchers as the government funding mechanism for their detailed and large-scale model of a comprehensive and thoroughly religious alternative to conventional welfare programs. Their plan also incorporates a host of other features designed to ensure that a local government could adopt it without violating the constitution: any government that agreed to this Christian proposal would also have to offer to work with any other religious group that desired to emulate the model; the central agency would be not a church but a Christian nonprofit organization; welfare recipients could enter and leave the program at their own choice; and so on. This is a promising model of a practical way to put the religious dynamic at the center of the helping relationship.

However, despite their optimism, it is not a foregone conclusion that either government policymakers or the courts would agree that their plan is acceptable. The idea of a high wall between church and state, between religious organizations and government, remains powerful in American society, policymaking, and jurisprudence. It is difficult to imagine that the many citizens, officials, and interest groups dedicated to a "naked public square" will find a plan like this acceptable, despite its voucher foundation. Critics will surely say that it must be unconstitutional to deliver a welfare family into such a religious total environment, notwithstanding the supposed guarantee of free entry and exit! As Stronks notes, the more an organization or structure appears to be "pervasively" religious, the stronger the courts' aversion to any government support for it; furthermore, the more the activities of an organization and the character of its relationship with recipients are religiously transformative, the stronger the courts' impulse to keep it away from government funds.

The careful analyses offered by Stronks and Monsma strongly suggest

15. For further discussion of vouchers, see, e.g., James W. Skillen, ed., *The School-Choice Controversy: What is Constitutional?* (Grand Rapids, Mich.: Baker Books, 1993), and E. S. Savas, *Privatization: The Key to Better Government* (Chatham, N.J.: Chatham House, 1987).

the need for a new understanding of the First Amendment's religious clauses and of the appropriate government stance toward organizations and activities that are shaped by and express religious commitments. When the prohibition of a government establishment of religion is interpreted to be a prohibition of government assistance to religious organizations and activities, then government is not taking a stance of neutrality between religions and between religion and secularism but rather discriminating against particular groups and practices just because they are religious. What the First Amendment requires is equal treatment by government of all groups, religious or secular, and not a de facto establishment of secularism. Monsma points us in the right direction with his suggestion of the concept of "positive neutrality."[16]

This is a critical area for further constitutional analysis and for the creative design of new models for the relationship between government and what we might call the "religious social sector."[17] Religiously inspired social service providers that carry out programs in the public interest should be eligible for government support on the same basis as secular nonprofit service providers. Neither the receipt of government funds nor a recommendation as a worthy program should require an artificial segmentation of services into secular and religious components or otherwise constrict an organization's ability to carry out its work in accordance with its religious vision. The same point may be put in another way: Needy people who choose to seek assistance from religious providers should not suffer discrimination from government, but that is what results when government's policies keep funds from going to such providers or hamper the integrity of their work.[18]

The question at stake is not only the critical one of how rightly to interpret government's obligation to treat equally, without discrimination, all citizens and organizations under its jurisdiction — what we might term the question of *confessional pluralism.* There is the equally pressing issue of how government should relate to nongovernmental institutions, in this case religious — and secular — social service providers. We can call this the issue of *structural pluralism,* to use a neo-Calvinist term, or the question

16. See Monsma's *Positive Neutrality: Letting Religious Freedom Ring* (Westport, Conn.: Greenwood Press, 1993), and also Luis E. Lugo, ed., *Religion, Public Life, and the American Polity* (Knoxville: Univ. of Tennessee Press, 1994).

17. Cf. Peter F. Drucker, "The Age of Social Transformation," *Atlantic Monthly,* Nov. 1994, 72ff.

18. See the draft statement, "Justice for Diverse Faiths in American Public Life," *Public Justice Report* (Center for Public Justice), Mar.–Apr. 1995, 3.

of *subsidiarity*, to use the Catholic term for a similar concept.[19] When should a service be carried out by government, and when should government, instead, either leave it to nongovernmental groups to perform the service or fund them to carry out the service? If a needed service is not being carried out by a nongovernmental institution, must government step in to perform the service itself or instead act to support and require the original agent to resume its responsibility? Responses to such questions are woven through this volume and are given particular attention in *A New Vision for Welfare Reform*. These are complex issues about which, as Glendon says, our typical American ideologies can give us little reliable guidance.

If religious service providers need to be at the center of society's efforts to help persons, families, and neighborhoods gripped by poverty and devastated by social problems, then one of the most important "welfare reforms" is not a change in welfare programs at all. Rather, the needed reform is at the level of government's relationship with nongovernmental helping institutions, and in particular religious social ministries. Government should cooperate with, rather than displace, such institutions both as a matter of justice in its relationships with the structures of society and because, as Glendon points out, such groups have proven themselves able to provide schooling and social services "more efficiently, effectively, and humanely than the state."

Glendon's observation that it is in the institutions of civil society that people become "prepared to take significant responsibility for themselves and their own dependents" points us to a second key "welfare" reform that transcends welfare policy in the narrow sense. It is in and through families, religious congregations, civic organizations, neighborhood groups, political party locals, unions, and other such social institutions that the values, habits, and patterns of responsible living are not only put into practice but also learned. If government's concern is that people assume or resume their varied responsibilities, then a key goal should be to strengthen these "fragile social groups" (Glendon's phrase).

19. For these various concepts of pluralism, see esp. James W. Skillen and Rockne M. McCarthy, eds., *Political Order and the Plural Structure of Society* (Atlanta: Scholars Press, 1991); Skillen, *Recharging the American Experiment: Principled Pluralism for Genuine Civic Community* (Grand Rapids, Mich.: Baker Books, 1994); and Stanley W. Carlson-Thies, "Democracy in the Netherlands: Consociational or Pluriform?" (Ph.D. diss., University of Toronto, 1993).

How can government strengthen the institutions of civil society and encourage people to fulfill their varied responsibilities? Charles Glenn gives us a case study, focusing on schools in their relationship with parents, and through the parents, with the neighborhoods in which they are located. A thorough reform of school governance and school financing will improve inner-city schools and also inner-city neighborhoods, he argues.

Because of the importance of education and the credentials that education yields, a reform of inner-city schools to make them more effective centers of learning ought to be a high priority in the battle against poverty. The key is to deepen the involvement of parents in their children's education. That requires two major changes, Glenn argues. The existing public schools, with their bureaucratic structures that relate to parents as clients, need to be replaced by schools governed as associations of parents, teachers, and staff. And as a matter of both freedom of education and freedom of conscience and as a way of empowering poor parents to exercise real choice concerning their children's schooling, the public's education money should flow not just to the schools operated by government but also to "those nongovernment schools that provide an effective education to poor children." Children are much more likely to be able to learn in school if their parents and their school are partners in education.

Glenn also argues that comprehensive reform of school governance and financing will facilitate the rebuilding of the shattered civil society of inner-city neighborhoods. A "restructured relationship" that maximizes the opportunities for parents to take real responsibility for and in their children's schooling can "help to provide a context of mutual responsibility within which more adults in these distressed neighborhoods will begin to live productive lives and to function effectively as parents, workers, and citizens." The recommended school reforms cannot guarantee that parents will become activated in such ways, of course. Government, however, can enlarge the opportunity for expanded responsibility by changing the rules that dictate how government and nongovernment schools are governed and financed. "[B]y making it much easier for parents, teachers, and community institutions like churches to establish and maintain schools that will not only respond to the needs of children but also serve to develop new habits of cooperation and problem solving among adults," Glenn concludes, government can enable a start to be made in "reviving urban communities." School changes, in other words, may be among the most important "welfare" reforms that government can devise.

As Glenn emphasizes, radical reform of school governance and school financing is important for the sake of education and not only to encourage reweaving the social fabric of inner-city America. Using the language of *A New Vision for Welfare Reform,* then, we can say that while comprehensive school change is an example of a "regenerative reform that seeks to overcome structural patterns of injustice," the outcome — a system of associational schools and school vouchers — is the pattern that should have been supported in the first place by government's "standard operating policies." For government's "first mode of responsibility for public justice" is to "uphold a just social order," that is, a society that maximizes the opportunities for people to fulfill their varied responsibilities.[20] That is to say, when there are unhealthy patterns, government's reforming action will be designed to encourage the emergence of the healthy patterns that its standard operating policies should uphold.

Do American governments also need to undertake regenerative reform of their economic policies and to establish new standard economic policies? There is no bureaucratic rigidity in this arena comparable to the entrenched government role in education.[21] Corporations in the United States are largely free to carry out the important tasks highlighted by Max Stackhouse of "generat[ing] the resources necessary to overcome poverty and dependency" and nurturing in their employees positive patterns of work and cooperation. But for many reasons they carry out these roles largely outside those urban and rural areas that have the most concentrated and persistent poverty.

Stackhouse proposes that government should actively support the inner-city economic development activities that are sprouting from the soil of religious congregations. Should government policy go further than this? The marketplace undoubtedly should remain free from a domineering government, but that does not mean that businesses may be treated as autonomous actors existing without a legal framework of accountability. As Stephanie Baker Collins points out, if the only goal of government's economic policy is the promotion of material gain, then government is likely inadvertently to be promoting in the economic sector practices and outcomes that will require of it expanded welfare rescue efforts. It may be counterproductive for government through its economic policies to foster job-shedding technological advance when it is attempting through welfare

20. Center for Public Justice, 574, 570; emphases deleted.

21. A case can be made, however, that various forms of overregulation perpetuate poverty by making it difficult for the poor to start and run small businesses such as hairdressers, alternative taxi services, and sidewalk vending.

reform to move more recipients into the workplace. If welfare policy is in reality to move people to the fulfillment of their varied responsibilities, government may need to undertake major policy changes to stimulate the economic revitalization of depressed urban and rural areas.

Justice and Grace

Endow the king with your justice, O God . . .
He will defend the afflicted among the people
and save the children of the needy;
he will crush the oppressor.

— Psalm 72:1, 4 (NIV)

Stephanie Baker Collins's proposal that economic and social or welfare policies must be considered in relation to each other reminds us that to fight poverty effectively requires a comprehensive approach that calls not only the poor but also government and the many institutions of a differentiated society to fulfill their responsibilities. Persistent poverty and urban degradation "are the expression of a multifaceted responsibility crisis" that is caused by "the moral failures of social institutions, government, and individuals."[22]

The most important policy question in dealing with poverty and welfare, Charles Glenn says in his chapter, is "how to build on the strengths that already exist among poor people, rather than to continue to treat the needy as helpless victims." We must "learn how to recognize the signs of grace" among the poor, he urges. But we cannot stop there. Injustice, mistakes, and negative patterns must be rooted up and replaced. We must prepare the way for grace to bear fruit "by removing the barriers that human sinfulness (and not that of poor people alone) has put in the way. This sinfulness is evident both in personal irresponsibility and in structural arrangements that systematically devalue those whom God values highly."

The design of American welfare programs has been predominantly shaped instead by the idea that government must add to the poor what

22. Center for Public Justice, Thesis 3, 565; emphasis deleted.

they are lacking: more money, more services, more skills. The intent has often been compassionate, but the practice has treated the poor not so much as actors but as victims. The reaction that has now arrived, however, also misinterprets the poor, society, and the tasks of government. The emphasis now is on enforcing personal responsibility by trimming or ending programs that might serve to buffer the poor from mistaken choices.

Human sinfulness cannot be reduced to the bad choices that each person willfully makes. The example of schooling is instructive. When young people reach the end of their high-school years without being prepared to assume the adult responsibility of employment, it may be because they chose not to learn. But it may also be because their teachers lost enthusiasm for their vocation and their parents neither required them to learn nor helped them to do so. Unpreparedness for adult life may also be due to patterns of school governance and financing that result in schools that discourage learning, teaching, and parental responsibility. The young ought not to be excused from adult responsibilities because they are ill prepared. But they may now need to be equipped for responsibility as well as pushed into it, and any reform strategy must address not only them but also the dysfunctions in the school and the distorted structure of schooling.

The argument of this book is that if government's efforts to address persistent poverty and social distress are to become fruitful, then reforms in three distinct domains are required. (1) Welfare programs themselves need to be modified so that they encourage and require recipients to fulfill as fully as possible their varied responsibilities. (2) A new relationship needs to be established between government and religious social service providers in order to bring them into the center of the nation's helping effort. (3) The rules governing schools should be changed so that schools can educate better and also become a means of facilitating the renewal of persons and neighborhoods; economic policies may also require change in some places so that the poor may take up their employment responsibilities.

"In a highly differentiated and interdependent society" such as ours, "the only answer to human degradation is to seek the recovery of responsibility on all fronts simultaneously."[23] To carry out its high calling of ensuring that justice is done when the poor cry out for help, government should seek to restore the poor and the institutions surrounding them to the fulfullment of their manifold responsibilities and opportunities.

23. Center for Public Justice, 569.

Appendix

A New Vision for Welfare Reform: An Essay in Draft

Preface

This essay is the fruit of a project still in progress. The final version will not be published until 1995. With this draft we invite comments and criticisms. The three-year project from which it arises — "Welfare Responsibility: An Inquiry into the Roots of America's Welfare Policy Crisis" — is conducted by the Center for Public Justice under the auspices of the Christian College Coalition with the help of a major grant from The Pew Charitable Trusts.

The project as a whole aims both to understand the moral and religious roots of the welfare policy dilemmas and to sketch out the contours of a public philosophy able to address the subject at its deepest level. More than thirty scholars, policy experts, and practitioners have been working diligently as writers, advisers, consultants, and critics. A small leadership team has guided the effort. One major product anticipated at the end of the project will be a volume of about two dozen essays written by members of the leadership team and other contributors. . . .

Another major product will be the final version of this essay, which we hope will encourage creative thinking, intense debate, further scholarship, and innovative policy making long after the project has ended. This preliminary draft is brief and compact. It offers no detailed policy proposals; it does not provide an extensive critique of existing and proposed

This appendix contains the text of the booklet *A New Vision for Welfare Reform: An Essay in Draft* (Washington, D.C.: Center for Public Justice, 1994), except for a list of "Commissioned Papers" and a list entitled "Essential Reading on Poverty and Welfare." A sentence in the Preface referring to the commissioned paper list has been deleted.

welfare policies; it does not try to evaluate the vast literature on poverty and welfare. Rather, it attempts to introduce a particular vision, a distinctive outlook on reality, which might help citizens, policy makers, and leaders in many different walks of life to engage one another in a fresh way over the issues of poverty and welfare.

We firmly believe that the viewpoint presented here can, after refinement under fire, lead to creative innovations in policy making. But what is most important at this stage is that a significant number of people — both poor and not so poor — begin talking together about poverty in a new way. Creative policy making does not fall from the sky or bubble up automatically from interest-group pressures. If both poverty and the welfare policy crisis are as serious as they appear to be, then nothing less than a profound change in public outlook will be sufficient to bring about enduring reforms.

We are grateful for criticisms of earlier drafts of this essay offered by members of the leadership team, none of whom, however, is responsible for this penultimate draft. The team members are: Charles L. Glenn, Bob Goudzwaard, Jerry S. Herbert, Gina Barclay McLaughlin, John Mason, Lawrence M. Mead, Max L. Stackhouse, and Mary Stewart Van Leeuwen. We also wish to thank others who offered comments and criticisms, including Hank Allen, Harold Bratt, Richard Chewning, Roy Clouser, Bill Gram-Reefer, Karen Hosler Kispert, Valerie McWilliams, Hebron Morris, Jr., Larry Murphy, Cynthia Neal, Carol Veldman Rudie, Wendy Sereda, and Gary Visscher.

We hope this small contribution to the welfare debate will be helpful to many different groups of people — in government as well as in churches, in colleges and universities as well as on the street. We welcome critical responses that can help us produce a better final version.

Stanley W. Carlson-Thies
and James W. Skillen for the
leadership team
May 19, 1994

Introduction

Vibrant hope seems to be missing from American life today, even in the circles of those who are relatively prosperous. For many desperate people — including millions of youngsters who most need care and encouragement — life may appear to be hopeless, marked as it is by a dangerous neighborhood, a failing school, a broken family, and little connection to the ordinary world of work.

Discouragement and even hopelessness are also evident among some who hold political power and promise to solve society's problems. Policy makers cannot agree on how to deal with the worst kinds of poverty taking deep root across America. One reason for this paralysis is that earlier visions that guided anti-poverty efforts have not delivered as promised.

However, at the very moment when more and more people are giving up hope for the future and losing confidence in government's ability to do anything about the worst forms of poverty, pressures are mounting on local, state, and federal authorities to do something new, something better, something more, something different to assist the poor. The "something different" that one group of critics proposes is simply to cancel current welfare programs. Others urge government to do "something more" on behalf of the poor. Despite wide differences in opinion about what should be done, and in face of growing skepticism about whether anything will work, the cries grow louder: Create jobs! Stop the surge in out-of-wedlock births! Break the cycle of poverty! Stop welfare dependency! Halt crime!

The Argument of This Essay

The authors assume from the start that the poverty-and-welfare crisis should not be attributed to poor people alone or to failed public policies alone but to many institutions and individuals *together, at the same time,* in a global and not only a national context. In fact, what Americans and people of many other nations now face is a widespread "responsibility crisis" with deep moral and religious roots. Solutions will not come merely from welfare policy reforms, because policy making takes place in a context of assumptions, institutional patterns, and cultural conditions that are themselves part of the problem.

We begin this essay by taking a critical look at American political culture, which, at least in part, appears to be implicated in the poverty-and-welfare conundrum. Against the backdrop of that critical analysis we next articulate a vision of human identity and purpose that might open the way to a different kind of thinking about government's responsibility in relation to the diverse range of other human responsibilities. People simultaneously exhibit different talents and vocations in a variety of relationships and organizations. Institutions themselves — including governments — have their own callings, with distinct types of obligations. Both poverty and welfare policy need to be seen in a new light that illuminates the entire landscape of diverse personal and institutional responsibilities.

From the vantage point of this "new vision" we then try, in the third place, to show why the poverty crisis cannot be assessed narrowly as an income crisis of poor people and why citizens should not expect the solution to come solely from the assistance programs of federal and state governments. The arena of government and politics certainly cries out for reform, and we direct our attention to it in the final section. But the source of difficulty is not solely the design and size of government welfare programs. The problem lies deeper. It has to do with the way governments act in relation to citizens and society. It has to do with the way people use governments and expect them to act. Our political culture itself is part of the crisis.

Four Propositions

Our argument is built on four theses.

> **Thesis 1.** *Fruitful welfare reform depends on an accurate understanding of human dignity and the nature of diverse human vocations and obligations. American politics is hampered by problematic assumptions and patterns that all too often push aside important aspects of the truth about human responsibility in a complex society in a rapidly shrinking world.*

> **Thesis 2.** *A dependable vision of human life in society comes most clearly into focus from a biblical point of view. Human beings are created in God's image with many talents and vocations. Every task, including government's calling to do justice, has the character of a response to the Creator. God's love for this world, which is now radically marred by evil,*

is being revealed in ways that expose our sin and misery and offer healing for our brokenness.

Thesis 3. *The distressing conditions associated with poverty, particularly in the most degraded urban areas, are the expression of a multifaceted responsibility crisis. These tragic conditions cannot be measured by poverty statistics alone, for they represent the moral failures of social institutions, governments, and individuals.*

Thesis 4. *Governments are called to establish and enforce public justice by (a) upholding a just social order, (b) assisting with relief in emergencies, and (c) acting to bring about fundamental reforms where patterns of injustice exist. Public policies should not serve to legitimize irresponsibility. Instead, government should call people and institutions to healthy patterns of life in society.*

We wish to emphasize that this essay represents a brief and preliminary venture into highly complex matters of public policy, philosophy, ethics, and the religious foundations of human life. We do not presume that the argument is sufficient to deal adequately with all of these matters. Our aim is simply to try to expand and deepen the American debate about poverty and welfare.

Welfare Policy in a Bind

American welfare policy faces serious dilemmas today. At least three signs point to difficulty at a fundamental level.

A. Practical Failure. Significant efforts by the federal government to fight poverty began during the Great Depression and were expanded in the 1960s into a sweeping program to lift all citizens into the Great Society. But despite decades of effort and a major commitment of resources, poverty persists and in some places is deepening. Even worse, chronic poverty coupled with permanent dependence on government's direct assistance seems to have become endemic for some people in many inner cities and in some rural areas. These problems, in turn, appear to be tied to various personal and institutional dysfunctions among people who experience a growing sense of hopelessness.

B. Crisis of Legitimacy. Although motives and goals are mixed, government welfare programs aim to assist neighbors in need. But public programs to help the poor no longer hold the confidence of most people, including many who depend on them. In fact, more and more people now believe that welfare programs actually aggravate rather than alleviate poverty.

C. The Impasse of Policy Reform. In response both to the failures of past programs and to growing doubts about government's ability to deal with persistent poverty, reformers have advanced a wide range of proposals to resolve the crisis. But there is little agreement on a comprehensive framework for reform. Arguments at the two extremes are mutually exclusive: to expand and to eliminate the welfare system.

Awareness of the bind that welfare policy is in today leads to our first thesis:

> **Thesis 1.** *Fruitful welfare reform depends on an accurate understanding of human dignity and the nature of diverse human vocations and obligations. American politics is hampered by problematic assumptions and patterns that all too often push aside important aspects of the truth about human responsibility in a complex society in a rapidly shrinking world.*

The Prevailing Climate of American Public Life

What do we mean by "problematic assumptions and patterns" that keep us from gaining an accurate understanding of human life in society? Let us try, somewhat impressionistically, to characterize the present climate.

> A. First, Americans generally believe that individuals ought to be as free as possible from imposed obligations in order to be able to pursue their interests and to choose their own means of self-realization.
>
> B. Public policies, shaped at three levels of government under strong interest-group pressures, are typically built on the assumption that human beings are self-interested individuals whose socially important actions need to be channeled by means of material incentives and penalties that play to that self-interest.
>
> C. Politicians act on the assumption that the economic market-

place is the primary public arena of self-determination and self-realization. In the normal operation of the free market, self-interested pursuits are supposed to lead not only to individual happiness but also to the greater good of the entire nation and even of the world.

D. In the atmosphere of these assumptions and patterns, most people see government's responsibility as one of protecting citizens in their civil rights and their pursuit of happiness while it tries to promote the greater national good by means of economic growth.

E. Within a framework of policies designed to protect individual freedom and to promote economic growth, government should also do something, most Americans believe, to assist the poor who do not benefit from the nation's economic progress or who may be suffering negative consequences from it.

Obviously, welfare policies do not stand alone. They are embedded in a larger political and economic context. Debates over welfare, therefore, are bound up with controversies about the task of government, about the nature and purpose of a market economy, and about human nature itself.

Consider this question, for example: Are individuals poor because they have not diligently used their freedom to succeed in the market? If so, then they do not deserve special help from government, do they? Or, to the contrary, are individuals poor because of social and economic forces beyond their control? If so, then surely they are not responsible for their poverty and should be eligible for government's help, right?

The inevitable, unavoidable question here is how to justify welfare programs. Is government's primary obligation to reinforce market rules so that economic incentives and penalties can function optimally to teach people how to succeed on their own? Or, to the contrary, can welfare programs be justified as a legitimate correction to market forces, which when left untouched produce unjust outcomes for some members of society?

These questions lead to an even deeper one: Should we assume that each individual is primarily "free" (self-governing and responsible) or that each is "determined" (socially conditioned and thus not individually responsible)? Our culture holds high the ideal of freedom from imposed obligations. But do individuals really exercise freedom in that self-defining, self-governing sense? Or is that an illusion? Perhaps humans are so conditioned by past and present environments that they cannot be held accountable for their actions, especially if they are very poor.

Unresolvable Dilemmas

In our estimation, the dilemmas reflected in these crucial questions cannot be resolved within the framework of the problematic assumptions and patterns outlined above. Nor will we find within that framework an adequate explanation of the relative impotence of the war on poverty. The dilemmas are due, we believe, to a mistaken understanding of human life in society. The crisis in many of our inner cities and depressed rural regions is not poverty defined as a statistical abstraction. And relief from that poverty will require more than government's delivery or withdrawal of meager assistance to statistically poor people, whether considered "free" or "determined."

People whose income puts them below the poverty line cannot be reduced to the category of "poor people." Their qualifying identification as human beings is not, in the final analysis, their poverty. A statistical definition of the poor, or of the middle class, or of the wealthy does not get at the full identity of human beings who may or may not be meeting their obligations in various capacities and relationships. Furthermore, to recognize the existence of statistical poverty does not tell us who is responsible for it and who should do what to address which aspects of it.

At precisely this point the dominant assumptions and patterns of our political culture leave us stranded. If the poverty-and-welfare crisis does not consist merely of too many low-income people depending on government assistance, but instead reflects the failure of various institutions, the misdeeds of some individuals, and the mistaken judgments of government policy makers, then antiseptic adjustments in current welfare programs cannot be an adequate response to that crisis. Serious policy reform demands judgments about human responsibility in various arenas. But the prevailing political climate allows for few of those judgments in the policy making process.

Our tentative conclusion, therefore, is that the poverty-and-welfare dilemmas represent, in the deepest sense of the term, a *moral* crisis. This crisis is bred of human error at many levels. It is in part a crisis of public confusion bred of misguided public policies shaped by the problematic assumptions and patterns of our political culture. It is also a crisis bred of human mistakes and misdirections in many of our families, schools, churches, businesses, media, and interest groups.

If we are correct in this assessment, then the answer to persistent poverty will not be found in either more or fewer anti-poverty programs within the current framework. We need a new vision, a more accurate understanding of human life, and revised patterns for politics and law making. This leads to our next thesis.

In Search of a Better Worldview

Thesis 2. *A dependable vision of human life in society comes most clearly into focus from a biblical point of view. Human beings are created in God's image with many talents and vocations. Every task, including government's calling to do justice, has the character of a response to the Creator. God's love for this world, which is now radically marred by evil, is being revealed in ways that expose our sin and misery and offer healing for our brokenness.*

With this thesis, a framework of thought and action comes into view that contrasts strongly with the assumptions and patterns that control much of our American political culture.

A. In contrast to the prevailing emphasis on individual freedom from imposed obligations, a biblical perspective holds high the view of human beings as God's stewards, created in God's image, who are dignified by their moral responsibility for one another. Many human vocations may be accepted or rejected voluntarily (choosing to marry or accepting a particular job, for example) while others are inescapable (a child's accountability to parents or a citizen's obligation to live within the law). But whether or not obligations are freely chosen, the people who bear them are creatures accountable to one another and to God according to standards not devised by humans themselves.

B. In contrast to a largely behavioral picture of self-interested individuals, the biblical view of human beings is much richer, resisting reduction. Humans are, to be sure, constituted in part by their genetic make-up and social and environmental conditions. But their creative and highly diversified decision-making capability is part and parcel of their moral nature.

C. In contrast to a market-centered conception of social interaction, the biblical view envisions a more diversified and complex society. The market should be seen as one among many important arenas of modern social life. Moreover, an open market, which is increasingly global in character, entails its own distinct moral obligations on the part of individuals, corporations, governments, and other actors. Honesty, careful management, and wise stewardship of the creation should be recognized as binding principles of economic life.

D. In contrast to the popular view of government, a biblical view emphasizes government's divinely appointed vocation to establish and uphold justice. This includes not only protecting individual rights and property, but also recognizing the diverse kinds of moral obligation people bear for one another in many institutions, organizations, and relationships. Democratic procedures coupled with a free-market economy do not by themselves constitute a just state, nor can separate states any longer respond adequately, each by itself, to the demands of justice for a shrinking world.

E. In contrast to current approaches to poverty, a biblical perspective suggests that in order for governments to fulfill their own moral obligation to do justice, they must do more than react to the negative economic effects of social degradation. They must do more than simply redistribute material resources to those beneath the poverty line or withhold such resources in order to propel unemployed individuals back into the marketplace. Rather, governments should pursue more fundamental reforms, seeking to restore effective action on the part of all who bear responsibility for poverty.

No Parochial or Partisan Aim

Our appeal here to a biblical point of view comes not from a parochial theological purpose or with any partisan aim to rally Christians and Jews against Americans who live by other commitments. Rather, in addressing the common concerns of American public life, we simply wish to bring to the conversation those things we believe most deeply to be true. Many different points of view now contend with one another in the public square both in this country and around the world. Let others come openly from their points of view to the common discussion we all need to have about these most urgent and fundamental issues. But let us leave no stone unturned, no avenue of possible insight unexplored, as we address the problems of poverty in the United States and the world today.

Much from the biblical tradition has shaped American society, but only in a highly synthetic fashion. American life represents a volatile amalgam of biblical and nonbiblical traditions, both ancient and modern — an amalgam that increasingly manifests critical instability and inner conflict. Perhaps this is one reason why so many adherents to the biblical tradition have been seeking anew to understand the Bible's message for contemporary public life. Catholic bishops and mainline Protestants, Orthodox Christians and Orthodox Jews, Evangelicals and Anabaptists have all been engaged in efforts to discover the contemporary relevance of biblical revelation for political and economic justice.

Nevertheless, Americans who identify themselves in one way or another with the biblical tradition are spread across the entire spectrum of the debate over welfare policy. Consequently, our appeal to a biblical worldview as guide to socio-economic thinking does not imply that we think the policy implications of that worldview are already lying on the table fully developed and ready to use. Our appeal to the biblical tradition is therefore also, and especially, an appeal for serious, self-critical debate within circles where biblical authority is acknowledged.

The High Dignity of Being Human

The welfare debate is paralyzed in part, we contend, by what appears to be an irreconcilable tension between the assumption that poor people are responsible for their poverty and the assumption that they are helplessly trapped by adverse conditions. Individual autonomy is pitted against social determinism. From a biblical point of view, that false dilemma cannot stand. Individuals are neither autonomously self-determining nor fully determined by genetic and environmental conditions. The human ability to take genuine and creative action, to make judgments and decisions, is always in response to God's commandments. Human freedom is a responsive freedom. From a biblical point of view, human dignity, freedom, and responsibility hang together as inherent character traits of the image of God.

It is true that men and women give culturally diverse shapes to their societies and governments. But in devising their rules and standards, they are not the authors of the ultimate principles by which all human efforts are judged. The structures and rules humans devise will work well or poorly, they will turn out to be legitimate or illegitimate, acceptable or unacceptable, moral or immoral, just or unjust, depending on their compliance with standards of justice, love, and stewardship that originate with the Creator. An important degree of originality and free-forming creativity will always be apparent in human activity, but human freedom to shape the world is always a response to divine ordinances.

Just as the human capacity for responding freely to divine standards should not be mistaken for unbounded individual autonomy, neither should the real contextual and historical constraints on human action be mistaken for social or biological determinism. Human behavior, from a biblical point of view, is not reducible to biological and social conditioning, although human choices and actions are always structured in part by those conditions.

Any person who becomes a responsible adult undergoes a long maturation process from helplessness at birth to what can become a high degree of independence if the right kind of nurturing and education takes place in the family and in wider community. Human beings are interdependent, mutually responsible creatures, never self-sufficient individuals. Social interdependency, moreover, is a multigenerational, historically extensive, and increasingly global reality. The languages we speak, our family habits, the characteristics of our music, cuisine, clothing, government, and worship, all speak of cultural development over time. None of us acts out of complete self-direction, self-definition, or self-determination. Those who have been made in God's image are multigenerational, history-shaping creatures. Nevertheless, this entire creational context does not reduce people to deterministic automatons. Rather, it provides the setting for each person's exercise of genuine responsibility.

In the course of history, human activity has given rise to an increasing differentiation of talents and vocations into the wide-ranging complexity we experience in our society today. That widening array of human relationships and organized specialties is also contributing to the experience of a shrinking globe in which people throughout the world find themselves linked ever more closely by transnational corporations, communication networks, religious organizations, scientific projects, environmental dangers, and much more. The meaning of this world as a single, integral creation order is becoming clearer and clearer even as human talents, vocations, and institutions continue to proliferate. Increasingly, each person holds responsibility in many different relationships and organizations at the same time. It is true that corporations and financial markets operating worldwide have more and more influence — both for good and for ill —

on our domestic economic conditions, all the way down to the shape of our inner cities. But these global dynamics neither deprive nor relieve our domestic governments, businesses, schools, families, churches, and urban residents of their own responsibilities.

Accountability and Culpability

Men and women are able to make judgments and exercise diverse responsibilities because, in the final analysis, they have been created to respond to the Creator's will for human life. God's commands to work, to do justice, to love neighbors, to care for the creation, to honor parents, and to rest on the Sabbath are commands from our Creator, not rules concocted out of our own autonomy or generated out of biological necessity. People are also capable of violating these commands, of perpetrating injustice, of hating and killing their neighbors. We can misuse other creatures, become indolent, and turn our backs on the Creator.

From a biblical point of view, what we recognize today as injustice and degradation are the fruits of human sinfulness — the expression of disregard for, or defiance of, God's commands for healthy and responsible life in the creation. Evil amounts to more than individual sinfulness leading to individual unhappiness. We all inherit the consequences of the sins of earlier generations, and none of us is untouched by the failings of our ancestors, co-workers, fellow citizens, political and business leaders, neighbors, cultural idols, and others who are co-responsible for shaping the organizations and institutions of our society.

However, this does not mean that we may treat some individuals or institutions as innocent and without responsibility because they have been the victims of the sins of others. In biblical terms, each individual and each institution bears real responsibility for its own actions, even though those actions occur in contexts that are influenced by factors beyond its control.

For example, a local bank may find itself in difficulty due to an increase of crime in the neighborhood, a shrinking number of well-qualified employees, population flight to other neighborhoods, and competition from larger banks. But none of this gives the endangered bank's managers a justification for defrauding customers, employees, or the government for the benefit of the owners and stockholders. The bankers must do what is right and suffer punishment for any wrongdoing even if the choices they face are highly limited and even unpalatable.

Or take a very different example. An unwed teenage mother without a job or neighborly support may be in her predicament for many reasons: the irresponsibility of the father of her child; the failures of her own parents; the bitter legacy of American racism; the decline of the local school; the greed of industry; and the carelessness of government. But none of this allows us to treat the young woman as if she were not responsible for her child and her own actions. Her human dignity requires that we honor her as a responsible person even as we demand that the father of her child, the school, her parents, the government, and others fulfill their obligations toward her.

A Firm Basis for Hope

Finally, we may say that the biblical story offers hope for human renewal and restoration, but not on the basis of self-designed programs of salvation. Ultimate self-realization will not be achieved by economic, political, technological, sexual, or any other human means. Heaven will not be brought to earth by human insistence and ingenuity. Historical development throughout the world has shown the deepening of sin and degradation as well as an increase in the opportunities for human beings to exercise their talents in thankful response to God. Life is possible because of divine providence and mercy, revealed through God's own act of sacrificial love. Genuine hope, from this point of view, is grounded in God's firm promise to redeem the creation and to triumph over evil and lawlessness on earth.

If we put aside false hopes of autonomous self-realization and of a human-made heaven on earth, we can find genuine comfort and encouragement in the biblical story. If we view all of human life, including government and economic activities, as arenas of human responsibility before God, the full scope of human experience appears in a different light. Because God's grace can turn people from despair to hope, from disobedience to obedience, we are set free to face up to our failings and to seek the proper means of exercising our talents and capabilities.

In the strength of this hope, we can also turn a truly critical eye toward the diverse responsibilities God has given governments and other institutions. We will not expect one institution to pick up all the pieces produced by the failures of others. We will deny neither individual responsibility nor social responsibility for poverty. Nor will we assume that government bears all the social responsibility by itself. But we will approach government seriously as the institution called to uphold public justice rather than as a catch-all, save-all institution that many want it to be. Moreover, we will call government to fulfill its obligation to uphold justice by doing more than simply translating interest-group pressures into law. We will demand more of our politicians than the pursuit of what is "politically possible" in a bargaining process that leaves the poor and helpless at the mercy of the rich and mighty. Indeed, we will call governments to act with all the strength and authority God has given them, to do justice and to fight without compromise against injustice.

A Responsibility Crisis

From the viewpoint just introduced, the manifold character of human responsibility comes into clear view and the poverty-and-welfare crisis appears in a new light.

> **Thesis 3.** *The distressing conditions associated with poverty, particularly in the most degraded urban areas, are the expression of a multifaceted responsibility crisis. These tragic conditions cannot be measured by poverty statistics alone, for they represent the moral failures of social institutions, government, and individuals.*

The prevailing climate of American political and economic life leads policy makers to interpret the condition of the poor far too narrowly and abstractly as a lack of income. Welfare policies then aim, through various means of assistance, to lift the poor above the poverty line but without giving sufficient attention to the reasons for their poverty. Today, after decades of welfare programs and continuing economic growth, the development of what now appears to be concentrations of intractable poverty seems to prove that anti-poverty programs are a failure. But are they?

Not every type of assistance program has failed. Programs such as unemployment insurance, Social Security, tax-supported education, and medical insurance for the elderly generally work to help people *avoid* poverty. Whatever the flaws of these programs, they do not so often raise highly charged questions about responsibility and irresponsibility on the part of either government or the beneficiaries.

However, the matter appears in a different light when it comes to government programs such as Aid to Families with Dependent Children (AFDC) that are specifically targeted to the poor. On the one hand, most welfare recipients utilize the assistance as an indispensable, temporary stepping stone in their journey to overcome impoverishment caused by some tragedy or low-paying work. However, the programs themselves neither require responsible action nor facilitate it. Recipients who need help to pull their lives together do not receive it. Those with no desire to change find their irresponsibility supported. In some cases, therefore, the assistance actually works to entrench poverty.

More Than an Income Crisis

How shall we explain both the apparent successes and the apparent failures of welfare programs? An answer to this question begins with the recognition that long-term, hard-core poverty cannot be explained in economic terms alone. Rather, it is tied to deeper and more extensive problems, both personal and social. The problems are typically those of multiple personal and institutional failures: deficient schooling; insufficient connection between able-bodied adults and available jobs; asocial, antisocial, or criminal behavior on the part of some individuals; family breakdowns; out-of-wedlock births; careless, unjust governments; and more. If these debilitating circumstances and patterns are not due merely to low incomes, then there is good reason to believe that government's direct assistance programs may, in some cases, be misconceived and misdirected. The inadequacy of some programs may be due to their failure to discriminate between people who can responsibly use the benefits and those who cannot or will not do so.

We must not simply point the finger at questionable welfare policies, however. As long as we focus on those policies alone, we continue to think only of government's duty in a narrow, reactive sense. The argument of this essay is not that government alone should reform or that government should get out of the welfare business altogether. Rather, it is that other people and institutions, including welfare recipients themselves, should be expected, along with government, to fulfill their God-given responsibilities. Government policies should take fully into account the responsibilities of others and aim to strengthen them. Furthermore, government has the special responsibility to confront the structural causes of poverty in society and not merely to react to their effects on poor people. If government simply concentrates on promoting economic growth and giving a little aid to the needy, it may remain blind to the ways in which even its growth and assistance policies may contribute to the forces of greed and corruption that help cause poverty.

A New Consensus on Workfare?

Current debates over welfare reform suggest that some of the old simplicities are giving way to a more sophisticated understanding of the interplay between government and poor people. A new group of politicians and policy experts argues that welfare benefits should be tied to a work requirement for able-bodied welfare recipients, since their poverty is due to non-work. Government may need to assist with job training and in other ways, but welfare recipients must be expected to go to work.

But this new approach has not yet entirely resolved the policy dilemmas. Why should work be required? Is work good for welfare recipients because it forces them back into the disciplines of the market and can help them break with dependency? Or is work a payment to society for the welfare benefit? In the latter case, should welfare recipients be required, as a social duty, to accept whatever work the market provides, or must government supply jobs to those who are unable to find "decent" work in the market? And should welfare recipients be required to work in every case or only if the work they find yields a better package of income and benefits than does welfare? In other words, who owes what to whom?

There is also now a broad agreement that giving birth out of wedlock is undesirable. But many unanswered questions remain here as well. Should government discourage out-of-wedlock births by refusing to grant or increase welfare benefits when those births occur? Or would that show unjustified retribution against some women and reveal an impermissible government bias in favor of marriage and against single-parent families?

On closer examination, it appears that the new consensus has not yet settled on the range of behavior for which people ought to be held accountable or on how government should go about holding them accountable. The idea that public assistance should be combined with changes in the behavior of welfare recipients does not, by itself, escape the deeper bind in which welfare policy is caught.

Multiple, Simultaneous Vocations

Here is where a wider, deeper view of human identity and responsibility is so important. Think, for instance, of schools where students are passed along to a new grade level each year regardless of their abilities and actual achievements. Some argue that this is necessary to avoid inflicting psychological damage on children who might otherwise begin to see themselves as failures. But when a young person is certified as a high school graduate and yet cannot adequately read, write, count, or think, what will that person's sense of worth be over the long term? And who bears responsibility for that person's unemployment, poverty, anti-social behavior, and lack of motivation?

Surely we must judge in this case that the school, and not just the student, has failed. Other people may also be implicated. The student's parents may bear important responsibility for their child's attitude, motivation, and work habits. Of course, the long-term reform of school governance is not going to address the immediate needs of the desperately poor person who has already reached an age of maturity without an adequate education. But the illustration shows why government may not construct its welfare policies with a focus only on poor people after they have become poor, abstracted from the full context of diverse responsibilities that others bear for them and that they also bear. Schools have an important obligation to nurture children to maturity. Other institutions cannot fully substitute for failing schools any more than schools can substitute for failing homes and governments. In an interdependent, diversified society, we may not ignore or discount one set of human responsibilities simply because another set has not been fulfilled.

To recognize, for instance, that international economic competition may put domestic companies under greatly increased pressure cannot justify illegal or immoral business practices. The fact that slavery and legal discrimination had a terrible impact on African Americans does not mean that African American workers today should be exempted from the standards that apply to other employees. It is true, of course, that a school which serves a neighborhood with a high percentage of broken homes, or a domestic corporation in decline, or a member of a long-oppressed minority group may need support, advice, and encouragement not required by institutions and individuals in better circumstances. However, each of these still has responsibilities that are not transferable and that may not be discounted.

Restoring People to Their Callings

In a highly differentiated and interdependent society, such as the one in which we live, the only answer to human degradation is to seek the recovery of responsibility on all fronts simultaneously. The approach we have suggested here demands recognition of the multiplicity of human vocations so that no single aim or purpose in society is allowed to overwhelm others. A government that ignores some of its own duties, or that tries to take on obligations that do not belong to it, will not be acting to fulfill its vocation to do justice to a richly differentiated society.

In this light, it makes sense, then, to expect that government's attempts to overcome or ameliorate poverty should take the *primary* course of trying to strengthen the accountability structures that constitute the warp and woof of society. Why should we not see welfare policies as having the aim of restoring people and institutions to their diverse responsibilities in a healthy society, rather than aiming directly and abstractly to lift the income of poor people above a certain poverty line? Could it be that part of the problem with many welfare policies is that they have skirted, ignored, and even denied the most important sources of both deprivation and recuperation, of both degradation and restoration, in the hope of offering to individuals (whether considered "free" or "determined") a direct, governmentally created escape route from poverty? We believe that government's primary aim should be to call people and institutions to their own responsibilities.

To Do Justice

Thesis 4. *Governments are called to establish and enforce public justice by (a) upholding a just social order, (b) assisting with relief in emergencies, and (c) acting to bring about fundamental reforms where patterns of injustice exist. Public policies should not serve to legitimize irresponsibility. Instead, government should call people and institutions to healthy patterns of life in society.*

Our conviction that human beings develop their talents and callings in a variety of relationships and institutions leads to a particular understanding of government's responsibility in and for society. Family life and education, science and art, business and commerce, worship and leisure — all of these and more comprise the rich fabric of society. But this diversity cannot exist apart from a framework of public law and order that gives each its due, making it possible for all to thrive simultaneously in the same territory. Political community under government, therefore, is itself an essential arena of human moral responsibility before God.

We may conceive of the exercise of government's responsibility in at least three different ways: (A) upholding a just social order, (B) assisting with relief in emergencies, and (C) acting to bring about fundamental reforms where patterns of injustice exist.

A. Upholding Society

Government's first mode of responsibility for public justice is to *uphold a just social order* by protecting and encouraging citizens in the fulfillment of both their civic and non-civic vocations. Government's most basic duty is to establish and enforce the public rules for peaceful living, to encourage those who are doing right and to punish those who are doing wrong. This should be the goal of its normal operations, the substance of its "standard operating policies." This has meant, for example, authorizing and administering the public infrastructure of transportation, water, and sewage systems, as well as providing fire and police protection. With regard to human resources, it has meant policies such as funding education and using the tax code to support families and others who care for dependents. Upholding a just society has also meant sustaining a court system for the peaceful resolution of conflict and encouraging entrepreneurial activity for the enhancement of the commonwealth.

Government efforts to uphold a just society make it possible for people and institutions to work out their diverse vocations simultaneously in a common order. To play this role, government must be able to take for granted that parents are rearing their children, that businesses are employing people, that teachers are educating students, and that farmers are producing food. It is vital, therefore, that government always consider whether its policies in any way fail to do justice to the diverse range of obligations people bear. If current laws ignore or actually encourage destructive activity, and if such irresponsibility lies at the root of some of the misery and degradation associated with chronic poverty, then welfare reform should go back, first of all, to a reexamination of government's standard operating policies.

1. For example, a key area of law that should be revised concerns the recognition and support of parenting. A healthy future for children is highly dependent on how well parents rear them. Government's standard policies should uphold family integrity and the good order of the parental covenant. A man and a woman who produce children should both fulfill the responsibility of caring for their offspring even if they are not married and do not live together. Fathers as well as mothers should be held accountable. And if minors bear children, then the grandparents and possibly other members of the extended family should bear some responsibility for these children of their children.

This has nothing to do with penalizing single-parent welfare families. Any and all parents should be held accountable for their own children, and the law should recognize and work to strengthen the family covenant across the board. If government cannot or will not do this, then welfare policy will inevitably fail. If welfare policy tries to compensate for parental irresponsibility, while allowing that irresponsibility to continue, it will not be able to save children from the dire consequences of these failures.

To uphold parenting, government must, of course, do more than enforce accountability laws. To fulfill their covenant, parents need sufficient income, jobs, a place to live, good schools, protection against crime, and more. Families alone cannot provide these things. Some of the responsibility here falls directly to government. Some of it is indirectly affected by public policies. To the extent that parenting is jeopardized because of failing schools, joblessness, and crime, government bears a major burden of responsibility.

2. With regard to government's positive encouragement of parents and others who care for dependents, we believe there should be a much greater public investment in the primary and secondary institutions that offer such care. This could come by way of direct public allowances for children and dependents, as is done in many European countries. Or it could be provided by a considerable increase in the income tax code's standard deduction for dependents. If the latter were coupled with a correspondingly large increase in the earned income tax credit for those who are

working but not earning enough to support their families, the change could be of great assistance to poorer working families. It would be the right way to encourage parents both in their work and in the fulfillment of their family vocations.

B. Responding to Emergencies

A second mode of government responsibility is that of *emergency relief.* The most obvious services are those we see when the police arrive at a highway accident; when state and federal governments organize a relief operation after a natural disaster; when the military defends the country against foreign aggression; when someone receives temporary support after a job loss; or when a failed business is allowed to declare bankruptcy. An earthquake or job loss does not destroy the ability of parents to raise their children or the ability of people to work. But if emergency relief does not arrive quickly, the probable consequence will be that all of these abilities will be stymied or paralyzed, thus compounding and extending the disaster. The presupposition of emergency relief is the basic soundness of both the people and the institutions temporarily engulfed by an emergency.

This role of government also underlies social insurance programs such as unemployment insurance and Social Security. By means of these programs, government both requires and enables employees and their families to make provision for times when income from employment will be interrupted. Future emergencies are thereby anticipated, and government's ability to uphold the just order of society is further enhanced.

1. At least one aspect of health-care reform should be seen as a means of providing for emergency relief. A serious health crisis that requires expensive treatment may hit any person or family. In the absence of catastrophic health insurance, either the inability to obtain treatment because of its high cost or a financial disaster following expensive treatment is likely to have serious social as well as personal consequences. Making sure that there is universal insurance against catastrophic costs of health care represents a legitimate exercise of government's responsibility to help with emergency relief.

2. We also believe that government should carefully re-evaluate its current mode of response to severe social disorder. Have the conditions in

some of our central cities, for example, degenerated to the point where normal policing is insufficient to withstand gangs and drug rings? Under those circumstances, neither welfare nor other social programs can hope to succeed. It is not right for responsible people to have to go about their work, rear their children, and try to pursue the ordinary duties of life while living in war zones. In that case, governments have failed to fulfill their obligations to uphold the good order of society. If some urban circumstances represent a state of emergency, then emergency measures may be required.

This is one area in particular where the inadequacy of our federal system is most clearly on display. In many respects urban problems are metropolitan problems, not confined within city boundaries and often extending across state lines. If the reason for ineffective response to emergency circumstances (and to many nonemergency injustices as well) is that governments are not organized properly to exercise that responsibility, then the critical fault lies within government itself.

3. A reexamination of government's emergency responsibilities should also lead us to ask whether certain policies first designed to promote recovery from an emergency have now become ongoing supports for irresponsibility. This appears to be the case with certain aspects of the AFDC program. The program was originally designed as emergency relief for widowed mothers who, it was thought at the time, ought not to work outside the home. But AFDC has become, for some recipients, a permanent alternative to work and marriage. AFDC has not required mothers to perform gainful work, nor have the fathers or the grandparents been held accountable for support of the mother and child. Consequently, AFDC has, for a few, become a public prop for irresponsibility rather than a form of emergency assistance to help them step back into the ordinary vocations of life.

In some cases, then, government may be failing to take adequate emergency measures to deal with emergency circumstances, while on the other hand it may be continuing to deliver certain relief services that no longer serve an emergency purpose. On one side we see responsible people who are unable to live a normal life because government is not responding adequately with emergency services to restore public health and safety. On the other side, we see people capable of fulfilling ordinary duties but not doing so because they have become permanently dependent on what should have been only temporary, emergency assistance.

C. Pursuing Fundamental Reforms

The third mode of government action, to which we turn in conclusion, might be described as long-term *regenerative reform* that seeks to overcome structural patterns of injustice. This has to do with complex networks of interrelated responsibilities for which a system change is required.

The end of slavery represented such a challenge. Federal and state governments needed to do more than simply recognize former slaves as free persons within the existing legal, economic, and political order. Governments also needed to do more than offer temporary emergency assistance to former slaves leaving the plantations and to former slave owners trying to cope with the demise of the slave-based economy. Beyond those actions, a more extensive and extended process of reform was needed to help change the entire fabric of society. Much of this was not achieved until the civil rights movement a century after the Civil War.

In the case of chronic poverty and the deepening crisis of many inner cities today, we need a multilevel movement for structural reform. Some new emergency efforts may be necessary at the start, but if so, they can serve only a temporary purpose. Fundamental reforms must change the ways that many institutions and individuals relate to one another. No single element of change will be enough by itself. Every dimension of human responsibility is important; none can be discounted.

Efforts to change distorted social and cultural patterns present the greatest challenge to policy makers, in part because those changes have to be made over the long term and in part because government cannot, by its own strength, accomplish all that is needed. If people are not renewed in their hearts; if spouses do not commit themselves to one another; if parents do not love their children; if schools do not offer quality education; if workers do not have the means and motivation to work; then government will achieve relatively little. Nevertheless, government may not shrink from its obligation on the grounds that others are failing to fulfill theirs.

1. One of the complex networks of injustice that is aggravating persistent poverty is our "system" of health care. The current Medicaid program for the poor, for example, is part of a system that is caught in the contradictory framework of prevailing assumptions and patterns criticized earlier. With Medicaid, government has put itself in a position of reaction, offering inadequate health-care services to people after they have become poor. It should, instead, address the structural causes of poverty and deal

with the absence of adequate medical insurance. Some of the poor who remain tied to welfare programs, for example, do so because it is the only way they can obtain a measure of health-care for themselves and their families. Dependency compounds dependency.

Properly structured, a national system of health insurance would function, much like Social Security and unemployment insurance, as a means of promoting, rather than negating, responsibility. Government-mandated health insurance must, of course, be organized in a way that encourages parental responsibility for children, emphasizes preventive health care, inhibits or penalizes bad habits that lead to health problems, and promotes employment for the able bodied. Having said only this much, it is obvious that health-care reform entails significant changes in the interdependent responsibilities of health insurance companies, hospitals, doctors, employers, families, and many departments of government.

2. Another critical area calling for system reform is schooling. Here we think especially of the interconnected responsibilities of families, schools, governments, and the workplace.

Government support of a free education for every child is, we believe, a sound standard operating policy. But the means of rendering that support should be revised on several counts. First, it is increasingly obvious that the property-tax system of support for education delivers highly inequitable funding to different school systems, further increasing the distance between rich and poor. Many states along with the federal government try to compensate for that inequity by targeting funds to poorer school districts. But this hodgepodge of reactive programs, involving billions of dollars in administrative expense alone, requires radical reform. Greater equity not only in the delivery of funding, but also in giving opportunity to all students, is essential. Since both the tax system and the governance of education are largely in the hands of state, local, and federal governments, any system reform must begin with action by public authorities.

Another aspect of inequity in education takes us back to the question of parental responsibility for children. Parents who have the means to do so invariably consider the school they want for their children when they decide where to buy a house. Often those parents select an independent school if they think it will better serve their children. However, the poorest Americans are unable to make these choices. For the most part they can neither choose where to live nor make a selection from among different schools. Even the most responsible parents are trapped, forced by government's own laws to submit their children to a process that in some cases amounts to outright miseducation. We suggest that long-term reform will require a fundamental change in the law to allow all parents to exercise real responsibility in choosing schools for their children, having at their disposal a fair share of education dollars.

Education reform should also lead to a better connection between the schools and future employment. Too many children are passed along through a general system of schooling that aims for nothing beyond getting them to the next grade and out of the system. Many businesses now have to provide essential remedial education to prepare new employees for work. Those who have endured deficient schooling suffer more than others when it comes to finding employment. We need schools that are better able to help students build from sound basics up through apprenticeships and on to real jobs. We need schools that are better able to cooperate with employers in the work-a-day world as well as with families in the neighborhood.

Also crucial here is a better approach to life-long reeducation and retraining. Technological changes and global economic restructuring are combining to render more and more jobs impermanent and to demand very specialized training for the performance of some jobs. Public investment in life-long learning and retraining, coupled with greater opportunity for practical apprenticeships while in high school, could open new doors to those currently unemployed or underemployed. Rather than allow today's schools to fail some students and then try to pick up the pieces by means of low quality, low-success, remedial training for the poor, government should instead change its laws to make schools, from the start, more accountable to families and more prepared to guide students to future employment and/or higher education.

3. A third arena in which long-term system reform is necessary is that of remediation and relief services for people facing urgent and immediate needs. These are the needs ordinarily met within families, friendship networks, and church communities — needs such as food, clothing, shelter, counseling, and temporary financial support for those without jobs or income. In this regard, significant regenerative reforms are needed to reorder the relationships among governments, churches, families, schools, hunger and shelter ministries, and various counseling and rehabilitation programs.

Return for a moment to the epidemic of fatherlessness — the other side of the growing number of single mothers. Some of our severest social problems are linked with, if not produced by, child rearing in the absence of fathers. To be sure, a response to absent fathers ought to include government-backed efforts to establish paternity and to enforce child-support. But this is not enough. The real solution is for fathers to accept and work at fulfilling their paternal responsibilities.

To bring about this kind of change requires something governments cannot guarantee or deliver: direct, personal contact with the absent (or soon-to-be absent) father by someone with sufficient concern, resources, and moral authority to be of help. The best help is to be found in the surrounding primary and secondary institutions of society — families, churches, schools, and helping organizations. Counseling and other kinds of assistance that may be needed involve judgments about moral accountability, about the rights and wrongs of marriage, family life, single parenthood, promiscuity, teenage pregnancy, and more. The kind of help that is most successful comes from people with deep moral and religious commitments, and very often from those who work for explicitly religious organizations.

Government should recognize the preeminence of these institutions and organizations and support them vigorously in its effort to reverse the poverty and degradation spiral. Direct public assistance through government agencies cannot substitute for the original and remedial services offered within primary and secondary institutions, many of which are overtly religious.

For governments to achieve major reform at this level, they must end all religious discrimination against independent institutions and organizations. Insofar as government authorizes funding for education, job training, counseling, adoption, rehabilitation, food for the hungry, shelter for the homeless, or any number of other services, it should revise its laws and programs to channel its funds proportionately to the independent institutions and agencies that deliver those services.

In the case of nonprofit service organizations, perhaps this can best be done by means of matching grants that complement the funds raised privately by nongovernment organizations. The federal government now does this with foreign relief and development assistance, which goes to explicitly religious organizations, among others. The same pattern should hold in the domestic arena. There is, in our view, no violation of the First Amendment if public funds go to support families, schools, churches, and various relief and remediation efforts, in proportion to their service and without regard to their confessional basis. In fact, the opposite is true; to discriminate against self-professed religious organizations is to violate the First Amendment.

The issue of ending discrimination against confessional institutions and service providers may seem a small matter in itself, but it is connected with the larger question of how government should properly seek to help those in need. From the beginning, we have been critical of the approach that abstracts the poor, as a general class, from their full context of multiple responsibilities to make them direct clients of the government. This is a fundamental injustice built into much welfare legislation. We must call our governments to change their orientation, to recognize that, in most cases, the primary institutions and secondary organizations of society are the ones that can and should bear responsibility for people in special need. Government policies should not sidestep or displace families, churches, schools, and independent service agencies. To the contrary, the law and public funds should go, first of all, to support the institutions and organizations that can (and in many cases should) minister directly and personally to people, helping them recover their own accountability. All of this will require renewed appreciation for religious freedom and new ways of promoting cooperation between government and non-government agencies without threatening the independence of the latter.

Conclusion

This brief essay can serve only as an introduction to a new vision for welfare reform. What we have called the responsibility crisis in the United States is severe. Radical changes in public welfare policy are necessary. But those reforms cannot be made in abstraction from the wider social, economic, and political dynamics of American and global society in which various system reforms are urgently needed.

We have argued that the reform of welfare policy appears to be stymied today because it is caught on the horns of dilemmas fostered by a faulty vision of human responsibility. Trying, by contrast, to take seriously the implications of a biblical worldview, we have exposed a multifaceted responsibility crisis, which is often overlooked by those who focus their attention on the problem of low incomes. To address the responsibility crisis, it will be necessary for governments to change their mode of operation from one of taking on clients to one of strengthening the multiple accountability structures in society. Government should do its part by fulfilling its own obligations to uphold justice in society, to respond to emergencies, and to work for the fundamental reform of unjust social patterns.

This argument now needs to be tested in public discussion and debate. The policy implications of our approach need to be worked out and compared to policy proposals fashioned on the basis of other assumptions. We have offered only a few suggestions in this regard about where our argument might lead. We await your comments and criticisms.

Contributors

STANLEY W. CARLSON-THIES, Director, Welfare Responsibility Inquiry, and Fellow of the Center for Public Justice, Annapolis, Maryland.

CLARKE E. COCHRAN, Professor of Political Science and Adjunct Professor of Health Organization Management at Texas Tech University, Lubbock, Texas.

STEPHANIE BAKER COLLINS, Researcher, Citizens for Public Justice, Toronto, Ontario, Canada.

JEAN BETHKE ELSHTAIN, Laura Spellman Rockefeller Professor of Ethics, the School of Divinity, the University of Chicago, Chicago, Illinois.

MARY ANN GLENDON, Learned Hand Professor of Law, Harvard Law School, Cambridge, Massachusetts.

CHARLES L. GLENN, Professor of Educational Policy and Chairman, Department of Administration, Training, and Policy Studies, School of Education, Boston University, Boston, Massachusetts.

BOB GOUDZWAARD, Professor of Economics, the Free University, Amsterdam, The Netherlands.

Contributors

ANNE MOTLEY HALLUM, Associate Professor of Political Science, Stetson University, Deland, Florida.

JOHN HIEMSTRA, Assistant Professor of Political Studies, The King's University College, Edmonton, Alberta, Canada.

PAUL MARSHALL, Senior Fellow in Political Theory, Institute for Christian Studies, Toronto, Ontario, Canada.

JOHN D. MASON, Chairman, Department of Economics, Gordon College, Wenham, Massachusetts.

LAWRENCE M. MEAD, Professor of Politics, New York University, New York City, and Weinberg Visiting Professor of Public Policy, Woodrow Wilson School of Public and International Affairs, Princeton University, Princeton, New Jersey.

STEPHEN V. MONSMA, Professor of Political Science, Pepperdine University, Malibu, California.

STEPHEN CHARLES MOTT, Professor of Christian Social Ethics, Gordon-Conwell Theological Seminary, Wenham, Massachusetts.

CYNTHIA JONES NEAL, Assistant Professor of Psychology, Wheaton College, Wheaton, Illinois.

HEIDI ROLLAND, Charles Finney Scholar in Evangelism and Social Change at Evangelicals for Social Action, Wynnewood, Pennsylvania.

RONALD J. SIDER, President, Evangelicals for Social Action (ESA), and Professor of Theology and Culture, Eastern Baptist Theological Seminary, Wynnewood, Pennsylvania.

JAMES W. SKILLEN, Executive Director, the Center for Public Justice, Annapolis, Maryland.

MAX L. STACKHOUSE, Stephen Colwell Professor of Christian Ethics, Princeton Theological Seminary, Princeton, New Jersey.

JULIA K. STRONKS, Assistant Professor of Political Studies, Whitworth College, Spokane, Washington.

MARY STEWART VAN LEEUWEN, Professor of Psychology and Resident Scholar at the Center for Christian Women in Leadership, Eastern College, St. Davids, Pennsylvania.

MARY P. VAN HOOK, Associate Professor, School of Social Work, the University of Central Florida, Orlando, Florida.